# www.Brooks/Cole.com

*Brooks/Cole.com* is the World Wide Web site for Wadsworth and is your direct source to dozens of online resources.

At *Brooks/Cole.com* you can find out about supplements, demonstration software, and student resources. You can also send email to many of our authors and preview new publications and exciting new technologies.

**Brooks/Cole.com**
Changing the way the world learns®

# COUNSELING CHILDREN

## SIXTH EDITION

### Charles L. Thompson
*The University of Tennessee, Knoxville*

### Linda B. Rudolph
*Austin Peay State University*

### Donna A. Henderson
*Wake Forest University*

**THOMSON**

**BROOKS/COLE**

Australia • Canada • Mexico •
Singapore • Spain • United Kingdom • United States

# THOMSON

## BROOKS/COLE

*Executive Editor:* Lisa Gebo
*Acquisitions Editor:* Julie Martinez
*Assistant Editor:* Shelley Gesicki
*Editorial Assistant:* Amy Lam
*Technology Project Manager:*
Barry Connolly
*Marketing Manager:* Caroline Concilla
*Marketing Assistant:* Mary Ho
*Advertising Project Manager:* Tami Strang
*Project Managers, Editorial Production:*
Stephanie Zunich, Katy German

*Print/Media Buyer:* Kris Waller
*Permissions Editor:* Elizabeth Zuber
*Production Service:* Graphic World
*Photo Researcher:* Graphic World
*Copy Editor:* Graphic World
*Cover Designer:* Roy Neuhouse
*Printer:* Phoenix Color Corp
PHOTO CREDITS: **1.** © 1998 Comstock;
**73.** © M. Siluk/The Image Works; **405.**
© J. Fossett/The Image Works.

For more information about our products, contact us at:
Thomson Learning Academic Resource Center
1-800-423-0563
For permission to use material from this text, contact us by:
**Phone:** 1-800-730-2214
**Fax:** 1-800-730-2215
**Web:** http://www.thomsonrights.com

**Brooks/Cole—Thomson Learning**
10 Davis Drive
Belmont, CA 94002
USA

**Asia**
Thomson Learning
5 Shenton Way #01-01
UIC Building
Singapore 068808

**Australia/New Zealand**
Thomson Learning
102 Dodds Street
Southbank, Victoria 3006
Australia

**Canada**
Nelson
1120 Birchmount Road
Toronto, Ontario M1K 5G4
Canada

**Europe/Middle East/Africa**
Thomson Learning
High Holborn House
50/51 Bedford Row
London WC1R 4LR
United Kingdom

Library of Congress Control Number: 2002117214
ISBN 0-534-55685-X

# About the Authors

**Charles L. Thompson** is a professor of Counselor Education and Educational Psychology at The University of Tennessee at Knoxville. He received his bachelor's and master's degrees in science education and educational psychology from The University of Tennessee and his Ph.D. degree in counselor education and developmental and counseling psychology at The Ohio State University—where he held NDEA and Delta Theta Tau fellowships. Charles is a former teacher and counselor for grades 7 to 12. He holds memberships in the American Counseling Association, The American School Counselor Association, The American Mental Health Counselors Association, The Association for Counselor Education and Supervision, and the American Psychological Association. He is a licensed psychologist and a licensed school counselor and is board certified by the National Board of Certified Counselors. His research interests are in counselor education and individual counseling. He has published articles in *The Journal of Counseling & Development, The Elementary School Guidance & Counseling Journal, The School Counselor, Counselor Education and Supervision, Professional School Counseling, Journal of Mental Health Counseling,* and *The Journal of Counseling Psychology,* and he has co-written five books on counseling. He is co-author of *Educational Psychology: For Teachers in Training* and *Classroom Management for Teachers in Training* with Steven Banks. Charles was editor of the IDEA Exchange in the *Elementary School Guidance & Counseling Journal* from 1979 to 1997. Charles received the American Mental Health Counselors Association's Counselor Educator of the Year Award for 1996 and the Writer of the Year Award from The American School Counselor Association in 2001. His Website can be accessed at http://web.utk.edu/~thompson.

**Linda Rudolph** is professor emeritus of psychology from Austin Peay State University, Clarksville, Tennessee. From 1995 to 1998, she served as commissioner of the Tennessee Department of Human Services, appointed by Governor Don Sunquist. During her tenure as commissioner, Linda led the state's welfare reform initiative and focused on the need to improve child care. In January 1999 she accepted the position of senior officer for policy and planning with the Tennessee Higher Education Commission. She earned undergraduate and master's degrees in psychology and holds a doctorate in counselor education with a cognate area in psychology. She has taught psychology and counseling. She is a licensed professional counselor in the State of Tennessee and has served as both vice president and president for the state licensing Board for Professional Counselors and Marital and Family Therapists. Linda holds a membership in the American Counseling Association, the Tennessee Counseling Association, and the Association for Counselor Education and Supervision. She has been active in state, regional, and national counseling associations, presenting workshops on counseling with children as well as on her research into women's career choices. Her research has focused primarily on children of divorce, assessment, and the effects of women's backgrounds, values, and choices on their professional advancement. She has published numerous articles in professional journals and has co-written a chapter on women's career development in a textbook on counseling with women.

**Donna A. Henderson** is an associate professor of counselor education in the Department of Education at Wake Forest University in Winston-Salem, NC. She received her bachelor's degree in English from Meredith College, her master's degree from James Madison University and her Ph.D. degree in counselor education from the University of Tennessee, Knoxville. She is a former teacher and counselor for grades 7 to 12. She is a licensed school counselor and a licensed professional counselor. She holds memberships in the American Counseling Association and has been active in national, regional, and state counseling associations. She has been president of the North Carolina Counseling Association and the Southern Association for Counselor Education and Supervision. She has also served as Governing Council representative and is president-elect of the Association for Counselor Education and Supervision. Her research interests include counseling children, particularly in the school setting, and counselor education concerns. She is co-author for *The Handbook of School Counseling and Counselor Preparation,* 11th edition. She has written chapters on legal and ethical issues, developmental issues, creative arts and counseling, and other topics. She has had articles published in *The Journal for Specialists in Group Work, Arts in Psychotherapy, Journal of Family Therapy,* and *Elementary School Guidance and Counseling.*

# Dedicated to Our Families

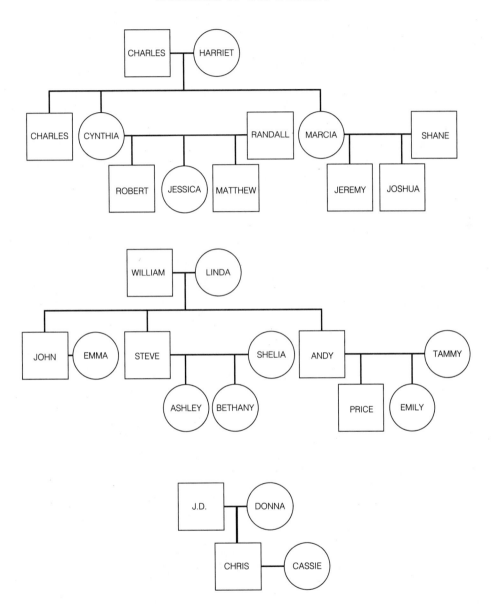

# Contents

✪

## Part One

## Introduction to Counseling Children    1

### Chapter 1
### *Introduction to a Child's World*    3

Indicators of Well-Being    4
   What Causes Our Children's Problems?    5
A Changing World    6
   The American Home    7
   Societal Crises    7
   Changing Values    8
   Summary of Children's Difficulties    8
The Personal World of the Child    9
Child Development    11
A Child's Cognitive World    12
The Child's World of Social Development    15
   Resilience    19
What is Counseling?    21
   How Does Counseling Differ from Psychotherapy?    21
   What Is an Appropriate Working Definition of Counseling?    21
What Counseling Can Do    22
   What Specific Types of Assistance Can Be Expected from the
      Counseling Session?    23
Who Are the Mental Health Professionals?    25
Websites for Understanding a Child's World    28
   References    28

### Chapter 2
### *The Counseling Process*    31

Which Approaches to Counseling Are Effective?    31
Classifying Counseling Theories    33
Preparing for the Interview    36
What Are Some Things to Consider During the First Interview?    37
   Children's Resistance to Counseling    37
A General Model for Counseling    42
   Step 1: Defining the Problem Through Active Listening    42
   Step 2: Clarifying the Child's Expectations    42
   Step 3: Exploring What Has Been Done to Solve the Problem    43
   Step 4: Exploring What New Things Could Be Done to Solve the
      Problem    43

Step 5: Obtaining a Commitment to Try One of the Problem-
    Solving Ideas    44
Step 6: Closing the Counseling Interview    44
Questions Counselors Ask    44
    What Does the Counselor Need to Know About Counseling
        Records?    44
    How Much Self-Disclosure Is Appropriate for the Counselor?    45
    What Types of Questions Should the Counselor Use?    46
    How Can Silences Be Used in Counseling?    49
    Should Counselors Give Advice?    49
    Should Counselors Give Information?    51
    How Does the Counselor Keep the Client on Task During the
        Counseling Session?    51
    What Limits Should Be Set in Counseling?    52
    What About the Issue of Confidentiality?    53
    Is This Child Telling Me the Truth?    53
    What Can Be Done When the Interview Process Becomes
        Blocked?    54
    When Should Counseling Be Terminated?    54
How Can Counseling Be Evaluated?    55
How Do Professional Counselors Work With Managed Health
    Care?    60
    Step 1: Problem Identification    66
    Step 2: Problem Definition    66
    Step 3: Goal Development    66
    Step 4: Measurable Objectives    66
    Step 5: Creating Interventions    67
    Step 6: Diagnosing    67
Websites for the Counseling Process    68
Websites for Information on Managed Care    69
    References    69

✹

_____ Part Two _____

**Counseling Theories and Techniques:
Adaptations for Children    73**

Chapter 3
*Psychoanalytic Counseling*    75

Sigmund Freud    75
The Nature of People    77
Theory of Counseling    79
    Structural Concepts    80
    Dynamic Concepts    81
    Developmental Concepts    82
    Psychosexual Stages    85

Psychoanalytic Counseling and Development of Self-Esteem    87
Object Relations Theory    90
Counseling Methods    92
Catharsis    93
Free Association    93
Interpretation    94
Analysis of Transference    95
Analysis of Resistance    96
Analysis of Incomplete Sentences    96
Bibliocounseling    97
Storytelling    97
Psychoanalytic Play Therapy and the Expressive Arts    98
Case Studies    101
Cross-Cultural Applications of Psychoanalytic Counseling    106
Psychoanalytic Counseling and Managed Health Care    106
Summary    107
Websites for Psychoanalytic Counseling    107
References    108

Chapter 4
*Reality Therapy*    110

William Glasser    110
The Nature of People    111
Choice Theory and the Nature of People    112
Theory of Counseling    116
Counseling Method    117
The Reality Therapy Process    121
Case Study    123
The 10-Step Reality Therapy Consultation Model    126
Cross-Cultural Applications of Reality Therapy    129
Reality Therapy and Managed Health Care    130
Summary    130
Websites for Reality Therapy    131
References    131

Chapter 5
*Brief Counseling: Solution-Focused and Paradoxical
Counseling Strategies*    133

Background    133
Solution-Focused Brief Counseling    134
The Nature of People    134
Theory of Counseling    135
Counseling Method    137
Setting Counseling Goals    138
Using the Miracle Question to Formulate Goals    140

Case Study    142
    Reviewing the Steps in Solution-Focused Brief Counseling    146
    Erickson Play Therapy    150
Paradoxical Counseling Strategies    150
    The Nature of People    150
    Theory of Counseling    151
    Counseling Method    152
    Case Examples    152
Cross-Cultural Applications of Brief Counseling    153
Brief Counseling and Managed Health Care    154
Summary    155
Websites for Brief Counseling    156
    References    156

## Chapter 6
### *Person-Centered Counseling*    *158*

Carl Rogers    158
The Nature of People    160
Theory of Counseling    160
Counseling Method    163
Case Study    169
Person-Centered Counseling and Development of Self-Esteem    171
    Integrating Self-Esteem–Building Activities with the Child's
        Life    172
Child-Centered Play Therapy    174
Cross-Cultural Applications of Person-Centered Counseling    175
Person-Centered Counseling and Managed Health Care    177
Summary    178
Websites for Person-Centered Counseling    180
    References    180

## Chapter 7
### *Gestalt Therapy*    *182*

Fritz Perls    182
The Nature of People    184
Theory of Counseling    186
Counseling Method    187
    Gestalt Techniques    188
    Gestalt Play Therapy    195
Case Studies    196
Cross-Cultural Applications of Gestalt Therapy    199
Gestalt Therapy and Managed Health Care    200
Summary    201
Websites for Gestalt Therapy    203
    References    203

Chapter 8
*Rational-Emotive-Behavior Therapy and
Cognitive-Behavior Therapy*    205

Albert Ellis    205
The Nature of People    206
Theory of Counseling    208
Counseling Method    212
    Rational-Emotive-Behavior Education    217
Cognitive-Behavioral Therapy    218
Case Study    221
    Applications of Cognitive-Behavioral Therapy    224
    Cognitive-Behavioral Play Therapy    227
Cross-Cultural Applications of REBT and CBT    228
REBT, CBT, and Managed Health Care    229
Summary    230
Websites for Rational-Emotive-Behavior Therapy    231
    References    232

Chapter 9
*Behavioral Counseling*    235

B. F. Skinner    235
The Nature of People    236
Theory of Counseling    237
    Behavior Analysis    238
    Steps in Behavior Analysis    239
    Schedules of Reinforcement    241
Counseling Goals    242
Counseling Methods    242
    Contingency Contracts    243
    Self-Management    244
    Shaping    245
    Behavioral Momentum    245
    Biofeedback    246
    Modeling    246
    Token Economics    247
    Behavior-Practice Groups    247
    Role-Playing    248
    Counseling Homework Assignments    249
    Assertiveness Training    250
Classical Conditioning Methods    250
    Ivan Pavlov    250
    Systematic Desensitization    251
    Flooding    254
    Hypnosis    255
    Counterconditioning    255
    Aversive Conditioning    255

Case Study    256
Applications of Behavioral Counseling    259
    Response Cost    260
    Eating Disorders    260
    Multimodal Approaches    261
Cross-Cultural Applications of Behavioral Counseling    261
Behavioral Counseling and Managed Health Care    262
Summary    262
Websites for Behavioral Counseling    263
    References    263

Chapter 10
*Transactional Analysis*    265

Eric Berne    265
The Nature of People and Theory of Counseling    266
    Structural Analysis    267
    Transactional Analysis    269
    Script Analysis    270
    Game Analysis    272
    Life Positions    272
    Games Clients Play    274
    The Pursuit of Strokes    276
    Rackets    279
Counseling Method    279
Case Studies    288
Cross-Cultural Applications of Transactional Analysis    290
Transactional Analysis and Managed Health Care    291
Summary    292
Websites for Transactional Analysis    292
    References    292

Chapter 11
*Individual Psychology*    294

Alfred Adler    294
The Nature of People    295
    The Need for Success    297
    Goals of Behavior    297
    Lifestyle    297
    Social Interest    298
    Family Environment    299
    The Family Constellation    299
    The Family Atmosphere    302
Theory of Counseling    304
    Goals of Misbehavior    306
    Attention    306

Power    307
Revenge    307
Inadequacy or Withdrawal    308
Counseling Method    309
Early Recollections    312
Interventions for the Four Goals of Misbehavior    314
Natural and Logical Consequences    318
Case Study    319
Adlerian Play Therapy    322
Adlerian Family Counseling    323
Cross-Cultural Applications of Individual Psychology    325
Individual Psychology and Managed Health Care    326
Websites for Individual Psychology    327
References    327

Chapter 12
*Family Counseling*    *330*

How Does Family Counseling Differ from Individual Counseling?    330
What Defines a Family?    331
How Does General Systems Theory Relate to Families?    331
The Systems Approach to Family Therapy    332
Murray Bowen    332
The Spousal Relationship    333
Differentiation of Self    333
Detriangulation of Self from the Family Emotional System    334
Nuclear Family Emotional Process    334
Family Projection Process    335
Multigenerational Transmission Process    335
Sibling Position    335
Emotional Cutoff    336
Emotional Process in Society    336
Emotional Systems of the Family    340
Modeling Differentiation    340
Structural Family Therapy    340
Salvador Minuchin's Contributions to Structural Family
Therapy    342
Strategic Family Therapy    345
Paradoxical Interventions    346
Contributions of Milton Erickson, Jay Haley, and Cloé Madanes to
Strategic Family Therapy    347
The Communications Approach to Family Therapy    351
John Gottman's Behavioral Interview Method    351
Virginia Satir's Conjoint Family Therapy    353
The Nature of People    354
Theory of Counseling    357
Counseling Method    361

An Example of Satir's Method    362
The Importance of Including Children    362
Three Keys to Satir's System    364
Satir's Technique    364
The Counselor's Role    367
Case Studies    367
Play Therapy with Families    369
Dynamic Family Play Therapy    370
Filial Therapy    370
Strategic Family Play Therapy    371
Theraplay    372
Cross-Cultural Applications of Family Counseling    372
Family Counseling and Managed Health Care    373
Summary    374
Websites for Family Therapy    375
Websites for Parenting    375
References    375

Chapter 13
*Personality Type*    378

Carl Jung    378
The Nature of People    380
Theory of Counseling    380
Psyche    380
Psychic Energy    381
Consciousness    381
The Personal Unconscious    381
The Ego    381
The Ego Gatekeeper    382
Complexes    383
Individuation    384
Dreams    384
Progression and Regression    384
The Collective Unconscious    385
Archetypes    385
Word Association    387
Psychological Types    387
The Type Table    394
Dominance    395
Temperament    395
Usefulness in Counseling    395
Psychological Diversity in Children    396
Theory of Type Development    397
Counseling Method    398
Case Study    400
Cross-Cultural Applications of Jung    403

Summary    403
Websites for Personality Type    403
    References    404

Part Three

# Counseling with Children: Special Topics    405

Chapter 14
*Play Therapy*    *407*

Defining Play Therapy    407
Advantages of Play Therapy    408
Cross-Cultural Applications of Play Therapy    409
Personal Qualities of a Play Therapist    411
Theories of Play Therapy    411
    Ecosystemic Play Therapy    411
    Jungian Play Therapy    412
Group Play Therapy    413
Prescriptive Play Therapy    414
Play Therapy With Families    414
    Dynamic Family Play Therapy    414
    Filial Therapy    415
    Strategic Family Play Therapy    416
    Theraplay    416
Considerations in Play Therapy    417
    Therapist    417
    Appropriate Clients    417
    Effectiveness of Play Therapy    418
    Play Stages    418
    Play Therapy and Managed Health Care    420
Play Therapy Media and Strategies    420
    Art    421
    Puppets    423
    Sand    424
Case Study    426
Summary    428
Websites for Play Therapy    429
    References    429

Chapter 15
*Counseling with Children from Different Cultures*    *434*

Introduction    434
Competence    435
    Multicultural Counseling Competencies    437
    Skills    441

Children    443
    African American Children    445
    Native American Children    447
    Asian American Children    449
    Latino Children    451
    Biracial Children    453
Summary    453
Websites for Counseling with Children from Different Cultures    454
    References    454

Chapter 16
*Consultation, Collaboration, Teamwork*    459

Consultation    459
    Models of Consultation    460
    Consulting Process    465
Collaboration    468
Teamwork    470
Combinations    472
Consultation Interventions    473
    Role Shift    473
    Listing of Behaviors    474
    Logical Consequences    474
    Isolation Techniques    474
    Assessment as a Consulting and Counseling Intervention    475
Case Histories    477
Summary    480
Websites for Consultation, Collaboration, Teamwork    480
    References    481

Chapter 17
*Group Counseling with Children*    484

Definition of Group    484
Types of Groups    485
Theoretically Oriented Group Counseling    486
Group Leadership Skills    488
Getting Started    489
    Group Focus    489
    Selecting Group Members    491
    Forming a Group    492
    Screening Interview    493
    Size of Group    493
    The Group Setting    494
    Group Stages    494
The Group Counseling Process    495
    The First Session    495
    Guidelines for the Remaining Sessions    496

Implications for Different Ages    497
Evaluation of Groups    499
Group Crisis Intervention    502
Summary    504
References    504

Chapter 18
*Counseling Children with Special Concerns*    508

Child Maltreatment    508
Psychological Maltreatment    510
Physical Abuse    511
Child Sexual Abuse    511
General Counseling Strategies for Working with Abused Children    515
Children's Memories of Abuse    517
Children of Alcoholics    519
Children in Cults    521
Death and Bereavement    523
Depression and Suicide    527
Family Structures    532
Children of Divorce    532
Children in Stepfamilies    538
Children in Single-Parent Homes    541
Homeless Children    542
Latchkey Children    544
Children and Violence    545
Gangs    549
Websites for Counseling Children with Special Concerns    552
References    553

Chapter 19
*Counseling with Exceptional Children*    559

The Situation of the Exceptional Child    559
History    561
Categories of Exceptionality    562
Methods for Counseling with Exceptional Children    569
The Gifted Child    570
Children with Emotional or Behavioral Disorders    573
The Child with a Learning Disability    575
Attention Deficit–Hyperactivity Disorder and Attention Deficit
Disorder    578
The Child with Mental Retardation    581
The Child with a Physical Disability    583
General Guidelines    584
Counseling with Parents of Exceptional Children    585

Summary    586
Websites for Counseling with Exceptional Children    587
    References    587

Chapter 20
*Legal and Ethical Considerations for Counselors*    589

Competence    591
Parental Permission    591
Confidentiality    592
    Confidentiality of Files    595
    Breaching Confidentiality    596
    Confidentiality in Groups    597
Child Abuse Reporting    597
Summary    598
Test Your Ethical Knowledge    598
Summary    604
Websites for Legal and Ethical Considerations for Counselors    605
    References    605

❂

Appendixes

Appendix A
*Children's Conflicts with Others: Alternatives for Intervention*    609

Appendix B
*Children's Conflicts with Self*    626

Appendix C
*Conversion Tables*    642

Appendix D
*Questions for Licensing*    647

# Preface

The Sixth Edition of *Counseling Children* is a significant event marking the changing of the guard. Linda Rudolph, a most valued friend and partner in the authorship of five editions of *Counseling Children* has turned her portions of our book over to Donna Henderson of Wake Forest University. Linda has retired and is now Emeritus Professor of Psychology at Austin Peay State University. Donna Henderson, like Linda Rudolph, is a former doctoral student of mine who has made significant achievements in the counseling profession. The very best part of being a professor occurs when students partner with their professors on research and other scholarship efforts. I have been blessed to have had the privilege of working with two such graduates as Linda Rudolph and Donna Henderson.

The strength of *Counseling Children, Sixth Edition* rests on our goal of putting theory into practice for established professionals and for people preparing to work with children and their families. Counselors, psychologists, social workers, and teachers will find the book useful in developing approaches for teaching children how to meet their needs in ways that do not infringe on the rights of others to meet their needs. We integrate the best ideas from research and practice into straightforward, up-to-date methods and interventions for helping children with specific developmental, social, educational, personal, or behavioral problems. We have included specific suggestions for counseling children who are exceptional; who are experiencing divorce, death, abuse, homelessness, or drug and alcohol problems; and who are victims of AIDS, cults, bullying, or violence. Cross-cultural adaptations for the various theories and interventions are made throughout the book, as are developmental considerations for the differing stages of child development.

The sixth edition of *Counseling Children* is dedicated to the principle that effective counselors and therapists adapt their system of counseling to the clients they serve rather than forcing clients to adapt to one rigid system they may prefer. That is, effective counselors are integrative in their counseling as they adapt interventions and techniques from a variety of theoretical systems into their counseling system. Therefore, one of our goals is to present accurate descriptions of a variety of theories from which our readers can develop their own approaches to counseling.

Mental health service providers will find this edition especially useful with our expanded coverage of managed care health programs and how to work with them. Brief counseling theories, techniques, and interventions that are adaptable to the limited number of sessions imposed by MCOs are discussed. School counselors, as well as mental health counselors, will find the chapters on brief counseling, choice theory reality therapy, behavioral counseling, rational emotive behavioral counseling, individual psychology, and family counseling particularly well-suited to the time limitations that they face in their daily work.

## ORGANIZATION

We have updated each chapter. Our evaluation of current trends in counseling children have resulted in the following changes.

In Part One, we look at some of the causes of children's problems as well as the resiliency of the majority of young people. We try to describe the world of the child by looking at theories of child development—Piaget's stages of cognitive development, Erikson's theory of social development, Freud's psychosexual stages of development, Havighurst's developmental tasks, and Selman's description of changes in perspective taking. Next we explore best practices that contribute to counseling being effective and consider counseling as a remedial, preventive, or developmental activity. The definition and description of counseling, as well as some questions counselors often ask about the process, are discussed in this section also. Finally, one way of evaluating counseling progress and working with managed health companies are addressed.

The order of presentation of the counseling theories in Part Two of the book was based on the following logic. Psychoanalytic counseling theory was presented first because many of the prominent approaches to counseling were developed in opposition to principles in Freud's theory. Also, in spite of their opposition to Freud, many theorists have retained some key ideas from Freud's system. Reality therapy and solution-focused brief counseling were included next because they offer students some practical counseling skills early in the semester that they can use in their work and in their field experiences. These two models also meld with the managed care realities of the mental health counseling profession and with the time restrictions faced by school counselors. We also want to teach active listening skills in person-centered counseling early in the term to help our students do a better job with reality therapy and solution-focused counseling.

A primary objective of the theory and practice of counseling class is to provide our students with a basic counseling game plan to prepare them for their practicum. Our experience has been that active listening in tandem with reality therapy and solution-focused counseling provides the basic skills counselors need to be successful in their first counseling experience.

Gestalt therapy is offered next for its unique counseling interventions which are helpful additions to the beginning counselor's repertoire. Rational emotive behavior therapy, cognitive behavioral therapy, and behavior therapy follow next to add skills for working with clients who respond well to cognitive and behavioral interventions. Transactional analysis is presented next to provide students with a series of techniques to help children, adolescents, and adults understand (1) how they transact their communications and business with other people, (2) how their personality developed, and (3) how life scripts can be rewritten when the need arises. The Adlerian and family counseling chapters are presented to provide students with a wide choice of methods for working with families ranging from individual psychology and conjoint family therapy to structural, strategic, and systems approaches to family counseling. The Jung chapter, a new addition to the book, is presented next because it offers a different view of personality development, and it provides a nice introduction to play therapy in part three. We have found in our surveys that all professors have different preferences for the order in which they prefer to present the material in the chapters. We encourage each of you to continue doing what works best for you.

Part Three begins with a chapter about play therapy techniques and theories that have not been included in the theories chapters. An expanded discussion of counseling children from different cultures includes multicultural competencies, identity development, and other general concepts as well as information specific for particular populations of children. We talk about three interventions that might be useful when working with parents, teachers, or other adults in the chapter on consultation, collaboration, and teamwork. Ways of working with children in groups are outlined, as are the legal and ethical guidelines that guide a counseling practice. An extended discussion on working with children with special concerns rounds out the topics covered in Part Three.

## ACKNOWLEDGMENTS

We appreciate the encouraging support of our work from many people at our universities and in our communities. We also acknowledge our reviewers, who gave us expert advice and constructive criticism: Sally Murphy, George Mason University; Steven Berman, Lewis & Clark College; Thomas Trotter, University of Idaho; Elizabeth Ciaravino, University of Scranton; Jan Jirouch, Northern State University; John Worzbyt, Indiana University of Pennsylvania; John Felton, University of Evansville; and Mary Stinson, Jacksonville State University. We especially appreciate the top-drawer assistance given to us by our editor, Julie Martinez. Julie, like her predecessor at Brooks/Cole, scheduled the arrival of her son, Nathan, about the same time we began the sixth edition of *Counseling Children*. Well done, Julie! Thanks also to our assistant editor, Amy Lam, for her valuable help in moving our book through the completion stages. We wish to acknowledge Julie Harden for her manuscript preparation and editorial assistance.

Finally, we offer our spouses, Harriet, Bill, and J.D., our love and appreciation for their continuing patience, support, understanding, and encouragement. To our children, now adults of whom we are very proud, we extend our thanks for teaching us about children, parenting, and unconditional love. More recently, our education has been refreshed and enriched through the joys of grandparenting for Linda and Charles and the addition of a daughter-in-law for Donna (see our genograms)!

Charles L. Thompson
Linda B. Rudolph
Donna A. Henderson

*Go to the people*
*Learn from them*
*Love them*
*Start with what they know*
*Build on what they have*
*But of the best leaders*
*When their task is accomplished*
*Their work is done*
*The people will remark:*
*"We have done it ourselves."*

2000-year-old Chinese Poem

One hundred years from now it will not matter what my bank account was, the sort of house I lived in, or the kind of car I drove . . . but the world may be different because I was important in the life of a child.

Author Unknown

# PART ONE

# INTRODUCTION TO
# COUNSELING CHILDREN

# Chapter 1

# Introduction to a Child's World

*The honor of one is the honor of all.*
*The hurt of one is the hurt of all.*
—Creek Indian Creed

According to the most recent census (Child Trends, 2002), in 2000 there were 70.4 million children under the age of 18 in the United States. That number represents 26% of the total population. By 2020 that number is projected to be 77.2 million. We pride ourselves on being a child-oriented nation. Laws have been passed to prevent children from being misused in the workplace, to punish adults who physically or psychologically harm children, to provide means for all children to obtain an education regardless of their mental or physical condition, and to support programs for medical care, food, and clothing for children in need. Politicians have debated "save our children" issues such as educational reform, sex and violence on television, an adolescent girl's right to an abortion without parental consent, family-leave policies in the workplace, and ways of providing a more environmentally safe world for our children's future.

Indeed, what could possibly be considered more precious than children? They enrich our lives and contribute to our delight. Certainly the unbounded joy of children frolicking on a playground brings smiles to the eyes of the beholder. Most teachers and other adults who interact often with young people have a storehouse of the humorous sayings and extraordinary wisdom of their charges. Children help us remember the wonder of the world. Many of us have had chances to refine our "mature" views after considering a careful answer to a question stemming from the curiosity of a younger one. Children bring us delight in these and so many other ways.

Furthermore, we know what children need to thrive. They need a place to live, adequate food and clothing, affordable health care, and safety. They need freedom from stress, caring relationships with family and friends, and positive role models. They also need opportunities to succeed in school and at other activities. Children need support and guidance as they move to adulthood.

Yet forces that impede their opportunities for a childhood of manageable cares scar the days of too many children and adolescents. Pietrzak, Petersen, and Speaker (1998) reported that when asked to rank student behaviors that had increased or greatly increased within the last 2 years, the top 10 chosen were verbal intimidation or threats (61%), increase in biologically damaged children (60%), punching and/or hitting (50%), rumors among peers/peer escalation of rumors (46%), punching and/or hitting (open or closed hand) (42%), sexual harassment including inappropriate sexual behavior (36%), classroom vandalism (34%), kicking (34%), lack of conflict resolution skills/other people skills (30%), and possession of knives/ice picks/razors (23%). Data from the Children's Defense Fund (2002) further delineate the difficulties in childhood. According to that organization, every day in America

5 children or youth under 20 commit suicide
9 children or youth under 20 are homicide victims
9 children or youth under 20 die from firearms
34 children and youth die from accidents
180 children are arrested for violent crimes
367 children are arrested for drug abuse
1,329 babies are born to teen mothers
2,019 babies are born into poverty
2,861 high school students drop out
4,248 children are arrested
7,883 children are reported abused or neglected (www.childrensdefense.org)

Barriers to the well-being of young people contribute significantly to these grim statistics. Every adult could discover ways to ameliorate those difficulties—ways as distant as casting an informed vote or as up close and personal as becoming a volunteer Big Brother or Big Sister. Mental health professionals have myriad possibilities for making the world healthier for children and more supportive of positive, productive development. Counselors who work with children learn to balance an appreciation for the gifts of childhood with the reality of a world of challenges. Knowledge of indicators of well-being, supportive factors, healthy environments, and productive working alliances allows counselors to work for the mental health of children.

## INDICATORS OF WELL-BEING

The behaviors of mentally healthy children include their functioning well at home, in school, and in their communities (Surgeon General, 2000). Children must be understood in the contexts of these social settings—with their family, peers, and others. Brazelton and Greenspan (2000), a pediatrician and a child psychiatrist, wrote about what they call the "irreducible needs" for a child to grow, learn, and thrive. Their list of the fundamental components for children's health include the following:

- Continuing, nurturing relationships
- Physical protection and safety with regulations to safeguard those needs

- Experiences tailored to individual differences for each child's optimal development
- Developmentally appropriate opportunities as building blocks for cognitive, motor, language, emotional, and social skills
- Adults who set limits, provide structure, and guide by having appropriate expectations
- A community that is stable and supportive and consistent

Some children are born into warm and loving homes that provide excellent environments for growth and development. Many children pass successfully through the developmental stages of childhood and adolescence and become well functioning adults. Other children overcome the adversities of their childhoods and go on to lead productive and meaningful lives. These children have the resilience to carry them through neglect, abuse, poverty, and other unfavorable home conditions. A later section in this chapter discusses that ability to ward off potentially negative forces, barriers that we will discuss next.

## What Causes Our Children's Problems?

Tommy is a fifth grader referred for counseling because of "lack of motivation." He is a loner who does not seem to want friends. He appears unenthusiastic about life—nothing interests or excites him. He has begun to exhibit signs of aggressiveness—increased fighting and abusive language. His teachers are concerned about this trend in his behavior.

Rochelle is a first grader whose parents have recently divorced. Her mother and father have found other partners, and in the excitement of their new lives, they have little time for Rochelle. She is very confused about whom she can rely on and trust. At this very crucial point in her school life, she is floundering in an unstable world. Her grades are falling, and she is withdrawing from interactions with adults and peers.

Stacie's family lives in abject poverty. Neither parent completed high school. Neither has been able to hold a steady job. Stacie's few clothes are too small for her and sometimes not clean. She often does not have lunch or lunch money, and she complains about being hungry at home. At school, she seems to be in her own dream world.

Carlos, a fourth grader, has been acting out since the first grade, and no one has been able to work with him effectively. He comes from a family that has obvious wealth, and his parents have tried to provide him with care and loving support. Carlos is constantly in trouble for hitting, lying, and name-calling. He has now begun to fight in class, on the playground, and with children in his neighborhood. There are rumors about spouse abuse in his family.

Mike has been diagnosed as having attention deficit–hyperactivity disorder (ADHD), but his parents refuse to accept the diagnosis. They blame the school for Mike's learning and behavior problems. Mike is two grades behind in reading and a constant disruption in his classroom. The teacher has given up, saying that she cannot help Mike unless his parents cooperate with her educational plan.

## A CHANGING WORLD

Parents like to think that children are immune to the stressful complexities and troubles of the rapidly changing adult world. They see childhood as a carefree, irresponsible time, with no financial worries, societal pressures, or work-related troubles. Many adults who consider themselves child advocates do not understand children's perceptions. They do not believe a child's concerns matter much and see children as largely unaware of what is happening politically and economically. Adults who underestimate children's awareness of the world may also misjudge children in other matters. Our experience in working with children has been that they are effective problem solvers and decision makers when they have the opportunity to be listened to and guided in a nonthreatening counseling atmosphere.

Normal child development involves a series of cognitive, physical, emotional, and social changes. Almost all children at some time experience difficulty in adjusting to the changes, and the accompanying stress or conflict can lead to learning or behavior problems. Normal child development tasks include achieving independence, learning to relate to peers, developing confidence in self, coping with an ever-changing body, forming basic values, and mastering new ways of thinking and new information. Numerous factors in children's lives require them to adapt, including changes in home or school locations, death or divorce in the family, and major illnesses. A high degree of stress has been found to be strongly associated with behavior symptoms. Add the stresses and conflicts of a rapidly changing society—which even adults find difficult to understand—to normal developmental concerns, and the child's world does not look so appealing.

Orton (1997) detailed the world as having many faces of poverty. She discussed the poverty of resources with more than 14 million U.S. children as victims. Hunger, poor housing, unemployment, and homelessness are evidence of this type of poverty. The impact is staggeringly dismal. Orton also talked about the poverty of tolerance for each other and for anyone who is dissimilar. Intolerance and the ignorance and fear it engenders reduce the quality of life for us all. The poverty of time relates to the widespread fatigue of a life too fast and of demands too great. Finally, Orton pointed out what she considers a poverty of values. Her examples include the high incidence of abuse, crime, and violence. Her explanation of these difficulties of the world helps us understand the stresses of childhood.

Herr (1998) stated that four primary challenges in the coming years will influence counselors' work: technology and the global economy, the changing American family, cultural diversity, and working with at-risk populations. Herr reminded counselors that they do not practice in a vacuum. Their work is influenced by political, social, cultural, and economic factors that affect the nation at large or a group within the nation. Counselors need to heed these contextual dimensions of the child's world.

In summary, counselors will need to be prepared to work with issues of separation, divorce, and differing family structures; increased stresses and differences among cultures; the effect of a changing world on the family and work environment; poor parenting and home conditions that lead to academic, social, and emotional problems in children; the need for sex education at younger ages to protect children from disease and early pregnancy; gangs and the violence that accompanies membership in them; and violence in general that results from societal influences such as abuse, alcohol and drugs, television, role modeling, anger, and other factors.

## The American Home

According to developmental psychologists, children need warm, loving, and stable home environments in order to grow and develop in a healthy manner. Brazelton and Greenspan (2000) have emphasized that environment as an irrevocable need. Years ago, children lived in large, stable, extended families. Fathers worked on the land, mothers labored in the home, and often grandparents or an unmarried aunt or uncle lived with the family. Many adults were around when a child needed to talk or needed to feel special to someone. Decisions about social activities, careers, and marriage were relatively simple: The choices were restricted, and the expectations were clear.

In today's society the home is not so simple. Family constellations include intact families, single-parent homes, teen-parent families, intergenerational families, and blended families. Grandparents may live 3,000 miles away and be almost unknown to their grandchildren. Aunts and uncles seldom live nearby; in any case, they are often busy pursuing individual interests and careers. Parents may work long hours to provide financial security for their families and then are expected to attend meetings or other community events at night. Mothers still shoulder the primary responsibility for the care of the home, so they are often occupied at night with washing, ironing, or cleaning. Single parents assume the roles of both mother and father, doubling the burden on the parent and leaving little time free for children. Garbarino (1997) reported some estimates of a 50% decrease in the last 30 years of constructive parent–child time. Children may not be able to find someone to listen or to provide the care and guidance they need, even though adults are present.

## Societal Crises

Not only do many children live in unstable homes but also they are continually confronted by conflict-ridden society. The media report the high cost of life's necessities—food, shelter, clothing—almost daily. The war on poverty has not been won, and children are some of the most vulnerable victims. Job markets change rapidly, and career planning is hampered by uncertainties about future demand for specific skills. Those adults with jobs are often dissatisfied. Crime seems to be everywhere, and many neighborhoods are no longer safe for children or adults. The cost of vandalism to schools and other private and public property is astronomical. People are increasingly cynical and distrustful of local, state, and federal government. Once-respected public figures, corporate leaders, and government agencies have engaged in criminal or highly unethical practices. Finally, we live in a world full of tensions, war, and the threat of terrorism that can strike anywhere at any time.

## Changing Values

Although change can be frightening or confusing, especially for a child, it can also be wondrous and exciting. It can bring new discoveries in medicine, new ideas for recreation, different jobs, new ways of living—all areas of life may be affected.

The children of today are forming values in a constantly and rapidly changing world. What is right or wrong seems to change daily or vary with the person. Who is right concerning standards of sexuality, cohabitation, alternative lifestyles, or abortion? Are the various liberation movements good or bad? How does a person behave in a world with changing gender roles? Will drugs really harm a person? Should society condone mercy killing? Is capital punishment justified? Adults with mature thinking processes and years of life experience have trouble making rational judgments on such ethical and moral issues.

## Summary of Children's Difficulties

No simple answer to what causes our children's problems emerges. The home, society, and changing values contribute to both the well-being and the difficulties of childhood. The impact of poverty may cause children to do without a home, food, or medical care. Families under stress may abuse or neglect children, may not adequately supervise the young person, and may provide a dearth of learning opportunities. Children need to feel loved and valued at home, at school, and in their communities; a truth that deserves emphasis.

Children in today's world are expected to grow, mature, and make critical decisions at a very young age. Counselors are now seeing psychosomatic symptoms—stomachaches, headaches, fevers, and other physical symptoms—in children who feel pressured by adults or society.

Some children enjoy secure childhoods that prepare them to meet the challenges of contemporary society. We encourage adults to investigate the increase in learning, behavioral, and emotional problems; drinking and drug abuse; runaways; suicides; lack of commitment; and the numerous other problems children face. Although every adult was once a child, as early as the days of Socrates and Aristotle, adults felt that the younger generation was "going to the dogs." However, past generations did not have to deal with a gap in understanding compounded by the complexities of today's society.

# THE PERSONAL WORLD OF THE CHILD

The various social and cultural conditions we have been discussing can have a profound effect on the child's personal and psychological world. Maslow (1970) believed we all have certain basic needs that must be met for us to become "self-actualizing" and reach our potential in all areas of development (Figure 1-1). If our lower-level basic needs are not met, we will be unable to meet higher-order needs. His ideas suggest why our children are experiencing more learning and behavior problems.

The first level of Maslow's hierarchy is physiological needs for food, shelter, water, and warmth. We might be tempted to pass these needs by and believe that the children of today are fed well and have adequate shelter and clothes. However, we must consider the number of children who participate in breakfast programs in schools or who do not get breakfast either at home or at school, as well as the poor diet of some children who may consume an adequate quantity of food. We are just beginning to learn about the relationship between diet and academic and behavioral problems, such as hyperactivity and inability to learn. Some recent research has focused on the possibility that an inadequate diet may contribute to mental illness in adolescents. Are we truly meeting the physiological needs of our children?

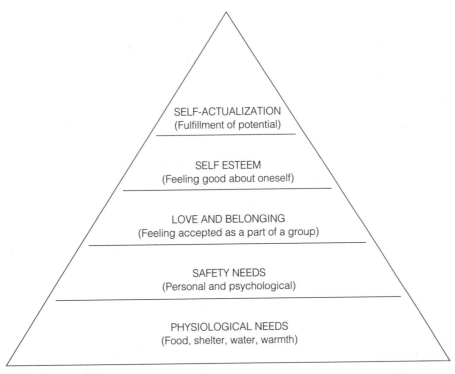

FIGURE 1-1   Maslow's hierarchy of needs

Maslow's second level is the need for safety. Again, we may be tempted to ignore this level at first glance. However, can we say that our children really feel safe, that they have little to fear? Some children feel afraid for their physical safety in their own homes. Because their own needs are not adequately met, parents may take out their frustrations on the child through physical or psychological abuse. Some adults who would not think of hurting children physically will psychologically abuse them with demeaning and damaging words. Children may receive similar treatment in school, where teachers may use children as a safe target for their personal or professional frustration. Children are afraid not only of adults but also of their peers. Consider Antonio, who is small for his age, is rather shy, and has few friends. As Antonio enters school one morning, several bigger guys tell him they will be waiting to get him this afternoon. Antonio cannot be expected to learn his multiplication tables with this problem weighing on his mind! Antonio's fear may not be limited to home and school. For some children, a high crime rate makes the neighborhood threatening. In addition, television news vividly portrays the dangers of natural disasters such as hurricanes, tornados, and earthquakes as well as other all too prevalent acts of violence. Finally the threat of war also seems ever present, and recent acts of terrorism threaten everyone's sense of personal safety.

Even if Antonio feels safe and protected, his learning or behavior may be influenced by the need to feel loved and to belong—the third level need that emerges, according to Maslow, after physiological and safety needs have been met. Humans are social beings who want to feel part of a group, a need fulfilled by children's cliques, gangs, and clubs, as well as in the family. Wherever we are, most of us want to be loved and accepted and to fit in with the group. Antonio may not be getting positive attention from adults or peers, and he may think that no one likes him. Children sometimes hide their feelings of rejection or compensate for the rejection with antisocial behavior; either defense can hurt learning and personal relationships.

Perhaps children have the most trouble satisfying their need for self-esteem—the fourth need in Maslow's hierarchy. Children are ordered, directed, commanded, criticized, devalued, ignored, and put down. An adult treated like a child feels annoyance, inferiority, defensiveness, and anger and may rebel, fight, or leave the scene. Such responses are not considered acceptable in children. All people—adults and children—need to be respected as worthwhile individuals, capable of feeling, thinking, and behaving responsibly. Children can be treated with the warmth and respect needed to encourage their learning within firm guidelines and expectations. Cruel and thoughtless remarks can be avoided, criticisms can be reduced, and positive interactions can be accentuated to build self-respect and self-confidence.

Satisfaction of needs at the first four levels contributes to achievement of the fifth need in Maslow's hierarchy—self-actualization. Maslow stated that a self-actualized person is moving toward the fulfillment of his or her inherent potential. Fulfilling this need implies that the child is not blocked by hunger, fear, lack of love or feelings of belonging, or low self-esteem. The child is not problem-free but has learned problem-solving skills and can move forward to become all that he or she can be.

According to Glasser (see Chapter 4), society is not meeting our children's needs, and thus they are failing in school and in life, academically and behaviorally. He listed five needs of all persons: (1) the need to survive and reproduce, (2) the need to belong and love, (3) the need to gain power, (4) the need to be free, and (5) the need to have fun. Glasser stated that children's problems relate to their inability to fulfill these needs and emphasized teaching reality, right and wrong, and responsibility.

Adlerian psychologists believe that children often attempt to meet their needs in a mistaken direction. They suggest that adults examine the goals of misbehavior and redirect the behavior toward achieving more satisfying results.

Behavioral psychologists see academic and behavior problems as resulting from faulty learning. The child has learned inappropriate ways of behaving through reinforcement or from poor models. Unlearning or extinguishing inappropriate patterns and learning more appropriate behaviors help the child succeed.

Bronfenbrenner (1993) proposed an ecological systems theory of human development. That model suggests the complex system within which a person exists and grows. Any person lives within nested systems that include an immediate environment with expanding connections beyond the home, school, and other settings. Bronfenbrenner called the closest level of the environment the microsystem, the activities and interactions in a child's immediate surroundings. He emphasized that those interactions are bidirectional; for example, the parent's child-rearing practices affect the child, and the child's temperament affect parenting practices. The mesosystem refers to the connections between the immediate environment and other systems that support the child—for example, the parent's workplace. The exosystem relates to social settings yet another step removed from the individual, such as health policy and unemployment. The outermost level of this model is the macrosystem, not a specific context but rather the laws, customs, and resources of the society in which the child lives. Bronfenbrenner delivered a comprehensive look at the many factors that influence childhood as well as a way to categorize those variables.

Whatever the factors contributing to children's learning, behavioral, and social problems, parents, counselors, and other professionals must assist and support children as they grow and develop in this complex, changing world. Understanding the process of development helps adults provide that support. The following section of this chapter includes a review of a few of the developmental theories of cognitive, psychosocial, moral, and optimal development.

## CHILD DEVELOPMENT

Children and adolescents bound through physical, cognitive, social, and emotional changes almost daily. A critical aspect in defining their mental health is their successful movement through the normal developmental milestones. As noted previously, other indicators of success are their secure attachments, satisfying relationships, and effective coping skills. Development can be understood as periods of transition and reorganization—a lifelong process of growing, maturing, and change. One challenge in working with children is the different interpretations of behaviors according to different ages. LeVine and Sallee (1992) explained that one child may display certain symptoms at one stage of development and completely different symptomatic behavior at another stage. They cited an example of a child expressing anger with a temper tantrum at age 3 and with drug abuse at 13. Counselors must be steeped in knowledge of normal development to understand mental health in children. The following sections review just a few of those important concepts.

## A CHILD'S COGNITIVE WORLD

Cognitive development refers to the thinking skills of the child. According to Jean Piaget (Piaget & Inhelder, 1969), children move to increasingly sophisticated thought processes as they progress through four stages (Table 1-1). Those distinct patterns of thought occur in the stages of sensorimotor (birth to age 2), preoperational (2–7), concrete operations (7–11), and formal operations (after 11).

The work of Piaget and Inhelder (1969) established that children aged 5 to 12 may function in as many as three stages of cognitive development. Although age is no guarantee of a child's stage of development, 5- and 6-year-olds are on the verge of moving from the preoperational to the concrete stage of cognitive development, and 11-year-old children are moving into the formal stage. The counselor must know the child's level of cognitive development, particularly the degree to which a child is able to engage in abstract reasoning, a characteristic of the formal thinking stage. Children in the concrete thinking stage need explicit examples, learning aids, and directions. For example, the concrete thinker can walk through a series of directions but cannot draw a map of the same route.

Counseling methods need to be matched with the child's cognitive ability if counseling is to be effective. Piaget characterized the preoperational child's behavior and thinking as egocentric; that is, the child cannot take the role of or see the viewpoint of another (see Wadsworth, 1989). Preoperational children believe that everyone thinks the same way and does the same things they do. As a result, preoperational children never question their own thoughts; as far as they are concerned, their thoughts are the only thoughts possible and consequently must be correct. When they are confronted with evidence that is contradictory to their thoughts, they conclude that the evidence must be wrong because their thoughts cannot be. Thus, from the children's point of view, their thinking is always logical and correct. This egocentrism of thought is not egocentric by intent; children remain unaware that they are egocentric and consequently see no problem in need of resolution.

Wadsworth (1989) added that not until about age 6 or 7, when children's thoughts and those of their peers clearly conflict, do children begin to accommodate others and egocentric thoughts begin to give way to social pressure. Peer group social interaction and the repeated conflict of the child's own thoughts with

TABLE 1-1   Piaget's four stages of cognitive development

| Stage | Type of development | Age | Cognitive traits |
|-------|---------------------|-----|------------------|
| Infancy | Sensorimotor | 0–2 | Children:<br>• Learn through their senses by touching, hitting, biting, tasting, smelling, observing, and listening<br>• Distinguish between "me" and "not me" world<br>• Learn about invariants in their environment (e.g., chairs are for sitting)<br>• Form language<br>• Develop habits<br>• Begin to communicate symbolically<br>• Can distinguish self and other objects<br>• Have the ability to think about things and engage in purposeful behavior<br>• Achieve a sense of object permanence<br>• Begin trial-and-error problem solving |
| Childhood | Preoperational | 2–7 | Children:<br>• Are not able to conserve in problem solving<br>• Have greatest language growth<br>• Are trial-and-error problem solvers who focus on one stimulus at a time<br>• Can classify objects more than one way (i.e., by shape, color, size, texture)<br>• Have trouble with reversible thinking<br>• Prefer to learn things in ascending rather than descending order<br>• Are egocentric thinkers<br>• Are able to use mental images, imagination, and symbolic thought<br>• Are capable of understanding simple rules—regarded as sacred and unchangeable |

*Continued.*

TABLE 1-1    Piaget's four stages of cognitive development *(continued)*

| Stage | Type of development | Age | Cognitive traits |
|---|---|---|---|
| Preadolescence | Concrete | 7–11 | Children:<br>• Have conversation skills<br>• Can do reversible thinking<br>• Have difficulty with abstract reasoning<br>• Can appreciate views of others<br>• Need concrete aids for learning<br>• Move toward logical thought<br>• Are less egocentric<br>• See rules as more changeable<br>• Can distinguish reality from fantasy<br>• Have greater capacity for concentration, attention, and memory<br>• Are capable of understanding that distance equals rate times time |
| Adolescence through adulthood | Formal | 11+ | Children:<br>• Have no need to manipulate objects to solve problems<br>• Are capable of abstract thought and scientific experimentation<br>• Are capable of understanding and applying ethical and moral principles<br>• Are capable of self-reflective thought and high levels of empathic understanding<br>• Have a sense of what is best for society |

those of others eventually jar the child to question and seek verification of his or her thoughts. The very source of conflict—social interaction—becomes the child's source of verification. Thus, peer social interaction is the primary factor that acts to dissolve cognitive egocentrism.

Elkind (1984, 1994) explained ways abstract thought affects the adolescent. Teenagers can combine facts and ideas to build an argumentative case as well as multiple reasons to invalidate any contradictions. He also discussed adolescent egocentrism. This self-centered nature of adolescent thinking may make communication processes difficult. One characteristic of adolescent thinking is the "imaginary audience," a concept involved in teenagers' self-consciousness that results from their belief that they are always at the center of everyone's attention. Public criticism can be devastating to a teenager. Another characteristic is the "personal fable," the belief that leads teenagers to feel invincible and immune from harm. That may lead to exaggerated expectations for self and to unwise risk taking. Adults need to recognize these tendencies when working with adolescents.

Other theorists (Selman, 1976; Selman & Bryne, 1974) also offered explanations of a child's and an adolescent's perspective taking, the capacity to imagine what someone else may be thinking and feeling. That ability supports important social skills needed to build and maintain relationships. In the first stage (ages 3–6), children have undifferentiated perspective taking. They may recognize that other people can have different thoughts and feelings than their own, but they confuse the separation. In social-informational perspective taking (4–9), children comprehend that other people may have different information and therefore different perspectives. Self-reflective perspective taking (ages 7–12) involves children being able to step into another person's views and see their own thoughts, feelings, and actions from the other person's perspective. They also recognize that other people have the same ability. For third-party perspective taking (ages 10–15), children move beyond the two-person situation and can imagine how they and others are seen from the view of a third, impartial party. With the last type, societal perspective taking (14 to adult), people understand that third-party perspective taking can be influenced by systems of societal values. Thus children move from a limited idea of what others might be thinking to a more differentiated view of the thoughts and feelings of others.

## THE CHILD'S WORLD OF SOCIAL DEVELOPMENT

Psychosocial development relates to the attitudes and skills needed to become a productive member of society. Erikson (1963, 1968) and Havighurst (1961) have written extensively about these stages of human development. Erikson described eight stages of human development from birth through adulthood beyond the age of 50. Havighurst, in a similar vein, described expectations and developmental tasks over the life span. Effective counselors are well informed about human development and know how to incorporate this knowledge into their methods.

Using Erikson's (1963, 1968) and Havighurst's (1961) systems as a frame of reference, counselors can compare expectations, human needs, and developmental tasks across the childhood years. Table 1-2 shows developmental tasks and necessary interventions for each of the eight stages of human development.

The two basic tasks are (1) coping with others' demands and expectations that conflict with people's own needs and (2) meeting these demands with the limited abilities they have in each developmental stage. Newman and Newman (1999) have extended Erikson's eight stages of human development to include three additional stages: prenatal, from conception to birth; later adolescence, from ages 18 to 22;

TABLE 1-2   Development tasks and interventions for the eight stages of human development

---

### STAGE I: BIRTH TO AGE 1½
*Basic Trust versus Basic Mistrust*

Task:

- Develop trust in their parents and environment
- Learn the world is safe, consistent, predictable, and interesting

Interventions:

- Children need responsive, affectionate, consistent caregivers who meet their basic needs in order to bond with others

### STAGE II: AGES 1½ TO 3
*Autonomy versus Shame and Doubt*

Task:

- Gain a sense of self-control as well as control over their environment

Interventions

- Children have gained trust, need to experience success in doing things for themselves
- Overly restrained or overly punished children develop a sense of shame and doubt

### STAGE III: AGES 3 TO 6
*Initiative versus Guilt*

Task:

- Develop a sense of initiative as opposed to feelings of guilt about never doing anything right

Interventions:

- Children begin to set goals and take leadership roles in carrying out projects
- Parent should empower children by giving them choices and allow them to participate in family activities
- Unacceptable behavior is corrected in a loving, caring manner
- Discipline is based on logical consequences
- Expectations are realistic in order to prevent guilt and anxiety

### STAGE IV: AGES 6 TO 12
*Industry versus Inferiority*

Task:

- Learn range of academic, social, physical, and practical skills needed in an adult world

Interventions

- Encouragement and praise will help children achieve competence and be productive
- Nurturing can help children develop special talents and abilities

---

TABLE 1-2   Development tasks and interventions for the eight stages of human development *(continued)*

### STAGE V: AGES 12 TO 18
#### Identity versus Role Confusion

Task:

- Develop a self-image, know who they are and how their roles will fit into their future

Interventions:

- Adults should make teens feel accepted as they develop their identity through group activities, work, or play
- Key questions are: "Who am I?" and "Where am I going?"
- Period of exploration for further education, training, jobs, career, and marriage

### STAGES VI, VII, AND VIII
#### Adult Stages

Tasks:

- Achieve intimacy through sharing a close friendship or love relationship in young adulthood
- Middle adulthood tasks are proper care of children and productive work life
- Older adults are concerned with ego integrity—acceptance of past life, a search for meaning in the present, and continued growth and learning in the future

Interventions:

- Must match young adult's counseling to learning style
- Adults may use concrete or abstract thinking in problem solving
- Issues in counseling often center on relationships, careers, and the search for meaning and purpose in life

and old age, from 75 until death. They pointed out that theories of human development emerge and change as development is shaped by biological and psychosocial evolution within the context of cultural, environmental, and genetic influences.

To become a contributing member of the world, a person must build relationships. A way of understanding that ability has been provided by some other developmental theorists. John Bowlby (1969) introduced the concept of attachment when studying the bond between a mother and infant. Bowlby stated that the pattern of early attachment formed the basis for later relationships. Attachment or these secure ties of affection give us pleasure and joy when we interact, as well as comfort in their nearness when we are stressed. Out of the experiences infants have with their caretakers, children build a set of expectations about the availability of attachment figures and the likelihood that those figures will provide support. Those expectations guide close relationships through childhood, adolescence, and adult years (Bretherton, 1992). Bowlby (1988) suggested that a therapist becomes an attachment figure who inspires trust in a client. That relationship then would become a secure base for clients to explore themselves and their relationships with others.

Ainsworth (1989) discussed attachments beyond infancy and related caregiving relationships to future friendships, kinship bonds, and intimate relations. Berk (2001) summarized support for the importance of attachment relationships. Researchers (Bartholomew & Horowitz, 1991; Kirkpatrick & Davis, 1994; Shaver & Brennan, 1992) asked adults to discuss their early bonds with parents, their attitudes toward intimate relationships, and their actual experiences with romantic partners. Consistent with Bowlby's (1969) premise, the memories and interpretations of childhood attachment indicated relationship experiences. Three models explain different types of attachments. People who report secure attachment had parents they described as warm, loving, and supportive. The adults considered themselves likable and easy to get to know. They were comfortable with intimacy and rarely worried about being abandoned or about someone getting too close to them. They talked about loving relationships in terms of trust, happiness, and friendship. Peers of people with secure attachments talk about competent, charming, cheerful, and likable young adults (Kobak & Sceery, 1988).

The two types of insecure attachments are avoidant and resistant. People who report avoidant attachment described their parents as demanding, disrespectful, and critical. As adults, they mistrusted partners and had anxiety about people getting too close to them. They believed that others did not like them and that love is elusive. Their intimate relationships were apt to include jealousy, emotional distance, and lack of acceptance. Finally, adults who discussed resistant attachment characterized their parents as unpredictable and unfair. Those adults wanted to merge with their significant others. They worried about intense feelings overwhelming them and about being abandoned by those they love. Their relationships included jealousy, emotional highs and lows, and desperation (Berk, 2001).

Children must build relationships with siblings and peers as well as with adults. These bonds also change over time. Toddlers have few social skills. Time with others involves playing side by side. As children mature, they learn the give-and-take of relationships. Children who can form close friendships have highly developed social skills. They can interpret and understand other children's nonverbal cues. They can respond appropriately to what other children say. They use eye contact and the other person's name and may touch the other person to get attention. If they disagree with a peer, they can explain why their plan is a good one. They are willing to forgo their desires to reach a compromise and may even change their stated belief. When they are with strange children, they observe until they have a sense of the group. Children without these skills tend to be rejected. They are withdrawn, do not listen well, and give few reasons for their wishes. They rarely praise others and have trouble participating in cooperative activities (Dodge, 1983; Dodge & Feldman, 1990; Putallaz, 1983).

These brief descriptions of a child's cognitive, personal, and interpersonal development illustrate the multiple factors that must be taken into account in constructing healthy environments. Developmental psychology also provides a base for understanding the range of normal and abnormal behaviors at various times in life. Many professionals in the mental health field rely on those areas of knowledge as they work with children.

The Surgeon General (2000) discussed principles necessary for understanding children's mental health. First, professionals must acknowledge the complexity of all of these: interactions within the child (biological, psychological, and genetic factors), the child's environment (parents, siblings, family relations, peers, as well as neighborhood, school, community, and national factors), and the way these factors interact. Therefore, the history of the child is crucial. Second, the report identifies the child's innate abilities to adapt. These "self-righting" and "self-organizing" tendencies allow a child to cope with the world. Third, the importance of age and timing in a professional's understanding of normality is stressed. Crying after separation from a caretaker seems normal for a 2-year-old and perhaps a disturbing symptom in a 10-year-old. A final point is that the difference between mental health and mental illness often involves only differences in degrees. These guidelines help professionals by identifying factors for recovery, reducing a tendency to oversimplify, offering perspectives to multiple targets for intervention, and highlighting windows of opportunity during a child's development. Counselors will be well served to take advantage of those possibilities.

## Resilience

One emerging research trend in child counseling is the concept of resiliency. Rak (2001) explained that counselors often question whether to help clients overcome problems or instead to focus on clients' strengths and resiliency. He provided some guidelines for focusing on resilience.

In a comprehensive article, Rak and Patterson (1996) defined resiliency in children as the ability "to continue to progress in their positive development despite being 'bent,' 'compressed,' or 'stretched' by factors in a risky environment" (p. 368). They stated that resiliency is not an uncommon phenomenon, citing many studies that found only a minority of children exposed to such high-risk factors as illness, disadvantage, poverty, parental alcoholism, family dysfunction, and other negative conditions experienced serious difficulties in their development. Many of those who did have difficulties were coping well with these issues by the time they reached middle adulthood, according to these researchers.

Resiliency tendencies can be augmented. Some authors (Benson, 1997; Garmezy, 1991; Hauser, 1999; Lowenthal, 1998; Werner & Smith, 1982) have studied resiliency and developed lists of protective factors or variables that act as buffers for the many children who overcome their difficulties to grow and lead well-adjusted lives. Those assets include personal factors, family factors, supportive other adults, and self-concept factors. The following list summarizes those supportive dimensions.

Resilient children have some common personal factors (Rak, 2001). They participate in an active approach to problem solving as they negotiate their world. As infants and beyond, they demonstrate the capacity to gain positive attention from other people. They tend to view experiences optimistically and maintain a positive vision of life's meaning. These young people seek out new experiences and have a proactive perspective toward life.

Some family factors alleviate the effects of multiple stressors. One factor is the age of parents—young mothers for resilient males and older fathers for females who are resilient. Another helpful asset is a family with no more than four children who are separated by more than 2 years. Resilient youth are apt to have had a nurturing first year with limited separation from caregivers. They have a network of relatives with similar values and beliefs who are available for counsel and support. The other family factor that protects young folks is having structure and rules in the home during their adolescence. Having a supportive group of other adults or a number of significant role models outside the family plays a critical part in building resilient youth. Those role models might be teachers, counselors, coaches, clergy, good neighbors, and other adults who serve as friends or mentors. The final area Rak (2001) discussed is the young person's ability to cope and to build a sense of victory over adversity. Werner (1984) described this more fully. He stated that these young people had at some time performed a role of "required helpfulness" by protecting another person from distress or discomfort. The result was an enduring sense of positive change. He further described resilient young people as having confidence in a reasonably good outcome that surmounts the odds against it.

In their explanation of resiliency, Rak and Patterson (1996) provided a set of questions to guide counselors in uncovering the patterns of helpful habits children have. Rak (2001) proposed that the counselor use this set of questions with follow-up responses to develop "an assessment that minimizes judgment, enhances salutogenesis [origins of health], and evaluates the client's life space, support systems, and capacity to endure and overcome" (p. 229). With this understanding of the child's historical pattern of resilience, counselors provide interventions to reinforce those patterns. Counselors also teach or model self-management and effective coping skills for problems and stressors.

1. Role plays that help young people learn to express themselves
2. Conflict resolution techniques to help through interpersonal difficulties
3. Nurturing, empathy, authenticity, realistic reinforcement, and genuine hope from the counselor
4. Modeling healthy interactions
5. Peer support interventions
6. Creative imagery
7. Bibliotherapy (Rak & Patterson, 1996)

Rak (2001) noted that counselors who work with resilience in mind do not focus on arriving at solutions or resolving conflicts. Rather, that type of counseling emphasizes the "client's reservoir" of resilient behavior.

Although some children do have the resiliency to survive a poor home environment, a growing number have emotional, behavioral, social, and other problems that warrant mental health treatment. Resources for counselors and others who work with children are increasing; however, clinical, agency, and school professionals have felt frustrated because information about specific counseling procedures for developmental, learning, and behavioral problems has been limited and difficult to obtain. This book provides people in clinical, agency, school, and other counseling situations with suggestions for counseling children with specific learning or behavioral problems.

## WHAT IS COUNSELING?

The American Psychological Association, Division of Counseling Psychology, Committee on Definition (1956), defined *counseling* as a process "to help individuals toward overcoming obstacles to their personal growth, wherever these may be encountered, and toward achieving optimum development of their personal resources" (p. 283). The National Conference of State Legislatures and the American Counseling Association (Glosoff & Koprowicz, 1990) defined *counseling* as "a process in which a trained professional forms a trusting relationship with a person who needs assistance. This relationship focuses on personal meaning of experiences, feelings, behaviors, alternatives, consequences, and goals. Counseling provides a unique opportunity for individuals to explore and express their ideas and feelings in a non-evaluative, non-threatening environment" (p. 8).

### How Does Counseling Differ from Psychotherapy?

Distinctions between counseling and psychotherapy may be superficial in that both processes have similar objectives and techniques. Table 1-3 summarizes some differences, which are often lost in the common ground they share. The key question about the domain of each process rests with counselors and therapists, who must restrict their practice to their areas of competence.

### What Is an Appropriate Working Definition of Counseling?

Counseling involves a relationship between two people who meet so that one person can help the other resolve a problem. One of these people, by virtue of training, is the counselor; the person receiving the help is the client. The terms *coun-*

TABLE 1-3   Comparison of counseling and psychotherapy

| *Counseling is more for:* | *Psychotherapy is more for:* |
|---|---|
| 1. Clients | 1. Patients |
| 2. Mild disorders | 2. Serious disorders |
| 3. Personal, social, vocational, educational, and decision-making problems | 3. Personality problems |
| 4. Preventive and developmental concerns | 4. Remedial concerns |
| 5. Educational and developmental settings | 5. Clinical and medical settings |
| 6. Conscious concerns | 6. Unconscious concerns |
| 7. Teaching methods | 7. Healing methods |

*selor* and *client,* which some view as dehumanizing, can be replaced by words such as *helper* and *helpee, child, adolescent, adult,* or *person.* In fact, Carl Rogers (see Chapter 6) referred to his client-centered counseling approach as *person-centered.* We see counseling as a process in which people learn how to help themselves and, in effect, become their own counselors. Counseling may also be a group process, in which the role of helper and helpee can be shared and interchanged among the group members. The group counselor then functions as a facilitator as well as a counselor.

Coleman, Morris, and Glaros (1987) credit David Palmer of the Student Counseling Center at UCLA with one of the best definitions we have found:

> To be listened to & to be heard . . .
> To be supported while you gather your forces & get your bearings.
> A fresh look at alternatives & some new insights; learning some needed skills.
> To face your lion—your fears.
> To come to a decision—& the courage to act on it & to take the risks that living demands. (p. 282)

## WHAT COUNSELING CAN DO

Mental health incorporates the way we think, feel, and act; how we look at ourselves, our lives, and other people; how we evaluate and make choices; and how we handle stress, relate to others, and make decisions. Mental health exists along a continuum from good to not so good to poor. A person may be mentally healthier at some times than at others. At certain times an individual may seek help for handling problems. A young person's performance in schoolwork, relationships, and physical health may suffer during difficult times. Mental health problems in children and adolescents may lead to school failure, violence, suicide, family distress, drug abuse, and a host of other difficult situations.

Approximately 1 in 5 children and adolescents may have a mental health problem (Surgeon General, 2000), and 1 in 10 may have a serious functional disturbance. That amounts to as many as 6 million children and adolescents. Mental illness occurs in all social classes and in all backgrounds.

If you were to ask elementary classroom teachers to estimate how many of their students are experiencing learning, emotional, or behavioral problems, how many do you think they would name? Then ask these teachers to predict how many of the approximately 30 students in each class will have serious trouble with the law or other adjustment problems in the future. Multiply these figures by the number of classrooms throughout the United States, and the estimates are overwhelming. We can change these statistics by becoming more effective professionals.

Counseling with children is a growing area of interest for people in the helping professions. Developmental theorists have studied children's growth and development and the effect of childhood experiences on the adult, whereas child psychiatry has focused on seriously disturbed children. However, children with learning, social, or behavioral problems who are not classified as severely disturbed have been largely overlooked. Counseling can prevent "normal" problems from becoming more serious and resulting in delinquency, school failure, and emotional disturbance. Counselors can work to create a healthy environment to help children cope with the stresses and conflicts of their growth and development. Counseling can also help children in trouble through appraisal, individual or group counseling, parent or teacher consultation, or environmental changes.

The principles of counseling with children are the same as those used with adults; however, the counselor needs to be aware of the world as the child sees it and adjust counseling procedures to suit the child's cognitive level, emotional and social development, and physical abilities. Each child is a unique individual with unique characteristics and needs. Childhood should be a time for healthy growth, for establishing warm and rewarding relationships, for exploring a widening world, for developing confidence in self and others, and for learning and experiencing. It should contain some fun and carefree times, and it should also provide a foundation and guidance for the maturing person.

## WHAT SPECIFIC TYPES OF ASSISTANCE CAN BE EXPECTED FROM THE COUNSELING SESSION?

Counseling generally involves three areas:

1. The client's thoughts and feelings about life at present
2. Where the client would like to be in life
3. Plans to reduce any discrepancy between (1) and (2)

The emphasis given to each area varies according to the counseling approach used. Nevertheless, most counseling approaches seem to share the ultimate goal of behavior change, although they may differ in the method used to attain that goal.

Perhaps the most important outcome for counseling occurs when clients learn how to be their own counselors. By teaching children the counseling process, we help them become more skilled in solving their problems and, in turn, become less dependent on others. In our view, counseling is a reeducative process designed to replace faulty learning with better strategies for getting what the child wants from life. Regardless of the counseling approach, children bring three pieces of information to the counseling session: (1) their problem or concern, (2) their feelings about the problem, and (3) their expectations of the counselor. Failure to listen for these points makes further counseling a waste of time.

Most problems brought to the counselor concerning children can be classified in one or more of five categories:

1. *Interpersonal conflict, or conflict with others:* The child has difficulty in relating with parents, siblings, teachers, or peers and is seeking a better way to relate to them.
2. *Intrapersonal conflict, or conflict with self:* The child has a decision-making problem and needs some help with clarifying the alternatives and consequences.

3. *Lack of information about self:* The child needs to learn more about his or her abilities, strengths, interests, or values.
4. *Lack of information about the environment:* The child needs information about what it takes to succeed in school or general career education.
5. *Lack of skill:* The child needs to learn a specific skill, such as effective study methods, assertive behavior, listening, or how to make friends.

In summary, counseling goals and objectives can range from becoming one's own counselor to positive behavior change, problem solving, decision making, personal growth, remediation, and self-acceptance. The counseling process for children often includes training in communication, assertiveness, and effective study; however, counselors choose the focus that seems most appropriate to the child and the child's situation. Some counselors prefer to work on developing meaning and purpose in everyday living, whereas others work toward solving specific problems (Figure 1-2). Of course, many counselors try to accomplish both ends. Conceivably, Child A could start at point –5 on both the *x*-axis and the *y*-axis and move toward +5 on both axes.

In counseling children in their middle childhood years (ages 5–12), for example, counselors may choose to work with problem areas in any or all of the quadrants represented in Figure 1-2. Some counselors prefer to work with the developmental and personal growth concerns found in Quadrant 1. The children in Quadrant 1 are solving their problems and seem to be finding purpose in living. They are sometimes referred to as stars because they get along well with their friends, teachers, and family.

Quadrant 1 children seem to have a winner's script for achieving their goals in academic, athletic, social, and artistic endeavors. Working with these children is often a matter of staying out of their way, helping them develop their full potential, and ensuring that they receive the appropriate teaching and parenting necessary for the development of their gifts and talents. This developmental model, emphasizing problem prevention over remediation, was pioneered by Herman J. Peters (Peters & Farwell, 1959), who encouraged counselors to focus on their clients' strengths as a way to facilitate their next steps up the developmental ladder. The developmental emphasis continues to be popular in counseling literature.

Quadrant 2 children find purpose in life but are not able to solve many of their problems. The counselor's role with these children is remedial in that counseling is directed toward establishing problem-solving strategies. Frequently these Quadrant 2 children have good interpersonal relationships but experience problems with academic achievement and self-concept. They lack the success identity found in Quadrant 1 children.

Quadrant 4 children do very well with their everyday problem solving but do not seem to find life exciting or challenging. Frequently these introverted children have little fun and few high points in their lives. A recent fourth-grade classroom discussion on the topic, "My High Points from Last Week," led by one of the authors, revealed that 20% of the class had difficulty finding one high point! Counseling plans for this group are more developmental than remedial in that they are directed toward building high points for each day of the child's life.

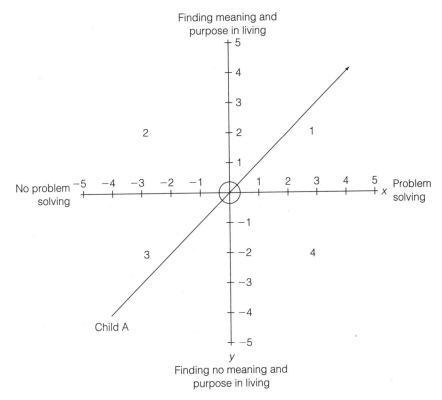

FIGURE 1-2    Counseling focus scale

Quadrant 3 children represent the toughest counseling cases. They are not solving their problems, and they find little value in living their lives. Children in this group suffer from depression, have a very poor self-concept, and may be potential suicides. Frequently no one really loves and cares about these children, and they have no one to love and care for in return. These children have experienced a world of failure at home and at school. Counseling with these children is a highly remedial process directed toward encouragement and, as in all counseling, establishing a positive, caring relationship between counselor and child. Once a helpful relationship has been established, the counseling focus can be directed toward building success experiences in the child's life.

## WHO ARE THE MENTAL HEALTH PROFESSIONALS?

Those seeking help for children need to choose the counselor best suited to the child's and family's needs and the particular type of problem. Various people trained in the helping professions—counselors, school counselors, school psychologists, social workers, marriage and family counselors, counseling psychologists, clinical psychologists, rehabilitation counselors, child development counselors—work with children (Table 1-4). Their duties may include individual counseling, group counseling, and/or consultation in a school, agency, clinic, hospital, criminal justice facility, or other institutional setting to assist children with their personal, social, developmental, educational, or vocational concerns; collecting and analyzing data (personality, interests, aptitude, attitudes, intelligence, and so on) about an individual through interviews, tests, case histories, observational techniques, and other means; and using statistical data to carry out evaluative functions, research, or follow-up activities. A counselor can serve in an administrative role as the director of a school guidance unit or the head of an institutional counseling division or can be engaged primarily in teaching or research. Wagner (1994) encouraged counseling psychologists to become more involved with children, pointing out that "by applying a developmentally based health-oriented model that recognizes sociocultural influences, counseling psychologists can, through their work with children, families, schools, and community, effect structural changes in the lives of young people and thereby facilitate more optimal development" (p. 394).

Some counseling positions require only a 4-year baccalaureate degree with a major in psychology, social work, or a related area; however, most positions require a master's or doctoral degree.

Accreditation standards and state laws governing the certification and licensure of counselors and psychologists are moving toward requiring a 2-year master's degree, including a supervised practicum or internship. Doctoral programs, too, are raising their degree requirements to require additional supervised practicum and internship experiences. Doctoral programs generally require 5 years of study beyond the baccalaureate degree.

Many professionals use counseling skills in their jobs (for example, teachers use behavior-modification procedures; ministers and nurses use active listening), but using these skills does not make them professional counselors who have completed degree and credentialing requirements in their counseling specialty. Many states define and regulate the practice of counseling, psychology, and social work through certification (protection of title) and licensure (protection of practice).

The Council for Accreditation of Counseling and Related Educational Programs (CACREP), an accrediting body associated with the American Counseling Association (ACA), recommends a graduate training program including 48 semester hours of master's-level training and competency in such areas as human growth and development, social and cultural foundations, helping relationships, group work, lifestyle and career development, appraisal, research and evaluation, and professional orientation. Its recommendations for doctoral training build on these competencies and include additional internship experiences.

The National Board for Certified Counselors (NBCC) administers the National Counselor Examination (NCE) as a component of the NBCC national professional counselor certification program. The National Academy of Certified Clinical Mental Health Counselors (NACCMHC), a branch of the ACA, publishes a registry of certified mental health counselors. Special credentialing associations provide information about the recognition of counselors in many specialties.

TABLE 1-4  Mental health professionals

| Professional | Minimum degree requirement | Work setting |
|---|---|---|
| Human service worker | Baccalaureate | Human service agencies |
| Juvenile justice counselor | Baccalaureate | Juvenile justice system |
| Child-development specialist | Master's | Community agencies |
| Clinical social worker | Master's | Private practice<br>Community agencies<br>Hospitals |
| Community agency counselor | Master's | Private practice<br>Community agencies |
| Marriage and family therapist | Master's | Private practice<br>Community agencies |
| Mental health counselor | Master's | Private practice<br>Community agencies |
| Pastoral counselor | Master's | Churches<br>Counseling centers<br>Private practice |
| Rehabilitation counselor | Master's | Rehabilitation agencies<br>Hospitals |
| School counselor | Master's | Elementary, middle, and secondary schools |
| Social worker | Master's | Community agencies<br>Hospitals<br>Schools |
| School psychologist | Educational specialist/ doctorate | Schools |
| Child psychologist | Doctorate | University<br>Private practice<br>Community agencies<br>Hospitals |
| Clinical psychologist | Doctorate | University<br>Private practice<br>Community agencies<br>Hospitals |
| Counseling psychologist | Doctorate | University<br>Private practice<br>Industry<br>Community agencies<br>Hospitals |
| Counselor educator | Doctorate | University<br>Private practice<br>Industry |
| Psychiatrist | Medical degree | Private practice<br>Hospitals |

# W E B S I T E S for Understanding a Child's World

Annie E. Casey Foundation
www.aecf.org

Children's Defense Fund
www.childrensdefense.org

Child Welfare League of America
www.cwla.org

Resiliency in Action, Bouncing Back from Risk and Adversity: Ideas for Youth, Families, and Communities
www.resiliency.com

## REFERENCES

Ainsworth, M. D. (1989). Attachments beyond infancy. *American Psychologist, 44,* 709–716.

American Psychological Association, Division of Counseling Psychology, Committee on Definition. (1956). Counseling psychology as a specialty. *American Psychologist, 11,* 282–285.

Bartholomew, K., & Horowitz, L. M. (1991). Attachment styles among young adults: A test of a four-category model. *Journal of Personality and Social Psychology, 61,* 226–244.

Benson, P. L. (1997). *All kids are our kids.* Minneapolis, MN: Search Institute.

Berk, L. E. (2001). *Development through the lifespan* (2nd ed.). Boston: Allyn & Bacon.

Bowlby, J. (1969). *Attachment and loss: Vol. 1. Attachment.* London: Hogarth.

Bowlby, J. (1988). Attachment, communication, and the therapeutic process. In J. Bowlby (Ed.), *A secure base: Clinical applications of attachment theory* (pp. 137–157). London: Routledge.

Brazelton, T. B., & Greenspan, S. I. (2000). *The irreducible needs of children: What every child must have to grow, learn, and flourish.* Cambridge, MA: Perseus.

Bretherton, I. (1992). The origins of attachment theory: John Bowlby and Mary Ainsworth. *Developmental Psychology, 28,* 759–775.

Bronfenbrenner, U. (1993). The ecology of cognitive development: Research models and fugitive findings. In R. H. Wozniak & K. W. Fischer (Eds.), *Development in context* (pp. 3–44). Hillsdale, NJ: Erlbaum.

Child Trends. (2002). Demographic characteristics. www.childtrendsdatabank.org/demo/basic/ Retrieved August 6, 2002.

Children's Defense Fund. (2002). Every day in America. www.childrendefense.org. Retrieved August 6, 2002.

Coleman, J., Morris, C., & Glaros, A. (1987). *Contemporary psychology and effective behavior.* Glenview, IL: Scott, Foresman.

Dodge, K. A. (1983). Behavioral antecedents of peer social status. *Child Development, 54,* 1386–1399.

Dodge, K. A., & Feldman, E. (1990). Issues in social cognition and sociometric status. In S. R. Asher & J. D. Coi (Eds.), *Peer rejection in childhood* (pp. 119–155). Cambridge, MA: Cambridge University Press.

Elkind, D. (1984). *All grown up and no place to go.* Reading, MA: Addison-Wesley.

Elkind, D. (1994). *A sympathetic understanding of the child: Birth to sixteen* (3rd ed.). Boston: Allyn & Bacon.

Erikson, E. (1963). *Childhood and society.* New York: Norton.

Erikson, E. (1968). *Identity, youth, and crisis.* New York: Norton.

Garbarino, J. (1997). Educating children in a socially toxic environment. *Educational Leadership, 54,* 12–16

Garmezy, N. (1991). Resiliency and vulnerability to adverse developmental outcomes associated with poverty. *American Behavioral Scientist, 34,* 416–430.

Glosoff, H., & Koprowicz, C. (1990). *Children achieving potential: An introduction to elementary school counseling and state-level policies.* Washington, DC: National Conference of State Legislatures; Alexandria, VA: American Association for Counseling and Development.

Hauser, S. T. (1999). Understanding resilient outcomes: Adolescent lives across time and generations. *Journal of Research on Adolescence, 9,* 1–24.

Havighurst, R. (1961). *Human development and education* (2nd ed.). New York: David McKay.

Herr, E. (1998). *Counseling in a dynamic society: Contexts and practices for the 21st century.* Alexandria, VA: American Counseling Association

Kirkpatrick, L. A., & Davis, K. E. (1994). Attachment style, gender, and relationship stability: A longitudinal analysis. *Journal of Personality and Social Psychology, 66,* 502–512.

Kobak, R. R., & Sceery, A. (1988). The transition to college: Working models of attachment, affect regulation, and perceptions of self and others. *Child Development, 88,* 135–146.

LeVine, E., & Sallee, A. (1992). *Listen to our children: Clinical theory and practice* (2nd ed.). Dubuque, IA: Kendall-Hunt.

Lowenthal, B. (1998). The effects of early childhood abuse and the development of resiliency. *Early Child Development and Care, 142,* 43–52.

Maslow, A. (1970). *Motivation and personality* (2nd ed.). New York: Harper & Row.

Newman, B., & Newman, P. (1999). *Development through life: A psychosocial approach.* Pacific Grove, CA: Brooks/Cole.

Orton, G. L. (1997). *Strategies for counseling with children and their parents.* Pacific Grove, CA: Brooks/Cole.

Peters, H., & Farwell, G. (1959). *Guidance: A developmental approach.* Chicago: Rand McNally.

Piaget, J., & Inhelder, B. (1969). *The psychology of the child.* New York: Basic Books.

Pietrzak, D., Petersen, G., & Speaker, K. (1998). Perceptions of school violence by elementary and middle school personnel. *Professional School Counseling, 1,* 23–29.

Putallaz, M. (1983). Predicting children's sociometric status from their behavior. *Child Development, 54,* 1417–1426.

Rak, C. F. (2001). Understanding and promoting resilience with our clients. In E. R. Welfel & R. E. Ingersoll (Eds.), *The mental health desk reference* (pp. 225–231). New York: Wiley.

Rak, C. F., & Patterson, L. E. (1996). Promoting resilience in at-risk children. *Journal of Counseling and Development, 74,* 368–373.

Selman, R. L. (1976). Social-cognitive understanding: A guide to educational and clinical practice. In T. Lickona (Ed.), *Moral development and behavior: Theory, research, and social issues* (pp. 299–316). New York: Holt, Rinehart and Winston.

Selman, R. L., & Bryne, D. F. (1974). A structural-developmental analysis of levels of role taking in middle childhood. *Child Development, 45,* 803–806.

Shaver, P. R., & Brennan, K. A. (1992). Attachment styles and the "big five" personality traits: Their connections with each other and with romantic relationship outcomes. *Personality and Social Psychology Bulletin, 18,* 536–545.

Surgeon General. (2000). Children and mental health (pp. 124–220). In *Mental health: A report of the Surgeon General.* www.surgeongeneral.gov/library/mentalhealth/toc.html. Retrieved August 6, 2002.

Wadsworth, B. (1989). *Piaget's theory of cognitive and affective development.* New York: Longman.

Wagner, W. G. (1994). Counseling with children: An opportunity for tomorrow. *Counseling Psychologist, 22,* 381–401.

Werner, E. E. (1984). Resilient children. *Young Children, 40,* 68–72.

Werner, E. E., & Smith, R. S. (1982). *Vulnerable but not invincible: A longitudinal study of resilient children and youth.* New York: McGraw-Hill.

# Chapter 2

# The Counseling Process

*We shall not cease from exploration*
*And the end of all our exploring*
*Will be to arrive where we started*
*And know the place for the first time.*
—T. S. Eliot

The type of help counselors offer children may vary according to the model of counseling used. Theories of counseling help practitioners understand patterns and causes of difficulties. Theories explain behavior change and provide details about relationship factors, counseling goals, techniques, process, and outcomes. Counselors use theory to make sense of their observations and to organize information (Gladding, 2000). The following chapters will help you understand counseling theories, the foundation of a helping relationship.

Counseling theories often differ more in name and description than in actual practice. However, some counseling situations and some children are better suited to one approach than to another. Counseling is basically a learning situation, and people have favorite styles of learning.

## WHICH APPROACHES TO COUNSELING ARE EFFECTIVE?

According to Seligman (2001), 350 counseling and psychotherapy forms have been described. However, these myriad systems can generally be classified in four intervention categories: cognitive, behavior, affective, and some combination of categories, referred to as eclectic or integrative. In comparison studies of the different systems of counseling and psychotherapy, no one system has emerged as consistently most effective. Rather, various counseling approaches based on different theories and emphasizing different methods have been found effective for a wide range of people and their problems.

Kazdin (2000) reviewed meta-analyses of child and adolescent therapy to conclude the following:

- Treatment appears to be better than no treatment.
- The positive effects with children and adolescents are equivalent to the benefits obtained with adults.

Based on their review of counseling effectiveness, Lambert and Cattani-Thompson (1996) likewise concluded that counseling is more effective than no treatment, that the positive effects are lasting, and that improvement can occur relatively quickly. Those authors and others (Kazdin, 1994; Sexton & Whiston, 1996; Smith, Glass, & Miller, 1980) found little evidence for specific techniques being consistently more effective than others. In fact, Sexton (2001) supports the notion that common factors across counseling approaches contribute to effectiveness. Those factors can be grouped as support factors, learning factors, and action factors (Lambert & Cattani-Thompson, 1996). Support factors include variables such as a positive relationship with the counselor, a working alliance, warmth, empathy, and trust. Some of the learning factors are corrective emotional experiencing, affective experiencing, and assimilating problem experiences. Some examples of the third category, action factors, are gaining cognitive mastery, facing fears, and regulating behaviors. Understanding those common factors can help counselors build essential skills, and their theoretical knowledge will allow them to use those skills wisely.

Training counselors in a variety of approaches has considerable support. Thompson and Campbell (1992), in a phenomenological study, surveyed 500 people on what type of self-help interventions they chose to alleviate mild depression. These interventions were spread fairly equally across affective, behavior, cognitive, and eclectic categories, with a slight but significant preference for affective remedies. The authors attributed these results to the preponderance of women in the sample and to their expressed preference for affective interventions. Men, by contrast, tended to favor cognitive interventions. The study indicates that effective counselors should be able to adapt to the client's preferred learning style rather than expecting the client to adapt to the counselor's preferred counseling style.

An individualized counseling plan is usually superior but possible only when the counselor can draw on a vast array of theory and technique, an eclectic approach, and is not bound by any single approach. Lazarus (1981, 1990, 2000) made essentially the same point in his argument that not only is behavior therapy not behaviorism, but also neither behavior therapy nor behaviorism can account for all the events that occur in the counseling process. He recommended a multimodal, or comprehensive, eclectic framework for counseling that can be adapted to meet the needs of individual children. Lazarus developed his BASIC ID model to describe seven problem areas often treated in counseling:

**B** *Behavior:* Fighting, disruption, talking, stealing, procrastination
**A** *Affect:* Expression of anger, anxiety, phobias, depression
**S** *Sensation/School:* Headaches, backaches, and stomachaches; school failure; perceptual/motor problems
**I** *Imagery:* Nightmares, low self-esteem, fear of rejection, excessive daydreaming and fantasizing

**C** *Cognition:* Irrational thinking, difficulty in setting goals, decision-making problems, problem-solving difficulties

**I** *Interpersonal relationships:* Withdrawing from others (shyness), conflict with adults, conflict with peers, family problems

**D** *Drugs/Diet:* Hyperactivity, weight-control problems, drug abuse, addictions

The Lazarus BASIC ID model covers most of the problems that counselors working with children, adolescents, or adults are likely to encounter.

Gerler (1990) and Gerler, Drew, and Mohr (1990) reviewed multimodal research, applications, and changes and cited considerable research support for this eclectic counseling method. Keat (1990a, 1990b) specialized his multimodal writing on counseling children. He converted the BASIC ID model into the acronym HELPING:

**H** refers to *health* issues (pain and sickness).

**E** stands for *emotions* (anxiety, anger, feeling down).

**L** is for *learning* problems (deficiencies, failing, and sensory shallowness).

**P** stands for *personal relationships* (adult and peer relationships).

**I** refers to *imagery* (low self-worth and poor coping skills).

**N** is the *need* to know (despair, faulty thinking, lack of information).

**G** stands for *guidance* of actions, behaviors, and consequences (behavior and motivation problems).

After identifying the problem areas, counselors design interventions to strengthen weak areas before those areas become more serious problems. The counseling approaches presented in this book offer possibilities for helping counselors work with one or more of the seven areas presented in the BASIC ID model and/or the HELPING model.

## CLASSIFYING COUNSELING THEORIES

One way to classify counseling theories is to examine how the practitioners of each theory encounter their clients. Some counselors focus on the client's feelings, whereas others intervene with thinking or behavior. Change in any one of these three areas is likely to produce change in the other two. Therefore, rather than a two-dimensional continuum, we propose a model showing the integrative relationship that exists among thoughts, feelings, and behaviors (Figure 2-1).

Counselors may also choose to work beyond the individual or on a systemic level. At that level, counselors may intervene with families, institutions, teachers, healthcare professionals, communities, or other systems that have an impact on the lives of children. For this book we will focus on the point of intervention, classifying the theories and interventions presented in this book as follows:

Affective (feeling)
    Person-centered counseling
    Gestalt therapy

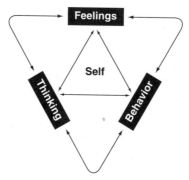

FIGURE 2-1   Classification of counseling approaches

Behavior (behaving)
  Behavioral counseling
  Reality therapy
  Brief counseling
  Individual psychology
Cognitive (thinking)
  Rational-emotive behavioral therapy
  Cognitive behavioral therapy
  Psychoanalytic counseling
  Transactional analysis
  Systemic interventions
  Family therapy
  Consultation, collaboration, teamwork

Our intention is not to isolate feeling, thinking, and behaving or systems. Failure to integrate feelings, thoughts, and behaviors is a symptom of schizophrenia, a diagnosis that describes a loss of contact with the environment, a split from reality, and a disintegration of personality. Rather, we attempt to describe how effective intervention in one of the three areas helps the individual integrate the other two areas into a more fully functioning lifestyle.

Counseling theories can also be classified as belonging to one of two broad categories. In the first, the focus is on observable events and data: behavior, antecedents to behavior, consequences of behavior, behavioral goals, and plans. The second category is focused on the unobservable events and data surrounding counseling: feelings, thoughts, motivation, and causes of behavior (Figure 2-2).

Category 1 counselors believe that if you feel bad at Point A (in Figure 2-2), the only way to feel better at Point B is to make a positive change in your behavior, which, in turn, leads to better feelings at Point B. Additional positive change in behavior leads to even better feelings at Point C.

Category 2 counselors believe just the opposite. If you feel bad at Point A, you need to work through these feelings and/or thoughts with your counselor until

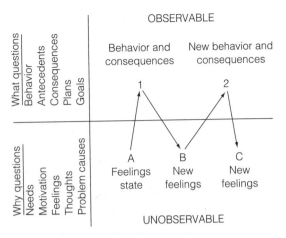

FIGURE 2-2    Focus points for counseling interventions

you have sufficient strength to make a behavior change at Point 1. You then examine the resulting thoughts and feelings at Point B for meaning and significance, which help you gather sufficient strength to tackle the next behavior change.

Classifying the various approaches to counseling creates a framework for examining their similarities and differences. These approaches have a variety of techniques adaptable to learning style differences. The cognitive, affective, and behavior classifications should help counselors provide children with appropriate counseling methods.

Attending to the points of intervention helps counselors make treatment plans. Counselors also need to pay attention to particular skills to allow the counseling process to succeed. Erdman and Lampe (1996) identified critical adaptations to basic counseling skills for working with children. They urged counselors to attend to the following:

- The child's developmental level of cognitive and emotional understanding
- The presentation of information that matches that understanding
- The utilization of concrete examples, hands-on activities, clear interpretation of rules, and careful explanation of consequences
- The recognition that the egocentric child will be unable to see another point of view and will not question his or her own thoughts or reasons
- The lack of a child's clarity about time, amount, and frequency
- The knowledge that the recollections and expectations of the child may be distorted
- The reality that children often lack control over many aspects of their existence
- The acknowledgment that reluctance to change may be expected; that may involve crying, silence, laughing, fidgeting, and fighting

To address these characteristics in counseling settings, counselors work to establish appropriate physical environments, build trust in the relationship, maintain a helpful attitude, and use questions appropriately (Erdman & Lampe, 1996). Additional information about these practices follows.

## PREPARING FOR THE INTERVIEW

Effective counselors create a relaxed counseling environment and build rapport with their clients. The counseling environment should contribute to a client's feelings of comfort and ease. A cluttered, stimulating, busy room can distract children, whose attention is easily drawn to interesting objects in the room and away from the counseling interaction. Restless, distractible children may be affected by brightly colored objects, mobiles, ticking clocks, outside noise, or even darting fish in an aquarium. Inasmuch as counselors are part of the environment, you should also check yourself for distracting jewelry, colorful ties, or patterns in clothing that may affect children.

The furniture in the counseling room should be comfortable for both adults and children. We suggest that the counselor not sit behind a desk or table that can act as a barrier between child and counselor. Children see people sitting behind desks as authority figures, such as teachers, principals, and caseworkers. Keep in mind that children prefer chairs that are low enough to allow them to keep their feet on the floor.

Counseling seems to work better if children can control the distance between themselves and the counselor. Adults are often too aggressive in trying to initiate conversations with children. Children prefer to talk with adults at the same eye level, so some care needs to be given to seating arrangements that allow for eye-to-eye contact and feet on the floor. Of the various possible seating arrangements (Figure 2-3), two seem to be *least* effective: (1) having a desk between the counselor and child and (2) having no barrier at all between counselor and child. The preferred seating arrangement (3) is to use the corner of a desk or table as an optional barrier that allows the child to retreat behind the desk or table corner or to move out around the corner when he or she feels comfortable doing so.

A thick carpet, comfortable chairs, floor pillows, puppets, dollhouses, and other toys to facilitate communication are also recommended for the counseling room. Many counselors conduct all of their interviews with children on the carpet in a play therapy room (see Chapter 15). Play media have developed a relaxed atmosphere with younger children, and a few counselors have employed large, friendly dogs as icebreakers, with child and counselor sitting on a rug and playing with the dog during the session (Burton, 1995; O'Brien, 1993; Trivedi & Perl, 1995).

Counselors should be models of promptness for scheduled sessions. Children (and adult clients) dislike being kept waiting. Tardiness may be interpreted as lack of interest or cause restlessness, fatigue, or irritability.

The counselor should be free from distracting worries and thoughts and ready to devote full attention to the child. Children are extremely sensitive to adult moods and can recognize insincerity or lack of concern quickly. Many counselors reschedule appointments when they do not feel well rather than risk hurting the

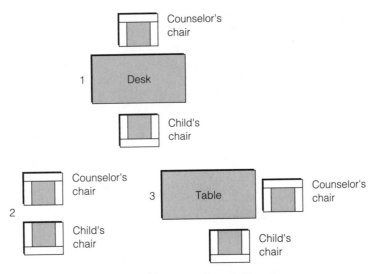

FIGURE 2-3  Seating arrangements for counseling children

counseling relationship. If you have a cold, headache, or other minor ailment, you may want to admit to the child that you are not feeling up to par rather than have the child misinterpret your behavior as a lack of interest.

## WHAT ARE SOME THINGS TO CONSIDER DURING THE FIRST INTERVIEW?

### Children's Resistance to Counseling

Children who are clients are still children, with their own feelings, behaviors, problems, and expectations of counselors. Like adults, children have a fear of the unknown. To be frightened of new faces in new places with new activities and mystery outcomes is very natural. Children may not know why they are being taken to a counselor's office. In fact, parents or teachers may have given them misinformation that could result in mistrust of the counselor who does not meet a child's expectations. Questions children may have about counseling include:

1. What is counseling, and why do I have to go there?
2. Did I do something wrong? Am I being punished?
3. Is something wrong with me?
4. Do Mom and Dad think something is wrong with me? Do they love me?
5. Will my friends think something is wrong with me? Will they make fun of me if they find out?
6. Will it hurt? Is it like going to the doctor?
7. How long does it take? When will I get to come home?

8. If I don't like it, will I have to go back?
9. What am I supposed to say and do? What if I say something wrong?
10. Should I tell bad things about my family?
11. Will the counselor tell anybody what I say?

Effective counselors understand the full range of fears, concerns, and questions children might have about visiting a counselor's office for the first time. In addition, children as well as adults naturally resist situations in which they might lose their autonomy or freedom to choose what they would like to say and do. When children are forced to do things, they become angry, resistant, and oppositional in an attempt to regain control. Children may also get angry because they view the trip to the counselor's office as unfair. They may think they are being blamed for the family's problems.

Children are generally not motivated to seek counseling. Children are drawn to pleasurable thoughts, feelings, and behavior and tend to avoid negative feelings, thoughts, and activities. A first visit to the counselor would ordinarily not be a favorite activity. The exception to the rule occurs in those elementary and middle schools that are fortunate enough to have talented counselors who lead regular group meetings with all of their children. Children will and do refer themselves to these trusted counselors.

Children do many of the same things adult clients do to resist counseling:

- Refuse to talk, refuse to share anything of importance, deny there is a problem, or talk about irrelevant topics
- Avoid eye contact
- Are late for or miss their appointments
- Exhibit negative body language and make hostile verbal comments
- Act out and refuse to cooperate (e.g., hide behind the furniture)

This list is certainly not exhaustive. People can be very creative in devising ways to resist anything, and counselors ought to rely on their feelings as indicators of client resistance. Frustration and anger are common reactions counselors have to uncooperative clients. Counselors need considerable patience and high levels of frustration tolerance to work with difficult children. Their major task is to get on the same team with their child clients and try to help them find better ways to get what they want and need. Remember that resistant children are reacting normally, as anyone would do, to someone who is trying to change them. Many children are not self-referred, and counselors are often viewed as extensions of the system that has been unhelpful and even painful to them. Resistant children are protecting themselves from the counselor's agenda, which they are unwilling or scared to follow.

## Steps to Overcoming Children's Resistance

The first step in the successful application of all counseling theories is the development of a good counseling relationship, a therapeutic alliance between counselor and client. The relationship-building process begins with the counselor as a person. *Friendly, warm, interested, genuine,* and *empathic* are the key descriptive words used to define successful counselors. For children, such a person truly listens and understands how they think and feel about things. Children view effective counselors as caring, protective, safe, and on their side. "On the child's side" means the child's advocate rather than best friend. Taking the role of a child's advocate would not excuse the counselor from maintaining the empathy–objectivity balance requisite to successful counseling. Effective counselors are also able to strike a healthy balance between adult–adult and parent–child activities in the counseling session. From transactional analysis (see Chapter 9), adult–adult activities are the problem-solving and decision-making parts of counseling; the parent–child activities are the nurturing and relationship-building parts of counseling. Finally, the counselor should offer children as many choices as possible to restore to them some of the control children thought they lost by coming to counseling.

As a second step, the counselor's office should seem like a friendly, comfortable, relaxed, safe place to be. Children find security in consistency, limits, and predictability. Counseling appointments should be regularly scheduled for the same time and day. Counseling time is the child's time and is not interrupted by phone calls or knocks on the door. Children should not be kept waiting for their appointments.

Attention to these scheduling details makes children feel worthy and important. Behavioral limits should be set and enforced with logical consequences; for example, "the sand must stay in the sandbox, and sand play has to stop until the sand is swept up and put back in the box." Misbehavior is handled best by redirecting it to appropriate activity; for example, "People are not for hitting; punching bags are for hitting."

Third, children need to understand what counseling is and what they can expect from it. Some counselors prefer to ease the anxiety of the initial meeting by engaging in general conversation with the child for a few minutes. After initial introductions, the counselor may start to talk with the child about home, school, friends, hobbies, or other interests. For nonverbal or extremely anxious children, the first session or two may include play therapy. The counselor can begin to build a good relationship with the child while learning something about the child's world through these methods. Other counselors prefer to go directly to the problem: "Would you like to tell me why you have come to see me?" During the initial interview, a counselor may want to explain to the child the process of counseling and the counselor's expectations. The following is a sample dialogue for middle-school children:

*Counselor:*  Do you know what counseling is?
*Child:*  No.
[If the child answers yes, the counselor might say, "Tell me your ideas about what counseling is."]
*Counselor:*  Well, at some time during our lives, most of us have things that worry or upset us—things we would like to talk to someone about. It could be something about school that concerns us, like another student in our class

or our teacher; it could be a problem at home with our brothers or sisters, or perhaps we feel that our parents don't really understand how we feel. It could be that we are having trouble with friendships or we have some thoughts or feelings that it would be helpful to discuss with someone. A counselor listens and tries to help the other person work these things out. A counselor tries to think with that person about ways to solve these worries. Your job is to tell me whatever is bothering you. My job is to listen carefully and try to help you find ways to solve these problems.

The preceding statement is too long and wordy for children under the age of 7. Counselors should adjust their explanations of the process to the developmental level of the child and use sentences with fewer words.

For children others have referred for counseling, the counselor can begin with a statement such as "Mrs. Jones told me that you were very unhappy since you moved here and that you might want to talk to me about it," or "Mr. Clifford told me that you would be coming by," and wait for the child to respond by saying what the trouble is.

In the first example, the counselor has informed the child that he or she is aware of the problem and is ready to discuss it. In the second example, the counselor is less directive, provides less structure, and allows the child to explain the problem, which may or may not be the one for which the child was referred. The counselor will want to consider the child's age, culture, and cognitive, social, and emotional development, as well as the type of presenting problem, before deciding which type of opening statement to use. The counselor may find this general guideline helpful: the younger the child, chronologically and developmentally, and the more specific the problem, the greater the probability that the child will respond more readily to a structured approach.

Carlson (1990) preferred a direct approach for counseling "other-referred" children. For example, a counselor might say, "Let me tell you what your teacher shared with me that led to your being asked to see me." The counselor states the teacher's concern in a way that lets the child know that the counselor is there to help and not punish. The counselor could say, for example, "Mr. Thompson is concerned about your behavior in class. He is afraid you will not learn all you need to know if you don't change what you are doing." Carlson also believed that counseling needs to be defined for "other-referred" children in language they can understand. For example, "Counseling is a time when you can talk to me about things that bother you. We can also talk about what we need to do to make things better."

Children need to know how much of what they say in counseling is confidential and what is not. Counselors are required by law to report any evidence of homicidal or suicidal ideation, child sexual or physical abuse, and child neglect. Counselors may also disclose information that children have given permission to share.

Counselors need to assure children that what they talk about is confidential or "just between you and me unless I have to stop someone from getting hurt. I will not tell anybody about anything else unless you say it is okay to tell something."

These examples of what counselors might say can be modified to fit the situation, the age and maturity of the child, and the counselor's personality. The counselor may not think it necessary to define the counselor's role; however, many children and counselors feel more comfortable with structure, and clearly defining expectations facilitates the counseling process.

## First Interview Goals and Observations

The counselor's main task is to build bridges between the child's world and the counseling office. Friendly, confident counselors who seem in control help children feel safe and secure in the new counseling environment. Counselors can begin by asking children what name they want to be called. Fun activities are helpful in getting the first session off to a relaxing start. A child who feels anxious about separating from a parent can have the parent join the activity. Serving a snack, reading a favorite story, and playing a game are good ways to reach the child. A parent may be included in all of these introductory activities. Some children, having been told not to speak to strangers, need assurance from their parents that the counselor can be trusted and that it is okay to speak to him or her.

If parents oppose counseling, children may feel disloyal if they participate in it or cooperate with the counselor. These children need reassurance that it is okay for them to work with the counselor.

Children differ from adults in several ways that affect counseling and play therapy:

- Children, lacking elaborate adult defenses, regress very quickly and easily into spontaneous and revealing play activities.
- Children have rich fantasy lives that reveal their thoughts, feelings, and expectations.
- Lacking adult formal thinking skills, insight, and verbal skills, children communicate through acting out their fantasies.

Once the relationship is established, the counselor can focus on how children conduct themselves in the counseling session. The counselor's work is to evaluate the climate of each counseling session. Was it happy, sad, pleasant, neutral, stormy, or productive? What seemed to set the tone? Next, counselors should look for patterns in the child's behavior or play. Hyperactive and attention deficit–disordered children act out their disorganization and impulsive behavior. Obsessive-compulsive children, by contrast, are rigid and structured in their play activities.

Children's choices of toys provide another rich area of data for counselors. Toys can be classified as passive or aggressive, masculine or feminine, and constructive or destructive; however, many toys may be neutral. Observe what the child does with each toy. Counselors search for themes and patterns in children's behavior and play therapy activities in the effort to learn the motivation directing their behavior.

More important than the themes uncovered in counseling is the intensity with which these themes are played out in the sessions. The play themes of unstable or disturbed children are more variable and unreliable.

Counselors' accurate reflection of content, feelings, expectations, and behavior helps focus children's attention on their actions and stimulates the self-observation needed to gain insight about their lifestyle and motivational incentives. Play therapy methods are presented in detail in Chapter 15. The following six-step counseling model combines the best of reality planning with person-centered, active listening for children receiving general counseling or a combination of counseling and play therapy.

# A GENERAL MODEL FOR COUNSELING

## Step 1: Defining the Problem Through Active Listening

The way the counselor listens to the child is important in building rapport. An open, relaxed body posture is the best way to invite a child to talk. It is often helpful to suggest a time limit for your interview, which should vary according to the attention span of the child.

One way to start might be to say, "Jimmy, we have 20 minutes today to talk about anything you'd like to discuss." In fact, several 20-minute periods might be used to build a friendship with Jimmy. Individualizing the counseling process to fit each child you counsel is very important.

When the child wishes to discuss a concern or problem with you, it is necessary to listen for three significant points: (1) a problem that has not been solved, (2) feelings about the problem, and (3) expectations of what the counselor should do about the problem. The counselor can assume the role of student and let the child teach these three topics, since people learn best when they teach something to another person.

Counselors have the responsibility of letting the child know what they have heard and learned as their clients teach them. For example, the counselor should periodically respond with a statement such as "In other words, you are feeling _____ because _____, and you want _____." This feedback to the child is referred to as *active listening;* it promotes better communication and lets the child know you are paying attention. The active listening process continues throughout the interview, but it is most important in helping to clarify the nature of the child's problem. When the child confirms your response as an accurate understanding of the problem, counseling can move to the next phase (see Chapter 5 for a detailed explanation of the active-listening process).

## Step 2: Clarifying the Child's Expectations

Counselors also need to let children know if they can meet their expectations for counseling. The counselor probably cannot have an unpopular teacher fired, for example. However, counselors can inform children and their parents what they are able to do and let them determine if they want to accept or reject the service available. If the service is rejected, the counselor may want to explore other alternatives with the family about where or how the child can obtain the service.

## Step 3: Exploring What Has Been Done to Solve the Problem

In looking at past attempts to solve the problem, remember that open-ended questions generally elicit the best responses. Closed questions that yield one-word answers such as *yes, no,* and *maybe* make the counselor's job much more difficult. As noted in this text, many approaches to counseling avoid heavy questioning, and others rely on a series of questions. Statements often work better than questions; they empower the client by letting the client maintain the pace and direction of the interview. For example, rather than asking the child, "What have you done to solve the problem?" the counselor would say, "If you feel ready, we could begin by looking at what you have tried to do to solve the problem." In exploring the child's efforts to solve the problem, we find it helpful to have the client who can write make a list of these behaviors; otherwise, the child can dictate the answers to the counselor. The list becomes important if we want the child to make a commitment to stop behaviors that are not helping to solve the problem. It is helpful to explore the possible rewards or payoffs the child derives from ineffective or unhelpful behaviors. Change is facilitated when both the pluses and the minuses are examined. A profit and loss statement can be prepared to see if the behavior is actually worth the cost the child is paying. If it is not, the child may discard the behavior in favor of a more productive alternative.

## Step 4: Exploring What New Things Could Be Done to Solve the Problem

The next step could be a brainstorming session in which the counselor encourages the child to develop as many problem-solving alternatives as possible. Judgment is reserved until the list is finished; quantity of ideas is more important than quality in this first step. Thompson and Poppen (1992) recommended drawing empty circles on a sheet of paper and then seeing how many circles the child can fill with ideas. If children are blocked from thinking of possible new ideas, the counselor can fill two circles with ideas as a way of encouraging the child to get started. The counselor thus allows the child to become a partner in the problem-solving process by choosing one of the counselor's two suggestions.

Children seem to do best with a plan they have made or helped make. For example, if the plan involves learning a new skill such as assertion, effective study, or making friends, the counseling interview can be used for teaching and role-play rehearsal. After the brainstorming list is complete, children are asked to evaluate each alternative in light of its expected success in helping them get what they want.

## Step 5: Obtaining a Commitment to Try One of the Problem-Solving Ideas

Building commitment to try a new plan may be difficult. Children must achieve success with their first plan because they may be quite discouraged by their previous failures to solve the problem. We suggest that the child not set impossible goals in this first attempt; the first plan should be achievable. Children do better if they are asked to report the results of their plan to the counselor. When plans do not work, the counselor helps the child write new ones until the child achieves success. Plans can include a program of reinforcement when the child succeeds in meeting daily or weekly goals.

## Step 6: Closing the Counseling Interview

A good way to close the interview is to invite the child to summarize or review what was discussed in the session; for example, the summary might include what progress was made and what plans were developed. Summarizing by the child is also helpful when the interview becomes mired and the child cannot think of anything to say. Because the process seems to stimulate new thoughts, summarizing at the close of the interview should be limited to 2 to 4 minutes. We also recommend asking the child to summarize the last counseling interview at the start of each new interview.

These counselor requests to summarize teach children to pay attention in the session and to review counseling plans between sessions; they have the effect of an oral quiz without the threat of a failing grade. The summary also helps counselors evaluate their own effectiveness. Finally, the counselor and the child make plans for the next counseling interview or for some type of maintenance plan if counseling is to be terminated.

## QUESTIONS COUNSELORS ASK

### What Does the Counselor Need to Know About Counseling Records?

Most counselors keep some record of interviews with their clients. Notes that summarize the content of sessions and observations the counselor makes can assist in recalling previous information. Before deciding on a method of taking notes, counselors are wise to become knowledgeable about their state's laws regarding privileged communication and the regulations contained in the Family Educational Rights and Privacy Act (also known as FERPA and as the Buckley Amendment) (1974), which gave parents and young people of legal age the right to inspect records, letters, and recommendations about themselves. Personal notes do not fall under these regulations; however, for their own protection, counselors in institutional settings will want to become aware of the full requirements of the law.

Videotaping or audiotaping counseling sessions is also common practice. This procedure not only provides a record of the interview but also aids counselors in gaining self-understanding and self-awareness. Counselors can listen to or watch their tapes with another counselor and continue to grow and learn by evaluating their own work. In addition, listening to and discussing some sessions with the client may promote growth. Permission to record should be obtained from the child and the parents before the procedure is begun. If the material is to be used for instruction or if anyone other than the counselor will hear the client, written permission should be obtained. Regarding use and storage of these records, reading state laws pertaining to privileged communication and the Buckley Amendment is advised.

When introducing a recording system to children, show them the recorder, perhaps allow them to listen to themselves for a minute, and then place the equipment in an out-of-the-way place. Occasionally, children are unable to talk when they are being recorded; most, however, quickly forget the equipment. Should a child resist being recorded, the counselor may wish to pursue the reasons for this resistance. If circumstances indicate that recording is inhibiting the counseling process, the counselor may choose to remove the equipment. At the other extreme, some children become so excited and curious about the taping equipment that counseling becomes impossible. Again, the counselor may prefer to remove the equipment, or a contract may be made with the child such as "After 30 minutes of the counseling work, Mickey may listen to the tape for 5 minutes." It is usually best to give as little attention to the recorder as possible after a brief initial explanation of its purpose and uses.

## How Much Self-Disclosure Is Appropriate for the Counselor?

Children are often interested in their counselors as people. They ask their age, where they went to school, where they live, and whether they have children, and counselors are faced with the perplexing problem of how much personal information to share. Counselors who refuse to answer any personal questions run the risk of hurting the counseling relationship or being viewed as a mysterious figure, bringing forth more questions. If counselors answer all personal questions, however, the interview time may center on the counselor rather than the client.

With seriously disturbed or acting-out clients, revealing your address or where your children go to school could be bothersome or even dangerous. A general guideline might be to share some personal information (favorite sport or TV show, number of children) and, when the questions become too personal or continue too long, reflect to the child, "You seem to be very interested in me personally" and explore the child's curiosity and pursuit of the subject. Understanding the child's curiosity about the counselor could promote understanding the child as a person. Questioning the counselor can be a defense for children who wish to avoid discussing their own problems.

A second problem concerning self-disclosure relates to the counselor's feelings and emotions. Counselor training programs are founded on the assumption that people are unique, capable of growth, and worthy of respect. These programs focus on listening and responding to clients with empathic understanding and respect.

The programs also emphasize being genuine; however, genuineness is often interpreted as showing only genuine *positive* emotions and feelings. Counselor trainees are sometimes quite surprised when their supervisors encourage them to admit to the client their negative feelings, such as frustration or anger. Obviously, admitting emotions does not mean attacking and degrading the client; rather, it means admitting that the counselor is a person with feelings and is frustrated or angry over what is occurring ("I am really frustrated that we seem to be talking about everything except what occurred with your friend today").

The counselor's proper level of self-disclosure is a controversial issue in the profession. Some feel comfortable being completely open and honest about their feelings (high levels of self-disclosure); others think such openness interferes with the counselor–client relationship and prefer low levels of self-disclosure. However, most counselors agree that self-disclosure is not "true confessions." Poppen and Thompson (1974) summarized the arguments on both sides of the issue. The principal arguments in favor of high levels of self-disclosure are as follows:

- Counselors who are open and honest about their thoughts and feelings encourage similar behavior by their clients.
- Knowing that the counselor has had similar adjustment problems helps clients feel more at ease to discuss their own.
- Children learn by imitation and can learn to solve their own problems through hearing about the experiences of others.
- Counselors could be models for behavior.

On the other side of the issue, those opposing high levels of self-disclosure claim the following:

- Clients are in the counselor's office for help with their problems, not to hear about the counselor's problems.
- Counseling could become a time for sharing gripes or problems rather than a working session for personal growth.
- Counselors can lose objectivity if they identify too strongly with the child's concerns.

According to Poppen and Thompson (1974), self-disclosure is more beneficial when it takes a here-and-now focus—that is, when self-disclosure becomes an open and authentic expression of the counselor's or student's [child's] thoughts and feelings experienced at a particular time. Self-disclosure, when examined in the here-and-now context, means much more than dredging up the dark secrets of the past.

## What Types of Questions Should the Counselor Use?

Adults often think they must ask children several questions to get the "whole story." Usually, these questions are of the "who," "what," "when," "where," and "what did you do next" variety. These questions may or may not be asked for the purpose of helping the child or for clarification; too often they arise out of general curiosity. Some questions may even be irrelevant and interrupt or ignore the child's thoughts and expressions. Questions can also be used to judge, blame, or criticize.

*Child:*   The teacher called me a dummy in front of the whole class today!
*Adult:*   (sarcastically) What did you say this time to make him call you that?

At that particular moment, the important fact is not what the child said but the fact that the child was embarrassed, hurt, and possibly angered. By listening and understanding feelings and expressions rather than probing for details of who said what and when, the adult will get the whole story eventually and maintain a much friendlier relationship with the child. Counselors who listen and respond with understanding learn the child's important thoughts or problems. In other words, questions rephrased as statements work better. Some counselors, in their efforts to help the child, take over the counseling interview.

Counselors who direct the interview risk missing important feelings and thoughts. The counselor may guide the conversation in a totally meaningless direction.

*Child:*   I hate my brother.
*Counselor:*   Why do you hate your brother?
*Child:*   Because he's mean.
*Counselor:*   How is he mean?
*Child:*   He hits me.
*Counselor:*   What do you do to make him hit you? [accusation]
*Child:*   Nothing.
*Counselor:*   Come on, now. Tell me about when he hits you—and what your mother does when he hits you.

This example sounds more like an inquisition than a counseling session. The hitting and what the mother does may or may not be what is really troubling the child. What could be more important is the feeling that exists between the child and her brother. Is it really "hate" because he hits her, or could there be other problems in the relationship that the counselor will miss by focusing on hitting rather than listening to the child tell about her relationship with her brother? It is also possible that "hating brother" could have been a test problem to see if the counselor really would listen and be understanding. A counselor who guides the interview by questions could overlook the true problem entirely.

In the preceding example, the child answered the counselor's questions but offered no further information. Children easily fall into the role of answering adults' questions and then waiting for the next question. Rather than being a listener and helper, the counselor assumes the role of questioner. If this pattern has been established, the interview may die when the counselor runs out of questions.

Obviously, there are times in counseling when direct questions should be asked. The counselor may need factual information or clarification. However, counselors can probably get more information from children with open-ended questions. An open-ended question does not require a specific answer. It encourages the child to give the counselor more information about the topic but does not restrict replies or discourage further communication in the area. Suppose a counselor was interested in learning about a child's social relationships. Rather than asking the direct, closed question "Do you have friends?" the counselor might elicit more information about the child's social relationships by saying, "Tell me about what you like to do for fun—things that you enjoy doing in your free time." In this way, the counselor could learn not only about friends but possibly also about the child's sports interests, hobbies, and other activities (or lack of activities).

Another open-ended question that might help the counselor understand what is going on in the child's life is "Tell me about your family," out of which could come answers to such unasked questions as "Do both your mother and father live in the home?" "How many people live in the household?" and "What are your feelings about various members of the household?" One further point should be made about questioning in counseling. Adults should be careful about the use of "why" questions with youth because they are associated with blame. "Why did you do that?" is often interpreted in the mind of a child as "Why did you do a *stupid thing* like that?" These questions put people on the defensive; when asked why we acted a certain way, we feel forced to find some logical reason or excuse for our behavior. Glasser (see Chapter 4) suggested that a better question might be a "what" question. Most of us are not really sure *why* we behaved a certain way, but we can tell *what* occurred. A "what" question does not deal with possible unconscious motives and desires but focuses on present behavior; the client and counselor can look at what is happening now and what can be done.

Garbarino and Stott (1989) reminded counselors that effective questions must be appropriate for the developmental level of their clients. They made the following suggestions for interviewing preschoolers and probably for most elementary school–aged children.

- Use sentences that do not exceed by more than five words the number of words in a sentence the child uses.
- Use names rather than pronouns.
- Use the child's terms.
- Do not ask, "Do you understand?" Ask the child to repeat your message.
- Do not repeat questions children do not understand because they may think they have made errors and attempt to "correct" their answers. Rephrase the question instead.
- Avoid time-sequence questions.
- Preschoolers, being very literal, may give us answers that are easy to over interpret.
- Do not respond to every answer with another question. A short summary or acknowledgment encourages the child to expand on his or her previous statement.

In summary, counselors learn more by listening and summarizing than by questioning. The habit of questioning is difficult to break. When tempted to question, counselors might first ask themselves whether the questions they ask will (1) contribute therapeutically to understanding the child and the child's problems or (2) inhibit the further flow of expression.

## How Can Silences Be Used in Counseling?

Most of us are uncomfortable with silences. We have been socially conditioned to keep the conversation going; when conversation begins to ebb, we search through our thoughts for a new topic of interest to introduce to the group. Although silences can be very productive in a counseling interview, counselors often find them difficult to bear. Silence may be helpful, however. A child may need a few moments of silence to sort out thoughts and feelings. The child may have related some very emotional event or thought and may need a moment of silence to think about this revelation or regain composure. The child or the counselor may have behaved or spoken in a confusing manner, and sorting things out may take time and silence.

On the other hand silence can be a way of resisting counseling. The child may be reluctant to open up and talk with this stranger who promises acceptance, or the child may not be willing to admit and deal with the problem. Techniques such as play therapy, role playing, and confrontation may be necessary to establish a better relationship and deal with the resistance.

Silences can be used for problem solving and therefore be productive, but how long should the counselor allow the silence to last? Obviously, an entire session of silence between child and counselor is not likely to be helpful. The child may spontaneously begin to speak again when ready. Children's nonverbal behavior may provide counselors with clues that they are ready to begin. The counselor may test the water by making a quiet statement reflecting the possible cause of the silence: "You seem a little confused about what you just told me." The child's response to this reflection should indicate whether he or she is ready to proceed.

## Should Counselors Give Advice?

The role of a counselor has often been interpreted as advice giver, and some counseling theorists advocate giving advice to clients. Their rationale is that the counselor, who is trained in helping and more knowledgeable, should advise the less knowledgeable client.

We prefer to view the role of the counselor as using skills and knowledge to assist another person in solving his or her own problems or conflicts. Counselors who believe in the uniqueness, worth, dignity, and responsibility of the individual and who believe that, given the right conditions, individuals can make correct choices for themselves are reluctant to give advice on solving life's problems. Instead, they use their counseling knowledge and skill to help clients make responsible choices of their own and, in effect, learn how to become their own counselor.

An illustration of the difference between giving advice and assisting in problem solving may clarify the point. Consider this example:

Tony was threatened by neighborhood bullies who were going to beat him up on the way home from school. Tony confided his fear of fighting to the counselor, who advised him to talk this over with his parents, who, he said, will understand and probably talk to the neighborhood boys' parents, and everything will work out fine. Tony was reluctant to talk to his parents, but the counselor persuaded him they would understand and help. Tony returned later to relate that his father lectured him for being a "sissy" and instructed him to "go out and fight like a man." Tony was more terrified than ever because neither his parents nor the counselor understood his dilemma or could be counted on to support him. In this case, the counselor, not considering the client's home and culture, gave advice that intensified the problem. The counselor might have been more helpful by assisting Tony to think of ways of solving the problem—ways that Tony would choose.

Another possible disadvantage of counselors' advice is the problem of dependency. Counselors want their clients to become responsible individuals capable of solving their own problems. Children have a multitude of adults telling them how and when to act, but only a few assist them to learn responsible problem-solving behavior. In counseling, children learn the problem-solving process; they learn that they do not have to depend entirely on adults to make all decisions for them. The process can develop confident, mature, and independent individuals moving toward self-actualization.

Excessive advice giving in counseling can foster dependency, overconformity, and low self-esteem. Counselors who encourage excessive dependency might investigate their own motivations and needs. Most counselors become extremely frustrated by clients who depend on them for decisions. A dependency relationship inevitably breeds hostility: The dependent person resents having to depend on the counselor; the counselor resents having to support the dependency of the client.

This conflict is analogous to the typical adolescent struggle for independence. Because many people see the counselor's role as that of advice giver, some clients may become frustrated and angry when counselors will not give advice. Talking about the role of the counselor and working with the client to negotiate realistic expectations would ease the tension and begin building a working alliance with the client. This is an imperative step when the counselors and the children are from different cultures.

When asked what they think they could do to work out the conflict or problem, children typically are unable to think of possible solutions. It is a new experience for many children to be involved in solving their own problems. When pressed to give advice, a counselor could reflect the feeling that the child is not sure what to do and would like to have an answer and then suggest again that they explore possibilities together. If the child is persistent and demands an answer, the counselor may wish to explore the reasons for this demand.

We need to point out, however, that counselors have a duty to protect their clients from any harm they might do to themselves as well as to prevent them from harming others. Therefore, counselors may need to give advice in emergency situations and to act on the advice they give.

## Should Counselors Give Information?

Beginning counselors, believing that giving information is the same as giving advice, often give neither. Clients need good information to make good decisions, and counselors help clients by sharing what good information they have. For example, counselors should inform their clients of community and school resources where clients can receive assistance. The decision to seek assistance should be the client's. In other words, advice often takes the form of a suggestion to perform a certain behavior or to take some course of action. Information giving, however, means providing data, facts, general knowledge, and, to some extent, alternatives.

Two primary causes of problems are lack of information about self and the environment. The counselor's role is to help clients find the information they need to solve their problems. Once again, we believe that the more active clients are in seeking their own information, the better their learning experience.

## How Does the Counselor Keep the Client on Task During the Counseling Session?

Children soon discover that the counselor is a good listener who gives them undivided attention. Because many children are not listened to by adults, they often take advantage of the counseling situation to talk about everything except the reason for coming to counseling. With the least suggestion, the counselor may find the child rambling on about a TV show, last night's ball game, a current movie, tricks a pet dog can do, or any number of other irrelevant topics. Children, like adults, can ramble excessively when they wish to avoid a problem. Talkativeness then becomes a diversionary tactic either to avoid admitting what is troubling them or to avoid coping with the conflict. The conflict could be too traumatic or painful to face.

Another possible reason for losing focus in a counseling session is that children do not understand their role in the counseling interview. If the purpose of counseling and expectations of the people involved are clearly defined in the initial interview, pointless chatting is less likely.

Counselors who discover themselves being led into superficial or rambling conversations may want to bring the conversation back to the problem at hand by reflecting to the child, "We seem to be getting away from the reason for our time together. I wonder if you could tell me more about. . . ." If a child consistently wanders, state that you notice the wandering and then explore possible reasons for the avoidance. A tape recorder can be an excellent means of determining when, how, and why the distractions occur. A contract might be drawn up, such as "[The counselor] and I will work on [the problem] for 25 minutes. I can talk to [the counselor] about anything else for the last 5 minutes."

## What Limits Should Be Set in Counseling?

In training, most counselors are taught to be empathic, respectful, genuine, accepting, and nonjudgmental—characteristics that writers such as Carl Rogers and Robert Carkhuff defined as essential for a facilitative counseling relationship. Counselors may follow many other theories during the counseling process, but most believe that establishing a therapeutic relationship based on these ingredients is a necessary first step for effective counseling. Based on their synthesis of outcome literature, Orlinsky, Grawe, and Parks (1994) concluded that the counseling relationship is the best predictor of counseling outcome and is critical to its success. The characteristics of empathy, respect, and genuineness have been operationally defined by Carkhuff (1969), and many training institutions teach counselors these behaviors according to his model.

To define the counseling attitudes and behaviors involved in being accepting and nonjudgmental may not be quite so easy. Acceptance implies that counselors believe individuals have infinite worth and dignity, the right to make choices and decisions for their lives, and responsibility for their own lives. Accepting an individual as a person of worth and potential is possible without accepting that person's behavior. Children should be viewed as unique and responsible individuals, capable of making wise choices; however, adults cannot totally accept all child behaviors. Acceptance does not imply total permissiveness. Respect for the rights of all individuals involved must accompany acceptance, and counselors cannot allow children to infringe on their rights as people or on the rights of other family members, friends, or acquaintances.

Being accepting and nonjudgmental can be difficult for some counselors, especially regarding moral and ethical issues. Counselors are human beings with their own attitudes, values, and beliefs. Remaining open-minded enough to really hear the client's entire story is difficult if the client's values and those of the counselor conflict.

Being nonjudgmental does not mean that anything goes. Rather, it is withholding those judgments we ordinarily make and allowing clients to tell the whole story without being threatened by the counselor's condemnation. Counselors attempt to refrain from blaming, accusing, criticizing, and moralizing, but they also attempt to teach responsible, reality-oriented behavior to their child clients. The counselor does not tell children they are wrong; the counselor's job is to help children explore the consequences, advantages, and disadvantages of their choices and, perhaps, discover better methods of resolving the conflict. For instance, rather than sermonizing to Tony that fighting is wrong, the counselor might be more helpful by thinking with him about what would happen if he challenged the bully to a fight and whether he could gain his father's acceptance and respect in other ways.

In summary, accepting and nonjudgmental attitudes are essential for good counseling, but they must be combined with respect for the rights of others, the reality of the situation, and responsibility for one's own behavior.

## What About the Issue of Confidentiality?

Most counselors have been taught that whatever is said in a counseling interview should remain confidential unless there is danger to the client, another person, or property. Many explain the principle of confidentiality to their clients during the first interview; others discuss confidentiality only if the child asks whether what is said will be told to parents or teachers. Should information indicating danger to a person or property be revealed during later interviews, counselors remind children of the counselor's obligation to report such danger to the proper authorities. Counselors do not have privileged communication in their counselor–client relationships unless they are licensed by a state regulatory board. Counselors' records can be subpoenaed, and counselors can be called to testify in court proceedings if the information they possess is deemed necessary for a court decision. If counselors think that revealing the information required in their testimony could harm the child, they can request a private conference with the judge to share both the information and their reasons for wanting to keep the information confidential. See Chapter 19 for more information on confidentiality and privileged communication.

Some counselors maintain that children and adults should be encouraged to communicate more openly and that the counselor can facilitate this process in the family counseling interview. They further contend that parents and other adults can provide insight and needed information about the child; the significant adult in the child's life can become a co-counselor. A signed contract with the parents to protect the confidentiality of the child's counseling sessions, although not legally binding, may help establish the interview content's confidentiality. Talking with the parent about the counseling relationship may also allow the counselor opportunities to involve the parent in the out-of-session activities of the client, such as homework assignments or information gathering.

Careful evaluation of the child's presenting problem and the adults involved may help the counselor decide whether strict confidentiality should be maintained or if others should be included. To avoid misunderstanding and maintain the trust necessary for the counseling relationship, the decision to include others or share information should always be discussed with the child. The child may agree and, in fact, lead the discussions.

## Is This Child Telling Me the Truth?

Another counseling problem is whether the child is telling the counselor the truth or enhancing or exaggerating to get attention or sympathy. Children often tell their counselors of seeing shootings, raging fires, and robberies. Unfortunately, many of these stories are true; however, children have vivid imaginations, and it is difficult to know how much to believe. Counselors do not want to encourage children to lie. If counselors doubt the truth of what they are hearing, soliciting more details of the incident (for example, by saying, "Tell me more") may clarify whether the story is truth or fiction. When asked to give specifics, children may admit they were "only kidding" or "making it up." Counselors might also admit their genuine concerns: "I am really having trouble with this because I have never heard anything like it." An admission of this sort by a counselor expresses a genuine feeling and avoids labeling the child a liar or possibly denying a true story. It also provides the child with an opportunity to change the story while saving face.

## What Can Be Done When the Interview Process Becomes Blocked?

In some counseling sessions, the child does not feel like talking. It is possible that things have been going well for the past few days and the child really has nothing to discuss. There may be a lull before new material is introduced. One way to avoid these unexpected empty periods is to be prepared for a session. Some counselors have general goals for their client (for instance, to increase assertiveness) and also define specific short-term goals for each session as counseling proceeds. Whether the counselor prefers to define objectives or not, notes of the previous session can be reviewed and a tentative plan made for the coming interview. Obviously, this plan is subject to change, according to the content of the interview.

When the child seems highly distracted, a short summary of the previous conversation by the counselor or child may stimulate further communication. If the child does not seem to want to talk, the techniques of play therapy (drawing, clay, games) may be beneficial. At times (illness, extreme excitability, or apathy) ending the session short of the designated time is best. The length of counseling sessions can vary from a few minutes to an hour, depending on the client's age and presenting problem.

When sessions become blocked, evaluate what is happening. Again, the tape recorder assists in assessing the lack of progress. Blocking may be a sign that the child is ready for the counseling to conclude. It could be resistance on the part of the child. It could come from the counselor's inadequate skills or lack of planning. Unproductive sessions occur occasionally for all counselors, but frequent periods of nonproductivity should signal the counselor to investigate what is happening.

## When Should Counseling Be Terminated?

How does a counselor decide when to end counseling? Does the counselor or the client decide? How does either party know the client is ready to stand alone? If the counselor and client have clearly defined the problem brought to counseling and the goal to be accomplished, the termination time will be evident—when the goal is accomplished. The counselor may also want to look for any of the following signs:

- Is the child more open?
- Does the child accept responsibility for feelings and actions?
- Is the child more tolerant of self and others?
- Is the child more independent and self-directing?
- Is the child less fearful, less unhappy, and less anxious than when the relationship began?

Termination may be difficult for children, who usually find the sessions to be a time when a caring adult gives them undivided attention. Deep friendships are often formed between counselor and child, and the child (and possibly the counselor) does not wish to end this pleasant relationship. To ease the break, client and counselor can discuss a possible termination date several weeks ahead of time. Plans can be made and rehearsed about how the child will react should problems recur. The child can be left feeling that the counselor still cares and will be available should trouble arise. Counselors may even consider building in a follow-up time when they ask their child clients to drop them a note or call to let them know how things are going. The counselor may want to schedule a brief follow-up visit. Any informal method of showing the child that a counselor's caring does not end with the last interview can signal the counselor's continued interest in the child's growth and development. Most successful counselors use a plan for maintaining the gains their clients have achieved during counseling. Such maintenance plans require periodic follow-up contacts—for example, 30 days or 6 months.

## HOW CAN COUNSELING BE EVALUATED?

In these times when accountability has become a high priority because of budgetary pressures, counselors are being asked to demonstrate their effectiveness by specific and measurable outcomes. In addition, providers of mental health services working with clients enrolled in managed care plans are under pressure to deliver services in the most cost-effective way possible (Steenbarger & Smith, 1996).

*Consumer Reports* (cited in Seligman, 1995) conducted a survey to determine the efficacy of therapy and concluded that no single measure of effectiveness sufficed. However, three areas for assessment were suggested: "How much did treatment help with the specific problem?" "How satisfied was the consumer with services received?" and, overall, "How much did the client improve?"

Steenbarger and Smith (1996) recommended similar measures. They propose a measure evaluating the degree to which clients feel they have received services that are convenient and useful and recommend several scales. Unfortunately, most scales that have been validated and that have established reliability are constructed for adults. They would have to be adapted for the developmental age of the child client, and validity and reliability would need to be reestablished.

A second measure suggested by Steenbarger and Smith (1996) is outcome measures taken at two or more points. Outcome measures are related to the goals of counseling and are statements about the counselors' and clients' expected outcomes from counseling that are written in measurable terms. Measures could be evaluated by both client and counselor. Again, most published measures are for adults and usually assess symptoms that are indicative of pathology rather than growth and development, and they may not be individualized to the clients' particular goals. Steenbarger and Smith (1996) and Ahn and Wampold (2001) also report that standards of care can be used as measures of effectiveness if professionals agree on the *best practices* of the profession and *common factors*, including the healing context, the working alliance, and the rationale of the treatment. Counselors would be required to document in their notes how and when they engaged in these practices. The writers conclude that professionals in counseling need to assess and document client satisfaction, outcomes, and counselor performance on selected criteria in order to demonstrate effectiveness. The challenge for counselors working with children is to develop age-appropriate satisfaction scales, to develop outcome measures from initial goals set early in counseling, and to work with other professionals to establish *best practices* and *common factors* for highly effective care.

Goal-attainment scaling is another method of evaluation designed for evaluating counseling outcomes. Goal-attainment scaling (Kiresuk, Smith, & Cardillo, 1996; Yarbrough & Thompson, 2002) allows counselor and client the opportunity to establish counseling goals cooperatively. The counselor's task is to help the child clarify these goals in measurable terms as a way of evaluating the distance between "What I have" and "What I would like to have." The tabulation and calculation of the data are the counselor's responsibility. Generally one to five goals are set, with five levels of attainment defined for each goal (Table 2-1). In addition, each goal is given a weight to represent its importance to the client. Clients establish priorities for their goals and assign weights to the most important and least important. For instance, Goal 1 may be three times more important than Goal 2. Intermediate goals are assigned weights representing their relative importance to the client. For example, if the most important goal is three times as important as the least important goal, it would receive a weight of 30 compared to a weight of 10 for the least important goal. Goals are then weighted on a scale of 10, 20, or 30 depending on their relative importance to the client.

Levels of attainment for each goal range from a "+2" for the best anticipated success to a "−2" for the least favorable outcome. A "0" value is assigned for the middle level of expected outcome success. Values of "+1" and "−1" represent "more than" and "less than" expected levels of success, respectively.

The goals are defined in measurable and observable terms, with the level of entry checked on the goal-attainment follow-up guide. Following counseling, an asterisk is placed on the guide indicating where the client is after counseling. Follow-up data can also be recorded periodically on the chart.

TABLE 2-1 Goal-attainment scale

| Scale attainment level | Scale 1: on task $W_1 = 20$ | Scale 2: behavior $W_2 = 30$ | Scale 3: punctuality $W_3 = 10$ | Scale 4: relationships $W_4 = 30$ | Scale 5: grade improvements $W_5 = 10$ |
|---|---|---|---|---|---|
| a. Most unfavorable counseling outcome expected (−2) | Daydreams, leaves desk; ignores assignments [ | Breaks classroom rules 4 or more times/day | Late to class 4 times/week [ | Child gets into three fights per week | Child continues to fail [ |
| b. Less than expected success with counseling (−1) | Completes one assignment per day | Breaks rules 3 times/day [ | Late to class 3 times/week | Child gets into at least one fight per week [ | Child demonstrates D work |
| c. Expected level of counseling success (0) | Completes two assignments per day | Breaks rules 2 times/day | Late to class 2 times/week | Child avoids all fights | Child demonstrates C work |
| d. More than expected success with counseling (+1) | Completes three assignments per day φ | Breaks rules 1 time/day φ | Late to class 1 time/week φ | Child develops one new friend φ | Child demonstrates B work φ |
| e. Most favorable counseling outcome expected (+2) | Completes four assignments per day | Follows all rules | Late to class 0 times/week | Child develops three new friends | Child demonstrates A work |

NOTE: Level at intake: [; level at follow-up: φ.

Goal-attainment scores can be calculated for both the intake and follow-up levels. A follow-up goal-attainment score of 50 or better is considered successful. Kiresuk and Sherman (1968) adopted a conventional T-score scale with the mean set at 50 and a standard deviation set at 10 for their goal-attainment scale. The following formulas are used to derive the goal-attainment scores for the guide in Table 2-1 (Kiresuk & Sherman, 1968). Using the numbers from the guide in Table 2-1, the reader will find that the formula is not as difficult to use as it might appear to be. However, T-score tables are provided for those who wish to avoid calculating the scores (see Appendix C).

*Goal-Attainment Score Calculation: Level at Intake*

| | |
|---|---|
| $\overline{X}$ = mean | $\overline{X}$ = 50 |
| $s$ = standard deviation | $s$ = 20 |
| $\rho$ (rho) = probability of interscale correlation | $\rho$ = 0.3 |
| | $1 - \rho$ = 0.7 |
| $w_1$ = weight value | $w_1$ = 10 to 30 |
| $x_1$ = scale value | $x_1$ = −2 to +2 |

Goal-attainment score (T) $= 50 + \dfrac{10\Sigma w_1 x_1}{\sqrt{(0.7\Sigma w_1{}^2) + 0.3(\Sigma w_1)^2}}$

$50 + 10\,[(20 \times -2) + (30 \times -1) + (10 \times -2) + (30 \times -2) + (10 \times -2)]$

$50 + \dfrac{10 \times -170}{\sqrt{0.7(20^2 + 30^2 + 10^2 + 30^2 + 10^2) + 0.3(20 + 30 + 10 + 30 + 10)^2}}$

$50 + \dfrac{10 \times -170}{\sqrt{0.7(2{,}400) + 0.3(10{,}000)}}$

$50 + \dfrac{10 \times -170}{\sqrt{3{,}276}}$

$50 + \dfrac{10 \times -170}{57.23}$

$50 + \dfrac{(-1700)}{57.23}$

$50 + (-29.7)$

T = 20.3

Z score $= \dfrac{50 - 20.3}{10} = 2.97$ standard deviations below the mean

*Goal-Attainment Score Calculation: Level at Follow-Up*

| | |
|---|---|
| $\overline{X}$ = mean | $\overline{X} = 50$ |
| $s$ = standard deviation | $s = 10$ (standard deviation) |
| $\rho$ (rho) = probability of interscale correlation | $\rho = 0.3$ |
| $w_1$ = weight value | $w_1 = 10$ to $30$ |
| $x_1$ = scale value | $x_1 = -2$ to $+2$ |

Goal-attainment score $(T) = 50 + \dfrac{10\Sigma w_1 x_1}{\sqrt{(0.7\Sigma w_1{}^2) + 0.3(\Sigma w_1)^2}}$

$$50 + \dfrac{10\,[(20 \times 1) + (30 \times 1) + (10 \times 2) + (30 \times 1) + (10 \times 1)]}{\sqrt{0.7(20^2 + 30^2 + 10^2 + 30^2 + 10^2) + 0.3(20 + 30 + 10 + 30 + 10)^2}}$$

$$50 + \dfrac{10 \times 140}{}$$

$$50 + \dfrac{10 \times 110}{\sqrt{0.7(2{,}400) + 0.3(10{,}000)}}$$

$$50 + \dfrac{10 \times 110}{\sqrt{4{,}680}}$$

$$50 + \dfrac{10 \times 110}{68.41}$$

$$50 + \dfrac{(1100)}{68.41}$$

$$50 + (16)$$

$$T = 66$$

$$Z \text{ score} = \dfrac{66 - 50}{10} = \dfrac{16}{10} = 1.6 \text{ standard deviations below the mean}$$

Goal-attainment scaling (Dowd & Kelly, 1975) can be graphed to show weekly progress (Figure 2-4). The graph can also be used to chart the results of periodic follow-up checks on the maintenance of counseling gains.

Martin and Thompson (1995) also found the goal-attainment scale effective in helping student athletes balance their responsibilities between school, sports, and other areas in order to fulfill their expectations of success. Yarbrough and Thompson (2002) used goal-attainment scales in tracking elementary school students on improving their on-task behaviors.

T-scores and average scale scores may be obtained from the conversion tables in Appendix C if you wish to avoid doing the arithmetic required to work the T-score formula. Both before- and after-treatment scores can be obtained from the

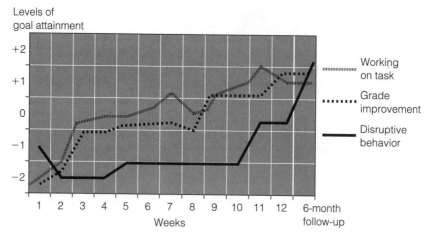

FIGURE 2-4   Weekly goal-attainment scale

conversion tables. Simply sum the individual scale scores prior to treatment and enter the conversion table corresponding to the number of scales on the goal-attainment scale. For example, the goal-attainment scale on page 57 has five scales and a sum of –9 on the individual pretreatment scale scores $[(-2) + (-1) + (-2) + (-2) + (-2) = -9]$. So, entering conversion Table C-5 in Appendix C we find that the pretreatment T-score is 22.86, with an average scale score of $-1.8$ for the five scales. Following treatment, the scale scores totaled $+6$, found by summing the individual scale score of $(1 + 1 + 2 + 1 + 1)$. Again, checking conversion Table C-5, we find the post treatment scale score to be 68.09, with an average scale score of 1.2. Therefore, with a mean T-score of 50 and a standard deviation of 10, the client on the goal-attainment scale improved from $\dfrac{50 - 22.86}{10} = 2.7$ standard deviations *below* the mean to $\dfrac{68.09 - 50}{10} = 1.8$ standard deviations *above* the mean. Improvements of at least one step on a scale are considered to be significant gains. In this case, the child improved 4.5 standard deviations on his full scale score.

## HOW DO PROFESSIONAL COUNSELORS WORK WITH MANAGED HEALTH CARE?*

Approximately 71% of Americans (excluding individuals over age 65) are covered by private insurance, and about 80% of the plans are administered by a managed care organization (MCO) (American Counseling Association, 1997). One major study

*The authors appreciate Dr. Laura Veach, Wake Forest University, for contributing this section.

(Ringel & Sturm, 2001) found that 1998 costs for treating mental health in children, ranging in age from 1 to 17, were conservatively estimated at $11.68 billion, or $172 per child. In addition, Ringel and Sturm found major changes in the delivery of care since previous 1986 estimates—namely, a much higher use of outpatient mental health services (57% of the total 1998 cost) than previous dominant trends of inpatient or residential services prior to managed care. Their work illustrated that adolescents, ages 12 to 17, use 60% of the total dollars spent on mental health for children and youth. At least one managed behavioral health organization (MBHO), United Behavioral Health (UBH), provided data for the study. UBH is the third largest MBHO, with approximately 18 million covered lives in the United States (Ringel & Sturm). The findings indicated that utilization was lower than the study average, and outpatient visits for covered UBH members aged 1 to 17 was notably lower than other groups, including public-sector mental healthcare recipients. This study determined that "a sizable amount of mental health services are provided outside the specialty settings covered by insurance . . . the education sector likely accounts for a large portion of the difference" (Ringel & Sturm, 2001, p. 326). That statement implies that the mental health needs of many school-aged youth may too often be addressed only in school settings. Another important finding was that 9% of the total costs for 1998 mental health care for children were for psychotropic medications. Not surprisingly, the authors further concluded that the majority of children who could respond favorably to mental health care do not receive the needed services. They also point to the significant trend of primary care medical settings providing a substantial amount of mental health care for children (Ringel & Sturm).

In both the private and public sectors, significant changes have resulted in more counseling services for children and youth being managed by specialized behavioral health insurance organizations (Stein & Orlando, 2001). The majority of these specialty behavioral health organizations are deemed carve-outs because they are contracted out to oversee and manage only the behavioral health benefits of those insured by the contracting health maintenance organization (HMO). This practice separates the management of medical benefits and frees the HMO to delegate behavioral health issues to its contracted MBHO. Throughout the 1990s, one HMO might have contracted with two different MBHOs within the same year. Competition among the MBHOs for the increasingly shrinking healthcare dollar resulted in many buyouts and consolidations of MBHOs. Currently, there are three major MBHOs that manage behavioral healthcare for more than half of all managed behavioral health in the United States. These MBHOs or carve-outs are now dominating the management of counseling services in the United States. The past decade has witnessed extensive MBHO contracting by the public sector for Medicaid-covered individuals. Each state determines how Medicaid services are administered by the selected MBHO, and numerous problems occurred with contract administration. Currently, MBHOs are more selective in bidding for managing public-sector behavioral healthcare because of hidden costs and difficulties with satisfaction by some stakeholders.

At present, the most influential and largest MBHO is Magellan Behavioral Health. As of 2001, they reported a total enrollment of 69.3 million individuals, covering one of every three insured citizens (Magellan Behavioral Health, 2002). They reported $1.76 billion net revenue for their fiscal year 2001. However, currently even the leading MBHO has experienced serious financial pressures attributed to rising outpatient behavioral health costs, increased utilization, and a loss of approximately 1.8 million members in 2002 as a result of contract changes (Open Minds On-Line News, 2002). Major changes and economic pressures continue in the managed care industry with significant impact on the counseling children now receive.

Patterson, McIntosh-Koontz, Baron, and Bischoff (1997) have painted managed care as the primary shaper of the new world environment that counselors and therapists will be facing in trying to succeed in private practice. They outlined some of the problems counselors face that result from the change in access and cost of care. In addition, increased penetration by managed care into community and school counseling settings has also complicated how counseling is provided throughout the continuum of care. An extensive case study by Heflinger and Northrup (2000) examined differences in delivery of mental healthcare for CHAMPUS-covered children and youth after a contract with a for-profit MBHO. The related trends revealed less access to mental health services (a 50% reduction in eligible clients receiving services), a pattern of referral of more troubled cases to the public sector after case management deemed clients "non-responsive" and therefore unlikely to benefit from costly levels of care, poor ratings related to coordination of care, and significant lags of payment for contracted services by the MBHO. A clash of philosophy between containing costs and best care for the client often contaminates authorizations for the type, level, and duration of counseling and stresses the need for independent review of MBHO practices and authorization patterns. Even projects aimed at prevention of serious mental health problems in young children met with significant frustration for clinicians trying to work with a managed care approach and Medicaid (Hocutt, McKinney, & Montague, 2002).

Some other problems with managed behavioral healthcare include restrictions placed on counselors and their clients regarding dollar amounts and time limits for certain types of therapy. Decisions on diagnosis and treatment are often influenced by managed care administrators and case reviewers rather than by the actual counselor(s). The best possible treatment for a particular client may not be available under the client's health insurance.

Patterson, McIntosh-Koontz, Baron, and Bischoff (1997) were concerned that graduate programs are not preparing their students to deal with the managed realities of today's counseling. The world of managed care is characterized by the complications caused by added record keeping, general paperwork, emphasis on treatment cost over treatment quality, panel appointments, network inclusion, and recognition of licensure.

Murphy (1998) raised the questions of whether managed care is ethical and whether counselors can engage in ethical practice within the managed care system. Her response to both questions was that counselors have the responsibility to ensure that they practice within the codes and laws that govern the counseling profession and within the limits of their training and competence, regardless of managed care restrictions. She pointed out that the answer to the question of how to be an ethical practitioner within the context of managed care lies in our ability to hold the line—what we consider to be "good enough" counseling. She recommended that counselors work as a group to advocate changes of those aspects of managed care that breach the limits of our ethical codes.

English and Marino (1998) provided a thorough update and analysis of how professional counselors were letting managed healthcare influence their practice. Somewhat surprising was the finding that counselor attitude toward managed care ranged from enthusiasm to outright hostility and opposition. However, the wide range of counselor attitudes is not all that dissimilar from that of other healthcare professionals. Reports of cheating or fraud in the use of managed care programs by professional counselors did not appear in the survey. Some counselors, having adapted to managed care, were actually thriving within the limits and restrictions placed on their practice. Other counselors, though, completely frustrated with the paperwork, restrictions, and guidelines posed by managed care, have chosen to exempt their practice from managed care.

Successful counseling practices have been built within and without managed care plans. However, practices fail under both approaches. English and Marino (1998) cited a survey conducted by Howard Smith, chair of the American Counseling Association (ACA) Professionalization Committee. Sixty-five percent of 1,200 counselors surveyed received one quarter or less of their income from managed care. Several complaints about managed care were registered in the survey. These included lower fees, delays in payments, and concerns about possible breaches of clients' confidentiality. Also reported in the survey, fees paid by managed care programs have failed to keep pace with the rather low rate of inflation and have, in some cases, actually decreased in the range of 10 to 15% over the past 4 years for all nonphysician mental health professionals. Other complaints included difficulty in getting authorization for treatment, excessive paperwork, and the expense involved in purchasing software to generate claim forms and record forms for tracking patient outcomes.

During the past two decades, we have recommended that all counselors find a system for tracking their clients' progress and outcomes. We have found that managed healthcare company administrators, as well as school administrators, have been very impressed with the system we recommend in this chapter: goal-attainment scaling. We have found no better instrument than the goal-attainment scale for documenting success as a counselor with either managed healthcare or school administrators. Even without calculating the Z scores for each client, which can be done with simple arithmetic, the chart is quite effective in showing client change from the first to the last counseling session.

English and Marino (1998), in an interview with Warren Throckmorton, past president of the American Mental Health Counselors Association (AMHCA), found counselors were more concerned about how to fight MCOs than with how to work with them. He believed the trend toward working with managed care would continue to increase. Apparently, significant numbers of people have managed care plans yet want to seek counseling without involving the plan or the panel of providers provided by the plan. Several counselors are marketing their services toward this group. Reports from professional counselors in our area reflect similar data. Many people are quite aware that having counseling or psychotherapy listed in their treatment records may not be beneficial to their careers. Unfortunately counseling and psychotherapy still carry the stigma of not being "normal" health care. Mental health professionals working outside MBHOs can and do offer confidentiality to protect against the misuse of clients' health and insurance records.

O'Hara (1996) wrote a very positive article on how she has been successful in her practice outside managed care. We strongly recommend her article for all who currently are in private practice or contemplating it. O'Hara believes the key to her success is marketing her services outside the medical model for treating mental illness. Her focus, much like the focus of our entire book, is to further personal growth and development through concentrating on fostering mental health rather than treating mental illness. People come to her for self-improvement and education rather than to cure an illness. Campbell (2003) has followed a similarly successful plan over the past two decades. Her office, an attractive, refurbished small house, contains a waiting room, counseling office, and play-therapy room. The sign in the front yard reads: "Educational Development Center." Her counseling philosophy defines counseling as an educational process directed toward helping her clients find better ways to meet their needs. Campbell's philosophy is quite compatible with ours, which undergirds each chapter in this book.

Not all the data on counseling and managed care are negative. Definite benefits for the profession have accrued from managed care. First, professional counselors have been recognized as viable providers of mental health services. The number of MBHOs recognizing counselors continues to increase each year. The ACA Office of Public Policy and Information was successful in achieving recognition of professional counselors by managed healthcare's leading accrediting body, the National Committee for Quality Assurance (NCQA). NCQA is also the developer of the primary assessment instrument used by the government and businesses to measure the quality of care provided by MCOs. The American Mental Health Counselors Association has also been successful in increasing recognition of professional counselors by MCOs.

Second, the Balanced Budget Act of 1997 stipulates that Medicare managed care administrators cannot discriminate against providers on the basis of their type of license. The Mental Health Parity Act of 1998 prohibits health plans from using annual or lifetime dollar limits on coverage for mental health services that are different or less than those provided for medical services. These two acts have their problems and loopholes, but they do represent significant first steps in bringing parity to counselors as recognized providers of mental health services. Senate Bill 1754, the Health Professions Education Partnership, included mental health counselors among the list of health service providers that could be trained under their legislation. In addition, the bill would recognize professional counselors as "core mental health professionals" by the Health Resources and Services Administration, thereby making professional counselors eligible for participation in the National Health Service Corps scholarship and loan repayment program. The program was established to ensure an adequate supply of health professionals, including mental health professionals, in areas designated as health professional shortage areas (Powell, 1998).

Third, MCOs have helped counselors make their practice more time- and cost-effective with their demands for quality care documentation. Increasingly, studies are finding that counselors and therapists are cost-effective. For example, Stein and Orlando (2001), using data from UBH, the third largest MBHO in the United States, found in a study of youth under the age of 15 being treated for ADHD that the fewest counseling sessions (7.6) were provided by therapists and the duration of counseling was the shortest when the therapist was the only mental health practitioner working with the young person. MBHO personnel have also started to reduce some of the red tape, paperwork, and pretreatment procedures in response to consumer and provider pressure. For example, ValueOptions is an MBHO that offers certain plans that provide outpatient counseling benefits, and the total 26 sessions are authorized at the beginning of treatment. An additional benefit to counselors has been the referral sources offered by the MBHOs. The current trend is to offer consumers more choices for their mental health care providers.

English and Marino (1998) suggested several ways counselors can work successfully with MCOs. First, counselors need to be good marketers, distinguishing themselves and what they do from other providers. English and Marino interviewed Brett Steenbarger, executive director of Prime Care, a multispecialty group practice in Syracuse, New York, on the question of how to succeed in working with MCOs. Steenbarger emphasized the importance of having a specialty, such as solution-focused brief counseling or group psychotherapy, that is favored by MCOs. Any therapy with time-limited and goal-directed foci is quite popular with the MCOs. Cummings (1996) predicted that psychotherapists of the future would be doing one-on-one psychotherapy with only about 25% of their clients. The remaining 75% would be group counseling and therapy, with up to 50% of that total being done with counselors and other therapists following a psychoeducational model. He cites one example in which five-session psychoeducational treatment plans were found to reduce costs of medical treatment for chronic conditions such as asthma, emphysema, and diabetes.

Competing on cost appears to be a good way to work within managed care and also a good way to compete outside of it. Steenbarger (English & Marino, 1998) also recommended (1) that counselors consider joining a group practice or network to increase their chances of being appointed to MBHO panels and (2) that counselors keep their MBHOs appraised of their specialties and any new training obtained in performing one of their approved specialties. Most important, providers' success in remaining on panels will be determined by report card records on such factors as customer service, documented outcome success, and length of client time in treatment. In short, professional counselors will need to be highly accountable for quality and cost whether they choose to work with or without managed healthcare systems.

Davis (1998) summarized six steps for developing effective treatment plans that meet MCO specifications. They are explained in the next section. The steps were taken from a presentation by Judy Stone, manager of training and development for Value Behavioral Health. Stone echoed the treatment philosophy of today: "Treatment is very focused on solutions and doing it in the shortest amount of time."

## Step 1: Problem Identification

Concentrate on those problems that are within the realm of managed care's short-term treatment focus. Describe client problems with descriptor words for behaviors that occur with excessive or deficient intensity, frequency, and duration. Examples include the terms "acting out," "compulsive drinking," and "physically assaultive." Descriptor words for frequency and duration include "prolonged excitement," "daily worry," and "consistent dread." Examples of behavioral deficits include the terms "social withdrawal" and "lack of concentration."

## Step 2: Problem Definition

Following identification of the problem, the counselor needs to define the problem in terms that are consistent with the Diagnostic and Statistical Manual of Mental Disorders (4th ed., text revision) (DSM-IV-TR) (American Psychiatric Association, 2000). Definitions should include the cognitive process that motivates the problem behaviors of the client and a description of the history of the problem. For example, for an anger-management problem, the report could read that the client has a history of explosive, aggressive behaviors disproportionate to any precipitating stressors, leading to assaultive acts and destruction of property.

## Step 3: Goal Development

Write broad goals that are more general in scope and may be long term. For example, "stabilized mood" or "sustained abstinence" are broad goals that help focus on the overarching, larger picture for which the client aims.

## Step 4: Measurable Objectives

Steps or objectives need to be developed for each goal, with projected time lines for meeting them. Objectives help the client and counselor have specific, brief, measurable steps to reach the broad goal. For example, if a client had attempted suicide, objectives leading to the overall goal of preventing future attempts could be the development of future plans to build relationships with others and to find a job. These steps could be broken down into joining an organization such as a church to meet people and developing a resume to use in job applications. Again, the goal-attainment scale described in this chapter is an excellent instrument for meeting managed care guidelines. Having goals for which small steps in progress can be charted is crucial.

## Step 5: Creating Interventions

Develop at least one intervention for every outcome objective. Regardless of one's personal orientation to counseling, treatment plans need to include specific, well-defined steps that are understood by MBHO personnel. For example, a counselor practicing reality therapy would list how the reality therapy steps were to be used to get the client to explore better alternatives to meet personal needs, the intervention frequency, and the duration of the intervention. For example, "individual counseling once per week for 8 weeks" and reevaluate as needed.

## Step 6: Diagnosing

Diagnoses must fit the DSM-IV-TR system for treatment to be reimbursed by MCOs. Decisions to certify the treatment provided will be based on what is written for the five DSM-IV-TR axes. Counselors have to walk the tightrope between defining the client's problem as too severe for brief treatment to be effective or not severe enough to be reimbursed. An example of a too severe definition would be schizophrenia, and an example of a not severe enough definition might be school absenteeism.

We also found that MBHOs are not especially interested in having the public know about the differential rates given to various groups and individuals. We found the best way to collect data on companies was to survey individuals on the particular plan under which they are covered or contact the related state department of insurance. We also noted that many plans, dependent on employee premiums not matched by any employer contributions, are nothing more than enforced savings plans that charge for the privilege of forcing employees to save money for mental health care. Obviously, clients under such plans would be much better served by developing their own direct bank deposit savings plans that earn interest. The following figures represent some typical limits placed on mental health coverage by various MBHOs. Many MBHOs have a 30-day limit per benefit period for inpatient care. Mental health parity continues to be a legislative and administrative challenge, but in 2002 President Bush announced support for mental health parity and the creation of the New Freedom Commission on Mental Health to improve the delivery of mental health care in the U.S. (Bush, 2002). Examples of disparity include some plans paying as much as 90% of the inpatient care costs and others limiting inpatient care to a ceiling of $10,000 per year and a lifetime limit of $50,000. One company we researched had no limit on psychological therapy, whereas others did not cover marriage counseling. The critical factor was the type of license held by the provider of mental health services. Many MBHOs include licensed counselors on their in-network panels. Outpatient benefits paid to out-of-network providers are considerably less in a managed care environment. Outpatient visits may be limited as follows: Visits 1 to 26 are covered with a co-payment by the client ranging from $10 to $30. Some MBHOs may require more extensive utilization reviews of outpatient care, which requires the counselor to contact the MBHO to authorize additional visits or more intensive levels of care. Although some MBHO panels may be closed in general to additional counselors, further investigation with the director of provider relations for the MBHO may reveal a need for services in specialized areas, especially in counseling services for children or in rural areas. Quality standards of NCQA indicate, for example, that services be available within a specified time range. That standard could be specified with a statement such as a counselor should be available no more than 30 minutes in travel time from the client's location. Therefore, as mentioned before, prudent licensed counselors would do well to become members of as many MBHO provider panels as feasible. And, while building a private practice, keeping a salaried position as a counselor in a community agency might be a good idea. Our contention is that professional counselors have overlooked a viable resource in developing their private practices.

In summary, we have noted the positive and negative implications managed healthcare has for the mental health profession in general and professional counselors in particular. The limitations placed on treatment, time, and cost are disadvantages to counselors. Some advantages include efficiency, more accountability, professional recognition, and, for some counselors, the challenge to succeed outside the traditional medical model and managed healthcare.

## W E B S I T E S  for the Counseling Process

Counseling is a challenging field because the world is changing so rapidly. The need for new information about how to handle counseling cases confronts counselors on an almost daily basis. There are hundreds of Websites with specific kinds of information available to help counselors with these challenges. Some sites for general information include:

American Counseling Association
www.counseling.org

American Psychological Association
www.apa.org

American School Counselor Association
www.schoolcounselor.org

Clinical Social Work Federation, Inc.
www.cswf.org

National Mental Health Association
www.nmha.org

National Alliance for the Mentally Ill
www.nami.org

W E B S I T E S for Information on Managed Care

At Health, Inc.
www.athealth.com

Managed Care—Medscape
www.medscape.com/Home/Topics/psychiatry/psychiatry.html

Mental Health Patient's Bill of Rights
www.apa.org/pubinfo/rights/rights.html

Clinical Social Work Federation (CSWF)
www.cswf.org/lobby/updates.html

National Coalition of Mental Health Professionals and Consumers
www.nomanagedcare.org

## REFERENCES

Ahn, M., & Wampold, B. (2001). Where oh where are the specific ingredients? A meta-analysis of component studies in counseling and psychotherapy. *Journal of Counseling Psychology, 48,* 251–257.

American Counseling Association. (1997, December 7). Managed care: A primer on issues and legislation. www.tmhca.org/mgdcare.htm. Retrieved August 13, 2002.

American Psychiatric Association. (2000). *Diagnostic and statistical manual of mental disorders* (4th ed., text revision). Washington, DC: Author.

Burton, L. (1995). Using a dog in an elementary school counseling program. *Elementary School Guidance and Counseling, 29,* 236–240.

Bush, G. W. (2002, April). *President says U.S. must make commitment to mental health care.* Speech given at University of New Mexico, Continuing Education Conference Center, Albuquerque, NM. www.whitehouse.gov/news/releases/2002/04/20020429-1.html. Retrieved February 7, 2002.

Campbell, S. (2003). Personal communication.

Carkhuff, R. (1969). *Helping and human relations* (2 vols.). New York: Holt, Rinehart & Winston.

Carlson, K. (1990). Suggestions for counseling "other-referred" children. *Elementary School Guidance and Counseling, 24,* 222–229.

Cummings, N. (1996). Now we are facing the consequences. *The Scientist Practitioner, 6,* 9–13.

Davis, J. (1998). Managed care forum offers counselors advice on how to gain the competitive edge. *The Advocate, 21,* 5, 9, 12.

Dowd, E., & Kelly, F. (1975). The use of goal attainment scaling in single case study research. *Goal Attainment Review, 2,* 11–21.

Eliot, T.S. (1943). *Four quartets.* New York: Harcourt, Brace and Company.

English, S., & Marino, T. (1998). Update: Professional counselors and managed care. *Counseling Today, 40,* 18–19.

Erdman, P., & Lampe, R. (1996). Adapting basic skills to counsel children. *Journal of Counseling and Development, 74,* 374–377.

Family Educational Rights and Privacy Act. (1974). 20 U.S.C.A. §1232g. [Buckley Amendment.] (1991). Implementing regulations 34 C.F.R. 99.3. Fed. Reg. 56, §117, 28012.

Garbarino, J., & Stott, F. (1989). *What children can tell us.* San Francisco: Jossey-Bass.

Gerler, E. (1990). Multimodal approaches to counseling in schools. *Elementary School Guidance and Counseling, 24,* 242.

Gerler, E., Drew, N., & Mohr, P. (1990). Succeeding in middle school: A multimodal approach. *Elementary School Guidance and Counseling, 24,* 263–271.

Gladding, S. T. (2000). *Counseling: A comprehensive profession.* Upper Saddle River, NJ: Merrill.

Heflinger, C., & Northrup, D. (2000). What happens when capitated behavioral health comes to town? The transition from the Fort Bragg Demonstration to a capitated managed behavioral health contract. *Journal of Behavioral Health Services and Research, 27,* 390–406.

Hocutt, A., McKinney, J., & Montague, M. (2002). The impact of managed care on efforts to prevent development of serious emotional disturbance in young children. *Journal of Disability Policy Studies, 13,* 51–61.

Kazdin, A. E. (1994). Psychotherapy for children and adolescents. In A. E. Bergin & S. L. Garfield (Eds.), *Handbook of psychotherapy and behavior change* (pp. 543–594). New York: Wiley.

Kazdin, A. E. (2000). *Psychotherapy for children and adolescents: Directions for research and practice.* New York: Oxford University Press.

Keat, D. (1990a). Change in child multimodal counseling. *Elementary School Guidance and Counseling, 24,* 248–262.

Keat, D. (1990b). *Child multimodal therapy.* Norwood, NJ: Ablex.

Kiresuk, T., & Sherman, R. (1968). Goal attainment scaling: A general method for evaluating comprehensive community mental health programs. *Community Mental Health, 4,* 443–453.

Kiresuk, T., Smith, A., & Cardillo, J. (Eds.). (1996). *Goal attainment scaling: Applications, theory, and measurement.* Hillsdale, NJ: Erlbaum.

Lambert, M. M., & Cattani-Thompson, K. (1996). Current findings regarding the effectiveness of counseling: Implications for practice. *Journal of Counseling and Development, 74,* 601–608.

Lazarus, A. (1981). *The practice of multimodal therapy.* New York: McGraw-Hill.

Lazarus, A. (1990). Multimodal applications and research: A brief overview and update. *Elementary School Guidance and Counseling, 24,* 243–247.

Lazarus, A. (2000). Multimodal therapy. In R. Corsini (Ed.), *Current psychotherapies* (6th ed.) (pp. 340–375). Itasca, IL: F. E. Peacock.

Magellan Behavioral Health. (2002, July 31). Fast facts. www.magellanhealth.com/mbh/about_us/fast_facts.html. Retrieved September 3, 2002.

Martin, S., & Thompson, C. (1995). Reality therapy and goal attainment scaling: A program for freshman student-athletes. *Journal of Reality Therapy, 14,* 45–54.

Murphy, K. (1998). Is managed care unethical? *International Association of Marriage and Family Counselors, 11,* 3.

O'Brien, M. (1993). Pets as counselors. *Elementary School Guidance and Counseling, 4,* 308.

O'Hara, M. (1996). Divided we stand. *The Family Therapy Networker, 20,* 46–53.

Open Minds On-Line News. (2002, September 2). Magellan reports drop in profits from last year. www.openminds.com/hot.htm. Retrieved September 3, 2002.

Orlinsky, D. E., Grawe, K., & Parks, B. K. (1994). Process and outcome in psychotherapy-Noch einmal. In A. E. Bergin & S. L. Garfield (Eds.), *Handbook of psychotherapy and behavior change* (pp. 270–378). New York: Wiley.

Patterson, J., McIntosh-Koontz, L., Baron, M., & Bischoff, R. (1997). Curriculum changes to meet challenges: Preparing students for managed care settings. *Journal of Marital and Family Therapy, 23,* 445–459.

Poppen, W., & Thompson, C. (1974). *School counseling: Theories and concepts.* Lincoln, NE: Professional Educators.

Powell, B. (1998). Professional counselors included in Federal Health Professionals Training Bill. *The Advocate, 21,* 5, 1, 8.

Ringel, J. S., & Sturm, R. (2001). National estimates of mental health utilization and expenditures for children in 1998. *Journal of Behavioral Health Services and Research, 28,* 319–334.

Seligman, M. (1995). The effectiveness of psychotherapy. *American Psychologist, 50,* 965–974.

Seligman, L. (2001). *Systems, strategies, and skills of counseling and psychotherapy.* Upper Saddle River, NJ: Merrill.

Sexton, T. L. (2001). Evidence-based counseling intervention programs. In D. C. Locke, J. E. Myers, & E. L. Herr (Eds.), *The handbook of counseling* (pp. 499–512). Thousand Oaks, CA: Sage.

Sexton, T. L., & Whiston, S. C. (1996). Integrating counseling research and practice. *Journal of Counseling and Development, 74,* 588–589.

Smith, M. L., Glass, G. V., & Miller, T. I. (1980). *The benefits of psychotherapy.* Baltimore, MD: Johns Hopkins University Press.

Steenbarger, B., & Smith, H. (1996). Assessing the quality of counseling services: Developing accountable helping systems. *Journal of Counseling and Development, 75,* 145–150.

Stein, B., & Orlando, M. (2001). ADHD treatment in a behavioral health care carve-out: Medications, providers, and service utilization. *Journal of Behavioral Health Services and Research, 28,* 30–42.

Thompson, C., & Campbell, S. (1992). Personal intervention preferences for alleviating mild depression. *Journal of Counseling and Development, 71,* 69–73.

Thompson, C., & Poppen, W. (1992). *Guidance activities for counselors and teachers.* Knoxville, TN: Author.

Trivedi, L., & Perl, J. (1995). Animal facilitated counseling in the elementary school: A literature review and practical considerations. *Elementary School Guidance and Counseling, 29,* 223–234.

Yarbrough, J., & Thompson, C. (2002). Using single-participant research to assess the efficacy of two brief counseling approaches on children's off-task behavior. *Professional School Counseling, 5,* 308–314.

# PART TWO

# COUNSELING THEORIES
# AND TECHNIQUES
Adaptations for Children

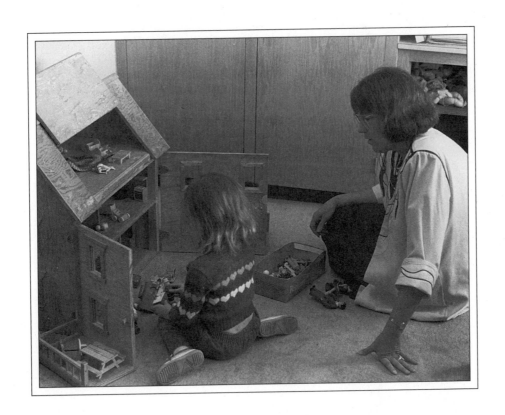

# Chapter 3

# Psychoanalytic Counseling

*A moment's insight is sometimes worth a life's experience.*
—Oliver Wendell Holmes

## SIGMUND FREUD

Sigmund Freud was born in Freiberg, Moravia, in 1856 and died in London in 1939. However, he is considered to have belonged to Vienna, where he lived for nearly 80 years. Freud was the first of his mother's eight children; he had two half-brothers more than 20 years his elder.

Freud graduated from the gymnasium at 17 and, in 1873, entered the medical school at the University of Vienna. He became deeply involved in neurological research and did not finish his M.D. degree for 8 years. Never intending to practice medicine because he wanted to be a scientist, Freud devoted his next 15 years to investigations of the nervous system (Hall, 1954). However, the salary of a scientific researcher was inadequate to support the wife and six children he had by then. In addition, the anti-Semitism prevalent in Vienna during this period prevented Freud from achieving university advancement. Consequently, Freud felt forced to take up the practice of medicine.

Freud decided to specialize in the treatment of nervous disorders; at the time, not much was known about this particular branch of medicine. First, he spent a year in France learning about Jean Charcot's use of hypnosis in the treatment of hysteria (Stone, 1971). Freud (1925/1963) was dissatisfied with hypnosis because he thought its effects were only temporary and did not get at the center of the problem. Freud then studied with Joseph Breuer, learning the benefits of the catharsis (or "talking out your problems") form of therapy.

Noticing that his patients' physical symptoms seemed to have a mental base, Freud probed deeper and deeper into the minds of his patients. "His probing revealed dynamic forces at work which were responsible for creating the abnormal symptoms that he was called upon to treat. Gradually there began to take shape in Freud's mind the idea that most of these forces were unconscious" (Hall, 1954, p. 15). According to Stone (1971), this finding was probably the turning point in

Freud's career. To substantiate some of his ideas, Freud decided to undertake an intensive analysis of his own unconscious forces in order to check on the material he had gathered from his patients. "On the basis of the knowledge he gained from his patients and from himself he began to lay the foundations for a theory of personality" (Hall, 1954, p. 17).

Freud's early support of Charcot and his new and revolutionary ideas cost him the support of most scholars and doctors. Eventually, however, Freud was accepted as a genius in psychotherapy. Many influential scientists, including Carl Jung, Alfred Adler, Ernest Jones, and Wilhelm Stekel, recognized Freud's theory as a major breakthrough in the field of psychology; however, these scientists broke with Freud early on. Freud's academic career with the University of Vienna began in 1883; however, he did not receive the rank of full professor until 1920. Freud's recognition in academic psychology came in 1909, when he was invited by G. Stanley Hall to give a series of lectures at Clark University in Worcester, Massachusetts. According to Fancher (2000), Hall single-handedly made Freud's name a household word in America by ensuring full press coverage for all of Freud's lectures on psychoanalysis. It was Clark University's 20th anniversary, and Hall marked it by bringing Freud to America for his first and only trip. Freud's name began to appear in popular songs, and *Time* magazine featured him on the cover.

Freud's writing career spanned 63 years, during which time he produced more than 600 publications. His collected works have been published in English in 24 volumes as *The Standard Edition of the Complete Psychological Works of Sigmund Freud* (1953–1964). Among his more famous works are *The Interpretation of Dreams* (1900/1965a), *The Psychopathology of Everyday Life* (1901/1971), and *New Introductory Lectures in Psychoanalysis* (1933/1965b).

Freud seemed never to think his work was finished. "As new evidence came to him from his patients and his colleagues, he expanded and revised his basic theories" (Hall, 1954, p. 17). As an example of his flexibility and capability, at 70 Freud completely altered a number of his fundamental views: He revamped motivation theory, reversed the theory of anxiety, and developed a new model of personality based on id, ego, and superego.

Freud developed his psychoanalytic model of people over five decades of observing and writing. The major principles were based on the clinical study of individual patients undergoing treatment for their problems. Free association became Freud's preferred procedure after he discarded hypnosis.

Just as Sigmund Freud was the father of psychoanalysis, he was the grandfather of child psychoanalysis. His therapy with adults conducted at the Vienna Psychoanalytic Institute was continuous and lengthy, often requiring several years to complete. A school for children was established adjacent to the institute. Anna Freud, Sigmund Freud's daughter, began to take a great interest in these children and eventually devoted herself almost exclusively to the study of children. She stands today as the outstanding pioneer in the field. The institute also trained other prominent child analysts, most notable among them Peter Blos, Marianne Kris, and Erik Erikson. Erikson is best known for his theory of sequenced tasks as the means to develop one's identity.

Psychoanalysis includes theories about the development and organization of the mind, the instinctual drives, the influences of the external environment, the importance of the family, and the attitudes of society. As useful as psychoanalysis is as a therapeutic tool, its impact and value reach far beyond medical applications. It is the only comprehensive theory of human psychology. Psychoanalytic theory has proved helpful to parents and teachers in the upbringing and education of children.

Although psychoanalytic theory has been modified in some areas, its basic concepts remain. The fact that almost all counseling theories include some of the basic premises from the psychoanalytic method shows the influence and durability of the theory.

## THE NATURE OF PEOPLE

The concept of human nature in psychoanalytic theory found its basis in psychic determinism and unconscious mental processes. Psychic determinism implies that mental life is a continuous manifestation of cause-related relationships. Mental processes are considered the causative factors of human behavior. Mental activity and even physical activity may be kept below the conscious level. Analysis on the basis of unconscious determinism is the base of psychoanalytic counseling. Counseling leading to catharsis then leads to confronting the unconscious mind in ways that promote learning, understanding, and growth in mental development and coping skills.

Freud viewed people as basically evil and victims of instincts that must be balanced or reconciled with social forces to provide a structure in which human beings can function. To achieve balance, people need a deep understanding of the forces that motivate them to action. According to Freud, people operate as energy systems, distributing psychic energy to the id, ego, and superego; human behavior is determined by this energy, by unconscious motives, and by instinctual and biological drives. Psychosexual events during the first 5 years of life are critical to adult personality development.

Sugarman (1977), in the belief that Freud's concept of human nature is often misinterpreted, presented a contrasting view of Freudian theory in which a humanistic image of people is recognized in the following eight ideas:

1. People have a dual nature, biological and symbolic.
2. People are both individuals and related to others simultaneously.
3. People strive for goals and values.
4. One of the strongest human needs is meaning in life.
5. One's internal world, including the unconscious, is more important than overt behavior.
6. People are social creatures whose need for interpersonal relationships is supreme.
7. People are always evolving, always in process.
8. People have a certain amount of autonomy within the constraints of reality.

In summary, according to psychoanalytic theory, the basic concepts of human nature revolve around the notions of psychic determinism and unconscious mental processes. Psychic determinism simply implies that our mental function or mental life is a continuous logical manifestation of causative relationships. Nothing is random; nothing happens by chance. Although mental events may appear unrelated, they are actually closely interwoven and depend on preceding mental signals. Closely related to psychic determinism are unconscious mental processes, which exist as fundamental causative factors in the nature of human behavior. In essence, much of what goes on in our minds and hence in our bodies is unknown, below the conscious level, so we often do not understand our feelings or actions. The existence of unconscious mental processes is the basis for much of what is involved in psychoanalytic counseling.

Freud believed that unresolved conflict, repression, and free-floating anxiety often go together. Painful and stressful conflicts that cannot be resolved in the conscious may be buried and forgotten in the unconscious. Later on, a person may experience anxiety that cannot be readily traced to any ongoing situation in the person's life. Relief from such anxiety may come only from accessing the unconscious and uncovering and resolving the original conflict. Recall and integration of repressed memories into one's conscious functioning often provide symptom relief from free-floating anxiety.

Freud also was interested in how people handled the tension of being pulled in opposite directions by the polarities in life. He saw people as born with the pleasure principle, or the will to seek pleasure; however, people are confronted with an opposite force, the reality principle, which demands that the will to pleasure be bridled. The tension that results from being pulled in opposite directions by the pleasure principle and the reality principle becomes the essential, motivating force in one's life. People can either find productive ways to reduce the tension or give in to the tension and be destroyed by it. The task of humankind is to find a way to integrate the polarities into synergistic choices that neither compromise nor deny the opposing polarities. For example, taking your textbook to the beach on spring break may be an attempt to find a middle ground between doing what you want and what you should. A synergistic solution might be completing the work before leaving on the trip, which would probably result in higher quality work and play. Living becomes a process of either mastering or succumbing to the tension resulting from life's polarities. A brief list of life's polarities is presented in Chapter 6.

As noted in Figures 3-1 and 3-2, the *unconscious* holds about 85% of the material in our minds. The concept of the unconscious is the foundation of psychoanalytic theory and practice. It holds that, in a part of the mind that we are not aware of, drives, desires, attitudes, motivations, and fantasies exist and exert influence on how people think, feel, and behave in the conscious area of functioning. The *conscious* refers to the part of mental activity that we are aware of at any given time. The *preconscious* refers to thoughts and material that are not readily available to the conscious but can be retrieved with some effort. Students may struggle to find an answer to a test question lost in the preconscious. The *subconscious* refers to those involuntary bodily processes such as digestion and breathing that have been with

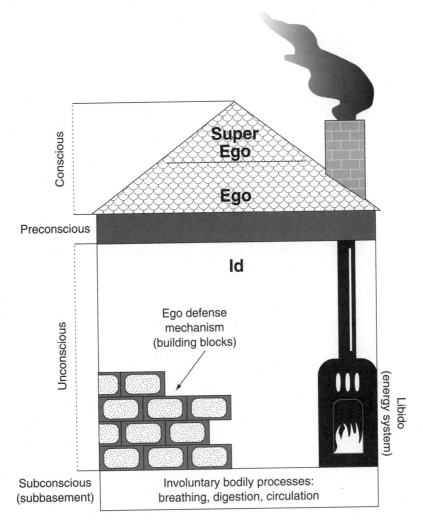

FIGURE 3-1    Freud's psychoanalytic model

the person since birth. Carl Jung's *collective unconscious* refers to the vast reservoir of inherited wisdom, memories, and insights that we share with all humankind (see Figure 3-2).

## THEORY OF COUNSELING

Freud's concepts of personality form the basis of a psychoanalytic counseling theory. The principal concepts in Freudian theory can be grouped under three topic headings: structural, dynamic, and developmental. The structural concepts are id, ego,

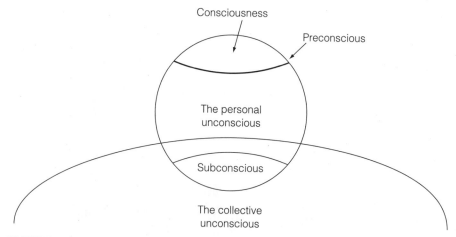

FIGURE 3-2   The relative importance of the conscious, preconscious, unconscious, subconscious, and collective unconscious

and superego. The dynamic concepts are instinct, cathexis, anticathexis, and anxiety. The developmental concepts are defense mechanisms and psychosexual stages.

## Structural Concepts

Freud believed human behavior resulted from the interaction of three important parts of the personality: id, ego, and superego.

### Id

The id contains our basic instinctual drives, including thirst, hunger, sex, and aggression. These drives can be constructive or destructive. Constructive, pleasure-seeking (sexual) drives provide the basic energy of life (libido). In Freud's system, anything pleasurable is labeled sexual. Destructive, aggressive drives tend toward self-destruction and death. Life instincts are opposed by death instincts. The id, working on the pleasure principle, exists to provide immediate gratification of any instinctual need, regardless of the consequences. The id is not capable of thought but can form, for example, mental pictures of hamburgers for a hungry person. The formation of such images and wishes is referred to as *fantasy* and *wish fulfillment* (the *primary process*).

### Ego

Often called the "executive" of the personality, the ego strives to strike a balance between the needs of the id and the reality of the external world and transforms the mental images formed by the id (the hamburgers, for example) into acceptable behavior (purchasing a hamburger). These reality-oriented, rational processes of the ego are referred to as the *secondary process*. The ego, operating under the *reality principle,* is in line with environmental constraints and adjusts behavior to meet these constraints.

### Superego

Composed of two parts—the *ego ideal* (developed from the child's idea of what parents and significant others thought was good) and the *conscience* (what parents and significant others thought was bad)—the superego is, in essence, a personal moral standard. Often thought of as the judicial branch of the personality, the superego can act to restrict, prohibit, and judge conscious actions.

In summary, the id, the basic unit in Freud's personality structure, contains the basic human instincts plus each person's genetic and constitutional inheritance. As a result of interacting with reality, the id developed a liaison between itself and the environment that Freud labeled the ego. The ego's primary mission is self-preservation, which is accomplished by mediating the demands of the id (instinctual demands) with the realities of the environment. The well-functioning ego is able to achieve the right balance between seeking pleasure and avoiding the consequences of immoderate infringement on the societal rules and mores. As noted in Figure 3-3, children are generally dependent on their parents to a large extent during the first two decades of their lives. During this time, the ego develops a superego that continues the parents' influence over the remainder of the person's lifetime. Within the superego are two subsystems: the conscience and the ego ideal. The conscience holds the parents' conceptions about what is bad; the ego ideal holds the parents' conceptions about what is good. The ego is left with the task of mediating a balance between the demands of the id, superego, and reality.

## Dynamic Concepts

### Instinct

An instinct is an inborn psychological representation, referred to as a *wish,* that stems from a physiological condition referred to as a *need*. For example, hunger is a need that leads to a wish for food. The wish becomes a motive for behavior. Life instincts serve to maintain the survival of the species. Hunger, thirst, and sex needs are served by life instincts. Freud believed that human behavior is motivated by basic instincts.

> *Libido:* Libido is the energy that permits life instincts to work.
> *Cathexis:* Cathexis refers to directing one's libidinal energy toward an object, person, or idea that will satisfy a need.
> *Anticathexis:* Anticathexis refers to the force the ego exerts to block or restrain the impulses of the id. The reality principle or superego directs this action of the ego against the pleasure principle emanating from the id.

Dependency–autonomy continuum

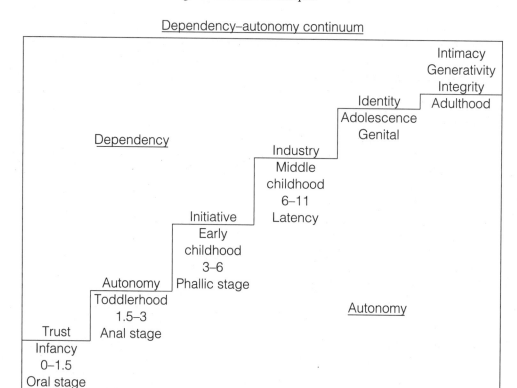

FIGURE 3-3   Developmental stages and the dependency–autonomy continuum

*Anxiety:* Anxiety refers to a conscious state in which a painful emotional experience is produced by external or internal excitation—a welling up of autonomic nervous energy. Closely akin to fear, but more encompassing, is the anxiety that originates from internal as well as external causes. Freud believed there were three types of anxiety: reality, neurotic, and moral. Reality anxiety results from real threats from the environment. Neurotic anxiety results from the fear that our instinctual impulses from the id will overpower our ego controls and get us into trouble. Moral anxiety results from the guilt we feel when we fail to live up to our standards.

## Developmental Concepts

### Defense Mechanisms

The ego protects itself from heavy pressure and anxiety with defense mechanisms. Patton and Meara (1991) pointed out that defenses are any operations of the mind that aim to ward off anxiety and depression. The healthy, high-functioning ego attempts to cope with anxiety, depression, and stress with effective, reality-based, task-oriented coping skills. When the load becomes too heavy, the ego may resort to defense-oriented coping methods that provide short-term relief but deny or distort reality and generally cause more problems in the long run.

Clark (1991) defined *defense mechanisms* as unconscious distortions of reality that reduce painful affect and conflict through automatic, habitual responses. Defense mechanisms are specific, unconscious, adjustive efforts used to resolve conflict and provide relief from anxiety. Counselors are generally able to detect their clients' defense mechanisms. Borrowing from Clark, we have provided examples of how a child might express a preference or lifestyle built around one, two, or a combination of defense mechanisms.

*Identification.*    Identification is the development of role models that people identify with or imitate. They may choose to imitate either a few traits of the model or the total person. Identification often occurs with the same-sex parent and may be born out of love or power—for example, "I love Dad so much I want to be just like him" or "If I can't beat him, I'll join him until I get big, too." The underachieving child might say, "I know a high school student who dropped out and is making a lot of money. He says school is a waste of time."

*Displacement.*    Displacement means redirecting energy from a primary object to a substitute when an instinct is blocked. For example, anger toward a parent may be directed toward a sibling or another object because of the fear of reprisal from the parent. The underachieving child might say, "The stuff we study is so boring I'll never make good grades." The child may be redirecting hostile feelings from the teacher to the subject matter.

*Repression and suppression.*    Repression forces a dangerous memory, conflict, idea, or perception out of the conscious into the unconscious and places a lid on it to prevent the repressed material from resurfacing. In repression, the person unconsciously bars a painful thought from memory. Suppression is a conscious effort to do the same thing. An underachieving child might have repressed painful memories about failure in a prior school experience.

*Projection.*    Projection is attributing one's own characteristics to others or to things in the external world. For instance, a teacher may find it uncomfortable to admit he does not like the children in his class, so instead he says the children do not like him. In this way, he projects his dislike for his students onto the students. An underachieving child may say, "My teacher doesn't like me; he thinks I'm stupid."

*Reaction formation.*    Reaction formation refers to the development of attitudes or character traits exactly opposite to ones that have been repressed. Anxiety-producing impulses are replaced in the conscious by their opposites; for example, "I love booze" is replaced by "Liquor should be declared illegal." An underachieving child may say, "I don't want to be a nerd; nerds suck up to the teacher just to make good grades."

*Rationalization.*   Rationalization is an attempt to prove that one's behavior is justified and rational and is thus worthy of approval by oneself and others. When asked why they behaved in a certain manner, children may feel forced to think up logical excuses or reasons. An underachieving child may say, "I could finish my homework if my little brother would stop bothering me."

*Denial.*   Denial is a refusal to face unpleasant aspects of reality or to perceive anxiety-provoking stimuli. Children may deny the possibility of falling while climbing high trees. An underachieving child may say, "Things are going fine; my grades will be much higher this time." Counselors need to remember that denial is common in young children but is maladaptive for adolescents.

*Fantasy.*   Fantasy is a way of seeking gratification of needs and frustrated desires through the imagination. A fantasy or imagined world may be a more pleasant place than a child's real world. An underachieving child may say, "Just wait, one of these days I'll become a doctor and show that teacher. She'll be sorry she made fun of my bad test score."

*Withdrawal.*   Withdrawal means reducing ego involvement by becoming passive or learning to avoid being hurt; examples of withdrawn children include the shy child or school-phobic child. A withdrawn, underachieving child will probably not say much as he or she tries to avoid "risky" situations.

*Intellectualization.*   Intellectualization is the act of separating the normal affect, or feeling, from an unpleasant or hurtful situation; for example, a child whose dog has been hit by a car might soften his or her grief by saying, "Our dog is really better off dead; he was feeble and going blind." An underachieving child may say, "I learn best from doing things outside school" or "I don't learn from the boring things we do at school."

*Regression.*   Regression is a retreat to earlier developmental stages that are less demanding than those of the present level. An older child may revert to babyish behavior when a baby arrives in the family. An underachieving child may say, "All we do is work; recess and lunch should be longer."

*Fixation.*   Fixation differs from regression in that the individual does not always regress to a more pleasant stage of development to avoid the pain or stress in a current developmental stage but rather might decide to remain at the present level of development rather than move to the next stage, which poses more difficulties and problems to solve. The tendency is to stay with a situation that is pleasurable and comfortable and in which the person has been successful. Counselors are often confronted with dependent, underachieving children who have a difficult time, first, in developing alternative problem solutions and, second, in making commitments to try their new alternatives.

*Undoing.*    Undoing is engaging in some form of atonement for immoral or bad behavior or for the desire to participate in such behavior. For instance, after breaking a lamp, a child may try to glue it back together. An underachieving child may say, "I get in a lot of arguments with my teacher, but I always try to do something to make up for it."

*Acting out.*    Acting out means reducing the anxiety aroused by forbidden desires by expressing them. The behavior of a revenge-seeking child is one example. An underachieving child may engage in violence, vandalism, or theft to express forbidden hurt feelings.

*Compensation.*    Compensation is covering up a weakness by emphasizing some desirable trait or reducing frustration in one area of life by overgratification in another area; for example, the class clown may compensate for poor academic performance by engaging in attention-getting behavior. An underachiever may be an attention-getting clown of the first order or may overachieve in another area (for example, sports, hobbies, or gang activities) to compensate for low grades.

*Sublimation.*    Sublimation has often been referred to as the backbone of civilization. Through it, people redirect their libidinal desires and energy into productive and acceptable activities and outlets. Often the products of this redirected energy have resulted in significant advances in the arts, sciences, quality of life, and civilization in general. We might speculate that surgeons and butchers found more useful and acceptable outlets for their libidinal desires than did Jack the Ripper. Parents and teachers would do well to help children find productive outlets for their great energy. An underachieving child does not need a lot of unstructured time to fill with negative addictions such as television, gang activity, overeating, and drugs.

## Psychosexual Stages

Freud (1940/1949) viewed personality development as a succession of stages, each characterized by a dominant mode of achieving libidinal pleasure and by specific developmental tasks. How well one adjusts at each stage is the critical factor in development. Freud believed that personality characteristics are fairly well established by the age of 6. Gratification of need during each stage is important if the individual is not to become fixated at that level of development. The key to successful adjustment in each stage is how well parents help their child adjust to that stage and make the transition to the next stage. The difficulty with Freud's system comes when counselors emphasize the extremes rather than the normal range of behaviors. The key seems to lie in maintaining a balance between extremes. The five developmental stages are oral, anal, phallic, latency, and genital.

## Oral Stage (Birth to 1½ Years)

The oral-erotic substage is characterized by the sucking reflex, which is necessary for survival. The child's main task in the oral-sadistic substage is to adjust to the weaning process and learn to chew food. The mouth is characterized as an erogenous zone because one obtains pleasure from sucking, eating, and biting. Adult behaviors, such as smoking, eating, and drinking, and the personality traits of gullibility, dependency (oral-erotic), and sarcasm (oral-sadistic) originate in the oral period.

Winnicott (1971, 1977, 2001) and Piaget and Inhelder (1969) believed that children at 12 to 18 months old begin to form an identity based on their "me" and "not me" worlds during this oral or trust-building stage. The process of developing an identity begins when infants see their image reflected in their mothers' expression as they look at their babies. Mothers who are depressed or under stress and have difficulty expressing their love by their looks and expressions send a disturbing message to their infants. The infant begins to sense, "If Mother seems not to love me or be pleased with what she sees, I may be unlovable."

## Anal Stage (1½ to 3 Years)

During this time, the membrane of the anal region presumably provides the major source of pleasurable stimulation. There are anal-expulsive and anal-retentive substages. The major hurdle is the regulation of a natural function (bowel control). Toilet training requires the child to learn how to postpone immediate gratification. Again, the manner in which the parents facilitate or impede the process forms the basis for a number of adult personality traits. Stubbornness, stinginess, and orderliness (anal-retentive) and generosity and messiness (anal-expulsive) are among adult traits associated with the anal stage.

## Phallic Stage (3 to 6 Years)

Self-manipulation of the genitals provides the major source of pleasurable sensation at this age, and the Oedipus complex occurs during this stage. The female version is sometimes referred to as the *Electra complex*. Sexual and aggressive feelings and fantasies are associated with the genitals. Boys have sexual desires for their mothers and aggressive feelings toward their fathers; girls develop hostility toward their mothers and become sexually attracted to their fathers. Attitudes toward people of the same sex and the opposite sex begin to take shape. Criticisms of Freud's castration complex concept range from labeling them ridiculous to calling them projections of his own fears. In any case, Freud believed that boys are afraid that their fathers will castrate them for loving their mothers. Girls' castration complexes were thought to take the form of penis envy; compensation for lacking a penis came with having a baby.

### Latency Stage (6 to 11 Years)

Sexual motivations presumably recede in importance during the latency period as the child becomes preoccupied with developmental skills and activities. Children generally concentrate on developing same-sex friendships. Sexual and aggressive impulses are relatively quiet during this phase. (As for aggression, Freud obviously never worked with a group of children in this age group!)

### Genital Stage (Adolescence)

After puberty, the deepest feeling of pleasure presumably comes from heterosexual relations. The major task of this period is developing opposite-sex relationships, a risky task involving rejection and fear of rejection that has a tremendous impact on future heterosexual relationships.

Oral, anal, and phallic stages are classified as narcissistic because children derive pleasure from their own erogenous zones. During the genital stage, the focus of activity shifts to developing genuine relationships with others. The goal for the young person is to move from a pleasure-seeking, pain-avoiding, narcissistic child to a reality-oriented, socialized adult.

In summary, overgratification of the child's needs could result in the child's fixation at a particular stage; deprivation may result in regression to a more comfortable developmental stage. For example, a 3-year-old only child, suddenly finding a rival for his parents' attention in the form of a new baby sister, regresses to his pre–toilet-training period in an effort to compete. Too much frustration in coping with a particular developmental stage could also result in fixating the child at that stage. Residue from regression and fixation may reappear in adult personality development.

Finding the healthy balance between unhealthy extremes is the key to mental health and a theme that runs throughout this book. Parents always have the difficult task of walking the thin line between too much and too little gratification of their child's needs. How much is too much or too little help in assisting a child in advancing to a new developmental stage? Perhaps the answer lies in the nurturing and preservation of the child's self-esteem, confidence, and trust.

## PSYCHOANALYTIC COUNSELING AND DEVELOPMENT OF SELF-ESTEEM

Psychoanalytic counselors often search for repressed, traumatic events in the lives of their clients as possible causes for the symptoms and problems brought to counseling. Severe trauma is often associated with damaged egos, low self-esteem, and anxiety disorders; however, counselors can overlook the devastating effects on self-esteem of the daily onslaught of negative criticism heaped on some children throughout their developing years. Because such behavior falls short of legally being abuse and because it occurs in relatively small doses, it often goes unnoticed and unchecked. Therefore, we are presenting two systems for evaluating how well a child's self-esteem, mental health, and other personal needs are being supported by the family and, to a great extent, by the school.

Simon (1988) presented six conditions for nurturing and maintaining self-esteem and mental health in children and adults. Self-esteem is a by-product of our productive activity and our relationships. It is not a goal that can be attained through self-affirmation activities. Programs designed to build self-esteem tend to fall short unless the participants take steps to improve their productivity and relationships. Freud believed that love and work are the keys to mental health. For children, the keys to mental health are their schoolwork and their relationships with family, peers, and other significant people. Simon's (1988) six conditions complement the productivity and relationship equation for self-esteem.

Belonging: Children need to feel connected to their family or to a family of their own creation if the family of origin did not work out. As children grow older, they need to feel connected to a peer group.

Child advocacy: Children need at least one advocate who can be trusted to help them through crisis periods.

Risk management: Self-esteem increases as children are able to take risks and master challenging tasks. The difficulty is finding tasks that are challenging yet not impossible. Children need to believe that they are successful if they have given a task their best effort and that it is okay to take risks and fail.

Empowerment: Children need to exercise developmentally appropriate amounts of control over their own lives. Opportunities to make choices and decisions contribute to empowerment.

Uniqueness: Children need to feel they are special. Simon (1988) suggested that we work with children in constructing lists of 100 sentences validating their unique and positive qualities, which he calls "anti-suicide" lists.

Productivity: As children get things done, they feel better. Encouragement and reinforcement of productive activity can move children toward finding intrinsic rewards in accomplishment.

Simon's six conditions are as relevant for adults as they are for children. Adding more risk to one's life can improve one's mental health, providing that the risk falls within rational limits. Closely related to self-esteem is the degree to which children are meeting their other human needs.

Counseling children through Freud's five stages of development often requires an assessment of how well their basic needs are being met. A rating scale of 0 to 10 (0 for unmet needs and 10 for fully met needs) can be used to assess the child's progress in each level of Maslow's (1970) hierarchy, including self-esteem (Table 3-1).

Problems in adult development are often traced to childhood frustration from failure to meet basic human needs during the developmental years. Psychoanalytic counseling can focus on the child's level of human needs attainment in past years as well as in the present. Questions of how children handle the pain of not getting what they want can be treated in psychoanalytic counseling. Are conflict and stress

**TABLE 3-1   Child's needs assessment**

*Physiological needs*

| | 0 | 5 | 10 |
|---|---|---|---|
| Nutrition, sleep, exercise, general | | | |

*Safety needs*

| | 0 | 5 | 10 |
|---|---|---|---|
| Safety within the family and peer group settings | | | |

*Love and belonging needs*

| | 0 | 5 | 10 |
|---|---|---|---|
| Affection shown to the child | | | |
| Promises made and kept to the child | | | |
| Someone listens to the child | | | |
| Family follows a dependable schedule | | | |
| Child has own space, possessions, and a right to privacy | | | |
| Someone is there when the child arrives home | | | |
| Child is loved unconditionally | | | |
| Child has a place and role in the family | | | |
| Child has found acceptance and a place in his/her peer group | | | |

*Self-esteem needs*

| | 0 | 5 | 10 |
|---|---|---|---|
| Someone affirms the child's worth | | | |
| Child is given the opportunity to achieve and accomplish tasks | | | |
| Child is given the opportunity to make choices | | | |

*Self-actualization needs*

| | 0 | 5 | 10 |
|---|---|---|---|
| Child is not blocked by unmet needs in the previous four levels | | | |
| Child is developing potential abilities, strengths, and skills | | | |
| Problem-solving skills enable the child to engage in developmental rather than remedial activities | | | |

repressed in the unconscious or handled in the conscious area of functioning? Are depression and anxiety handled in task-oriented or defense-oriented ways? Both are good questions for psychoanalytic counselors to address.

## Object Relations Theory

As mentioned earlier, love and work are important concepts in Freud's system. He believed that a quick assessment of mental health could be based on how well people were managing their relationships and careers. Object relations theory is a natural progression from his earlier work on how well children resolved the conflict surrounding competition with the same-sex parent for the love and attention of the opposite-sex parent. Object relations theory focuses on how the early family relationships affect the type of relationships formed outside the family. For example, missing a solid father figure during her childhood years may motivate a woman to seek the love and attention she did not get from her father from older, fatherly types of men. Object relations theorists use the word *object* to refer to people other than the self. Family relationships that model appropriate and healthy models for future relationship development are the best assistance children can have in learning to build relationships outside the family. Children who receive proper nurturing during their dependent years do not seek parent figures in their adult relationships. Parents who facilitate their children's movement through the developmental stages toward the achievement of independence and identity provide them with blueprints for fulfilling and healthy adult relationships. As children begin differentiating themselves from their families, they carry their internalized view of how relationships operate to their peer group and eventually to their adult world. For example, a woman might carry a repressed image of her father as a hostile and rejecting person who did not provide the love and nurturing she needed and project this image of her father on all men in general. Seeing this hostile father image in her husband, she reacts accordingly, causing him to act out the hostile role of her father. Treatment for children educates parents to be better models of how to provide the right amounts of love and nurturing. Treatment for adults accesses the unconscious to find the history of the unresolved conflicts with their parents and to find out how the repressed conflicts contribute to their difficulties in establishing and maintaining the relationships they would like to have.

Donald Woods Winnicott (1896–1971) was a British psychoanalyst who, through his clinical experience as a pediatrician and child psychiatrist, came to believe that the first few months of a child's life were critical to the development of good mental health and adjustment in the future life of the child. He strongly emphasized the mother's role in her child's development. Winnicott's view was that mothers did not have to be extraordinary in their duties and that the "good enough mother" would be sufficient in facilitating the development of good mental health in her children. He believed that most mothers instinctively know how to meet their children's needs through providing the love, caring, and support needed to get their children started on the road to mature independence—providing they do not let themselves become misguided by child-rearing books. Winnicott (1971, 1977, 2001) recognized the importance of physical holding by the mother when the child is totally dependent and the "holding environment" mothers create through their empathy, which meets the child's physiological and emotional needs in reliable and consistent ways. He viewed holding as a form of ego support that is needed for children, adolescents, and adults when they are under stress. Well-cared-for infants do not experience the anxieties produced by environmental failure that some children experience during their stage of total dependence. These anxieties include feelings of falling forever, depersonalization, and generalized insecurity. To handle these intolerable feelings and anxieties, children create elaborate defenses such as repression to avoid having to face these difficulties on a day-to-day basis. Splitting themselves from reality (schizophrenia) would be an extremely costly, but not uncommon, measure for developing a position of invulnerability to defend against these anxieties. Winnicott believed that the analyst should "stand in" for the important people (objects) in a person's psychological history who literally let the person down. He used these transference relationships in treatment to help people relive and reevaluate their past. The analyst assumes the "holding" role the child never experienced, including the environmental support or holding that was lacking in the person's past. Such environmental support was the forerunner of case management, which includes helping people meet their basic survival needs so that they can benefit from counseling.

What about father? Two recent reports in the popular press have caught our attention (Dobson, 2002). Although we do not believe animal psychology always translates to human behavior, we noted that in Pilansberg National Park in South Africa, park rangers have reported that young bull elephants have become increasingly violent, especially to white rhinos. They attack the rhinos, knock them over, kneel, and gore them to death. Such has not previously been typical elephant behavior. Apparently, according to the game wardens, the aggressiveness is the result of a government program to reduce the elephant population by killing the older animals, including the dominant, older males who kept the young bulls in line and served as role models. The question is: "Are boys reared without the influence of a strong and positive father figure more likely to become violent teenagers and adults?"

The second news report focused on a past Mother's Day project by a greeting card company to furnish free cards and postage to all of the male inmates who wanted to send their mothers cards. The response was overwhelming, and the sponsor had to bring in additional cards. Since the Mother's Day project was so successful, the company decided to repeat it for Father's Day. You guessed right: Nobody showed up for the cards. Approximately 2 million people are serving time in jail; 94% of them are men. Again, the question is: "How much influence does a father-absent home have on violent behavior in men?" Westen (1998) notes that childhood experiences are critical to the development of the adult personality. Children must have stability in their relationships to develop stable, mature personalities as adults. Children lacking healthy interactions with a stable family will have to look no further than their childhood to find their source of pain and suffering. Mental representations formed in childhood of self, others, and relationships, for better or worse, may determine our interactions with others throughout the adult years unless corrective adjustments are made.

## COUNSELING METHODS

The primary goal of counseling within a psychoanalytic frame of reference is to make the unconscious conscious. All material in the unconscious was once in the conscious. Once brought to the conscious level, repressed material can be dealt with in rational ways by using any number of methods discussed in this book.

Several methods are used to uncover the unconscious. Detailed case histories are taken, with special attention given to the handling of conflict areas. Hypnosis, although rejected by Freud, is still used to assist in plumbing the unconscious. Analyses of resistance, transference, and dreams are frequently used methods, as are catharsis, free association, interpretation, and play therapy. All these methods have the long-term goal of strengthening the ego. The principal counseling methods discussed in this chapter are catharsis, free association, interpretation, analysis of transference, analysis of resistance, analysis of incomplete sentences, bibliocounseling, storytelling, and play therapy.

Much of what is practiced in psychoanalytic counseling depends on the spirit and process of play therapy. Successful outcomes depend on voluntary engagement and participation. By definition, play is voluntary, and when it is not, it ceases to be play. Free association rests on spontaneous, uncensored engagement in a type of voluntary play. If censorship occurs in the free association game, an important rule is broken, and progress in counseling stops. Rather than admonishing clients for censoring their thoughts, the counselor makes an interpretation of why the censorship may have occurred, which helps the client gain insight.

Play in counseling helps the child, as well as the adult, suspend reality, thus allowing children to direct a make-believe gratification for those areas found wanting in their lives. In cases in which fantasy has become delusion, totally detached from reality, the client may be experiencing the results of failed attempts to play. If counseling is to work for these clients, they will have to be taught how to play. In addition to being taught how to play, some clients will have to be taught how to trust, and others will need to be taught about the limits to be observed in play therapy. Working through transference is an exercise in fantasy and imagination requiring a form of role playing.

Psychodrama with older children and adolescents who have lived in chaotic and dysfunctional families can be a very effective counseling play method. Successful psychodrama for these clients depends on providing very structured directions stated clearly in an exact manner, with as little room as possible for misinterpretation. The counselor has to take charge of the session with confidence and leadership. The drama should be kept in the first person so that it is effective in working through personal concerns. Do not terminate the drama until the important objectives have been achieved. Provide ample time for sharing what the group learned from the drama. Both play and the expressive arts, including psychodrama, allow thoughts and feelings in the unconscious to return to the conscious, where they can be treated—especially in children who have limited skills and ability to reason by nature of their stage of cognitive development, be it the preoperational or concrete stage. Some blocks to cognitive development can be overcome in psychoanalytic counseling by using metaphors to explain how the unconscious works.

## Catharsis

Freud, along with Breuer, first discovered the benefits of catharsis through hypnosis. Freud found that if, under hypnosis, hysterical patients were able to verbalize an early precipitating causal event, the hysterical symptoms disappeared. Freud soon discarded hypnosis because he was not able to induce in everyone the deep hypnotic sleep that enabled the patient to regress to an early enough period to disclose the repressed event. Freud discovered that for many people the mere command to remember the origin of some hysterical symptom worked quite well. Unfortunately, many of his patients could not remember the origin of their symptoms even upon command. Freud thus decided that all people were aware of the cause of their illness but that for some reason certain people blocked this knowledge. Freud believed that unless this repressed traumatic infantile experience could be retrieved from the unconscious, verbalized, and relived emotionally, the patient would not recover. Because not everyone had the ability to find this unconscious material, the analyst had to use more indirect means to gain access to the unconscious mind. Freud developed free association and interpretation to bring everyone to the emotional state of catharsis that was necessary for cure.

## Free Association

In traditional psychoanalysis, the client lies on a couch and the analyst sits at the head of the couch beyond the client's line of vision. The analyst then orders the client to say whatever comes to mind. Through this means, the unconscious thoughts and conflicts are given freedom to reach the conscious mind. A great struggle takes place within the client to keep from telling these innermost thoughts to the analyst. The analyst must constantly struggle against this resistance. The fundamental rule of psychoanalytic counseling requires clients to tell the counselor whatever thoughts and feelings come into their minds, regardless of how personal, painful, or seemingly irrelevant.

While the client is trying to associate freely, the counselor must remain patient and nonjudgmental and insist that the client continue. The counselor must also look for continuity of thoughts and feelings. Although the client may appear to be rambling idly, psychoanalytic counselors believe there is a rational pattern to this speech. To interpret what the client is saying, the counselor must pay attention to the affect, or feeling, behind the client's verbalization, noting the client's gestures, tone of voice, and general body language during free association. The counselor, at this point, offers some interpretations of the client's statements to try to open another door for free association.

## Interpretation

Free association, in turn, leads to another important technique—interpretation. Three major areas of interpretation are dreams, parapraxia, and humor.

### Dreams

To Freud, dreams expressed wish fulfillment. To correctly interpret the power of the id, the analyst must learn about and interpret the client's dreams. According to Freud, there are three major types of dreams: those with meaningful, rational content (almost invariably found in children); those with material very different from waking events; and those with illogical, senseless episodes. According to Freud, all dreams center around a person's life and are under the person's psychic control. Every dream reveals an unfulfilled wish. In children's dreams, the wish is usually very obvious. As the individual matures, the wish, as exposed in the dream, becomes more distorted and disguised. Freud said that the ego fights the initial conscious wish, which thus is pushed back to the unconscious mind; it brings itself back into the conscious mind by means of a dream.

According to Freud, the dream guards against pain, and humor serves to acquire pleasure. When people are sleeping, repressive defenses are lower, and forbidden desires and feelings can find an outlet in dreams. Freud referred to dreams as the royal road to the unconscious. The counselor's role is to listen to the client's dream and help the client by interpreting the dream's symbolism.

Freud's method of dream interpretation was to allow the client to free associate about the dream's content. Certain objects in dreams were universal symbols for Freud. For example, a car in someone's dreams usually represented analysis, the number 3 represented male genitals, jewel cases and purses were vaginas, peaches and twin sisters were female breasts, woods were pubic hair, trees and steeples were penises, and dancing, riding, and flying were symbols for sexual intercourse. Dreams about falling are related to fears about falling from one's moral standards.

Freud (1901/1952) believed every dream to be a confession and a by-product of repressed, anxiety-producing thoughts. Freud thought that many dreams represented unfulfilled sexual desires and that many expressed the superego's guilt and self-punishment. Nightmares result from the desire for self-punishment. Because we are consciously and unconsciously aware of those things that we fear most, we put these things into our nightmares to punish ourselves.

### Parapraxia

Parapraxia, or "Freudian slips," are consciously excused as harmless mistakes, but through them the id pushes unconscious material through to the conscious. The counselor must be very aware of any slips of the tongue while dealing with a client. The Freudians also believe there are no such things as "mistakes" or items that are "misplaced." According to psychoanalytic thinking, everything we do—forgetting a person's name, cutting a finger while peeling potatoes—has unconscious motivation. The analyst must take all these unconscious mistakes and arrange them into a conscious pattern.

### Humor

Jokes, puns, and satire are all acceptable means for unconscious urges to gain access to the conscious. The things we laugh about tell us something about our repressed thoughts. One of the fascinations of humor, according to psychoanalytic theory, is that it simultaneously disguises and reveals repressed thoughts. Repressed thoughts, released by humor, usually generate from the id or superego. Because sexual thoughts are usually repressed, many jokes are sexually oriented; because aggressive thoughts are usually repressed, they are expressed in humor by way of satire and witticisms.

Again, the counselor must watch for patterns and themes. What does the client think is funny? How does the client's sense of humor fit into a pattern from the unconscious?

## Analysis of Transference

Transference occurs when the client views the counselor as someone else. Freud was genuinely surprised when his patients first regarded him as someone other than an analyst, helper, or adviser. During the course of psychoanalytic counseling, clients usually transfer their feelings about some significant individual from the past to their therapist. Transference generally is a product of unfinished business with a significant person from the client's childhood. Clients commonly transfer their feelings, thoughts, and expectations about the significant other to the counselor. Counseling provides a stage for reenacting unresolved conflicts with the counselor, who can help clients deal with them in more effective and functional ways. Transference relationships can become a real battleground when love feelings directed toward the counselor are rejected and the client, in turn, rejects the counselor by resisting the counselor's every effort to be helpful. Both transference and resistance can be analyzed for cause-and-effect implications for the client's life. Countertransference occurs when the counselor begins to view a client as someone other than a client. Referral to another competent professional is recommended for a counselor who loses his or her balance on the objectivity–empathy continuum.

## Analysis of Resistance

Freud was also surprised by the amount of resistance his patients mounted against his attempts to help them. Resistance took the form of erecting barriers to free association, thus breaking Freud's rule against censoring or holding back material; Freud's patients were often unwilling or unable to talk about some of their thoughts during free association or descriptions of their dreams. Resistance prevents painful and irrational content from reaching the conscious, and it must be eliminated in order for the person to have the opportunity to face and react to these repressed conflicts in realistic and healthy ways. Therefore, the essential task of any counselor is building a trusting relationship with clients that undermines their need to resist the counselor's attempts to be helpful. Analysis of resistance can also provide valuable information regarding the client's need to withhold information from the counselor.

## Analysis of Incomplete Sentences

Psychoanalytic counselors often use projective techniques such as the House/Tree/Person or Children's Apperception Test in an attempt to understand their clients' thoughts, behaviors, and feelings. For counselors not trained in test interpretation, asking children to complete stimulus statements about likes, dislikes, family, friends, goals, wishes, and things that make the child happy or sad helps counselors understand children and find problem areas. This procedure may be especially helpful in acquainting counselors with children and in establishing better rapport with those who are anxious, fearful, or reluctant to talk.

*Examples*

The thing I like to do most is _____.
The person in my family who helps me most is _____.
My friends are _____.
I feel happiest (or saddest) when _____.
My greatest wish is _____.
The greatest thing that ever happened to me was _____.
I wish my parents would _____.
When I grow up, I want _____.
Brothers are _____.
Sisters are _____.
Dad is _____.
Mom is _____.
School is _____.
My teacher is _____.

## Bibliocounseling

Bibliocounseling—reading and discussing books about situations and children similar to themselves—can help clients in several ways. Children unable to verbalize their thoughts and feelings may find them expressed in books. From selected stories, children can learn alternative solutions to problems and new ways of behaving; by reading about children similar to themselves, clients may not feel so alone or different.

In an article citing the benefits of bibliocounseling for abused children, Watson (1980) suggested that children may become psychologically and emotionally involved with characters they have read about. Vicarious experiences through books can be similar to the child's own thoughts, feelings, attitudes, behavior, or environment. Directed reading can lead to expression of feelings or problem solving. Watson listed the goals of bibliotherapy as (1) teaching constructive and positive thinking, (2) encouraging free expression concerning problems, (3) helping clients analyze their attitudes and behaviors, (4) looking at alternative solutions, (5) encouraging the client to find a way to cope that is not in conflict with society, and (6) allowing clients to see the similarity of their problems to those of others.

With bibliocounseling, discussion focused around characters' behaviors, feelings, thoughts, relationships, cause and effect, and consequences is more effective than just asking the child to relate the story. Discussion also clears up questions that arise from the reading. Counselors can guide children to see how the story applies to their own lives.

Bibliocounseling is also a means of educating children about certain areas of concern such as sex, physical disabilities, divorce, and death. Once children have enough information about a problem, their attitudes and behaviors tend to change. Books suggested for bibliocounseling with exceptional children and children with special concerns are listed in the *Student Manual* for this textbook.

## Storytelling

Richard Gardner developed the mutual storytelling technique as a therapeutic means for working with children (Schaefer & Cangelosi, 1993). It uses a familiar technique to help children understand their own thoughts and feelings and to communicate meaningful insights, values, and standards of behavior to children. The counselor sets the stage and asks the child to tell a story, which is recorded on tape. The counselor instructs the child that the story should have a beginning, a middle, and an ending and that the child will be asked to tell the moral (lesson) of the story at the end. The counselor may need to clarify some points of the story after the child has finished. The counselor then prepares a story using a similar theme and setting and including the significant figures from the child's story. The counselor's story, however, provides the child with better alternatives or responses to the situation.

We have found storytelling to be an excellent counseling technique to help children cope with feelings, thoughts, and behaviors they are not yet ready to discuss in a direct manner with the counselor. Storytelling has also been useful in helping children realize possible consequences of their behavior. (See the case study of Pete later in this chapter.)

In examining mutual storytelling as a viable therapeutic method, Kestenbaum (1985) presented three cases. In two cases, the child dictated the stories and the teacher wrote them down. In the third case, the child spoke into a tape recorder as though an original radio play was being produced. Transcripts from each case were typed, and the tapes were listened to during subsequent sessions. Story plots and characters were found to parallel events in the children's lives. The children's answers to questions about the characters, their backgrounds, and their motives were recorded for use in future sessions.

Lawson (1987) presented a helpful method of using a story within a story in working with an overweight 8-year-old girl who was acting out in an attempt to handle rejection by her peers. The therapist told a story about a similar girl who had no friends. No name was used in the story, but the counselor mentioned the client's name in nearly every sentence; for example, the counselor would say, "Ann, I once knew a little girl. . . ." Next, the counselor began another story within a story with the same theme: "Ann, this little girl had a dream about a little brown, black, and white puppy who had no friends because she was different than the other puppies who were all white, all black, or all brown." The second story worked out a solution around the theme that being different and special is good. When the girl wakes from her dream about the puppy, she is excited about being special and can hardly wait to take her new feelings to school because, as in the puppy story, what the other children thought about her did not matter as long as she felt special.

## Psychoanalytic Play Therapy and the Expressive Arts

Anna Freud (1926) adapted psychoanalysis for the treatment of children by incorporating play activities into therapy. She used toys and games to put the child at ease, create an alliance with the child, and discover clues about the child's inner life. The therapist engages the child, entering the fantasy or dramatization or free play by going along with the child's make-believe. Thus, Anna Freud used play to enhance the relationship and as a diagnostic tool. Melanie Klein (1932) also recognized the value of play in understanding the child's wishes, fears, and fantasies. She saw children's play as significant symbolic communication and interpreted the meaning of play in sessions with children (Lyness-Richard, 1997). Klein used play to accomplish with children the effect of free association used with adults (Fall, 1994).

Neubauer (1987) listed ways that play can affect therapy. Play involves a mental act, unconscious or conscious, that contains a fantasy and a wish. It has a physical component that is an observable enactment. Finally, play is an exploration, a "trying on"; play is pretending. The role of the therapist is to establish and maintain an alliance by interpreting, empathizing with, and understanding the child. Frankel (1998) examined processes essential in psychoanalytic play therapy. Play is the first process. The interrelated aspects of play include the emergence and integration of the dissociated self-states, symbols, and recognition. The second process proposed is renegotiation of relationships with self and others. The goals of psychoanalytic play therapy are to resolve fixations, regression, developmental deficiencies, and other impediments to the child's normal development (Lee, 1997).

Play is a universal activity that people of all ages need. Both spectator and participative play and recreation activities fill important human needs. Play provides needed change from our daily school or work routines. Play provides opportunities to work through emotional problems and release pent-up emotions in ways that are acceptable to society. It also allows rest for our bodies and minds. Play has been identified as preparation for adulthood in that it provides children with a medium in which to act out the roles they will—or hope to—live as adults: spouse, parent, hero, doctor, lawyer, and star athlete. The theory has even been advanced that play provides a theater for children to reenact the drama of the development of civilization. Young children begin learning about the "not me" world by biting, hitting, and pushing anything and anyone they can without regard to consequences and rules. Gradually, as children move through the socialization process, they do approximate, in brief form, the steps humankind took in moving from primitive to advanced civilizations.

From a Freudian view, play provides the medium for moving through the five psychosexual stages and the corresponding development of the ego and superego superstructures from the id structure. Exercise of the pleasure principle, such as hitting, biting, pushing others, and doing what the child pleases, gradually comes up against the reality principle, which tells the child that games have rules and that sometimes it is necessary and even best to postpone pleasurable activities. Play is useful in working through healthy identification with the same-sex and opposite-sex parent. The development of relationships with same-sex peers and, eventually, with opposite-sex friends is facilitated through play activities.

For children, play therapy is the treatment of choice for bringing both conscious and unconscious material into the counseling session. Play is the natural mode of communication for children. Limited verbal ability prevents children from being able to verbally express their thoughts, feelings, and behavior. Play is the natural way for children to express themselves and learn about their world. Many counseling techniques, including the expressive arts of painting, drawing, playing and singing music, and dancing, can be used with play therapy to adapt the process to the particular child's developmental level. Self-portrait drawings are good indicators of how well children are doing with their lives. See Figure 3-4 for a drawing done by a 10-year-old girl who has love and support from her family, does well in school, makes friends easily, and excels in her sport of gymnastics. Contrast this drawing with Pete's drawing in Figure 3-5.

Winnicott (1971, 1977, 2001), in his extensive work with children from the 1920s through the early 1960s, developed a squiggle game play technique that combined drawing and storytelling. He would begin by drawing a few neutral

FIGURE 3-4   Self-portrait drawing by a 10-year-old girl. (Reprinted by permission of Jessica Marie Martin.)

lines (a "squiggle") and then passed the paper to the child to make it into a picture. Next, the child would start a squiggle for Winnicott to finish. Each time a drawing was finished, the "artist" made up a story about the completed picture. Through the storytelling and conversation surrounding the squiggle game, children were able to express thoughts, feelings, and ideas from their unconscious that previously were not accessible to them.

Of course, most general theories of counseling can be adapted to fit the play therapy setting. Some counselors use dogs and other pets in their play therapy and regular sessions (Burton, 1995; Levinson, 1962; O'Brien, 1993; Trivedi & Perl, 1995).

As is true with the counselor's office, children must perceive the play therapy room as a safe place to discuss anything they wish without fear of criticism or punishment. The counselor's role is to interpret the child's symbolic play in words that are meaningful to the child. Successful play therapy should result in higher levels of self-esteem, communication, trust, confidence, and problem-solving ability. (See Chapter 14 for a full discussion and presentation of play therapy.)

In summary, Freud viewed the personal unconscious as the repository of *the primitive, the antisocial, and the evil within us.* Repressed below the conscious area of functioning, these three forces tend to cause anxiety and tension through conflicts that affect our behavior in negative ways. The solution is to bring these three forces into conscious awareness.

Psychoanalytic counselors are interested in accessing the personal unconscious to bring these repressed conflicts into conscious awareness, where they can be treated. The most common means of returning unconscious content to the conscious are dream interpretation, free association, analysis of resistance, analysis of transference, hypnosis, meditation, journaling, reflection, and analysis of slips of the tongue, selective remembering and forgetting, and accidents. Play therapy, in combination with the expressive arts, provides the preferred treatment modality for any theoretical orientation for younger children.

## CASE STUDIES

### Identification of Problem I*

Dennis, age 9, was considered a disturbed, slow, resistant boy who had to be pushed into doing everything he was supposed to be doing. He rarely participated in any family activities and had no friends in the neighborhood. His school records listed such problems as regression, playing with much younger children, thumb sucking, daydreaming, soiling, bullying, and tardiness. An excerpt from the first counseling session begins with Dennis entering the playroom.

### Transcript

*Dennis:*  Well, what are we going to do today?

*Counselor:*  Whatever you'd like. This is your time.

*Dennis:*  Let's talk.

*Counselor:*  All right.

*Dennis:*  Let's go back in history. We're studying about it in school. I'm going to be studying about Italy next week. I can't think of anything to talk about. I can't think of one thing to say. Can you?

*Counselor:*  I'd rather discuss something you suggest.

*Dennis:*  I can't think of a thing.

*Counselor:*  We can just sit here if you like.

*Dennis:*  Good. Do you want to read?

*Counselor:*  Okay.

*Dennis:*  You be the student, and I'll be the teacher. I'll read to you. Now you be ready to answer some questions. I don't like spelling. I like social studies, and I like history more than any other subject. I'd like being the teacher for a change. [Dennis asks counselor questions from a reading text.]

*Counselor:*  You like to ask questions you think I'll miss.

*Dennis:*  That's right. I'm going to give you a test next week. A whole bunch of arithmetic problems, and social studies, and other questions.

*Counselor:*  You like getting to be the teacher and getting to be the boss.

*Dennis:*  Yeah, I never get to be the boss.

*Counselor:*  You would like to have a chance to tell people what to do.

*Dennis:*  Yeah, I hate getting bossed around all the time.

*Counselor:*  It would be nice if you got to be your own boss sometimes and not have to take orders from your teacher and your parents.

---

*The case of Dennis was contributed by Michael Gooch and is reprinted by permission.

*Dennis:* Right, I never get to do anything I want to do.

*Counselor:* It would be really nice if your teacher or parents would let you choose some things to do.

*Dennis:* Yeah, but they don't let me.

*Counselor:* It's hard for you to get your own way at school and home.

*Dennis:* Sometimes I do.

*Counselor:* How were you able to do that?

*Dennis:* I raised a fuss.

*Counselor:* You mean you got what you wanted by making a lot of noise.

*Dennis:* I cried, kicked, and screamed.

*Counselor:* So one time you got what you wanted.

*Dennis:* I got punished, too—I couldn't play Nintendo for a week.

*Counselor:* So you need a better way to get to do something you want to do.

*Dennis:* I don't know what to do.

*Counselor:* Well, we can practice in here on how to get things you want.

*Dennis:* How?

*Counselor:* Kind of like you are doing now, when you are the teacher and I am the student.

*Dennis:* Okay. Now, I'm going to read like my friend does. . . . Notice how he reads?

*Counselor:* He seems to read fast without pausing.

*Dennis:* Yes.

*Counselor:* You'd like to be able to read like that.

*Dennis:* Not much. Let's name the ships in the books. [Dennis names each type of boat.] I have so much fun making up those names. That's what we'll do next week. [Dennis begins reading again.] Stop me when I make a mistake or do something wrong.

*Counselor:* I'd rather you stop yourself.

*Dennis:* The teacher always stops me.

*Counselor:* I'm a listener, not a teacher.

*Dennis:* Be a teacher, all right? [Dennis begins reading again.] That reminds me, I have three darts at home. The set cost me three dollars. Two have been broke. [The session is about to end. Counselor examines some darts and a board.] Oh boy, darts. Maybe we can play with them next week.

*Counselor:* You're making lots of plans for next time.

*Dennis:* Yeah.

Several counseling sessions followed this one. Dennis showed marked improvement at school and at home. Dennis's mother and teacher spoke more positively of him. The counselor gave Dennis his complete, undivided attention, participating in his games, tasks, projects, and plans. Here was someone with whom Dennis could talk and share his interests and ideas at a time when no one else would understand and accept him. He needed someone who would let him lead the way and be important in making decisions and plans. Dennis played the role of the initiator, the director, and the teacher. He needed to have someone else know how it felt to be the follower who is told what to do, ordered into activity, and made to meet expectations. He needed to gain respect as well as confidence in his ability to face tasks and problems and see them through successfully. In short, he used the therapy experience to improve his relationships and his skills. He became a competent, self-dependent person by practicing behavior that gave him a sense of adequacy and self-fulfillment.

### *Identification of Problem II**

A family sought therapy for problems with Pete, their rebellious 12-year-old son. The boy and his younger sister had been adopted 5 years earlier after a series of foster care arrangements. The adopting couple had no children before the adoption.

A history-gathering first session with the adoptive parents revealed that Pete had been physically abused by his biological mother and by at least one subsequent foster mother. The parents described Pete as rebellious and disrespectful, especially toward his mother. During the second session, the counselor met separately with Pete to establish rapport and continue assessing the context of the presenting problem. Although the boy was 12 years old, his social and emotional development appeared to be more like that of a 6- or 7-year-old. The counselor wanted to help Pete feel comfortable, as well as elicit more information about his inner thoughts. With these objectives in mind and in view of Pete's apparent developmental stage, the counselor asked him to draw a picture of a person. Pete drew a hypermuscular, threatening-looking young adult (Figure 3-5). Then the counselor asked Pete to make up a story about the picture. Pete then told the following

---

*The case of Pete was contributed by Robert Lee Whitaker, Ph.D., and is reprinted by permission.

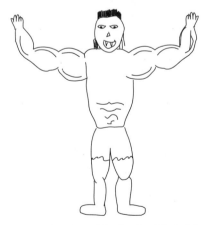

FIGURE 3-5   Pete's drawing (Contributed by Jessica Marie Martin, reprinted by permission.)

story. Note how the story's themes metaphorically describe Pete's experiences and his frustrated efforts to cope with them.

### Pete's Story

He was born in a hollow tree. His mom was a dog; his dad was a cat. He was green, and he was the strongest person who ever lived. People called him Starman. He could throw a car, and it wouldn't come down for a week.

Then one day he met a baby. The baby had a race with him in the Olympics and beat him. The baby asked if he thought he could beat him again. For 2 years, they competed, and the baby always won. So the guy trained for 2 more years to beat the baby, but by that time, the baby was so big his head went out of the earth. He could jump out the earth. The guy knew he couldn't do anything about it, so he retired and went off to be a wimp and was never seen again. There were stories that he was beat up, killed, shot. And that was the last they saw of him.

A week later, the counselor asked Pete to tell the story of Starman's early life.

He lived in a jungle and helped his dad fight off the beasts that tried to attack his family. He's been alive 300 billion years. He was a god and a very powerful prince of the world then. His dad was the king. The prince made up the rules for the kingdom (which was communist). People could only work when the prince wanted them to work, and no family could have over $700. If so, they had to see him, and they couldn't leave the country.

The queen was named Laura. She was as skinny as a toothpick, and she was so powerful she could make it rain or snow or any kind of weather when she wanted. She could make people feel like they were dying and could make them grow old real fast. She could make them have nine lives or make them look ugly. She could change their bodies into beasts. She was very wicked.

The prince didn't like her because she was trying to overrule him and get all the power he had. So, the prince got all the other gods in all the world or universe and his dad and formed all their powers together and killed her. When she died, she turned into a planet called Saturn (her remains). The queen is dead now.

The prince grew up, and his dad died because of Zeus. Zeus gave him poison, and the prince was in charge from then on, except for Zeus (the god over all). The prince enforced all the laws the same way the lady did, and Zeus threatened to kill him. The lady had enforced the laws because Zeus threatened to kill her. The prince killed her because he didn't like the rules and what she was doing to the people, but he didn't know Zeus was making her do it by threatening to kill her.

The prince went on doing things the way Zeus wanted until he died. Now he is just a strong person.

### Interpreting the Story

This story suggested to the counselor a need to explore issues of anger and powerlessness with Pete. "Starman," or "the prince," felt powerless against the exceptional power and influence of the queen and the baby. Queen "Laura" had absolute control over the environment and could make whatever kind of weather she wanted (usually bad), make people grow old quickly, make them experience a feeling of death, make them ugly, and even turn them into beasts. Leadership, no matter who was in power, was always threateningly authoritarian. The prince's battle for power or control is described as a violent act against the leader, made possible by combining the power of all oppressed victims.

The story appears to reflect the trauma of Pete's upbringing and the particularly negative feelings he has toward females with power over him. Further, the story seems to parallel closely his history of abuse and development into an aggressive person involved in a power struggle with his adoptive mother. The information elicited from the story alerted the counselor to Pete's experience of the reported historical events. It is unlikely that Pete could have conveyed the impact of his history and its present relevance to his life in a form more insightful and descriptively meaningful than the story he told.

## Intervention

On the basis of the initial assessment interview with Pete's parents and the issues identified within the story, the counselor chose the following initial interventions: First, he decided to continue combining direct assessment procedures with picture-drawing and storytelling strategies to identify additional problematic areas for Pete. Second, the counselor began formulating a story to be used later about an abused person or animal who learned to adapt to a new environment by gradually learning to trust. Third, he asked Pete's permission to share with Pete's parents the story and the counselor's impressions of it. He then used the story to show the parents the relationship between Pete's present behavior and the trauma of his early experiences. The parents appeared to expect Pete to behave like any normal 12-year-old and not manifest any significant behavioral deficits related to the care he received during the first 7 years of his life. The counselor suggested that Pete was attempting to cope with these early experiences and that his parents might be able to help him and themselves by reconsidering the long-range impact of such an experience, adjusting their expectations, mutually deciding upon and concentrating on just a few rules, giving Pete choices within limits they could accept, and selecting the roles each of them wanted to serve in Pete's life in light of what the story might suggest. Finally, the counselor suggested they try an experiment to begin their exploration of the new roles they wished to assume in Pete's life by letting the mother have a vacation from her job as the primary disciplinarian.

## Rationale

The therapeutic intentions of this plan were, first, to reinforce consistency in the parents' rules and expectations; second, to empower Pete with choices his parents could accept; third, to empower Pete's mother by providing more involvement and support from his father in parenting; fourth, to foster an expectation of trust rather than distrust ("I know he'll do the right thing" instead of "I know he'll do the wrong thing"); fifth, to focus less on punishment and more on logical consequences for Pete's misbehavior; and, finally, to do away with any "mystery" rules or consequences.

## CROSS-CULTURAL APPLICATIONS OF PSYCHOANALYTIC COUNSELING

Many of the adaptations psychoanalytic counselors are making to meet managed care guidelines will also assist them in adapting the system to a wider variety of clients representing many different cultures. Long-term treatment focused on attainment of intrapsychic insight to bring more of the unconscious into conscious awareness does not hold much appeal for clients from cultures that do not have the resources, patience, or desire for such treatment and outcomes. However, being the oldest treatment approach and having been developed in Austria, it has a classical acceptance worldwide that many American counseling theories do not. As psychoanalytic counselors move toward treating families, their acceptance among other cultures should increase (see Chapter 13). Likewise, moving from stressing the individual to focusing on the welfare of the family and community should appeal to those cultures where group needs are considered over individual needs.

Catharsis, the process of talking out painful feelings and emotions, does not enjoy universal appeal across all cultures. The use of the analysis of transference and countertransference is rendered impossible when the counselor lacks awareness of the cultural realities of their clients. These cultural realities are presented in Chapter 13 with some guidelines on how to use the information in counseling.

Yi (1998) pointed out that psychoanalytic counseling had its birth in European culture and has been shaped by values such as a bounded, autonomous self with an affect-filled inferiority, assertiveness of personal needs, personal achievement, personal identity, democracy, introspection, and interpersonal equality. Practitioners of psychoanalytic counseling traditionally hold that the truths on which psychoanalysis was founded are objective and universally applicable to all cultures. However, as noted by Imber-Black (1997), this view is being modified by the realization that, to be effective, counselors need to understand differing cultural constructs and to de-center themselves from their own cultural values.

## PSYCHOANALYTIC COUNSELING AND MANAGED HEALTH CARE

For psychoanalytic counselors to meet the managed care guidelines presented in Chapter 2, they will have to move to briefer treatment periods. Such a move will necessitate a clearer focus on problems with the setting of definite, measurable goals and the development of definite counseling strategies and treatment plans. Attention will shift from the past and unconscious conflicts to current environmental stresses. More attention will be given to children and how they interact with their families. There will also be a shift from interpretation of intrapsychic mechanisms to reliance on the counselor–client relationship as the main treatment agent. The use of play therapy and the expressive arts will continue to increase in counseling children.

## SUMMARY

Freud (1918) identified the task of analysts as bringing to patients' knowledge their unconscious, repressed material and uncovering the resistances that oppose this extension of their knowledge about themselves. He believed that frustration made his patients ill and that their symptoms served them as substitute satisfactions. Freud (1918) clearly noted the harm that may come to patients who receive too much help and consolation from their therapists but also pointed out that many patients lack the strength and general knowledge to handle their lives without some mentoring and instruction, in addition to analysis, from their therapists.

Freud's theory continues to be criticized for its lack of sound research support. Freud considered his theory of repression to be the cornerstone of the entire structure of psychoanalysis. However, Grünbaum (1993) noted that more research is needed to validate the link between such things as repressed childhood molestation and adult neurosis. He pointed out that a first event followed by a second event does not prove causality between the events. The theories of dreams and parapraxia also suffer from lack of hard data to prove causality.

In Freud's defense, much of his data collecting was similar to what passes today for acceptable, phenomenological research. In fact, data collecting through free association has many similarities to the open-ended, phenomenological interviewing method in which participants are encouraged to free-associate about the topic under study. Moreover, much of what is being done in counseling today has its roots in his many contributions to the theory and practice of counseling.

### W E B S I T E S  for Psychoanalytic Counseling

D. W. Winnicott
home.online.no/~vals/winni.html

National Psychological Association for Psychoanalysis
www.npap.org

Psychoanalysis
www.umdnj.edu/psyevnts/psa.html
www.questia.com

Sigmund Freud Museum, Vienna Homepage
freud.t0.or.at

## REFERENCES

Burton, L. (1995). Using a dog in an elementary school counseling program. *Elementary School Guidance and Counseling, 29,* 236–240.

Clark, A. (1991). The identification and modification of defense mechanism in counseling. *Journal of Counseling and Development, 69,* 231–236.

Dobson, J. (2002, June 29). If father wasn't there, life probably isn't full, happy. *Knoxville News Sentinel,* C-3.

Fall, M. (1994). Physical and emotional expression: A Combination approach for working with children in small areas of a school counselor's office. *The School Counselor, 42,* 72–77.

Fancher, R. (2000). Snapshots of Freud in America. *American Psychologist, 55,* 1025–1028.

Frankel, J. B. (1998). The play's the thing: How the essential processes of therapy are seen most clearly in child therapy. *Psychoanalytic Dialogues, 8,* 149–182.

Freud, A. (1926). *Psychoanalytic treatment of children.* London: Imago.

Freud, S. (1918). *Lines of advance in psychoanalytic therapy.* Paper presented at the fifth International Psychoanalytic Congress, Budapest, Hungary.

Freud, S. (1949). *An outline of psychoanalysis* (J. Strachey, Trans.). New York: Norton. (Original work published 1940)

Freud, S. (1952). *On dreams* (J. Strachey, Trans.). New York: Norton. (Original work published 1901)

Freud, S. (1963). *An autobiographical study* (J. Strachey, Trans.). New York: Norton. (Original work published 1925)

Freud, S. (1965a). *The interpretation of dreams* (J. Strachey, Trans.). New York: Norton. (Original work published 1900)

Freud, S. (1965b). *New introductory lectures in psychoanalysis* (J. Strachey, Ed. and Trans.). New York: Norton. (Original work published 1933)

Freud, S. (1971). *The psychopathology of everyday life* (A. Tyson, Trans.). New York: Norton. (Original work published 1901)

Grünbaum, A. (1993). *Validation in clinical theory of psychoanalysis.* Madison, CT: International Universities Press.

Hall, C. (1954). *A primer of Freudian psychology.* New York: Mentor.

Imber-Black, E. (1997). Developing cultural competence: Contributions from recent family therapy literature. *American Journal of Psychotherapy, 51,* 607–610.

Kestenbaum, C. J. (1985). The creative process in child psychotherapy. *American Journal of Psychotherapy, 39,* 479–489.

Klein, M. (1932). *The psychoanalysis of children.* London: Hogarth.

Lawson, D. (1987). Using therapeutic stories in the counseling process. *Elementary School Guidance and Counseling, 22,* 134–142.

Lee, A. C. (1997). Psychoanalytic play therapy. In K. O'Connor & L. M. Braverman (Eds.), *Play therapy theory and practice: A comparative presentation* (pp. 46–78). New York: Wiley.

Levinson, B. (1962). The dog as co-therapist. *Mental Hygiene, 46,* 59–65.

Lyness-Richard, D. (1997). Play and perfectionism: Putting fun back into families. In H. G. Kaduson, D. Cangelosi, & C. E. Schaefer (Eds.), *The playing cure: Individualized play therapy for specific childhood problems* (pp. 29–60). Northvale, NJ: Jason Aronson.

Maslow, A. (1970). *Motivation and personality* (2nd ed.). New York: Harper & Row.

Neubauer, P. (1987). The many meanings of play. *Psychoanalytic Study of the Child, 42,* 193–203.

O'Brien, M. (1993). Pets as counselors. *Elementary School Guidance and Counseling, 4,* 308.

Patton, M., & Meara, N. (1991). *Psychoanalytic counseling.* New York: Wiley.

Piaget, J., & Inhelder, B. (1969). *The psychology of the child.* New York: Basic Books.

Schaefer, C., & Cangelosi, D. (Eds.). (1993). *Play therapy techniques.* Northvale, NJ: Aronson.

Simon, S. (1988). *Six conditions for nurturing self-esteem.* Paper presented at the American School Counselors Association convention, Breckenridge, CO.

Stone, I. (1971). *Passions of the mind.* New York: Doubleday.

Sugarman, A. (1977). Psychoanalysis as a humanistic psychology. *Psychotherapy: Theory, Research, and Practice, 14,* 204–211.

Trivedi, L., & Perl, J. (1995). Animal facilitated counseling in the elementary school: A literature review and practical considerations. *Elementary School Guidance and Counseling, 29,* 223–234.

Watson, J. (1980). Bibliotherapy for abused children. *School Counselor, 27,* 204–208.

Westen, D. (1998). The scientific legacy of Sigmund Freud toward a psychodynamically informed psychological science. *Psychological Bulletin, 124,* 333–371.

Winnicott, D. W. (1971). *Playing and reality.* London: Tavistock.

Winnicott, D. W. (1977). The piggle: An account of the psychoanalytic treatment of a little girl. New York: International University Press.

Winnicott, D. W. (2001, February 16). D. W. Winnicott, 1896–1971: His life and work. home.online.no/~vals/winni/html. Retrieved August 15, 2002.

Yi, K. (1998). Transference and race: An intrasubjective conceptualization. *Psychoanalytic Psychology, 15,* 245–261.

# Chapter 4

# Reality Therapy

*Nothing strengthens the judgment and quickens*
*the conscience like individual responsibility.*
—Elizabeth Cady Stanton

*Restlessness and discontent are the first necessities of progress.*
—Thomas A. Edison

## WILLIAM GLASSER

William Glasser graduated from Case Institute of Technology as a chemical engineer in 1944, at the age of 19. He enrolled at Case Western Reserve University and, at 23, earned a master's degree in clinical psychology. At 28 he received a medical degree from the same institution. While serving his last year of residency at the University of California at Los Angeles School of Psychiatry and in a Veterans Administration hospital, Glasser discovered that traditional psychotherapy was not for him. Glasser voiced reservations about psychoanalysis to his last teacher, who reputedly responded, "Join the club," although such an attitude was not common or popular among his colleagues. Denied a promised teaching position because of his rebellion against Freudian concepts, Glasser said he would have made about $8,000 in the first 16 years of his practice if he had relied on referrals from his alma mater, as most beginning psychiatrists do.

In 1956, Glasser became head psychiatrist at the Ventura School for Girls, an institution operated by the State of California to treat seriously delinquent adolescent girls. For 12 years Glasser conducted a successful program at the Ventura School; the theory and concepts of reality therapy evolved out of this program. In his first book, *Mental Health or Mental Illness?* (1961), he laid the foundation for the techniques and concepts that became reality therapy.

Glasser used the term *reality therapy* for the first time in April 1964 in a manuscript, "Reality Therapy: A Realistic Approach to the Young Offender." His widely read *Reality Therapy* was published in 1965. In 1966, Glasser began consulting in California public schools for the purpose of applying reality therapy in education. These new ideas for applying reality therapy to teaching later became his third book, *Schools Without Failure* (1969).

In 1968, Glasser founded the Institute for Reality Therapy in Los Angeles. It offers training courses for physicians, probation officers, police officers, nurses, lawyers, judges, teachers, and counselors. Introductory and advanced courses and programs are offered on a regular and continuing basis. Following the publication of *Schools Without Failure,* the Educator Training Center, a special division of the Institute for Reality Therapy, was established in Los Angeles in 1971. In 1970, the William Glasser La Verne College Center was established at the University of La Verne in southern California to provide teachers with an off-campus opportunity to gain graduate and in-service credits while working within their own schools to provide an exciting educational environment for children.

The Schools Without Failure Seminars, sponsored by the Educator Training Center, drew large followings across the country. Glasser's other books include *The Identity Society* (1972), *Positive Addiction* (1976), *Stations of the Mind* (1981), *Control Theory* (1984), *Control Theory in the Classroom* (1986), *The Quality School: Managing Students Without Coercion* (1990), *The Quality School Teacher* (1993), *Staying Together* (1995), *Choice Theory: A New Psychology of Personal Freedom* (1998), *Getting Together and Staying Together* (2000), *Reality Therapy in Action* (2000), *Every Student Can Succeed* (2000), and *Unhappy Teenagers: A Way for Parents and Teachers to Reach Them* (2002). Glasser has made approximately 75 speaking appearances a year in addition to television interviews, writing, and videotaping.

## THE NATURE OF PEOPLE

Glasser believed that, despite varying manifestations, psychological problems are the result of one factor: inability to fulfill one's basic needs. Glasser (1965) saw a correlation between people's lack of success in meeting their needs and the degree of their distress. He maintained that all psychological problems can be summed up by people's denial of the reality of the world around them. *Denial of reality* in the reality therapy system refers to the tendency of people to try to avoid the unpleasant natural and logical consequences of their irresponsible behavior. People also are viewed as getting into trouble when they behave in irresponsible ways. In Glasser's system, *irresponsible behavior* is defined as attempts by people to satisfy their basic needs in ways that infringe on the rights of others to meet their needs. Glasser believed that people have five of these basic needs: survival, freedom, power, fun, and love and belonging. Joining reality and responsibility is the third R—right and wrong. As is true with the other two *R*s, the issue of doing the right behavior is addressed in the practice of reality therapy. Glasser struggled more with the definition of the right behavior than he did when defining behavior in touch with reality and responsible behavior. For Glasser, feelings are the one indicator that our behavior is on the right track. That is, if people feel good about their behavior and if others also feel good about it, chances are they are doing the right thing. More recently, in his incorporation of choice theory into reality therapy, Glasser (1998) stated that all problems brought to counseling are relationship problems. Behavior in opposition to the three *R*s is likely to lead to an abundance of relationship problems.

Borrowing from Maslow's hierarchy of human needs, Glasser focused his early treatment plans on teaching people to love and be loved and to feel valued by themselves and by others. Successful attainment of these two needs leads to a success identity (Figure 4-1). In fact, success in these two important areas can be a quick index of mental health. Both are key to healthy self-esteem; this theme runs through Kronick and Hargis's book, *Dropouts: Who Drops Out and Why—and the Recommended Action* (1998). They echo many of Glasser's points in their prescriptions for preventing school failure and school dropouts. They focus on teaching children basic social skills to help them interact more effectively with their peers and with adults in the school setting. Building a network of friends and supportive people puts a child on the road to achieving a healthy sense of self-esteem, a journey to be completed through success in the classroom. Kronick and Hargis also recommended treating children who have failure identities by teaching them time management and study skills as a way of ensuring their academic success. "Schools without failure" has been a principal theme throughout Glasser's work, which has been continued in his writing on quality schools and quality schoolteachers. The Chestnut Ridge School described by Beilharz in Kronick and Hargis (1998) is a successful adaptation of many of Glasser's principles.

## Choice Theory and the Nature of People

Choice theory is based on the proposition that the only behavior we can control is our own. Glasser (1998) pointed out that people get into trouble when they try to control other people. He believed that the practice of control psychology is re-

FIGURE 4-1    Failure and success identities

sponsible for the widespread belief that people and their behaviors can be controlled. Consequently, people waste considerable energy and time trying to get other people to do things they do not want to do. Equal amounts of time and energy are expended on resisting the efforts of others to get you to do things you do not want to do. Glasser (1998) sees these efforts to get others to do things they do not want to do as responsible for the breakdown of good relationships. In fact, Glasser believed that all long-lasting psychological problems brought to counseling are relationship problems resulting from attempts to get people to do things they do not want to do. The remedy for fixing the damage done by the practice of control psychology is to teach choice theory psychology to as many people as possible. Choice theory psychology practitioners teach their clients that they can control only their own behavior and that they have the freedom to make choices that lead to better-quality lives. Glasser (1998) held that each of us maintains mental images of what and whom we would like to have in our quality world. The best way to bring reality to our quality world image is to make the changes in our lives that help us find better ways to meet our needs.

Glasser believed that all we can give or get from other people is information. What we do with that information is our choice, as are the type and amount of information we give to others. We are responsible only for what we choose to do with our behavior. Relationships become progressively better as people focus on changing their own behavior as opposed to trying to get other people to change their ways.

Glasser (1998) pointed out that relationship problems are at least partial causes of many other problems, such as pain, fatigue, weakness, and some chronic diseases commonly referred to as autoimmune diseases. He believed that people choose misery and depression rather than facing the problem of what they are doing to destroy an important relationship that is not working the way they want. In fact, Glasser insists that his clients refer to personal depression as "I am choosing to depress or I am depressing" rather than "I am depressed or suffering from depression."

Consistent with reality therapy philosophy, Glasser stated that problem relationships are part of our present life. He never found them in a person's past relationships or in future aspirations for relationships. Although past painful events and relationships have significant influence on a person's present life, Glasser believed to revisit the past is not nearly as productive as focusing on what needs to be done to improve a current, important relationship.

As mentioned previously, reality therapists practicing choice theory psychology believe that people are driven by five genetic needs: survival, love and belonging, power, freedom, and fun. Glasser did not define his list of needs in a Maslow-like hierarchy. That is, filling a particular need does not depend on filling a prerequisite lower-level need. It could be argued that filling the survival need would necessarily always precede filling other needs, with the exception of a person who chooses suicide over survival. Glasser believed all five needs have to be satisfied. Failure to satisfy a particular need often results in choosing a symptom behavior such as depression. These needs are satisfied only by satisfying an image or picture

*Needs circle*

we have included in our quality world. Hence, we see the importance of being able to visualize ourselves achieving the important and realistic goals we have set for ourselves. The amount of freedom we have in our lives is directly proportional to the success we have in satisfying the pictures and images we hold in our quality worlds. We give up freedom when we put pictures in our quality worlds that we cannot satisfy. Glasser (1998) viewed all behavior as total behavior consisting of four integrated components: acting, thinking, feeling, and physiology. Interventions with any one of the four components will affect the other four. Glasser believed that all behavior is chosen, but that direct control is limited to acting and thinking. Feelings and physiology can be controlled indirectly by how people choose to think and act.

Glasser has been influenced by W. Edwards Deming's (1966) philosophy that high-quality work is dependent on eliminating the fear that prevents people from getting along well with each other. You cannot get good work from people when there is an adversarial relationship between management and labor, teachers and students, and counselors and clients. To be successful, managers, teachers, and counselors must become a part of the quality worlds of the people with whom they work. Glasser believed that the practice of control psychology—punishing wrong behavior and rewarding right behavior—is responsible for most of the human misery and adversarial relationships we have worldwide. The problem is compounded by the fact that those who have power—government agencies, parents, teachers, business managers, and religious leaders who define right and wrong—totally support the practice of control psychology.

In *Choice Theory* (1998), Glasser described methods for taking control of one's life. The theory is based on the idea that people are responsible for their own choices, decisions, goals, and the general degree of happiness in their lives. We are not controlled by external events and people unless we choose to let them take over. To a person who said, "Mary Sue hurt me when she rejected me, and I am too depressed to want to continue my life," Glasser would point out that the person is "depressing" (using *depression* as a verb) as a last, desperate, ineffective effort to regain control of a large part of his life that seems to be slipping away. He would recommend reframing the mental image of life to include something more than a relationship with Mary Sue as a raison d'être. This concept is similar to the methodology used in rational-emotive-behavior therapy and cognitive therapy, which focus on reframing of thoughts, self-talk, and visualization as ways of treating undesired emotional states such as depression. In fact, many points Glasser raised are similar to those in Gestalt and existential theory regarding self-responsibility for living life. For example, rather than saying, "I have a cold," one would say, "I am doing a cold." Presumably, taking control over having a cold enables one to take control over stopping it. Two themes run through *Choice Theory:* (1) We control our mental images or pictures. We can put them in, exchange them, add to them, or throw them out. We can also choose which picture or goal we can and want to satisfy. (2) Whenever we choose to depress or develop a psychosomatic illness, we have the option of choosing something more satisfying. The chapter on choice theory and rearing children, in which Glasser integrates his choice theory points into the standard steps of reality therapy, is particularly relevant for counseling children. Perhaps the greatest help to parents, counselors, and teachers is the idea that we need to empower rather than overpower children to win their cooperation when they grow too big to overpower.

The notion of empowering children is central to *Control Theory in the Classroom* (1986). In his best work for educators since *Schools Without Failure* (1969), Glasser made a strong case for the teacher as manager, who motivates students by empowering them with the responsibility for learning. Note that Glasser now uses choice theory rather than control theory. The principal motivation method is two- to five-member learning teams designed to meet student needs for belonging, power, friendships, and achievement. The team idea has been presented elsewhere (Thompson & Poppen, 1972) and found successful. Glasser draws a parallel between successful managers in business and successful managers (teachers) in education and presents examples of how lead managers connect with people. He has been highly critical of stimulus–response (S–R) learning; however, the team-learning approach, if well designed, seems an excellent example of creating the proper stimulus conditions to foster the desired learning response. Much of the research and writing on reality therapy is related to the school environment because counselors and teachers find the theory and practice of reality therapy useful in working with student problems.

Glasser continued his educational model in four other books: *The Quality School: Managing Students Without Coercion* (1990), *The Quality School Teacher* (1993), *Every Student Can Succeed* (2000a), and *Unhappy Teenagers: A Way for Parents and Teachers to Reach Them* (2002). These books emphasize the business metaphor derived from Deming's work with Japanese factories. The message is that managers and teachers have a lot in common in that the results depend on how people are treated. The book presented two managerial models: the boss manager and the lead manager. Boss managers motivate by punishment rather than encouragement and reinforcement, tell rather than show, overpower rather than empower, and rule rather than cooperate. Lead managers do the reverse. In short, Glasser makes a case for cooperative teachers rather than controlling ones. Glasser (2002) believes that teachers can connect with their students if they give up the 7 deadly habits that destroy all relationships. These are criticizing, blaming, complaining, nagging, threatening, punishing, and rewarding to control. The model works equally well in homes, schools, businesses, community agencies, and government because, regardless of setting, we are all in the business of managing people.

In summary, Glasser's views on the nature of people are based on the following principles.

1. The only person whose behavior we can control is our own. Behavioral psychologists would disagree, pointing out that we can control the behavior of others with reinforcement, punishment, and extinction. Glasser's response would be that the practice of behavioral methods to control the behavior of others will cost you a positive working relationship with the person whose behavior you are trying to control.

2. All long-lasting psychological problems are relationship problems that result from attempts of people to control other people. Disagreement comes from those who point out that problems also originate from inner conflicts with the self, lack of information, and lack of skill.

3. Past events have everything to do with what we are today, but we can satisfy our basic needs only in the present and make plans for the future. Psychodynamic theorists disagree, stating that insight into how we became the people we are is helpful in bringing about change.

4. Satisfying the needs represented by the pictures of our quality world is the way we meet our needs for survival, fun, freedom, power, and love and belonging. Failure to meet these needs often results in choosing a symptom as a way of rationalizing or excusing this failure. Third force psychologists side with Maslow's hierarchy of human needs, positing the necessity to satisfy lower-level needs before higher-level needs.

5. Total behavior is all that we do, including acting, thinking, feeling, and physiology. We have direct control over acting and thinking; however, we can control our feelings and physiology indirectly by how we choose to act and think. That is, if we feel bad on Monday, we will feel bad on Tuesday unless we change our behavior or thinking. Disagreement would come from those counselors who believe that exploration of feelings precedes changes in thinking and behavior.

## THEORY OF COUNSELING

Glasser was reacting against some of the principles of psychoanalytic theory when he developed reality therapy. Reality therapy differs from traditional psychoanalytic therapy in six ways.

First, reality therapists discard the concept of mental illness in favor of the concept of responsibility. Traditionally, people behave irresponsibly because they are mentally ill, whereas Glasser believed that people become mentally ill because they behave irresponsibly.

Second, reality therapists focus on the moral issue of right and wrong—an issue often ignored in counseling because many believe that people already feel too guilty about various unresolved conflicts. In Freud's time, everyone talked about doing the right thing, so Freud thought it best to make psychotherapy a sanctuary free of moral judgments to avoid increasing his patients' feelings of guilt. In reality therapy, moral issues are addressed head-on.

Third, reality therapists largely ignore the past in favor of dealing with the present and future. Most discussion in reality therapy evaluates how present behavior is helping to meet one's needs. If present behavior is not working, future alternatives are examined, and commitments to change are made.

A fourth difference involves transference. In traditional psychoanalytic practice, transference is frequently used as a therapeutic mechanism for living through unresolved conflicts. In reality therapy, the counselor relates to the client on a person-to-person basis and does not encourage the client to relate to the counselor as someone else; for example, the child does not relate to the counselor as a parent, teacher, or other authority figures (objects).

Fifth, reality therapists largely ignore the unconscious, whereas it is generally the primary focus in psychoanalytic practice. According to Glasser, the unconscious is a fertile ground for excuses for misbehavior; the counselor is advised to look at *what* is going on rather than *why*.

The sixth and perhaps most significant feature of reality therapy distinguishing it from traditional practice is the aspect most dear to educators, whose philosophy is that the counseling performed with children is primarily a teaching–learning situation. Glasser said about reality therapy that it is a teaching process, not a healing process. Counselors are in the business of teaching children better ways to meet their needs. From the reality therapy point of view, counseling is a matter of learning how to solve problems—teaching children, in effect, to become their own counselors.

## COUNSELING METHOD

The biggest challenge counselors face in the practice of reality therapy based on choice theory is to teach their clients that control psychology will not work for them any better than it has worked for the rest of the world. Glasser (1998, 2000c) believes that our attempts to control others are largely responsible for the misery in so many people's lives. When people do not do what we want them to do, we have a long history of turning to coercion and control to get them to follow our wishes.

The primary focus of choice theory in reality therapy is to prevent problems before they happen. Regardless of the skill of the counselor, it is often impossible to rescue failing students who have never been willing to put school and teachers in their quality world vision. People do not admit those who try to control them to their quality world. Glasser (1998, 2000a) believed that a good way to learn choice theory is to treat others in your life like you treat your best friend, your boss, and most strangers. You rarely try to force these people to do anything. Ownership contributes to the problem of trying to control others. People tend to believe that they own their spouses, children, students, and employees. For example, I have a right to control the people I own, and when they do not do what I want, I have a right to force them to do it. Consequently, we often have better relationships with those not so close to us because we do not try to own them and force them to do things they do not want to do. Glasser (1998, 2002) recommended that parents treat their children like the grandparents do, but he recognized that there must be limits; natural or logical consequences should result when limits are breached.

In concert with Albert Ellis's rational-emotive-behavior therapy, Glasser (1998, 2000c) identified three faulty beliefs that undergird the control psychology that essentially rules the world.

First belief: Much of my behavior is a response to an external signal, such as answering a ringing phone.

Second belief: I can make people do what I want them to do even if they do not want to do it, and other people can control how I think, act, and feel.

Third belief: I have a right and a duty to punish those who do not do what I tell them to do and to reward those who do.

So, reality therapy based on choice theory now includes an examination of the client's belief system. Clients will be challenged to prove the rationality of what they believe, as well as the utility of what they do when they act on their beliefs. It is Glasser's contention that acting on the faulty beliefs of control psychology will make every situation or problem immediately worse.

Each person has a quality world vision made up of the pictures of the people we want to be with, the things we want to own and experience, and the ideas or belief systems that govern our behavior. The closer our reality world approaches our quality world, the happier we will be. The further apart our reality and quality worlds are, the more pain we experience from not getting what we want. Choice theory and reality theory treatment plans are directed toward helping people handle the pain from not getting what they want. Treatment often involves changing strategies to help people get what they want and/or reviewing the pictures in their quality world. In all cases, counseling is focused on changing the client rather than on how the client should try to change others. However, it must be noted that change in the client's behavior often influences change in others. The idea is to place one's quality world totally in one's hands and not have quality world objectives under the control of others. In choice theory reality therapy, the focus is on improving present relationships through personal change while disregarding past relationships. The success of the counseling process depends on creating a good relationship between the client and the counselor. The trust level between client and counselor needs to be high enough to handle confrontations such as the following:

*Counselor:*   What do you think caused the problem?
*Client:*   It's hard to say. It's really hard to say.
*Counselor:*   (In a friendly tone of voice) Well, say it anyway. This is the place to say hard-to-say things.

Clients sometimes choose to depress themselves when they do not get what they want. When this happens, the counselor confronts them with four choices:

1. Continue to depress yourself.
2. Change what you are doing to get what you want.
3. Change what you want.
4. Both (2) and (3).

Glasser held that choosing to depress, no matter how strongly or how long the duration, is not a mental illness. Like all behavior, it is a choice.

The practice of reality therapy follows eight steps. Step 1 is building good relationships with clients. Glasser calls this first step becoming involved, although *in-*

*volvement* may not be the best word to describe this stage of counseling because it implies entangled or complex rather than positive, honest, open, unencumbered relationships. Any approach to counseling children should build the kind of trust and climate in which children feel free to express their innermost fears, anxieties, and concerns.

In Step 2, children describe their present behavior. In Step 3, children evaluate what is going on in their lives and how they are helping themselves. In other words, is their behavior helping them get what they want from life? If not, the counselor asks, "Do you want to change what is going on?" However, people do not change old behaviors until they are convinced that they are either not helping them or are actually harming them. So, if in Step 3 counselors do not get negative evaluations from their clients about their current behaviors, counseling is not likely to generate any behavior change. Glasser believed that the only way for a person who feels bad to feel better is to make a positive change in behavior (see Figure 2-2). Reality therapy focuses on working with observable content, including behavior, plans, and goals. "What" questions are preferred to "why" questions, which encourage people to find excuses for irresponsible behavior.

In Step 4, the counselor and child begin to look at possible alternatives for getting what the child wants in life. A brainstorming format is used in which children look at better ways of meeting their needs. In Step 5, children select alternatives for reaching their goals. The child then makes a commitment to try the alternative. A key process in counseling children is helping them make commitments. When they are able to carry out present commitments, counselors can help them build on these successes to get more from life. Therefore, children are first asked to make a relatively small commitment; they can then achieve success and have a foundation on which to build further behavioral changes.

In Step 6, counselor and client examine the results of the commitment. Children returning for a second interview often say, "Well, I made a commitment to turn in one homework paper a day, and I did not meet my commitment" and then begin to list all the reasons why they failed. Reality therapists do not dwell on rationalizing "whys." At this point, the counselor and child discuss writing a new contract the child can handle; maybe one homework paper per day is too much for now, and a less demanding contract is needed. Counselors do not accept excuses if children do not meet the commitments they made. Excuses are designed to avoid punishment, and when children learn they will not be punished for not meeting a commitment, they have no need for excuses.

In Step 7, logical consequences are used—for example, a lower grade for failing to turn in a homework paper. Additional penalties that are not logical or natural consequences of failing turn in the paper, such as paddling, are considered neither effective nor humane; however, logical and natural consequences are not permissively removed.

In Step 8, perseverance is required. How long should counselors stick with children who seem bent on destroying their self-esteem? Glasser recommends working with such children three or four times longer than they expect. "Never give up" does not mean a lifelong commitment but rather building on whatever relationship has been established in Step 1 and continuing to build this relationship through the entire eight-step process.

To review, the three key terms in reality therapy are *reality, responsibility,* and *right and wrong. Reality* is generally defined as willingness to accept the logical, natural consequences of one's behavior. Trying to avoid these consequences denies reality and makes people prone to act irresponsibly. Glasser defined *responsibility* as the ability to meet one's needs without infringing on other people's rights to meet their needs. The third term is difficult to define, and Glasser's definition is on somewhat shaky ground. Glasser defined *right and wrong* as something people know by how they feel; feelings are good indicators of responsible and correct behavior. For example, if we feel good about what we are doing and most other people also feel good about it, then we are probably doing the right thing. One problem with defining right and wrong in terms of others' opinions is that mass criticism is not always right. In essence, Glasser defines the right behavior as behavior you would like done to or for you (the Golden Rule). The question becomes: How should these three concepts be treated in counseling children, adolescents, and adults? Piaget (1973) described three broad stages of moral development, which match his stages of cognitive development:

1. Preconventional (preoperational stage)
2. Conventional (concrete stage)
3. Postconventional (formal stage)

Kohlberg (1981) expanded Piaget's three stages to six by defining two substages within each of Piaget's stages. The questions on which people make their moral judgments, choices, and decisions are listed for each substage.

*Preconventional morality*

| | |
|---|---|
| Stage 1 | Will I get caught? |
| Stage 2 | What is in it for me? |

*Conventional morality*

| | |
|---|---|
| Stage 3 | What will the neighbors think? |
| Stage 4 | What is the rule or law? |

*Postconventional morality*

| | |
|---|---|
| Stage 5 | What is best for society? |
| Stage 6 | What is best for humankind? |
| | Is human life at risk? |

A strong case can be made that most problems brought to counseling are actually disorders of responsibility. Neurotic individuals assume too much responsibility; people with character disorders assume too little. Most people find themselves, at times, doing a little of both, depending on the situation. Sometimes knowing how much responsibility to take is difficult. Perhaps Glasser's answer would be to consult your brain first and then, second, the feelings you are getting as indicators of whether you are doing the right behavior. Feelings are often the product of your brain's attempt to communicate with you when you fail to consult it.

## The Reality Therapy Process

The first step—one that must continue throughout the counseling process—is to build a warm relationship. Glasser refers to building a relationship as having the counselor work toward becoming included in the client's quality worldview of what is important in his or her life. Development of a warm and trusting relationship is also referred to as establishing a therapeutic alliance between counselor and client, when both join forces to help the client meet those needs he or she is having difficulty meeting. For example, when resistant clients are sent for counseling or are court-ordered to attend counseling, the alliance between counselors and clients would work toward meeting the conditions for termination of counseling.

Next, a series of five questions is often asked in reality therapy: (1) What are you doing? (2) Is what you are doing helping you get what you want? (3) If not, what might be some other things you could try? (4) Which idea would you like to try first? (5) When? The following dialogue is an example:

*Counselor:*  Mary, can you tell me a little bit about your life right now here at school?

*Mary:*  What do you mean?

*Counselor:*  Well, Mary, it seems as though you get sent to the office a lot to talk to me about problems you're having with your teachers. Tell me what you're doing, and let's talk about it.

*Mary:*  Well, I guess I talk out of turn in class too much sometimes. But my classes are so boring.

*Counselor:*  Okay, so you talk a lot in class, and the teachers don't like what you're doing. Do you do anything else that seems to get you in trouble with Mr. Thompson and Mrs. Rudolph?

*Mary:*  No, I don't think so.

*Counselor:*  Are you happy with what happens to you when you do these things?

*Mary:*  I do the same old things that keep getting me in trouble, but I feel good for the moment.

*Counselor:*  I know you do feel better for a while. Are the good feelings worth the price you have to pay for them?

*Mary:*  I guess not, because I'm sure tired of spending so much time in the office.

*Counselor:*  Would you like to work on a better plan?

*Mary:*  Okay. Why not?

*Counselor:*  Let's start by thinking of some things you could do to get along better in your classes and some ways to make them less boring, too.

*Mary:* Well, I could stop talking out of turn! I know the teachers would like that.

*Counselor:* Stopping unhelpful things is usually a good way to start. What about some things you could begin doing in class?

*Mary:* Doing more assignments would please the teachers, but I don't like all the work.

*Counselor:* Your two suggestions will probably help you with the teachers, but they won't do much to make the class more enjoyable for you. Can you think of something to help you like school more?

*Mary:* Some of the kids get free time or get to go to the library when they turn in their work. Could I do this, too?

*Counselor:* We can ask your teachers about that today. That might be a way to please both you and the teachers. Can you think of other ideas to try?

*Mary:* I guess that's about all for now.

*Counselor:* Okay, Mary, how many of these ideas do you want to try?

*Mary:* I think I can do all of them if I can get free time, too.

*Counselor:* When do you want to start?

*Mary:* Today, if I can.

*Counselor:* We can try. Can you go over these with me one time before we leave?

*Mary:* I think so. No more talking out of turn, and do enough work to earn some free time.

*Counselor:* That sounds good to me. Do you want to shake hands and make this an agreement between you and me?

*Mary:* Okay.

*Counselor:* Good. I'd like to talk with you a little each day to see how your plan is working. If it doesn't work, we'll have to make another plan. See you tomorrow?

*Mary:* Okay, see you tomorrow.

This is a typical reality therapy interview. Identifying and evaluating present behavior are followed by making a plan and building a commitment to follow through on it. Each step in the reality therapy process is supported by a relationship of trust, caring, and friendship between the counselor and the child.

As mentioned in Chapter 2, the counseling process works better when the counselor uses statements rather than questions. Questioning moves the interview from a dialogue toward a teacher–student question-and-answer session that develops the counselor's plan rather than one for which the child feels ownership. More important, statements by the counselor allow the client more options in shaping the direction of the interview. As Carl Rogers said, given the opportunity to take charge of the counseling interview, clients may gradually begin to take charge of their lives outside the counseling session as well. Examples of questions changed to reality therapy statements follow:

1. What are you doing to solve the problem?
   If you are ready to do this, we can begin by looking at what you have been doing to solve the problem.

2. How is what you have been doing helping? Is your behavior getting you what you want?

   It might be helpful to evaluate your behavior to see how each method is working for you if you feel ready to move to the next step.

3. If what you have been trying is not working, what are some things you could do that would help?

   We could look at some new alternatives to try when you are more comfortable about moving toward a plan.

4. Which of these new alternatives would you like to try?

   You have several alternatives listed. I am not sure what you think about committing yourself to any of them.

5. When can we meet again to find out how well your plan worked out?

   It might be helpful to schedule a time for a follow-up of your plan. [Shake hands and sign a written plan if necessary.]

We have included a second transcript from a case brought to a counselor as a way of demonstrating how reality therapy can be put into practice.

## CASE STUDY

### Identification of the Problem

Wendy was a 12-year-old girl in the seventh grade at White Oak School. She was referred to the counselor because she cheated on a mathematics test.

### Individual and Background Information

Academic: School records indicate that Wendy is a high achiever, with an overall A average on her elementary school record. She also has an A average for the first two grading periods in the seventh grade. During the third grading period, which is almost over, Wendy has had some erratic test scores in mathematics. The test she was caught cheating on was an important test that could have brought up her low grades, had she done well on it.

Family: Wendy is the only child of older parents, both of whom are professionals. Teachers have indicated that the parents seem to expect Wendy to make the highest grades in her class.

Social: According to teachers' reports on cumulative records, Wendy was well liked by most of the children in her classes in elementary school. She did not seem to have a close friend then, but this year she has developed a close friendship with a girl in her class. A sociogram done in her sixth-grade class indicated she was well accepted by her peers.

*Counseling Method*

The counselor used the reality therapy counseling method to help Wendy evaluate her behavior and identify some things she could do to meet more of her needs socially and emotionally without creating problems in other areas of her life.

The five basic steps followed by the counselor in this case are (1) establishment of a relationship, (2) identification of present behavior (what is being done or has been done), (3) evaluation of present behavior (is it helping the client get what he or she wants?), (4) development of plans that will help, and (5) commitment from the client to try at least one of the plans.

*Five basic steps*

*Transcript*

*Counselor:* Wendy, I understand that there has been a problem in your math class. Would you like to talk about it?

*Wendy:* I guess so.

*Counselor:* You're feeling somewhat embarrassed about the problem and uncomfortable about talking with me.

*Wendy:* Yes, I am, but I know I need to talk about it.

*Counselor:* Would you like to tell me what happened?

*Wendy:* Miss Waters caught me cheating on my math test. I have some bad grades in math this period. I knew I had to do well on this test, but I wasn't ready for it.

*Counselor:* How did you see cheating as helping you?

*Wendy:* I was feeling a lot of pressure because I wasn't prepared, and my parents expect me to do well.

*Counselor:* Can you tell me what you've been doing that kept you from being prepared for the test?

*Wendy:* I'm just getting to know Susan, and I've been spending a lot of time talking with her and not enough time studying.

*Counselor:* Susan's friendship is very important to you.

*Wendy:* Yes. I've never had a really close friend before.

*Counselor:* What might be some ways you could still be friends with Susan and also keep up with your studies?

*Wendy:* Well, I guess I could spend less time talking to her and more time studying.

*Counselor:* You believe that you can spend less time with Susan and still be close friends?

*Wendy:* Yes, I'm sure she'd understand.

*Counselor:* What are some other things you could do that might help?

*Wendy:* Maybe we could spend time together studying instead of talking so much.

*Counselor:* Would you like to try one of these plans for the next week and see how it works?

*Wendy:* Okay. I'd like to try studying with Susan.

*Counselor:* All right. Let's meet next Tuesday at one o'clock and see how well your plan worked.

---

As pointed out in Chapter 1, counselors must adapt their counseling style and language to their clients' developmental levels. A suggested reality therapy format for counseling younger children follows.

1. What did you do?
2. What is our rule about this?
3. Was what you did against our rule?
4. What were you supposed to do?
5. What are you going to do next time?
6. Do you want to write your plan for next time, or do you want me to write it?
7. Let's check tomorrow to see if your new plan is working. [Shake hands and sign names.]

Following is an outline of basic reality therapy for older children and teenagers who are capable of formal reasoning and abstract thinking.

1. Let's begin by talking about what you have been doing to solve the problem.
2. It would be helpful if you could give me an idea of how all of what you have been doing has been helping you or the situation. We may want to consider some questions: Is your behavior in touch with *reality*? Is your behavior the *responsible* thing to do? Is your behavior the *right* thing to do? From a cost-analysis point of view, is your behavior cost-effective? (All of these questions would be addressed one at a time).
3. If your behavior is not getting you what you want, what would you like to do differently?
4. What plan would you like to develop?
5. When can we follow up on your plan?

As suggested in these questions, much of reality therapy becomes a cost-analysis procedure of helping clients determine if their behavior is giving them fair value for the price they are paying. A good question to investigate is, "Are you getting your money's worth?"

For example, in counseling children and their parents going through divorce, Oz (1994) presented a reality-based intervention that can facilitate discussion during any stage of the divorce process. Briefly, her method provides a cost-analysis system of the benefits and costs of each alternative related to a particular problem. Following a brainstorming session for generating a list of alternatives for solving a problem, clients move to evaluate each alternative in light of the costs they are willing and prepared to pay. How costs can be reduced for selected alternatives is considered. After narrowing the choices to the most cost-effective alternative, clients may be asked to role-play the situation with the chosen alternative. Likely impedi-

*Questioning*

ments and worst-case scenarios are considered in the clients' implementation plan. A secondary advantage accrues to the clients in reframing "difficult to do" alternatives as the least expensive and most cost-effective choices.

In summary, reality therapy is such a straightforward approach to counseling that some of our students question its utility for counseling difficult cases. Glasser's *Reality Therapy in Action* (2000c) is a strong answer to those who believe that while reality therapy may be the treatment of choice for regular problems of adjustment, it is not sufficient for treating people suffering from major disturbances in their lives. In *Reality Therapy in Action,* Glasser presents 18 of his most challenging cases from his 50-year career as a psychiatrist. These cases range from chronic depression to an extreme obsessive-compulsive disorder. Regardless of the various symptoms presented by these clients, they all had some things in common. Each of the clients had problems with establishing and maintaining relationships. All of them also lacked meaning in their careers or in their lives. Glasser believes that when people have difficulty meeting their basic needs of survival, freedom, power, fun, and love and belonging, they often choose a symptom as a way of compensating for failure to meet one or more of these basic needs. Choosing a symptom has the reinforcing effect of excusing the person for living an unproductive or even irresponsible life. After all, what can be expected from a person who has problems or who is "mentally ill"? If the symptom is sufficiently severe, further reinforcement for keeping the symptom is provided if the person receives total care for the disability. The road back to living a responsible life begins with a reality therapy type of plan to commit to doing those tasks or homework assignments the client can do and gradually increasing the tasks until the client decides, "I do not need my symptom anymore, and there are better ways to meet my basic needs." Therefore, treatment, via reality therapy, is geared toward taking the steps needed to put clients on track to finding better ways to meet their needs. The stuff of life is building loving relationships and a solid career or other meaningful activities that contribute to society. For students, academic progress is their career. Likewise, the stuff of choice theory reality therapy is building and maintaining relationships and improving academic or career performance to meet one's basic needs. Glasser presents a blueprint for how to use reality therapy to treat the most difficult cases you will ever have in your counseling career, and, yes, it is the same basic choice theory reality therapy that you use with children who are not completing their math assignments.

## THE 10-STEP REALITY THERAPY CONSULTATION MODEL

The 10-step reality therapy consultation model is an effective tool for counselors to use with teachers and parents who seek the counselor's assistance with their children's behavior and motivation problems. Glasser (1998, 2000a, 2002) no longer endorses his own version of the 10-step model. He believes his version to be an application of the control psychology he now views as a harmful attempt to get people to do things they do not want to do. We believe our current model to be more consistent with Glasser's choice theory model. The 10 steps are divided into three phases, each with a special objective. Phase I, consisting of three steps, is designed to assist a teacher or parent in building a better relationship with the child.

**Step 1.** List what you have already tried that does not help. Stopping these ineffective interventions often stimulates a positive change in the child's behavior.

**Step 2.** If Step 1 is unsuccessful, make a list of change-of-pace interventions to disrupt the expected interactions between the adult and the child. For example, catch the child behaving appropriately, act surprised when the child repeats the same old irritating behavior, ask yourself what the child expects you to do and then do *not* do it, or try a paradoxical counseling strategy, such as asking the child to increase the behavior you would like to eliminate (see Chapter 5).

**Step 3.** If Step 3 is necessary, make a list of things you could and would do to help the child have a better day tomorrow. For example, give the child at least three 20-second periods of your undivided positive attention, ask the child to run an errand for you, give the child some choices in how to complete a task or an assignment, ask the child's opinion about something relevant to both of you, give the child an important classroom or household chore, or negotiate a few rules (fewer than five) that you and the child think are fair to both of you.

Phase II, consisting of three steps, is devoted to counseling the child. In most cases we find that successful interventions happen in the first phase. When this does not occur, we ask the adult to move to Step 4.

**Step 4.** Try one-line counseling approaches such as the following:
- Ask the child to stop the undesirable behavior. Use as few words as possible, relying instead on nonverbal gestures. Do not use threats.
- Try the "Could it be?" questions recommended by the practitioners of individual psychology (see Chapter 11).
- Acknowledge the child's cooperative efforts, but do not thank the child for behaving responsibly as if this behavior is a favor to you.

**Step 5.** Use reality therapy questions that emphasize the rules on which agreement was reached in a previous negotiation.
- What did you do?
- What is our rule?
- What were you supposed to do?
- What will you do?

**Step 6.** Use the standard reality therapy questions that end with a written contract or a handshake.
- What did you do?
- How did it help you?
- What could you do that would help you?
- What will you do?

Have the child dictate or write and sign a contract; have a follow-up meeting. If the contract is broken, have the child write or dictate a contract that he or she can meet. Eliminate punishment in favor of letting the child experience the logical consequences of appropriate and inappropriate behavior.

Phase III, consisting of four steps, is designed for children whose behavior makes teaching and learning difficult for everyone else in the classroom. In the home setting, Phase III is used when the child's behavior infringes on the rights of other family members. We hope to solve our consultant problems in the six steps before Phase III, in which the primary intervention is isolation.

**Step 7.** In-class time-out is recommended. A quiet corner, study carrel, or private work area may be used. Time-out should not be in a punishment area or a "dunce's corner." The child has two choices: be with the group and behave or be outside and sit. When the misbehavior occurs, send the child to the quiet area firmly with no discussion. The rest of the group does not have to be aware of the intervention. Have the child make a plan before returning to the group. The child's room may be used for time-out at home.

**Step 8.** Some children may require a time-out outside the classroom. The procedure is basically the same one described in Step 7. Some schools use a time-out room, and others use an in-school suspension room. Contracts or plans for making a successful return to the classroom group can follow the questions employed in the reality therapy method.

**Step 9.** Some children have difficulty getting through the entire school day without disrupting the class. Individual educational plans (IEPs) for these students may list four or five expectations or rules that the school has for all students. If the child fails to meet one of these rules, have the child's parents remove the child from school for the remainder of the day. Allow the child to return the next day and remain as long as he or she follows the rules. Community agencies have been used when home isolation was not possible. Once again, no punishment in addition to the logical consequence of isolation needs to be administered. Such IEPs require the input of teachers, parents, administrators, the child, and the counselor.

**Step 10.** Step 10 often involves taking the child on a field trip to juvenile court to observe the probable consequences of continuing present behavior patterns. Interviews with the judge, other court officials, counselors, teachers, and inmates increase the child's awareness of logical consequences existing outside the home and school settings. Failure to meet consultation goals with a child who has not reacted positively to the 10-step method may mean that the child should be referred to a community agency better equipped to solve the child's problem.

The basic consultation model can be adapted to any situation in which the counselor is consulting with a client about how to work with a third person. (See Chapter 15 for more information about consultation.)

Consultation may be done with clients who come in or have been sent to you for counseling. McFadden (1991) used several principles of reality therapy to teach students how to train the teacher *not* to pick on you. She begins by discussing with the student how the student has managed to train the teacher to look his or her way whenever there is a disturbance in the classroom. Next, McFadden points out that when teachers get a new group of students, they tend to classify them in one of two groups: the workers and the disturbers. "How did you train your teacher to put you in the disturbers' group?" is the question. Finally, after a good discussion of how one gets in the disturbers' group, the topic turns to how to get into the workers' group that the teacher has pictured in his or her quality world. The following clues are given.

1. Does the student make eye contact with me when I am teaching?
   Inference: The student is listening.

2. Does the student answer and ask questions on the topic?
   Inference: The student is interested.

3. Does the student get to class on time with all of the right equipment and books?
   Inference: The student cares about the class and subject.

4. When work is assigned, does the student begin before I count to 10?
   Inference: The student wants to learn and cares about success.

5. Does the student complete quality work?
   Inference: The student wants to succeed.

6. Does the student treat me and others well?
   Inference: The student is a nice person who behaves well.

7. Does the student find something to do when finished working or when disturbed by others?
   Inference: The student is responsible.

The message is that the students who are in the teacher's "worker" group get more privileges and "get away" with more things than the students in the "disturbers" group do. And, to be in the worker's group, you do not have to do all seven things all of the time.

## CROSS-CULTURAL APPLICATIONS OF REALITY THERAPY

Glasser (1965) has always held the view that all humans have the same basic needs; these needs do not vary with age, gender, or race. A Chinese infant girl has the same basic needs as a Swedish king. Reality therapy was designed to help all types of people meet two basic needs: the need to love and be loved and the need to feel worthwhile to ourselves and others. Glasser (1998) has revised his list of human needs to include the needs for survival, freedom, power, fun, and love and belonging. However, we need to keep in mind that different cultures shape different images in the quality worldview of the people growing up in those cultures. We are not suggesting that cultural influence destroys the freedom to choose, only that different values and philosophies are part of these different cultures. Even within cultures, individuals hold different quality worldviews. Therefore, for each client we counsel, we must examine the individual's spiritual values, oral traditions, nonverbal behaviors and communication, family values, and healing practices. Counseling has always been based on treating each client as a unique individual. Cunningham (1995) pointed out that counseling theories originating in Western culture may contain inherent cultural biases that are not always appropriate for culturally dissimilar clients. However, reality therapy can be adapted for clients from most cultures, providing the counselor is familiar with the values and traditions of the cultures in question. Wubbolding and Brickell (2000) point out that reality therapy has been well received in Asia, the Middle East, and South Africa. See Chapter 13 for descriptions of differences and similarities within and between cultures.

## REALITY THERAPY AND MANAGED HEALTH CARE

Reality therapy, based on choice theory, fits very well into the managed care framework. It is goal directed and easily evaluated for progress. The process generally can be terminated successfully in 10 or fewer sessions. Building current, trusting relationships with others is the focus of reality therapy, with little attention given to the past. The focus remains on what the client is choosing to do now. Practitioners of choice theory reality therapy do not deny their clients have real pain, but very little time is allowed for clients to complain about their symptoms. They teach clients that the only people they can control are themselves. Glasser (1998) believes that it is no kindness to treat unhappy people as helpless, hopeless, or inadequate, no matter what has happened to them. Glasser sees kindness as having faith that people can handle the truth and to do so is to their benefit. True compassion is helping people help themselves.

In opposition to Freud, Glasser (1998) wrote that counseling should always move forward, never backward. He believes there are more than enough problems in the present to keep the counselor and client busy. Reference to the Chapter 2 section on managed care confirms that reality therapy fits managed care guidelines.

## SUMMARY

Perhaps the best validation of reality therapy is Glasser's success at the Ventura School for Girls. Before his tenure, the school's recidivism rate approached 90%; in a relatively short time, this rate fell to 20%. What was the secret of changing the orientation of these young women into success identities? Glasser gave them the experience of personal responsibility and success by assigning them tasks they could handle and by making each girl responsible for her own behavior. He discarded punishment in favor of logical consequences, gave generous amounts of praise, and showed sincere interest in each girl's welfare. Glasser's approach at the

Ventura School included individual and group counseling conducted within the reality therapy model and framework presented in this chapter. Regardless of one's theoretical outlook, it would be difficult to argue with Glasser's formula for success. In fact, most counseling approaches are effective under Glasser's conditions, as described earlier in the chapter.

Reality therapy is simple and easy to understand but difficult and demanding to implement. The key is helping people accept responsibility for what they are doing now. A pessimistic counselor cannot be a successful reality therapist. Considerable effort, persistence, and optimism are required from both the client and the counselor to make the reality therapy process work. The definition of behavior should expand to include feelings and thoughts, as well as what we actually do. The focus remains on what we can change about these three behavior components.

As is true with all counseling approaches, reality therapy has its supporters and critics. As might be expected, Glasser continues to find his greatest following among counselors, educators, psychologists, and social workers.

## W E B S I T E S for Reality Therapy

The William Glasser Institute
www.wglasser.com

## REFERENCES

Beilharz, C. (1998). Chestnut Ridge Learning Center: An innovative solution. In R. Kronick & C. Hargis (Eds.), *Dropouts: Who drops out and why—and the recommended action* (pp. 115–126). Springfield, IL: Charles C Thomas.

Cunningham, L. (1995). Control theory, reality therapy and cultural bias. *Journal of Reality Therapy, 15,* 15–22.

Deming, W. E. (1966). *Some theory of sampling.* New York: Dover.

Glasser, W. (1961). *Mental health or mental illness?* New York: Harper & Row.

Glasser, W. (1965). *Reality therapy.* New York: Harper & Row.

Glasser, W. (1969). *Schools without failure.* New York: Harper & Row.

Glasser, W. (1972). *The identity society.* New York: Harper & Row.

Glasser, W. (1976). *Positive addiction.* New York: Harper & Row.

Glasser, W. (1981). *Stations of the mind.* New York: Harper & Row.

Glasser, W. (1984). *Control theory.* New York: Harper & Row.

Glasser, W. (1986). *Control theory in the classroom.* New York: Harper & Row.

Glasser, W. (1990). *The quality school: Managing students without coercion.* New York: Harper & Row.

Glasser, W. (1993). *The quality school teacher.* New York: HarperCollins.

Glasser, W. (1995). *Staying together.* New York: HarperCollins.

Glasser, W. (1998). *Choice theory: A new psychology of personal freedom.* New York: HarperCollins.

Glasser, W. (2000a). *Every student can succeed.* Chatsworth, CA: Author.

Glasser, W. (2000b). *Getting together and staying together.* New York: HarperCollins.

Glasser, W. (2000c). *Reality therapy in action.* New York: HarperCollins.

Glasser, W. (2002). *Unhappy teenagers: A way for parents and teenagers to reach them.* New York: HarperCollins.

Kohlberg, L. (1981). *The philosophy of moral development: Moral stages and the idea of justice.* New York: Harper & Row.

Kronick, R., & Hargis, C. (1998). *Dropouts: Who drops out and why—and the recommended action.* Springfield, IL: Charles C Thomas.

McFadden, J. (1991). Behavior lotto or how to train the teacher not to pick on you. *Journal of Reality Therapy, 10,* 16–19.

Oz, S. (1994). Decision making in divorce therapy: Cost-cost comparison. *Journal of Marital and Family Therapy, 20,* 77–81.

Piaget, J. (1973). *The moral judgment of children.* New York: Free Press.

Thompson, C., & Poppen, W. (1972). *For those who care: Ways of relating to youth.* Columbus, OH: Merrill.

Wubbolding, R., & Brickell, J. (2000). Misconceptions about reality therapy. *International Journal of Reality Therapy, 19,* 64–65.

C h a p t e r   5

# Brief Counseling: Solution-Focused and Paradoxical Counseling Strategies

*If you want truly to understand something, try to change it.*
—Kurt Lewin

## BACKGROUND

Brief counseling could be labeled "counseling for the millennium." Quicker, faster—the watchwords for the past several decades—have now moved from fast foods, faxes, and faster computers into the world of managed health care. Counseling is one of the healthcare services. However, the recent popularity of brief counseling cannot be attributed solely to the insurance company underwriters who seem to be running our country's healthcare systems. Deviations from long-term, analytic therapy have been developing over the last 50 years, beginning with Rogers's person-centered counseling, which was followed by a number of new therapies designed to help people reach their counseling goals in shorter and more efficient ways. Even Freud himself, the architect of long-term analysis, described several of his single-session therapy cases that resulted in successful outcomes. As noted in Chapter 4, in addition to advocating shorter-term therapy, Glasser (1965) was one of the first psychiatrists to take a stand against psychotherapy and counseling as being a cure for emotional problems. Instead, he viewed counseling and psychotherapy as an educative process directed toward helping people find better ways to meet their psychological needs of being successful and loved. Behavioral counseling methods were directed toward these same goals. The case can be made that brief counseling has been evolving since the beginning of the 20th century and is well positioned to take its place in the 21st century. To date, two types of brief counseling have emerged. First came the paradoxical counseling strategies focusing on symptom reduction, introduced by Dunlap (1928, 1932) in the 1920s and 1930s, developed by Viktor Frankl (1975) in the 1930s, and refined and popularized by Milton Erickson, Jay Haley (1973, 1976, 1984), and Watzlawick, Weakland, and Fisch (1974). Then came the work of de Shazer (de Shazer, 1985,

133

1988, 1994; de Shazer & Molnar, 1964), which was focused on solutions rather than on the client's problem. Both types of brief counseling are discussed in the next section, beginning with the most recent form of brief counseling, solution-focused brief counseling (SFBC).

## SOLUTION-FOCUSED BRIEF COUNSELING

### The Nature of People

Counselors practicing SFBC fall into the top half of the chart presented in Chapter 2, Figure 2-2. They believe that people feeling bad at Point A on the chart will continue to feel bad if they do not make positive behavior changes in their lives. Merely discussing "why" people feel as they do will not help, nor will focusing on such unobservables as feelings, thoughts, and motivations. The key to feeling better is to focus on "what" people are doing that seems to be helpful and to set goals with plans on how to accomplish them. SFBC counselors believe that their clients will do better with a present *and* future orientation. In fact, SFBC may be the only counseling theory in which a future orientation takes precedence over a present orientation. The SFBC philosophy seems to be that clients can become mired in their past unresolved conflicts and failures and blocked when focusing on present problems rather than on future solutions.

SFBC counselors view their clients as being free to make choices and not victimized by their heredity or environment. They hold a positive view of people that rivals that held by Rogerians. People are seen as being basically good, with the power to overcome evil and to make good behavioral choices. SFBC counselors believe that people are also basically rational, having the capacity to solve their own problems and overcome the irrational influences in their culture. It would be difficult to find an approach to counseling holding a more humanistic view of nature than that embodied in SFBC. In SFBC, the biggest exception to the humanistic philosophy is in the high activity level of the counselor in directing the client's thoughts toward building on the positive things that are happening in formulating counseling goals and plans for reaching them. Even then, the client's input is always sought, with most of the counselor's activity directed to holding the counseling focus on the positive, rather than the negative, side of the client's situation.

The tremendous faith SFBC practitioners have in their clients' ability to work through their own problems is highlighted in the words of an old song, "Accentuate the positive, eliminate the negative, and say no to Mr. In-Between." In other words, people do better when they concentrate on their successes rather than on their failures. Positive and helpful changes are more likely to grow from exploring strengths rather than weaknesses or deficits. It is human nature for clients to prefer talking about what is going right in their lives over what is going wrong.

SFBC counselors cater to whatever common sense is found in their clients' thinking. For example, the test of any good idea is whether it will work for the client. Sklare (1997), Bruce (1995), Walter and Pellar (1992), Berg and Miller

(1992), and de Shazer (1986) emphasized the appeal to their clients' common sense in the following pragmatic points stated in colloquial, if not overused, everyday language:

1. "If it ain't broke, don't fix it."
2. "If it works a little, build on it and try to do more of the part that is working."
3. "If it is broke, do something different to fix it."

In other words, once you know what works and what does not, do more of what works and stop doing what does not work.

In summary, SFBC practitioners base their work on the following concepts about the nature of people:

1. People are viewed as basically good, capable of rational thought, and free to make choices. However, without direction from the counselor, people seem by nature to want to focus on the negative aspects of their lives.

2. Once the counseling focus has shifted from the negative to the positive, people prefer to talk about what is going well in their lives.

3. People have the capacity to act on common sense if given the opportunity to identify commonsense problem-solving strategies.

4. People respond better to counseling when they make positive changes in their behavior as opposed to working on the cognitive and affective components of their situation. For children who may have difficulty in handling some of the abstract thinking involved in cognitive and affective counseling, the behavior change focus is most useful.

5. People will respond better to a present and future counseling orientation than they will to a past orientation focused on why they have a problem they cannot solve.

## Theory of Counseling

SFBC practitioners might well adopt the 4-H club motto: "Make the best better." The method is based on the theory that people will respond better to building up the positive aspects of their lives. Every problem is viewed as having identifiable exceptions that can be transformed into solutions. For example, a child who is having trouble making friends in her classroom might be asked to look at those times when she was able to initiate some contact. She might say, "Well, one day Jane Ann asked me to eat lunch with her, and that made me feel good." The counselor would build on that by asking how that happened and how she could make it happen more often.

SFBC is based on the theory that small changes in behavior lead to bigger changes in behavior. Small behavior changes build momentum in a person's life, much like the momentum defined in Newton's laws of motion: A body at rest tends to remain at rest, and a body in motion tends to remain in motion. Many of our clients come for counseling because they are bodies at rest. Small behavior changes are used to get them moving. For example, John might be asked to complete a small portion of his math assignment rather than the entire assignment, based on the theory that he needs encouragement and success to get some momentum started in his life. In addition, SFBC methods are helpful to counselors wanting to capitalize on role-shift theory. Small shifts in role by one person in a relationship will cause a role shift by others in that relationship. For example, Mary notices that when she says something nice to her brother, he is more likely to be nice to her. George may notice that his parents are more cooperative with him when he does his homework and chores without being nagged.

SFBC is also based on the theory that goals need to stated in positive and observable terms to be effective. People do better in attaining goals that are quantifiable and specific. For example, the goal of "completing one homework assignment per day at school" is far superior to the goal "to study harder." Behavioral counselors and reality therapists would concur that clients respond better to accomplishments they can observe and record. Goals stated as "Thou shalt not . . ." have less chance for success than goals stated positively. For example, the goal of "I will not cause anybody to become angry with me" is better stated as "I will say something nice to one person each day." "Thou shalt not . . ." goals may have the paradoxical effect of making clients want to do the things they are trying to quit doing. For example, the worst goal a dieter could have would be the self-admonition, "Don't think about food!" Former President Clinton's initiative to curb teenage smoking by making smoking the forbidden fruit may have been responsible, in part, for the sudden upsurge in teenage smoking that occurred at that time.

Bruce (1995) identified the following four main components of SFBC:

1. Development of a working alliance in which the counselor and client work together in attacking the problem and its causes

2. Identification of clients' strengths as foundations on which to build their confidence in their ability to make positive changes in their lives

3. Implementation of active, eclectic counseling strategies and interventions, including role playing, homework assignments, confrontations, interpretations, visualization, and reframing, to help clients achieve their goals

4. Establishment of clear, concrete, measurable goals that serve to help counselors and clients evaluate their progress

The emphasis in SFBC counseling is on creating concrete word pictures to describe the problem and the problem setting. Clients are asked to describe exactly what happens, who is there, and what is said and done. Bruce (1995) detailed four useful intervention tasks:

1. "Do something different" for the client who tends to repeat the same ineffective reaction in problem situations.

2. "Pay attention to what you do when you overcome the urge to . . ." for the client who has trouble controlling impulsive behaviors.

3. "Tell me about a time when you had a good day at school" for clients who have taken on the victim mentality of believing that nothing good ever happens to them.

4. "Observe and take notes" for clients who have trouble avoiding problem situations and interactions. The observations help the client identify the good and bad things that happen in the problem setting; however, the most beneficial outcome is the client's role shift from interactor to observer. A role shift by one person in a group leads to role shifts by the other interacting members.

Finally, the SFBC method is based on the theory that more (counseling) is not better. Better is better—that is, counseling works best when the focus shifts from the number of counseling sessions to increasing or expanding the best parts of clients' lives. The current status of managed health care is certainly favorable to the SFBC philosophy, and SFBC practitioners might even owe a debt of gratitude to insurance companies and HMOs for promoting brief counseling. However, the authors caution that many people require longer-term counseling than what is generally implied by brief counseling. Such cases include clients who are suicidal or psychotic and those with schizophrenia, manic-depression, and various addictions. This is not to say, however, that SFBC strategies could not be incorporated into longer-term counseling and psychotherapy.

## Counseling Method

### Orientation Statement

Brief counseling generally requires more structuring than most methods because it differs radically in counselor activity and the number of sessions required. While it is of prime importance to clarify any counseling process to new clients and to children, it is a must as a first step in doing SFBC. The SFBC focus and goal-setting strategies begin to take shape with the counselor's orientation statement about how the process works. For example, your opening statement to your client might be:

> Our purpose in talking together will be to help you find out what you need to do to solve a problem. We will look at some things you are good at doing and see if we can use them to figure out what you want to do and what steps you should take next. I will be asking you several questions. Some of these questions will be hard to answer. I will be writing things down about what we are talking about. After we finish our talk, I will leave for a few minutes and write you a message from the notes I have been taking. I will make a copy for you and keep a copy for me. Does all of this sound okay with you?

### Statement of the Problem

As is true with any other approach to counseling, we recommend that counselors use active listening from person-centered counseling before embarking on the preferred counseling interventions. Failure to use active listening often results in the counselor and client working on the wrong problem; therefore, we suggest that counselors remain in the active listening mode until clients agree that their counselors understand four important things about their situation:

1. The problem
2. The feelings associated with the problem
3. The intensity of those feelings on a 1 to 10 scale (10 is the best feeling: high; 1 is the worst feeling: low)
4. The client's expectations of what he or she would like to have happen in counseling and the goals the client would like to accomplish

Regarding the third point, rating intensity of feelings on a 10-point scale, this activity can result in a goal statement. When the client says, "I am about a 6 on a 10-point scale in feeling good," the counselor can focus the interview on those good things the client is doing and the things that are happening in the client's life that make the client's rating as high as a 6. Then, the interview can be directed to discovering how the client can make more of these good things happen.

As noted in Chapter 1, children in the upper range of the preoperational stage of cognitive development will need visual presentations of such a rating scale. Five smiley faces ranging from a very happy smile to a deeply frowning, unhappy face help younger children identify how good or bad they are feeling. Some counselors use a "feel-o-meter" constructed like a regular outdoor thermometer and let the child color in how high the mercury level has risen on the feelings scale. Smiling and frowning faces can also be used on the feel-o-meter to depict how the child is feeling. The same rating scale can be used throughout the SFBC process for setting goals and measuring the child's progress. Note that many children set behavioral goals to jump all the way from a low rating of a 3 to a high rating of 10 in just a day or two. Counselors will do well to focus on helping children move from a 3 to a 4 on behavioral goals (what the child will actually be doing at the 4 level) to ensure early success with the SFBC process. Gains of 10% are good when they are defined in observable, positive behavior changes.

## Setting Counseling Goals

The heart of many counseling methods is to set good or productive goals. Good goals have some of the following common properties:

1. Goals owned or set by the client work best because clients are more likely to achieve the goals for which they hold ownership.

2. If clients need assistance in goal setting—and they probably will with SFBC—be sure that the goals are cocreated and are not the counselor's goals.

3. Set goals that are behavioral. Goals work best when they are positive, concrete, and reduced to small steps.

4. State a goal in terms of what behavior will occur, how often it will occur, and under what conditions it will occur.

For example, Frank's goal is to earn an A average in English. To earn an A, Frank has agreed to request that his seat be moved to the front row, attend class every day, complete each day's homework assignment, and answer at least one question per day during class discussion.

## *The Skeleton Key Question/Statement for Goal Setting*

de Shazer (1985) recommended starting goal setting by asking clients to think about the good things rather than the bad things that have been happening in their lives. For example, "I would like to have you think about your life recently and the things that have happened to you that you would like to have happen more often in the future" or "Please think about what you would like to get done in counseling and how you will know if counseling is helping." The client's thoughts on either of these statements will help the counselor determine what the client's goals might be.

## *Working with Unproductive Client Goals*

Unproductive goals will scuttle the SFBC approach before it leaves the harbor. The three most common unproductive client goals are negative goals, harmful goals, and "I don't know" goals. Sklare (1997) did an excellent job in describing how each of these three types of unproductive goals can be reframed into productive, positive goals. Remember that SFBC is focused on the solutions and not the problem.

*Negative Goals.*   Negative goals are stated as "thou shalt not . . ." goals, goals that are "stop-doing-things" goals and goals to get others to stop doing things—for example, "I would like to stop getting so many detentions." All of the preceding goals need to be reframed to describe what it is the client will be doing rather than not doing—for example, "I need to raise my hand in class to get permission to speak, and that will lower the number of detentions I have been getting."

Negative goals need to be refocused on what clients *will* be doing instead of what they will *not* be doing. The refocused goal can be derived from the things the client will be doing—for example, "If you stop doing all those things that you said cause you to fail English, what will you be doing instead?" Nature abhors a vacuum, and something is sure to rush in and fill the void in a person's life when an activity is stopped. So, clients can be asked how they plan to fill the free time they will have when they stop doing an unproductive behavior such as arguing excessively with their parents.

*Harmful Goals.*   Harmful goals are those goals that, when achieved, will bring either harm to the client or harm to others. More often than not, these goals will also lead to violations of the law or school rules, such as selling drugs or engaging in other criminal acts. The counselor can approach harmful goal statements by exploring with clients how achieving such goals would get the clients what they want. For example:

*Counselor:*  So, dropping out of school and selling drugs to make a living is what you really want. How will this help you?

*Client:*  Well, I hate school because I don't do the work and I get Fs.

*Counselor:*  So you are saying if you did the work you would get better grades and then you might like school a little better?

*Client:*  Maybe.

*Counselor:*  Maybe a goal for you would be to find out how you could do the work and do better on your grades.

Finally, in discerning harmful counseling goals, it is incumbent on the counselor to inform their clients about the conditions under which counselor–client confidentiality cannot be maintained. Harming of the self or others, property damage, and other violations of the law will have to be reported, and the counselor will have to take whatever steps possible to prevent the client from doing harmful acts.

*"I Don't Know" Goals.*  "I don't know" goals are most likely ploys by the client to engage the counselor in some type of resistance activity. The client usually has been sent for counseling by parents, teachers, or judges and is determined to resist any effort by the counselor to help in any way. As noted in Chapter 2 on overcoming a child's resistance, the counselor can begin by saying:

*Counselor:*  What would have to happen to get your parents off your back and say you don't need counseling?

*Client:*  They want me to try harder at school.

*Counselor:*  What would I be seeing you doing at school that would let your parents know that you were trying harder?

By following this script, the counselor becomes an ally who is working on the same team with the client to figure out how to help her or him avoid the need for counseling.

## Using the Miracle Question to Formulate Goals

The miracle question, developed by de Shazer (1990) in his frustration with some clients' inability to form good behavioral goals, is used to help clients visualize and hypothesize what their problems would be like if suddenly they were solved. For example, a counselor might ask, "Should a miracle occur this evening while you were sleeping and when you woke up, you suddenly realized that your problems were solved, what would you be doing that would indicate to you that the miracle had actually taken place?"

Children may respond better to the question stated in magic terms (Sklare, 1997)— for example, "If I were to wave a magic wand or rub a magic lamp and wish all your problems away, what would we see you doing if we could videotape you for a day?" Older children, teenagers, and adults might respond better with a visualization about what their life will look like 6 months or a year from now if the problem brought to counseling were solved—for example, "If the problem you brought to counseling were solved in the next 6 months, how would you know things were okay, and what would you be doing differently?" Again, active listening is a good way to help clients put their hypotheses about their problem-free futures in good behavioral goal language. Here is where the future orientation parts of SFBC stand out. The counselor's job is to keep the focus on what the client *will* be doing when the problem is solved.

Frequently, clients still use ineffective goal statements and generalizations in stating their hypotheses about their problem-free futures, such as, "Well, I would feel good, I would be happy, or my parents would be nicer to me." When this happens, the counselor tries to identify the client's specific behavior: "When you are feeling this good feeling, what would you be doing that would let you know that you are feeling good, or that you are happy?" Other examples are: "What would your parents be doing that would let you know that they are treating you nicer?" and "What would you be doing that would cause your parents to be nicer to you?" Again, visualization of the "new" behavior in the client's future, problem-free environment can be assisted with the metaphor of what a video tape would show the client doing and with inquiries about what others would see him or her doing. Others who would be observing the client could be the counselor, family members, classmates, teachers, and friends. For example, you could ask, "What would your friends see you doing differently?"

Sklare (1997) pointed out that clients often respond to the miracle question with improbable (if not impossible) miracles and "I want others to be different" miracles. For the former, the counselor's job is to reframe the improbable answer into what might be probable. For example, in the case of a divorce, the child might say:

*Client:* I want my Mom and Dad to get married again.
*Counselor:* How would that help you?
*Client:* I would feel like I was part of a real family.
*Counselor:* So, feeling a part of your family would be a goal for you.
*Client:* Yes, because now it doesn't seem like I am.
*Counselor:* What would you be doing to let you know that you were a part of your family?
*Client:* I would like to be doing things that would help Mom and Dad out—like I did before they got divorced.
*Counselor:* So, finding out how you could help both your Mom and Dad could be another goal for you.

For the latter "I want others to be different" goal, the counselor would continue to keep the focus on what the client will be doing to cause others to behave differently. For example:

*Client:* I would like other kids in my class to be friends with me.
*Counselor:* Well, if that miracle occurred, what would we see on a videotape of what was going on in your classroom?

*Client:* Other kids would choose me to work with them on stuff.

*Counselor:* So, if the other kids were choosing you for a work partner, what would you start doing differently?

*Client:* I guess I would be nice about sharing my stuff with them.

*Counselor:* That sounds like a good goal for you to have. What else would you be doing?

*Client:* I would be working hard to do my share of the work.

*Counselor:* That sounds like a better goal, because you would know right away if you did at least your share of the work.

# CASE STUDY

## Identification of the Problem

George was an 8-year-old boy in the second grade at Mountain Springs School. He was brought to private counseling by his parents, who were concerned because of his anxiety about going to school.

## Individual and Background Information

*Academic.* George's school records were a small road map of low achievement beginning midway through the first grade, when he began to fall behind the others in reading and mathematics concepts. Testing by the school psychologist did not reveal any learning disabilities, and his verbal and performance IQ was calculated to be within the 110 to 120 range. The school psychologist concluded that George's poor academic progress was more of a case of not *wanting* to do the school work rather than not being *able* to do it.

*Family.* George was the middle child between an older sister, age 10, and a younger brother, age 5. His parents indicated that George's older sister had always made top grades and that his younger brother enjoyed going to kindergarten.

*Social.* George's first-grade teacher had reported in his records that he had some difficulty in making friends with most of the other children. He seemed to gravitate toward two boys who were causing most of the classroom discipline problems, and George frequently had to be disciplined because of his own misbehavior, as well as misbehavior with the other two boys. The pattern has continued in the second grade.

## Counseling Method

The counselor used SFBC to help George identify some specific behavioral goals for himself. Following identification of the goals, the counselor had periodic follow-up sessions with him to coordinate his progress with the school counselor, who was working with George's teachers in reinforcing progress on his goals. Behavioral contingency contracts and reality therapy used by the school counselor had not been successful with George.

### Transcript

Following about 5 minutes of getting to know each other and giving the structuring speech about what the SFBC counselor does, the counselor began:

*Counselor:*  Well, George, do you know why your parents wanted you to see me?

*George:*  I don't know.

*Counselor:*  That is one of the hard questions I told you I would be asking. So, I would like to have you pretend for a moment that you do know why your parents brought you here.

*George:*  Well, it's probably about school, isn't it?

*Counselor:*  That was a good guess. What do you think they want to have happen to you in school?

*George:*  Probably make better grades on my schoolwork.

*Counselor:*  George, I have a thermometer-type thing here that goes from a low of 1 to a high of 5. The 1 would be for very low grades, like all Fs, and the 5 would be for very high grades like all As. Which number on my thermometer is most like your grades?

*George:*  I think I am about a 2½, because my grades are Cs and Ds.

*Counselor:*  I wonder how good your grades will have to be to get your parents to stop bringing you here for counseling.

*George:*  Bs and Cs might make Mom and Dad happier with me, and that would be about a 3½ on your scale.

*Counselor:*  So raising your grade one level would be a good goal for you. I would like to do another "let's pretend" with you. Suppose I had a magic lamp like in the genie story, and I could rub it and make a wish and a miracle happened. Imagine that your parents said, "George, your grades are good enough, and you don't have to go back to see the counselor." What would you be doing in your classroom the next day?

*George:*  I would be really happy, and so would my teacher and Mom and Dad.

*Counselor:*  If I could videotape you in your classroom, what would I see you doing that would let me know you were happy about your grades?

*George:*  I wouldn't be getting into trouble.

*Counselor:*  That's right, George, but what would you be doing instead?

*George:*  I would be doing my schoolwork at my desk and raising my hand before talking in class.

*Counselor:*  These things sound like two good goals for you to work on this week. What else would you be doing that we could see on a videotape?

*George:*  I would be finishing nearly all of my work at school so I wouldn't have to bring it home.

*Counselor:* These goals are getting better all the time. Do you think this would be a good goal that you could do?

*George:* Yes, I could if I could sit away from some guys who always get me into trouble.

*Counselor:* So changing your seat might be another goal for you. Where do you see yourself sitting?

*George:* I think I would do better in the front row.

*Counselor:* What else would we see you doing?

*George:* Making mostly B grades and no more than two C grades.

*Counselor:* What would that videotape show you doing to make mostly B grades and just two Cs?

*George:* Well, like I said, I would be getting nearly all my work done at school, and I would be working away from the troublemakers.

*Counselor:* Okay, George, it looks like you have two good goals to work on this week. Would it be okay if I talked to the school counselor about getting your seat moved so that you can get your work done at school, or do you want to talk this over with your teacher?

*George:* I'll ask my teacher.

*Counselor:* What if she asks you why you want to move?

*George:* I'll tell her that it will help me get my work done.

*Counselor:* Well, George, I have asked you about all the questions I have for you, and you have given me some really smart answers. I am wondering if you have any questions for me. [pause] If not, I have two last questions: What other things do I need to know about that might help you reach your goals? [pause] If there isn't anything else, we need to look at what might happen to stop you from meeting your goals. [pause] If there is nothing you can think of, I need to leave you for a few moments to think about my notes and all the answers you gave me and to write you a message that you can take with you. You can play with any of the toys in the room and read any of the magazines while I am gone for a few minutes.

While they write these messages, some counselors prefer to remain in the room with younger children. Sklare (1997) recommended that messages should contain at least three compliments, with each compliment bridged to a task that will indicate that the child has met his or her goal.

In George's case, the counselor would refer to the notes taken during the session.

### George's Goals

1. Wants to raise his grades to all Bs and Cs.
2. Wants to improve his classroom behavior.
3. Wants to do well enough in school to get out of having to come for counseling.

*Miracle*

I would be completing most of my homework at school and finishing the rest of my assignments at home.

My grades would be all Bs and Cs.
My classroom behavior would be good.
My parents would be happy with my school behavior and grades, and I would not have to have more counseling.

*FirstSign(s) the Miracle Had Happened*

I would be doing my work in a front-row seat away from the guys who got in trouble with me.
I would be completing all of my school assignments, and my teacher would notice that I am doing better.
I would be raising my hand for permission to speak in class, and that would make my teacher happy.

*Instances or Exceptions When the Miracle Has Happened a Little Bit*

When I ignore the two boys who try to get me to break the rules.
When I do my assignments during work periods.

*Scaling*

Currently at a 2½ because grades are all Cs and Ds.
To get to a 3½ on a 5-point scale, all grades have to be a C or better.
To get a 5, all grades will have to be at least half Bs and half As.
Classroom behavior is at a 2, because George had to go to three time-outs for disrupting class last week. To get to a 4, he would have to go to no more than one time-out each week.

The counselor's written message to George was as follows:

[Compliment] I think you were really smart in coming up with some good ways to let your parents know that you won't need to come in here for more counseling. You figured out a good way to stay out of trouble and an even better way to raise your grades. Getting your seat moved to the front row, doing most of your homework assignments at school, turning in all of your assignments, and raising your hand to get permission to speak are four excellent ideas that should help you meet all your goals.

[Bridges] Because of your promise to do your four ideas at school,

[Task] I would suggest that you begin by asking the teacher if she would move your seat to the front and tell her why you want to do this. Then, I would suggest that you start doing the three other ideas and move up to a 3½ on your 5-point scale for grades and a 4 for classroom behavior.

George may have trouble reading the message, so the language may need to be simplified for him to understand the compliments and how those are bridged to the tasks he needs to do. Sklare (1997) recommended having children draw pictures of their miracles, showing what will be happening when the miracle occurs. Discussion of the events depicted in these miracle drawings provides an excellent review of the session and leads into the counselor's message. For children who are not able to read the counselor's message, it might also be a good idea to draw a picture of their messages showing the complimented behaviors and the tasks to be done. Pictures help children visualize outcome goals being met and hence contribute to the child's ability to meet these goals.

## Reviewing the Steps in Solution-Focused Brief Counseling

No theory of counseling has more steps or interventions than SFBC. In fact, the prudent approach to using SFBC would be to select from the menu those interventions you think will take your clients where they want to go. Our purpose here is to present a menu of SFBC interventions discussed by several key authors on the subject: Daughhtree and Grant (2002), Fleming and Rickford (1997), Littrell (1998), Murphy and Duncan (1997), Cade and O'Hanlon (1993), Selekman (1997), and Sklare (1997). All have contributed steps and questions typically used in conducting SFBC counseling interviews.

### Orientation to the SFBC Process

Tell the child that you will be asking some hard questions and that you will be taking notes so that you can remember the answers. Explain that the answers will help you write a note to the child at the end of the talk.

### Setting Goals for Counseling

Begin by asking, "What is your goal in coming in for counseling?" or "What would you like to have happen from our counseling?" The focus is on goals and positive information, rather than on problems and negative aspects of the problem.

### Active Listening

Use active listening to help clients
1. Clarifying:
   a. "What my goal is and what I will be doing when my goal is reached"
   b. "My feelings about my situation"
   c. "How strongly I feel about my situation"

2. Scaling:
   a. For example: On a 10-point scale where 10 is very good and 1 is very bad, where are you on the scale of 1 to 10?
   b. If clients indicate they are a 4, ask what is happening that keeps their bad feelings from being a 1. Focus on how they can make more of these good things happen.

## Working with Negative Goals

Negative goals are an absence of something, as in:

*Client:*  "I don't want to. . . ."
*Counselor:*  "So, what would you be doing instead?"

Or

*Client:*  "I want others to stop. . . ."
*Counselor:*  "What difference would this make?"

> Or

> "How will that help you?"

> Or

> "What will you do if they don't change?"

## Working with Positive Goals

Positive goals are the presence of something, as in:

*Client:*  "I would like to make better grades."
*Counselor:*  "What would you be doing that would show you have gotten what you want?"

## The Miracle Question

1. "If a miracle happened overnight and your problem were solved, what would you be doing differently?"
2. "If we videotaped you after the miracle happened, what would we see you doing?"
3. "Who would be the first to notice the difference in your behavior?"
   a. "What would they notice?"
   b. "How would they respond to you?"
   c. "How would you respond to them?"
   d. "What would be different/happening after this miracle?"

Repeat this question three or four times to get more indicators of what the counseling goals should be for your client.

## The Relationship Questions

1. "What will your [parents, brother or sister, teacher, friend] say that will be different after the miracle?"
   a. "How will they act when they see you are different after the miracle?"
   b. "When they act differently toward you, what will you do differently in response to them?"

## Exceptions to the Problem Situation

1. Ask about some instances when some of the miracle has already happened a little bit.

2. Reinforce these exceptions to the problem situation.

3. Fleming and Rickford (1997) recommended the EARS approach, which stands for *Elicit, Amplify, Reinforce,* and *Start again* when exceptions to the problem, other positive thoughts, and positive behaviors are mentioned.

## Positive Blame

Use positive blame when exceptions to the problem situation are identified. For example, say, "How in the world were you able to make that happen?"

## Scaling Progress Toward the Goal

1. "On a scale of 1 to 10 where 1 is the worst that things could be and 10 is the day after the miracle, where are you right now?"

2. Again, if the client says 4, ask what is going on that keeps it from being a 1.

3. Focus on talking about how to make more of these good things happen.

4. Again, reinforce any indicators that the client is already doing some helpful things that can be increased.

## 10% Improvements

1. Ask clients what they need to do to go up one step or 10% on the scale.

2. Develop a plan for making the 10% improvement. Operational goals work best because they can be documented—for example, complete mathematics homework the next 5 days.

*Flagging the Mine Field*

1. Ask clients what things might prevent them from moving up 10% on the scale or what might sabotage their plan.

2. Ask your clients what they could do to prevent their plan from being sabotaged.

*Closing the Session*

1. Ask clients to draw a picture of what will be happening after the miracle occurs (visualization).

2. Ask clients if they have any questions or if there is anything else you (the counselor) should know.

*Writing the Note*

1. Write the client a message with at least three compliments and a bridging statement from each compliment to one of the tasks the client needs to accomplish to raise the scale score 10% or one level from a 4 to a 5.

2. The counselor has the option of drawing a picture of what the client will be doing the day after the miracle occurs.

In summary, additional SFBC sessions can follow the same pattern of interventions and questions to build on progress made or to recycle the process if little or no progress occurred. Most SFBC sessions will not require all of the steps mentioned here. In fact, Daughhtree and Grant (2002) only use five questions or steps in their practice of SFBC.

1. Ask clients, "How do you experience the problem?"

2. Ask clients, "When do (or did) you not experience the problem? What were you doing then?"

3. Have clients rate their current progress on solving the problem on the 1–10 scale.

4. Ask the miracle question.

5. Set goals based on increasing what works for the client.

Campbell, Elder, Gallagher, Simon, and Taylor (1999) present five SFBC statements that assist clients in moving away from the problem impasse toward solutions:

1. *Normalizing statements* to let clients know they are not alone in experiencing their problem—for example, "No wonder you are feeling. . . ." Although this state-

ment seems to be in conflict with our philosophy of not using "level one, discount of feelings" statements in person-centered counseling, it does have the possibility of offering clients the hope that others have worked their way out of similar difficulties and that they are not "crazy" for experiencing the feelings they are having.

2. *Restructuring statements* to rephrase the impasse as directions for the future, as in, "You have reached a decision point in your life."

3. *Affirmation statements* about the positive steps the client has already taken and attributes the client can marshal to achieve personal goals.

4. *Bridging statements* that connect client attributes with the next steps in achieving goals.

5. *Between-session homework statements* that the client will be doing, which serve to connect the sessions and remind students of when times are better. Homework will also move clients toward their goals.

## Ericksonian Play Therapy

Marvasti (1997) discussed the characteristics of Ericksonian play therapy in the following terms: This therapy relies on the child's strengths rather than weaknesses. It focuses on the present and future rather than the past. The child's potential is utilized, and the current symptoms are transformed into solutions. The therapy uses trance without the child's awareness. The counselor communicates through metaphor and storytelling, not interpreting play and not necessarily searching for insight. The counselor uses a doll or puppet to play the role of an older, wiser self, telling a therapeutic story that includes suggestions, metaphors, and happy endings.

The type of play therapy is modified for each child and relies on the flexibility and creativity of the counselor for success. Diagnosis is used to determine the child's potential, resources, assets, interpersonal issues, and favorite hero. The solution-oriented aspect of this therapy requires well-defined goals with a present and future focus. The recognition that change is constant and inevitable, often a ripple effect, is a crucial principle. The counselor searches for exceptions, times when the problem was not present. The counselor uses the miracle question (de Shazer, 1988) as well as reframing and positive connotations to the problem situation in the Ericksonian approach to play therapy.

## PARADOXICAL COUNSELING STRATEGIES

### The Nature of People

Practitioners of paradoxical brief counseling (PBC) strategies differ in one significant way from practitioners of SFBC in how they view the nature of people: They view people as having a drive toward independence that makes them want to resist compliance with counselors' suggestions and directives. Not only do people resist cooperating with their counselors but also they often do the opposite. The resistance can be either passive or active. Working on this principle, practitioners of PBC methods try to harness this resistance and make it work for the client rather than against the counselor. Actually, this drive toward independence is viewed as a very positive trait in human nature. It becomes difficult in counseling only when the client is resisting just for the sake of resisting, much like the 2-year-old who says "no" to all requests. In other words, these are times when resistance is the right choice based on the logic that to not resist would result in an undesirable outcome. Also, there are times when resistance is an attempt to impede progress toward making changes that would lead to a good outcome.

## Theory of Counseling

The goal of all brief counseling methods is to help clients resolve a problem that is preventing them from moving on in their lives. There is a slight shift in focus when comparing SFBC with PBC methods. In SFBC, the focus is on solutions. In the PBC method, the focus is on problem formation and elimination. PBC methods are as specific and eclectic as the particular client requires. Counseling is focused, with the counselor taking an active role in initiating brief counseling interventions. However, the clients are still responsible for making behavior changes in their lives. Positive outcome is valued over the counseling process. Counseling is designed to make each session productive and to end counseling as soon as possible. Clients can return for additional sessions when they are needed.

PBC practitioners believe that they will perform best by staying out of conflict with their clients. Such power struggles are not helpful to the client, counselor, counseling process, or counseling outcome. Rather, the client's resistance can be used as a source of energy that can be redirected, helping the client make positive behavior changes. Not using the client resistance as an energy resource would be viewed as very inefficient as well as ineffective in helping clients change their behavior. Clients seem to respond best when they can show the counselor that they know more about their lives than their counselors do. Therefore, given the opportunity to prove their counselors wrong, clients often will take the path opposite to that directed by the counselor.

PBC practitioners have two basic ways to approach their clients. One way is to take a "one-down" position, which elevates the client to the expert and drops the counselor to the "less than expert" role. For example, the counselor might say to an underachieving, bright adolescent, "I'd like to put you into the college-prep English class for a while to see how it goes, but I'm afraid you might have trouble understanding some of the things they are reading in there. They have a spot open in third period—do you know anybody who might like to give it a shot?" Given a golden opportunity to prove the counselor wrong, many highly resistant students will beg for the chance. The counselor's role is to remain skeptical and show utter amazement when the student actually does well in the class. The PBC counselor may choose to approach the client from a "one-up" frame of reference in which the counselor, as expert, prescribes the behavior the client is to follow. For example, the counselor might prescribe the client to do more of his symptomatic behavior, which puts the resistant client into the double bind of having to obey the counselor or choose to do the appropriate behavior. The resistant client will nearly always choose to disobey the counselor. For example, the clients having difficulty in losing weight can be directed by the counselor to gain 20 pounds just to see if they have control of their bodies. Resistant clients will often lose weight under the directive to gain weight.

## Counseling Method

In addition to prescribing symptoms from the "one-up" position and pleading a "less than expert" knowledge solution from the "one-down" position, PBC counselors employ several variations on the same paradoxical theme. Problems are often reframed as opportunities. For a person who has trouble sleeping, the counselor might reframe the problem as an opportunity to get those extra household chores done. Since the client is sleeping only 2 hours per night, she is only giving up about 14 hours of sleep per week, and that would be a small price to pay for curing the sleep problem and getting so much work done. Of course, the counselor would emphasize the point that the intervention would be for 1 week only. In any case, it would be important for the client not to sleep for the next 7 nights; she was to continue to do whatever she ordinarily did during the day. Shifting the emphasis from "I must sleep" to "I must not sleep" generally has the desired effect of returning people to their normal sleep routine without the aid of medication. Tantrum-throwing children can be instructed to schedule their tantrums—for example, at 2 P.M. in a time-out area.

Performance anxiety can be successfully treated by de-reflection. Students with test anxiety can be instructed to fail their next six examinations to get used to taking tests. However, the counselor would not do the intervention without working with the student's teachers to ensure that the student would not suffer during the intervention period.

Students who are afraid to make speeches in their speech classes for fear of showing how nervous they are can be instructed to actually show the class how scared they are by sweating and trembling during their next speech. Of course, students find that they can show the symptoms only when they try *not* to show them. It is similar to trying to blush on cue—the only time you can do it is when you try not to blush.

## Case Examples

In a recent consultation, a high school teacher of a computer class described how one of her senior girls liked to get up and walk out of class without permission. She did this two or three times each class period. When asked how the problem was handled, the teacher said that she would go after her and bring her back. Detention was threatened, the bluff was called, and detention was served. Worst of all, the student–teacher relationship had become quite adversarial, and the teacher herself realized that she could not get quality work under such conditions. Power struggles like this one are right up the PBC counselor's alley. The solution was to assign errands for the girl to run when she had the urge to walk out of class. The first day when the student started to leave, the teacher said, "Would you please drop this note off to Ms. Brown in Room 303?" The girl looked puzzled but did the errand, which took her to one of the building's farthest points from the classroom. When she returned, the teacher said, "Let me know when you need to leave again because I always have several errands you can help me do." After the third "errand," which didn't happen until the next day, the girl complained that she should not be the only errand person in the class. The teacher responded that everybody else was too busy with their work to go. That marked the end of the problem. Not every symptom can be prescribed, but leaving class was one that worked especially well.

Some time ago the authors had the opportunity to replicate a case reported many years ago by Viktor Frankl (1975):

> A sixth-grade boy discovered that he could keep his entire class and the teacher in a minor uproar all day long by selectively staring at individual students until they reported him to the teacher. The teacher would tell him to quit staring at the student, whereupon he would select another student and the sequence would be repeated. Various punishments and a behavior modification program had not helped the situation. Our PBC intervention was to have the teacher make out a staring schedule for our student. The schedule was presented to him with instructions that he was to spend the day staring at the students on his list. He was to switch students every 20 minutes, and if he forgot to stare or switch students, the teacher was to remind him. Placed in the double bind of doing the appropriate behavior or obeying his teacher, he chose the appropriate behavior and refused to stare at the students. He said if he did the staring, he wouldn't get his work done. He still refused to stare even when his teacher offered him a day off from his work.

Our next brief case study involved a third-grade boy who refused to stay in his seat. Rather than labeling him attention deficit–hyperactivity disorder (ADHD) and sending him to a special education resource room, the teacher had his desk removed. When he came in the next day and reported his desk missing, the teacher explained there was a shortage of desks in another room and since his was not being used, she donated it to the other teacher. The flabbergasted boy sputtered a protest, to which the teacher replied that she could not keep moving desks back and forth between rooms all year, so he would have to make a commitment that the desk would be occupied at all the appropriate times for the rest of the year. The boy readily agreed to sign a "desk lease" under those terms.

## CROSS-CULTURAL APPLICATIONS OF BRIEF COUNSELING

Brief counseling will work most effectively with cultures and individuals with preferences for engaging in direct behavior change rather than interventions focusing more on cognitive or affective material. Thompson and Campbell (1992) found that people in American culture were equally divided in preferences for behavioral, cognitive, affective, and integrative self-help interventions to deal with depression. It could be that similar findings regarding preferences for counseling interventions might be found in all cultures. Keeping in mind the dangers involved in generalizing from cultural norms to all individuals within that cultural setting, we refer the reader to Chapter 13 for a more complete description of what counseling methods work best in certain cultures.

Brief counseling methods appeal to cultures and individuals who prefer their counselors to act as consultants who dispense useful information on what is needed to solve the presenting problem. Brief counseling has a present-time orientation with very little, if any, time given to talking about the past. In fact, very little time is given to discussing the presenting problem itself. Rather, attention is centered on the problem's solution and ways the client can do more of the behaviors that will make the solution happen. Brief counseling, true to its name, is just that. It is generally completed in fewer than 10 sessions and appeals to those cultures and individuals who want their counseling to be a down-to-earth, all-business approach to making things better as soon as possible. As such, brief counseling should have wide appeal for African, Hispanic, and Asian clients as well as African American, Latino, Asian American, and European American clients. However, Native American clients could have difficulty with the practice in brief counseling of de-emphasizing the past. Practitioners of brief counseling should be aware of clients who want their counselors to function as expert advisors and guard against the possibility that they could exert too much control over what these clients decide to do about their presenting problems.

Brief counseling enjoys wide appeal among cultures and clients who emphasize individual responsibility over the family and the community. Sue and Sue (1999) point out that in Western cultures when one does something wrong, the most common reaction is guilt, yet in non-Western cultures, the emotion most often expressed is shame. Sue and Sue hold that guilt focuses on the individual whereas shame appears to focus on the group, as in "I did something wrong and let my family down." Once again, the authors believe that it is dangerous to overgeneralize such statements on guilt and shame across cultures to all individuals within them. Western cultures have not cornered the market on guilt nor have non-Western cultures cornered the market on shame. Although brief counseling does take an individual approach, considerable attention is given to how the client's family, friends, and colleagues will be reacting when the problem's solution is achieved. In fact, brief counseling is being used to counsel families. Park (1997) reports success in using the SFBC model to provide counseling for families in a teaching hospital in Seoul, South Korea.

## BRIEF COUNSELING AND MANAGED HEALTH CARE

Fleming and Rickford (1997) observe that managed care organizations (MCOs) want to do business with providers who can deliver high-quality care with the lowest possible cost to them and to their clients. In short, MCOs want to reduce recidivism, as well as time spent on treatment waiting lists, while increasing client satisfaction with their treatment. Brief counseling methods practiced by trained counselors are well positioned to meet all of these MCO preferences. In fact, brief counseling practitioners are eagerly sought for panel membership by MCOs that fund mental health services. As mentioned in Chapter 2, MCOs prefer to work with counselors who limit their treatment to 10 or fewer sessions; who identify short-term, behaviorally stated counseling goals; and who are able to measure session-by-session progress by their clients. Accountability of counselors to their clients and to third-party payers is the watchword of the day. Therefore, we feel confident in stating that competent practitioners of brief counseling should do very well in today's MCO system. Brief counseling methods infused into the other approaches presented in this book can provide counselors with the tools they need to be successful in helping their clients meet their goals in the fewest number of sessions. Fleming and Rickford (1997) point out that an additional benefit accruing to brief counseling practitioners is witnessing their clients discover what they need to do more often to improve their lives and then watching them do it.

Levenson and Evans (2000), concerned that training in the brief therapies was not keeping pace with the demand for their use, surveyed 1250 psychologists across the nation on their training and use of brief therapy. With a response rate of 87%, the authors found that 90% of the psychologists reported using brief therapy in their practice; however, 50% of the respondents had not had any coursework in brief therapy. The authors also surveyed 165 training directors of clinical psychology programs and 370 training directors of internship programs on the number of programs providing brief therapy training. Only 59% of the graduate programs offered training in brief therapy; however, 85% of the professional schools of psychology offered brief therapy training. In summary, the good news is that a majority of training programs are providing brief therapy training. The bad news is that 40% are not providing any training. With 90% of the psychologists in private practice using brief therapy, more training and continuing education in brief therapy needs to be made available to students and practitioners.

## SUMMARY

Solution-focused brief counseling and paradoxical counseling have much to offer counselors who are working under the constraints of managed health care and who are working with large client loads in K–12 school systems and community agencies. Numerous studies on the efficacy of SFBC with children and adolescents have been reported. Corcoran and Stephenson (2000), Franklin, Biever, Moore, Clemons, and Scamardo (2001), Williams (2000), and Yarbrough and Thompson (2002) used SFBC successfully in a school setting with children. Singleton and Pope (2000) found SFBC to be effective in successful smoking cessation by adults and adolescents. We are not suggesting brief counseling as the recommended treatment for all clients and all problems, but we do think the method is a valuable addition to our scope of practice, which is built on the philosophy that counselors should adapt to their clients' learning styles and not force clients to adapt to their preferred counseling and learning styles.

The brief counseling approaches appear to be deceptively easy to master. However, such is not the case. As is true with any other approach to counseling, therapists and counselors of all orientations will need to study and practice brief counseling under expert supervisors if they are to do it well and not harm their clients. While organizational demands from MCOs may be forcing therapists into shorter-term counseling, this does not absolve therapists who practice outside their area of competence and training.

## W E B S I T E S for Brief Counseling

What Is Possibility Therapy?
www.brieftherapy.com/faq/whatis.htm

## REFERENCES

Berg, I., & Miller, S. (1992). *Working with the problem drinker.* New York: Norton.

Bruce, M. (1995). Brief counseling: An effective model for change. *School Counselor, 42,* 353–364.

Cade, B., & O'Hanlon, W. (1993). Negotiating the problem. In *A brief guide to brief therapy* (pp. 49–63). New York: Norton.

Campbell, J., Elder, J., Gallagher, D., Simon, J., & Taylor, A. (1999). Crafting the "tap on the shoulder": A compliment template for solution-focused therapy. *American Journal of Family Therapy, 27,* 35–47.

Corcoran, J., & Stephenson, M. (2000). The effectiveness of solution-focused therapy with child behavior problems: A preliminary report. *Families in Society, 81,* 468–474.

Daughhtree, C., & Grant, D. (2002). Stress management. *ASCA School Counselor, 39,* 17–19.

de Shazer, S. (1985). *Keys to solutions in brief therapy.* New York: Norton.

de Shazer, S. (1986). Minimal elegance. *Family Therapy Networker, 59,* 57–60.

de Shazer, S. (1988). *Clues! Investigating solutions in brief therapy.* New York: Norton.

de Shazer, S. (1990). What is it about brief therapy that works? In J. K. Zeig & S. G. Gilligan (Eds.), *Brief therapy: Myths, methods, and metaphors* (pp. 90–99). New York: Brunner/Mazel.

de Shazer, S. (1994). *Words were originally magic.* New York: Norton.

de Shazer, S., & Molnar, A. (1964). Four useful interventions in brief family therapy. *Journal of Marital and Family Therapy, 10,* 297–304.

Dunlap, K. (1928). A revision of the fundamental law of habit. *Science, 67,* 360–362.

Dunlap, K. (1932). *Habits: Their making and unmaking.* New York: Liveright.

Fleming, J., & Rickford, B. (1997). Solution-focused brief therapy: One answer to managed mental health care. *Family Journal, 5,* 286–294.

Franklin, C., Biever, J., Moore, K., Clemons, D., & Scamardo, M. (2001). The effectiveness of solution-focused therapy with children in a school setting. *Research on Social Work Practice, 11,* 411–434.

Frankl, V. (1975). Paradoxical intention and de-reflection. *Psychotherapy: Theory, Research, and Practice, 12,* 226–237.

Glasser, W. (1965). *Reality therapy.* New York: Harper & Row.

Haley, J. (1973). *Uncommon therapy: The psychiatric techniques of Milton H. Erickson, M.D.* New York: Norton.

Haley, J. (1976). *Problem-solving therapy.* New York: Norton.

Haley, J. (1984). *Ordeal therapy: Unusual ways to change behavior.* San Francisco: Jossey-Bass.

Levenson, H., & Evans, S. (2000). The current state of brief therapy training in American Psychological Association–accredited graduate and internship programs. *Professional Psychology: Research and Practice, 31,* 446–452.

Littrell, J. (1998). *Brief counseling in action.* New York: Norton.

Marvasti, J. A. (1997). Ericksonian play therapy. In K. O'Connor & L. M. Braverman (Eds.), *Play therapy theory and practice: A comparative presentation* (pp. 285–309). New York: Wiley.

Murphy, J., & Duncan, B. (1997). *Brief interventions for school problems: Collaborating for practical solutions.* New York: Guilford.

Park, E. (1997). An application of brief therapy to family medicine. *Contemporary Family Therapy, 19,* 81–88.

Selekman, M. (1997). *Solution-focused therapy with children: Harnessing family strengths for systematic change.* New York: Guilford.

Singleton, M., & Pope, M. (2000). A comparison of successful smoking cessation interventions for adults and adolescents. *Journal of Counseling and Development, 78,* 448–453.

Sklare, G. (1997). *Brief counseling works: A solution-focused approach for school counselors.* Thousand Oaks, CA: Corwin.

Sue, D., & Sue, D. (1999). *Counseling the culturally different: Theory and practice.* New York: Wiley.

Thompson, C., & Campbell, S. (1992). Personal intervention preferences for alleviating mild depression. *Journal of Counseling and Development, 71,* 69–73.

Walter, J., & Pellar, J. (1992). *Becoming solution-focused in brief therapy.* New York: Brunner/Mazel.

Watzlawick, P., Weakland, J., & Fisch, R. (1974). *Change: Principles of problem formation and problem resolution.* New York: Norton.

Williams, G. (2000). The application of solution-focused brief counseling in a public school setting. *Family Journal, 8,* 76–78.

Yarbrough, J., & Thompson, C. (2002). Using single-participant research to assess counseling approaches on children's off-task behavior. *Professional School Counseling, 5,* 308–314.

# Chapter 6

# Person-Centered Counseling

*If you bring forth what is within you, what you bring
forth will save you. If you do not bring forth what is
within you, what you do not bring forth will destroy you.*
—Saint Thomas

*I'm looking for the angel within.*
—Michelangelo

## CARL ROGERS

Carl Rogers (1902–1987) was born in Illinois, the fourth of six children. His early
home life was marked by close family ties, a strict religious and moral atmosphere,
and an appreciation of the value of hard work. During this period, Rogers thought
his family was different from others because they did not mix socially. In fact,
Rogers had only two dates during his high school years.

When Rogers was 12, his parents moved to a farm to remove the young family
from the "temptations" of suburban life. From raising lambs, pigs, and calves,
Rogers learned about matching experimental conditions with control conditions
and about randomization procedures, and he acquired knowledge and respect for
the methods of science. Rogers's thinking was influenced by teachers who encouraged him to be original.

Rogers started college at the University of Wisconsin to study scientific agri-
culture. After 2 years, however, he switched his career goal to the ministry as a result of attending some emotionally charged religious conferences. In his junior
year, he was chosen to go to China for 6 months for an international World Student Christian Federation conference. During this period, two things greatly influenced his life. First, at the expense of great pain and stress within his family relationships, he freed himself from the religious thinking of his parents and became
an independent thinker, although he did not abandon religion entirely. Second, he
fell in love with a woman he had known most of his life. He married her, with re-

luctant parental consent, as soon as he finished college so that they could attend graduate school together.

Rogers chose to go to graduate school at Union Theological Seminary, where Goodwin Watson's and Marian Kenworthy's courses and lectures on psychology and psychiatry interested him. He began to take courses at Teachers College, Columbia University, across the street from Union, and found himself drawn to child guidance while working at Union under Leta Hollingsworth. He applied for a fellowship at the Institute for Child Guidance and was accepted; he was well on his way to a career in psychology.

At the end of his internship at the Institute for Child Guidance, Rogers accepted a job in Rochester, New York, at the Society for the Prevention of Cruelty to Children. He completed his Ph.D. at Columbia Teachers College and spent the next 12 years in Rochester. His son and daughter grew through infancy and childhood there. Rogers once said that his children taught him far more about the development and relationships of individuals than he ever learned professionally.

Rogers spent his first 8 years in Rochester immersed in his work, conducting treatment interviews, and trying to be effective with clients. Gradually, he began teaching in the sociology department at the University of Rochester. He was also involved in developing a guidance center and writing a book, *The Clinical Treatment of the Problem Child* (1939). At this time, Otto Rank's work influenced Rogers's belief in people's ability to solve their own problems, given the proper climate.

In 1940, Rogers accepted a full professorship at Ohio State University. Realizing he had developed a distinctive viewpoint, he wrote the then-controversial *Counseling and Psychotherapy* (1942), in which he proposed a counseling relationship based on the warmth and responsiveness of the therapist. Rogers believed that, in such a relationship, clients would express their feelings and thoughts. This first truly American system of psychotherapy was a radical change in a field that had been dominated by psychoanalysis and directive counseling. He and his students at Ohio State made detailed analyses of counseling sessions and began to publish cases in "client-centered therapy." The theory developed as Rogers and his colleagues began to test the hypotheses they formed from their case studies.

In 1945, Rogers moved on to the University of Chicago, where he organized the counseling center and spent the next 12 years doing research. While he was associated with the University of Chicago, he wrote his famous *Client-Centered Therapy*, published in 1951. Rogers described his years at Chicago as very satisfying but accepted an opportunity at the University of Wisconsin, where he was able to work in both the departments of psychology and psychiatry; he had long wanted to work with psychotic individuals who had been hospitalized.

Rogers moved to the Western Behavioral Sciences Institute in La Jolla, California, in 1966. In 1968, he and several colleagues formed the Center for Studies of the Person, also in La Jolla. Through the 1970s and into the 1980s, Rogers spent most of his time working with and writing about person-centered therapy with groups. As noted in Chapter 2, Rogers came to prefer the term *person-centered* to *client-centered* in writing about his approach.

# THE NATURE OF PEOPLE

Carl Rogers, with his person-centered school of thought, viewed people as rational, socialized, forward-moving, and realistic beings. He contended that negative, antisocial emotions are only a result of frustrated basic impulses; this idea is related to Maslow's hierarchy of needs. For instance, extreme aggressive action toward other people results from failure to meet the basic needs of love and belonging. Once people are free of their defensive behavior, their reactions are positive and progressive.

People possess the capacity to experience—that is, to express rather than repress—their own maladjustment to life and move toward a more adjusted state of mind. Rogers believed that people move toward actualization as they move toward psychological adjustment. Because people possess the capacity to regulate and control their own behavior, the counseling relationship is merely a means of tapping personal resources and developing human potential. People learn from their external therapy experience how to internalize and provide their own psychotherapy.

In summary, a person-centered counselor believes that people:

- Have worth and dignity in their own right and therefore deserve respect
- Have the capacity and right to self-direction and, when given the opportunity, make wise judgments
- Can select their own values
- Can learn to make constructive use of responsibility
- Have the capacity to deal with their own feelings, thoughts, and behavior
- Have the potential for constructive change and personal development toward a full and satisfying life (self-actualization)

Perhaps Rogers's view of human nature is best revealed by a quote from him:

One of the most satisfying experiences I know—is just fully to appreciate an individual in the same way that I appreciate a sunset. When I look at a sunset . . . I don't find myself saying, "Soften the orange a little on the right hand corner, and put a bit more purple along the base, and use a little more pink in the cloud color. . . ." I don't try to control a sunset. I watch it with awe as it unfolds. (1994, p. 189)

# THEORY OF COUNSELING

Rogers (1992), in a reprint of his classic 1957 article, addressed the question, "Is it possible to state in clearly definable and measurable terms what is needed to bring about personality change?" Accepting the behaviorists' challenge, Rogers proceeded to answer in descriptive terms. His six conditions for personality change, listed next, have become the classic conditions for person-centered counseling:

1. Two persons are in psychological contact.
2. The client is in a state of incongruence.
3. The therapist is congruent and involved in the relationship.

4. The therapist experiences unconditional positive regard for the client.
5. The therapist experiences empathetic understanding of the client's frame of reference.
6. The communication of empathetic and positive regard is achieved.

Rogers believed that each condition is necessary to create optimal opportunity for personality change. Condition 6, the basis for trust between counselor and client, is especially vital to the therapy process. We agree with Rogers that the six conditions, which need not be limited to the person-centered method of counseling, provide a sound foundation for most standard methods of counseling children and adults.

Rogers first called his process *nondirective therapy* because of the therapist's encouraging and listening role. Later he adopted the term *client-centered,* because of the complete responsibility given to clients for their own growth, and then *person-centered,* in hopes of further humanizing the counseling process.

To maintain himself in the nondirective role of the person-centered counselor, Rogers refrained from giving advice, asking questions, and making interpretations of the client's message, thoughts, feelings, and behaviors. All three of these counselor behaviors tend to shift the counseling process from person-centered to counselor-centered. When pressed for advice, a common Rogers response would be, "I would like to know the advice you would like to hear from me." Rogers believed that one way people get themselves into trouble is letting other people direct their lives and that a counselor who does likewise makes the client's problem situation worse. Therefore, Rogers believed he could facilitate his clients' progress if he would put them in the position of charting the direction of their counseling interviews. He was successful in doing so by replacing advice, interpretations, and questions with the active listening process of limiting his responses to summaries and clarifications of the content, feelings, and expectations for counseling presented in his clients' interviews. Hence, the direction of person-centered interviews is left to the client. Visualize two people riding side by side in a horse-drawn carriage with the reins lying on the floor of the driver's seat. Each rider is waiting for the other to pick up the reins and drive the horse. Finally, out of clear frustration, if not fear, one of the riders picks up the reins and guides the horse. Rogers will not be the one to pick up the reins unless possible bodily injury demands it. Some people are not all that sure that he would have done it even then. Rogers believed that directing the counseling interview would be an important first step for clients to begin directing their lives outside the counseling interview. A second important benefit accrued from person-centered counseling escaped even Rogers's awareness. That is, the person-centered approach puts clients in the role of teachers as they teach counselors about their situations in life. As all teachers know, when you teach something you learn more about it in greater depth than you have ever previously known. Clients receiving person-centered counseling learn more about themselves and their unsolved problems than they have ever known before because they are in the teaching role of trying to help counselors understand their situations. The task of person-centered counselors is to take periodic oral quizzes on how much they are learning and understanding their clients' teaching. Person-centered counselors do not need a script or list of questions to follow because all of their "lines" comes from listening to their clients. As Myers (2000) concludes from her phenomenological study on the experience of being heard, "As comforting as it might be for therapists to have a perfect model or recipe for empathic listening, the experience of being heard requires an interpersonal, relational context."

Reflecting Rogers's view of human nature, if the counselor creates a warm and accepting climate in interviews, people trust the counselor enough to risk sharing their ideas about their lives and the problems they face. During this sharing with a nonjudgmental counselor, people feel free to explore their feelings, thoughts, and behaviors as they relate to their personal growth, development, and adjustment. Such explorations should, in turn, lead to more effective decision making and to productive behavior. Rogers (1951) wrote that the counselor operates from the point of view that people have the capacity to work effectively with all aspects of their lives that come into conscious awareness. Expansion of this conscious awareness occurs when the counseling climate meets Rogers's standards and clients realize that the counselor accepts them as people competent to direct their own lives.

Person-centered counseling deals primarily with the organization and function of self. The counselor becomes an objective, unemotional "mirror" who reflects the person's inner world with warmth, acceptance, and trust. This mirroring allows people to judge their thoughts and feelings and begin to explore their effects on behavior. Thus, people are enabled to reorganize their thoughts, feelings, and behaviors and function in a more integrated fashion.

The Rogerian model for helping, as modified by Carkhuff (1973), involves three general stages through which the client proceeds. In the first phase, self-exploration, people examine exactly where they are in their lives, including a type of self-searching in which they question themselves concerning their status at the present moment. In the second phase, people begin to understand the relationship between where they are in life and where they would like to be. In other words, they move from a type of discovery in self-exploration to an understanding. The third phase involves action. In this context, action is goal-directed; people engage in some program or plan in order to reach the point where they want to be. The only exception to the logical order of these three stages might be in helping children; their movement through the process may be more meaningful if action is followed by understanding and then self-exploration. Children problem-solve better when they can move from concrete to abstract thinking. Self-exploration is the most abstract area of the process in Rogers's system.

One can think of person-centered counseling in two dimensions: (1) responsive and facilitative, which includes attending, observing, and listening, and (2) initiative, which includes initiating, personalizing, and responding. The counselor is the "expert" in creating the nonthreatening environment vital to the counseling process. Empathy, respect, warmth, concreteness, genuineness, and self-disclosure all facilitate change in client behavior. As mentioned previously, the process works best when counselors let clients direct the interviews—a first step in teaching clients how to direct their lives. Clients are the experts whose task is to teach the counselor about their life situation. Clients thereby learn more about themselves, because teaching generally helps the teacher learn. The teaching factor may be the main reason that person-centered therapy helps many people.

The main goal of person-centered therapy is assisting people in becoming more autonomous, spontaneous, and confident (Rogers, 1983). As people become more aware of what is going on inside themselves, they can cease fearing and defending their inner feelings. They learn to accept their own values and trust their own judgment rather than live by the values of others. Expectations of person-centered therapy include the discussion of plans, behavioral steps to be taken, and the outcome of the steps; a change from immature behavior to mature behavior; fewer current defensive behaviors; more tolerance for frustration; and improved functioning in life tasks.

The ultimate goal of person-centered therapy is to produce fully functioning people who have learned to be free and who can counsel themselves. According to Rogers (1983), learning to be free is the essential goal of education "if the civilized culture is to survive and if individuals in the culture are to be worth saving." People who have learned to be free can confront life and face problems; they trust themselves to choose their own way and accept their own feelings without forcing them on others. Such individuals prize themselves and others as having dignity, worth, and value.

## COUNSELING METHOD

The counselor as a person is vital to person-centered counseling. The conditions the counselor models become the ultimate counseling goals for all clients. Optimally, effective person-centered counselors must possess openness, empathic understanding, independence, spontaneity, acceptance, mutual respect, and intimacy. After clients move through the immediate counseling goals of self-exploration and subgoals such as improving a math grade or making a new friend, they begin to work toward achieving the ultimate counseling goals for the effective person-centered counselor—developing the same traits modeled by person-centered counselors.

Perhaps the strongest techniques in the person-centered counselor's repertoire are attitudes toward people: *congruence* (genuineness), *unconditional positive regard* (respect), and *empathy.* Congruence implies that the counselor can maintain a sense of self-identity and can convey this identity to clients. In other words, the counselor is not playing an artificial role. Unconditional positive regard implies that the counselor accepts clients as people who have the potential to become good, rational, and free. Because people have self-worth, dignity, and unique traits as individuals, they require individualized counseling approaches. Thus, people direct their own counseling sessions. For the process to succeed, clients must feel they can reveal themselves to the counselor in an atmosphere of complete acceptance. Empathy is the attitude that holds the counseling process together. By attempting to understand, the counselor helps convince people that they are worth hearing and understanding. Rogers (1995), in a reprint of a 1956 speech, identified six principles he believed helped him become more effective in understanding and showing empathy in counseling. He believed that acceptance and understanding of his clients kept him from trying to fix their problems. Once he came to believe that people have a basic positive direction, he wanted his clients to discover their own paths to resolving their problems.

Rogers's first principle: "In my relationships with people I have found that it does not help, in the long run, to act as though I am something I am not." He found it harmful to pretend to be feeling a certain way with a client if he actually felt differently. Constructive relationships could not be built on pretense.

Rogers's second principle: "I have found it effective in my dealings with people to be accepting of myself." He learned to trust his reactions to clients, which he thought made his relationships with clients much more authentic. He believed that real relationships were always in the process of change and never static.

Rogers's third principle: "I have found it to be of enormous value when I can permit myself to understand another person." This principle became the cornerstone for his theory of person-centered counseling. He believed a therapist should be completely open to hearing exactly what the client is trying to relate. He believed that most people had an opinion formed before hearing what another person was trying to communicate. Consequently, Rogers thought that the best counselors could do was listen. He placed great value on learning from his students' reactions to each of his classes. Any success he enjoyed as a teacher was attributed to understanding each student's point of view.

Rogers's fourth principle: "I have found it to be of value to be open to the realities of life as they are revealed in me and in other people." He believed there was balance to life, the fragile as well as the tough.

Rogers's fifth principle: "The more I am able to understand myself and others, the more that I am open to the realities of life and the less I find myself wishing to rush in." That is, he was less likely to try to manipulate people into meeting certain goals or conforming to certain modes of living. Rogers did not believe clients should learn what a therapist thought they should learn but did hold that other people change as the therapist changes.

Rogers's sixth and final principle: "It has been my experience that people have a basically positive direction." He believed that the more individuals felt they were being understood and well received, the more they would drop false pretenses. Having seen the negative side of human behavior—immaturity, destructiveness, regression, and antisocial behavior—he still maintained that people in general were positive, constructive, moving forward toward self-actualization, and growing toward maturity. Most rewarding to Rogers were the times when his clients discovered their positive directions in life.

In summary, the person-centered counselor refrains from giving advice or solutions, diagnosing, interpreting, moralizing, and making judgments, which would defeat the plan for teaching clients how to counsel themselves and imply that the counselors know and understand their clients better than the clients know themselves—an assumption totally out of line with Rogers's view. Instead, person-centered counselors use the methods of (1) active and passive listening, (2) reflection of thoughts and feelings, (3) clarification, (4) summarization, (5) confrontation of contradictions, and (6) general or open leads that help a client's self-exploration.

The major technique for person-centered counseling is active listening, which lets the client know that the counselor is hearing and understanding correctly all that the client is saying. As we said in Chapter 2, active listening is especially important for counseling children. If the counselor fails to receive the correct message, the child attempts to reteach it to the counselor. Once counselor and child agree that the counselor has the story straight and that the counseling service will be helpful, counseling can continue.

Carkhuff (1973, 1981) systematized Rogers's concept of active listening (reflection) into a highly understandable, usable model (Table 6-1). Carkhuff believed that counselors typically respond on any one of five levels relating to the three phases of counseling: (I) where you are now in your life, (II) where you would like to be, and (III) planning how to get from Phase I to Phase II. He classified Levels 1 and 2 as harmful, Level 3 as break even, and Levels 4 and 5 as helpful. It is often assumed that the worst thing that can happen in counseling is that clients show no change. However, this is not true. Clients who receive a preponderance of Level 1 and 2 responses could grow worse as the result of counseling.

Level 1 and 2 responses in Carkhuff's model also appear in Gordon's (1974) "dirty dozen" list of responses that tend to close or inhibit further communication:

1. Ordering; directing
2. Warning; threatening; stating consequences
3. Moralizing; shoulds, oughts

TABLE 6-1    Five levels of communication

| Levels | *Phase I* | *Phase II* | *Phase III* |
|---|---|---|---|
| | *Thoughts and feelings about where you are now* | *Thoughts and feelings about where you would like to be* | *Plans for getting from where you are to where you would like to be* |
| 1 | | | |
| 2 | | | X |
| 3 | X | | |
| 4 | X | X | |
| 5 | X | X | X |

NOTE: The X's indicate which phase of counseling is treated by each of the five levels of communication.

4. Advising; giving suggestions and solutions
5. Messages of logic; counterarguments
6. Judging; criticizing
7. Praising; buttering up
8. Name-calling; ridiculing
9. Psychoanalyzing
10. Reassuring; giving sympathy; consoling
11. Probing: "who, what, when, where, why?"
12. Humor; distracting; withdrawing

Level 1 responses tend to discount what a person is feeling and thinking with statements such as the following:

- "Oh, don't worry about that. Things will work out."
- "If you think you have a problem, listen to this."
- "You must have done something to make Mrs. Jones treat you that way."

Level 1 responses may also be an indication that the counselor simply was not listening. As such, Level 1 responses do not help with any of the three counseling phases in Table 6-1.

Level 2 responses are messages that give advice and solutions to problems. These responses are relevant in Phase III, but they are not considered helpful because they do not allow the counselor and the client to fully explore the problem situation. Ignoring the active-listening process deprives clients of the opportunity to work out their own solutions to their problems. Level 2 responses keep clients dependent on the counselor's authority and prevent clients from learning to counsel themselves. Typical Level 2 responses include the following:

- "You need to study harder."
- "You should eat better."
- "You should be more assertive."
- "Why don't you make more friends?"
- "How would you like your brother to treat you the way you treat him?"

Even though the advice may be excellent, the client—child or adult—may not have the skill to do what you suggest. Moreover, rebellious children may work especially hard to show that your advice is ineffective, just to receive the satisfaction of knowing that an "expert" counselor is no more successful than they are in solving day-to-day problems.

Level 3 responses are classified as break-even points in the counseling process—neither harmful nor helpful. However, these responses provide bridges to further conversation and exploration in the counseling process; they are the door openers and invitations to discuss concerns in more depth.

Level 3 responses reflect what the client is thinking and feeling about the present status of the problem, for example, "You are feeling *discouraged* because *you haven't been able to make good grades in math.*" Such responses are checkpoints for counselors in determining if they are hearing and understanding the client's problem. Either the client acknowledges that the counselor has understood the message correctly, or the client makes another attempt to relate the concern to the counselor. At this point in counseling, clients are teaching the counselors about their problems and are thereby learning more about their problems themselves.

According to Carkhuff's model, an aid to counselors in making Level 3 responses is to ask themselves if the client is expressing pain or pleasure. The next task is to find the correct feeling word to describe the pain or pleasure. Seven feeling words are listed later in Figure 6-1. To build your counseling vocabulary, add three synonyms of your own under each word. In reflecting the client's feeling and thoughts, do not parrot the exact words of the client. Time out for a summary is often helpful; say to your client, "Let's see if I understand what you have told me up to now."

Remember that the focus on feelings is to help clients to recognize and be aware of their feelings so that they can use them as indicators of whether they are making good decisions or doing the behaviors they need to be doing. To ignore feelings is much like driving a car without paying attention to the red lights and gauges on the car's dashboard. Feelings are the one of the best indicators we have for helping us find direction in our lives. Children may prefer to discuss their feelings by selecting one of the faces on the feelings chart in Figure 6-1. In fact, they may prefer to draw a face that represents how they feel.

Level 4 responses reflect an understanding of Phases I and II in Carkhuff's model—for example, "You are feeling discouraged because you haven't been able to make good grades in math, and you want to find a way to do better." Rephrase the responses in your own words as you summarize the client's thoughts and feelings.

Level 5 responses are appropriate when the client agrees that the counselor understands the problem or concern. Now it is time to assist the client in developing a plan of action. Reality therapy provides a good framework for planning after

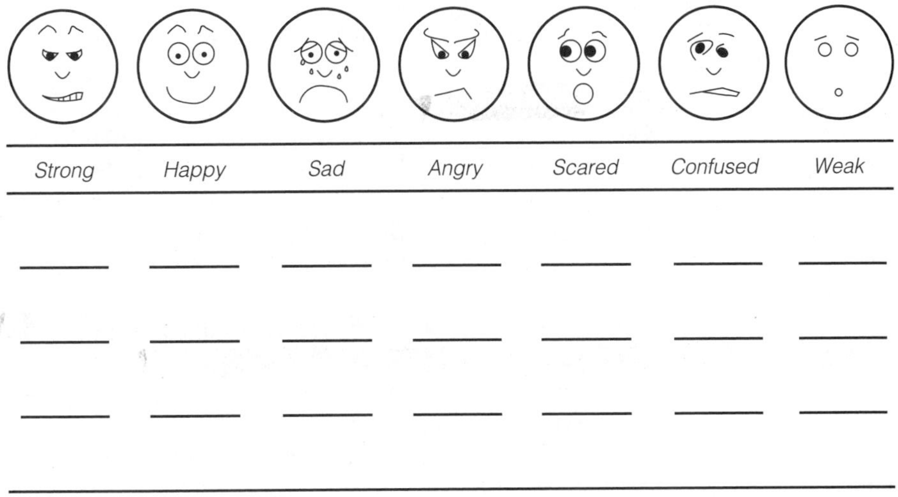

| Strong | Happy | Sad | Angry | Scared | Confused | Weak |
|--------|-------|-----|-------|--------|----------|------|

FIGURE 6-1

person-centered counseling has helped the client relate the concern to the counselor. An example of a combined Level 5 response is the following:

> Person-centered (PC) therapy: You feel _____ because _____, and you want _____.
>
> Reality therapy (RT): Let's look at what you have been doing to solve your problem.
>
> PC and RT: You feel *discouraged* because *you haven't been able to make good grades in math,* and you want to *find a way to do better.* Let's look at what you have been trying to do *to make good grades in math.*

The entire counseling interview cannot be accomplished in one response. Several sessions of Level 3 and 4 responses may be necessary before the problem is defined well enough for solving.

Because the success of the person-centered approach to counseling depends so much on the relationship between counselor and client, this approach may be *unsuccessful* with young children. Not every adult is capable of establishing true empathy with children or even of liking children. Children, to a greater degree than adults, are sensitive to the real feelings and attitudes of others. They intuitively trust and open up to those who like and understand them. Phony expressions of understanding do not fool a child for very long. A good example of a person-centered counseling method used with play therapy is presented in Virginia Axline's *Dibs: In Search of Self* (1964).

To help children effectively, the counselor must provide a warm, caring environment in which children can explore their emotions and verbally act out the consequences of alternative means of expressing them. Together, counselor and child—or the child alone if he or she possesses sufficient maturity—can evaluate the alternatives and select the one most likely to be appropriate and productive.

In using the person-centered approach with young children, the counselor may have to assume a more active role. Still, even young children can distinguish between positive and negative behaviors and are able to choose the positive once the counselor has established an open dialogue in which feelings and emotions can be aired and conflicts resolved.

Again, the counselor uses active listening to give children an opportunity to release feelings without feeling threatened by the counselor. Listening carefully and observing the child increase the counselor's ability to understand what the child is trying to communicate. All clients convey both verbal and nonverbal messages, and the counselor needs to be alert to them. Because a child's verbal skills may be limited, nonverbal messages may be the most important clue to what the child is really feeling and trying to communicate.

Once again, the person-centered approach is most successful when clients take the role of teaching their counselors about their problem situations. The counselor's job, as the "student" being taught, is to take periodic oral quizzes (counseling summary or reflection statements) to let the client (teacher) know how well the subject matter is being understood. The subject matter consists of the problem, type and depth of feelings about the problem, and expectations the client has for its solution. Clients learn by *teaching* their counselors about themselves and their lives. In addition, through active listening the counselor also helps clients clarify problems clouded by the *overgeneralizations, distortions,* and *deletions* commonly brought to counseling. The focus on feeling is done to help clients learn how to recognize and use their feelings as indicators of whether they are making good choices and decisions in their lives. Lacking the verbal skills of most adults, children can benefit from bibliocounseling, storytelling, and play therapy (see Chapter 14) as aids to teaching about their problem situations.

## C A S E   S T U D Y *

### *Identification of the Problem*

Ginger Wood, an 11-year-old girl in the sixth grade at Hill Middle School, was referred to the school counselor because her grades had recently fallen and she seemed depressed.

### *Individual and Background Information*

*Academic.*   School records show that Ginger is an A student who was chosen to be in an advanced group in third grade. On her last report card, however, her grades dropped to a C average.

*Family.*   Ginger is the elder of two children; her younger brother is 9. Her mother is an elementary school teacher, and her father is a systems analyst; they have recently separated.

*Social.*   Ginger is approximately 30 pounds overweight. She has a friendly personality, and teacher reports do not show that she has a problem relating to her peers.

### *Counseling Method*

The counselor chose to use Rogers's (1965) person-centered counseling method. The counselor believes that Ginger's problem originates from emotional blocks. Her goal is to establish a warm relationship with Ginger, aid her in clarifying her thoughts and feelings, and enable her to solve her problems.

In this method, the counselor uses five basic techniques:

1. Unconditional positive regard
2. Active listening

---

*The case of Ginger was contributed by Anne Harvey.

3. Reflection
4. Clarification
5. Summarization

*Transcript*

*Counselor:*  Hi, Ginger. I'm Susan Morgan. Your teacher, Ms. Lowe, told me that you might come to talk to me.

*Ginger:*  Yeah, I decided to.

*Counselor:*  Do you know what a counselor's job is?

*Ginger:*  Yeah, Ms. Lowe told me that you help people with their problems.

*Counselor:*  That's right. I try to teach people how to solve their own problems. Do you have something on your mind that you'd like to talk about?

*Ginger:*  Well, I haven't been doing so well in school lately.

*Counselor:*  Yes, Ms. Lowe said you are normally an A student.

*Ginger:*  I used to be, but not now. I made Cs on my last report card. My mom was really upset with me; she yelled at me and then grounded me.

*Counselor:*  It sounds as though she was angry with you because your grades went down.

*Ginger:*  Well, not so much angry as unhappy. [She looked ready to cry.]

*Counselor:*  So she was disappointed that you weren't doing as well in school as you usually do, and this made you feel bad, too.

*Ginger:*  I guess so. She probably blamed herself some, too, and that could have made her feel worse.

*Counselor:*  You mean that she felt responsible for your grades going down.

*Ginger:*  Well, maybe. Things aren't going so well at home. Mom and Dad aren't living together right now, and they may get a divorce. She hasn't had a lot of time for us lately. I guess she's really been worried.

*Counselor:*  The problem at home has made it tougher for you to do well at school because you're worried about what's happening.

*Ginger:*  Yeah, I think about it a lot. It's harder to study when I'm worrying about it.

*Counselor:*  It would be for me, too. This must be a very hard situation for you to go through.

*Ginger:*  It sure is; everybody's mad. My little brother doesn't understand what's going on, and he cries a lot. Mom does, too.

*Counselor:*  So the whole family is upset.

*Ginger:*  Well, I guess so. My dad doesn't seem to be, but why should he be? It's all his fault. He's getting what he wants.

*Counselor:*  I guess he's the one who wants the divorce. It doesn't seem fair to the rest of you.

*Ginger:*  Yeah. He's got a girlfriend. My mom didn't even know anything about her until Daddy said he was leaving. I hate him! [Starts to cry.] And that makes me feel even worse cause I know I shouldn't hate my father. I wish he were dead!

*Counselor:* [Handing her a tissue] So you're all torn up between the way you feel and the way you think you should feel.

*Ginger:* Yeah. It's so hard to sort everything out. Do you think that makes me a bad person for me to hate my father?

*Counselor:* I think you are a good person who doesn't know what to do with all of her feelings right now. I'm wondering if you think you are a bad person.

*Ginger:* No, I guess not. I mean, I think most of my friends would feel about the same way I do if they were in my shoes.

*Counselor:* Sure, it's a tough thing to handle.

*Ginger:* And I guess they're not all bad people. Thanks, Ms. Morgan. I'm glad we talked about it. I feel a little better now.

*Counselor:* I'm glad, Ginger. It sounds like you're beginning to work out your problems. Would you like to make another appointment to talk with me?

*Ginger:* Okay. Could I come back during free time next week?

*Counselor:* That will be fine. You can see me any day when you want to talk.

*Ginger:* Bye, Ms. Morgan, and thanks.

*Counselor:* You're welcome.

## PERSON-CENTERED COUNSELING AND THE DEVELOPMENT OF SELF-ESTEEM*

Self-esteem development has been a centerpiece of person-centered counseling. Building self-esteem in children is receiving increasing emphasis. Our position is that self-esteem is a by-product of achievements and relationships and can be increased by helping clients improve these two important areas in their lives.

Radd (2003) developed a process to integrate self-esteem development into life skills education, a theme consistent with the application of person-centered theory to education. The process includes a series of activities that focus on teaching children about self-esteem and ways of applying that information to daily living.

The activities each have three steps. The counselor may choose to teach these statements in the first person or in the format given. The counselor begins by saying:

1. "All people are special and valuable because they are unique." This statement is discussed to teach the concept of unconditional valuing of people simply because they are people. For children in kindergarten through fourth grade, the words *special* and *different* are effective. "No matter what you do, you are still special because you are a person." For children in grades 5 through 8, variations of the words *unique* and *valuable* are effective. "If everyone were the same, it would be boring." "It is impossible for people to be better than other people because everyone is unique." In other words, "I'm the best me there is." The counselor continues:

2. "Because people are special and unique, they have a responsibility to *help* and *not hurt* themselves. People *show* if they remember that they are important by

*Tommie R. Radd, professor in the College of Education, University of Nebraska at Omaha, contributed this section.

the way they *choose* to act. If people choose to hurt themselves or others, they are forgetting that they are special. Likewise, if people choose to help themselves or others, they are remembering that they are special. What is special to you? How do you treat it? Do you *help* or *hurt* the things you think are special? Are your toys and computer games more important to you than people? Toys and games can be replaced, but people are different and not replaceable. If you are remembering that you are as special as your toys, will you help or hurt yourself? When people help others, they are helping themselves. People hurt themselves when they hurt other people by forgetting that all people are special and unique. Possible consequences of hurting others include feeling bad about oneself and losing positive relationships, which result in self-esteem erosion. What people give is generally what they receive. The point we want to teach is that if we like ourselves, we do not hurt ourselves or others." The counselor continues:

3. "People are responsible for 'watching' their actions to determine if they are remembering the *truth* that they are special. People are 'with' themselves at all times and are accountable for remembering to treat themselves as important people. When people blame others for their actions, they are forgetting their responsibility to value themselves. Who is with you all the time? Who will live with you forever? Who decides what happens to you? Who is the only one you can change?"

## Integrating Self-Esteem–Building Activities with the Child's Life

After the self-esteem activities are introduced into all environments children experience, the concepts are related to the children's daily life experiences and associated with various situations, interactions, and other skills, such as decision making, self-control, and group cooperation.

The continuing process of relating self-esteem activities to a child's life is the *self-esteem series weave*. Picture the self-esteem activities being introduced to children. After this information is taught and processed, the children experience the integration of these concepts into their daily life experiences. The weaving process makes the concepts about self alive and relevant for children.

The self-esteem series weave process is implemented consistently, regardless of the counseling approach or setting. The self-esteem activities and weave can become the core of classroom group guidance, small-group counseling, individual counseling, and positive behavior management. The self-esteem activities are introduced and taught. Then, each subsequent session begins with a brief review of the self-esteem activities and a weave of the self-esteem activities into the process of the group or individual session.

An example of the self-esteem series weave process follows. Although it is part of the second individual counseling session with a third-grade student, the same process is used in classroom group guidance, in small-group counseling, and within the classroom behavior plan.

In the first session, the self-esteem activities were introduced and woven throughout the session. Bill was referred to counseling because of his problems with work completion.

*Bill:* I'm still in trouble with my teacher this week.

*Counselor:* You are not feeling very good about this.

*Bill:* I think my teacher doesn't like me. She thinks I'm dumb.

*Counselor:* Your feeling bad comes from what your teacher thinks about you. I'm wondering how this fits in with what we talked about last week.

*Bill:* You said that I am special, no matter what I do, because no one else is like me anywhere in the world.

*Counselor:* It seems this week you are feeling as though you're not special.

*Bill:* I don't know. My teacher doesn't think so.

*Counselor:* So you think you are not important or special because you think your teacher does not think you are special.

*Bill:* Yeah. I know you think I'm special, but it is hard for me to think so when my teacher doesn't like me.

*Counselor:* You may be showing that you forget you are special by the way you have been acting in your class. You and your teacher told me you have been deciding not to complete your work. I'm wondering if you have been hurting yourself with your choices.

*Bill:* I've been hurting myself because I'm not doing my work. But other people aren't doing their work, and they don't get picked on.

*Counselor:* It sounds as though you feel cheated because the teacher likes the other children better than you and does not treat you fairly. Let's see if we can figure this out with the ideas we learned last week.

*Bill:* Okay.

*Counselor:* I wonder if you remember what we said about whom children hurt when they choose not to do their work.

*Bill:* I think they are hurting themselves.

*Counselor:* So, we could take a look at what happens to you when you don't do your work.

*Bill:* I guess it hurts me.

*Counselor:* If you want to, we can think of some ways to help you stop hurting yourself.

*Bill:* Okay. Maybe. I can ask the teacher for help when I get lost on my work, or I can get a friend to help me. I can ask for help remembering the homework, too.

*Counselor:* These ideas might help you. We need to know which ones you want to try.

*Bill:* I guess I just need to do what it takes to turn in all my assignments.

*Counselor:* Next week we can see if you've been remembering to do all those things you need to do to help yourself. Maybe you could show me the work you get done each day.

*Bill:* Okay.

The process of integrating self-esteem building with life skill development is most effective if it becomes the focus and foundation of group guidance, group counseling, behavior management, and individual counseling (Radd, 1996). The consistent exposure of children to self-concept activities related to life experiences clarifies and personalizes these difficult concepts so that they become part of the children's knowledge base. Once again, however, self-esteem development is best served by helping children improve their academic performance and develop more friendships.

## CHILD-CENTERED PLAY THERAPY

Virginia Axline translated the nondirective counseling approach of Carl Rogers to work with children. Her book *Dibs: In Search of Self* (1964) describes this play therapy model. Landreth (1993) and Landreth and Sweeney (1997) provided further details on the child-centered approach to play therapy. This model is based on beliefs in the child's innate desire for growth and capacity for self-direction. In child-centered play therapy, the child leads. The counselor focuses on the child's strengths, reflects the child's feelings, and recognizes the power of a warm, accepting, and empathic relationship. Basic principles of the child-centered relationship are as follows:

1. The counselor has a genuine interest in the child and builds a warm, caring relationship.

2. The counselor accepts the child unconditionally, not wishing the child were different.

3. The counselor institutes a feeling of safety and permissiveness in the relationship, allowing the child freedom to explore and express.

4. The counselor maintains sensitivity to the child's feelings and reflects them in a way that increases the child's self-understanding.

5. The counselor strongly believes in the child's capacity to act responsibly and solve personal problems, and allows the child to do so.

6. The counselor trusts the inner direction of the child, allowing the child to lead the relationship and refusing to override the child's direction.

7. The counselor does not hurry the therapeutic process.

8. The counselor uses only the limits necessary for helping the child accept personal and appropriate responsibility (Axline, 1947, pp. 77–78; Landreth & Sweeney, 1997, p. 22).

The counselor who practices child-centered play therapy expresses an attitude of being completely with the child, an emotional and verbal participant. The process involves the counselor being open to the child's experience by living out these messages: *I am here* (nothing will distract me), *I hear you* (I am listening carefully), *I understand you,* and *I care about you* (Landreth, 1991). *Play Therapy: The Art of the Relationship* (Landreth, 1991) contains details about accomplishing these goals.

Moustakas (1998) explained relationship play therapy as the creation of play dramas. Within the relationship, the counselor demonstrates acceptance, receptiveness, and openness, along with the skills of "listening and hearing, teaching and learning, directing and receiving, participating actively and quietly observing, confronting and letting be" (p. 2). He discussed the use of play therapy as a prevention strategy in which parents and teachers participate. The brief therapy—one to four play sessions—is supportive. The relationship and counseling process encourage self-disclosure, expression of feelings, and limits.

Johnson, McLeod, and Fall (1997) studied client-centered play therapy with children who had special needs. Six children were identified in two rural Midwestern elementary schools. Six weekly 30-minute play therapy sessions were held. The transcripts and videotapes of the sessions were analyzed for expression of feelings and of control. They concluded that nondirective child-centered play therapy was effective in allowing the children chances to express feelings, experience control, and develop coping skills. They also noted that therapists' perceptions were altered more favorably toward the children. Griffith (1997) discussed a client-centered empowerment model of play therapy for working with children who had been sexually abused. Her report also documented the effectiveness of child-centered play therapy.

## CROSS-CULTURAL APPLICATIONS OF PERSON-CENTERED COUNSELING

Kincade and Evans (1996) pointed out that person-centered counseling can be problematic for clients from cultures who expect their "counselors" to be experts who will advise and guide them regarding decisions to be made and problems to be solved. In other words, when expectations are not met, then clients are likely to become frustrated with the person-centered process and drop out of counseling. Asian and Native American clients, operating from a value system that stresses seeking help from older, wiser adults, are likely to become frustrated with the nondirective quality of person-centered counseling. However, the authors know from experience that similar expectations are held by some clients from the American culture who work mightily to move counseling from an adult–adult encounter to a parent–child relationship in which the counselor advises the client on what decisions should be made. As mentioned in Chapter 2, clients from all cultures may need orientation by the counselor on how counseling will be conducted and why it is done that way.

For working with clients from all cultures, a strong point in favor of the person-centered approach is the therapeutic conditions established by the counselor. These conditions of genuineness, unconditional positive regard, accurate empathic understanding, and nonjudgmental interest in the client show the respect for others that is important in many cultures (see Chapter 13). People in action-oriented cultures who are frustrated with the person-centered process will need to be told that person-centered counseling is designed to solve immediate problems by teaching clients how to be their own counselors. Clients from cultures that value group interests over individual interests find the individual freedom offered by competent, person-centered counselors very appealing. Person-centered counseling has enjoyed wide acceptance across many cultures. The emphasis on individual freedom and self-directed thinking and behavior featured in person-centered counseling is quite popular with people who, because of their cultures, have not always been free to make choices and speak their minds.

Follensbee, Draguns, and Danish (1986) studied the differential effects of affective responses and closed questions on adult client responses in an analog counseling setting. Affective responses were superior to closed questions in facilitating client verbalizations focusing on the present, the client, and the client's feelings. This finding held true for African, African American, Puerto Rican, and Anglo American clients.

In an attempt to evaluate person-centered counseling across cultures, Usher (1989) examined person-centered counseling against 10 possible problems with cultural bias arising from the method. The point is made that, although not a perfect method for all cultures, person-centered counseling has some advantages. There is less risk of being judged by the dominant culture's definition of *normality* because the client defines the goals and evaluates the process. Rogers also allowed for circularity of thinking, which allows culturally different clients to express feelings and thoughts within an open, nonjudgmental setting. Possible cross-cultural disadvantages of person-centered counseling include an emphasis on individualism that fails to accommodate the healthy dependencies on family members fostered in other cultures. Focusing on the self, subjective experience, and the "here and now" may be truly foreign or offensive to other cultures. The level of abstraction required in person-centered counseling conducted in English may also be too difficult to be helpful.

Waxer (1989), in an effort to research the multicultural implications for person-centered counseling, compared Cantonese and Canadian college students' reactions to Rogers and Ellis in *Three Approaches to Psychotherapy* (Shostrom, 1965). The Canadians preferred Rogers, and the Cantonese chose Ellis. Although both groups of students viewed Ellis as more directive, paternalistic, and authoritarian than Rogers, the Cantonese students did not rate him as harshly as the Canadians did. The Asian preference could be for counselors who are more autocratic, paternalistic, and directive; North Americans may view counseling as an open, exploratory, and democratic process.

Nevertheless, Hayashi (1992) and Hayashi, Kuno, Osawa, Shimizu, and Suetake (1998) report that person-centered counseling is viewed in a positive light in Japan. Person-centered counseling and theory are highly regarded by students in the Japanese university system; however, cultural differences have deterred full understanding of Rogerian theory, and the Japanese Focusing Institute has been established to provide insight and self-help through person-centered therapy. In addition to university settings, in Japan the approach is used in schools, hospitals, and companies. Hayashi, Kuno, Osawa, Shimizu, and Suetake (1998) write that the nondirective nature of person-centered counseling is quite compatible with Taoism, which holds that no individual can directly guide, educate, or give advice to others. As such, person-centered counseling should become more compatible with Japanese culture as people begin to understand and learn about it. Jenni (1999) made a similar point regarding person-centered counseling in China. She writes that Chinese philosophical, religious, and literary themes run parallel to the tenets of humanistic psychology and person-centered counseling.

A significant indicator of person-centered counseling as a viable cross-cultural counseling method was Rogers's work with South Africans. In an interview with Carl Rogers shortly before his death in 1987, Hill-Hain (Hill-Hain & Rogers, 1988) explored some of the basic challenges involved in a large-scale, cross-cultural application of person-centered group work that Rogers had started in 1986 with white and black South Africans. Rogers believed that the facilitator must not only accept a great deal of responsibility for learning about the culture of the participants but also be ready for surprises. Rogers also stressed the goal of relinquishing any attempt to control the outcome of the group experience, direction, or mood. However, group members were not to physically or psychologically abuse other group members. Rogers reported that his method seemed to accomplish its goals. The interview ended with Rogers posing the question: "Can I really be open to any little clue that might open up doors of new understanding?" That is how Rogers worked with individuals and groups.

Stipsits and Hutterer (1989) detailed another account of person-centered approaches in another culture. They found that after two decades of experience with person-centered approaches, Austrian professionals and their clients were moving toward this U.S. system of working with people. One survey revealed that 35% of the professionals in Austria who work in psychosocial areas have a person-centered orientation, and 40% of all clients in Austria had been in person-centered therapy. The person-centered numbers are most impressive when considered in light of the fact that they were compiled in the homeland of psychoanalysis, individual psychology, and logotherapy. Finally, Combs (1988), in writing about current issues in person-centered therapy, summarized Rogers's work in cross-cultural settings by pointing out how people from groups with supposedly irreconcilable differences and prejudices apparently learned to appreciate and communicate with one another in Rogers's encounter groups.

Rogers was actively working on world peace projects at the time of his death in 1987. Soloman (1990) pointed out that Rogers devoted the last 15 years of his life to working on ways to bring emotional honesty and personal congruence into international dialogue. Rogers firmly believed that the methodology of person-centered theory could be successfully applied to the negotiation process needed to achieve peace between people and nations.

## PERSON-CENTERED COUNSELING AND MANAGED HEALTH CARE

Person-centered counselors will be hard-pressed to meet some of the managed care guidelines presented in Chapter 2. Having fewer counseling sessions, establishing behavioral goals, and monitoring goal-attainment progress tend to work against clients proceeding at their chosen rate or clients who have rather indefinite or undefined goals. Key to the person-centered process is letting clients structure the sessions to meet their own needs. In other words, the person-centered process typically does not initiate moving into the third stage of counseling, which is initiating a plan to help clients move from where they are to where they would like to be. Such a move will not occur until the client makes a move toward putting a plan together. Perhaps the problem can be solved by ensuring that clients know the limitations of their health coverage and adjust person-centered methods to fit the plan. To that end, some counselors are cutting cost to their clients by:

1. Conducting 25-minute sessions rather than 50-minute sessions
2. Doing more group counseling
3. Informing their clients about the necessity to set and work toward meeting counseling goals
4. Offering reduced fees to clients who are self-paying or choose to continue after their coverage lapses
5. Supporting medical-savings-account legislation that rewards people for being proactive in maintaining their medical and physical health

## SUMMARY

Criticisms of person-centered counseling call it too abstract for young children and for adults who have not attained the ability to do formal thinking. The perfect clients for person-centered counseling have often been described as having the "YAVIS" syndrome—that is, they are *y*oung, *a*ttractive, *v*erbal, *i*ntelligent, and *s*ensitive. Such people may not need much counseling. Who, then, we might ask, will counsel tough, nonverbal children? Others criticize the approach as becoming mired in feelings and not moving quickly enough into planned behavioral change. Another criticism is Rogers's distaste for diagnostic tools and tests; critics argue that valuable data may be lost to counselors who do not use diagnostic methods. He also had a strong aversion to diagnosis, prognostication, and prescription. Critics of person-centered counseling hold that counselors are experts who can dispense valuable advice as well as predict future behavioral patterns and personality development in their clients.

In rebuttal, Rogers (1977) pointed out how person-centered counseling relates to a wide variety of individual and group concerns that span diverse populations, including the areas of family counseling, couple relationships, education, politics, government, and business administration.

Quinn (1993) challenged the person-centered approach of Carl Rogers as being too soft to provide the motivation clients often need to move ahead in their lives. Further, he contended that it does not allow the confrontation needed to help clients see the contradictions and inconsistencies in their thinking and behavior. Quinn stated that people develop best when they interact with and confront their environment and that counselors should provide the same opportunities. Person-centered counselors, he argued, avoid interactive confrontation with their clients. We believe that Quinn missed the point that Rogers was trying to create a counseling environment in which clients felt safe and could begin directing their own lives within the context of the therapy setting. Rogers's hope was that, given this opportunity, the inner-directed behavior would generalize to life outside the counseling interview. Counselors who take an active and directive role in counseling deprive their clients of the opportunity to practice directing their own lives. In a response to Quinn, Graf (1994) wrote that Quinn did not understand Rogers's approach to genuineness. Graf argued that Quinn's recommendation on what genuineness should be was actually what Rogers intended it to be: counselor and client communicating their thoughts and feelings honestly and openly. According to Graf, Rogers never intended to restrict person-centered counseling to active listening and expression of empathy. However, Myers (2000) found that clients in her phenomenological study on the experience of being heard put high values on their therapists' active listening, feedback, and expressions of empathy. They reported that these methods gave them room for self-exploration, the opportunity to move further and deeper into their own experience, and the feelings of safety, trust, and being understood, all of which were reported as being necessary to give them the freedom to examine their personal experiences. In a similar vein, Siebert (2000) studied the efficacy of empathy on the "recovery" of an 18-year-old woman who had been diagnosed as an "acute paranoid schizophrenic" upon her commitment to a hospital by her parents. She was telling her parents that God told her she was to have his baby. Her physician and the hospital staff thought she should be committed to the state psychiatric hospital, where they predicted she would spend the rest of her life. Siebert viewed this as an opportunity to try something different in his interview with her, because she was headed to what he termed "the snake pit" anyway. It was definitely a "What have you got to lose?" situation for him. Prior to his interview with the patient, he developed a game plan of four questions for himself. What would happen if:

1. I just listened to her and did not allow my mind to put any psychiatric labels on her?
2. I talked to her believing that she could turn out to be my best friend?
3. I accepted everything she reports about herself as being the truth?
4. I questioned her to find out if there is a link between her self-esteem, the workings of her mind, and the way others have been treating her?

Siebert, following the person-centered counseling model he designed for himself, brought about dramatic improvement in his patient, and she was not committed to the state hospital. Several days after that first session, she mentioned to Siebert that she had been doing a lot of thinking about what they had talked about. She asked, "I've been wondering, do you think I imagined God's voice to make myself feel better?" This case led Siebert to do a lot of thinking also.

On a concluding note, Rogers (1985) was an early supporter of utilizing phenomenological research methods and hermeneutics to answer the difficult questions about the inexact human science of the person. He believed these approaches would require researchers to indwell the perceptions, attitudes, feelings, experiences, and behaviors of the participants, whom he referred to as *co-researchers*. We concur with Rogers on the value of phenomenological research.

## W E B S I T E S for Person-Centered Counseling

The Association for the Development of the Person Centered Approach (ADPCA) Home Page
www.adpca.org/

Carl Rogers
oldsci.eiu.edu/psychology/Spencer/Rogers.html

## REFERENCES

Axline, V. (1947). *Play therapy: The inner dynamics of childhood.* Boston: Houghton Mifflin.

Axline, V. (1964). *Dibs: In search of self.* Boston: Houghton Mifflin.

Carkhuff, R. (1973, March). *Human achievement, educational achievement, career achievement: Essential ingredients of elementary school guidance.* Paper presented at the National Elementary School Guidance conference, Louisville, KY.

Carkhuff, R. (1981, April). *Creating and researching community based helping programs.* Paper presented at the American Personnel and Guidance Association convention, St. Louis.

Combs, A. W. (1988). Some current issues for person-centered therapy. *Person-Centered Review, 3,* 263–276.

Follensbee, R. W. Jr., Draguns, J. G., & Danish, S. J. (1986). Impact of two types of counselor intervention on Black American, Puerto Rican, and Anglo-American analogue clients. *Journal of Counseling Psychology, 33,* 446–453.

Gordon, T. (1974). *Teacher effectiveness training.* New York: Wyden.

Graf, C. (1994). On genuineness and the person-centered approach: A reply to Quinn. *Journal of Humanistic Psychology, 34,* 90–96.

Griffith, M. (1997). Empowering techniques of play therapy: A method for working with sexually abused children. *Journal of Mental Health Counseling, 19,* 130–143.

Hayashi, S. (1992). The client-centered therapy and person-centered approach in Japan: Historical development, current status, and perspective. *Journal of Humanistic Psychology, 32,* 115–136.

Hayashi, S., Kuno, T., Osawa, M., Shimizu, M., & Suetake, Y. (1998). Client-centered therapy in Japan: Fujio Tomoda and Taoism. *Journal of Humanistic Psychology, 38,* 103–124.

Hill-Hain, A., & Rogers, C. (1988). A dialogue with Carl Rogers: Cross-cultural challenges of facilitating person-centered groups in South Africa. *Journal for Specialists in Group Work, 13,* 62–69.

Jenni, C. (1999). Psychologists in China: National transformation and humanistic psychology. *Journal of Humanistic Psychology, 39,* 26–47.

Johnson, L., McLeod, E. H., & Fall, M. (1997). Play therapy with labeled children in the schools. *Professional School Counseling, 1,* 31–34.

Kincade, E., & Evans, K. (1996). Counseling theories, process, and interventions within a multicultural context. In J. Delucia-Waack (Ed.), *Multicultural counseling competencies: Implications for training and practice* (pp. 89–112). Alexandria, VA: Association for Counselor Education and Supervision.

Landreth, G. L. (1991). *Play therapy: The art of the relationship*. Bristol, PA: Accelerated Development.

Landreth, G. L. (1993). Child-centered play therapy. *Elementary School Guidance and Counseling, 28,* 17–29.

Landreth, G. L., & Sweeney, D. S. (1997). Child-centered play therapy. In K. O'Connor & L. M. Braverman (Eds.), *Play therapy theory and practice: A comparative presentation* (pp. 17–46). New York: Wiley.

Moustakas, C. (1998). Relationship play therapy. http://www.aronson.com. Retrieved August 26, 2002.

Myers, S. (2000). Empathic listening: Reports on the experience of being heard. *Journal of Humanistic Psychology, 40,* 147–173.

Quinn, R. (1993). Confronting Carl Rogers: A developmental-interactional approach to person-centered therapy. *Journal of Humanistic Psychology, 33,* 6–23.

Radd, T. R. (1996). *The Grow with Guidance Manual,* ed. 2. Omaha: Grow with Guidance.

Radd, T. R. (2003). *Teaching and counseling for today's world: Pre-K-12 and beyond.* Omaha: Grow with Guidance.

Rogers, C. R. (1939). *The clinical treatment of the problem child.* Boston: Houghton Mifflin.

Rogers, C. R. (1942). *Counseling and psychotherapy.* Boston: Houghton Mifflin.

Rogers, C. R. (1951). *Client-centered therapy.* Boston: Houghton Mifflin.

Rogers, C. R. (1965). *Client-centered therapy: Its current practice, implications, and theory.* Boston: Houghton Mifflin.

Rogers, C. R. (1977). *Carl Rogers on personal power: Inner strength and its revolutionary impact.* New York: Delacorte.

Rogers, C. R. (1983). *Freedom to learn for the 80's.* Columbus, OH: Merrill.

Rogers, C. R. (1985). Toward a more human science of the person. *Journal of Humanistic Psychology, 25,* 7–24.

Rogers, C. R. (1992). The necessary and sufficient conditions of therapeutic personality change. *Journal of Consulting and Clinical Psychology, 60,* 827–832.

Rogers, C. R. (1994). Rogers's quote. *Journal of Humanistic Education and Development, 32,* 189.

Rogers, C. R. (1995). What understanding and acceptance mean to me. Illinois Personnel and Guidance Association Meeting (1956, Urbana, IL). *Journal of Humanistic Psychology, 35,* 7–22.

Shostrom, E. (Producer). (1965). *Three approaches to psychotherapy* [Film]. Orange, CA: Psychological Films.

Siebert, A. (2000). How non-diagnostic listening led to a rapid "recovery" from paranoid schizophrenia: What is wrong with psychiatry? *Journal of Humanistic Psychology, 40,* 34–58.

Soloman, L. N. (1990). Carl Rogers' efforts for world peace. *Person-Centered Review, 5,* 39–56.

Stipsits, R., & Hutterer, R. (1989). The person-centered approach in Austria. *Person-Centered Review, 4,* 475–487.

Usher, C. H. (1989). Recognizing cultural bias in counseling theory and practice: The case of Rogers. *Journal of Multicultural Counseling and Development, 17,* 62–71.

Waxer, P. H. (1989). Cantonese versus Canadian evaluation of directive and non-directive therapy. *Canadian Journal of Counseling, 23,* 263–271.

# Chapter 7

# Gestalt Therapy

*Making mental connections is our most crucial learning
tool, the essence of human intelligence: to forge links; to
go beyond the given; to see patterns, relationship, context.*
—Marilyn Ferguson

*I learned to make my mind large, as the universe
is large, so that there is room for paradoxes.*
—Maxine Hong Kingston

## FRITZ PERLS

Fritz Perls's estranged wife, Laura, once referred to him as half prophet and half bum, and Perls considered this description accurate. In his autobiography, *In and Out the Garbage Pail* (1971), Perls wrote that, at the age of 75, he liked his reputation of being both a dirty old man and a guru. Unfortunately, he continued, the first reputation was on the wane and the second ascending.

Born in a Jewish ghetto on the outskirts of Berlin on July 8, 1893, Friedrich Salomon Perls was the third child of Amelia Rund and Nathan Perls. He later Anglicized his first name to Frederick but is remembered more commonly as Fritz.

Perls disliked his eldest sister, Else. He thought of her as a clinger and was uncomfortable in her presence. Else also had severe eye trouble, and Perls disliked the thought that he might have to take care of her someday. He did not mourn much when he heard of her death in a concentration camp. Shepard (1975) speculated that Perls resented the extra attention and favor his mother offered Else because of her partial blindness. He did seem to like his second sister, Grete.

After a difficult first few weeks of life, Perls seems to have led a happy and healthy life for his first 9 years. About the age of 10, Perls became rebellious. His parents were having bitter fights, and his father was away from home quite often. Perls described himself as mother loving, ambitious, loving the arts, and hating his father. He described his father as hating Amelia and loving other women. Perls began to doubt his paternity and suspected that his biological father was a much-respected uncle; this question remained open for Fritz until his death. His marriage was not much happier than his childhood, although he and Laura remained married and worked together in the development of Gestalt therapy. Perls came to realize that the roles of husband and father gave him little satisfaction.

Perls first attended school at the Humanistic Gymnasium in 1910. From his late teens through his university schooling, Perls studied and acted with the Reinhard School of Drama, earning money to pay for most of his education. He earned his M.D. degree from the Friedrich Wilhelm University in 1921. He was in psychoanalysis with Karen Horney, Clara Happel, and Wilhelm Reich and studied with Helene Deutsch at the Psychoanalytic Institute in Vienna.

After some hard times in Europe, Perls found success as a training analyst in Johannesburg, South Africa. There he founded the South African Institute for Psychoanalysis in 1934. He learned to fly and got his pilot's license. In 1936, Perls flew to Czechoslovakia to deliver a paper to the Psychoanalytic Congress. He met with his hero, Sigmund Freud, but was given only a cool reception—a brief 4-minute audience while he stood in Freud's doorway. Perls experienced another disappointment when most of the other analysts gave his paper an icy reception. From then on, Perls challenged the assumptions and directions of Freud and the psychoanalysts. In his final years, many people began to listen. Perls thought he had four main "unfinished situations" in his life: not being able to sing well, never having made a parachute jump, never having tried skin diving, and never having had the opportunity to show Freud his mistakes.

Perls spent 12 years in South Africa, during which time he formulated all the basic ideas underlying what he would later call Gestalt therapy. At 53, he moved his family to New York, where the "formal birth" of Gestalt therapy took place. The people involved debated what to call the new theory. Perls held out for *Gestalt,* a German term that cannot be translated exactly into English, but the meaning of the concept can be explained as:

> a form, a configuration or a totality that has, as a unified whole, properties which cannot be derived by summation from the parts and their relationships. It may refer to physical structures, to physiological and psychological functions, or to symbolic units. (English & English, 1958, p. 225)

In late 1951, Perls's *Gestalt Therapy: Excitement and Growth in the Human Personality* was published. Perls is listed as one of the authors, although Ralph Hefferline wrote nearly all of the first half of the book and Paul Goodman the second. Perls's other writings included *Ego, Hunger, and Aggression: The Beginnings of Gestalt Therapy* (1969a), *Gestalt Therapy Verbatim* (1969b), *The Gestalt Approach and Eye Witness to Therapy* (1973), *Gestalt Is: A Collection of Articles about Gestalt Therapy and Living* (1975), and, with Patricia Baumgardner, *Gifts from Lake Cowichan and Legacy from Fritz* (1975).

At first, the new therapy had almost no impact. Perls began traveling to cities such as Cleveland, Detroit, Toronto, and Miami to run groups for professionals and laypeople interested in the new idea. As he traveled throughout the United States, he discovered that he was received far better on the road than he was in

New York. After 10 years in New York, Perls decided to leave the city—and his wife—for the warmth of Miami. Laura Perls's interpretation of Fritz's reason for leaving was that he was not the leading psychotherapist—or even the leading Gestaltist—in New York.

Miami was very important to Perls because there he met "the most significant woman in my life," Marty Fromm. In Florida he also found LSD and became involved in the drug subculture. He then moved to California in 1964, eventually Big Sur, where he became widely known. At the Esalen Institute, he had to compete with people such as Virginia Satir, Bernard Gunther, and Will Schutz. Perls contended that the techniques Gunther and Schutz employed used other people's ideas and offered "instant joy." Perls, who opposed quick cures and respected only originality, established his own Gestalt Institute of Canada at Cowichan on Vancouver Island in British Columbia in 1969.

Nine months after the center in Canada was begun, Fritz Perls died. An autopsy disclosed advanced cancer of the pancreas. Perls died as he had lived. On the last evening of his life, March 14, 1970, Perls was sitting on the edge of his bed in the intensive care unit getting ready to light a cigarette. His nurse rushed in, took his cigarettes and lighter, and said, "Dr. Perls, you can't smoke in here." Fritz glared at her, said, "Nobody tells Fritz Perls what to do," fell back on his bed, and died.

Perls viewed Gestalt theory as being in progress at the time of his death. He thought that theory development, like human development, was a process of becoming. He was not one to close the book on his theory and treat it as gospel. Rather, Perls revised the theory to fit his observations of human behavior.

## THE NATURE OF PEOPLE

According to Gestalt theory, the most important areas of concern are the thoughts and feelings people are experiencing at the moment. Normal, healthy behavior occurs when people act and react as total organisms. Many people fragment their lives, distributing their concentration and attention among several variables and events at one time. The results of such fragmentation can be seen in an ineffective living style, with outcomes ranging from low productivity to serious accidents. The Gestalt view of human nature is positive: People are capable of becoming self-regulating beings who can achieve a sense of unity and integration in their lives.

Perls (1969b) saw the person as a total organism—not just as the brain. His saying that people would be better off losing their minds and coming to their senses meant that our bodies and feelings are better indicators of the truth than our words, which we use to hide the truth from ourselves. Body signs such as headaches, rashes, neck strain, and stomach pains may indicate that we need to change our behavior. Perls believed that awareness alone can be curative. With full awareness, a state of organismic self-regulation develops, and the total person takes control.

Mentally healthy people can maintain their awareness without being distracted by the various environmental stimuli that constantly vie for our attention. Such people can fully and clearly experience their own needs and the environmental alternatives for meeting them. Healthy people still experience their share of inner conflicts and frustrations, but, with their higher levels of concentration and awareness, they can solve their problems without complicating them with fantasy elaborations. They likewise resolve conflicts with others when it is possible and otherwise dismiss them. People with high levels of awareness of their needs and their environment know which problems and conflicts are resolvable and which are not. In Perls's theory, the key to successful adjustment is the development of personal responsibility—responsibility for one's life and response to one's environment. Much of the Perls's doctrine is summarized in his famous Gestalt Prayer:

> *I do my thing and you do your thing.*
> *I am not in this world to live up to your expectations,*
> *And you are not in this world to live up to mine.*
> *You are you and I am I*
> *And if by chance we find each other, it's beautiful.*
> *If not, it can't be helped. (Perls, 1969b, p. 4)*

The healthy person focuses sharply on one need (the figure) at a time while relegating other needs to the background. When the need is met—or the Gestalt is closed or completed—it is relegated to the background, and a new need comes into focus (becomes the figure). The smoothly functioning figure–ground relationship characterizes the healthy personality. The dominant need of the organism at any time becomes the foreground figure, and the other needs recede, at least temporarily, into the background. The foreground figure is the need that presses most sharply for satisfaction, whether the need is to preserve life or is related to less physically or psychologically vital areas. For individuals to be able to satisfy their needs, close the Gestalt, and move on to other things, they must be able to determine what they need, and they must know how to manipulate themselves and their environment. Even purely physiological needs can be satisfied only through the interaction of the organism and the environment (Perls, 1975).

Perls defined neurotic people as those who try to attend to too many needs at one time and, as a result, fail to satisfy any one need fully. Neurotic people also use their potential to manipulate others to do for them what they have not done for themselves. Rather than running their own lives, they turn them over to those who will take care of their needs. In summary, people cause themselves additional problems by not handling their lives appropriately in the following six categories:

1. Lacking contact with the environment: People may become so rigid that they cut themselves off from others or from resources in the environment.

2. Confluence: People may incorporate too much of themselves into others or incorporate so much of the environment into themselves that they lose touch with where they are. Then the environment takes control.

3. Unfinished business: People may have unfulfilled needs, unexpressed feelings, or unfinished situations that clamor for their attention. (This situation may manifest itself in dreams.)

4. Fragmentation: People may try to discover or deny a need, such as to show aggression. The inability to find and obtain what one needs may be the result of fragmenting one's life.

5. Topdog/underdog: People may experience a split in their personalities between what they think they "should" do (topdog) and what they "want" to do (underdog).

6. Polarities (dichotomies): People tend to flounder at times between existing, natural dichotomies in their lives, such as body–mind, self–external world, emotional-real, infantile-mature, biological-cultural, poetry–prose, spontaneous-deliberate, personal-social, love–aggression, and unconscious-conscious. Much of everyday living seems to be involved in resolving conflicts posed by these competing polarities.

Assagioli (1965) identified five types of polarities:

1. Physical: masculinity–femininity and parasympathetic-sympathetic nervous system
2. Emotional: pleasure–pain, excitement–depression, love–hate
3. Mental: parent–child, eros (feeling)–logos (reason), topdog–underdog
4. Spiritual: intellectual doubt–dogmatism
5. Interindividual: man–woman, black-white, Christian–Jew

## THEORY OF COUNSELING

An adaptation of Perls's system to counseling children should incorporate the five layers of neuroses proposed by Perls (1971). Perls devised these five layers to depict how people fragment their lives and prevent themselves from succeeding and maturing. The five layers form a series of counseling stages, or benchmarks, for the counseling process; in fact, they could be considered as five steps to a better Gestalt way of life.

1. The phony layer: Many people are trapped in trying to be what they are not. The phony layer is characterized by many conflicts that are never resolved.

2. The phobic layer: As people become aware of their phony games, they become aware of their fears that maintain the games. This experience is often frightening.

3. The impasse layer: This is the layer people reach when they shed the environmental support of their games and find they do not know a better way to cope with their fears and dislikes. People often become stuck here and refuse to move on.

4. The implosive layer: People become aware of how they limit themselves, and they begin to experiment with new behaviors within the counseling setting.

5. The explosive layer: If experiments with new behaviors are successful outside the counseling setting, people can reach the explosive layer, where they find much unused energy that had been tied up in maintaining a phony existence.

Perls believed that progress through the five layers of neuroses is best achieved by observing how psychological defenses might be associated with muscular position, or what he called *body armor.* He believed the client's body language would be a better indicator of the truth than the client's words and that awareness of hidden material could be facilitated by acting out feelings. Perls asked people to project their thoughts and feelings upon empty chairs representing significant people in their lives. People were often asked to play several roles in attempting to identify sources of personal conflict. Perls expanded on Rogers's idea of feedback as a therapeutic agent by including body posture, voice tone, eye movements, feelings, and gestures.

Gestalt therapists emphasize direct experiences. They focus on achieving awareness of the here and now and block the client in any attempt to break out of this awareness. As an experiential approach, Gestalt therapy is not concerned with symptoms and analysis but rather with total existence and integration. Integration and maturation, according to Perls, are never-ending processes directly related to a person's awareness of the here and now. A "Gestalt" is formed in a person as a new need arises. If a need is satisfied, the destruction of that particular Gestalt is achieved, and new Gestalts can be formed. This concept is basic in Gestalt therapy. Incomplete Gestalts are referred to as "unfinished situations."

Perls (1969b) wrote that the aim of his therapy was to help people help themselves to grow up—to mature, take charge of their lives, and become responsible for themselves. The central goal in Gestalt therapy is deeper awareness, which promotes a sense of living fully in the here and now. Other goals include teaching people to assume responsibility for themselves and facilitating their achievement of personal integration. These goals are consistent with those of most counseling systems.

The aim of integration is to help people become systematic, whole persons whose inner state and behavior match so that little energy is wasted within the system. Such integration allows people to give their full attention and energy to meeting their needs appropriately. The ultimate measure of success in Gestalt therapy is the extent to which clients grow in awareness, take responsibility for their actions, and move from environmental support to self-support.

## COUNSELING METHOD

The function of the Gestalt counselor is to facilitate the client's awareness in the "now." Awareness is the capacity to focus, to attend, and to be in touch with the now. The Gestalt counselor is an aggressive therapist who frustrates the learner's attempts to break out of the awareness of here and now. The counselor stops client's attempts to retreat into the past or jump into the future by relating the content to the immediate present.

Miller (1989) pointed out that Perls often used sarcasm, humor, drama, and shock to rouse people from neurosis. For Perls, Gestalt therapy was a search for a workable solution in the present. The counselor's job is to assist the client in experimenting with authentic new behaviors rather than to explain and maintain the unhelpful or harmful behaviors of the past. Dolliver (1991), attacking "inconsistencies" in Perls's philosophy and style in the often-reviewed *Three Approaches to Psychotherapy* (Shostrom, 1965), concluded that none of the counselor's objectives in Miller's statement were met with Gloria. Actually, after viewing the Gloria interviews with Rogers, Perls, and Ellis, it is fairly obvious that Perls is the only one of the three therapists who is successful in getting Gloria to deal with her core issue of trying to please others by being the person she thinks others want her to be. Her lifestyle was a textbook, phony layer of neuroses. Perls, confronting Gloria with the inconsistencies in her verbal and nonverbal behavior, was able to penetrate her well-defended lifestyle of playing roles she thought others would prefer to the actual person she was trying to conceal. Basically, the point of Gestalt therapy is to treat the client's lifestyle rather than fragments of the client's life. To Perls, spending time talking with Gloria about her daughter, father, ex-husband, boyfriends, and transference issues would be like trying to put a jigsaw puzzle together, one piece at a time, without looking at the picture of the completed puzzle before starting. Perls wanted to work with the whole Gestalt person, not fragments of the person's life.

The general reaction students have to watching Perls working with Gloria is, first, they cannot visualize themselves counseling a client in the same confrontational manner. Second, they do not see a counseling framework or guideline, such as those provided in reality therapy, solution-focused brief counseling, and rational emotive behavior therapy. However, they do become interested in various Gestalt methods that help clients work through impasses in their personal development. In many ways, these Gestalt interventions are breakthrough mechanisms that help clients reframe their problems into manageable projects, resolve decision-making conflicts, and find a reasonable balance between taking too much or too little responsibility in their lives. Descriptions of these and other Gestalt interventions follow. Miller and others, no doubt, disagree, and the controversy over the film will most likely continue well into the 21st century. Fritz Perls—in person or on film—never left anyone feeling neutral; he made everyone think and react.

## Gestalt Techniques

Several language, game, and fantasy methods may be used to maintain the present-time orientation of the counseling interview. We have used some of the following techniques with 5- to 12-year-old children, as well as with adolescents and adults.

### "I" language

Encourage the use of the word *I* when the client uses a generalized *you* when talking, for example, "*You* know how it is when *you* can't understand math and the teacher gets on *your* back." When *I* is substituted for *you,* the message becomes,

"*I* know how it is when *I* can't understand math and the teacher gets on *my* back." The client tries on such substitutions of *I* for *you* like a pair of shoes to see how they fit. "I" language helps children take responsibility for their feelings, thoughts, and behaviors.

### Substituting Won't for Can't

Again, the client tries on the "shoes" for comfort, substituting "I *won't* pass math" for "I *can't* pass math." How much of the responsibility the child will own is the question to be answered.

### Substituting What and How for Why

"*How* do you feel about what you have just done?" "*What* are you doing with your foot as we talk about your behavior?"

### No Gossiping

If the child must talk about someone not present in the room, let the talk, all in the present tense, be directed to an empty chair. For example, the child might say, "I think you treat me unfairly, Ms. Clark. I wish you would be as nice to me as you are to the other kids." The child can then move to the other chair and answer for Ms. Clark. "Joan, I would find it easier to like you if you would be more helpful to me during the day." The dialogue between Joan and Ms. Clark would continue until the child finished her complaint and the anticipated responses from her teacher. Person-to-person dialogues not only update the material into the present but also increase the child's awareness of the problem. Side benefits include a better picture of the situation for the counselor and rehearsal time for the child, who may wish to discuss the problem later with the teacher. Some appreciation for the teacher's side of the conflict may also emerge from the dialogue.

### Changing Questions into Statements

This method has the effect of helping children to be more authentic and direct in expressing their thoughts and feelings. For example, rather than asking, "Don't you think I should stop hanging around those guys?" the child should say, "I think I should stop hanging around those guys" or "I think you want me to stop hanging around those guys." Perls believed that most questions are phony in that they are really disguised statements.

## Taking Responsibility

Clients are asked to fill in sentence blanks as another way of examining personal responsibility for the way they manage their lives. For example, "Right now I'm feeling _____, and I take _____ percent responsibility for how I feel." The exercise is quite an eye opener for those clients who tend to view outside sources as the total cause of their good and bad feelings.

## Incomplete Sentences

These exercises, like the exercise on taking responsibility, help clients become aware of how they help and hurt themselves. For example, "I help myself when I _____" or "I block or hurt myself when I _____."

## Bipolarities

Perls applies the term *differential thinking* to the concept of thinking in terms of opposites. Much of everyday life appears to be spent resolving conflicts posed by competing polarities, such as "I should" versus "I want" when one is confronted with a difficult decision.

*Topdog Versus Underdog.* One of the most common bipolarities is what Perls (1969b) labeled *topdog* and *underdog*. The topdog is righteous, authoritarian, and knows best. The topdog is a bully and works with "you should" and "you should not." The underdog manipulates by being defensive or apologetic, wheedling, and playing crybaby. The underdog works with "I want" and makes excuses such as "I try hard" and "I have good intentions." The underdog is cunning and usually gets the better of the topdog because the underdog position appeals to the pleasure-seeking side of our personality.

Two chairs can be used to help children resolve "I want" versus "I should" debates. Label one chair topdog (I should) and the other chair underdog (I want). Children are asked to present their best "I should" argument while sitting in the topdog chair and facing the empty underdog chair. Upon completing the first "I should" point, the child moves to the underdog chair to counter with an "I want" argument. The debate continues back and forth until the child completes all arguments from both points of view. Processing the activity often reveals in which chair (or on which side of the argument) the child feels that the greatest integration of shoulds and wants occurs, thus allowing the client to have the best of both sides.

The topdog–underdog technique works for individuals and groups. To use the technique in a group, the counselor can divide the clients into two subgroups, the topdogs and the underdogs. The topdog group members list reasons they *should* do a certain thing, while the underdog group members think of reasons they *want* to do something. The lists generally lead to much discussion. Children respond very well to this activity.

The best outcomes from the topdog–underdog debate occur when children can identify areas in their lives where the "I shoulds" and "I wants" agree, for example, "I love to read, and I should read." These synergistic solutions help children integrate the polarities in their lives.

*The Empty Chair Technique.*  The Gestalt technique of the empty chair is often used to resolve a conflict between people or within a person (Paivio & Greenberg, 1995). The child can sit in one chair, playing his or her own part; then the child can sit in the other chair, playing out a projection of what the other person is saying or doing in response. Similarly, a child may sit in one chair to discuss the pros of making a decision and then argue the cons of the decision while sitting in the opposite chair.

For example, Sharon was having trouble deciding whether to tell of her friend's involvement in destruction of property. She thought her friend had behaved wrongly and should not let other children take the blame for the incident, yet she was reluctant to tattle on the friend and get her in trouble. The counselor suggested that Sharon sit in one chair and talk about what would happen if she did tell on her friend and then move to the other chair to describe what would happen if she did not. The technique helped Sharon to look at the consequences of both acts and make her decision. In this instance, Sharon decided to talk with her friend to give her the opportunity to confess and make amends for the damaged property.

The empty chair technique is a powerful intervention for working with clients of all ages who are in conflict with a third party who is not present in the session. For example, the conflict might be with a spouse, sibling, teacher, parent, friend, or boss. Rather than having clients talk on and on about how awful this other person is, the client is asked to speak directly to the offending person as if she or he were sitting in the empty chair. Then, because the client knows this person well, the client is asked to sit in the empty chair and reply the way the offending person would respond. The back-and-forth dialogue continues until clients finish expressing all of their thoughts and feelings on the subject.

Three productive things happen with this version of empty chair. First, the counselor gets a better, firsthand account of the dynamics of the relationship. Second, the client may develop some empathy for the offending party's position, and third, the client receives some rehearsal practice for confronting the absent person. The counselor might even model some possible methods of confronting the third party by taking the client's role and having the client play the part of the other person. Then, the client can practice confronting the offending third person, with the counselor taking the role of that person. This method has been particularly useful in helping students complain effectively to their teachers when they have questions about their grades.

The empty chair method has also been useful with clients of all ages who have "unfinished business" with a departed loved one. They talk to their lost loved one as though that person were sitting in the chair and, in many cases, sit in the empty chair and reply as they "know" this person would reply. For example, a son might say to his deceased father, "Dad, I always wanted to tell you how much I loved you, and I was never able to do this." Speaking for his father from the other chair, the reply is almost always, "Son, you didn't have to say it. I knew all along that you loved me." Counselors have only to witness such an event one time to "see" the heavy burden of guilt rise from the shoulders of their client.

Alexander and Harman (1988) reported a successful application of a Gestalt approach to group counseling with middle school classmates of a student who committed suicide. Using the empty chair, writing, and artwork, children said goodbye and discussed their own fears and anxieties about suicide.

In a variation of the empty chair, a problem can be explored in an individual or group situation by introducing the empty chair as a hypothetical person with behaviors and characteristics similar to those of the child and his or her particular problem. It is sometimes easier for children to discuss a hypothetical child and how this child feels or could change than to discuss their own feelings and behaviors. While discussing an imagined person, children learn about themselves.

The empty chair method is useful for angry children, who can talk to the angry self in another chair and find out why they are so upset. It can also serve as projection for the child who is afraid of an ugly monster. The child can become the monster and allow that creature to explain its motives for scaring children. Retroflection also may be used to help students express difficult or frightening thoughts and feelings. Retroflection is giving voice to that part of the body that is exhibiting muscular tension. The counselor may ask a child who tightens up his or her mouth to say what the mouth would like to say.

Engle and Holliman (2002) write that the expression of emotional experiences allows for the formation of a new Gestalt when people are in conflict over opposing values or over what they should do versus what they want to do. Experiments such as the empty chair dialogue are useful in developing new schematic structures for bringing the conflict into focus so that they can be integrated into a workable solution. Greenberg and Malcolm (2002) present a six-step method for using the empty chair. The intervention begins with clients addressing an individual with whom they have unfinished business, followed by clients responding as they believe the other person would respond. The dialogue continues until clients reach a point of resolution in completing the unfinished business, which, in effect, moves the issue of "unfinished" business from figure to ground in the client's field of awareness.

## My Greatest Weakness

In another exercise, clients are asked to name their greatest weakness and write a short paragraph on how this weakness is really their greatest strength, for example, "My greatest weakness is procrastination, but I'll never give it up because by putting things off I create the motivation I need for completing unpleasant tasks."

Once clients realize that their greatest weakness may, in fact, be the greatest strength they have going for them, they begin to realize that they control the weakness rather than vice versa. Clients also realize that the counselor who uses this technique is not pushing them to fix their "weakness." Maybe all that is needed is to just manage the weakness more efficiently, such as by not procrastinating too long.

### *Resent, Demand, and Appreciate: The Integration of Opposing Thoughts, Feelings, and Beliefs*

Have your clients list the three people they are closest to and, for each of them, write one thing they resent about the person, one thing they demand, and one thing they appreciate. Such an exercise helps clients become more aware of the mixed feelings they have about others, how it is possible to resent and appreciate a person at the same time, and how opposing thoughts and feelings can be integrated.

The purpose of working with these bipolarities, or splits in the personality, is to bring each side into awareness so reorganization that does not exclude either side can take place. Gestalt therapy is directed toward making life easier by integrating the splits in existence; each side is necessary and has its place in the well-integrated personality.

| Name | I resent | I demand | I appreciate |
|------|----------|----------|--------------|
| John | that you don't spend enough time with me | more time | your company and friendship |
| Mary | | | |
| Sue | | | |

### *Fantasy Games for Creating Awareness*

Fantasy games can be great fun for children of all ages while enabling them to become aware of their feelings right now. As a group activity, the children choose an animal they would like to be and then move around as they think this animal would. The children sit down in pairs and discuss what they would feel if they were this particular animal. As a culmination of the activity, they write stories about how they would feel, think, and behave if they were actually the animal. By the end of the exercise, children should have a real awareness of how they feel and think and be able to discuss this with their counselor, teacher, or parents.

Fantasy games can be devised from almost any object or situation. The rosebush and wise-person fantasies are two favorites. In the first, the client pretends to be a rosebush and then considers the following points:

1. Type of bush—strong or weak?
2. Root system—deep or shallow?
3. Number of roses—too many or too few?

4. Number of thorns—too many or too few?
5. Environment—bad or good for growing?
6. Does your rosebush stand out?
7. Does it have enough room?
8. How does it get along with the other plants?
9. Does it have a good future?

The wise-person fantasy involves asking a fantasized source of wisdom one question, which the wise person ponders for a few minutes before answering—speaking through the client, of course. Both question and answer should add some awareness and understanding to the client's life. For example, a client might ask, "What should I do with my life?" and answer, as the wise person, "Develop all your talents and skills as much as you can."

Clients are asked to discuss their fantasies in depth with the counselor in individual sessions and with groups of two to four if a group is meeting. A good follow-up procedure for clients is to complete the statement "I learned that _____" after each exercise. The fantasy games are enhanced if clients lie down and participate in relaxation exercises before the experience and continue to lie down and relax in a comfortable spot during the fantasy exercises.

Heikkinen (1989) wrote a helpful article on reorienting clients from altered states of consciousness (ASC), used in Gestalt and other therapies, in a way that avoids uncomfortable aftereffects, such as unusual cognitive or emotional functioning and atypical body reactions. As clients may experience an ASC during activities such as the rosebush or wise-person fantasies, these activities should end with the counselor counting backward slowly from 10 or in the direction opposite to that used to reach the ASC. Imagining a walk up steps, a swim to the top of the lake, or a return from a journey is a useful method for reorienting clients. Directing clients in a group setting to look slowly around the area and become reacquainted with their environment is also effective.

## Dreamwork

Dreaming is a way of becoming aware of the world in the here and now. Because awareness is the dominant theme of Gestalt, dreaming and Gestalt seem to work well together. Dreaming is a guardian of one's existence because the content of dreams always relates to one's survival, well-being, and growth; therefore, Gestalt therapists have helped clients overcome impasses in their lives through serious consideration of dreams. The Gestalt approach to dreams is helpful not only to people suffering from dilemmas in their lives but also to the average "healthy" person. Most people spend many of their waking hours out of touch with the here and now by worrying compulsively about the future or by doting on memories of failure or past pleasures.

Spontaneity is an important feature of Gestalt therapy, and, according to Perls, dreams are the most spontaneous expression of the existence of the human being. The Gestalt approach is concerned with integration rather than analysis of dreams.

Such integration involves consciously reliving a dream, taking responsibility for being the objects and people in the dream, and becoming aware of the messages the dream holds. According to Perls, all parts of the dream are fragments of the dreamer's personality that must be pieced together to form a whole. These projected fragments must be reowned; thus, hidden potential that appears in the dream is also to be reowned. As clients play the parts of all the objects and persons in the dream, they may become more aware of the message the dream holds. They may act out the dream until two conflicting roles emerge—for instance, the top-dog and the underdog. This want-should conflict is essentially the conflict from which the dreamer suffers. Gestaltists believe that dreams have hidden existential messages that, once discovered, can fill the voids in people's personalities. In the Gestalt system, dreamwork holds many possibilities for solving the problems of life or for developing a better self-awareness.

Basically, the Gestalt method for working with dreams requires clients to describe the dream and then list all the parts of the dream, including people, objects, animals, buildings, rooms, and trees. Clients are asked what, if anything, the dream might mean to them. Interpretation is left to the client, based on the philosophy that to interpret the client's dream for the client would suggest that the counselor would know the client better than the client does. Next, the client is asked to speak or give voice to each part of the dream, much like an animated movie in which trees and animals talk. Each object in the dream offers clients the opportunity to project parts of their personality onto that object. For example, a client might say, "I am the bedroom in Harriet's house and I like being her bedroom. She is very particular about keeping me clean, neat, and orderly." These projections are done for all of the things in the client's dream. The counselor might suggest that Harriet's bedroom have a conversation with Harriet's house and ask the client to role-play the dialogue for such a conversation. Following the talking exercise for each object in the dream, the client is again asked for an interpretation of the dream. It may come in the form of a best guess. Regardless of the interpretation or best guess about the dream's meaning, the client is not likely to have this dream again. This method has a way of finishing up unfinished business that retires the dream to the background of the client's experience. We have found this method to yield spectacular results in ending unpleasant recurring dreams and nightmares. The therapist's task in the integration of dreams is to concentrate on what clients are avoiding in their present existence and to help them act out painful situations and reintegrate the alienated parts of their personality into their lives.

## Gestalt Play Therapy

Carroll and Oaklander (1997) explained that Gestalt therapy is a humanistic and process-oriented approach. The concern of the therapy is the integrated functioning of all aspects of the person so that senses, body, emotions, and intellect are well coordinated in a creative adjustment. They stated that the child's capacity to represent experiences in symbolic fashion allows a self-reflective manner that helps the child develop a greater sense of self. Oaklander described (Campbell, 1993) the process of Gestalt play therapy as like a dance that sometimes the counselor leads and other times the child leads. Meeting the child where she or he is and suggesting but not pushing are Oaklander's admonitions for the counselor.

She also explained the important concept of *contact* in Gestalt play therapy. Contact is having the ability to be completely present in a situation by using one's senses that connect with the environment, such as looking, listening, and smelling. Being aware of feelings and using the intellect are also part of making contact. Recognizing what is being done and how it is being done is the contacting process. When children are anxious or troubled, they do not use their senses fully. They block emotions and inhibit contact. Gestalt play therapy includes exercises and experiences that involve the senses and the expression of feelings. Oaklander's book *Windows to Our Children: A Gestalt Therapy Approach to Children and Adolescents* (1988) contains examples of these exercises in which she uses various creative activities and explains how they work. Enhancing the self increases a person's ability to be in contact. The goal of the therapy is to restore the child's natural functioning and self-regulatory processes. Experiencing the contacting process leads to integration, choice, and change. Oaklander (1978, 1993) also adapted several Gestalt techniques for children. She recommended projection through art and storytelling as a way of increasing the child's self-awareness and cited fantasy and imagery, such as the wise-person fantasy, as good ways to tap intuitive thought in children and adults. Oaklander has also frequently used the empty chair method as a helpful way to handle unfinished business, frustration, and anger.

### Confidence Courses for Play Therapy

This gentle form of obstacle course, designed to build confidence, uses combinations of pit jumps, incline balances, boxes, barrels, ladder climbs, rope slides, and the like. (Children can also be involved in constructing such a course.) As children attain better motor coordination and balance, they form better self-images, a feeling of mastery, and an "I can do it" attitude about themselves. They begin to feel they can solve problems and deal with their world competently.

## CASE STUDIES

Many short-term counseling sessions can be conducted with children using the empty chair technique. For example, consider the following method for working with anger:

*Child:* I hate my dad. He's mean. I hate his guts.

*Counselor:* Let's pretend your dad is sitting in that empty chair. What do you want to say to him? You can walk over there and say whatever you want.

*Child:* Get off my back! Leave me alone! I cleaned my room just as good as I could.

*Counselor:*   Now sit in the other chair. Pretend to be your dad.

*Child:*   I've told you and told you that this room looks like a pigpen.

*Counselor:*   Now be yourself again.

*Child:*   I cleaned my room good, Dad! Then you came in and said it still isn't good enough. Nothing was left out in the room but my toys!

*Counselor:*   Now be your dad.

*Child:*   This is the last time I'm telling you, Son. The room better be finished when I get back. That means toys, too.

*Counselor:*   Now be you.

*Child:*   You don't care about me! You don't care about how I feel. You just worry about the house being messed up. You get mad when I get out my toys. Kids are supposed to have toys! It's MY ROOM! Quit buggin' me! [accompanied by much nonverbal expression of anger as well as the overt angry verbal content]

The child has expressed his strong thoughts that his room should be his territory, that it should be okay to have his toys out. A global "hatred" for the father has been reduced to anger about a specific recurring problem (the differing standards for the room held by the parent and the child). After release of the built-up anger, some problem solving could achieve a compromise about the room situation.

Another sample counseling session involves the topdog–underdog debate, using an empty chair for each "dog." This technique is useful when the child has a decision-making problem. Most decision-making problems involve a debate between the inner voice of "I should do . . ." (topdog) versus "Yes, but I want to do . . ." (underdog). An empty chair is assigned to each point of view.

### Identification of the Problem

Susan is experiencing a conflict over whether to live with her mother or with her father when their divorce is final.

### Individual and Background Information

Susan Adams is a 10-year-old in the fourth grade. Her mother and father are getting a divorce, and she has to decide whether to live with her mother or her father. Susan is the second of three children. This marriage was the second for Susan's mother and the first for Susan's father. Her elder brother is not her father's son. Both parents work in factory jobs, but their income seems to be limited by the fact that Susan's father spends most of his paycheck on alcohol. Susan is an average student in school; she is quiet and has never been a behavior problem. She gets along well with her peers at school. Susan's physical health is good, but she has a vision problem that requires a new pair of glasses, which her parents say they do not have the money to buy.

*Transcript*

*Counselor:* Susan, we have the next 30 minutes for our talk. Where would you like to start?

*Susan:* Well, you know my problem about having to decide whether to live with Mom or Daddy after their divorce is final. I just don't know what I'm going to do.

*Counselor:* I know that when we talked about this the other day, you were feeling really upset about this situation of having to choose between your mom and dad. I can tell you still feel this way.

*Susan:* Yes, I do. I did all the things we talked about—like talking to both of them. That made it even harder to decide because they both want me. I still don't know what to do. I wish they would stop the divorce.

*Counselor:* Well, it's a good feeling to know that they both want you, but a bad feeling to know you have to choose. You would really like to have them stay together.

*Susan:* Yes, I really would, but that's impossible! I've tried every way I can to keep them together.

*Counselor:* Susan, would you try an exercise with me that might help clarify your thinking about this decision?

*Susan:* I'll try anything to help.

*Counselor:* [explains and demonstrates the topdog–underdog technique] So, when you are in the topdog chair, you say, "I should . . ." and when you are in the underdog chair, you say, "I want. . . ." Okay?

*Susan:* Okay [goes to the topdog chair first].

*Topdog:* I should go with Daddy because he'll be all alone.

*Underdog:* Yes, but I want to stay with Mom because I hate to give up my room, and I want to stay with my sister.

*Topdog:* What is Daddy going to do without anyone to cook for him and clean house?

*Underdog:* Why can't he hire a maid, and I can visit him a lot, too?

*Topdog:* If I don't live with Daddy, he won't have anybody, because he doesn't want Jake, and Sally is too young to move away from Mom.

*Underdog:* Well, Daddy goes out and drinks a lot with his friends, and sometimes he gets sick and is not nice to be around when he gets drunk.

*Topdog:* I think I should take care of him when he gets sick.

*Underdog:* I think it is better not to be near him when he drinks. I would like to visit him when he is not drinking.

*Topdog:* How can I live with Mom and help Daddy, too?

*Underdog:* I just know things will be better if I live with Mom in my room and see Daddy as often as I can.

*Counselor:* Do you think you've finished with this argument, Susan?

*Susan:* Yes, I've said all I can think of.

*Counselor:* I'm wondering what you learned from doing this exercise.

*Susan:* Well, I think things will be better if I stay where I am with Mom. But I'll need to see a lot of Daddy—as much as I can. I love them both so much [starts to cry].

*Counselor:* I know this has to be a sad and rough time for you. It really hurts, doesn't it?

*Susan:* It sure does. I need to be brave about this and not let it make me so sad.

*Counselor:* Its okay to feel sad about this. You can always come in here to talk to me when you want to.

[Counselor terminates the interview and schedules another session for the next day.]

## CROSS-CULTURAL APPLICATIONS OF GESTALT THERAPY

Gestalt therapy has certain aspects that appeal to some cultures and others that the same cultures might find offensive. Gestalt therapy is directed more toward total lifestyle change than it is to individual problems that are mere pieces of the total puzzle that represents a person's life and style of interacting with the environment. Most people from all cultures coming to counseling for the purpose of getting help for specific problems are frustrated when they find the Gestalt counselor taking a global focus of examining the total picture rather than its fragments that define the presenting problem. In short, Gestalt counselors believe that teaching clients how to behave in an authentic, honest, and open manner will be sufficient for handling any problem that might arise. Having studied Chapter 15, the counselor should be prepared to meet the cultural expectations of each client.

Gestalt therapy is the most present-oriented therapy discussed in this book; however, old, unfinished business can be updated to the present by having clients confront their "problem" people in the empty chair. Even unfinished business with deceased people can be addressed with the empty chair method. Techniques such as the empty chair might present problems for clients from cultures where emotions are not expressed.

Gestalt therapy practitioners do not believe in victimhood. People are viewed as being responsible for how well they are handling their lives. The focus on individual responsibility may be more difficult for some cultures than it is for others. Gestalt therapists would argue that no matter how difficult personal circumstances might be, people are still responsible for finding ways to lift themselves out of an oppressive situation in which they might find themselves. Gestalt therapists would not quarrel with the concept of organizing a group or using any legal resource available for getting oneself out of the ditch. All of these issues raise the ethical question of the counselor's role when a client brings the baggage of some individual cultural ideas to counseling—and every culture has these. Does preservation of irrational cultural ideas take precedent over helping a client who might be suffering from trying to live by such ideas?

Specifically, people suffering from oppression might be put off by the Gestalt emphasis on individual responsibility. For instance, Native American clients may not like discounting the past. Asian clients might not appreciate the emphasis on confrontation and the expression of honest feelings. Clients from African cultures might appreciate the emphasis on the expression of true and honest feelings. Hispanic clients, like Asian clients, may not appreciate the emphasis on expression of feelings that could happen in Gestalt therapy.

Saner (1989) voiced concerns about possible cultural bias in U.S. Gestalt therapy. He suggested several ways to make Gestalt therapy valid across cultures: Drop the ethnocentric emphasis on the individual in favor of stressing reciprocal interaction by all participants in a social setting, use psychodrama in group therapy rather than the hot-seat method of individual therapy within the group setting, and incorporate contributions from other disciplines in Gestalt theory and practice.

In the end, it is the counselors' responsibility to be aware of possible difficulties clients from other cultures might have with the interventions and theories the counselor practices. Each client, regardless of cultural background, should be respected and treated as a unique individual.

Practitioners of Gestalt therapy and other methods of counseling would do well to adapt their counseling approach to fit the particular learning styles and worldviews of their clients. The traditional approaches to counseling have always been focused on the uniqueness of each client. This unique quality of each client is not to be lost in groups and cultural stereotyping. However, as Bingham, Porche-Burke, James, Sue, and Vasquez (2002) point out, counselors must avoid disrespecting the worldview of their clients, either from ignorance of their cultural norms or from insensitivity to their values. They remind us that there is no one way to conceptualize human behavior, no all-inclusive theory that captures and explains the experience of all diverse cultures, and no counseling method that has proven efficacy across all cultures.

## GESTALT THERAPY AND MANAGED HEALTH CARE

Managed healthcare administrators might have difficulty accepting the rather general goals of Gestalt therapy—general, that is, to the novice and layperson points of view that focus on counseling interventions with behavioral, measurable, and concrete goals, such as getting and holding a job, having one social date per week, running a mile each day, and making a B average in school. These goals, while quite laudable, represent to the Gestalt therapist mere pieces of the complicated jigsaw puzzle that makes up a person's life and the way that person reacts to the environment. Rather than examining each individual piece in a person's jigsaw puzzle, the Gestalt therapist prefers to work with the total person. What this means is that discussion of how to get a job will take a back seat to interacting with the counselor with the goal of teaching the client to interact with people in an open, authentic manner while discarding phony behavior designed to portray a personality different than the one the client is trying to cover up. The Gestalt counselor believes the key to solving day-to-day problems is to relate to others in an open, honest manner and to invest the energy, formerly used to play phony roles, into more productive activities, such as getting and holding employment. In addition, the Gestalt counselor trains clients to trust the feelings their brains are sending to their bodies. In other words, people need to give their attention to those feelings that are indicators they are about to do the right or wrong thing, make the right or wrong decision, stay in the right or wrong job, or stay in the right or wrong relationship. These global counseling outcome goals are more difficult to sell to managed care organizations. However, Harman (1996) wrote that there is definitely a future for the here-and-now approach to personal development as practiced by Gestalt counselors.

Because Gestalt techniques facilitate discovery, confrontation, and resolution of the client's major conflict, often in a dramatically short time, the inexperienced therapist, observer, or client might assume that Gestalt therapy offers an "instant cure." Even experienced counselors are tempted to push the client to a stance of self-support too fast, too soon. Group Gestalt therapy is common, but frequently it amounts to individual counseling in a group setting. Another hazard is the counselor's assumption of excessive responsibility for the direction of the group by too much activity, thus fostering client passivity and defeating the goal of client self-support. Extensive experience with Gestalt therapy may actually make clients less fit for or less adjusted to contemporary society; at the same time, however, they may be motivated to work toward changing the world into a more compassionate and productive milieu in which human beings can develop, work, and enjoy their full humanness.

As noted in Chapter 2 and by Anderson (2000), the key terms defining preferred treatments by managed care organizations include *brevity, accountability, low cost, quantifiable outcomes,* and *client satisfaction.* Gestalt counseling can compete well on cost and client satisfaction but not as well as other therapies on accountability, quantifiable outcomes, and brevity.

## SUMMARY

Caution is urged regarding the misuse of popular Gestalt techniques with fragile children, adolescents, and adults who cannot handle the emotional intensity some of the methods generate. Additional caution, patience, and sensitivity are also recommended regarding Gestalt counseling with severely disturbed or psychotic clients. Therapeutic activity should be limited to procedures that strengthen clients' contact with reality, their self-confidence, and their trust in the counselor and the counseling process. With trust established between counselor and client, Gestalt counseling can be directed toward working with the painful, unfinished business of past as well as current conflicts.

Greenberg (1989) echoed similar concerns about using traditional Gestalt therapy with people who have borderline personality disorder. He recommended interactive group therapy over talking to a dead parent in an empty chair and "hot-seat" confrontations. Therefore, the question of who should receive Gestalt therapy is as important as the skill, training, experience, and judgment of the therapist. A counselor who uses this approach must be neither afraid nor inept in allowing the client to follow through and finish the experience of grief, rage, fear, or joy. Without such skill, the counselor may leave the client vulnerable.

Another issue hinges on the questions of when, with whom, and in what situations Gestalt therapy should be used. In general, Gestalt therapy is most effective with overly socialized, restrained, constricted individuals. Less organized, more severely disturbed clients require long-term counseling. Limiting activities at first to those that strengthen a client's contact with reality is preferable to role-playing situations further removed from the here and now. Individuals whose problems lie in lack of impulse control, acting out, and delinquency require a different approach. For these people, Gestalt therapy could reinforce the activities that are causing the problems.

Misconceptions surround the use of Gestalt methods for quick and exciting results, whereas Gestalt therapy was developed as a lengthy, time-consuming process. Effective practitioners of Gestalt therapy use small steps to help clients heighten their own awareness. Too much awareness too soon can have an adverse effect on clients. Clients cannot be expected to drop elaborate defenses and "walk without these crutches" after just a few sessions. Living without defenses requires considerable rehearsal and practice within the therapy session.

Laura Perls (1992) discussed her concerns about the misconceptions surrounding Gestalt therapy. She noted that many therapists who had attended Fritz's workshops began to attach Gestalt therapy to whatever they happened to be working on at the time. People began holding workshops on such topics as sensitivity training and Gestalt therapy or transcendental meditation and Gestalt therapy. Laura Perls noted that Gestalt therapy has been useful in working with a variety of subject areas and client treatment programs. However, she pointed out that Fritz Perls realized that Gestalt methods were not effective in working with every type of disorder and would not work with people who had paranoid or schizoid disturbances.

Laura Perls discussed other misconceptions about Gestalt therapy. Contrary to popular belief, Gestalt therapy is not limited to treating the here-and-now aspects of the client's life. The focus of Gestalt therapy is on the here-and-now present occurring within the therapy session; however, a person's past and present life outside therapy is also valued by Gestalt therapists. Fritz Perls believed that the past is very real in defining our life experiences and memories.

Laura Perls reminded her readers that Fritz Perls thought that tension was too valuable to waste. Tension is an indicator that something in a person's life is not working or that some unfinished business needs attention. Yet, many therapists use Gestalt methods to rid their clients of tension. Tension, as a resource, can provide the motivation and energy to make adjustments and changes in one's life.

Perls seems to have done well in his attempt to establish the philosophy and practice of Gestalt therapy. The approach is well grounded in and consistent with the principles of human behavior. By removing the mystique of professional jargon, he made Gestalt therapy comprehensible to the general public. Many counselors, while choosing not to become true believers or disciples of Gestalt therapy, use many of the procedures reported in the Gestalt literature. Most notable among these techniques are the two-chair dialogue, visualization, fantasy, and projection.

## W E B S I T E S  for Gestalt Therapy

A Life Chronology of Fritz Perls
www.gestalt.org/fritz.htm

Association for the Advancement of Gestalt Therapy (AAGT) Homepage
www.aagt.org/

Behavior OnLine: An Introduction to Gestalt Therapy
www.behavior.net/gestalt.html

Gestalt Theory: Society for Gestalt Theory and Its Applications (GTA)
www.enabling.org/ia/gestalt/gerhards/

The Gestalt Therapy Page
www.gestalt.org/index.htm

## REFERENCES

Alexander, J., & Harman, L. (1988). One counselor's intervention in the aftermath of middle school student's suicide: A case study. *Journal of Counseling and Development, 66,* 283–285.

Anderson, C. (2000). Dealing constructively with managed care: Suggestions from an insider. *Journal of Mental Health Counseling, 22,* 343–353.

Assagioli, R. (1965). *Psychosynthesis.* New York: Viking.

Baumgardner, P., & Perls, F. (1975). *Gifts from Lake Cowichan and legacy from Fritz.* Palo Alto, CA: Science and Behavior Books.

Bingham, R. P., Porche-Burke, L., James, S., Sue, D. W., & Vasquez, M. J. T. (2002). Introduction: A report on the National Multicultural Conference and Summit II. *Cultural Diversity and Ethnic Minority Psychology* [online version], *8,* 75–87.

Campbell, C. A. (1993). Interview with Violet Oaklander, author of *Windows to Our Children. Elementary School Guidance and Counseling, 28,* 52–61.

Carroll, F., & Oaklander, V. (1997). Gestalt play therapy. In K. O'Connor & L. M. Braverman (Eds.), *Play therapy theory and practice: A comparative presentation* (pp. 184–203). New York: Wiley.

Dolliver, R. (1991). Perls with Gloria re-reviewed: Gestalt techniques and Perls's practices. *Journal of Counseling and Development, 69,* 299–304.

Engle, D., & Holliman, M. (2002). A Gestalt-experiential perspective on resistance. *Journal of Clinical Psychology, 58,* 175–183.

English, H., & English, A. (1958). *A comprehensive dictionary of psychological terms.* New York: Longmans, Green.

Greenberg, E. (1989). Healing the borderline. *Gestalt Journal, 12,* 11–55.

Greenberg, L. S., & Malcolm, W. (2002). Resolving unfinished business: Relating process to outcome. *Journal of Consulting and Clinical Psychology* [online version], *70,* 406–416.

Harman, R. (1996). Is there a future for the here and now? *Journal of Gestalt, 19,* 101–108.

Heikkinen, C. (1989). Reorientation from altered states: Please, more carefully. *Journal of Counseling and Development, 67,* 520–521.

Miller, M. (1989). Introduction to Gestalt therapy verbatim. *Gestalt Journal, 7,* 5–24.

Oaklander, V. (1978). *Windows to our children.* Moab, UT: Real People Press.

Oaklander, V. (1988). *Windows to our children: A Gestalt therapy approach to children and adolescents,* Highland, NY: Center for Gestalt Development.

Oaklander, V. (1993). From meek to bold: A case study of Gestalt therapy. In T. Kottman & C. Schaefer (Eds.), *Play therapy in action: A casebook for practitioners* (pp. 281–300). Northvale, NJ: Aronson.

Paivio, S., & Greenberg, L. (1995). Resolving "unfinished business": Efficacy of experimental therapy using empty chair dialogue. *Journal of Consulting and Clinical Psychology, 63,* 419–425.

Perls, F. (1969a). *Ego, hunger, and aggression: The beginnings of Gestalt therapy.* New York: Vintage.

Perls, F. (1969b). *Gestalt therapy verbatim.* Moab, UT: Real People Press.

Perls, F. (1971). *In and out the garbage pail.* New York: Bantam.

Perls, F. (1973). *The Gestalt approach and eye witness to therapy.* New York: Bantam.

Perls, F. (1975). *Gestalt is: A collection of articles about Gestalt therapy and living.* Moab, UT: Real People Press.

Perls, F., Hefferline, R., & Goodman, P. (1951). *Gestalt therapy: Excitement and growth in the human personality.* New York: Julian Press.

Perls, L. (1992). Concepts and misconceptions of Gestalt therapy. *Journal of Humanistic Psychology, 32,* 50–56.

Saner, R. (1989). Culture bias of Gestalt therapy: Made-in-U.S.A. *Gestalt Journal, 12,* 57–71.

Shepard, M. (1975). *Fritz.* New York: Saturday Review Press.

Shostrom, E. (Producer). (1965). *Three approaches to psychotherapy* [Film]. Orange, CA: Psychological Films.

# Chapter 8

# Rational-Emotive-Behavior Therapy and Cognitive-Behavior Therapy

*Our civilization is still in a middle stage, no longer wholly
guided by instinct, not yet wholly guided by reason.*
—Theodore Dreiser

*Nothing is so terrible as activity without thought.*
—Johann Wolfgang von Goethe

*We do not see things as they are; we see things as we are.*
—The Talmud

## ALBERT ELLIS

Albert Ellis is currently president of the Institute for Advanced Study in Rational Psychotherapy in New York, a community agency chartered by the regents of the State University of New York. He is widely known as the founder or developer of rational-emotive therapy, which he has renamed rational-emotive-behavior therapy (REBT) (Ellis, 1994a).

For the past five decades, Ellis has given individualized remedial instruction—what he calls *emotional education*—to several thousand adults, adolescents, and children. In addition, he has conducted group therapy with more than 3,000 adults and adolescents.

Ellis was born in Pittsburgh in 1913 and grew up in New York City. In spite of a difficult childhood, he earned a degree in business administration from the City University of New York in 1934. During the Depression he earned his living first by working with his brother in a business that located matching pants for still-usable suit coats, then as the personnel manager in a gift and novelty firm. Ellis's ambition was to write, which he did in his spare time. He collected material for two books on sexual adjustment that were eventually published: *The American Sexual Tragedy* (1954) and *The Case for Sexual Liberty* (1965). His friends began to regard him as an expert on the subject and often asked his advice.

He discovered he enjoyed counseling people as much as writing and decided to return to school. In 1942, Ellis entered the clinical psychology program at Columbia University and in 1947 was awarded his doctorate.

Ellis's early professional work as a therapist in state institutions in New Jersey employed classical psychoanalytic methods, but he has since set psychoanalysis aside completely. His change in philosophy came about when he discovered that clients treated once a week or even every other week progressed as well as those he saw daily. Ellis found that a more active role, interjecting advice and direct interpretation, yielded faster results than passive psychoanalytic procedures. His own theory of counseling, however, did not emerge until after he had received his doctorate from Columbia and later received training as a traditional psychoanalytic therapist. Consequently, some of the origins of REBT can be traced to Freud and others to disillusionment with Freudian psychoanalysis.

After discovering that rationalist philosophy fit his temperament and taste, Ellis began concentrating on changing people's behavior by confronting them with their irrational beliefs and persuading them to adopt more rational ones. He now considers himself a philosophical or educational therapist and sees REBT as uniquely didactic, cognition oriented, and explicative. He believes that REBT places people at the center of the universe and gives them almost full responsibility for their fate.

More than 400 books and articles, in addition to his Institute for Rational Living, have proceeded from Ellis's conceptualization of REBT. From its early days to the present, he has modified REBT. Writing in 1977, Ellis noted that REBT, once a limited rational-persuasive therapy, had grown into a therapy that consciously used cognitive, emotive, and behavioral techniques to help clients (Ellis, 1977). In 1957, he published his first REBT book, *How to Live with a "Neurotic"* (1957/1975), and in 1960 his first successful book, *The Art and Science of Love* (1969). Other books by Ellis include *Reason and Emotion in Psychotherapy* (1994b), *Better, Deeper, and More Enduring Brief Therapy* (1996), and *The Practice of Rational Emotive Behavior Therapy* (1996) (with W. Dryden).

## THE NATURE OF PEOPLE

Ellis based rational-emotive-behavior therapy on the philosophy of Epictetus (ca. A.D. 55–135): "What disturbs men's minds is not events, but their judgment of events." Generally speaking, very young children have limited emotional repertoires and tend to express emotions in a quick, unsustained manner. When children grow old enough to use language effectively, they acquire the ability to sustain their emotions and possibly keep themselves emotionally upset. Rather than concentrating on past events, REBT practitioners emphasize present events and how we react to them. The theory of REBT stresses that, as human beings, we have choices. We control our ideas, attitudes, feelings, and actions, and we arrange our lives according to our own dictates. We have little control over what happens or what actually exists, but we do have both choices and control over how we view the world and how we react to difficulties, regardless of how we have been taught to respond.

People are neither good nor bad if they respond to others with a rational belief system, according to REBT theory. If individuals react with irrational beliefs, however, they view themselves and others as evil, awful, and horrible whenever they or others fall short of their expectations. Ellis (1987, 1997) viewed humans as naturally irrational, self-defeating individuals who need to be taught to be otherwise. They think crookedly about their desires and preferences and escalate them in a self-defeating manner into musts, shoulds, oughts, and demands. In assimilating these irrational beliefs, people become emotionally disturbed and feel anger, anxiety, depression, worthlessness, self-pity, and other negative feelings that lead to destructive behavior. However, Ellis also stated that people can be "naturally" helpful and loving *as long as they do not think irrationally*. In other words, Ellis described a circular process, as depicted in Figure 8-1. Irrational thinking leads to self-hate, which leads to self-destructive behavior and eventually to hatred of others, which, in turn, causes others to act irrationally toward the individual and thus to begin the cycle again.

In the early years of the development of civilization, our very survival undoubtedly depended on our ability to face the environment, always expecting and preparing for the worst to happen. While it was a good way to survive, it was not a happy way to live. We may carry on this pessimistic way of life inherited from the Stone Age to today, when we tend to "catastrophize" the events that happen to us as a defense against being unprepared or caught off guard when the next "disaster" strikes. However, Ellis believes that we do have the potential to think rationally if we can master the ABCDE steps of REBT.

Ellis wrote that some of our irrational thoughts are biological in origin, but the majority stem from our upbringing (parents, teachers, and clergy). Ellis has de-

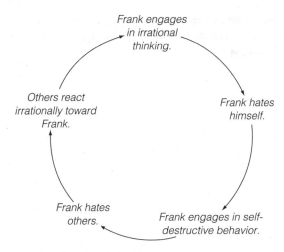

FIGURE 8-1   The circle of irrational thinking

scribed three areas in which people hold irrational beliefs: They must be perfect, others must be perfect, and the world must be a perfect place to live. The following examples describe in a nutshell what people tell themselves when they interpret events with an irrational belief system. A more rational replacement thought follows each irrational self-message.

1. Because it would be highly preferable if I were outstandingly competent, I absolutely should and must be; it is awful when I am not, and I am therefore a worthless individual.

Alternative: It would be nice if I were outstanding in whatever I do, but if I am not, it is okay, and I will try my best anyway.

2. Because it is highly desirable that others treat me considerately and fairly, they absolutely should and must, and they are rotten people who deserve to be utterly damned when they do not.

Alternative: I would prefer people to treat me considerately. However, I realize they will not always, so I will not take it personally when they do not, *and* I will make it my business to be considerate.

3. Because it is preferable that I experience pleasure rather than pain, the world should absolutely arrange this outcome, and life is horrible and I can't bear it when the world doesn't.

Alternative: I realize that in life there are both pleasurable moments and painful moments. Therefore, I will try to make the painful moments positive learning experiences so I can endure trials and even benefit from them.

## THEORY OF COUNSELING

Ellis (1998) postulated a system of inherently irrational beliefs or philosophies common to our culture that are conducive to maladjustment. When interpreting daily events with one or more irrational philosophies, the individual is likely to feel angry or hostile toward others or to internalize these feelings, with resulting anxiety, guilt, or depression. In essence, REBT theory holds that people are primarily responsible for their feelings about themselves, others, and the environment and for whether they want to be perpetually disturbed by them.

In their *Guide to Rational Living*, Ellis and Harper (1975) wrote that, because humans naturally and easily think crookedly, express emotions inappropriately, and behave in a self-defeating manner, it seems best to use all possible educational modes dramatically, strongly, and persistently to teach them how to do otherwise. Ellis and Harper compiled the following list of irrational beliefs that cause people trouble:

1. It is a dire necessity for people to be loved or approved by almost everyone for virtually everything they do.

2. One should be thoroughly competent, adequate, and achieving in all possible respects.

3. Certain people are bad, wicked, or villainous, and they should be severely blamed and punished for their sins.

4. It is terrible, horrible, and catastrophic when things are not going the way one would like them to go.

5. Human unhappiness is externally caused, and people have little or no ability to control their sorrows or rid themselves of their negative feelings.

6. If something is or may be dangerous or fearsome, one should be terribly occupied with and upset about it.

7. It is easier to avoid facing many life difficulties and self-responsibilities than to undertake more rewarding forms of self-discipline.

8. The past is all-important, and because something once strongly affected one's life, it should do so indefinitely.

9. People and things should be different from the way they are, and it is catastrophic if perfect solutions to the grim realities of life are not immediately found.

10. Maximum human happiness can be achieved by inertia and inaction or by passively and uncommittedly enjoying oneself.

11. My child is delinquent [or emotionally disturbed or mentally retarded]; therefore, I'm a failure as a parent.

12. My child is emotionally disturbed [or mentally retarded]; therefore, he or she is severely handicapped and will never amount to anything.

13. I cannot give my children everything they want; therefore, I am inadequate.

Consequences resulting from irrational or "stinking thinking" can be quite costly in the stress added to one's life. These include:

Work or career-related problems
Relationship problems
Low self-esteem
Depression over not getting what one wants
Anxiety from irrational fears
Overreacting to daily inconveniences
Negative addictions to overeating, drugs, and other useless behaviors
Physical illness

Crawford and Ellis (1989) provided further information on irrational beliefs and their consequences in their dictionary of 36 self-defeating feelings, accompanied by their corresponding rational and irrational beliefs. In the listing, the rational beliefs appear first and are often followed by sequential irrational beliefs to form a chain of irrational beliefs. Crawford and Ellis classified each irrational belief into one of five categories: (1) *self-defeating* beliefs that interfere with basic goals and drives, (2) highly rigid and *dogmatic* beliefs that lead to unrealistic preferences and wishes, (3) *antisocial* beliefs that cause people to destroy their social groups, (4) *unrealistic* beliefs that falsely describe reality, and (5) *contradictory* beliefs that originate from false premises.

In "What Rational-Emotive Therapy Is and Is Not," Ellis (1974) made the following points:

1. Anxiety is not "irrational" but an inappropriate feeling that stems largely from irrational ideas. Feelings should not be confused with ideas.

2. Clients have almost full or complete responsibility for their ideas and consequently for their feelings.

3. Clients mainly—not early environment or conditioning or contemporary conditions—choose to create their irrational ideas and consequent feelings. They can choose to change their ideas.

4. Do not blame, damn, denigrate, or condemn people for choosing irrational ideas, inappropriate feelings, or defeating behaviors.

5. Discourage absolutes, such as *must, should, always, never,* and *ought,* in clients' thinking. There are no absolutes (pun intended).

6. Therapists definitely do not determine whether clients' ideas or behaviors are rational or irrational.

Waters (1982, 1998) examined differences between the irrational beliefs of children, adolescents, and parents. Although she found some similarities between the three age groups, she also found some beliefs more prevalent in one group or another. The biggest commonality between groups is the resulting self-defeating emotions stimulated by the irrational beliefs of depression, anxiety, anger, and guilt.

*Common Irrational Beliefs of Children*

1. It is awful if others don't like me.

2. I am bad if I make a mistake.

3. Everything should go my way; I should always get what I want.

4. Things should come easily to me.

5. The world should be fair, and bad people should be punished.

6. I should not show my feelings.

7. Adults should be perfect.

8. There's only one right answer.

9. I must win; it's awful to lose.

10. I should not have to wait for anything.

### Common Irrational Beliefs of Adolescents

1. It would be awful if other kids did not like me, and if I were a loser.

2. I should not make mistakes, especially social mistakes.

3. It's my parents' fault that I'm so miserable.

4. I cannot help being the way I am. I'll always have to be this way.

5. The world should be fair and just.

6. It is awful when things do not go my way.

7. It's better to avoid challenges than to risk being a failure.

8. I must conform to my peers.

9. I cannot stand being criticized.

10. Others should always be responsible.

### Common Irrational Beliefs of Parents

1. It would be awful if my children did not like me.

2. I cannot stand it if others criticize my parenting.

3. I'm totally responsible for everything my children do, and if they behave obnoxiously, I must feel awful.

4. I must be a perfect parent and always know the right thing to do in every situation.

5. My children should always do what I want them to.

6. If my child has a problem, then I have to feel terrible, too.

7. Children should not disagree with their parents.

8. My children make me angry, depressed, and anxious.

9. If my children do not turn out the way I think they should, then I am a failure.

10. Parenting should be fun all the time.

Ellis (1998) recommended that people would do better to resist the tendency to rate themselves in favor of limiting themselves to rating only their deeds, traits, acts, characteristics, and performances. So, if a child made a bad grade on a math test, it would be okay to say, "I did poorly on the test" but *not* to say, "I am a stupid person." Ellis favored rating the effectiveness of how people think, feel, and behave. He also supported rating our progress toward goals we have set. Global, all-over ratings of the "self" or "ego" almost always create self-defeating, neurotic thoughts, feelings, and behaviors.

Ellis quarreled with the practice followed by the majority of psychotherapy systems that seem directed toward strengthening people's self-esteem. He took issue with Rogers's practice of trying to increase clients' self-esteem by providing them with vast amounts of unconditional positive regard. Ellis pointed out that self-acceptance would still be conditional on the therapists' uncritical acceptance of their clients. Ellis believed that we are more than our behavior and performances, and to rate ourselves bad because we had a bad performance would lead to an unhappy life. Ellis's goal for the people of the world is what he termed unconditional self-acceptance (USA). In other words, we are worthwhile persons regardless of how we did on the last test or in the last game. USA works better when it includes what Ellis called unconditional other acceptance (UOA) or acceptance of others. Ellis's (1998) view of healthy personalities is one that accepts others *and* ourselves with our virtues and our failings, with our important accomplishments and our nonachievements, simply because we are alive and because we are human.

The goal of rational-emotive-behavior therapy is to teach people to think and behave in a more personally satisfying way by making them realize they have a choice between self-defeating, negative behavior and efficient, enhancing, positive behavior. It teaches people to take responsibility for their own logical thinking and the consequences or behaviors that follow it.

## COUNSELING METHOD

In the past, counselors concentrated on either the developmental events in one's life or one's feelings about these events. Ellis did not believe these two main methods were totally erroneous, but he did not find either approach very effective. Neither approach explained why some people are rather well adjusted (that is, not too unhappy too much of the time, regardless of the passage of events) and others are emotionally dysfunctional much of the time with the same passage of events.

Ellis theorized that individuals' belief systems predicate their responses or feelings toward the same events. These individual belief systems are what people tell themselves about an event—in particular, an unfortunate incident. For example, 100 people may be rejected by their true loves. One of these people may respond: "I can't go on; I've lost my purpose in life. Because I've been rejected by such a wonderful person, I must really be a worthless slob. My only solution for getting rid of the unbearable pain I feel is to kill myself." Another may respond: "What a pain in the neck! I had dinner reservations and tickets for the show. Now I have to get another date for Saturday night. This surely sets me back. What an inconvenience!" Between these two extreme reactions are several other degrees of bad feelings growing from the various self-messages of the rejected 100. Such a wide variety of reactions to the same basic event suggests that one's view of the event and consequent self-message provide the key to the counseling strategy. The same process happens to children who experience bad feelings from school failure, peer conflicts, conflicts with adults, or rejection.

Thebarge (1989), in differentiating REBT from behavior modification, systematic desensitization, and traditional psychoanalysis, pointed out that REBT practitioners treat underlying causes (irrational beliefs) of symptoms and not the symptoms themselves. Therefore, successful REBT generates none of the symptom substitution that may occur when treatment is focused on symptoms only. Behavior modification and systematic desensitization are two therapies that are directed toward symptom removal.

Dryden (1989) discussed four types of chains people use to turn irrational beliefs into bad feelings and destructive behaviors. *Inference* chains occur when inferences are chained together and trigger emotions and irrational beliefs. The key to treatment is to find the most relevant inference. *Inference-evaluative belief* chains occur when a person holds an evaluative belief about each inference in the chain. The key to repairing this chain is to identify the earliest irrational belief that creates increasingly distorted beliefs. *Disturbance-about-disturbance* chains relate to how people become more upset by becoming upset about disturbances. In these cases, the client chooses the starting point in the chain. *Complex* chains are too difficult to handle by starting at the end of the chain. Clients are encouraged to start at the beginning and replay the entire process in slow motion to see the process of chain development.

DiGiuseppe (1990) detailed a method for using inference chaining as a technique for helping children reevaluate their automatic irrational beliefs. Children were asked to imagine or think about what would happen next if the automatic thought (for example, "I am stupid") were true and what it would mean to them. DiGiuseppe also recommended deductive interpretation with children. In this method, the counselor and the child form and test hypotheses concerning the irrational belief. Both methods allow self-discovery by the child.

The main goal of REBT is to increase happiness and decrease pain. In order to achieve a prevailing happier state, REBT has two main objectives. The first is to show the emotionally disturbed client how irrational beliefs or attitudes create dysfunctional consequences. These consequences might include anger, depression, or anxiety. The second objective is directively and intellectually teaching clients how to dispute or crumble their irrational beliefs and replace them with rational beliefs. Once counselors lead the clients to dispute the irrational ideas, they guide them into adopting new expectations for themselves, others, and the environment. Ellis reasoned that if the irrational, absolute philosophies and resultant feelings are replaced with more rational, productive thoughts, clients will no longer be trapped in a repetitious cycle of negative feelings. When children are no longer incapacitated by dysfunctional feelings, they are free to choose behaviors that eliminate the problem or at least lessen its disappointing impact.

Rational-emotive-behavior therapy is often referred to as the "A, B, C, D, and E" approach to counseling. A, B, and C show how problems develop; D and E are the treatment steps.

A is the activating event: "I failed my math test."
B is how you evaluate the event.

$B_1$—irrational message: "I failed the test; therefore, I'm a total failure as a person."

$B_2$—rational message: "I failed the test. This is unpleasant and inconvenient, but that is all it is. I need to study more efficiently for the next exam."

C represents the consequences or feelings resulting from your self-message at the B stage. The $B_1$ message will cause you to feel very depressed. The $B_2$ message won't make you feel great, but it will not be so overwhelming as to inhibit your performance on the next test.

D represents the disputing arguments you use to attack the irrational self-messages expressed in $B_1$. The counselor's function is to help you question these irrational self-messages once they have been identified.

E represents the answers you have developed to the questions regarding the rationality of your $B_1$ self-messages.

For example, counseling would proceed through the following steps:

A—Something unpleasant happens to you.
B—You evaluate the event as something awful, something that should not be allowed to happen.
C—You become upset and nervous.
D—You question your B self-message:
  1. Why is it awful?
  2. Why shouldn't it be allowed to happen?
E—You answer:
  1. It's a disappointment.
  2. It's a setback, but not a disaster.
  3. I can handle it.
  4. I would like things to be better, but that doesn't mean I'm always supposed to get things done my way.

Ellis (1972) provided another example of REBT in action in "Emotional Education in the Classroom." A student named Robert is so anxious about reciting in class, even though he knows the material, that he anticipates the event (A) and already feels the blocking and nervousness (C) just by anticipating the event (A). At point $B_2$ he tells himself: "It would be unfortunate if I did not recite well because the other children might think I did not know my lesson. They might even think I am a dummy, and I would not want that." At $B_1$, however, Robert usually adds another statement to his rational message: "It would be awful if I failed. No one would like me, and I would be a bum." The great anxiety felt at C caused by the $B_1$ message would sabotage Robert's efforts to recite in class the next time the teacher called on him.

Rational-emotive-behavior therapy is direct, didactic, confrontational, and verbally active counseling. Initially, the counselor seeks to detect the irrational beliefs that are creating the disturbance. Seven factors help to detect irrational thinking:

1. Look for *overgeneralizations*—"I made an F on the first math test; therefore, I will always do poorly on math tests."

2. Look for *distortions*—sometimes referred to as all-or-nothing thinking or black-and-white categorizing of things as all good or all bad: "I did not make all As on my report card; therefore, I will never be a good student."

3. Look for *deletions*—the tendency to focus on negative events or disqualifying positive events. "I struck out two times and got one hit; therefore, I will probably strike out the next time I bat."

4. Look for *catastrophizing*—Mistakes are exaggerated, and achievements are minimized: "I was just lucky to get that A on my last test."

5. Look for the use of absolutes such as *should, must, always, ought,* and *never*— "I should not make mistakes."

6. Look for statements *condemning* something or someone clients think they cannot stand—"He should be punished and should not be allowed to get away with that!"

7. Look for *fortune telling* or future predictions—"I just know my friends will not have fun at my party."

Once the irrational beliefs are recognized, the counselor disputes and challenges them. Ultimately, the goal is for children to recognize irrational beliefs, think them through, and relinquish them. As a result of this process and therapy, children, it is hoped, reach three insights. First, the present neurotic behavior has antecedent causes. Second, original beliefs keep upsetting children because they keep repeating these beliefs. Third, they can overcome emotional disturbances by consistently observing, questioning, and challenging their own belief systems.

People hold tenaciously to their beliefs, rational or not; consequently, the counselor vigorously attacks the irrational beliefs in an attempt to show the children how illogically they think. Using the Socratic method of questioning and disputing, the counselor takes a verbally active part in the early stages of counseling by identifying and explaining the child's problem. If counselors guess correctly, which often happens, they argue with and persuade the child to give up the old irrational view and replace it with a new, rational philosophy.

Waters (1980, 1982, 1998) wrote a classic book and article on helping children build tease tolerance that still works for children who do not handle teasing well. She recommended that counselors begin by teaching children there are two types of responses to being teased. One is what they *think* and *feel,* and the other is how they *behave.* Children are told they are in control of both things. Counseling is focused on these two points. First, children are taught that they can change what they tell themselves about being teased, and that will change how they feel about it. Second, when they feel less bad about being teased, they will be able to do things that will help them handle the teasing better. In other words, the immediate goal is to move from being angry, depressed, or anxious to irritated, displeased, or concerned. Children are taught that to continue with "stinking thinking" will result in more bad feelings and responses that encourage the teaser to keep on teasing. Also, the teaser will get the payoff he or she is after—causing the child to feel angry or depressed. Waters (1982, 1998) pointed out how irrational beliefs or stinking thinking exacerbates the resulting emotions of anger, depression, and anxiety.

*Anger*

> "I can't stand to be teased!"
> "He shouldn't tease me."
> "It's absolutely awful if others tease me."
> "She should be punished for teasing me."

*Depression*

> "If others tease me, I must be a total loser."

*Anxiety*

> "I'll always be teased forever, and I can't stand it."

Next, the irrational or stinking thinking responses are disputed or challenged and then answered with more rational responses.

*Anger*

> "How does Jim's teasing make your life terrible?"
> "What do you think Jim wants you to do when he teases you?"
> Answer: "Well, I don't like it when Jim teases me, but that does not have to ruin my life. I need to figure out a way to stop the payoff he gets from teasing me."

*Depression*

> "How does Sally's teasing you make you totally worthless?"
> Answer: "Well, it does make me feel sad when someone wants to make me feel that way, but that does not mean I am totally worthless. It just means that for the present, I don't have Sally's goodwill and that is just a minor pain, because I like myself. I do want to work on ignoring Sally's teasing."

*Anxiety*

> "How does teasing by those two girls mean you will always be teased?"
> Answer: "Well, I guess their teasing doesn't mean that I will always be teased. But I still don't like it, and I want to find out how to make teasing me no fun for them."

To the usual psychotherapeutic techniques of exploration, ventilation, excoriation, and interpretation, rational-emotive-behavior therapists add techniques of confrontation, indoctrination, and reeducation. Counselors are didactic in that they explain how children's beliefs (which intervene between an event and the resultant feelings), rather than events themselves, cause emotional disturbances. Because the counselor honestly believes that children do not understand the reason for their disturbance, the counselor enlightens and teaches. Counselors frequently assign homework—reading, performing specific tasks, and taking risks—for the child as an integral part of therapy.

There is little transference in REBT. Contrary to classical psychoanalysis, the counselor serves as a model of rational thinking and behavior and urges children to resolve problems with significant people in their lives. In addition, the counselor sometimes uses conventional methods, such as active listening, with the end result that the child's irrational thinking—which has led to irrational behavior—is destroyed, and a saner belief system replaces it.

Rational-emotive-behavior counselors believe that the development of a person's belief system (which is defined as the meaning of facts) is analogous to the acquisition of speech. Just as children learn language by imitation and modeling, they learn a belief system. Therefore, the belief system and attitudes children acquire are largely a reflection of the significant people in their lives. Furthermore, the belief systems incorporated into children's minds determine whether they think rationally about facts. Continuing the analogy, just as one continues to add vocabulary and modify one's speech, one can also change or replace one's belief system.

For children, REBT is modified because its style depends so much on verbal and abstract conceptualization skills. Working on the premise that people feel the way they think, the therapist attempts to change overt behavior by altering internal verbalization. A major disadvantage in using REBT with children is that children do not generalize well from one situation to another; that is, the improved behavior is limited to the specific circumstances. Furthermore, Piaget's research indicated that children in the preformal stages of cognitive development (see Chapter 1) might have difficulty relating to the REBT counseling method.

Role reversal is a very effective technique with children. In this technique, the child describes the activating event and the emotional consequences. Next, the counselor explains that thoughts are upsetting the child. Then they role-play the activating event, with the counselor playing the child. While acting out the event, the counselor demonstrates the appropriate behavior while uttering rational self-statements aloud. The roles are reversed again, with the child trying on new thoughts and being rewarded, preferably with social approval, as reinforcement for rational statements and behaviors. The child may need successive approximations of the appropriate REBT behaviors reinforced.

## Rational-Emotive-Behavior Education

An offspring of REBT is rational-emotive-behavior education (REBE). Its objectives are to teach how feelings develop, how to discriminate between valid and invalid assumptions, and how to think rationally in "antiawful" and "antiperfectionist" ways.

REBE programs have been effective in reinforcing rational verbal expressions with disturbed children. Children become more rational not only in their verbal expressions and belief systems but also in their behaviors. The following are examples of beliefs that can be reinforced by writing statements:

> I don't like school, but I can stand it.
> I did something bad, but I'm not a bad person.

I don't like being called insulting names, but being insulted is not awful. Just because someone calls you "stupid" does not mean you are.

Ellis (Ellis & Wilde, 2001) said that all children act neurotically simply because they are children. He stated that childish behavior cannot be differentiated from neurosis until the age of 5. At this point, many children have integrated into their belief system the irrational belief that one should be thoroughly competent, adequate, and achieving in all possible respects to be considered worthwhile. Strategies for undermining this philosophy in children can be summarized as follows:

1. Teach children the joy of engaging in games that are worthwhile because they are fun. De-emphasize the importance of winning at all costs by teaching children that you do not have to win to have fun and be a worthwhile person.

2. Teach children that significant achievements rarely come easily and that nothing is wrong with working long and hard to achieve their goals.

3. Teach children that they are not bad people when they do not meet their goals. Children must like themselves during periods of failure, even when they may not be trying their best to achieve their goals. Children also need to learn the difference between wants and needs. Wanting something we cannot get is not the same as not getting what we absolutely need.

4. Teach children that, although striving for perfectionism in performance is good, perfection is not required to be a worthwhile person. Making mistakes is not only okay but also a good way to learn why certain things happen and how to prevent them from happening again.

5. Teach children that popularity and achievement are not necessarily related, that to be liked by all people at all times is very difficult, and that being a worthwhile person does not require 100% popularity.

6. In summary, teach children not to take themselves and situations too seriously by turning minor setbacks into catastrophes. Balance corrective feedback with positive reinforcement in evaluating children's performances.

## COGNITIVE-BEHAVIORAL THERAPY

The movement toward integrative approaches to counseling is documented in the literature. These integrative approaches often involve the combination of two or more standard approaches into one treatment modality. We suggest that this has been happening in practice since the beginning of the counseling movement, and only now are some theorists willing to admit that they have been integrative all along. One such integrative combination is represented by the unification of cognitive and behavioral approaches into cognitive-behavioral therapy (CBT). The practice of cognitive-behavioral therapy combines behavior-change methods with thought-restructuring methods to produce behavior and feeling change in clients. Such a marriage between two approaches results from deficiency in one or both of the methods in bringing about the desired counseling outcomes. The terms *cognitive restructuring, cognitive behavior modification,* and *stress inoculation* all represent current descriptions of Ellis's original work and some related work by Beck (1976), Maultsby (1984), and Meichenbaum (1977, 1985). These techniques combine various cognitive and behavioral approaches (Bernard, 1990).

Stress-inoculation methods combined with role playing provide an example of a cognitive-behavioral technique. In cases of test anxiety, the client might be asked to practice the following examples of self-talk: (1) "Tests are no fun, but all I want is to do the best I can." (2) "Though it would be nice to make an A, it is not required for me to be a good and worthwhile person." (3) "All I need to do is prepare for the test and do the best I am able to do. If I fail, it will be inconvenient and no fun at all, but that is all it will be. For the moment, I just will not be getting what I want." Combining the self-talk with taking practice tests and visualization practice of the steps in the client's test-taking stimulus hierarchy (systematic desensitization) represents a typical cognitive-behavioral treatment plan.

Other stress-inoculation techniques include relaxation training, deep-breathing exercises, and reframing exercises that help children replace their anxiety with relaxation. Such reframing exercises help children perceive anxiety-provoking situations in a less threatening light. Rather than having the child focus on school as a place of potential failure and frightening teachers, for example, the counselor teaches the child to focus on the friends and fun available at school.

Stress-inoculation training programs, such as those designed by Meichenbaum (1977, 1985), have four categories of self-talk designed to help people master difficult and highly stressful situations and events:

1. Preparation for a stressor: "What is it you have to do? You can develop a plan to deal with it. Don't worry."

2. Confrontation and management of a stressor: "One step at a time; you can handle the situation. Relax, you are in control. Take a slow, deep breath."

3. Coping: "Don't try to eliminate fear totally; just keep it manageable. Keep the focus on the present; what is it you have to do?"

4. Reinforcing self-statements: "It worked; you did it. It wasn't as bad as you expected. It's getting better each time."

CBT treatment programs for such things as childhood depressive disorders are often quite elaborate. CBT models often consist of four levels of treatment: (1) behavioral procedures, such as contingent reinforcement, shaping, prompting, and modeling, to increase social interaction; (2) CBT interventions, which include pairing successful task completion with positive self-statements and reinforcement for those self-statements; (3) cognitive interventions, which are used with social-skills training, role playing, and self-management; and (4) self-control procedures, such as self-evaluation and self-reinforcement.

McGinn and Sanderson (2001) make the case that CBT belongs to the family of brief therapies. CBT sessions are formatted in a fashion similar to the time-efficient methods of solution-focused brief counseling, reality therapy, and behavioral counseling. CBT sessions follow a four-step process:

1. Review progress to bring counselor and client up to date on how much has been accomplished toward meeting the client's goals. Homework assignments are checked for completion. We like to use a four-quadrant structure that asks clients to review their past 7 days by listing high points in quadrant 1, low points in quadrant 2, how the week could have been better in quadrant 3, and plans for next week in quadrant 4.

2. Set the agenda for the current session based on the information gleaned from the high points–low points survey. For example, high points occur most often when plans are made in advance. Low points can often be avoided with similar planning.

3. Complete the current session by clarifying and setting specific behavioral goals for the next week.

4. Summarize the session (preferably done by the client) to provide a bridge to the next session by (a) reviewing next week's homework, (b) anticipating obstacles that might scuttle the client's plans, and (c) evaluating the current session.

Watkins (1983) adapted Maultsby's (1976) rational self-analysis format to fit the developmental level of children (Table 8-1). In Step 1, children write down what happened ("Jimmy called me a name because he doesn't like me"). In Step 2, children are asked to write, from the vantage point of a video camera, what they would see and hear ("Jimmy didn't like it when I didn't choose him for my team"). With the increased objectivity obtained in Step 2, children are then asked in Step 3 to write down their thoughts about what happened ("It's terrible when people talk mean to me" or "If people get angry at me, I'm a bad person"). In Step 4, children are asked to write how they felt (hurt, angry) and what they did ("I hit him"). In Step 5, children are asked to find out if they have been thinking "smart" thoughts by testing their thoughts with the five questions listed in Step 6 (for example, "Does my thought help me stay out of trouble with others?"). The answers are tabulated in Step 5. If "no" wins, the children go to Step 7 and list some of the feelings they want to feel (for example, a child may prefer to feel sad or disappointed instead of hurt, irritated, or angry). In Step 8, children are asked to write "smarter" thoughts that would help them feel better feelings ("I don't like it when others get upset with me, but things could be worse, and I don't have to let others control how I act"). Step 9 is reserved for a plan of action children can use the next time somebody does something to make them feel bad. Watkins's adaptation of Maultsby's model makes use of visualization in Step 2. Visualization is endorsed by Ellis (2001) as a way of experiencing the negative consequences of telling ourselves irrational messages and the positive consequences of telling ourselves rational messages about the events in our lives. In addition, goals that are not visualized as attainable are seldom achieved.

TABLE 8-1   Rational self-analysis for children

| **Step 1.** Write down what happened. | **Step 2.** Be a video camera. If you were a video camera and recorded a videotape of what happened, what would you see and hear? | **Step 3.** Write down your thoughts about what happened. What did you think?<br>A.<br>B.<br>C. |
|---|---|---|
| **Step 4.**<br><br>A. How did you feel?<br>B. What did you do? | **Step 5.** Decide if your thoughts are "smart." To do this, look at each thought you had and ask yourself the five questions in Step 6. Answer yes or no to each question and write your answers below.<br>A. 1.   B. 1.   C. 1.<br>   2.      2.      2.<br>   3.      3.      3.<br>   4.      4.      4.<br>   5.      5.      5. | **Step 6.** How do you know if you're thinking "smart" thoughts? Ask:<br>1. Is my thought really real? Say, "if I were a video camera, what would I see?"<br>2. Does the thought help me stay alive and in good physical shape?<br>3. Does the thought help me get what I want?<br>4. Does the thought help me stay out of trouble with others?<br>5. Does the thought help me feel the way I want to? |
| **Step 7.** How do you want to feel? | **Step 8.** Write down thoughts you could have that would be "smarter" than those listed.<br>A.<br>B.<br>C. | **Step 9.** What do you want to do? |

SOURCE: Watkins, 1983; adapted from Maultsby, 1976.

◆ ───────────────────────────────────────────

# CASE STUDY
Jeff is a quiet, serious, 12-year-old seventh-grader at Smith County Middle School. He was referred to the counselor because a failing grade on a language arts test left him very upset. After the test, Jeff seemed to be firmly convinced that he would fail the class.

## Individual and Background Information

*Academic.*   School records indicate that Jeff is a high achiever. He had excellent grades (B and above) in all his classes for the first two grading periods of the year. Except for an F on the last test, he has also maintained an above-average grade in language arts this grading period.

*Family.* Jeff is the youngest of three sons. His father is retired, and his mother works as a grocery store cashier. Both of Jeff's older brothers, one a high school senior and the other a college sophomore, are excellent students. The family expects (or appears to expect) Jeff to excel also.

*Social.* Jeff seems to get along well with his peers. He participates in group efforts and is especially good friends with one other student, John, also a good student with a quiet personality.

## Counseling Method

The school counselor used rational-emotive-behavior therapy as a counseling method to help Jeff recognize and evaluate the erroneous messages he was giving himself (and which upset him) about his low grade in language arts. The counselor also taught Jeff to replace the erroneous messages with "sane" messages and to recognize "insane" messages when he encountered them again. The basic steps the counselor used included having Jeff examine each step along the way to becoming upset and look at the real message he was telling himself at each step.

## Transcript*

*Counselor:* Jeff, why do you think you're going to fail language arts?

*Jeff:* Because I failed the last test.

*Counselor:* You mean if you fail one test, you're bound to fail the next one?

*Jeff:* Well, I failed that test, and I'm stupid!

*Counselor:* What are you telling yourself about your performance on that test?

*Jeff:* I remember thinking it was a really bad grade—not at all the kind I was used to getting. Then I thought how terrible it would be if I failed language arts and how my mom and dad and brothers would hate me and would think I was lazy and dumb!

*Counselor:* It would be unpleasant and inconvenient if you failed language arts, but would this make you a hateful and dumb person?

*Jeff:* It makes me really worried about passing the next test that's coming up. . .

*Counselor:* I can understand how you would be worried about the next test, but does a bad grade make someone a bad or hated person?

*Jeff:* No, but it's not the kind of grade I usually get.

*Counselor:* Okay, so a bad grade is unpleasant, and you don't like it, but it does not make you a bad person.

*Jeff:* My grade was an F and most of the other kids made As, so it made me look dumb.

---

*The case of Jeff was contributed by Sharon Simpson.

*Counselor:*   Okay, it *was* a bad grade compared with the rest of the class, but does this mean you are the dumbest kid around?

*Jeff:*   No, I make mostly As, a few Bs. One bad grade does not make me a dumb kid.

*Counselor:*   So, compared with your usual grade and the class's grades, this *was* a bad grade, and that is all it is, right?

*Jeff:*   Yeah.

*Counselor:*   What else are you telling yourself about the low test grade?

*Jeff:*   Well, like I said, I immediately thought how terrible it would be if I failed language arts, and. . . .

*Counselor:*   Stop there for just a minute, Jeff. Suppose you did fail language arts, even with your other high grades. It would be a bad experience, but would it be the end of the world?

*Jeff:*   No, I guess I'd have to repeat the class, that's all.

*Counselor:*   Right, it would be inconvenient and maybe embarrassing. It would not be pleasant, but you would go on living.

*Jeff:*   Well, I guess that's right.

*Counselor:*   Are you beginning to see what you told yourself about the consequences of *one* bad grade?

*Jeff:*   Yeah, I guess I believed that one bad grade was awful—the end of the world—and that I shouldn't even try anymore because I would fail the class anyway.

*Counselor:*   Was that the correct information to give yourself about your grade?

*Jeff:*   No!

*Counselor:*   Okay! Let's look at the rest of the message you gave yourself after you got that bad grade. Remember what was next?

*Jeff:*   I think I thought my family would hate me and think I was dumb and lazy because I failed that test and would probably fail language arts.

*Counselor:*   Do you think your family's love depends on your grades?

*Jeff:*   No, Jimmy made an F on a chemistry test the first part of the school year, and nobody hated him.

*Counselor:*   What did your parents do?

*Jeff:*   Let's see. Oh, yeah, they got him a tutor—a friend of Dad's knew a student who was majoring in chemistry.

*Counselor:*   What did your brother in college do when Jimmy failed the test?

*Jeff:*   He offered to help Jim on weekends. He's a brain—a physics major!

*Counselor:*   So when your brother failed a test, your family helped him out. They didn't say he was "dumb" or "lazy" or that they hated him for it!

*Jeff:*   No, they didn't. And I guess they wouldn't say it to me, either; in fact, Dad and Jim ask every night if I need help with my homework. I can usually do it okay by myself.

*Counselor:*   Okay. Let's go back over some of these bad messages you've been giving yourself about your bad grade.

*Jeff:*   I got a bad grade. I thought I would fail language arts no matter what I did. I decided my family would hate me and think I was dumb and lazy.

*Counselor:* Do you *still* believe those "crazy" messages you told yourself about failing and the way your family would react?

*Jeff:* No!

*Counselor:* Next time you mess up on something—maybe a ball game, maybe a test—what message will you give yourself?

*Jeff:* Well, I'm not exactly sure what I'll say, but I *won't* tell myself that it's a disaster and I'll never be able to do anything else. I'll probably say that I don't like what happened and that I'm not happy about it. That's all. Now I guess I'll go study and try to ace that next language arts test. Thanks a lot!

◆

## Applications of Cognitive-Behavioral Therapy

Kendall (1993) addressed the issue of how best to intervene to reduce or remediate cognitive, behavioral, and emotional difficulties in childhood that are associated with present psychological distress and later psychopathology. Specifically, Kendall presented a status report on the effectiveness of cognitive-behavioral therapies (CBT) in treating children in four diagnostic categories: aggression, anxiety, depression, and attention deficit–hyperactivity disorder (ADHD).

### Aggression

Kendall (1993) emphasized that aggressive children suffer from both distortions and deficiencies in their cognitive processing. Cognitive distortions result from dysfunctional thinking. Cognitive deficiencies result from insufficient cognitive activity in situations requiring cause–effect reasoning or the ability to visualize consequences of behavior. Kendall found support for the effectiveness of CBT treatments with aggressive psychiatric children in reducing their aggressive behavior. The treatments included problem-solving skills training and self-monitoring with self-instruction for monitoring their arousal states.

Lochman (1992) studied the effects of CBT on the behavior of 145 aggressive 10- to 12-year-old boys. The CBT interventions, ranging from watching video training tapes to role playing social problem-solving situations, had a long-term effect on some behaviors of aggressive boys. The most notable area of change was lower levels of substance abuse over a 3-year follow-up period. It did not prove to have as strong an impact on decreasing deviant behavior, however.

Davis and Boster (1993) proposed using CBT in combination with expressive interventions in working with aggressive and resistant youth. They viewed the combined approach as a way to modify the dysfunctional cognitive, affective, behavioral, and problem-solving skills seen in aggressive youth and considered several multimodal treatment interventions. Logbooks of perceptions were recommended as helpful for recording thoughts and reinforcing nonviolent appraisals. Art therapy techniques such as cartoons without captions helped to frame nonviolent appraisals. Art therapy, as well as the other expressive arts of music and movement, was also effective with violent clients, who are likely to be limited in requisite verbal skills and creative resources for expressing and testing alternative appraisals of life events. Instruction in social skills and conflict resolution was also recommended for the multimodal package for treating aggressive youth.

## Anxiety

Kendall (1993) found support for using muscle relaxation, deep breathing, and cognitive imagery (systematic desensitization) to reduce anxiety in anxious children. Anxious children exceed the norm by a significant margin with thoughts of being scared, hurt, and in danger. The same is true for self-critical thoughts.

Jay, Elliot, Woody, and Siegel (1991) investigated the effectiveness of CBT in combination with diazepam (Valium) for children undergoing painful medical procedures. The study was done with 83 children ages 3 to 12 who were suffering from leukemia. The purpose of the study was to find ways to reduce the anxiety and distress caused by the medical tests and procedures required for treatment. One group received CBT, and one group received CBT plus Valium. The CBT techniques included modeling, breathing exercises, imagery, positive incentives, and behavior rehearsal. The results showed that Valium did not increase the efficacy of CBT as hypothesized. In fact, the data, though not statistically significant, supported the possibility that Valium may impair the learning process of CBT. Used alone, CBT was found to decrease distress and to increase the children's rate of reporting their fears.

Beck, Sokol, Clark, Berchick, and Wright (1992) found that cognitive therapy was more effective than person-centered therapy for helping clients suffering from panic disorders. Cognitive strategies were used to break down the panic cycle. Person-centered strategies were nondirective and did not focus on the panic symptoms. Cognitive therapy resulted in a 71% rate of effectiveness in ending panic attacks, whereas only 25% of the person-centered participants succeeded. Clients could elect to cross over to the other treatment group. Crossover clients to cognitive therapy were successful in 79% of the cases.

Two treatments, CBT and CBT plus family therapy (FAM), were used with children suffering from anxiety disorders. In a 5- to 7-year follow-up of these children, Barrett, Duffy, Dadds, and Rapee (2001) found that 86% of the children no longer met the diagnostic criteria for any anxiety disorder. CBT and CBT plus FAM were equally effective at long-term follow-up. In a similar study comparing parent involvement in children's CBT treatment with no parent involvement, Spence, Donovan, and Brechman-Toussaint (2000) found that both groups improved significantly more than a wait-list group in the reduction of general and social anxiety and that there were no significant differences between the two CBT groups.

## Depression

Depressed children suffer from distortions in attributions, self-evaluation, and perceptions of past and present events. Silverman and DiGiuseppe (2001) found a significant correlation between self-reported depression and negative automatic thoughts in a study of 126 students in grades 4 through 8. Depressed children exhibit more external locus of control (an indication that they feel less capable) and low self-esteem, resulting from a perceived inability to succeed academically and socially. Effective help for depressed children included training in self-control, self-evaluation, assertiveness, and social skills. Social skills training included initiating and maintaining interactions and conflict resolution; specific CBT included relaxation, imagery, and cognitive restructuring.

### Attention Deficit–Hyperactivity Disorder

Children with ADHD show deficiencies in the mechanisms that govern (1) sustained attention and effort, (2) inhibitory controls, and (3) the modulation of arousal levels to meet situational demands. Kendall (1993) proposed CBT with medication to treat ADHD. Stimulant medication should improve attention, and CBT should improve cognitive functioning. Ronen (1992) discussed cognitive therapy with children and its suitability for children's needs and ability levels. She listed the most frequent behavior problems of children (from most common to least common): loss of temper, hyperactivity, fears, restlessness, sleep disorders, enuresis, food intake, nail biting, tics, and stuttering. Her review of the literature revealed that children with behavior problems such as hyperactivity, impulsivity, and aggression tend to (1) generate fewer alternative solutions to interpersonal problems, (2) focus on ends or goals rather than on the intermediate steps toward obtaining them, (3) see fewer consequences associated with their behavior, (4) fail to recognize causes of others' behavior, and (5) be less sensitive to interpersonal conflict. Ronen then outlined some successful applications of CBT, such as self-assessment, self-instruction, self-reinforcement, and self-punishment. Cognitive treatments require children's active participation in learning to identify irrational thoughts, initiate internal dialogues, halt automatic thinking, change automatic thoughts to mediated ones, and use CBT to change unwanted behavior. Ronen responded to the question of whether children have developed sufficient cognitive skills to benefit from a cognitive approach by citing the similarity in difficulty between early childhood tasks and understanding CBT; she compared changing one's behavior with learning to ride a bicycle, use computers, read, and write. Three keys to such learning were identified: (1) the knowledge of how to do it, (2) the desire to learn and practice, and (3) time to practice. Basically, our position is that good counselors should be able to teach children almost any skill that can be broken down into mediating steps that children can understand and find meaningful to the events in their everyday lives.

### Obesity

Duffy and Spence (1993) researched the effectiveness of cognitive self-management as an adjunct to behavioral interventions for childhood obesity. The study was done with 29 children ages 7 to 13. The traffic light system, which classified foods into three categories—green (eat freely), amber (eat in moderation), and red (stop, danger)—was used in behavior therapy (BT). The BT group also received training in exercise, and their parents were trained to use goal-setting and positive reinforcement strategies for facilitating behavior change. The CBT component included monitoring negative thoughts, restructuring negative or maladaptive thoughts, problem-solving skills, self-instructional training, and self-reinforcement. The results of the study confirmed the effectiveness of behavioral programs in the reduction of obesity in some children. The addition of CBT component did not add significantly to the BT approach.

As we have noted throughout the book, counseling children and adults who do not view themselves as having a problem is difficult. Such was true with children in this obesity reduction study.

### Children of Alcoholics

Webb (1993) endorsed CBT as a valuable method for school counselors to use with children of alcoholics (COAs). The principal benefit of CBT for COAs was help in dealing with situations beyond their control and thus help in avoiding responsibility for family issues that are, in reality, the responsibility of other family members. Moreover, CBT practitioners also provide their clients with the means for taking control of their lives and for improving those areas that are in their clients' control.

## Cognitive-Behavioral Play Therapy

Cognitive-behavioral play therapy is an adaptation of cognitive and behavioral therapies. Knell (1997) explained that cognitive-behavioral play therapy provides structured, goal-directed activities while allowing the child to engage in an unstructured, spontaneous way. The therapy is brief, directive, and problem oriented. In the cognitive-behavioral play therapy, the therapeutic relationship is educational and collaborative. The positive relationship is based on rapport and trust, with play activities being means of communication. Play techniques, as well as verbal and nonverbal communication, are used to help children change their behavior and participate in the therapy. The active intervention involves the child and the counselor working together to establish goals. Both choose play materials and activities. New skills are taught to the child. The counselor uses praise and interpretation to help the child learn new behaviors and increase understanding. The counselor focuses on the child's thoughts, feelings, fantasies, and environment. The counselor also provides strategies for developing more adaptive thoughts and behaviors. The behavioral techniques used by the counselor may include systematic desensitization, contingency management, self-monitoring, and activity scheduling. Cognitive techniques include recording thoughts, cognitive change strategies, coping self-statements, and bibliotherapy. To accomplish the educative process, counselors use techniques such as modeling, role playing, and using behavioral contingencies (Knell, 1996, 1998).

The counselor emphasizes the issues of control, mastery, and responsibility for the client's own behavior change. Knell (1996) believed that combining cognitive and behavioral interventions increased the potency of the intervention. The change proceeds first in calming the child through the counselor's empathy and acceptance. Relaxation techniques and verbal approval are also appropriate. In the second stage, children are given opportunities to experience and test the thoughts that are associated with their emotions. Next the children examine those distortions and learn to discern rational and irrational ideas in order to shift their perceptions. The counselor uses modeling tailored to the needs of the children to demonstrate adaptive coping skills. Cognitive change and adaptive behaviors are communicated indirectly (Knell, 1998).

The success of cognitive-behavioral play therapy has been discussed in work with children who are depressed (Briesmeister, 1997), who have ADHD (Kaduson, 1997), who express perfectionistic tendencies (VanFleet, 1997), and who have anxiety (Lyness-Richard, 1997). Friedberg (1996) gave some specific suggestions for using cognitive-behavioral games and workbooks with distressed children in schools. He stated that the flexibility and creativity of incorporating games and workbooks can promote the counseling relationship and augment the traditional counseling process. Utay and Lampe (1995) presented a cognitive-behavioral group counseling game designed to increase the social skills of children with learning disabilities. Their study supported the effectiveness of the cognitive-behavioral approach to play therapy.

## CROSS-CULTURAL APPLICATIONS OF REBT AND CBT

REBT and CBT are especially appealing to those cultures and to those individuals in all cultures who prefer strong, directive counseling and an active counselor who favors dispensing information about the "A, B, C, D, E" philosophy and approach to helping people think, feel, and behave better. REBT and CBT counselors are not shy in telling clients what they are doing wrong and what they need to do to correct it. REBT and CBT are education or reeducation methods that teach clients what they are doing to themselves to make themselves feel bad and what to do to make themselves feel better. Both therapies are especially effective with those who prefer to focus on reason and thinking rather than on affect or behavior to bring about a positive change in their lives. Likewise, these approaches are favored by cultures and individuals who want their counselor to be a strong and active consultant. In other words, these clients prefer reason over emotion and reason over behavior in solving their problems and resolving conflicts. As mentioned in Chapter 2, Thompson and Campbell (1992) found that 25% of their surveyed population of 500 people in American culture selected cognitive methods over affective, behavioral, and integrative counseling interventions when working through their own bad feelings. Again, it may be inaccurate to assign a specific learning style or problem-solving style to a culture that will be true for all groups and individuals within that culture. However, in general, we might expect REBT and CBT to be and CBT to be most accepted in cultures where people want their teachers and advisors to supply a strong, authoritative, and active presence in their lives. As noted in Chapter 15, African Americans, Hispanics, and Asian Americans are among those cultures favoring the direct approach offered by CBT and REBT. These same cultural groups appreciate the direct and immediate attention that cognitive-behavioral counselors give to their presenting problems. Asian Americans and Asians seem to prefer the CBT and REBT focus on thinking rather than on feelings. CBT and REBT practitioners offer an array of techniques and methods that can be taught to people from cultures favoring education and training that will, in turn, lead to empowering clients to solve problems and resolve conflicts more efficiently. All these three cultural groups respond well to learning new skills (Kincade & Evans, 1996; Pinderhughes, 1989; Sue & Sue, 1999). CBT and REBT methods include relaxation and stress-reduction techniques, assertiveness training, anxiety management, modeling, role playing, and goal setting. The counseling interview offers a "safe" environment for the counselor to explain and demonstrate each technique before giving clients a choice of which methods they would like to try. Clients feel safe in experimenting with the new methods they have been taught before using them in real-life situations. As for any client from any culture, the CBT or REBT counselor will want to be sure that the client's belief system is examined in the bright light of reality to see which beliefs are truly rational and irrational. For example, for a minority client, the belief that "I can't get a job" could very well be a rational belief in situations where discrimination against certain groups is practiced.

## REBT, CBT, AND MANAGED HEALTH CARE

As noted in the managed care guidelines presented in Chapter 2, any type of cognitive-behavior therapy, including rational-emotive-behavior therapy, fits nicely into the type of counseling treatments and interventions managed care organizations (MCOs) support. CBT and REBT are relatively short-term treatments that can be administered successfully in 20 or fewer sessions. They both have specific, behavioral objectives that can be tracked on a weekly basis and specific goals marking the end of treatment. CBT and REBT counseling outcomes and client satisfaction generally receive positive ratings. In addition, both types of treatment are generally near the top of the list when counseling outcomes are reported in comparative studies with other therapies. In summary, counselor accountability to the client and to the MCO are both high, the cost is reasonable, the treatment is one of the shorter-term interventions, the client's present-day conflicts and problems are addressed, considerable benefit is derived from homework assignments done by the clients on their own time, the treatment can be done well in groups, and the success rate is high. All of these characteristics make CBT and REBT quite compatible with managed health-care guidelines. CBT and REBT training delivered in psychoeducational groups could be one of the best preventive measures counselors have for addressing adjustment disorders before they become severe mental illness problems.

## SUMMARY

Replying to articles critical of rational-emotive-behavior therapy, Ellis (1981, 1984, 1998) wrote that REBT remains within the field of science while resting on some evaluative assumptions. For example, the REBT concept of unconditional humanistic self-acceptance is still valid, even though it requires an operational definition. The REBT concept of self-acceptance means that a person is more than a set of behaviors; that is, people are better off negating specific behaviors without labeling their entire selves as good or bad. Ellis (1993a) traced the development of his rational-emotive-behavior therapy from 1955 to 1993 and suggested directions where REBT might be taken in the future. He pointed out that in 1955 REBT, the first of today's cognitive-behavioral therapies, was highly cognitive, largely positivist, and very active-directive. Its ABC theory of human disturbance held that people experience undesirable activating events (A), that they have rational and irrational beliefs (B) about these events, and that they create *appropriate* emotional and behavioral *consequences* (aC) with their *rational beliefs* (rB) or they create *inappropriate* and dysfunctional *consequences* (iC) with their *irrational beliefs* (iB). Thus, REBT is directed to the client's belief system, which is the cause of the problem, not the activating event.

Ellis found support for his theory in the 1970s from the work of Berkowitz (1970) and Berkowitz & Alioto (1973) on aggression, which pointed out the danger and futility of "acting out" aggressive impulses as a way of relieving and treating aggression. Aggression begets more aggression. Therefore, treatment of aggression needs to be directed to the client's belief system that directs him or her to act on often irrational thinking, which leads to inappropriate aggressive acts.

Ellis made a distinction between general REBT, which he viewed as synonymous with general cognitive-behavioral therapy, and preferential REBT, which he described as a unique type of cognitive therapy that is distinctly constructivist and humanistic. He listed 10 points defining the unique style of preferential REBT (Ellis, 1994, 1996).

1. People, learning their expectations, preferences, and goals for success and culture, feel appropriately frustrated and disappointed when they fail and are disapproved. People make themselves neurotic by their innate tendencies to construct absolutist "musts" and demands on themselves, others, and their environments.

2. People make themselves more disturbed by creating exaggerated derivatives of their "musts" and demands. For example, "She absolutely must like me!" and when she ignores me, I rashly conclude and devoutly believe that (a) "She hates me!" (b) "It's awful that she hates me!" (c) "I'm worthless because she hates me!" and (d) "No decent person will ever like me!"

3. REBT contains the information to prevent people from making themselves neurotic.

4. REBT is multimodal and used in conjunction with a variety of cognitive, emotive, and behavioral methods, including imagery, shame-attacking exercises, coping statements, role playing, encouragement, and humor.

5. People are biologically predisposed to hold on strongly to their irrational beliefs. Therefore, REBT is designed to teach clients to think, feel, and act against these beliefs.

6. REBT tends to be more heavily behavioral than some of the other cognitive-behavioral therapies. Behavioral methods used in REBT include behavioral homework with reinforcements and penalties, in vivo desensitization, implosive counterphobic procedures, and response prevention.

7. REBT has always been psychoeducational and consequently includes a number of instructional and teaching methods to help people learn to survive within a dysfunctional system and change the system.

8. People are faced with two opposing creative tendencies: (a) to make themselves disturbed and dysfunctional or (b) to change and actualize themselves to reduce their self-disturbing tendencies and thus enjoy happier lives.

9. REBT opposes dogma, rigidity, "musturbation," and one-sidedness in favor of science, empiricism, and logic in constructing a healthy, rational belief system. The preceding statement defines *mental health* for Ellis.

10. Once people upset themselves, their emotional reactions of panic, depression, and self-hatred are so strong that they require an active-directive REBT approach to provide the instruction and guidance people need to pull themselves out of the hole they have dug.

In summary, Ellis's objective for all people is that they rate their performance in relation to the goals they have set. It is *healthy* to believe "It is good when I succeed and am loved" or "It is bad when I fail and am rejected." It is *unhealthy* to believe "I am good for succeeding" and "I am bad for getting rejected." Regarding unconditional positive regard, Ellis pointed out that REBT therapists try to give this type of acceptance to all clients but also teach them how to give it to themselves. Ellis (1993b) envisioned the main future of REBT in psychoeducational applications for the millions of people who do not have access to counseling services. In spite of some contradictory evidence, rational-emotive-behavior education still has promise as a preventive intervention for children, adolescents, and adults inclined to exaggerate negative events. REBT and CBT training may be the only hope for adding rationality to the emotion-driven culture in which we find ourselves living.

## W E B S I T E S for Rationale-Emotive-Behavior Therapy

A Life Chronology of Fritz Perls
www.gestalt.org/fritz.htm

Albert Ellis Institute
www.rebt.org/index.html

Cognitive-Behavior Therapy
www.rational.org.nz

Rational-Emotive-Behavior Therapy
www.threeminutetherapy.com/rebt.html

## REFERENCES

Barrett, P., Duffy, A., Dadds, M., & Rapee, R. (2001). Cognitive-behavioral treatment of anxiety disorders in children: Long-term (6-year) follow-up. *Journal of Consulting and Clinical Psychology, 69,* 135–141.

Beck, A. (1976). *Cognitive therapy and emotional disorders.* New York: International Universities Press.

Beck, A., Sokol, L., Clark, D., Berchick, R., & Wright, F. (1992). A crossover study of focused cognitive therapy for panic disorder. *American Journal of Psychiatry, 149,* 778–783.

Berkowitz, C. (1970). Experimental investigations of hostility catharsis. *Journal of Consulting and Clinical Psychology, 35,* 1–7.

Berkowitz, L., & Alioto, J. (1973). The meaning of an observed event as a determinant of its aggressive consequences. *Journal of Personality and Social Psychology, 28,* 206–217.

Bernard, M. (1990). Rational-emotive therapy with children and adolescents: Treatment strategies. *School Psychology Review, 19,* 294–303.

Briesmeister, J. M. (1997). Play therapy with depressed children. In H. G. Kaduson, D. Cangelosi, & C. E. Schaefer (Eds.), *The playing cure: Individualized play therapy for specific childhood problems* (pp. 3–28). Northvale, NJ: Jason Aronson.

Crawford, T., & Ellis, A. (1989). A dictionary of rational-emotive feelings and behaviors. *Journal of Rational-Emotive and Cognitive Behavior Therapy, 7,* 3–28.

Davis, D., & Boster, L. (1993). Cognitive-behavioral expressive interventions with aggressive and resistant youth. *Residential Treatment for Children and Youth, 10,* 55–67.

DiGiuseppe, R. (1990). Rational-emotive assessment of school aged children. *School Psychology Review, 19,* 287–293.

Dryden, W. (1989). Albert Ellis: An efficient and passionate life. *Journal of Counseling and Development, 67,* 539–546.

Duffy, G., & Spence, S. (1993). The effectiveness of cognitive self-management as an adjunct to a behavioral intervention for childhood obesity: A research note. *Journal of Child Psychology and Psychiatry, 34,* 1043–1050.

Ellis, A. (1954). *The American sexual tragedy.* New York: Twayne.

Ellis, A. (1965). *The case for sexual liberty.* Tucson, AZ: Seymour Press.

Ellis, A. (1969). *The art and science of love* (2nd ed.). New York: Lyle Stuart/Bantam.

Ellis, A. (1972). Emotional education in the classroom. *Journal of Clinical Child Psychology, 1,* 19–22.

Ellis, A. (1974). What rational-emotive therapy is and is not. *Counselor Education and Supervision, 14,* 140–144.

Ellis, A. (1975). *How to live with a "neurotic".* New York: Crown. (Original work published 1957)

Ellis, A. (1977). *How to live with—and—without anger.* New York: Reader's Digest Press.

Ellis, A. (1981). Science, religiosity and rational emotive psychology. *Psychotherapy: Theory, Research and Practice, 18,* 55–58.

Ellis, A. (1984). Rational-emotive therapy and pastoral counseling: A reply to Richard Wessler. *Personnel and Guidance Journal, 62,* 266–267.

Ellis, A. (1987). The impossibility of achieving consistently good mental health. *American Psychologist, 42,* 364–375.

Ellis, A. (1993a). Reflections on rational-emotive therapy. *Journal of Consulting and Clinical Psychology, 61,* 199–201.

Ellis, A. (1993b). *Rational emotive therapy.* Paper presented at the convention of the American Psychological Association, Toronto, Ontario.

Ellis, A. (1994a). Personal communication.

Ellis, A. (1994b). *Reason and emotion in psychotherapy* (Rev. ed.). New York: Birch Lane.

Ellis, A. (1996). *Better, deeper, and more enduring brief therapy.* New York: Brunner/Mazel.

Ellis, A. (1997). Must musterbation and demandingness lead to emotional disorders? *Psychotherapy, 34,* 95–98.

Ellis, A. (1998). *REBT diminishes much of the human ego.* New York: Institute for Rational-Emotive Therapy.

Ellis, A. (2001). Rational-emotive imagery. www.rational.org.nz. Retrieved August 23, 2002.

Ellis, A., & Dryden, W. (1996). *The practice of rational emotive behavior therapy* (Rev. ed.). New York: Springer.

Ellis, A., & Harper, R. (1975). *Guide to rational living.* Englewood Cliffs, NJ: Prentice-Hall.

Ellis, A., & Wilde, J. (2001). *Rational emotive behavior therapy with children and adolescents: Verbatim case studies.* New York: Prentice Hall.

Friedberg, R. D. (1996). Cognitive-behavioral games and workbooks: Tips for school counselors. *Elementary School Guidance & Counseling, 31,* 11–19.

Jay, S., Elliot, C., Woody, P., & Siegel, S. (1991). An investigation of cognitive-behavior therapy combined with oral Valium for children undergoing painful medical procedures. *Health Psychology, 10,* 317–322.

Kaduson, H. G. (1997). Play therapy for children with attention-deficit hyperactivity disorder. In H. G. Kaduson, D. Cangelosi, & C. E. Schaefer (Eds.), *The playing cure: Individualized play therapy for specific childhood problems* (pp. 197–228). Northvale, NJ: Jason Aronson.

Kendall, P. (1993). Cognitive-behavior therapies with youth: Guiding theory, current status, and emerging developments. *Journal of Consulting and Clinical Psychology, 61,* 235–247.

Kincade, E., & Evans, K. (1996). Counseling theories, process, and interventions within a multicultural context. In J Delucia-Waack (Ed.), *Multicultural counseling competencies: Implications for training and practice* (pp. 89–112). Alexandria, VA: Association for Counselor Education and Supervision.

Knell, S. M. (1996). Cognitive-behavioral play therapy. In *The Hatherleigh guide to child and adolescent therapy* (pp. 129–152). New York: Hatherleigh.

Knell, S. M. (1997). Cognitive-behavioral play therapy. In K. O'Connor & L. M. Braverman (Eds.), *Play therapy theory and practice: A comparative presentation* (pp. 79–99). New York: Wiley.

Knell, S. M. (1998). Cognitive-behavioral play therapy. *Journal of Clinical Child Psychology, 27,* 28–33.

Lochman, J. (1992). Cognitive behavioral intervention with aggressive boys: Three-year follow-up and preventive effects. *Journal of Consulting and Clinical Psychology, 60,* 426–432.

Lyness-Richard, D. (1997). Play and perfectionism: Putting fun back into families. In H. G. Kaduson, D. Cangelosi, & C. E. Schaefer (Eds.), *The playing cure: Individualized play therapy for specific childhood problems* (pp. 29–60). Northvale, NJ: Jason Aronson.

Maultsby, M. (1976). *Rational self-analysis format.* Lexington, KY: Center for Rational Behavior Therapy and Training, University of Kentucky.

Maultsby, M. (1984). *Rational behavior therapy.* Englewood Cliffs, NJ: Prentice-Hall.

McGinn, L., & Sanderson, W. (2001). What allows cognitive behavioral therapy to be brief: Overview, efficacy, and crucial factors facilitating brief treatment. *Clinical Psychology: Science and Practice, 8,* 23–36.

Meichenbaum, D. (1977). *Cognitive behavior modification: An integrative approach.* New York: Plenum.

Meichenbaum, D. (1985). *Stress-inoculation training.* New York: Pergamon.

Pinderhughes, E. (1989). *Understanding race, ethnicity, and power: The key to efficacy in clinical practice.* New York: Free Press/Macmillan.

Ronen, T. (1992). Cognitive therapy with children. *Child Psychiatry and Human Development, 23,* 19–30.

Silverman, S., & DiGiuseppe, R. (2001). Cognitive-behavioral and emotional problems. *Journal of Rational-Emotive and Cognitive-Behavioral Therapy, 19,* 119–134.

Spence, S., Donovan, C. & Brechman-Toussaint, M. (2000). The treatment of childhood social phobia: The effectiveness of a social skills training based cognitive-behavioral intervention with and without parent involvement. *Journal of Child Psychology and Psychiatry, 41,* 713–726.

Sue, D., & Sue, D. (1999). *Counseling the culturally different: Theory and practice.* New York: Wiley.

Thebarge, R. (1989). Symptom substitution: A rational-emotive perspective. *Journal of Rational-Emotive and Cognitive-Behavior Therapy, 7,* 93–97.

Thompson, C., & Campbell, S. (1992). Personal intervention preferences for alleviating mild depression. *Journal of Counseling and Development, 71,* 69–73.

Utay, J. M., & Lampe, R. E. (1995). Use of a group counseling game to enhance social skills of children with learning disabilities. *Journal of Specialists in Group Work, 20,* 114–121.

VanFleet, R. (1997). Play and perfectionism: Putting fun back into families. In H. G. Kaduson, D. Cangelosi, & C. E. Schaefer (Eds.), *The playing cure: Individualized play therapy for specific childhood problems* (pp. 61–82). Northvale, NJ: Jason Aronson.

Waters, V. (1980). *Rational stories for children.* New York: Albert Ellis Institute.

Waters, V. (1982). Helping children build tease tolerance. *RETwork, 1,* 1.

Waters, V. (1998). Irrational beliefs of children, adolescents, and parents. Personal communication.

Watkins, C. E. (1983). Rational self-analysis for children. *Elementary School Guidance and Counseling, 17,* 304–306.

Webb, W. (1993). Cognitive behavior therapy with children of alcoholics. *School Counselor, 40,* 170–177.

# Chapter 9

# Behavioral Counseling

*Not everything that can be counted counts,*
*and not everything that counts can be counted.*
—Albert Einstein

## B. F. SKINNER

Behavior therapy is rooted in the work of Ivan Pavlov's experiments in respondent or classical conditioning. Behavior modification stems from B. F. Skinner's work on instrumental or operant conditioning. Both scholars shared a common interest in using experimental methods to research abnormal behavior patterns. The field of behavioral psychology has had numerous other contributors over the years. The 1920s marked the time when the basic concepts of behavioral therapy were first used. It was not until the 1950s and 1960s, though, that systematic and comprehensive forms of behavioral therapy emerged. Primary contributors were Joseph Wolpe in South Africa, M. B. Shapiro and Hans Eyseneck in Britain, and B. F. Skinner in the United States. The name best known to the general public, as well as the most controversial, is B. F. Skinner. Although he did not develop new principles of behaviorism, Skinner did the most to translate the theories and ideas of other behaviorists into the methods that are now used by counselors and therapists around the world.

Burrhus Frederic Skinner was born in Susquehanna, Pennsylvania. He majored in literature at Hamilton College in Clinton, New York, with the goal of becoming a writer. After a few years with little success, Skinner regarded himself a failure as a writer. Reflecting later on this time in his life, Skinner commented that he failed because he had nothing to say. Skinner then entered Harvard University to study psychology. The behavior of humans and animals was of special interest to him. He received a master's degree in 1930 and a Ph.D. in experimental psychology in 1931. Following graduation, Skinner began his most productive career as a teacher and researcher, first at Harvard and then at the University of Minnesota in 1936. While there, he married Yvonne Blue. They had two daughters, the younger of which became famous for being reared in Skinner's air crib, a combination playpen and crib with a plastic mattress cover, glass sides, and air conditioning. In short, it resembled an aquarium for babies. It never caught on with crib-buying shoppers.

He was appointed chairman of the psychology department at Indiana University in 1945. He later returned to Harvard in 1948 to accept a professorship, which he held until his death. As he began to generate things to say in the field of behaviorism, Skinner's flair for writing returned. His numerous books include the following:

*The Behavior of Organisms* (1938)
*Walden Two* (1948)
*The Technology of Teaching* (1968)
*Beyond Freedom and Dignity* (1971)
*Skinner for the Classroom* (1980, edited by R. Epstein)
*A Matter of Consequences: Part III of an Autobiography* (1983)
*Upon Further Reflection* (1987)

Skinner's contribution to knowledge is not strictly confined to the laboratory. He made considerable contributions to solving educational problems. He developed and advanced the concepts of programmed instruction, operant conditioning in classroom management, and the teaching machine (first developed by Sidney Pressey in 1923). Perhaps the most controversial of Skinner's works is *Beyond Freedom and Dignity,* which pictures a society where behavior is shaped and controlled by a planned system of rewards. His most helpful contributions to classroom management are found in *The Technology of Teaching* and *Skinner for the Classroom.*

Skinner (1990a), in an article he completed the evening before his death, attacked those who would use introspection or brain analysis as methods for analyzing behavior. He asserted that behavior is the product of three types of variation and selection: natural selection, operant conditioning, and modeling. Skinner had little use for cognitive psychology because he contended it had not contributed, as behavior analysis, to the design of better environments for solving existing problems and preventing future problems. Summing up his 60 years in the profession, Skinner (1990b) said that the point he tried to make is that it can be demonstrated that people choose behavior based on anticipated consequences. According to Skinner, this selection by consequences has negative implications for the world and its future unless some vital changes are made. He concluded by saying that "any evidence that I've been successful in that [fostering needed changes] is how I should like to be remembered."

Skinner's death in 1990 ended six decades of significant contributions to behavioral psychology that began with the publication of his first paper in 1930. During his career, citations of Skinner's name in the literature exceeded those of the previous leader, Sigmund Freud (Banks & Thompson, 1995).

## THE NATURE OF PEOPLE

A broad statement of the behaviorist view of the nature of people is Skinner's (1971) belief that things that happen to children influence and change them as biological entities. He believed that the idea that the child of our past is still contained within us is a form of animism that serves no useful purpose in explaining present behavior. Behaviorists view human beings as neither good nor bad but merely as products of their environment. People are essentially born neutral (the blank slate or tabula rasa idea), with equal potential for good or evil and for rationality or irrationality.

Behaviorists view people as responders. They reject self-directing, mentalistic concepts of human behavior. Behaviorists contend that people can make only those responses they have learned, and they make them when the stimulus conditions are appropriate.

Behavioral counselors, then, view individuals as products of their conditioning. The stimulus–response paradigm is the basic pattern of all human learning. People react in predictable ways to any given stimulus according to what they have learned through experience. Humans react to stimuli much as animals do, except that human responses are more complex and organized on a higher plane.

Skinner regarded the human being as an organism who learns patterns of behavior, catalogues them within a repertoire, and repeats them at a later date. More specifically, the organism learns a specific response when a satisfying condition follows an action. The number of these responses mounts as time passes and satisfying conditions are repeated. The behaviorist's interest is in the science of behavior as it relates to biology. Skinner believed that:

> a person is a member of a species shaped by evolutionary contingencies of survival, displaying behavioral processes which bring him under the control of the environment in which he lives, and largely under the control of a social environment which he and millions of others like him have constructed and maintained during the evolution of a culture. The direction of the controlling relation is reversed: a person does not act upon the world, the world acts upon him. (1971, p. 211)

Because human behavior is learned, any or all behavior can be unlearned, and new behavior learned in its place. The behaviorist is concerned with observable events that, when they become unacceptable behaviors, can be unlearned. The behavioral counselor is concerned with this unlearning or reeducation process. Behavioral counseling procedures can be developed from social learning theory.

## THEORY OF COUNSELING

Behavioral counseling is an action therapy in much the same way that reality therapy, solution-focused brief counseling, and cognitive-behavior therapy are. Clients do something about their behavior rather than trying to understand it by talking about it. Clients learn to monitor their behavior, practice coping skills, and complete homework assignments to help them reach their goals.

Behavioral counseling is a reeducation or relearning process. Counselors help clients develop plans to reinforce adaptive or helpful behavior and extinguish maladaptive or unhelpful behavior. The counselor's role is, through reinforcement principles, to help clients achieve the goals they have set for themselves.

Behavioral counseling includes several techniques based on principles of learning employed to manage maladaptive behavior. Today, behavioral counseling is used with covert processes (cognitions, emotions, obsessive ideation), as well as with traditional, overt behavior problems. Behavioral counseling involves two types of behavior: operant and respondent.

In operant conditioning, *operant behavior* refers to behavior that operates on and changes the environment in some manner. It is also referred to as *instrumental behavior* because it is instrumental in goal achievement. People who use operant conditioning wait until the desired behavior or an approximation of the desired behavior occurs and then reinforce it with a rewarding stimulus known as *positive reinforcement* (praise, money, candy, free time, and attention). *Negative reinforcement* (different from punishment) occurs when the operant behavior is reinforced by its capacity to stop an aversive stimulus. For example, rats learn to press a bar to shut off an electric shock, and children take their seats at school to shut off the aversive sound of their teacher's scolding. *Punishment,* like positive reinforcement, occurs after the behavior is emitted but tends to decrease its occurrence. *Extinction* is the process of eliminating a learned behavior by ignoring the behavior or by not reinforcing it by withholding attention and other rewards. A comparison of these four terms is presented in Figure 9-1.

## Behavior Analysis

### *Why People Behave as They Do*

People behave in ways that maintain or enhance their self-images. They also behave in ways to achieve goals that meet the following hierarchy of needs (Maslow, 1970):

- Self-fulfillment (the need to develop skills, interests, and talents)
- Self-esteem (feeling worthwhile)
- Social (belonging to a group, giving and receiving love)

|  | Present | Withhold |
|---|---|---|
| *Positive stimuli:* Praise Tangible rewards | Positive reinforcement | Extinction |
| *Negative stimuli:* Criticism Unpleasant consequences and tasks | Punishment | Negative reinforcement |

FIGURE 9-1  Examples of operant conditioning

- Security (safety, shelter)
- Physiological (food, sleep, oxygen, water)

## Steps in Behavior Analysis

### *Principles of Behavior*

1. Behavior consists of three phases:
   - Antecedent: the stimulus or cue that occurs before behavior that leads to its occurrence
   - Behavior: what the person says or does (or doesn't)
   - Consequence: what the person perceives happens to him or her (positive, neutral, and negative) as a result of the behavior
2. Behavior problems are usually rooted in antecedents or consequences.
3. People usually prefer behavior for which the consequences are known to behavior for which the consequences are uncertain.

A behavior analysis designed to determine causes of and solutions to performance problems requires four steps:

1. Identify the problem category. Is it a problem of *performing a task,* or is it a problem of *dealing with people?*

2. Identify the problem type. Is it the person *unable* to do the task, or is the person *unwilling* to do the task? The acid test is whether the person could do the task if his or her life depended on it (not that we would go that far).

3. Determine the problem cause if the person is unable to do the task. Is it due to a *lack of knowledge* about what, when, and how the task should be done, or is there an *obstacle* in the environment that is preventing accomplishment of the task? If the person is *unwilling* to do the task, is it because there is a *lack of knowledge* about why something needs to be done, or is it simple *refusal?* Behavioral methods often fail because of their tendency to assume that all problems with people are rooted in somebody's refusal to do certain things.

4. Select a problem solution that is appropriate for the problem at hand. If the person is *unable* to perform the task and needs to know how to do it, *provide training.* If there is an *obstacle in the environment* (e.g., the child cannot see the marking board), fix the problem (move the child closer to the board) or *remove the obstacle.* If a person is refusing to do a task (e.g., shows up late every day), the counselor needs to determine what is reinforcing the *undesired* behavior and what is punishing the *desired* behavior. Then, the counselor must find a way to *decrease* or *eliminate* both of these things that maintain the *undesired* behavior and find a way to reinforce the *desired* behavior (showing up on time). Note that punishment of the undesired behavior is a last-resort option because it carries a possible side effect of damaging the relationship you are trying to build with your client. The behavior analysis process is outlined in Table 9-1 and Figure 9-2.

TABLE 9-1    Determining causes of and solutions to performance problems

| *What category of problem?* | *Is it a problem of:* | *Is it due to:* | *Approach it by:* |
|---|---|---|---|
| Performing a task | Being unable* | Lack of knowledge about what, when, how | Providing training |
| | | Obstacle in the environment | Removing the obstacle |
| Dealing with people | Being unwilling* | Lack of knowledge about why something needs to be done | Providing information/ feedback |
| | | Simple refusal | Changing the balance of positive and negative consequences |

*Could he or she do it if his or her life depended on it? No = unable; yes = unwilling.

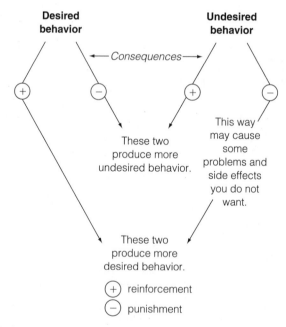

FIGURE 9-2    Balancing consequences

## Schedules of Reinforcement

Changing the balance of positive and negative consequences requires selecting an appropriate schedule of reinforcement. There are two schedules of reinforcement for the acquisition and establishment of a new behavior: continuous and intermittent. *Continuous reinforcement,* the reinforcement of each successful response, is best when the new behavior is first being learned. Once the new behavior has been learned, continuous reinforcement has the effect of extinguishing the behavior by satiating the learner. Reinforcement should be switched to one of four intermittent schedules: fixed interval, variable interval, fixed ratio, or variable ratio.

### Fixed Interval Schedule

Reinforcement is provided on the first response after a fixed time has elapsed. The interval could be set at, for example, 30 seconds. Hourly wages paid weekly and weekly tests given in a class each Friday are other examples of fixed interval schedules. Reinforced behavior increases before the reinforcement and decreases dramatically after reinforcement. Study behavior increases before the test and decreases after the test.

### Variable Interval Schedule

Reinforcement is provided on the first response after some average time period. For instance, intervals could range from 15 to 45 seconds, averaging 30 seconds over several successful responses. Unannounced pop quizzes given in class are excellent examples of an application of the variable interval schedule. Study behavior is highest for classes where pop quizzes are given, but the teacher's popularity may suffer. Study behavior increases as the time between quizzes increases.

### Fixed Ratio Schedule

The participant is reinforced for every 5, 10, or 20 correct responses made. The reinforcement rate is fixed at the same rate (e.g., every fifth correct response is reinforced). Piecework in a factory where people are paid according to the number of products produced is a good example of a fixed ratio schedule.

### Variable Ratio Schedule

Participants are reinforced on a schedule varying, for example, from 5 to 25 correct responses, with an average number of responses between reinforcements falling somewhere in midrange between 5 and 25. Playing slot machines is both a good example of how variable ratio reinforcement is applied and how strongly this method maintains the gambling addictions people have. Fishing is another good example of variable ratio reinforcement. An occasional bite will keep a fisherman "hooked" for hours.

## COUNSELING GOALS

As with most counseling, the ultimate goal of behavioral counseling is teaching children to become their own counselors by changing their behavior to better meet their needs. All behavior change, internal and external, can be attempted through behavioral counseling. Specific techniques reduce and eliminate anxiety, phobias, and obsessive thoughts, as well as reduce inappropriate, observable behaviors.

After the problem has been identified and the desired behavior change agreed on by the counselor and child, the behavioral counselor is apt to employ a variety of counseling procedures to help the child acquire the behaviors necessary to solve the problem. The ultimate outcome of behavioral counseling is to teach children to become their own behavior-modification experts—in other words, to program their own reinforcement schedules (self-management). Encouraging children to move from extrinsic to intrinsic reinforcement—to please themselves with their behavior rather than constantly seek the approval of others—is even more desirable. The success of behavioral counseling lies in the client's success in transferring from an extrinsic reward system to an intrinsic reward system for maintaining the target behavior. For example, a child who receives extra privileges at home for completing homework assignments reaches the intrinsic level when she realizes that her life is better when she does well at school and then continues the target behavior, reinforced only by the realization that her life is more pleasant. As her grades improve, she finds her parents more cooperative and nicer to be around, and she finds her teachers praising her efforts rather than nagging her about the missed homework assignments.

Because behavioral counseling differs from traditional counseling principally in terms of specificity, the behavioral counselor prefers to state goals as overt changes in behavior rather than as hypothetical constructs. The basic counseling function involved in behavioral counseling is defined as discrimination—differential responding to different situations (individuals, groups, institutions, and environmental settings). In behavioral counseling, continuing assessment of the effects on outcomes of each counseling intervention determines effectiveness of the procedure.

## COUNSELING METHODS

When using behavioral counseling (BC) methods with children, the counselor needs to match reinforcement to the child's developmental level and reward preferences. Social development is one good predicator of effective reinforcers. Egocentric children in the preoperational stage of development probably do not find sharing toys with siblings or friends to be a priority reward. Preoperational-stage children find playing alone with favorite toys or playing a game in which they can make up all the rules much more reinforcing.

## Contingency Contracts

Contracts are effective for children if they have a voice in writing the terms. Contract language must be simplified for understanding, and the goals should be quite clear, with as few steps as possible to meet the goals. Reinforcement should be immediate when the target behavior is being established. Readily available cost-free and developmentally appropriate rewards are preferable—being first in line, doing a favorite classroom job, being a student helper, running errands, tutoring a classmate— if they are reinforcing to the child.

The contingency contracting process can be broken down into six steps:

1. The counselor and the child identify the problem to be solved.

2. The counselor collects data to verify the baseline frequency rate for the undesired behavior.

3. The counselor and the child set mutually acceptable goals.

4. The counselor develops a contingency plan that identifies the target behaviors and the number of times the target behavior has to be performed to earn the reward for the client. For example, completion of one homework paper per day in math earns 20 minutes of playing a favorite video game at home. The counselor selects counseling interventions for attaining the goals.

5. The counselor evaluates the plan for observable and measurable change in the target behavior.

6. If the plan is not effective, the counselor repeats Step 4. If the techniques prove effective, the counselor develops a maintenance plan to maintain the new behavior and move the client from extrinsic rewards to the intrinsic reward of learning that life is better when math assignments are completed.

For example, Jerry completed no assignments in any of his school subjects. His teacher is lowering his grades because of his unwillingness to complete these assignments. He is referred to the counselor.

Step 1. The counselor talks with Jerry about the problem. Jerry is not happy with his grades but still has trouble concentrating on completing his work. He would like to do better on these assignments and make better grades.

Step 2. A 5-day period is set aside to determine the exact amount of work Jerry completes. The record verifies the teacher's report that Jerry does not complete any assignments, even though he starts about half of them.

Step 3. Jerry and the counselor agree that a good goal for a start would be to complete one assignment each day.

Step 4. For each assignment completed, Jerry will receive 10 points to be applied toward a total of 100 points, which can be exchanged for 30 minutes of free time during the school day.

Step 5. Evaluation of the contingency contract indicates that Jerry completed four assignments the first week, earning 40 points, and six assignments the second week, for a total of 100 points. He then received his 30 minutes of free time. The following week, he earned 100 points and received a second 30 minutes of free time. He was also successful during Week 3.

Step 6. The counselor and Jerry agree that continuing with the point system is not necessary. Jerry's grades are improving, and everyone seems happier—the teacher, Jerry, and his parents. As a maintenance procedure, Jerry agrees to check in with the counselor each Friday afternoon for reports on his completed assignments for the week, which he records on a pocket-sized scorecard. Of course, a good teaching procedure would be to continue to allow Jerry and his classmates to earn free time when they complete assigned work. It would also be helpful if Jerry's parents would award more privileges at home as Jerry's work improved.

## Self-Management

An adaptation of the six-step contingency contract method, the self-management plan, is for children who can take more responsibility for their behavior. These plans also follow a step-by-step process: defining a problem in behavioral terms, collecting data on the problem, introducing a treatment program based on behavior principles, evaluating the effectiveness of the program, and appropriately changing the program if the plan is not working. The major difference between self-management and other procedures is that children assume the major responsibility for carrying out their programs, including arranging their own contingencies or reinforcement when they have the skills to do so.

Steps in developing a self-management plan are as follows:

1. Choose an observable and measurable behavior you wish to change.

2. Record for at least 1 week (a) your target behavior, (b) the setting in which it occurs, (c) the antecedent events leading to the behavior, and (d) the consequences resulting from the behavior.

3. Set a goal you can achieve.

4. Change the setting and the antecedent events leading up to the target behavior.

5. Change the consequences that reinforce the target behavior.

6. Keep accurate records of your target behavior—your successes and failures.

7. Develop a plan for rewarding yourself when you meet your daily goal and a plan to punish or levy a fine on yourself when you fail to meet your daily goal.

8. Arrange a plan to maintain the goals you have reached.

Self-management contracts are generally not effective for younger children unless the plan is managed by both the child and an older person. Self-tracking and self-rewarding are usually difficult for children younger than 11. Children can set goals and choose consequences but need an adult monitor for tracking and reinforcing behavior. Training in self-management skills has been one of the best applications of behavioral principles to counseling children.

## Shaping

The basic operant technique of shaping is a general procedure designed to induce new behaviors by reinforcing behaviors that approximate the desired behavior. Each successive approximation of the behavior is reinforced until the desired behavior is obtained. To administer the technique, the counselor must know how to skillfully use (1) looking, (2) waiting, and (3) reinforcing. The counselor looks for the desired behavior, waits until it occurs, and reinforces it when it does occur. In essence, the counselor is catching the child in good behavior—a much more difficult task than catching the child in bad behavior. Shaping of successful approximations of the target behavior works well with children if the program is administered correctly. Small steps need to be reinforced immediately each time they occur. Shaping offers a method for teaching complex behaviors to children because mediating steps are identified and rewarded. Extrinsic reinforcers are more likely to be effective with children. Sugar-free candy, stickers, trinkets, and "good behavior" ink stamps on the hand all work well. Pairing intrinsic rewards with extrinsic rewards is always good practice to help children move away from the need for extrinsic rewards.

## Behavioral Momentum

Behavioral momentum is a relatively new concept in behavioral counseling. It operates on much the same principle of Newton's law of motion, which states that a body in motion tends to remain in motion. Behavioral momentum has been used mostly to reduce noncompliant behavior in children and adults. Momentum is established by making three to five short, easy requests, with a high probability of compliance, administered to a person just prior to a request having a low probability of compliance. Each high-probability request is reinforced by verbal praise upon compliance. The theory is that the reinforcement gained from doing the easy tasks builds momentum that carries over to completion of the more difficult or low-compliance task. Romano and Roll (2000) researched the level of compliance needed on the easy tasks to carry over for completion of the difficult task. High-probability tasks are generally defined as those having an 80% compliance rate. Romano and Roll investigated the momentum effect that requests with medium levels of compliance probability might have. Medium levels of compliance probability were set at 50% to 70% of the time. The researchers found that both high and medium levels of compliance probability were effective in increasing compliance to low-probability requests.

Ray, Skinner, and Watson (1999), in a related study on behavioral momentum, found that momentum could be established by having parents of an autistic child administer the easy tasks, followed by the teacher administering the difficult task. Prior to the intervention, the student had consistently displayed noncompliant behavior toward the teacher. In this case, stimulus control did transfer from the parents to the teacher.

## Biofeedback

In biofeedback, a machine accomplishes the three behaviors of looking, waiting, and reinforcing. Brain waves, muscle tension, body temperature, heart rate, and blood pressure can be monitored for small changes and fed back to the client by auditory and visual means. Biofeedback methods have been successful in, for example, teaching hyperactive children to relax. The more the child relaxes, the slower and lower the beeping sound on the monitor. The equipment may provide feedback with electric trains and recorded music. Both stop when the child stops relaxing and restart when the child takes the first small step toward relaxing again. An understanding of cause and effect by the children enhances biofeedback methods but is not a necessity.

## Modeling

Modeling consists of exposing the child to one or more individuals, either in real life or in film or tape presentations, who exhibit behaviors to be adopted by the child. Counselors may be the models to demonstrate certain behaviors to the child, or peers of the child may be used.

Peers are an important part of a child's world, and their influence can help children change. Children usually imitate the behaviors of people they like. A model may be presented to the child through the use of television, films, videotapes, or books. Other models include friends, classmates, adults, and the counselor.

For example, Charlene mentioned a friend, Patty, a number of times during the counseling sessions. She indicated that she would like to be like Patty because Patty had a lot of friends, made good grades, and got along well with her parents and teachers. The counselor asked Charlene to observe Patty's behaviors closely for 1 week and to write on an index card those she particularly liked and wanted to imitate. The next week Charlene brought back her list of six behaviors. The counselor and Charlene selected the most important one for Charlene (giving compliments) and began to work on that behavior. Role playing and behavior rehearsal were included in the counseling to help Charlene learn the new behaviors. The observed behaviors were practiced and modified until they were appropriate for Charlene. As counseling progressed, Charlene continued to observe her model and to practice new behaviors until she became more like her ideal self.

Modeling is a process for teaching children voluntary behaviors through observation and replication of desired behaviors. Modeling and shaping could be done in combination for younger children. Negative reinforcement is effective here if a new behavior is learned to avoid a consequence such as peer ridicule.

## Token Economies

Token economies are used on a group basis, as in a school classroom. The children earn tokens or points for certain target behaviors. These behaviors are classified as either on task or socially appropriate. Children also lose tokens or points for off-task and socially inappropriate behaviors. Children may periodically cash in tokens or points earned for rewards such as free time, game time, trinkets, and sugarless candy. Some teachers use token economies for their classroom groups. An empty jar sits on the teacher's desk. Every time something good happens in the class-room, the teacher drops some marbles in the jar. The marble noise becomes an auditory reinforcement to go with the visual image of the jar filling up. A full jar means all students get free popcorn during the lunch period. The case study on Sue in this chapter is an example of how to use a token economy contract.

## Behavior-Practice Groups

Behavior-practice groups have some advantages in counseling children. They provide a relatively safe setting for the child to practice new behaviors before trying them out in real-life situations. These groups are also useful in supporting and reinforcing children as they attempt new behaviors and reach goals. Behavior-practice groups may focus on any of several behavior changes, including the following:

- Weight loss
- Study habits
- Assertiveness training
- Communication skills
- Negative addictions such as drugs, alcohol, and smoking

In working with behavior-practice groups, the counselor needs to develop a lesson plan with behavioral objectives, instructional methods, reinforcement, and evaluation. A good lesson plan maintains a balance between three teaching strategies: (1) tell me, (2) show me, and (3) let me try it. For example, a lesson plan in assertiveness training might have the following objective: After 10 weekly group meetings, each child in the group will have demonstrated in at least three real-life settings the ability to do the following:

1. Make an effective complaint
2. Give negative feedback
3. Give positive feedback
4. Make a reasonable request
5. Say no to an unreasonable request

## Role Playing

Role playing is a counseling technique not restricted to one theory. Many counseling professionals use it. Behavioral counselors often find that role playing facilitates their clients' progress in self-management programs; for example, it can help clients see their behaviors as others see them and obtain feedback about these behaviors. Role playing can also provide practice for decision making and exploring consequences.

Negative role playing or rehearsal can be helpful in identifying what *not* to do. Role-playing negative behaviors and their consequences may help children evaluate objectively what is happening and the consequences of their behavior.

Role playing can help children learn about cause and effect and experience the consequences of their behavior in a relatively safe setting. Role playing is useful to children who are working toward developing a sense of empathy and beginning to modify their egocentric views of the world. Children can usually act out a problem scenario better than they can describe it.

### Role Playing to Define a Problem

Children often have trouble describing exactly what occurred in a particular situation, especially one involving interpersonal problems with parents, teachers, or peers. Moreover, they may be unable to see clearly how certain behaviors have evoked an unwanted response or consequence. For example, suppose Jerome tells the counselor that he and his mother are in constant conflict. She is unfair and never allows him to do *anything* he asks. Role playing could provide some insight into what occurs when Jerome asks for permission.

> *Counselor:*   I'll be your mother, and you show me exactly how you ask her to allow you, for instance, to have a birthday party. Talk to me exactly as you would to your mother if you were to ask her for the party.
>
> *Jerome:*   Mom, you never let me do anything! You always say no to anything I want. I want a birthday party, and you'll be mean if you don't let me have one this year!

The counselor can now readily see that if a conflict already exists between mother and child, this demand will increase the conflict and is unlikely to get Jerome his birthday party.

Children having trouble with peers might be asked to describe what happened and then to role-play one or more persons in the incident. Verbal and nonverbal behaviors not adequately described in relating the incident often become more apparent when they are role-played.

### Role Reversal

When conflicts occur between children, adults frequently ask one child, "How would you feel if he hit you like that [said that to you, bit you, and so on]?" The purpose of this admonition is to have the child empathize with the other. However, many cognitive theorists, especially Piaget, emphasized that young children up through the preoperational stage (2 to 7 years old) lack the cognitive development to be able to put themselves in another person's place. Because children understand better what they see, hear, or experience directly, role-playing other children's positions could promote a better understanding than a verbal admonition.

> *Counselor:* Barbara, I understand from your sister that you hit her on the head quite often. Would you agree that this is what happens?
>
> *Barbara:* Yeah, I can really make her move if I threaten to hit her on the head!
>
> *Counselor:* Would the two of you describe to me what happened the last time you hit Judy? [The girls describe the incident.] Now Barbara, I wonder if you would mind playing Judy and saying and doing exactly what Judy did. I would like Judy to say and do exactly what you did. [Remind the girls that hitting hard is not allowed in the role playing because people are not for hitting.]

The purpose of this role reversal is to help Barbara experience Judy's feelings when Barbara hit her, with the hope that Barbara will then want to explore better methods of relating to Judy.

Role reversal can be effective when communication breaks down between parents and children, between teachers and children, between peers, or between counselors and their clients. Each player can gain increased knowledge of the other's point of view.

### Role Playing Used as Behavior Rehearsal

To refine a speech and ensure a smooth delivery, most adults rehearse a speech before presenting it to an audience. Children, too, may feel more comfortable about trying a new behavior if they can practice it before actually facing the real world.

Dave is a shy little boy who has no friends. In an effort to help Dave make friends, the counselor may want to help him decide exactly how to approach another child and what to say to the child after the opening "Hello." To build confidence, the counselor could first role-play another child and allow Dave to practice his new behaviors in a safe atmosphere. When Dave feels secure in role-playing with the counselor, another child can be involved in the role play to help Dave gain more realistic experiences in meeting other children.

## Counseling Homework Assignments

Homework assignments may be given to children in counseling for a variety of reasons. Homework can build continuity between sessions and facilitate counseling by encouraging "work" on the child's problems between sessions. A homework assignment could be a commitment by the child to keep a record of some particular feeling or behavior, to reduce or stop a present behavior, or to try a new behavior. Homework assignments provide the child with an opportunity to try out new or different behaviors and discuss the consequences with the counselor. For example, after Dave (in the preceding example) has rehearsed approaching a new person within the counseling session, the counselor might ask him to approach one new person during the coming week and try out this new behavior. Dave could evaluate whether the new behavior was effective for him and discuss the results with the counselor; if it was not effective, they could explore other methods.

## Assertiveness Training

Some children's typical response to everyday interactions is withdrawal. Some of these children may have low self-esteem or feelings of inferiority that inhibit them; others, having experienced negative consequences as a result of speaking out, are inhibited from doing so by their anxiety. Children who are withdrawn and passive need to be encouraged to recognize their rights as people as well as accept the rights of others.

Tim and Charles were close friends. However, Tim always took from Charles whatever he wanted or needed—toys, pencils, food, and so on. Charles responded passively, always allowing Tim to have his way. The counselor asked Charles to describe in detail the latest incident, in which Tim had taken Charles's new bike, ridden it all afternoon, and brought it back scratched. The counselor encouraged Charles to formulate an assertive statement such as "I want to ride my new bike. Would you go and get your bike to ride?" Charles and the counselor took several incidents from the past, and Charles was encouraged to state (1) his needs and (2) what he would like to have happen in each situation. They then used behavior rehearsal to give Charles an opportunity to practice his assertiveness.

After several sessions, Charles made a commitment to try out his new response. He reported that he told Tim, "I want to use my Magic Markers now. Would you get your own?" and that it had worked. The counselor worked for several months on helping Charles learn how to become appropriately assertive. Each new situation was discussed and practiced in the counseling sessions before Charles actually tried it in daily living.

A word of caution is necessary to counselors teaching assertiveness to children. The adults in the child's life must be prepared for the child's new behavior. Parents who discipline children by authoritarian methods may not tolerate assertiveness on the part of their child. To avoid unpleasant consequences, the counselor has to determine the effect of the child's behavioral change on the child's significant others and on the child's culture and environment before teaching the child this new skill.

## CLASSICAL CONDITIONING METHODS

### Ivan Pavlov

Classical conditioning has its roots in the work of the Russian physiologist Ivan Pavlov. Born in 1849, Pavlov began his education in a seminary school but abandoned his pursuit of the priesthood for his fascination with science. He received his M.D. in 1883 from the University of St. Petersburg and was made director of several research facilities, including the Imperial Institute of Experimental Medicines (Windholtz, 1997). Pavlov was awarded the Nobel Prize in 1904 for his book, *Lectures on the Work of the Digestive Glands.*

Reminded that he had studied all the digestive juices of the body with the exception of saliva, Pavlov came out of retirement to research the question of how saliva contributed to the digestive process, if at all. In collecting saliva from dogs, he made several observations. He noted that the dogs salivated when they were fed and when they heard any noise that accompanied it, such as the click of opening the dog pen gate. This observation led to further experiments with Pavlov's classical, or respondent, conditioning model and to more efficient methods for collecting saliva for his research.

Classical, or respondent, conditioning can be defined as a form of learning that occurs when a neutral stimulus (the conditioned stimulus) elicits a response after multiple pairings with another stimulus (the unconditioned stimulus). In other words, respondent behavior is associated with classical conditioning, in which learning occurs when a stimulus that already elicits a response (an unconditioned stimulus) is presented along with a neutral stimulus that elicits no response or a different response. With repeated pairings of the two stimuli, the neutral stimulus begins to elicit the same response as the unconditioned stimulus. In the case of Pavlov's dogs, for example, Pavlov paired the unconditioned stimulus of food with the neutral stimulus of a bell. The response to the unconditioned stimulus was salivating. The neutral stimulus (the bell) became the conditioned stimulus, and the response to the conditioned stimulus became the conditioned response (salivating).

Wolpe and Plaud (1997) presented an overview of the development of behavior therapy, which featured the contributions of Pavlov through his work on animal conditioning. Pavlov and his students discovered experimental neurosis, which could be produced and eliminated in animals through conditioning and counterconditioning. Many of his counterconditioning techniques are in use today to treat neurotic and anxiety reactions. Pavlov found he could eliminate undesirable conditioned responses (CRS) and reduce associated anxieties by manipulating conditioned stimuli (CSS). As a footnote to history, Pavlov's Nobel Prize work on digestive juices has since been proved to be erroneous. The portion of his work that has withstood the test of time is his classical conditioning method first used to collect saliva from dogs.

## Systematic Desensitization

Systematic desensitization, developed by Wolpe (1958, 1969) from earlier work by Jacobsen (1938), is a procedure used to eliminate anxiety and fear. A response incompatible with anxiety, such as relaxation, is paired with weak and then progressively stronger anxiety-provoking stimuli. The approach is based on the principles of counterconditioning; that is, if all skeletal muscles are deeply relaxed, one cannot experience anxiety at the same time.

A child may be experiencing anxiety related to specific stimulus situations such as taking tests, performing in front of a group, being in high places, or seeing some animal. The first step is to develop a hierarchy of scenes related to the fear or phobia, with mildly aversive scenes at the bottom and progressively more aversive scenes at the top. The counselor then teaches the child the process of deep muscle relaxation and asks the relaxed child to visualize the various scenes in the hierarchy.

The relaxation exercises are successively tensing and relaxing 19 different muscle groups at 6-second intervals until a high level of relaxation is achieved. The process is usually performed with the child in a recliner chair or stretched out on a soft rug. The child is asked to go as high as possible on the hierarchy without feeling anxiety. When the child feels anxiety, he or she signals the counselor by raising one finger, and the counselor reverts to a less anxiety-provoking scene. Behavior practice facilitates the process. A child may successively practice giving a short speech in front of a mirror, with an audiotape recorder, with a videotape recorder, in front of a best friend, in front of a small group, and so on, until the child can give the speech in front of 25 classmates. The child's stimulus hierarchy might look like this:

0. Lying in bed in your room just before going to sleep—describe your room
1. Thinking about the speech alone in your room 1 week before you give it
2. Discussing the upcoming speech in class a week before it's due
3. Sitting in class while another student gives a speech 1 week before your speech
4. Writing your speech at home
5. Practicing your speech alone in your room or in front of your friend
6. Getting dressed the morning of the speech
7. Eating breakfast and thinking about the speech before going to school
8. Walking to school on the day of your speech
9. Entering the classroom on the day of the speech
10. Waiting while another student gives a speech on the day of your presentation
11. Standing in front of your classmates and looking at their faces
12. Presenting your speech before the class

The technique consists of asking the child to relax, imagine, relax, stop imagining, relax, and so on until, after repeated practice, the child learns to relax while visualizing each stage of the stimulus hierarchy.

Several relaxation exercises can be used with children. Following are two types of exercises frequently used.

1. Consciously "let go" of the various muscle groups, starting with your feet and moving to your legs, stomach, arms, neck, and head as you make yourself as comfortable as you can in a chair or lying down.
   a. Stop frowning; let your forehead relax.
   b. Let your hands, arms, and so on relax.
   c. Tighten 6 seconds, relax; tighten again 6 seconds, relax.

2. Form mental pictures.
    a. Picture yourself stretched out on a soft bed. Your legs are like concrete, sinking down in the mattress from their weight. Picture a friend coming into the room and trying to lift your concrete legs, but they are too heavy and your friend cannot do it. Repeat with arms, neck, and so on.
    b. Picture your body as a big puppet. Your hands are tied loosely to your wrists by strings. Your forearm is connected loosely by a string to your shoulder. Your feet and legs are also connected with a string. Your chin has dropped loosely against your chest. All strings are loose; your body is limp and sprawled across the bed.
    c. Picture your body as consisting of a bunch of rubber balloons. Two air holes open in your feet and the air begins to escape from your legs. Your legs begin to collapse until they are flat rubber tubes. Next a hole is opened in your chest, and the air begins to escape until your entire body is lying flat on the bed. Continue with your head, arms, neck, and so on.
    d. Imagine the most relaxing, pleasant scene you can remember—a time when you felt really good and peaceful. If you remember fishing in a mountain stream, pay attention to the little things, such as quiet ripples on the water and leaves on the trees. What sounds were present? Did you hear the quiet rustling of the leaves? Is your relaxing place before an open fireplace with logs crackling, or is it the beach, with a warm sun and breezes?

Continued practice facilitates achievement of these mental pictures and relaxation levels.

Systematic desensitization, a classical conditioning technique, could be too complex for younger children, who are not always capable of handling sequential behaviors. Conscious relaxation and visualization may also be difficult for younger children, who benefit more by actual practice of the steps in the stimulus hierarchy. For example, the following systematic desensitization program could be used to help a 6-year-old child who is experiencing school phobia: The child indicates that he would like to work toward getting a favorite video game. A chart is drawn up with spaces to star each day he followed the program and earned a dollar toward the purchase price of his video game. Steps in the hierarchy were small enough not to overwhelm the child. Each session lasted 30 minutes.

Step 1. Child and his mother working together alone in the schoolroom, the child reading or talking to his mother.
Step 2. Child, mother, and friend of the child in the schoolroom, with the child talking to his friend.
Step 3. Child, mother, friend, and familiar adult (not on the school staff) together in the schoolroom, with child talking while playing.
Step 4. Child, mother, friend, and teacher in the schoolroom, the child talking with the teacher; mother leaves them; friend leaves.
Step 5. Child and teacher together in the schoolroom, talking to each other.
Step 6. Child and teacher move to the classroom and talk to each other.

Step 7. Child joins the classroom for half a day.

Step 8. Child spends an entire day in the classroom.

In extreme anxiety, desensitization methods may need to be paired with appropriate medication to help the child relax. Going off the medication and performing the task becomes the final step in the hierarchy.

Classical conditioning and operant conditioning usually occur at the same time. A child is given after-school detention for disrupting her class. Detention has the operant effect of preventing the child's disruptive behavior; however, detention may also cause a classical conditioned response of hating school because more school is used as punishment. School time becomes associated with punishment. Associating being in school with a privilege would be much better. When the child misbehaves, she loses the privilege of being in class and has to spend her class time working in a time-out area or in the in-school suspension room. Additional school time (detention) would not be used as a punishment or consequence.

In summary, the technique of desensitization is based on a principle of learning referred to as *reciprocal inhibition;* that is, an organism cannot make two contradictory responses at the same time. If we assume that all responses are learned, relearning or reconditioning can extinguish them. Therefore, relaxation, being more rewarding than anxiety, can gradually replace anxiety as the response to the anxiety-evoking situation.

Wolpe (1989), attacking those who practiced cognitive therapy, made the point that if a habit has been acquired by learning, the logical approach is to treat it by a method based on learning principles. He wrote that the real difference between true behavior therapy and cognitive therapy is the cognitivists' failure to deny the possibility that some fears may be immediately triggered by a particular stimulus without the mediation of an idea of danger. Wolpe also criticized cognitive therapists for dispensing with the behavior analysis required for successful treatment of neurotic suffering.

## Flooding

Flooding, the opposite of desensitization, begins with the most feared stimulus in the stimulus hierarchy rather than the weakest or least feared. It is diving into cold water rather than getting used to it gradually. The clients are exposed to their strongest fears by putting themselves into the situation repeatedly over a short period of time. For example, a client might make several public speeches over a period of 2 weeks. The constant, concentrated approach has the effect of literally wearing out the stimulus. Flooding conducted during visualization exercises is referred to as *implosion.*

Flooding, also referred to as *reactive* or *internal inhibition,* is a process in which an anxiety-evoking stimulus is presented continuously, leading to fatigue and eventual unlearning of the undesirable response. When a parent told you to get back on your bike after a crash, you were exposed to the flooding technique. Another application might involve taking a child with a fear of riding in cars on a 4-hour trip. The initial response would be high anxiety or panic, which would, after a while, wear itself out as a stimulus. For example, the next time you find your eyelid blinking involuntarily when you are under too much stress, try blinking your eyelid 100 times without stopping (flooding). If the blinking continues, try again with 200 blinks of your eyelid.

## Hypnosis

A technique that incorporates deeper forms of relaxation, hypnosis has long been controversial; however, researchers have found that it can be a useful tool for working with children. Children seem to be fascinated with the procedure and, therefore, are usually easier to hypnotize than adults. Hypnotherapy has been used successfully with children experiencing anxiety, high blood pressure, asthma, and psychosomatic pain and to overcome such habits as nail biting, thumb sucking, tics, insomnia, and sleepwalking.

The danger of hypnotherapy, of course, comes when untrained persons attempt to use the procedure. Counselors may wish to investigate the availability of training in this area. Hypnotherapy appears to be a highly effective counseling tool for working with repressed conflicts, including memories of child sexual abuse. However, questions have been raised about hypnosis eliciting false memories of child sexual abuse. Therefore we suggest that counselors proceed with caution in selecting their training in hypnosis and in their practice of hypnosis after completing their training.

## Counterconditioning

In counterconditioning, a stronger, pleasant stimulus is paired with a weaker, aversive stimulus as a procedure for overcoming the anxiety the aversive stimulus evokes. For example, a child may be given his or her favorite candy while sitting in the classroom. If the candy is sufficiently rewarding to the child, the anxiety evoked by the classroom should be diminished.

## Aversive Conditioning

Aversive conditioning is the application of an aversive or noxious stimulus, such as a rubber-band snap on the wrist, when a maladaptive response or behavior occurs. For example, children could wear rubber bands around their wrists and snap them each time they found themselves daydreaming instead of listening to the teacher. Opportunity for helpful behavior to occur and be reinforced is recommended with this technique.

The following diagrams represent each of the four classical conditioning methods presented above:

Key: ⊕ pleasant stimulus; ⊖ aversive stimulus

1. Desensitization

   ⊖⊖⊖⊖⊖⊖⊖, where ⊖ is giving a speech.

   The aversive stimulus is handled in small steps by visualization or relaxation and by practice until increasingly larger steps can be handled.

2. Flooding (internal inhibition)

   ⊖⊖⊖⊖⊖⊖⊖⊖⊖, where ⊖ is getting back on the bike after falling off.

   The aversive stimulus is continually repeated until the fear response wears itself out.

3. Counterconditioning

   ⊕ and ⊖, where ⊕ is a candy bar and ⊖ is going to school.

   The larger, pleasant stimulus overcomes the anxiety or fear evoked by the smaller, aversive stimulus.

4. Aversive conditioning

   ⊖ and ⊕, where ⊖ is a snap of a rubber band on the wrist and ⊕ is daydreaming during class.

   The more painful stimulus overcomes the smaller reward gained from daydreaming in class.

## CASE STUDY

### *Identification of the Problem*

Sue is a 9-year-old in the fourth grade. She has exhibited some behavior problems in her classroom. She does not complete her classroom assignments, tells lies about her work and about things she does at home and at school, and is reported to be out of her seat constantly.

### *Individual and Background Information*

*Academic.*   Sue has an above-average IQ. She is an excellent reader and has the ability to do any fourth-grade assignment.

*Family.*   Sue is an only child. Her parents are in their 30s. Sue comes from an upper-middle-class family; her father and mother manage their own business.

*Social.*   Sue seems to get along relatively well with the other children but has only one close friend, Marie. Sue has been caught telling lies by the other children, and they tell her they do not like her lies. She brings money and trinkets to share with Marie and lets her wear her nice coats, sweaters, and jewelry. Sue has no other children to play with and is mostly around adults who let her have her own way.

## Counseling Method

The counselor in this case used a behavioral counseling technique to help Sue evaluate her behavior problems and to teach her to counsel herself. When using this method, a counselor has to determine carefully just how much right one has to influence the client's choices in modifying behavior. The criteria for determining when to use behavioral counseling are based on the frequency of the maladaptive behavior and the degree to which it hinders the child's healthy development and that of other children in the class.

In this case, the counselor used the following steps:

1. Established a warm, talking relationship (therapeutic alliance) with the child.

2. Wrote out the problems on paper.

3. Listed rewards and consequences of the plans.

4. Obtained a commitment from the client on the plan of action that would be most likely to help.

5. Used a behavior contract with positive reinforcement in the form of a social reward (praise) for desirable behavior and token reinforcement (points to exchange for fun-time activities). Positive reinforcers were withdrawn (by loss of points) when undesirable behavior occurred.

6. Drew up plans for a behavior contract. These plans were discussed with, agreed upon, and signed by the client, counselor, teacher, and parents because the child was exhibiting some of the undesirable behavior at home by not completing assigned tasks and telling her parents lies.

## Transcript

*Counselor:* Sue, your teacher sent you to me because you seem to be having some problems in class. Would you like to tell me what kind of problems you seem to be having? I'll write them down in a list so we can see what could be done to help you here and at home.

*Sue:* I just can't seem to get my work done or turned in on time.

*Counselor:* How do you stop yourself from doing this?

*Sue:* I just can't seem to be able to sit still long enough to finish, and then time is always up before I finish.

*Counselor:* Who else is affected by your getting out of your seat?

*Sue:* I guess I'm keeping the others from working when I go to their seats, and it bothers my teacher because she stops what she is doing and tells me to sit down and get busy.

*Counselor:* What happens when you don't finish your work?

*Sue:* Well, nothing really happens, except I try to get out of being fussed at and being kept in during play period for not doing my work.

*Counselor:* What do you mean, Sue?

*Sue:* I make up stories about I can't find my paper or somebody took it when I really hadn't even started it, or I hide what I have started in my desk or notebook and take it home and do it and then turn it in the next day and say I found it.

*Counselor:* What do you tell your mom and dad about your work for the day when they ask you?

*Sue:* Well, I tell a story to them, too. I tell them I did all my work, and usually the same things I tell the teacher I tell them, too.

*Counselor:* How do you feel about telling untrue stories?

*Sue:* I don't really feel good about it, but I want Mom and Dad to be proud of me and I really do want to do my work, but I just can't seem to do it, so I just tell a story.

*Counselor:* Okay, Sue, you say you want to change, so let's look at the list of things you want to change and see what you and I can work out together.

*Sue:* Okay, I'd like that.

*Counselor:* Let me read your contract terms to you. If you think there is anything you can't live with, we'll change it until we get it the way we think will help you the most. This contract tells you what will happen when you are able to finish your work. Your teacher, your mom and dad, you, and I will all sign it to show you we are all willing to help you live up to the terms. Will you go over it with your mother and father and see if there is anything that needs to be changed?

*Sue:* I think it's okay just the way it is.

*Counselor:* Okay, you and I will sign first, and I will send copies to your teacher and your parents to sign. We will try this for a week, and then you and I will meet at the same time next week to see how you are doing and if any changes need to be made.

*Sue:* Okay.

## Contract for Behavior and Learning

| Positive behaviors | Tokens |
|---|---|
| 1. Bringing needed materials to class | 5 |
| 2. Working on class or home assignment until finished | 5 |
| 3. Staying in seat | 5 |
| 4. Extra credit (reading assignments or laminated task sheets) | 1, 2, 3, 4, 5 |

You may exchange tokens earned for positive behavior for time to do "fun" activities.

| *Fun activities* | *Tokens* |
|---|---|
| 1. Writing on the small chalkboards | 15 |
| 2. Playing Phonic Rummy | 15 |
| 3. Playing with the tray puzzles | 15 |
| 4. Getting to be the library aide for a day | 15 |
| 5. Getting to use the computer | 15 |
| 6. Playing Old Maids with classmates | 10 |
| 7. Using the headphone and tape recorder to hear a story from audio or video tapes | 15 |
| 8. Using clay, finger paints, and other art supplies | 10 |

I, _____, agree to abide by the terms set forth in this contract. It is my understanding that tokens earned will depend on my classroom work and behavior.

_____

Signature

We, your teacher, your parents, and your counselor, agree to abide by the conditions specified in the contract. It is our understanding that we will assist you in any way we can with your tasks and behavioral problems.

_____

Teacher

_____

Parents

_____

Counselor

Behavioral counseling helps individuals look at what they are doing and what happens when they do it. The contract helps children try different behaviors to see which ones work for them. It encourages parents to adhere to the terms of the contract and positively reinforce all desirable behaviors at home. If the child continues to receive positive reinforcement for socially desirable and classroom-adaptive behavior, the counselor gradually implements a self-reinforcement system to help the child develop a sense of intrinsic reinforcement.

## APPLICATIONS OF BEHAVIORAL COUNSELING

Behavioral counselors have more supporting research data available than counselors practicing other counseling approaches. As noted previously, behavioral counselors must collect accurate data if their procedures are to operate with maximum efficiency. Therefore, they have done a thorough job of validating their claims of success.

The purpose of behavioral counseling is to change the client's overt and covert responses (cognitions, emotions, physiological states). Bandura (1974) reacted to the oft-repeated dictum "Change contingencies and you change behavior" by adding the reciprocal side: "Change behavior and you change the contingencies . . . since in everyday life this two-way control operates concurrently" (p. 866). Behavioral counselors work with behavior that is objective and measurable. Behavioral counseling methods, not confined to one stimulus–response theory of learning, are derived from a variety of learning principles.

The distinguishing features of behavioral counseling include the functional analysis of behavior and the development of the necessary technology to bring about change. Thus, behavioral counseling is the application of specified procedures derived from experimental research to benefit an individual, a group, an institution, or an environmental setting.

## Response Cost

Introducing response cost into behavioral programs is often necessary to modify difficult and well-established behavior patterns. One example is the treatment of enuretic children, in which a waking schedule is often a first-step method in solving the bed-wetting problem. When the first step fails, response cost is introduced as a second-step intervention. When the bed is wet, the child is required to change bed linens, clean urine-alarm pads, remake the bed, and reset the alarm after each wetting. The child receives monetary rewards for success in postponing urination. Following 14 dry days, overlearning is started by having the child drink 16 ounces of water before bedtime. Fourteen dry days following overlearning is defined as successful completion of the program. Encopresis is also successfully treated by response cost methods combined with reinforcement and punishment. Typical response cost contracts include washing dirty clothes, bathing immediately after soiling, doing extra chores, losing privileges, or a combination of such tasks. Reinforcement included spending time in favorite activities with parents or receiving a toy or money, or both.

## Eating Disorders

Behavioral counseling has been effective in treating eating disorders. Response prevention has been used to treat bulimia, in which eating is followed by vomiting or purging, which relieves the anxiety produced by eating and sustains the habit of binge eating because it removes the consequence of feeling guilty. The treatment plan is designed to allow the client to eat but not purge. The client is forced to tolerate the resulting anxiety and guilt by locking all nearby bathroom doors and remaining in the presence of other people, in front of whom the client is ashamed to vomit. This rather harsh treatment should be accompanied by plans to teach the client how to eat in moderation until it produces less anxiety and the client can eat normal amounts of food without vomiting.

Anorexic clients need positive reinforcement (social activities and visiting privileges) and punishment (isolation, bed rest, and tube feeding) to encourage eating and gaining weight. Friends and family often reward undesired behaviors with their attention and sympathy and need to be instructed how to reward the helpful and lifesaving behaviors of eating and gaining weight.

## Multimodal Approaches

Multimodal treatment plans are recommended for aggressive and violent youths, who present a wide range of learning styles and complex personalities that cannot be treated effectively with a single approach for everyone. We believe that the same argument holds true for all people. Suggested interventions for aggressive and resistant youths include CBT, the expressive arts, stress management, modeling of social skills, and the conflict-resolution skills of negotiation and compromise. Interventions for unwilling clients include (1) frequent group therapy with individual therapy as a contingency for refusal to participate in the group, (2) options for clients to terminate therapy after a set number of sessions, and (3) allowing them to know as much as possible about their cases by sharing case records and tapes of their counseling sessions, along with the privilege of sitting in on their own case conferences. Many of the recommendations rest on the assumption that aggressive and violent people are fascinated with themselves and that sharing their case data with them may draw them into the treatment process by making them active participants.

## CROSS-CULTURAL APPLICATIONS OF BEHAVIORAL COUNSELING

Behavioral counseling is most compatible with cultures that prefer behavioral interventions over working with the cognitive and affective parts of the problems brought to counseling. Behavioral counseling is focused on present behavior and on achieving short-term behavior changes leading to the attainment of specific, measurable goals. The behavioral counselor functions more as a directive, expert consultant than as a nondirective, active listener and facilitator for personal reflection. As noted in Chapter 15, with all of these characteristics, clients from African American, Latino, Asian American, African, Hispanic, and Asian cultures are likely to find behavioral counseling to be compatible with their preference for directive approaches focusing on current problems. Counselors using an active, direct, and expert approach should be cautious about exerting too much influence over the lives of clients from cultures that place a high premium on seeking advice from recognized experts.

Lee (1999) suggests that behavioral counselors beginning a counseling relationship would do well to be aware of the shame and guilt often felt by Asians, Native Americans, Latinos, and African Americans. Lee recommends selecting counseling techniques that focus on the positive things these clients bring to counseling rather than their maladaptive behaviors. Lee also points out that behavioral counseling might work well with Asian clients, who commonly believe that hard work, effort, and character development are the best cures for mental disorders.

## BEHAVIORAL COUNSELING AND MANAGED HEALTH CARE

As noted in Chapter 2, managed care organizations (MCOs) favor counseling treatments that hold the counselor accountable for session-to-session progress, culminating in reaching definite and specific goals in the shortest possible time. Behavioral counseling practitioners are well established to meet MCO requirements for third-party reimbursement. Treatment plans with specific, measurable goals can generally be implemented during the first session. Treatment periods are relatively brief, and client progress can be tracked on a daily or weekly basis. Costs for behavioral counseling treatments are relatively inexpensive, and client satisfaction with behavioral methods is generally high. Behavioral counseling, with accurate recording of baseline and posttreatment data, is well documented as an effective way to achieve rather impressive outcomes. In summary, behavioral counselors are apt to find themselves courted by MCOs for panel membership on their lists of approved and recommended counselors.

## SUMMARY

The same eclectic theme that runs through the current literature on behavioral counseling is found in all approaches to counseling. Behavioral counseling methods by themselves are inadequate to treat the full range of human problems. A more eclectic approach, such as multimodal counseling, discussed elsewhere in this book, may be preferable. However, behavioral methods are valuable tools in the counselor's repertoire.

Reinforcement methods may serve to extinguish desired behavior when the reward or token replaces any intrinsic reward a person might receive from engaging in the desired behavior. For example, if parents reward or reinforce a child's piano practice, the message to the child may be that piano playing is not worth doing without pay and therefore is not worthwhile in itself.

Children prefer independent group contingencies over interdependent and dependent group contingencies. Independent group contingencies require the same response of all individuals in the group, but access to reinforcement is based only on each individual's response (for example, everyone scoring 90% gets a reward).

Interdependent contingencies depend upon the collective performance of the group (for example, the entire group receives a reward if the group mean equals 90% or better). Dependent group contingencies are based on the performance of a selected member or selected members of the group (for example, if a paper drawn at random from a box containing all group members' test papers has a score of 90% or better, everyone receives a reward). Considerable evidence exists in the literature to support behavioral methods that use self-control, self-determination, and personal responsibility as motivators and reinforcers.

Behavioral counseling (BC), like most other counseling methods, is moving toward multimodal or integrative approaches that use it in combination with other counseling approaches. However, behavioral counselors do share several commonalities. Their work is based on research in experimental and social psychology. Like most of the other counseling orientations presented in this book, BC is focused more on present than past concerns and more on actions than on personality. Behavioral counselors operationalize terms referring to subjective states listed under such diagnostic categories as depression, anxiety, paranoia, shyness, obsession, and compulsion by describing these conditions as specific patterns of observable actions. For example, *depression* might be defined as loss of adequate reinforcement. Behavioral counselors are committed to defining problems precisely by breaking them down into observable and countable components of behavior. Behavioral goals are set in advance and systematically evaluated throughout the treatment process and follow-up period. Behavioral counselors view their work as reeducative rather than healing and reject diagnostic labels for behavior analysis. Often BC begins with a written contract outlining what the client is going to do and what outcomes are to be expected. Counseling begins with the behavior that is easiest to change, with accurate records maintained throughout the counseling experience. Counselors discard ineffective interventions in favor of new intervention plans.

## W E B S I T E S for Behavioral Counseling

Behavior OnLine: The Mental Health and Behavioral Science Meeting Place
www.behavior.net/

Positive Reinforcement
psych.athabascau.ca/html/prtut/reinpair.htm

## REFERENCES

Bandura, A. (1974). Behavior therapy and the models of man. *American Psychologist, 29,* 859–869.

Banks, S., & Thompson, C. (1995). *Educational psychology: For teachers in training.* St. Paul, MN: West.

Epstein, R. (Ed.). (1980). *Skinner for the classroom.* Champaign, IL: Research Press.

Jacobsen, E. (1938). *Progressive relaxation.* Chicago: University of Chicago Press.

Lee, W. (1999). *An introduction to multicultural counseling.* Philadelphia: Taylor & Francis.

Maslow, A. (1970). *Motivation and personality* (2nd ed.). New York: Harper & Row.

Ray, K., Skinner, C., & Watson, T. (1999). Transferring stimulus control via momentum to increase compliance in a student with autism: A demonstration of collaborative consultation. *School Psychology Review, 28,* 622–628.

Romano, J., & Roll, D. (2000). Expanding the utility of behavioral momentum for youth with developmental disabilities. *Behavioral Interventions, 15,* 99–111.

Skinner, B. F. (1938). *The behavior of organisms.* New York: Appleton-Century-Crofts.

Skinner, B. F. (1948). *Walden two.* New York: Macmillan.

Skinner, B. F. (1968). *The technology of teaching.* Englewood Cliffs, NJ: Prentice-Hall.

Skinner, B. F. (1971). *Beyond freedom and dignity.* New York: Knopf.

Skinner, B. F. (1983). *A matter of consequences: Part III of an autobiography.* New York: Knopf.

Skinner, B. F. (1987). *Upon further reflection.* Englewood Cliffs, NJ: Prentice-Hall.

Skinner, B. F. (1990a). Can psychology be a science of mind? *American Psychologist, 45,* 1206–1210.

Skinner, B. F. (1990b, August). *Cognitive science: The creationism of psychology.* Keynote address presented at the meeting of the American Pyschological Association, Boston.

Windholtz, G. (1997). Ivan P. Pavlov: An overview of his life and psychological work. *American Psychologist, 52,* 941–945.

Wolpe, J. (1958). *Psychotherapy by reciprocal inhibition.* Stanford, CA: Stanford University Press.

Wolpe, J. (1969). *The practice of behavior therapy.* New York: Pergamon.

Wolpe, J. (1989). The derailment of behavior therapy: A tale of conceptual misdirection. *Journal of Behavior Therapy and Experimental Psychiatry, 20,* 3–15.

Wolpe, J., & Plaud, J. (1997). Pavlov's contributions to behavior therapy: The obvious and the not so obvious. *American Psychologist, 52,* 966–972.

# Chapter 10

# Transactional Analysis

*The hardest thing to learn in life is which bridge to cross and which to burn.*
—David L. Russell

*We do not grow absolutely, chronologically. We grow sometimes in one dimension, and not in another, unevenly. We grow partially. We are relative. We are mature in one realm, childish in another. The past, present, and future mingle and pull us backward, forward, or fix us in the present. We are made up of layers, cells, constellations.*
—Anaïs Nin

## ERIC BERNE

Eric Lennard Bernstein was born May 10, 1910, in Montreal. His family consisted of his father, a general practitioner; his mother, a professional writer and editor; and a sister 5 years younger than he. Eric respected his father a great deal and was permitted to make house call rounds with him. He was 10 years old when his father died from tuberculosis, at which time his mother assumed responsibility for supporting the two children.

After receiving his medical degree from McGill University at the age of 25, Bernstein moved to the United States and began a psychiatric residency at Yale University. He became a citizen in 1938 and shortly thereafter changed his name to Eric Berne. Following service with the armed forces from 1943 to 1946, he began working to earn the title of psychoanalyst. His first book, *The Mind in Action,* was published in 1947. That same year, Berne began analysis with Erik Erikson.

Each of Berne's three marriages ended in divorce. He had seven children from his first two marriages; he found the role of parent rewarding and loved his children very much. Berne was said to be overly permissive and more nurturing than authoritarian or critical. One of the major rejections of his life occurred when, in 1956, the Psychoanalytic Institute denied his application for membership and recommended that he continue through 4 more years of personal analysis and then reapply for the coveted title. This action greatly discouraged Berne but at the same time motivated him, and he immediately began work on a new approach to psychotherapy.

Although Berne first published on the topic of the three ego states in "The Nature of Intuition" (1949), he formed the core of transactional analysis (TA) in 1954. At that time, Berne was involved in the psychoanalysis of a successful middle-aged lawyer he was treating by classic Freudian principles. During a session, the patient suddenly said, "I'm not a lawyer, I'm just a little boy," sparking the idea that each of us contains a child ego state accompanied by parent and adult ego states. After listening to his patients relating "games" for some 30 years, Berne decided to gather some of these into a catalog. Three years after its publication, *Games People Play* (1964) had been on the nonfiction best-seller list for 111 weeks—longer than any other book that decade. Some reviewers called the book psychiatric gimmickry, emphatically denying that it would ever be regarded as a contribution to psychological or psychiatric theory. Other reviewers found the book a real contribution to psychology and suggested that Berne had offered a thesaurus of social transactions with explanations and titles. In 1967, Berne attributed the book's success to the recognition factor—some of us recognize ourselves in it, while some of us recognize other people in it.

Poker was Berne's favorite game because people play it to win. He had little patience with losers and believed that players should play to win if they were going to play. Berne believed losers spent a lot of time explaining why they lost. In the final years of his life, Berne shifted his emphasis from games to life scripts.

Berne published 8 books and 64 articles in psychiatric and other periodicals and edited the *Transactional Analysis Bulletin*. In an article in the *New York Times* magazine in 1966, Berne renounced the therapeutic value of shock treatment, hypnosis, and medication in favor of his easy-to-understand approach to psychotherapy. Today TA is an international organization with more than 10,000 members. Eric Berne died in 1970.

## THE NATURE OF PEOPLE AND THEORY OF COUNSELING

The nature of people and the theory of counseling are covered together in this section because the TA theory of counseling is basically a statement describing the human personality.

Berne had a positive view of the nature of people. He believed children were born princes and princesses, but shortly thereafter their parents and the environment turned them into frogs. He believed that people had the potential to regain their royal status, providing they learned and applied the lessons of transactional analysis to their personal lives. Berne believed that the early childhood years were critical to personal development. During these early years, before children enter school, they form their basic life script and develop a sense of being either "OK" or "not OK." They also arrive at conclusions about other people's "OK-ness." In Berne's view, life is very simple to live. However, people upset themselves to the point that they invent religions, pastimes, and games. These same people complain about how complicated life is, while persisting in making life even harder. Life is a series of decisions to be made and problems to be solved, and Berne believed that people have the rationality and freedom to make decisions and solve their own problems.

Shahin (1995), taking a dim view of human nature and the "I'm OK, you're OK" model, writes that the model best reflecting society is: "I'm a jerk, you're a jerk, and that's OK." He expresses dismay with a society that defines bullies as just people with low self-esteem, mean people as misunderstood, and liars as insecure and acting out. To him, these people are jerks.

The TA theory of human nature and human relationships derives from data collected through four types of analysis:

1. Structural analysis, in which an individual's personality is analyzed
2. Transactional analysis, which is concerned with what people do and say to each other
3. Script analysis, which deals with the specific life dramas people compulsively enjoy
4. Game analysis, in which ulterior transactions leading to a payoff are analyzed

## Structural Analysis

In explaining the TA view of human nature and the difficulties people encounter in their lives, the first step is to begin with the structural analysis of personality. Each individual's personality is divided into three separate and distinct sources of behavior, the three ego states: Parent, Adult, and Child, or P, A, and C, for short. The ego states represent real persons who now exist or once existed and had their own identities. Therefore, the conflicts among them often cause inconsistencies as well as flexibility in people.

The Parent, Adult, and Child ego states Berne proposed are not concepts like the superego, ego, and id of Freud but rather phenomena based on actual realities. They each represent skeletal-muscular and verbal patterns of behavior and feeling based on emotions and experiences perceived by people in their early years. The Parent, Adult, and Child are all located in the conscious area of functioning and, as such, are readily available for use in our day-to-day living. In Freud's model, only the superego and ego are available to the conscious, with the id buried in the unconscious.

The Parent aspect of personality contains instructions, attitudes, and behaviors handed down mostly by parents and significant authority figures. It resembles a recording of all the admonitions, orders, punishments, encouragement, and so on experienced in the first years of life. Parents can take two different attitudes, depending on the situation: (1) Nurturing Parent manifests itself in nurturing or helping behavior, and (2) Critical Parent provides criticism, control, and punishment. The Parent feels and behaves as the one who reared you did—both critical and nurturing. The Parent admonishes, "you should" or "you should not," "you can't win," "boys will be boys," or "a woman's place is in the home." The Parent, wanting to be in control and to be right, acts with superiority and authority, but the Parent is also responsible for giving love, nurturance, and respect to the Child in you.

## Adult

The Adult ego state operates logically and unemotionally, providing objective information by using reality testing and a computerlike approach to life. Your Adult uses facts as a computer does to make decisions without emotion. The Adult says, "This is how this works" with mature, objective, logical, and rational thinking based on reality. The Adult ego state is not related to age. A child is also capable of dealing with reality by gathering facts and computing objectively. In fact, it is incumbent on the counselor to ensure that counseling sessions are conducted in an adult-to-adult format. Clients often work hard to shift communication to a parent-to-child format, where the counselor takes the parent role and tells the client what should be done. Counselors can deflect client attempts to shift the interview from adult to adult by using any of the counseling responses presented in this text. Active listening works, as do reality therapy and the other counseling responses to return the interaction to adult–adult.

## Child

All the childlike impulses common to everyone are in the Child state. The Child is an important part of personality because it contributes joy, creativity, spontaneity, intuition, pleasure, and enjoyment. The Child has two parts: (1) Adaptive Child emerges as a result of demands from significant authority figures and is marked by passivity, and (2) Natural or Free Child represents the impulsive, untrained, self-loving, pleasure-seeking part of the Child.

The Child part of us is an accumulation of impulses that come naturally to a young person and of recorded internal events or responses to what is seen and heard. It has an element of immaturity but also deep feeling, affection, adaptation, expression, and fun. Figure 10-1 presents the ego states and their divisions in graphic form.

The well-adjusted person allows the situation to determine which ego state is in control, striking an even balance among the three. A common problem is allowing one ego state to assume predominant control. For example, the Constant Parent is seen as dictatorial or prejudiced; the Constant Adult is an analytical bore; and the Constant Child is immature or overreactive. No age is implied by any of these states, because even the young child has Adult and Parent states, and older adults can evince a Child response. In fact, whenever you are having fun or jumping up and down cheering at a ballgame, you are in your child ego state. Berne believed you could diagnose the strength of a marriage relationship by how well a couple enjoyed playing together. Couples who play well together are likely to enjoy a wonderful love life together. Making love is a form of playing, and it is an ap-

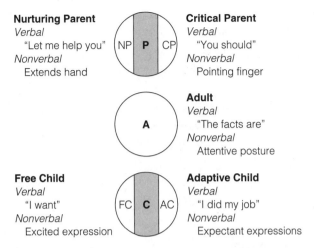

**Nurturing Parent**
*Verbal*
  "Let me help you"
*Nonverbal*
  Extends hand

**Critical Parent**
*Verbal*
  "You should"
*Nonverbal*
  Pointing finger

**Adult**
*Verbal*
  "The facts are"
*Nonverbal*
  Attentive posture

**Free Child**
*Verbal*
  "I want"
*Nonverbal*
  Excited expression

**Adaptive Child**
*Verbal*
  "I did my job"
*Nonverbal*
  Expectant expressions

FIGURE 10-1   Ego states

propriate time for the couple to be in their child ego states. To coin a phrase: "The couple who plays well together stays together."

## Transactional Analysis

The second type of analysis—the study of the transaction—is the heart of TA. Whenever a person acknowledges the presence of another person, either verbally or physically, a transaction has taken place. A *transaction* is often defined as a unit of human communication or as a stimulus–response connection between two people's ego states.

Transactions are grouped into three categories:

1. Complementary transactions, which Berne described as "the natural order of healthy human relationships," occur when a response comes from the ego state to which it was addressed (Figure 10-2).

*Sue:*   Billy, have you seen my bike?
*Billy:*   Yes, it is in the backyard.

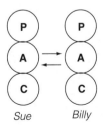

FIGURE 10-2   Complementary transaction

2. Crossed transactions break communications. They occur when a response comes from an ego state *not* addressed (Figure 10-3).

*Sue:* Billy, would you help me find my bike?
*Billy:* Can't you see I'm watching my favorite program?

3. Covert, or ulterior, transactions involve more than one ego state of each person and are basically dishonest. On the surface, the transaction looks and sounds like number 1 or 2, but the actual message sent is not spoken (Figure 10-4). For example, the ulterior message being sent in number 1 could be on a social or overt level:

*Sue:* Billy, why don't you help me find my bike so we can go riding?
*Billy:* Okay, it's a good day for a ride!

Or the ulterior message could be on a psychological, covert, or ulterior level:

*Sue:* I wish you would be my boyfriend.
*Billy:* I hope you like me better than the other boys.

## Script Analysis

The nature of people can be further described by script analysis. A psychological script is a person's ongoing program for a life drama; it dictates where people are going with their lives and the paths that will lead there. The individual—consciously or unconsciously—acts compulsively according to that program. As mentioned before, people are born basically OK; their difficulties come from bad scripts they learned during their childhood.

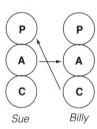

FIGURE 10-3   Crossed transaction

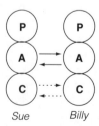

FIGURE 10-4   Covert transaction

Berne (1961) developed the theory of scripts as part of TA theory from its inception. A life script is that life plan your Child selected in your early years, based mostly on messages you received from the Child in your parents. For example, at the request of her mother, a little girl takes it upon herself to save her alcoholic father. The same script may emerge once again later in life as she tries to save an alcoholic husband in an attempt to regain some of the payoffs from the original experience. Although the Parent and Adult of your mother and father may have told you sensible things such as "Be successful," the unspoken injunction from the Child in your parents may communicate the message "You can't make it" (Figure 10-5). Injunctions are prohibitions and negative commands usually delivered from the parent of the opposite sex. Injunctions are seldom discussed or verbalized aloud. Values we hold as guidelines for living may have come from injunctions. These injunctions determine how we think and feel about sex, work, money, marriage, family, play, and people. For example, "Do not waste your time and money."

The best way to learn about scripts is to examine how we spend our time and how we relate (transactions) with others. Scripts have main themes, such as martyring, procrastinating, succeeding, failing, blaming, distracting, placating, and computing, and three basic types: winner, loser, and nonwinner. A small percentage of people seem to be natural winners; everything they touch turns to gold. Conversely, a slightly larger percentage seem to be natural losers; everything turns out badly for them. The majority, perhaps 80% or 85%, follow the nonwinners' script. Nonwinners are identified by a phrase they often use: "but at least . . ." ("I went to school and made poor grades, *but at least* I did not flunk out").

Transactional analysis borrows heavily from fairy tales for its terminology and analogies. For example, the Cinderella script is not an especially healthy plan because a prince or prize does not come to one who sits around waiting. Even martyrdom, as Cinderella did for her stepmother and stepsisters, does not help. The Santa Claus script is based on a similar myth. Because life scripts are formed in early childhood, selecting children's stories requires considerable care. We have included a comprehensive list of books in the Student Manual that we believe to be helpful to children and their families.

In summary, Berne believed that scripts have five components: (1) directions from parents, (2) a corresponding personality development, (3) a confirming childhood decision about oneself and life, (4) a penchant for either success or failure, and (5) a pattern for behavior.

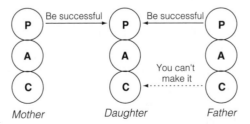

FIGURE 10-5   Life script: injunctions

## Game Analysis

Unfortunately, most people, in following their scripts, learn how to use ulterior transactions. In other words, they play games. A game is an ongoing series of complementary ulterior transactions progressing to a well-defined, predictable outcome. Like every ulterior transaction, all games are basically dishonest, and they are by no means fun. One of the first games a child learns is "Mine is better than yours." Its relatively benign outcome could range, in later years, to considerably more serious games. Three roles are played in games: persecutor, victim, and rescuer. There are no winners in these games, and every player loses. *Games People Play* (Berne, 1964) offers a vastly entertaining, chilling overview of what might happen to a not-OK child.

Berne (1964) believed that the general advantages of a game are its stabilizing (homeostatic) functions. He defined *homeostasis* as the tendency of an individual to maintain internal psychological equilibrium by regulating his or her own intrapsychic processes. Change is difficult for people who automatically accept only what reinforces or confirms their personal prejudices, values, and views, and many people are not open to new data. Game playing functions to maintain homeostasis in biological, existential, internal psychological, external psychological, internal social, and external social areas.

In reference to counseling, clients are ready to terminate counseling when their self-esteem is in order and they are able to exchange games for honest strokes from an "I'm OK, you're OK" view of human nature. In addition, fully functioning clients do confront and master the appropriate development tasks for age and stage. The ease with which children can understand TA concepts makes it a valuable approach for problem prevention.

In summary, games undermine the stability of relationships. Strokes are the motivation for games, and the need for strokes often turns an honest transaction into a game. Rackets are described as ego-state switches within the intrapsychic structure of an individual. Game analysis deals with transactions between two people. A racket could be the procrastination racket of "I'll do it tomorrow," in which the child masquerades as the adult. An example of a game is "Why don't you; yes but," in which a person says, "Help me," the helper gives advice, and the helpee says, "Yes, but that won't work."

## Life Positions

On the basis of the transactions and scripts, children develop life positions that summarize their concepts of self-worth and the worth of others. The four life positions are as follows:

1. I'm OK, You're OK. This position of mentally healthy people (mature independence) enables them to possess realistic expectations, have good human relationships, and solve problems constructively. It is a "winner's" position, defined as that of an authentic being. The extreme of this position is represented by a +5

on both the *x*- and *y*-axes in Quadrant I of Figure 10-6. Marriages, business partnerships, and friendships work best when both people hold to the I'm OK, you're OK orientation to life.

2. I'm not OK, You're OK. The universal position of childhood (total dependence) represents the introjective position of those who feel powerless. Adults in this position often experience withdrawal and depression. The extremes of this position are represented by a –5 on the *x*-axis and +5 on the *y*-axis in Quadrant II of Figure 10-6. Those who like to parent their partners will choose one from the I'm not OK, you're OK orientation.

3. I'm not OK, You're not OK. This life position is the arrival point of the child who cannot depend on parents for positive stroking (discussed later in this chapter). Already not OK, the child perceives Mom and Dad as not OK, too. Adults in this category are losers who go through a series of helpless, disappointing experiences and may even become suicidal or homicidal. The extreme of this position is represented by a -5 on both the *x*- and *y*-axes in Quadrant III of Figure 10-6. Partners from this category are dangerous to your health and theirs.

4. I'm OK, You're not OK. The individual feels victimized in this position. The brutalized, battered child ends up here. The position of the criminal and the psy-

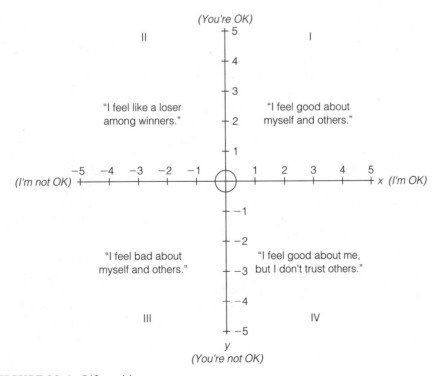

**FIGURE 10-6** Life positions

chopath is "Whatever happens is someone else's fault." The extreme of this position is a +5 on the *x*-axis and a -5 on the *y*-axis in Quadrant IV of Figure 10-6. If you like to be with a blamer or potential criminal, here is your person.

## Games Clients Play

Among the many games Berne identified, some are to be especially avoided in the counseling interview.

1. *Why don't you; yes, but. . . .* The counselor's Adult is tricked into working for the client's Child as the Parent when the counselor gives advice.

*Counselor:*  Why don't you ask your teacher to give you some extra help with math?

*Client:*  Yes, but what if she says she doesn't have time?

The payoff comes to the client in spreading bad feelings, as in the misery-loves-company game: "I am not okay, and you aren't either because you can't help me solve my problem."

Summerton (2000) writes that Berne began his study of game analysis with the "Why don't you—Yes, But" game. The overt communication appears to be adult to adult, but the covert communication is actually a one-upmanship move by the child ego state trying to hook the parent ego state of the "helper" into giving advice on what the "helpee" needs to do to solve a particular problem. However, in the game, the advice is always rejected as inadequate in an attempt to make the "helper" feel bad for not having the wisdom to be helpful. Woods (2000) distinguishes between the act of recognizing and confronting game playing and true game analysis. Recognition and confrontation of game playing is done to end the games. True game-playing analysis is done to explore how the client uses games as a defense and how games often communicate unconscious messages. Woods (2000) believes that people internalize the scenario of an early interpersonal relationship and unconsciously use it later as a template for further interpersonal interactions. One example is given of a client's father who always had a "Yes, but" statement for every self-assertive "I should" statement the client would make. In adulthood, client projected his father's role onto others by rejecting all feedback, suggestions, and advice in the "Why Don't You—Yes, But" game.

2. *I'm only trying to help you.* Counselors sometimes play this game with their clients. The message to the client is "You are not okay, and I know what is good for you." The payoff is for the counselor, who holds the faulty belief that "If I straighten my client out, then maybe I can get my own life in order." A truly helpful counselor offers help when it is requested but believes that help can be accepted or rejected. When help fails or is rejected, the helpful counselor does not respond derogatorily, "Well, I was only trying to help you."

3. *Courtroom.* The courtroom game puts the counselor in the position of judge and jury if two clients can manipulate the counselor into placing blame. The pay-

off is bad feelings for all—persecutor, victim, and rescuer—because the rescuer (counselor) usually ends up being victimized by the other two players.

4. *Kick me and NIGYYSOB*. Counselors may find that some clients enjoy playing "kick me" with the counselor, just as they do with their bosses, colleagues, and spouses. They seem to enjoy being victimized and work at getting themselves rejected. They even work at getting themselves terminated from counseling before any gains have been made. Kick-me players manipulate others into playing NIGYYSOB (now I've got you, you son of a bitch) when they react to the bids for negative attention the kick-me players make.

The NIGYYSOB game is played by itself if a person tries to trap others in a double bind: damned if you do and damned if you don't.

*Mother:* Johnny, do you love me?
*Johnny:* Yes, I do.
*Mother:* How many times have I told you not to talk with your mouth full!

5. *Gossiping*. Gossiping refers to talking about people who are not present. In a counseling interview, the counselor may wish to have clients role-play dialogue between themselves and a missing person, as was suggested in Chapter 7. For example, a child complaining about a teacher could role-play a conversation between the two of them, with the child playing the role of the teacher and then responding as the child would in the classroom. The technique uses an empty chair to represent the missing person. Role-playing and role-reversal methods have a way of limiting gossip while creating greater awareness of the problem situations and proper assignment of responsibility for the problem.

6. *Wooden leg*. The wooden-leg game is a display of the inadequacy pattern described in Chapter 11. Clients playing wooden-leg games work to increase their disabilities as a way of avoiding responsibility for taking care of themselves. These clients are experts at making people give up on them. Children are adept at convincing parents that they cannot handle certain chores and school subjects.

Paradoxical strategies, which are at times effective with these clients, focus on harnessing their rebellion into productive activity. The counselor might say, for example, "Frank, you've got me convinced that you really can't make it." The rebellious client, Frank, often rises to the occasion to show that the counselor is a total idiot and begins to succeed in the face of the prediction that he could not.

For clients who are really defeated and not rebellious, we recommend large doses of unconditional encouragement. Counselors of welfare and rehabilitation clients often find themselves in the wooden-leg game. The payoff goes to the clients, who justify not getting better, or even getting worse, as a way of increasing their benefits.

7. *If it weren't for you*. Related to the wooden leg, this game is another way of avoiding the assumption of responsibility for life and its unsolved problems. The client says, for example, "If it weren't for you and your good cooking, I could lose 10 pounds." The counselor may want to examine with the client the payoffs of be-

ing overweight and even develop a rationale of how being fat may be the preferred and "best" lifestyle for the client.

8. *Red Cross.* Red Cross happens when a person (the persecutor) pushes you (the victim) off a dock into deep water and then rescues you. This puts you (the victim) in debt to the rescuer. In this case, all three roles in the game are played by two people with the persecutor and rescuer role played by the same person. Red Cross happens when people get other people in trouble and then "jump in" to "rescue" them from peril.

9. *Make some sad.* One member of a couple decides to get more attention from the other person by making him or her jealous. The game works for a while until the victim discovers that the game can be played both ways. The result is that both people in the partnership end up hurting each other.

## The Pursuit of Strokes

A stroke is any act implying recognition of another person's presence. Human beings need recognition; in order to obtain it, they exchange what Berne called *strokes.* In acknowledging the presence of another person, people give a stroke, which can be either positive or negative. Which type is usually obvious, except in the case of ulterior transactions. Young children receive positive or negative physical strokes when they are cuddled or spanked, whereas adults obtain primarily symbolic strokes in conversations or transactions with others. Positive strokes, such as compliments, handshakes, open affection, or uninterrupted listening, are the most desirable, but negative strokes, such as hatred or disagreement, are better than no recognition at all. A middle ground is maintenance strokes, which keep transactions going by giving recognition to the speaker but neither positive nor negative feedback. All these strokes can be either conditional or unconditional—that is, given as a result of some specific action or given just for being yourself. Unconditional regard—"I like you"—has more positive stroke value than conditional acceptance—"I like you when you are nice to me." (See Figure 10-7.)

The pattern of giving and receiving strokes an individual uses most is determined by the person's life position, as explained in the section on life positions. How people view themselves and others controls their ability to give and receive conditional and unconditional positive and negative strokes. People engage in transactions to exchange strokes. According to Berne (1964), people have an inherent psychological hunger for stimulation through human interactions and stroking, and any act implying recognition of another's presence is a means of satisfying these hungers. Failure to fulfill these needs may cause a failure to thrive in infants and feelings of abandonment and not–OK-ness in both children and adults. Satisfied hunger yields feelings of OK-ness and release of creative energy. Awareness of psychological hungers and the satisfaction of them are important.

Negative strokes, such as lack of attention, shin kicking, and hatred, send "You're not OK" messages. Diminishing, humiliating, and ridiculing strokes all treat people as though they are insignificant.

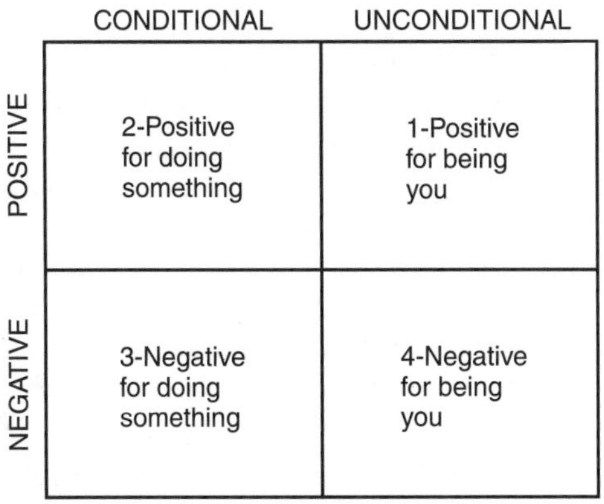

FIGURE 10-7   Types of strokes

Positive strokes are usually complementary transactions. They may be verbal expressions of affection and appreciation, or they may give compliments or positive feedback; they may be physical, like a touch, or they may be silent gestures or looks. Listening is one of the finest strokes one person can give another. All yield reinforcement to the "I'm OK, you're OK" position. Maintenance strokes, although lacking meaningful content, at least serve to give recognition and keep communication open.

## Structuring Time

People have six options for structuring their time in pursuit of strokes.

1. *Withdrawing,* in which no transaction takes place. It involves few risks, and no stroking occurs.

2. *Rituals,* which involve prescribed social transactions such as "Hello" and "How are you?" These transactions are fairly impersonal.

3. *Pastimes,* which provide mutually acceptable stroking. Pastimes are a means of self-expression but often involve only superficial transactions or conversations. Examples are baseball, automobiles, shopping, or other safe topics of conversation.

4. *Activities,* in which time is structured around some task or career. Activities are a way to deal with external reality and may involve more in-depth interaction with others.

5. *Games,* in which the need for strokes is met in a crooked way. Intense stroking is often received, but it may be unpleasant. Games are considered destructive transactions.

6. *Intimacy,* which provides unconditional stroking. It is free of games and exploitation.

Obviously, some of these ways of structuring time are healthy and some are unhealthy, depending on the time and energy given to each. One of the goals of TA therapy is to help people learn productive ways of structuring their time.

Withdrawing may be the Adult's decision to relax or be alone, the Parent's way of coping with conflict, or the Child's adaptation for protection from pain or conflict. It is fairly harmless unless it happens all the time or when a person needs to pay attention. Withdrawing into fantasy may allow one to experience good stroking when the present setting does not appear to hold any.

A ritual is a socially programmed use of time in which everybody agrees to do the same thing. Brief encounters, worship rituals, greeting rituals, cocktail party rituals, and bedroom rituals may allow maintenance strokes without commitment or involvement. The outcome is predictable and pleasant, but most people need more intense stroking.

Pastimes are, as they imply, ways to pass time. They are superficial exchanges without involvement that people use to size up one another. Conversations concerning relative gas mileage, the weather, or potty training may yield minimal stroking at the maintenance level while allowing one to decide whether to risk a more intimate relationship.

Doing work or activities is time spent dealing with the realities of the world. It is getting something done that one may want to do, need to do, or have to do. Activities allow for positive strokes befitting a winner.

Berne (1964) defined games as an ongoing series of complementary ulterior transactions progressing to a well-defined, predictable outcome. One who sends an ulterior message to another person, for some hidden purpose, is playing a game. The Adult is unaware that the Child or Parent has a secret reason for playing or wanting to play. Harris (1969) believed all games derive from the Child's "mine is better than yours" attempt to ease the not-OK feeling—to feel superior while the other feels put down. Games are differentiated from rituals and pastimes in two ways: (1) their ulterior quality and (2) the payoff. Games are a way, too, of using time for people who cannot bear the stroking starvation of withdrawal and yet whose not-OK position makes the ultimate form of relatedness—intimacy—impossible (Berne, 1964; Harris, 1969).

Intimacy is a deep human encounter stemming from genuine caring. Steiner (1974) viewed intimacy as the way of structuring time when there is no withdrawal, no rituals, no games, no pastimes, and no work. Conditions favorable for intimacy include a commitment to the "I'm OK, you're OK" position and a satisfying of psychological hungers through positive strokes. The traditional view of how people structure their time to meet their needs for emotional space between themselves and others has been unidimensional, with intimacy and self-definition on opposite ends of the same continuum. The healthy position is viewed as holding the middle ground between the two extremes of total withdrawal from people to the other extreme of being totally enmeshed in intimate relationships. Kaplan (2001), taking issue with the traditional view, suggests that the needs for self-definition (withdrawal) and intimacy exist on different dimensions, with their own continuums of high and low needs for each dimension. This bidimensional model, plotted on *x*- and *y*-axes, permits us to examine four lifestyles: (1) high needs for self-definition and intimacy, (2) high needs for intimacy and low needs for self-definition, (3) low needs for both self-definition and intimacy, and (4) high needs for self-definition and low needs for intimacy. The four-dimensional scale permits expansion of the two-scale model of high need for attachment versus fear of attachment to need for and fear of individuation and need for and fear of attachment. In other words, needs for intimacy and withdrawal are not opposite ends of a continuum on the need to affiliate with people.

## Rackets

Some people find themselves involved in what is known in TA theory as a "stamp-collecting enterprise," in which they save up archaic bad feelings until they have enough to cash in for some psychological prize. The bad-feelings racket, or stamp collecting, works in much the same way that the former supermarket stamp-collecting enterprise once worked. People save brown stamps for all the bad things others have caused them to suffer and gold stamps for all the favors others owe them. Gray stamps refer to lowered self-esteem, red stamps symbolize anger, blue stamps mean depression, and white stamps connote purity (James & Jongeward, 1971). The filled-up bad-feelings stamp books may be cashed in for such things as a free divorce, custody of children, nervous breakdown, blowup, drunken binge, depression, tantrum, runaway, or love affair. Good-feelings stamps are used to justify playtime, relaxation, and breaks from work. Stamp collecting is a racket learned from parents. The collector uses the stamps as excuses for behavior and feelings, and the suppliers may not even be aware they are giving them out. "I'm OK, you're OK" people do not need stamps because they need no excuses for their behavior, which is honest, open, and ethical.

## COUNSELING METHOD

Transactional analysis is the ideal system for those who view the counseling process as teaching. As is evident from this chapter, TA abounds with terms, diagrams, and models. Clients are taught the TA vocabulary so they can become proficient in identifying ego states, transactions, and scripts. The counselor's role includes teaching and providing a nurturing, supportive environment in which clients feel free to lift or eliminate restricting injunctions, attempt new behaviors, rewrite scripts, and move toward the "I'm OK, you're OK" life position. Contracting between counselor and client is a large part of the TA process.

TA practitioners teach the principles of transactional analysis to participants and then let them use these principles to analyze and improve their own behavior. TA concepts have been taught to people of all ages and ability levels, from the very young to the very old and from mentally retarded children to gifted children. The following TA points are most useful in counseling children:

1. Definition and explanation of ego states
2. Analysis of transactions between ego states
3. Positive and negative stroking (or "warm fuzzies" and "cold pricklies")
4. I'm OK, you're OK
5. Games and rackets
6. Scripts

Put simply, the primary goal in transactional analysis is to help the person achieve the "I'm OK, you're OK" life position. Various methods and techniques can accomplish this aim. Because children can easily learn and understand the terms and concepts of TA, the approach has become popular in helping school-age children.

The "I'm OK, you're OK" life position is one the child chooses to take. The other three positions more or less evolve of themselves; the child feels no sense of free choice in the matter. According to Harris (1969), the first three positions are based on feelings, and the fourth position—"I'm OK, you're OK"—is based on thought, faith, and initiation of action. The first three have to do with "why"; the fourth has to do with "why not." No one drifts into a new position; it is a decision a person makes. The graph in Figure 10-6 enables plotting a person's progress in moving from one quadrant to another, providing each step on the number axis is defined in operational terms. The $x$-axis refers to gains and losses in self-esteem; the $y$-axis indicates the same for relationships with others.

Ideally, the role of a transactional analyst is teacher. TA concepts have been taught successfully to children, preadolescents, and adolescents (see Alvyn Freed's books: *TA for Tots: And Other Prinzes,* 1973, 1998; with Margaret Freed, *TA for Kids: And Grown Ups Too,* 1971, 1998; *TA for Teens and Other Important People,* 1992). We recommend that counselors begin teaching the PAC model by showing children that all of us have these three parts that tell us what to do in certain situations. For example, our *Parent* tells us what we should do, our *Adult* tells us how to figure things out, and our *Child* tells us what to do for fun.

Once children have been taught how to speak the language of TA, the counselor can help them analyze their own transactions and see how their behavior affects others and vice versa. Children learn to identify the source of the reasoning that goes into their decisions; that is, they learn how to use their Adult in dealing with the demands of their Parent and Child.

Children can then be taught about the differences between the nurturing and critical parts of the Parent (P) part of their personality. The Critical Parent (CP) sounds a lot like our real parents, because it tells us the right thing to do. The nurturing parent tells us that we are OK and takes care of us in a loving way.

The Adult is compared to a computer. It helps us think for ourselves, solve problems, and learn new things. The Adult (A) can be contaminated by the Child (C). For example, when you are studying for a test using your Adult, your Child might say "Take time out for snack and watch some TV." Children can be taught to organize their study periods into shorter, concentrated periods with frequent breaks for snacks and bathroom. In fact, more learning occurs at the beginning and ending points in a study period; this augurs well for shorter study periods with more starting and stopping points.

Sometimes the Child part of our personality is divided into three parts: the adapted child, the little professor, and the free child. The adapted child is the part of you that might be the rebel who refuses to do what PICs (People In Charge—parents, teachers) want us to do. The adapted child seems to come alive at about age 2 and enjoys a rebirth during the adolescent years. However, the adapted child reaction is a natural reaction to any person, such as a peer or friend, who acts too bossy. The little professor is that part of the child that does the creative and clever planning to help the Child get what it wants. The little professor does the day-dreaming that stimulates the make-believe games that often lead to future careers and hobbies. The free (or natural) child is the part of the child that engages in spon-taneous fun. When we are playing in a fun game, we are in our natural child. The free child is also free to feel and express any emotion and feeling that may arise, in-cluding the negative feelings of hate and anger. Our free child does the playing, has the fun, and is often impulsive. However, it also needs to be monitored by our Adult and Parent to keep our behavior within the limits of responsible behavior.

The key to understanding PAC is to know which one is in charge at any particular moment and if that is the appropriate one for the situation. We know which ego state is in charge by how we talk, how we act, how others react to us, and how we feel. The Parent says things like "Shame on you," "That's stupid," or "I love you very much and you are pretty sharp." The Adult says things like "I can figure it out," "I'm going to do my homework," and "The answer is 64." The Child says things like "Cool," "I want," and "That sucks!"

After they understand how the PAC model works, children are ready to learn how positive and negative strokes are transacted between people. Positive strokes are identified as warm fuzzies (symbolized with soft balls of wool yarn) that in-clude pats on the back, hugs, compliments, and handshakes that make you feel warm and fuzzy all over when you get them. Strokes can be earned by doing good work, but the best strokes are the freebies you get for just being you. Negative strokes are taught by using hard, spiny plastic objects called cold pricklies that are not fun to hold in your hand. Cold pricklies are criticisms, punishments, insults, name calling, hitting, and kicking you might get from somebody.

Children are taught they were born as Prinzes (prince or princess) and later on, when they get some cold pricklies, may begin to think they have turned into Frozzes (girl and boy frogs). If we get too many cold pricklies about how we are not OK and everybody else is, we develop an "I'm not OK and you're OK" attitude, which could lead to developing and following a loser life script. The only cure for the "I'm not OK" position is to receive an abundance of unconditional, positive strokes and love from our parents and plenty of positive strokes (warm fuzzies) from our friends.

Stamp collecting is taught as a racket in which we save up incidents that hurt our feelings or made us angry and then trade these stamps in later for a guilt-free tantrum or blowup. As mentioned earlier, sometimes people use different colors to label the different bad feelings we collect, such as red for anger and blue for fear. However, brown stamps are now used to symbolize all bad feelings. The Adult has the task of acting rationally on these bad feelings to prevent them from being stored and saved for a later irrational act. These brown stamps can be saved or thrown away. In fact, our Adult can refuse to let us even print them.

These brown stamps can be avoided if you track them down. Children are taught to act as soon as they begin to feel uncomfortable because someone annoys them or hurts their feelings. The trackdown takes 30 seconds and consists of answering the following seven questions:

1. How do I hurt?
   anger, fear, or pain
2. Which part of me hurts?
   P, A, or C (usually it is the child)
3. Who did it?
4. With what?
   P, A, or C
5. Why did he or she do it?
6. What can I do now?
7. What can I do differently next time?

Children can be taught the three types of transactions: Complementary, Crossed, and Double (or hidden). Complementary transactions are parallel transactions where the arrows between your PAC and the other person's PAC do not cross. For example, the Adult question, "What was our math assignment?" is answered by the Adult response, "Page 104."

The transaction becomes crossed when the response to the Adult question comes from the Critical Parent: "You should have paid more attention in class." Another example of a crossed transaction might come from the Free Child, "Forget math, let's shoot some baskets." Crossed transactions often lead to arguments, fights, and other bad feeling activities. Double transactions have a hidden, unspoken meaning. For example, the Adult might appear to be saying to another Adult, "Let's play some ball." The Hidden Child to Child message might be, "Let's not do that math assignment for tomorrow."

Children are taught that TA games are not the same as fun games. TA games are played to get strokes, but they are crooked ways of getting them because the transactions are not open and honest. The first game children play is "mine is better than yours." Children play this game in an attempt to get rewarded with strokes when they do not believe they get strokes just for being. "Tattletale" often becomes the next game, when children realize they can get strokes from PICs by telling on their siblings or classmates. Both of these games are indications that children need to be reassured they are OK. PICs also can give strokes when children are trying to learn them by doing the right things and are not trying to earn them at the expense of others.

Rackets are taught as activities that can lead to games. Rackets are ways of trying to control others by making them responsible for the bad feelings you have that never seem to go away. An example PICs might use to get children to do what they want might go like this: "You really make me worried and nervous when you leave the house and go off with your friends" or "You know I have this heart condition and how upset I get when you don't make As and Bs."

Scripts are taught to children as what they are going to be when they grow up, but they are not written in stone. They can be changed (and often are) as we find out what we like to do and what we can do well. People can move from a loser's or nonwinner's script to a winner's script by being persistent in the pursuit of realistic, challenging goals that fall within their interest and ability levels. For children, the task involves moving from a failure identity to a success identity of "I am lovable and capable"—lovable because I have people in my life who care about me and whom I care about, and capable because I can do things like succeed in school and other activities. In short, "I am OK."

Children can be taught to inoculate themselves against people poisons, "putdown" remarks designed to make them feel bad. The Freeds (1971, 1998) recommended using parent shrinkers, actually critical parent shrinkers, to move the communication from the Critical Parent to the Adult. Some of these include:

1. Say, "You're right. What can we do about it now?"
2. Ask, "What did you say before you said that?"
3. Change the subject.
4. Say, "When you call me a name, I feel angry. So I wish you wouldn't do that."

Finally, children are taught about making and keeping contracts to make changes in their daily behavior. People do well when they keep their promises and hold to their contracts with friends and PICs. People who have difficulty in making and keeping their commitments to others get themselves into trouble. The way out of trouble is to commit to helpful behaviors they can and will do.

Probably the most important concept to remember when dealing with children is that everyone grows up feeling not OK. Children function on the basis of the OK-ness they see in their parents. If Mommy frequently responds to the child with *her* not-OK Child, the stage is set for the establishment of the "I'm not OK, you're not OK" position. In the case of the severely abused child, the extreme "I'm OK, you're not OK" position is a real possibility. One of the best ways for youngsters to develop strong Adult ego states is to observe how their parents use their Adults in handling inappropriate responses from the demanding Parent or Child.

Posters, pictures, humorous role playing, and stories are useful in teaching TA principles to children, such as how to be "prinzes" instead of "frozzes." Children also learn how to give and get warm fuzzies (positive strokes) and how to avoid giving and getting cold pricklies (negative strokes). Of course, in getting strokes, one must not play games.

As mentioned before, the goal of TA counseling with children is to help them learn to control their responses with their Adult, thereby achieving the "I'm OK, you're OK" life position. However, strengthening a child's Adult causes his or her family role to shift. The child becomes less active in playing the destructive games that dominate many families. Other family members' roles of necessity shift also. For this reason, the child's parents must be included in the counseling process to achieve lasting results.

Children can learn all about warm fuzzies and cold pricklies, but because of the tremendous influence of their parents, it is next to impossible, without effective intervention, for them to reverse a "loser" life script if their parents have given it to them. Everything parents do and say to children tells them they are OK or not OK, depending on what life position the parents themselves occupy. People attract not what they want but what they are. People also rear *not* the children they want but children who reproduce the parents.

Positive stroking and respect are two things everyone needs to build a winner's script. The child needs positive strokes, both conditional ("We'll have some ice cream after you put away your toys") and unconditional ("I love you no matter what"). Children come to see themselves as OK because their parents treat them that way.

As a positive stroke, respect is hard to beat. The conclusion a child reaches is this: If my OK parents think I'm OK, then I really must be OK.

Another useful TA principle for both teachers and parents is to teach "do" and *not* "don't." Parents' and other adults' attempts to teach appropriate behavior by catching children in *inappropriate* behavior baffle children. Because Mommy is OK, a child thinks, "It must be all my fault, and I must be not OK."

A slightly different aspect of the same idea is that children who are counseled and taught to "do more" or "do better" must also know *what*. The Parent in everyone admonishes us to "do better"; the Adult supplies the "do *what* better."

As children and their families become better acquainted with the whys of their relationships, they learn to avoid undesirable ways of structuring time. Again, the goal of TA is to help the individual learn to lead a full, game-free life, and everyone has that choice. The usefulness of the PAC model comes in creating awareness of how the Parent, Adult, and Child function in decision making.

As mentioned earlier, several techniques can teach TA to children. The concepts of positive and negative stroking have been taught with smiling and frowning faces as well as with fuzzy yarn balls and sharp, prickly plastic objects to connote warm fuzzies and cold pricklies. The following warm fuzzy, cold prickly fairy tale (Steiner, 1975) was written for the Child in everyone.

> There once existed a town where people shared their warm fuzzies without fear of running out of their supply of fuzzies. One day a wicked witch appeared and planted the idea that people should hoard their fuzzies in case there happened to be a shortage of fuzzies. When the townspeople did this, their backbones began to shrivel up. The witch cured the shriveling backbones by giving everybody a bag of cold pricklies to share. The sharing of cold pricklies continued until a good witch arrived and put the townspeople back on the right track, sharing their warm fuzzies.

Counselors and teachers can follow the story by bringing a bowl of sugar-free candy to class and telling the children that they can have a piece of candy only if someone gives them a piece. The counselor or teacher serves as a model in the exercise to make sure that each child receives a piece of candy, symbolizing a warm fuzzy or a positive stroke. The best way to get warm fuzzies is to give them.

Posters can be made with representations of the various ideas of TA (stroking, ego states, "I'm OK, you're OK," lists of games with appropriate illustrations, lists of scripting phrases, and so on). Puppets, dolls, and make-believe stories can be successful with younger children who cannot yet read.

A three-step process is effective in teaching TA to any child: First, explain the principle by using a story, a poster, puppets, or other age-appropriate methods. Second, ask the children to "read" back what they understand of the TA principle (correcting them as they go along). Third, ask the children to give examples of the principle from their own experience ("What positive strokes have you received today?") or to identify examples of the principle from the explanation ("'You must always go to bed early' comes from which ego state?").

Teach new stroking patterns to children who are having interpersonal conflicts. They first need to analyze the other person's behavior. What response does parent, teacher, or friend give to the child's positive or negative strokes? What strokes does the other person like? Teach children new ways of stroking from among these categories:

1. Self-strokes: doing nice things for yourself
2. Physical strokes: hugs, kisses, pats, backrubs, handshakes, "high fives" (be sure to distinguish between good and bad touching)
3. Silent strokes: winks, nods, waves, smiles
4. Verbal strokes: "I like you," "Good job," "Thanks"
5. Rewards or privileges: letting younger siblings go with you, playing with them, doing something for parents

Young children (up to 7 years) may not be able to symbolize stroking and ego states as well as older ones, and less technical language may be necessary. Young children can understand "warm fuzzy" if a stroke feels good and "cold prickly" if they feel bad after someone says or does something to them. They may need permission to ask for a warm fuzzy instead of manipulating for a cold prickly when they feel bad. Likewise, small children can understand "my bossy part," "my thinking part," "my angry part," or "my happy part" rather than the ego states, which they sometime confuse with actual people.

Ego-grams are bar graphs showing children "how much" of each ego state they use (Figure 10-8). An ego-gram can indicate what changes might be made. A child who wants to make a change can work on strengthening low ego states by practicing appropriate behaviors. See if the child thinks the ego-gram differs in various situations—at home, at school, playing with friends.

Once children understand ego states, they can learn to distinguish complementary, crossed, and ulterior transactions. If they bring in a situation that illustrates one of these, have them diagram it. In the case of crossed or ulterior transactions, encourage children to use their Adult to figure out ways to obtain a more successful result.

Some other methods for teaching the various TA techniques are described in the following list:

1. Talk about the feelings and behaviors that go with each ego state. Have children identify their own and others' ego states by relating the ego states to what children say about their experiences.

*Child:* My brother always tells me what to do. He's not my father.
*Counselor:* You feel rebellious when your brother acts like a bossy parent.

As children become aware of their ego states and can discriminate between them, their Adult can gain control of which ego state is expressed and give them permission to replace destructive ideas with constructive ones.

2. Figure 10-6 is useful in helping children identify how they feel and think about themselves and other people. Children are able to discuss what OK-ness and not–OK-ness mean to them in terms of specific behaviors.

3. Games intrigue children. Once they have the concept, they can readily pick up on games in themselves and others and describe them. Any time children describe a pattern of games or recognize that "this always happens to me," the counselor can introduce the concept of games as a way of getting negative strokes to replace the

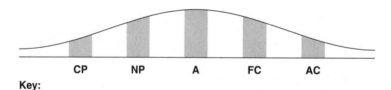

**Key:**

**P** The Parent refers to a person's values, beliefs, and morals.

   **CP** The Critical Parent finds fault, directs, orders, sets limits, makes rules, and enforces one's value system. Too much CP results in dictatorial or bossy behavior.

   **NP** The Nurturing Parent is empathic and promotes growth. The NP is warm and kind, but too much NP becomes smothering, and children will not be able to learn how to take care of themselves.

**A** The Adult acts like a computer. It takes in, stores, retrieves, and processes information. The A is a storehouse of facts and helps you think when you solve problems, but too much Adult is boring.

**C** The Child can be fun, expressive, and spontaneous, and sometimes it can be compliant and a follower of rules.

   **FC** The Free Child is the fun and spontaneous part of the child. When you cheer at a ballgame, you are in the Free Child part of your personality. However, too much FC might mean that you have lost control of yourself.

   **AC** The Adapting Child is the conforming, easy-to-get-along-with part of your personality. Too much AC results in guilt feelings, depression, other bad feelings, and robotlike behavior.

FIGURE 10-8  Ego-gram

positive strokes children think they cannot get: "You seem to mess up a lot. How do you manage that?" "What does this mean about you?" "How did it feel after it happened?" "What do you really want? How could you get it better?" "What 'bad' (scary) thing does this game prevent?" Children can also identify the three game roles of persecutor, rescuer, and victim and learn to stay out of them. The persecutor role can be demonstrated by having the child try to "put someone down" by pressing straight down on his or her shoulders. Putting people down this way is difficult unless they lean over or bend their knees. You can demonstrate the rescuer role by trying to pick up a limp person (of about the same size). Holding up a person who does not want to stand is also difficult. The victim role is demonstrated in relation to the other two by the partner's "giving in," lying down, and staying limp.

4. Racket feelings can be discussed in terms of stamp collecting. Children can usually identify the bad feelings they save up and the prize they get. Hypothetical situations such as the following create bad feelings: "Did you ever have a rotten day? Your mom yells at you at breakfast, your teacher catches you talking, the other guys play keep-away with your hat, and you drop your books in the mud when your dog jumps on you because he's so glad to see you home. All day long you have felt mistreated and hurt, and that is the last straw. So you pick a fight with your little sister." Talk about how cashing in stamps feels and how getting dumped on feels. As small people, children are often the target when stamps are cashed in. Awareness can help children stop collecting stamps (child abuse is the worst form of stamp cashing) by learning to talk about bad feelings with someone they can trust and by asking for and receiving the positive strokes they need.

5. For counselors working with script issues, useful questions for figuring out a child's script include many of the same questions used in the Adlerian lifestyle interview (see Chapter 11):

What are the "hurt" points in your family? (G)
Who is in your family? (BP)
What are the people in your family like? (BP)
Has anyone else ever lived with you? (BP)
What were they like? (BP)
Who is boss in your family? (PI, P)
What is your mother's (or father's) favorite saying? (PI, CI)
Describe yourself in three words. (BP, D)
What words would other people in your family use to describe you? (PI, CI, BP)
What bad feeling do you have a lot? (R)
What good feeling do you have a lot? (BP)
Who is your mother's favorite? (PI, CI)
Who is your father's favorite? (PI, CI)

The preceding questions are coded to fit parts of the life script.

BP—Basic life position regarding how I feel about myself and others
PI—Parental injunction (message from parent's Child): "Don't do as I do"

CI—Counterinjunction (message from parent's Parent): "Do at least try"
G—Games (getting strokes at others' expense)
R—Racket (bad feelings)
D—Decision (how I have chosen to live my life)
P—Program (how to obey injunctions)

6. At some time during their lives, most people have kept a diary or journal in which they have recorded their innermost feelings, thoughts, and other events. Children respond well to a homework assignment of keeping a diary. The diary provides the counselor and child with a record of feelings, thoughts, and life script to be explored. Keeping a journal or diary may also provide the child with a feeling of closeness to the counselor between sessions.

7. What *not* to do: The counselor who is not in a position to protect a child from negative consequences ought not interfere with script behavior that still serves a purpose in the family. Do not ask children to give up their games or rackets before they learn more appropriate ways to get strokes. Do not decide for children what they "should" do. Do not encourage children to play TA counselor with people who have power over them and may not appreciate their comments. However, scripts are not written in stone and can be modified or rewritten to help children and adults find better ways to meet their needs.

All the preceding exercises can be used in group and family counseling as well as in individual counseling. Role-playing and acting-out games are very effective group techniques. Families in TA counseling come to recognize where their transactions become crossed, how and when scripting occurs, and how stroking behavior can change family feelings.

## CASE STUDIES

### *Transcript I*

Jimmy, age 5, is being seen by the school counselor because he has recently begun fighting with other children in his kindergarten class.

*Counselor:*  Jimmy, remember when I came to your class and read the story about the warm fuzzies and the cold pricklies? [He nods.] Well, everybody, kids and grown-ups, needs to get some of these to live. Sometimes people do things to get cold pricklies like slaps or frowns, or being yelled at. Would you like to find out how to give yourself and other people nice warm fuzzies like smiles and hugs, and get them back from others?

*Jimmy:*  Yes. Everybody doesn't like me now.

*Counselor:*  What do you do to get hugs and smiles from your mommy?

*Jimmy:*  I don't do anything, she just gives them to me. Or sometimes I hug her first or say "I love you."

*Counselor:*  Sometimes mommies are busy. What do you do to get her attention then?

*Jimmy:*  Well, I get a hug from Grandma. But if I can't get one, I make my little sister yell. Then somebody comes to see what's happening.

*Counselor:*  If you can't get a warm fuzzy, you get them to give you a cold prickly?

*Jimmy:*  Yeah.

*Counselor:*  What do kids in your class have to do to get a hug?

*Jimmy:*  They hug you if you fall down. But I don't fall down, so nobody hugs me.

*Counselor:*  If you can't get a hug or other warm fuzzy when you want one, what do you do to get attention?

*Jimmy:*  I make one of the other kids yell.

*Counselor:*  Sometimes getting yelled at is better than nothing, huh?

*Jimmy:*  Yeah.

*Counselor:*  Do you think any of your teachers would give you a warm fuzzy?

*Jimmy:*  Miss Sally has a nice face.

*Counselor:*  So when you feel bad inside and need a warm fuzzy, you could get one from Miss Sally?

*Jimmy:*  Yeah, like when I miss my mommy. I could tell Miss Sally that and ask her to hug me.

*Counselor:*  That sounds like a good plan, Jimmy. And if you feel bad, or sad, or lonely, or angry, and need to talk about it, you can come here and talk to me about it.

*Jimmy:*  Okay.

*Counselor:*  [gives Jimmy a hug] I give warm fuzzies, too.

Counselor feedback to Jim's teacher should include talking about giving Jim some strokes when he is being good and not making a bid for attention in the form of negative feedback.

## *Transcript II*

The child in this interview is a 10-year-old boy.

*Counselor:*  Christopher, you've read the Freeds' book about stroking. Can you explain to me what they mean by strokes?

*Christopher:*  Stroking is when somebody does some type of action, physical or verbal, that makes you feel either good or not so good.

*Counselor:*  I think that's a very good definition. Can you give me some examples of a positive stroke?

*Christopher:*  Patting somebody, or hugging them, or saying something nice.

*Counselor:*  Like what?

*Christopher:*  "You really did well today."

*Counselor:*  Can you think of a positive stroke you've given someone today?

*Christopher:*  Not really.

*Counselor:*  How about when I came in, and you looked up and smiled?

*Christopher:*  I guess. I smiled at most everybody in the class today.

*Counselor:*  You have to remember that they don't have to be verbal; just a smile is a positive stroke. Can you think of any negative strokes you've given anyone today?

*Christopher:* No.

*Counselor:* That's good. Of course, the same holds true for negative strokes—if, without realizing it, you looked at someone and gave them a hard frown or something, that could be a negative stroke that you didn't realize you gave.

*Christopher:* I don't see why I would have given any, even by accident. There wasn't any reason to give any.

*Counselor:* Well, good. Can you think of any positive strokes anyone gave you today?

*Christopher:* When I got 100 on our test today, Mrs. Kincaid said that that was very good.

*Counselor:* I'm glad. Any negative strokes?

*Christopher:* No.

*Counselor:* Well, I told you your hands and face were dirty and I didn't like you coming downtown like that, right? You think you've got the idea about how positive and negative strokes work?

*Christopher:* Yes.

*Counselor:* How would you use stroking?

*Christopher:* Well, whenever I thought somebody did a good job on something, I could tell them.

*Counselor:* You know, there's such a thing as giving strokes that are not asked for, strokes that you just offer freely. Can you give an example of one of those, maybe?

*Christopher:* Just saying something nice when they don't even really need it . . . well, they do need it. Just saying it, but just saying it even if they haven't done anything.

*Counselor:* Be more specific.

*Christopher:* Well, if you meet somebody, you can say, "I like your shoes," or "Your hair looks nice," or something like that.

*Counselor:* Yes, those would be nice to hear. Can you tell me how you might use nonverbal positive strokes?

*Christopher:* By patting somebody, or smiling at them, or giving them a hug.

*Counselor:* How do you think you would feel if you started giving more positive strokes and getting more positive strokes?

*Christopher:* All covered over with strokes.

◆

## CROSS-CULTURAL APPLICATIONS OF TRANSACTIONAL ANALYSIS

Eric Berne believed that the concepts used in TA were universal. That is, all people possess Parent, Adult, and Child functions in their personality, and all people transact their business with others through communicating from each of the three ego states. The user-friendly nature of TA is a plus for transcending cultural barriers. Cultures and individuals within all cultures who prefer a direct, straightforward, educational approach to personal development over a healing approach to mental illness will find TA comfortable. TA practitioners offer the opportunity to learn new skills in both group and individual settings. As noted in Chapter 15, African Americans and Latinos have preferences for a psychoeducational context in which clients can learn useful skills. Asian Americans and Asians will find the emphasis on thinking an attractive feature of TA. Considerable thought is required to analyze transactions and communication patterns between people. Analysis of scripts, games, and rackets puts a premium on cognitive processes. However, the focus on feelings is not disregarded, especially in dealing with the giving and receiving of positive and negative strokes. Goal setting, role playing, and modeling, which can be used in Transactional Analysis, have been recommended as effective interventions for African Americans. Once again, we want to emphasize the point that vast, individual differences exist within each culture regarding preferences for counseling theory and practice.

In using Transactional Analysis across cultures, there is little variation in the method. Clients will learn the basic terminology and make contracts. TA has been used successfully in several different cultures. Mazzetti (1997) recommended TA for treating antisocial behavior by children of immigrant families in Italy. Robinson (1998) described a TA program for treating seriously disturbed clients in a small, residential therapeutic community in England. Guimaraes (1997) used TA to teach student doctors to communicate and work more effectively with patients from lower socioeconomic levels in Brazil. Beslija (1997) reported success with TA in working with the psychological problems of refugees from the former Yugoslavia.

## TRANSACTIONAL ANALYSIS AND MANAGED HEALTH CARE

Managed care organizations (MCOs) favor the group counseling format that transactional analysis practitioners often use. As noted in Chapter 2, the psychoeducational approach used by Transactional Analysis practitioners also finds favor in the managed care environment. Considerable work and progress toward counseling goals can be done in 10 group sessions, giving TA some plus points for brief treatment and a goal-attainment focus. Cost for Transactional Analysis treatments is low, and client satisfaction is generally high as people practice the new skills learned in group sessions. Goal setting may involve writing a new life script to replace the old script, which was not helping clients meet their needs. In fact, old, ineffective scripts are generally written out and destroyed in a "public" burning during a group session. TA enjoys some other advantages regarding MCO guidelines. It is a self-help psychology—people can be helped by reading about it because the concepts are easy to understand. In addition, people do not feel threatened by TA. It deals with observable behavior, the present, and the conscious area of functioning. The TA focus is on how people can change whatever they want to change; these changes often happen immediately as people learn how to communicate more effectively and develop contracts for behavior change. In summary, TA can be packaged in a format MCOs find attractive and worthy of support.

## SUMMARY

The practitioners of transactional analysis continue to enjoy wide popularity for improving relationship and communication skills between individuals and within groups of various types. TA training is useful in conducting group guidance classes or group counseling sessions with children in the 5 to 12 age range. However, TA training can be modified for use with any age group; the TA concepts are more user-friendly than the language of traditional psychotherapy. TA material is extremely well received in parent education groups, where the focus is on the positive things parents have been doing and how to increase the frequency of such helpful, positive parent behaviors. The TA focus is on reeducation rather than healing and, as such, is not based on the assumption that people are sick and need to be healed. Participants in TA groups appreciate their roles as learners over that of being patients. TA instruction helps people to become aware of what they do and how this affects other people in their families and in their circles of friends and acquaintances. This information supports decisions to make changes in behavior.

### W E B S I T E S for Transactional Analysis

International Transactional Analysis Association (ITAA) home page
www.itaa-net.org/index.htm

Institute of Transactional Analysis Psychotherapy Counseling
www.ita.org.uk

## REFERENCES

Berne, E. (1947). *The mind in action*. New York: Simon & Schuster.

Berne, E. (1949). The nature of intuition. *Psychiatric Quarterly, 23,* 203–226.

Berne, E. (1961). *Transactional analysis in psychotherapy*. New York: Grove.

Berne, E. (1964). *Games people play*. New York: Grove.

Beslija, A. (1997). Psychotherapy with refugees from Bosnia-Herzegovina. *Transactional Analysis Journal, 27,* 49–54.

Freed, A., & Freed, M. (1971, 1998). *TA for kids: and grown ups too*. Rolling Hills Estates, CA: Jalmar.

Freed, A. (1973, 1998). *TA for tots: And other prinzes*. Rolling Hills Estates, CA: Jalmar.

Freed, A. (1992). *TA for teens and other important people* (Rev. ed.). Rolling Hills Estates, CA: Jalmar.

Guimaraes, B. (1997). Medical omnipotence and transactional analysis: A pedagogical proposal. *Transactional Analysis Journal, 27,* 272–277.

Harris, T. (1969). *I'm OK—You're OK*. New York: Harper & Row.

James, M., & Jongeward, D. (1971). *Born to win*. Reading, MA: Addison-Wesley.

Kaplan, K. (2001, March 10). TILT and structural pathology. *Transactional Analysis Journal Internet, 4,* www.tajnet.org/articles/kaplan-tilt.html. Retrieved September 2, 2002.

Mazzetti, M. (1997). A transactional analysis approach to adjustment problems of adolescents from immigrant families. *Transactional Analysis Journal, 27,* 220–227.

Robinson, J. (1998). Reparenting in a therapeutic community. *Transactional Analysis Journal, 28,* 88–94.

Shahin, J. (1995). Hey, ya jerk. *American Way, 28,* 32, 37–38.

Steiner, C. (1974). *Scripts people live.* New York: Grove.

Steiner, C. (1975). *Readings in radical psychiatry.* New York: Grove.

Summerton, O. (2000). The development of game analysis. *Transactional Analysis Journal, 30,* 207–218.

Woods, K. (2000). The defensive function of the game scenario. *Transactional Analysis Journal, 30,* 94–97.

# Chapter 11

# Individual Psychology*

*Half of the harm that is done in this world is due to people who want to feel important. They don't mean to do harm. But the harm does not interest them.*
—T. S. Eliot

*It isn't that they can't see the solution. It's that they can't see the problem.*
—G. K. Chesterton

## ALFRED ADLER

Alfred Adler, the founder of individual psychology, was born in Vienna on February 7, 1870, the second of six children. When Adler was 10 years old, he was such a poor math student that his teachers suggested he be removed from school and assigned as an apprentice to a cobbler. As often happens with paradoxical counseling strategies, the boy became angry, studied harder, and placed first in his class. As a child, Adler suffered from rickets, pneumonia, and several accidents. The resulting frequent contact with doctors influenced Adler to study medicine.

Adler spent his entire youth in Vienna and received his medical degree from the university in 1895. In addition to medicine, Adler was also knowledgeable in psychology, philosophy, the Bible, and Shakespeare. Two years after his graduation, Adler married Raisa Timofeyeuna Epstein, an intellectual and friend of Freud's who had moved from Russia to study at the University of Vienna (Alexander, Eisenstein, & Grotjahn, 1966).

In the fall of 1902, Adler joined Sigmund Freud's discussion group, which was to become the first psychoanalytic society. Adler was not a proponent of Freud's psychosexual theory, and his writings about "feelings of inferiority" in 1910 and 1911 initiated a break with Freud. In 1910, in an attempt to reconcile the gap between himself and the Adlerians, Freud named Adler president of the Viennese Analytic Society and coeditor of a journal published by Freud. Nevertheless, Adler continued to disagree with Freud's psychosexual theory. Adler was the first psychoanalyst to

---

*We owe appreciation to Harold Mosak, PhD, of the Adler School of Professional Psychology in Chicago, for his contributions and his review of the fifth edition of this chapter.

emphasize human nature as being fundamentally social. Upon Freud's demand that his entire staff accept his theory without any conditions, Adler resigned, along with seven others, and founded the Society for Free Psychoanalytic Research. In 1912, Adler changed the name to the Society for Individual Psychology.

After World War I broke out, Adler served for 2 years as a military doctor and later was appointed to head a large hospital for the wounded and shell-shocked. In 1926, Adler accepted a visiting professorship at Columbia University in New York, and in 1935 he moved his family to the United States. His children, one son and one daughter, became psychiatrists and worked with the principles of individual psychology. On May 28, 1937, while giving a series of lectures in Scotland, Adler suddenly collapsed on the street and died of heart failure.

Adler's achievements included founding *Zeitschrift für Individualpsychologie* (1912), introducing the term *inferiority feelings,* and developing a flexible, supportive psychotherapy to direct those emotionally disabled by inferiority feelings toward maturity, common sense, and social usefulness. Individual psychology originated from the German word *Individualpsychologie,* meaning "psychology of the whole that cannot be divided." Basically, it is a psychology that is concerned at one and the same time with individuals as they are in themselves and in their relationships with the community.

Adler originated (1919) the network of child guidance clinics called *Erziehungs-beratungsstellen,* which means literally "places to come for questions about education"—parent-education centers. Their staffs included physicians, psychologists, and social workers. Because of his idea of group discussions with families, many people believe Adler to have been 50 years ahead of his time; the present-day emphasis on group counseling, parent education, and full-service schools supports this claim.

Parent education has been a significant part of Adler's system from the beginning. Several Adlerian parent-education packages have been published and used successfully over the past several years. In addition, Adlerian parent groups meet regularly around the country. Adler favored efforts directed toward prevention of mental illness through parent-education programs. He recognized the difficulty of undoing in adulthood the wrongs done to people in their childhood.

Rudolf Dreikurs contributed perhaps the most helpful adaptations and development of Adler's work. A leading proponent of individual psychology until his death in 1972, Dreikurs was a pioneer in music therapy and group psychotherapy, which he introduced into private psychiatric practice in 1929. His most significant contribution to counseling children was his ability to translate theory into practice. Dreikurs developed many of Adler's complex ideas into a relatively simple applied method for understanding and working with the behavior of children in both family and school settings.

## THE NATURE OF PEOPLE

If Freud had done nothing more than stimulate thinking and reactions in other theorists, he would have made a significant contribution to counseling and psychotherapy. Like many others, Adler reacted against Freud's ideas and developed a new theory. Freud attempted to interpret all behaviors and problems as extensions of sex, pleasure, and the death instinct; Adler believed that all people develop some sense of inferiority because they are born completely helpless and remain that way for a rather long childhood. Such feelings of inferiority may be exaggerated by body or organ defects (real or imaginary), by having older and more powerful siblings, or by parent neglect, rejection, or pampering. One way to cope with feelings of inferiority is compensation, or gaining power to handle the sense of weakness. The effects of organ inferiority are reduced through development of skills, behaviors, traits, and strengths that replace or compensate for these thoughts of weakness and powerlessness. Mosak (1992) pointed out that Adler introduced the theory of organ inferiority in 1907, when Adler was a Freudian, and that Freud complimented Adler on a major addition to Freudian theory. Although it is not a part of Adlerian theory today, Adlerians and others have observed that some people with organ inferiorities do compensate for them.

Adler viewed human behavior as falling on a continuum between his concepts of masculinity, representing strength and power, and femininity, symbolizing weakness and inferiority. What he called *masculine protest*, a striving for power, was common to both sexes, especially women. Adler replaced Freud's concept of sexual pleasure as the prime motivator of behavior with the search for power.

According to Adler, personality development progresses along a road paved with evidence of either personal superiority or inferiority. As infants—small, helpless, inexperienced—we are especially subject to others' whims and vulnerable to inferiority feelings. As we grow older, both family and society emphasize the advantages of size, beauty, and strength. Therefore, our wishes and dreams for superiority, our attempts to achieve it, and the social realities that make us feel inferior are in continual conflict. This striving for power (masculine protest) occupies a place in his theory similar to that of the Oedipus situation in Freudian theory. A person develops into a normal, neurotic, or psychotic adult as the result of this struggle between the masculine protest and social reality.

Freud believed that love and work were the two important indexes of mental health in that a person's mental health depends on how well these two areas are progressing. In a similar vein, Adler believed that problems brought to therapy reside in the areas of career (occupation), love relationships (intimacy), and friendships.

The following points are a summary of the Adlerian view on the nature of people:

- Beginning in childhood, people develop feelings of inferiority stemming from being totally dependent on their parents. Life becomes a process of believing in ways to become less inferior and more independent. People behave in ways to give themselves feelings of perfection or superiority.
- The future determines the present as people behave in ways to become the fictionalized ideal person they have established as a goal in their future. All parts of the person are directed toward achieving the goal of becoming the ideal self: cognitive, affective, behavioral, conscious, and unconscious. Psychological goals are often not known and have to be identified and explained to clients by their counselors as they examine the purposes of their clients' behavior.

- Individual perceptions of events and relationships are governed by one's own unique view of the world and its people. Understanding one's relationship to others is a first step to understanding oneself.
- People need to be educated to value and exhibit social interest. Children and adults make contributions to social interest when they make their neighborhood (and world) a better place to live.
- Unsolved problems of an individual may become problems for society if they are not treated before they become too difficult to solve.

## The Need for Success

Adler was struck by the importance of the hunger for success in human life—the ways people seek power and prestige and strive for goals associated with social approval. He was very concerned with the problems of competition, blocked ambition, feelings of resentment and hostility, and impulses to struggle and resist or to surrender and give in. Adler shifted his clinical attention from a primary focus on clients' psychosexual history to an examination of their success–failure pattern, or style of life. Adler's term *style of life* emphasizes the direction in which the individual is moving. Style-of-life analysis involves an assessment of children in terms of their habitual responses to frustration, to assumption of responsibility, and to situations that require exercising initiative.

## Goals of Behavior

Adler's individual psychology emphasizes the purposive nature of human strivings. All behavior, including emotions, is goal directed. According to Adlerian theory, the issue is not the cause of the behavior but determining what children want to accomplish, either in the real world or in their own minds. Behaviors do not continue over time unless they "work" for children. By looking at the consequences of children's behavior, adults can determine their goals. Adler's conception was that people are guided by a striving for ideal masculinity. Adler described what Horney (1950) termed the *neurotic search for glory:* Neurotics are characterized by an unrealistic goal of masculinity and mastery that they strive to overcome or attain. He also anticipated later psychoanalytic groups in his emphasis on the social as well as the constitutional determinants of one's style of life. To Adler, the term *individual psychology* emphasized the unity of personality as opposed to Freud's emphasis on instincts common to all people. An individual builds a style of life from interactions between heredity and environment; these lifestyle building blocks fit a person into life as that person perceives it.

## Lifestyle

Adler believed that a person's behavior must be studied from a holistic viewpoint. Usually by the age of 4 or 5, children have drawn general conclusions about life and the "best" way to meet the problems life offers. They base these conclusions on their biased perceptions of the events and interactions that go on around them and form the basis for their lifestyle. The style of life, unique for each individual, is the pattern of behavior that will predominate throughout that person's life. Only rarely does a person's lifestyle change without outside intervention. Understanding their lifestyle—that is, the basic beliefs they developed at an early age to help organize, understand, predict, and control their world—is important for adults, but children who have not reached the formal stage of cognitive development are incapable of understanding their lifestyles. Therefore, in working with children, Adlerians focus on the immediate behavior goals rather than on long-term goals. Socratic questioning methods help children learn their current lifestyle and goals through self-discovery.

Stiles and Wilborn (1992) developed a lifestyle instrument for children that describes those who responsibly cope with and solve problems and those who engage in social-interest activities that help others. Based on Adler's four lifestyle types, the scale reflected six lifestyle themes: *pleasing, rebelling, getting, controlling, being inadequate,* and *being socially useful.* They found that boys (age 8 to 11) scored higher than girls of the same age on rebelling; girls scored higher on pleasing.

## Social Interest

A person's amount of social interest is, according to Adler (1938/1964), a good barometer of mental health. Social interest is a feeling for and cooperation with people—a sense of belonging and participating with others for the common good. Ansbacher (1992) described how social interest and community feeling differ. He defined *social interest* as the more active of the two terms because it relates to how the individual handles the life tasks of love, friendship, and work in the social context. *Social interest* is the more concrete, workable term, whereas *community feeling* deals with the spiritual, universal order of a person's life.

Everyone has a need to belong to a group. Although social interest is inborn, it does not appear spontaneously but must be encouraged and trained, beginning with the relationship between the newborn and the mother. Children who feel they are part of a group do useful things that contribute to the well-being of that group; those who feel left out—and therefore inferior—do useless things in order to prove their own worth by gaining attention. From this concept comes the idea that misbehaving children are discouraged children—children who think that they can be known only in useless ways. Because children behave within the social context, their behavior cannot be studied in isolation. The study of human interaction is basic to individual psychology.

Many of life's problems center around conflicts with others. Solutions for these problems involve cooperating with people in the interest of making society a better place to live. A strong point in Adler's theory is his understanding of the implications of the social structure of life. Because every individual depends on other people for birth and growth; for food, shelter, and protection; and for love and companionship, a great web of interdependence exists among people. Thus the individual, Adler pointed out, owes a constant debt to society. Each person is responsible to the group, and those who do not learn to cooperate are destroyed. Adler believed that a person cannot violate the love and logic that bind people together without dire consequences for the health of one's personality. Pronounced egocentricity (the opposite of social interest) leads to neurosis, and the individual becomes healthy again only when this egocentricity is renounced in favor of a greater interest in the well-being of the total group. Critics of Adlerian theory who hold a less positive view of human nature point out that people know they should cooperate but ordinarily do not do so until forced. Cross-cultural research evidence supports this view.

Adler believed that social interest was exhibited through such qualities as friendliness, cooperation, and empathy. Social-interest development, being associated with so many good things, would seem to be a worthwhile pursuit for people of all ages.

## Family Environment

Three environmental factors affect the development of a child's personality: family constellation, family atmosphere, and the prevalent methods of training. Through the family atmosphere, children learn about values and customs and try to fit themselves into the standards their parents set. Children also learn about relationships by watching how their family members interact and about sex roles by seeing the patterns adopted by their parents. The family constellation is important in that children formulate personalities based on how they interpret their positions in the family relative to other siblings: The firstborn child dethroned by a new baby tries very hard to maintain the position of supremacy and seeks recognition by whatever means possible. The second child feels inadequate because someone is always ahead and seeks a place by becoming what the older child is not; this child may feel squeezed out by a third child and adopt the position that life is unfair. The youngest child may take advantage of being the youngest and become outstanding in some respect, good or bad, even by becoming openly rebellious or helpless.

In summary, Adler believed that the principal human motive, a striving for perfection, could become a striving for superiority and thus an overcompensation for a feeling of inferiority. Children are self-determining persons able to create a style of life in the context of their family constellation. By trial and error and by observation, children form their own conclusions about life and their place in it.

## The Family Constellation

One goal of counseling is to construct a picture of the family dynamics and the child's place in the family constellation. *Ordinal position* (the exact order in which the child was born, e.g., second or fourth) in the family constellation is a key to the lifestyle pattern being developed by the child, and it may have a significant effect on how that child perceives reality. Although certain characteristics are associated with each child's *birth order* (one of the Adlerian birth positions: first, second, middle, youngest, and only), there are many exceptions, and thus not all firstborns are alike. Mosak (Shulman & Mosak, 1977) has pointed out that the study of birth order and ordinal position has limited value because of the confounding variables of family size and number of children; for example, the second-born child is the youngest in a two-child family and the middle child in a three-child family.

However, in an effort to find their special place in the family, children tend to select different roles, behaviors, and interests. In general, some stereotypical behaviors based on birth order have been cataloged by Adlerians over the past century. Some of these generalizations are summarized in the following paragraphs.

### Only Children

The only child enjoys some intellectual advantages by not having to share mother and father with any siblings. Language development is usually accelerated because the child learns adult language patterns. However, the reverse is sometimes true in an extremely child-centered home where everyone talks baby talk. Only children may experience difficulties outside the home when peers and teachers do not pamper them, and only children may be skillful in getting along with adults but not in making friends with their peers. They enjoy being the center of attention. Observing how they gain the approval and attention to maintain their center-stage position can help a counselor understand these children. Have they developed skills, do they elicit sympathy by being helpless, or do they act shyly? Only children are more likely to have problems with the egocentrism block. They are usually interested only in themselves and may resort to tantrums and uncooperative behavior if their requests are not granted. They may depend too much on adults because they have not learned to do things on their own. Exceptions to the rule are those only children who learn to play ball and other games by themselves when they have not had an opportunity to be around friends. Shulman (Shulman & Mosak, 1977) wrote that only children never have rivals and that peers tend to be curiosities rather than rivals. Only children may not have learned how to share, compromise, and collaborate.

### Firstborn Children

Often considered the special child by the family, especially if male, firstborns enjoy their number-one ranking but often fear dethronement by the birth of a second child. Firstborns work hard at pleasing their parents. They are likely to be conforming achievers, defenders of the faith, introverted, and well behaved. Twenty-three of the first 25 astronauts were firstborn males. The National Aeronautics and Space Administration (NASA) was interested in recruiting high-achieving followers for the space program; it had no need for "creative astronauts" who might decide to take the scenic route home. Firstborns often find themselves functioning as substitute parents in larger families. Shulman (Shulman & Mosak, 1977) believed that firstborn children, having had it all at one time, still prefer to be first and foremost.

## Second-Born Children

Second-born children may be those extroverted, creative, free-thinking spirits that NASA was trying to avoid. More often than not, second-borns look at what is left over in the way of roles and behavior patterns that the firstborn child has shunned; picking another role is easier than competing with an older sibling who has a head start. Second-borns may get lower grades in school, even if they are brighter than number one. Parents are often easier on second-born children and show less concern with rules. In fact, second-borns may be the family rebels—with or without a cause! In any case, a second-born is usually the opposite of the first child. Second-borns are easily discouraged by trying to compete with successful, older, and bigger firstborns. The more successful firstborns are, the more likely second-borns are to feel unsure of themselves and their abilities. They may even feel squeezed out, neglected, unloved, and abused when the third child arrives.

## Middle Children

Some of the idiosyncrasies common to the middle-child position may affect second-born children. Middle children are surrounded by competitors for their parents' attention. They have the pace-setting standard-bearers in front and the pursuers in the rear. Middle children often label themselves as squeezed children. However, many younger children increase their skill in academic, athletic, and other pursuits through competition with older siblings.

## Youngest Children

Often referred to as Prince or Princess Charming, the youngest child could find a permanent lifestyle of being the baby in the family. Youngest children often get a lot of service from all the other family members. They may become dependent or spoiled and lag in development. Youngest children readily develop real feelings of inferiority because they are smaller, less able to take care of themselves, and often not taken seriously. The really successful charmers may learn how to boss subtly or to manipulate the entire family. They decide either to challenge their elder siblings or to evade any direct struggles for superiority. Then again, the path is marked and the trail is broken for the youngest child. Family guidelines are clear, and the youngest children always retain their position. Perhaps the downside is the child's perception that a lot of catching up is necessary to ever find a place in the family.

When a 5-year difference exists between two children in a family, the situation changes. With this large a gap, the next-born child often assumes the characteristics of a firstborn; apparently, the 5 years remove the competitive barriers found between children who are closer in age.

Extreme behavior patterns are often observed in children who find themselves the only boy or girl among siblings of the opposite sex. They may tend to develop toward extremes in either masculinity or femininity. Sex roles children assume often depend on roles perceived as most favored in our culture.

Large families appear to offer some advantages in child-rearing by making it tough for parents to overparent each child. Children in large families frequently learn how to solve their own problems, take care of themselves, and handle their conflicts because their parents cannot give personal service and attention to each and every problem. Large families are probably good training grounds for learning how to be independent.

The following factors influence the perceptions children have of their particular roles in their family:

1. The parents may have a favorite child.
2. The family may move.
3. Parents become more experienced and easygoing as they grow older.
4. Some homes are single-parent homes.
5. The children may have a stepparent living in the home.
6. The family climate changes with each addition to the family.
7. Chronic illnesses or handicaps may be a problem in the family.
8. A grandparent may live in the home.
9. Some families are blended families.

In summary, too much emphasis on birth order and ordinal position works in opposition to the Adlerian principle of free choice. People with the same birth order may share some commonalities, but they are not predestined to turn out the same. The key question for counselors is not birth order but how each child finds his or her place in the family.

## The Family Atmosphere

Adlerians stress the importance of the family atmosphere in the development of the child. Whereas the family constellation is a description of how family members interact, the family atmosphere is the style of coping with life that the family has modeled for the child (Dewey, 1971).

The following 12 family atmosphere profiles are indications of how a negative family atmosphere can adversely affect children:

1. *Authoritarian.* The authoritarian home requires unquestioned obedience from the children. Children have little or no voice in family decisions. Although these children are often well behaved and mannerly, they also tend to be more anxious and outer-directed. What was once a shy child may turn into a rebel with a cause in later life.

2. *Suppressive.* In tune with the authoritarian home is the suppressive family atmosphere, in which children are not permitted to express their thoughts and feelings. Expression of opinion is limited to what the parents want to hear. Frequently, children from such a family cannot express their feelings when they are allowed to in situations outside the home, such as counseling. This type of family atmosphere does not encourage close relationships.

3. *Rejective.* Children feel unloved and unaccepted in this family atmosphere. Some parents do not know how to show love and frequently cannot separate the deed from the doer. Children and parents need to know and understand that love can be unconditional and not tied to unacceptable behavior: "I love you, but I am still angered by your irresponsibility." A child can easily become extremely discouraged in the rejective family.

4. *Disparaging.* A child criticized by everyone else in the family often turns out to be the "bad egg" everyone predicted. Too much criticism generally leads to cynicism and inability to form good interpersonal relationships.

5. *High standards.* Children living in the high-standards atmosphere may think such things as "I am not loved unless I make all As." Fear of failure leads to the considerable distress perfectionist people experience. The tension and stress these children have often prevent them from performing as well as they are able.

6. *Inharmonious.* In homes with considerable quarreling and fighting, children learn the importance of trying to control other people and keep others from controlling them. Power becomes a prime goal for these children. Discipline may be inconsistent in these homes and depend on the mood of the parents.

7. *Inconsistent.* Inconsistent methods of discipline and home routines are often sources of confusion and disharmony in the home. Lack of self-control, low motivation, self-centeredness, instability, and poor interpersonal relationships are often attributed to inconsistency in parenting practices.

8. *Materialistic.* In this type of home, children learn that feelings of self-worth depend on possessions and on comparisons with what peers own. Interpersonal relationships take a back seat to accumulating wealth.

9. *Overprotective.* These homes often prevent children from growing up because parents do too much for them. They protect the children from the consequences of their behavior and, in doing so, deny the reality of the situation. This parental overindulgence leads to a child who feels helpless and dependent. Dependent children fall into the class of outer-directed people who rely on others for approval.

10. *Pitying.* Like overprotectiveness, pitying also prevents children from developing and using the resources they have for solving their problems. Such may be especially the case with handicapped children, who may be encouraged to feel sorry for themselves and to expect favors from others to make up for their misfortunes.

11. *Hopeless.* Discouraged and "unsuccessful" parents often pass on these attitudes to their children, who make hopelessness a part of their lifestyle. A pessimistic home atmosphere may be due to economic factors, especially if the breadwinners lack financial resources.

12. *Martyr.* People suffering from low self-esteem, hopelessness, and discouragement may have another pessimistic viewpoint, martyrdom. Once again, children may learn that life is unfair and that people should treat them better; martyrdom is a breeding ground for dependency.

Remember that atmosphere is not the total cause of behavior. Behavior is most influenced by the child's biased perceptions of the family climate.

## THEORY OF COUNSELING

Adler (1938/1964) held that four ties create reality and meaning in people's lives:

1. People are on earth to ensure the continuance of the human species.

2. Our survival depends on our need to cooperate with our fellow human beings.

3. Human beings each live in two sexes—the masculine, powerful side of our nature, and the feminine, weak side of our nature (perhaps Adler forgot that male babies have a higher infant mortality rate and women outlive men).

4. Human problems can be grouped into three categories: relationships, work life, and love life.

Adler viewed the counselor's job as helping the child substitute realistic goals for unrealistic life goals and instilling social interest and concern for others.

As with most approaches to counseling, the goal of establishing a positive sense of self-esteem is primary. To achieve this feeling of self-esteem, children need to feel good about finding a place in life and about their progress in overcoming the unpleasant sense of inferiority associated with the dependence, smallness, and vulnerability introduced in early childhood. In the Adlerian view (and we do not know where he found this child), the ideal or well-adjusted child exhibits the following qualities:

1. Respects the rights of others
2. Is tolerant of others
3. Is interested in others
4. Cooperates with others
5. Encourages others
6. Is courteous
7. Has a strong, positive self-concept
8. Has a feeling of belonging
9. Has socially acceptable goals
10. Exerts genuine effort

11. Is willing to share with others
12. Is concerned with how much "we" can get rather than how much "I" can get

In response to the specific pattern of inferiority feelings experienced by a child in a specific home situation, one unitary way of coping with the problem is discovered, one fundamental attitude is developed, and one mode of compensation is achieved. Thus, a person forms a style of life early in childhood—a style that is unitary, dependable, and predictable.

Adler recognized two fundamental styles of life: direct and indirect approaches to the good things, through strength and power or through weakness. A person usually tries power first; if power is blocked, a person chooses another road to the goal. The second road is paved with gentleness and bids for sympathy. If both roads fail, secondary feelings of inferiority arise. These secondary inferiority feelings, which Adler considered more serious than the primary, universal inferiority feelings, are ego problems, which can be the most burning problems of all. The focus of counseling, therefore, is harnessing this drive to compensate for weakness so that positive, constructive behavior results. Freud held that the backbone of civilization was sublimation. Adler thought that talent and capabilities arise from the stimulus of inadequacy. Adlerians believe that people are pulled by their goals and priorities. Knowledge of these goals is a major key to understanding behavior. For example, four priorities relate to the need to belong:

1. *To please others:* The main objective of pleasing others is to avoid rejection. Although other people may find a "me last" person quite easy to accept, the price for this behavior may be the rejection the person is trying to avoid. The "me last" position may also limit a person's growth and opportunities for learning, personal development, and general success in life. The pleasing attitude is supported by the faulty belief that "my meaningfulness and survival depend on whether I am loved by all" or that "life is good when my approval rating is high and bad when it is not."

2. *To be superior:* The main objective of trying to be superior is to avoid meaninglessness. Such an attitude of superiority tends to make others feel inadequate. The price for superiority may be an overloaded lifestyle. Children may become overly responsible and perfectionistic, with all the resulting worry and anxiety when things are not perfect. People holding superiority as their number-one priority attempt to avoid insignificance by influencing others through high achievement, leadership, and martyrdom. The superiority priority is supported by the faulty belief that "I am meaningful and therefore can survive only if I am better, am wiser, or know more than others."

3. *To control:* The main objective of trying to control oneself, others, and the environment is to avoid unexpected humiliation. Controlling others tends to make them feel challenged, with the resulting price of increased social distance. Too much self-control results in a very structured life with little spontaneity. Control people are best described as uptight, and their faulty belief is that "I am meaning-

ful and therefore can survive only if I can control my life and the events and people who are part of my life."

4. *To be comfortable:* Avoidance of stress and pressure is the main objective of those holding comfort as their number-one priority. At their extreme, comfort seekers specialize in unfinished business and unresolved problems and conflicts. They adopt a reactive rather than proactive stance toward life. Delayed gratification is not one of their strengths; they often give way to the self-indulgent attitude of "I want what I want now." The comfort-seeking priority is supported by the faulty beliefs that "I am meaningful and therefore can survive only if I am left alone, unpressured, and free to move" and "life is bad when I am uncomfortable."

Each priority has a price. As is done in the practice of reality therapy, the counselor can confront children and adults with a cost analysis of their chosen priorities. Because people are often reluctant to give up their number-one priority, counseling may focus on cost reduction by exploring how clients can manage their priorities in more cost-efficient ways. As is done in the practice of rational-emotive-behavior therapy, the counselor can ask clients to modify their faulty beliefs that meaningfulness and survival rest solely on the total and constant fulfillment of their number-one priority.

## Goals of Misbehavior

As children grow and interact with their environment, they gradually develop methods for achieving their basic goal, belonging. Several factors, including the child's place in the family, the quality of the parents' interaction with the child, and the child's creative reaction to the family atmosphere, are critical in the development of coherent patterns of behaviors and attitudes.

Dreikurs and Soltz (1964) made an especially insightful and useful analysis of the immediate goals by which children attempt to achieve their basic goal of belonging. Children with no pattern of misbehavior have an immediate goal of cooperation and constructive collaboration. They find their place and feel good about themselves through constructive cooperation. They generally approach life with the goal of collaborating, and their usual behavior is socially and personally effective. By contrast, children with a pattern of misbehavior are usually pursuing one of four mistaken goals: attention, power, revenge, and inadequacy or withdrawal. Understanding the goal for which a misbehaving child is striving helps put the behavior in perspective and provides a basis for corrective action.

## Attention

All children seek attention, especially those of preschool age. However, excessive attention-getting behavior should diminish in the primary school years before it becomes a problem to teachers, parents, and peers. The child's goal is to keep an adult busy, and the natural reaction is to feel annoyed and provide the service and attention the child seeks. Attention getting appears in four forms:

1. *Active constructive*. This child may be the model child, but with the goal to elevate self, not to cooperate. This is the successful student whose industrious and reliable performance is for attention only.

2. *Passive constructive*. This charming child is not as vigorous as the active-constructive child about getting attention. This child is a conscientious performer and a prime candidate for teacher's pet.

3. *Active destructive*. This nuisance child is the prime candidate for the child most likely to ruin a teacher's day—the class clown, show-off, and mischief-maker.

4. *Passive destructive*. This lazy child gets a teacher's attention through demands for service and help. This child often lacks the ability and motivation to complete work.

## Power

These children have an exaggerated need to exercise power and superiority. They take every situation, debate, or issue as a personal challenge from which they must emerge the winner; otherwise, these children think they have failed. The child's goal is to be the boss. A teacher's reaction ranges from anger to feeling threatened or defeated. The child acts in a stubborn, argumentative way and may even throw tantrums; this child leads the league in disobedience. The power struggle takes two forms:

1. *Active destructive*. This child is the rebel who has the potential of leading a group rebellion.

2. *Passive destructive*. This child is stubborn and forgetful and could also be the lazy one in the group.

## Revenge

These children feel hurt and mistreated by life. Their goal is to get even by hurting others. They achieve social recognition, although they usually make themselves unpopular with most other children. The child's goal, then, is to even the score, and the adult's reaction is usually to feel hurt. Revenge has two forms:

1. *Active destructive*. This child is violent and resorts to stealing, vandalism, and physical abuse to extract revenge. This child is a candidate to become a gang leader.

2. *Passive destructive*. This child is also violent but in a passive way: quiet, sullen, or defiant.

Both revenge types believe their only hope lies in getting even.

## Inadequacy or Withdrawal

These children often feel inferior and think they are incapable of handling life's problems. Their deficiencies may be real or imagined. By giving up, they hope to hide their inferiority and to prevent others from making demands on them. The child's goal is to be left alone, and the adult's reaction is helplessness and giving up. Inadequacy has only one form: passive-destructive. These children are usually described as hopeless. They often put on an act of being stupid just to discourage the teacher from asking them to recite and do work. They may have an unwritten contract with their teachers that says, in effect, "I'll leave you alone if you leave me alone."

Manly (1986) adapted the four goal questions into an informal inventory for use with students who have been referred to her for behavior or attitude problems. Manly tells her students that the inventory will help her know them better and know what they think. The inventory may be taken as a pencil-and-paper checklist or as an interview between counselor and client. Students are asked to indicate which of the following sentences are true for them:

### Goals Inventory

#### Attention

— I want people to notice me.
— I want people to do more for me.
— I want to be special.
— I want some attention.

#### Power

— I want to be in charge.
— I want people to do what I want to do.
— I want people to stop telling me what to do.
— I want power.

#### Revenge

— I think I have been treated unfairly.
— I want to get even.
— I want people to see what it is like to feel hurt.
— I want people to feel sorry for what they have done.

#### Display of Inadequacy

— I want people to stop asking me to do things.
— I want people to feel sorry for me.
— I want to be left alone. I can't do it anyway.
— I know I'll mess up, so there's no point in trying.

The questions may be intermixed or administered in these groupings. The four goal labels are not included on the inventory.

Adolescents are often confused in searching for their place in the world. Most teenagers move successfully through high school to become productive adults. However, some teens choose deviant behavior as a way to find their place in the world. The experiences children encounter and their interpretation of them lead to a life plan. The first social encounter is in the family. Children reared in democratic families understand how to meet life's challenges in meeting their needs for love, productive work, and friendship. Children reared in autocratic families often search for ways to fulfill their needs through attaining goals of misbehavior based on faulty reasoning (Ballou, 2002).

As mentioned before, the four goals of misbehavior are pursued by students who are having difficulty finding their place in their peer group by doing appropriate behaviors. All four goals are based on faulty logic by the students who resort to them to get what they want, whether it is attention, power, revenge, or avoidance of failure (withdrawal and giving up). Most misbehavior by children will be directed toward one or more of the four goals. However, adolescents begin to develop their capacity to incorporate more examples of faulty logic into their belief systems. Hence, each new faulty belief can result in a new goal of misbehavior. For example, the irrational idea "I must be perfect" could lead a student to engage in several types of perfectionistic behavior that make life miserable for the student. Most irrational messages produce failure because they lead to unattainable goals. Therefore, when counseling adolescent students, it is important to help them examine the faulty logic behind their behavior as well as the goal of the misbehavior. According to Ellis (1997), changing the word *must* to "it would be nice if" seems to help adolescents put irrational messages in better perspective. For example, "*it would be nice if* I were perfect, but since I'm human and humans make mistakes, it is okay to make mistakes, and I'm okay when I do."

## COUNSELING METHOD

Adler based the counseling methods he pioneered on his experience and philosophy about the nature of people. Later Adlerians, including Rudolf Dreikurs, Heinz Ansbacher, Harold Mosak, and Don Dinkmeyer, have used and modified many of Adler's original ideas.

Adlerian counseling makes no distinction between conscious and unconscious material. The counselor uses dreams, for example, to discover the lifestyle of adult clients—that is, the type of defense used to establish superiority. Many counselors use questions similar to adult lifestyle interviews with children as a means of assessing how well things are going for them. Although organ inferiority is not a part of modern-day Adlerian theory, counselors frequently analyze the inferiority feelings that stem from real or fancied personal deficiencies, particularly so-called organ deficiencies (such as defective vision) or organic inferiority (weak heart), some form of which everyone is assumed to possess. Next, the counselor proceeds to examine the client's academic, extracurricular, and social adjustments to see how the client has maintained or achieved superiority in each of these major areas of life and to examine the inferiority feelings that may plague the client. A primary goal of Adlerian counseling is to point out to the client the overcompensation and defensive patterns the client is using to solve problems and to find more successful ways of solving problems related to school, play, and other social concerns.

The establishment of the counselor–client relationship is the key step in the process. The counselor's job is to reeducate children who have developed mistaken ideas about some concepts of their lives. The counseling relationship assumes that the counselor and child are equal partners in the process and that the child is a responsible person who can learn better ways to meet personal needs. The positive view of human nature is indicated through the counselor's faith, hope, and caring attitude toward the child.

Adlerians believe that lives are holistic. Dinkmeyer, Pew, and Dinkmeyer (1979) referred to *teleoanalytic holistic theory,* which regards any troubled or troublesome behavior as a reflection of one indivisible, unified, whole organism moving toward self-created goals. The foremost task of Adlerian counselors is to prove this unity in people, in their thinking, feeling, and behavior—in fact, in every expression of their personality (Ansbacher & Ansbacher, 1956). Adlerians believe that children are the artists of their own personalities and are constantly moving purposefully toward self-consistent goals. An information interview based on questions used in the adult lifestyle analysis helps to reveal the pictures children have painted of their lives and their current personality development. The information interview consists of present and past (early) recollections of the children themselves and their families, how they fit into the family constellation, and how they perceive siblings and parents in relation to themselves. Questions often used include those in the following structured, interview guide:

*Information Interview Guide*

---

1. What type of concern or problem would you like to discuss, and how did this problem develop?

2. On a 5-point scale, how are things going for you? (Great, 1 or 2; medium, 3 or 4; poor, 5)

   In school? _____
   With your friends? _____
   With your hobbies? _____
   With your parents? _____
   With your brothers and sisters? _____
   With your fun times? _____

3. Can you tell me about your mother and father? (Separate the answers for mother and father or for any other parent figures living at home.)

   What do they do?
   What do they want you to do?

How do you get along with them?
How are you like your parents?
How are you different from your parents?

4. What things in your family would you like to be better?
5. Can you tell me about your brothers and sisters? (Make a list of children in the family, from eldest to youngest, with their ages.) Of all your brothers and sisters, who is:

Most like you? How?
Most different from you? How?

6. What kind of child are you?
7. What kind of child did you used to be?
8. What scares you most?
9. What used to scare you most?
10. Have any of your brothers or sisters been sick or hurt?
11. What do each of the children in your family do best?
12. Who is the smartest?

Best athlete?
Mother's favorite?
Father's favorite?
Hardest worker?
Best behaved?
Funniest?
Most spoiled?
Best in mathematics?
Best in spelling?
Best in penmanship?
Most stubborn?
Best looking?
Friendliest?
Strongest?
Healthiest?
Best musician?
Best with tools?

The counselor uses these and other questions initially to explore the pictures children have painted of their lives. The information is also helpful in assessing how children are developing their lifestyles. The interview can also help older adolescents and adults understand their lifestyles. Adlerian counselors hold that children and adolescents who have difficulty with mathematics may also have difficulty in solving their personal problems. They believe problem solving in mathematics and problem solving in life have some common elements. So, when students report difficulties with mathematics, Adlerians check to see how well they are solving their personal problems. In a like matter, Adlerians believe poor spelling and penmanship are symptomatic of the client's desire to rebel against authority and to break rules with a low response cost. Poor penmanship and spelling are fairly safe ways to rebel. Adlerians also believe that the sibling most different from you has the greatest impact on your lifestyle development.

Terner and Pew (1978) recommended examining the client's personality structure (the lifestyle). They divided the counseling process into the following four phases:

*Phase I:* The first phase includes an examination of the formative years of the person in his or her family constellation. For younger children, this phase is an ongoing or current event; it is an early recollection of an older adolescent or an adult.

*Phase II:* The second phase is focused on collecting early recollections (ERs) from the client's past, which are detailed in the next section of this chapter.

*Phase III:* The third phase's objective is to illustrate for clients what they are doing in their lives and the principles under which they are operating. Clients are confronted with the goals they are attempting to reach.

*Phase IV:* The fourth phase is reorientation toward living through an encouragement process designed to build clients' self-confidence. The counselor assesses strengths within clients in lieu of the problems that need to be solved and attends to how clients make themselves sick and what they need to recover. The counselor identifies discouragement, the loss of self-confidence, as the root of all deficiencies.

## Early Recollections

Counselors use early recollections (ERs) to understand the child's earliest impressions of life and how the child felt about them. They ask children to remember as far back as they can, particularly recollections of specific incidents, with as many details as possible, including the child's reaction at the time. "If we took a snapshot when that happened, what would we see? How did you feel?" Three to six of those early recollections help to show a pattern in the lifestyle. These recollections tend to reflect a prototype that is apparent in the lifestyle analysis. Although the occurrences children relate may not be factually accurate, they are true insofar as they reflect the children's memories and feelings. The counselor then has a clearer idea of the child's basic view of life and how some attitudes may have mistakenly crystallized. Examples of themes that may appear in these recollections and the child's accompanying mistaken beliefs include the following:

1. *Early Dangers:* Be aware of the many hostile aspects of life.
2. *Happy Times with Adults Around:* Life is great as long as many people praise and serve me.
3. *Misdeeds Recalled:* Be very careful that they do not happen again.
4. *Pleasure vs. Pain:* The easy way is best.
5. *Cheerful vs. Depressed:* It does not pay to be happy.
6. *Pampered vs. Mistreated:* I need someone to take care of me.
7. *Secure vs. Jeopardized:* People cannot be trusted.

8. *Reward vs. Punishment:* Life is good only when I get my way.
9. *Benevolent vs. Hostile:* Doing the right thing does not pay.
10. *Obedient vs. Defiant:* Stay out of trouble.
11. *Participant vs. Observer:* When in doubt, do something or when in doubt, do nothing.
12. *Praise vs. Blame:* It is never my fault.
13. *Confident vs. Inferior:* I will never be good at anything.
14. *We vs. I:* I should be able to do it by myself.
15. *Active vs. Passive:* It is always better to wait and see.
16. *Success vs. Failure:* Nothing ever works out well for me and never will.

Myer and James (1991) presented useful guidelines on ERs as an assessment technique to discern children's behavior patterns. A nonverbal child can produce ERs as drawings and in other types of play media. Counselors can make ERs a memory game or a "make up a story about when you were small" game. Modeling what the child is to do may be helpful. At least three ERs are needed to find a child's pattern of behaviors. The process should not be rushed. The counselor's job is to help the child teach the counselor about his or her situation by summarizing content and feelings. Open-ended statements are good if the counselor is not leading the child into one of the counselor's own ERs. Myer and James recommend paying attention to context (for example, a child alone may indicate isolation), content (for example, recurring topics such as food, water, animals, and wearing boots have special significance for the child), persons (for example, family members left in and out of the story), movement (for example, passivity and compliance may indicate discouragement), and feelings (for example, hot and cold feeling words tell much about the child's outlook on life). The counselor must be careful to avoid overinterpreting or underinterpreting ERs in planning interventions for children.

## Understanding

Counselors must be very understanding with children. No matter what children are doing, they are probably doing the best they can at the moment. Ways of relieving some anxiety and conflict include helping them interpret what is happening and giving the problem, child, or action a "handle." Use encouragement. Change negative situations to positive ones by telling fables where appropriate: "The Miller and the Donkey" helps children understand they can never please everyone, even by absurdly attempting the impossible. "The Frogs in the Milk" tells about two frogs who jumped into a barrel of milk and simply paddled until they made butter; they were then able to jump out easily.

## Confrontation

When children are unable to change the mistaken ideas behind their behavior, confrontation is necessary (Myer & James, 1986). A counselor can confront children with educated guesses about the goals they are trying to achieve at others' expense. Be aware also of the child who sees the counselor as an obstacle and is using depreciation. Typically, the child is unwilling to move in a direction indicated by the counselor and attempts avoidance or wastes time. Counselors are advised to stay out of these power struggles.

### Stages

Actual changes in children's perspectives occur in stages. First, children are limited to afterthoughts of insight: They can clearly see what they are doing to cause mistaken ideas or unhappiness to persist, but only after they have misbehaved. In the second stage, children become able to catch themselves in the act of misbehaving. Added awareness enables them to sensitize themselves to inappropriate behavior. In the next stage, children have developed a heightened sense of awareness that enables them to anticipate the situation and plan a more appropriate behavior or response. These three stages match the preconventional, conventional, and postconventional stages in Piaget's theory of moral development. Stage 3 may not occur to around age 11 if it occurs at all.

## Interventions for the Four Goals of Misbehavior

The four goals of misbehavior are intended to help parents, teachers, and counselors understand that how they feel about what the child is doing most clearly explains the child's mistaken goal (Dreikurs & Soltz, 1964). Analysis and description of the four mistaken goals (attention, power, revenge, and withdrawal), the ways of identifying them, and the methods of correction have resulted in an impressive array of guidance and counseling approaches to help discouraged children and their discouraged families. The steps outlined for determining a child's mistaken goals—learning the adult's corrective response to misbehavior and the child's reaction to the correction—are both penetrating and simple. The counselor who understands the child's goal can, through counseling the child and parents, help the child develop a constructive goal and appropriate behavior.

In describing and analyzing specific immediate goals, Dreikurs and his colleagues have focused primarily on preadolescents. Dreikurs noted that, in early childhood, the children's status depends on the impression they make on adults. Later, they may develop different goals to gain social significance in their peer group and, later still, in adult society. These original goals can still be observed in people of every age. However, they are not all-inclusive; teenagers and adults have additional goals of misbehavior based on irrational self-messages (see Chapter 8). Dreikurs reminded us that people can often achieve status and prestige more easily through useless and destructive means than through accomplishment.

Dreikurs advocated modifying the motivation rather than the behavior itself. When the motivation changes, more constructive behavior follows automatically.

The "four-goal technique" requires the following steps:

1. Observe the child's behavior in detail.
2. Be psychologically sensitive to one's own reaction.

3. Confront the child with the goal of the behavior.
4. Note the recognition reflex.
5. Apply appropriate corrective procedures.

Remember that misbehaving children are discouraged children trying to find their place; they are acting on the faulty logic that their misbehavior will give them the social acceptance that they desire. Goal 1, attention getting, is a manifestation of minor discouragement; Goal 4, display of inadequacy, is a manifestation of deep discouragement. Sometimes a child switches from one kind of misbehavior to another, which is often a signal that the discouragement is growing worse.

To identify young children's goals, the counselor's own immediate response to their behavior is most helpful. It is in line with their expectations. The following four examples of behaviors show how the adult may feel, what the child may be thinking, what alternate behaviors exist, and what questions may come to mind about the child's behavior.

### Attention

You are annoyed; you begin coaxing, reminding.

Charlie thinks he belongs only when he is noticed.

You can (1) attend to the child when he is behaving appropriately or (2) ignore misbehavior (scolding reinforces attention-getting behavior).

You can ask: Could it be that you want me to notice you and the only way you know how to do this is to interrupt me without permission?

### Power

You are angry, provoked, and threatened.

Linda thinks she belongs only when she is in control or is the boss.

You can withdraw or "take your sail out of her wind" by leaving the room.

You can ask: (1) Could it be that you want to be the boss? (2) Could it be that you want me to do what you want and the way you do this is to break our rules?

### Revenge

You are deeply hurt and want to get even.

Sally thinks her only hope is to get even.

You can (1) use group and individual encouragement and (2) try to convince her she is liked by building a positive relationship with her.

You can ask: Could it be that you want to hurt me because I or someone else has hurt you, and the only way to handle hurt feelings is to hurt back?

### Inadequacy

You are feeling helpless and don't know what to do.

Tom thinks he is unable to do anything and that he belongs only when people expect nothing of him.

You can show genuine faith in the child and use encouragement to help Tom begin having success in class every day.

You can ask: Could it be that you don't feel very smart and don't want people to know, and the way to hide this is to never do any work at all?

### *Sequence of the "Could It Be. . . ?" Questions*

A counseling interview that uses the four "Could it be?" questions might go as follows:

*Counselor:* Alice, do you know what you were trying to get when you did (the misbehavior)?

*Alice:* No. (This may be an honest response.)

*Counselor:* Would you like to work with me so that we can find out? I have some ideas that might help us explain what you are trying to get when you do _____. Will you help me figure this out?

*Alice:* Okay.

*Counselor:* (using one question at a time, in a nonjudgmental, unemotional tone of voice):

1. Could it be that you want Mr. Jones to notice you more and give you some special attention?
2. Could it be that you would like to be boss and have things your own way in Mr. Jones's class?
3. Could it be that you have been hurt and you want to get even by hurting Mr. Jones and others in the class?
4. Could it be that you want Mr. Jones to leave you alone and to stop asking you all those hard questions in math?

The counselor always asks all four of these questions sequentially, regardless of the child's answers or reflexes because the child may be operating on more than one goal at a time. The counselor observes the body language and listens carefully for the response in order to catch the "recognition reflex." An accurate disclosure of the child's present intentions produces a recognition reflex such as a "guilty" facial expression, which is a reliable indication of his or her goal, even though the child may say nothing or even "no." Sometimes the confrontation itself helps the child change. Another indication of the child's goal is the child's response to correction. Children who are seeking attention and get it from the teacher stop the misbehavior temporarily and then repeat it or do something similar. Children who seek power refuse to stop the disturbance or even increase it. Those who seek revenge respond to the teacher's efforts to get them to stop by switching to some more violent action. Instead of cooperating, a child with Goal 4 remains entirely passive and inactive.

Once the counselor suspects the goal of the child's misbehavior, confronting the child is most important. The purpose of this confrontation is to disclose and confirm the mistaken goal of the child. The emphasis is on "for what purpose," not "why."

The next step after identifying the goal of misbehavior is to choose and use appropriate corrective procedures, which may range from encouragement to logical consequences.

## Encouragement

Mosak and Maniacci (1998) wrote that Adler and his followers considered encouragement a crucial aspect of living, as well as a crucial part of the counseling process. Encouragement is the key to developing positive expectations in the people we counsel, which help clients to engage in wider varieties of adaptive behaviors with less stress and discomfort. Conversely, according to Mosak and Maniacci (1998), maladaptive, pathological behavior is viewed as a reflection of discouragement, which leads to a lack of confidence. Lacking confidence, clients are likely to cling to their old, unhelpful attitudes and behaviors that give them a false sense of security but get them into trouble. Encouragement becomes an important key in breaking the vicious cycle of discouragement, which causes the client to cling to unhelpful attitudes and behaviors that, in turn, perpetuate more discouragement and a repetition of maladaptive behaviors.

Dreikurs and Soltz (1964) wrote that encouragement implies faith in and respect for children as they are. One should not discourage children by having extremely high standards and ambitions for them. Children misbehave only when they are discouraged and believe they cannot succeed by other means. In fact, one evaluation of counseling is how far the child has moved from feeling discouraged toward feeling encouraged. Children need encouragement as plants need water and sunshine. Telling children they can be better implies they are not good enough as they are.

Problems with these ideas on encouragement arise when parents ask how they are supposed to *not* expect children performing below their ability levels to do better. The answer seems to be in loving children unconditionally in spite of their behavior and performance. However, one does not have to love their misbehavior or pretend to love it.

Encouragement is advocated in place of praise and reinforcement, but bribery is strongly discouraged. Adlerians see praise as a message that tells children that, under conditions determined by the adult, they are okay. Praise focuses on the product. Encouragement, however, accepts children where they are; it focuses on the process. Encouragement occurs *before* the child completes a task or even starts it.

- "I am proud of you."
- "That's a rough one, but I think you have what it takes to work it out."
- "I know you can do it; let me help you get started."

## Praise

Praise (reinforcement) occurs *after* the child performs a behavior or completes a task.

- "You certainly did a good job."
- "That was great work you did in math."

- "I like the way you handled that."
- "You played a good game."

### Bribery

Bribery often occurs *during* the child's misbehavior.

- "If you quiet down, I'll give you a candy bar."
- "I'll buy you a surprise if you stop fighting."
- "If you stop bothering me, you won't have to help with the dishes."

Adlerian counselors believe that extrinsic reward and illogical punishment have detrimental effects on the development of the child, particularly in the democratic atmosphere that prevails today. Only in an autocratic society are these reward-and-punishment systems an effective and necessary means of obtaining conformity; they presuppose a certain person is endowed with superior authority. Children may see rewards as one of their rights and soon demand a reward for everything they do if they are trained under this system. Adlerians agree with Kohn (1999), who writes in *Punished by Rewards* that an extrinsic reward system robs the child or adult of the intrinsic reward of simply engaging in an activity for its own enjoyment. Children rewarded for practicing the piano will begin to view playing the piano as work that nobody would do without pay. Children may interpret punishment as their right to punish others. In fact, children often are hurt more by their retaliation than by the punishment. They are experts in knowing how to hurt their parents, whether by getting into trouble or by making low grades. Therefore, Adlerians reject reward-and-punishment methods that focus on extrinsic reinforcement in favor of encouragement, intrinsic reinforcement, and logical consequences.

## Natural and Logical Consequences

Natural and logical consequences are Adlerian techniques favored over reward and punishment because they allow children to experience the actual consequences of their behavior.

### Natural Consequences

Natural consequences are a direct result of children's behavior. Careless children who touch the hot stove get burned and become more careful of stoves in the future. Natural consequences of irresponsible behavior are unfavorable outcomes that occur naturally without any prearranged plan or program. For example, if Sue leaves her baseball glove outside and it is ruined in a rainstorm, she has experienced a natural consequence. If I am late in making my airline reservation, I may find I cannot take the flight I want. Natural consequences to irresponsible behavior happen on their own, or naturally, without being planned and administered by others.

## Logical Consequences

Logical consequences, established through rules and family policy, are fair, direct, consistent, and logical results of a child's behavior. For example, if Frank comes home late for dinner, his family has assumed that he would have been home on time to eat or would have called if he had been hungry. Therefore, they removed his plate from the table. He is allowed to fix any food he can as long as he cleans up after himself.

As another example of a logical consequence, if Mary breaks someone's window, she is asked to repair the damage or pay to have the damage repaired. If Mary does not have the cash or skill required to repair the damage, she can work off her debt by performing other jobs. In school, if John interferes with someone's right to learn, he is moved to a place where he cannot continue to do so (some form of isolation). In other words, the consequence fits the misbehavior; it is a logical consequence. Punishment, as defined by Adlerians, is any illogical consequence for irresponsible behavior. For example, if Frank is late for dinner, he gets paddled and sent to bed. The punishment or consequence does not match the crime, but it teaches children that bigger people get to overpower smaller people. Children reared under a punishment-by-power system become very impressed with power and use it whenever they can to get what they want.

Both natural and logical consequences allow children to experience the results of their behavior instead of arbitrary punishment exercised through the parent's personal authority. These two techniques direct children's motivation toward proper behavior through personal experience with the social order in which they live. We are not recommending, however, that adults *not* protect children in dangerous situations, for example, teaching children about the dangers of street traffic through personal experience!

Natural and logical consequences focus on the Adlerian belief that people are responsible and capable of leading full, happy lives. Consequences allow the child to understand an inner message that is more likely to be remembered than punishment, which can harm the relationship with a child.

Natural and logical consequences give children the message that they are capable of making their own decisions. They have an opportunity for growth through weighing alternatives and arriving at a decision. Given overly severe limits, however, the child is deprived of making decisions that foster self-respect and responsibility. Children need to do for themselves what they are capable of doing.

◆ ────────────────────────────────────────────

# CASE STUDY

## Identification of the Problem

J. B., a 9-year-old boy in the fourth grade at Spoonbill Elementary School, is referred to our group by the teacher because of his classroom behavior. J. B. repeatedly leaves his seat and does not complete his work.

*Individual and Background Information*

*Academic.*   According to J. B.'s teacher, J. B. does less-than-average work. Most of his grades are Us. He does not usually complete his assignments; when he does, he hurries and commits many errors. His teacher believes that he is not working up to his potential in many areas: His test scores support her view that J. B. is an underachiever, and J. B. loves to read. His teacher reports that J. B.'s behavior sometimes annoys her and at other times makes her angry. She mentioned that she is discouraged about his schoolwork.

*Family.*   J. B. is the youngest son of an older father and stepmother. The sibling closest to his age is 19. He came to live with his father last year after spending time in a home for boys because of his abusive mother. Recently, his stepmother threatened to send him back to the home for boys if he did not behave in school.

*Social.*   J. B. has a friendly personality and seems to relate well with his peers.

*Counseling Method*

The counselor used the Adlerian counseling method to help J. B. identify the goals of his behavior and how well he was meeting his goals. They spent considerable time on helping J. B. understand what he did to get himself in trouble at school and what he could do to make his life more pleasant at school and home. They looked at ways J. B. could meet his goals without getting into trouble.

*Transcript*

> *Counselor:*   Well, J. B., it is good to see you again. We need to check up on how things are going with you in Ms. Johnson's room.
>
> *J. B.:*   Did she tell you I have been bad?
>
> *Counselor:*   She feels discouraged about your schoolwork.
>
> *J. B.:*   Sometimes it is just too hard.
>
> *Counselor:*   So sometimes you feel discouraged, too.
>
> *J. B.:*   Yeah, I sure do.
>
> *Counselor:*   It is sort of like sometimes you don't get the help you need.
>
> *J. B.:*   She won't look at me when I raise my hand to get her to help.
>
> *Counselor:*   That must be frustrating to you. Do you know what I mean by frustrating?
>
> *J. B.:*   Yeah, I get mad and go up by her desk, and she tells me to get back in my seat.
>
> *Counselor:*   So a lot of bad things seem to happen, one right after another one, and you just keep getting angrier.
>
> *J. B.:*   That's right!

*Counselor:*   Well, J. B., we've got some work to do. We need to figure out what you are trying to get and if you are getting what you want.

*J. B.:*   What do you mean?

*Counselor:*   If we can find out what goals you are trying to reach, we will be able to figure out what you need to do to get what you want without getting into trouble.

*J. B.:*   I'm not trying to get anything.

*Counselor:*   Could be; let's check it out.

*J. B.:*   Okay, I guess.

*Counselor:*   J. B., could it be when you do your work poorly or don't do it at all, you want to get Ms. Johnson to leave you alone?

*J. B.:*   What do you mean?

*Counselor:*   Maybe if you convince her you can't do the work, she and your parents will get off your back about making better grades.

*J. B.:*   Sometimes I really do try to do it all.

*Counselor:*   So, you really haven't given up on making better grades.

*J. B.:*   Oh, no, I haven't.

*Counselor:*   Well, could it be you would like to have Ms. Johnson pay more attention to you, and the way to do that is break rules about talking out of turn and leaving your seat?

*J. B.:*   Yeah, sometimes she really loses it and everybody laughs.

*Counselor:*   So, you end up getting a lot of attention, some good and some bad.

*J. B.:*   Yeah, but it's worth it.

*Counselor:*   You seemed pleased with having the attention and don't mind the consequences or bad stuff that happens to you.

*J. B.:*   Well, I do wish I could move back to my old seat. I don't like sitting right in front of the teacher's desk.

*Counselor:*   So attention is important to you, but sitting close to the teacher is not what you want.

*J. B.:*   You got that right! Can you get me moved?

*Counselor:*   You and I can work on it. We might be able to figure out how.

*J. B.:*   Let's go for it!

*Counselor:*   We have to figure out how to convince Ms. Johnson that you can be trusted to follow the class rules and do your work when you are sitting away from her desk.

*J. B.:*   How?

*Counselor:*   Well, J. B., you know her a whole lot better than I do. I would like to know what you think would work.

*J. B.:*   Maybe I can make a deal. She likes deals.

*Counselor:*   How would that work?

*J. B.:*   Well, I could ask her if I stay out of trouble and turn in all of my work for a whole week, could I move to my old seat?

*Counselor:*   I wonder what she will say about how well your work needs to be done.

*J. B.:*   I could tell her that I will make at least a B in everything.

*Counselor:* Well, I guess you could try that. I wonder what she should do if you go back to your old seat and the old behavior comes back.

*J. B.:* I guess I would have to go back to my old seat.

*Counselor:* Could be. Tell you what. If Ms. Johnson agrees to your plan, would you come by the office each day on your way home and give me the word on how your day went?

*J. B.:* Sure.

*Counselor:* If it doesn't work out, come back tomorrow, and we'll try to write a plan that will work.

*J. B.:* See you.

*Counselor:* Let's shake hands on this deal. Hope it works out. See you tomorrow.

As noted in the interview transcript, the Adlerian counseling method works well in concert with many of the other counseling approaches discussed in the text. Encouragement, group discussions, and logical consequences are often used with shaping (positive reinforcement and extinction) and reframing to bring about positive behavior change.

## ADLERIAN PLAY THERAPY

Kottman (1997) explained that a counselor using Adlerian play therapy begins by assuming that the children who have been referred are discouraged children. Discouraged children have negative convictions about themselves and the world. Their self-defeating goals, behaviors, and attitudes reflect those negative convictions. The goal of Adlerian play therapy is the reduction of this discouragement. Therefore, the counselor chooses play techniques to provide encouragement.

This type of play therapy has four phases. The first phase involves establishing a democratic, empathic relationship. The counselor then explores the child's lifestyle, highlighting the child's beliefs, attitudes, goals, emotions, and motives. The counselor's goal in the third phase is to interpret the lifestyle, faulty convictions, and self-defeating goals and behaviors. During the final phase, the counselor's objective is to help the child use the insight and convert it into action such as behavioral and attitudinal changes. Kottman (1997) cautioned the play therapist to recognize small shifts in attitude and behavior.

Kottman and Johnson (1993) discussed strategies to be used during the four phases of Adlerian play therapy. The counselor can use several approaches when establishing a relationship with the child. The counselor may choose to track the behavior of the child by giving a running account of what is being done and said. The counselor may also restate the content and reflect feelings so that the child knows that emotions, behaviors, and attempts to communicate are important to the counselor. The counselor also encourages the child by conveying respect for the child's strengths, faith in the child's abilities, and recognition of the child's attempts and improvement. During the first phase of Adlerian play therapy, the counselor sets limits to protect the child and others, to prevent toys or other things from being damaged, and to deter destructive behavior. In the second phase, the counselor explores the lifestyle of the child, examining the goals of the child's behavior. Considerations of the family atmosphere, family constellation, and the early recollections of the child are also important in this phase. Based on this information, the counselor begins to form a hypothesis about the child's beliefs and shares this understanding with the child. The third phase includes a deepening insight into the child's lifestyle. The counselor shares hypotheses and interpretations with the child and may use therapeutic metaphors. During the fourth phase—reorientation and reeducation—the counselor helps the child develop alternative behaviors that are practiced and encouraged. The counselor also consults with the adults in the child's life.

The Family Art Assessment Technique is a method of gathering information about a family. This three-part drawing activity starts with the family divided into teams that work on separate pieces of paper. The family is then united to work as a team on one sheet of paper. In the case described by DeOrnellas, Kottman, and Millican (1997), the family viewed the process as positive and enjoyable, and the therapists gathered helpful information about the family.

## ADLERIAN FAMILY COUNSELING

Adlerian methods are well suited for counseling the entire family. The following interview guide is suggested:

1. Interview the parents on the following topics (while their children are observed in a playroom situation):
   a. Describe your children—their respective ordinal positions, schoolwork, hobbies, athletics, and so on.
   b. How does each child find his or her place in the family?
   c. What problems revolve around getting up? Mealtime? TV? Homework? Chores? Bedtime?
   d. Does something in your family need to be better?
   e. Would you like to make a change? (Before the counselor gives suggestions, it is preferable that the parents admit they are bankrupt in child-rearing ideas; that is, nothing has worked in improving the particular family concern.)
2. Interview the children on the following topics with the parents not present. (Use "Could it be?" questions when appropriate. Ask who is in charge of discipline.)
   a. Do you know why you are here today?
   b. Does anything bother you in the family that you would like to change?
   c. How can we make things better at home?
   d. Who is the good child?
   e. Who is Father's favorite?
   f. Who is Mother's favorite?
   g. Who is best in sports?
   h. What do each of you do best?

    i. Which are your best school subjects?

    j. Which are your worst school subjects?

3. Interview the entire family. Summarize plans for the coming week, clarifying roles, behaviors, and expectations. Recommendations for each family generally include the following:

    a. Provide individual parent time for each child, each day.

    b. Have one family conference per week. Use collaboration and/or compromise to reach family consensus in making decisions. *No voting.* Three-to-two votes split the family, with the losing voters dragging their heels and not being enthusiastic supporters of the issue supported by the "winning" side.

    c. Do one family activity per week.

    d. Each family member does chores.

Dinkmeyer (1988) based "marathon family counseling" on Adlerian psychology. The process, completed in one 8-hour day, focuses on family constellation, mutual respect, encouragement, and taking responsibility for one's behavior. Dinkmeyer described the following four stages:

Stage I: Orientation and organization

    a. Determine if this type of counseling is suitable for the family.

    b. Obtain family background information.

    c. Arrange for family members to participate.

Stage II: Exploration

    a. Give overview and summary of Stage I.

    b. Obtain an overview of the family's life circumstances.

    c. Explore problems in more depth.

Stage III: Action

    a. Encourage family members to commit to doing something to improve the family situation.

    b. Confront family members who are reluctant to change.

    c. Encourage family members to take responsibility for their own behavior.

Stage IV: Termination

    a. Have family members talk about their commitments to change and how they will accomplish their goals.

    b. Thank family members for participating in the session.

    c. Talk individually with family members who want more counseling.

Pew (1989) outlined a different approach for conducting brief marriage therapy, Adlerian style, that may extend over several sessions.

1. The counselor and couple discuss why the couple is seeking counseling.

2. The counselor and couple discuss the couple's goals for counseling.

3. The counselor shares expectations.

4. The counselor draws a family constellation for each person and uses this and ERs to construct a lifestyle form for each client.

5. The couple works on the basic marriage skills of conflict resolution, communication, and doing fun things together.

6. The couple uses the paradoxical strategies of practicing at home those things that annoy each partner.
7. The couple keeps daily journal entries of feelings, thoughts, and behaviors.

## CROSS-CULTURAL APPLICATIONS OF INDIVIDUAL PSYCHOLOGY

Individual psychology by title alone would seem to suggest a focus on the individual above the family, group, or society in general. Such is far from the truth, however. Social-interest development has always been a main pillar supporting the practice of individual or Adlerian psychology. Therefore, as mentioned in Chapter 15, cultural groups favoring a family, group, and/or community emphasis in counseling will find individual psychology to be a comfortable and compatible way to examine their lives and behavior patterns for possible change.

Hispanic, Native American, Italian, and Middle Eastern cultures are among those favoring the family and community social-interest approach offered by the Adlerians. In fact, social-interest development is equated with one's mental health and level of personal development in the Adlerian system. The practice of Adlerian counseling does not require clients and families to share information that would infringe on the families' self-disclosure comfort level and breach the boundaries accorded to the level of respect shown to the family elders. Adlerian concepts have traditionally been more on the culture-free side than not. Birth order, goals of behavior, early recollections, lifestyles, and faulty reasoning problems transcend most cultures, and the client is never asked to fit a certain model described by the counselor (Carlson & Carlson, 2000).

Asian, African, African American, and American clients will enjoy the pragmatic aspects of Adlerian psychology. The opportunity to learn new skills and practical information is readily available in the educational approach Adlerians use. Learning is conducted in several modes, dividing the counseling time between listening, information gathering, telling, demonstrating, and practicing. As such, most clients find one of the instructional modes compatible with their particular learning style. Again, we emphasize the differences within cultures and realize that any one counseling style will not be universally accepted by an entire cultural group. We do know that people in some cultures accept the idea of receiving counseling much more readily than others. For example, a colleague once shared the following observation from his practice in a culturally diverse neighborhood. He said when he gets a call from a Jewish mother about coming in for counseling, he treats it more as a matter of fact. However, if he gets a call from an Irish mother, he becomes quite alarmed, treats the call as an emergency, and has her come to the office right away.

Among African American and Latino families, it is typical to find that parenting is often shared among a variety of individuals, including grandparents, aunts, uncles, neighbors, friends, and siblings. Flanagan and Miranda (1995) reported that this is especially true in times of family stress and that African Americans, Latinos, and Native Americans may select spiritual types of interventions over the services of a professional counselor. In addition to members of these three cultures, members of Appalachian cultures have more hesitancy in divulging familial or personal issues to professionals. Mosely-Howard (1995) reported that Appalachians are more likely to seek help from extended family or clergy. However, other Americans with European backgrounds are more likely to seek help from professional counselors.

Flanagan and Miranda (1995) reported that Asian fathers are publicly perceived as the figurehead and ruler of the family, while privately it is often the mother who decides the important child-rearing issues. Mosely-Howard (1995) noted that Filipinos and Japanese are much more protective of their children than are American families. Conversely, physical punishment is more acceptable among Appalachians, African Americans, and Samoans. Cultural awareness should help counselors work with the law requiring them to report anything resembling child abuse.

Compounding cultural differences is the changing nature of the family structure that was present when Rudolf Dreikurs was restructuring Adlerian theory to include his intervention strategies for families. Today there are more blended families and more families headed by single parents of either sex. The change in family structure presents unique difficulties for Adlerian counselors. Carlson (1995) found that in mother-headed, single-parent homes, problems causing unrest in the family were related to the mother's perceived or real inability to maintain the dual roles of parent–household manager and sole wage earner. These overburdened mothers were found to be more likely to suffer from depression, diminished parenting, and lack of social support from others. Male single parents are more likely to lack knowledge of child development and gender differences in development and to lack the ability to nurture as well as discipline children. The fathers, also lacking in social support, were found to minimize their thoughts and feelings about their parenting problems, and they were less likely to seek outside professional help. Again, counselors would do well to reestablish the Adlerian groups that were once more prominent. The added stresses of single parenting were found by Carlson (1995) to result in overpermissiveness or, in low-income, single, father-headed homes, high rates of violence. In addition, higher school dropout rates have been reported for daughters of single fathers and sons of single mothers. Clearly, stress reduction should be one focus of today's family counselors. We recommend involving churches and schools in providing meeting space and child care for parent-education groups led by trained counselors. The Adlerian parent-education model has proven to be one of the most useful ways to help ineffective parents become better parents.

## INDIVIDUAL PSYCHOLOGY AND MANAGED HEALTH CARE

Practitioners of individual psychology should find managed care guidelines easier to meet than practitioners of the longer, insight-oriented psychotherapies (see the managed care section in Chapter 2). Granted, some insight is used in the practice of individual psychology, but such methods are directed toward helping children and their parents understand the goals the children are trying to reach with their misbehavior. Individual psychology has always been one of the briefer approaches to helping people find interventions to bring about symptom relief and solutions to problems.

Adlerian counselors have a 100-year history of supporting a preventive approach to treating mental health problems. Adler himself created parent-education groups that met regularly to discuss managing family problems regarding child-rearing practices and interventions. Problem prevention, group counseling, and educational skill building, which Adlerian or individual psychology practitioners use in their work, are favored by managed care companies.

Adlerians typically can accomplish their goals in a relatively short time and have considerable follow-up success if families join a local parent group to reinforce what they have learned about child-rearing. Professional and school counselors may want to work together in reestablishing these Adlerian parent groups. Counseling goals are behaviorally stated and can be tracked on a weekly basis to termination of counseling. Client satisfaction typically runs high with recipients of Adlerian counseling because parents are largely bankrupt on what they should do about disciplining their children. They generally practice the ineffective interventions passed down through the generations to their own parents.

Adlerian, or individual, psychology has a lot to offer individuals who have presenting problems other than family issues. Lifestyle analysis is especially effective in helping people analyze their lives in light of how well their current behaviors are helping them get what they want. The Adlerians use a cognitive approach to help their clients identify the faulty logic underlying behavior goals that get them into trouble. Clients also receive some insight on how they got to be the way they are and what they need to do to break the cycle of their ineffective or self-defeating behavior patterns. Couples seeking counseling will find individual psychology useful in problem diagnosis and remediation. Individual psychology is also recommended for couples seeking a developmental approach to marriage enrichment.

## W E B S I T E S  for Individual Psychology

Alfred Adler
www.oldsci.eiu.edu/psychology/Spencer/Adler.html

Classical Adlerian Psychology: Alfred Adler Institutes
ourworld.compuserve.com/homepages/hstein/homepage.htm

## REFERENCES

Adler, A. (1964). *Social interest: A challenge to mankind*. New York: Capricorn. (Original work published 1938)

Alexander, F., Eisenstein, S., & Grotjahn, M. (1966). *Psychoanalytic pioneers*. New York: Basic Books.

Ansbacher, H. (1992). Alfred Adler's concepts of community feeling and social interest and the relevance of community feeling for old age. *Individual Psychology: The Journal of Adlerian Theory, Research, and Practice, 48*, 402–412.

Ansbacher, H., & Ansbacher, R. (1956). *The individual psychology of Alfred Adler: A systematic presentation in selections from his writings.* New York: Basic Books.

Ballou, R. (2002). Adlerian-based responses for the mental health counselor to the challenging behaviors of teens. *Journal of Mental Health Counseling, 24,* 154–165.

Carlson, C. (1995). Best practices in working with single-parent and step family systems. In A. Thomas & J. Grimes (Eds.), *Best practices in school psychology.* Washington: National Association of School Psychologists.

Carlson, M., & Carlson, J. (2000). The application of Adlerian psychotherapy with Asian American clients. *Journal of Individual Psychology, 56,* 214–225.

DeOrnellas, K., Kottman, T., & Millican, V. (1997). Drawing a family: Family art assessment in Adlerian therapy. *Individual Psychology: Journal of Adlerian Theory, Research, and Practice, 53,* 451–460.

Dewey, E. (1971). Family atmosphere. In A. Nikelly (Ed.), *Techniques for behavior change: Applications for Adlerian theory* (pp. 41–47). Springfield, IL: Charles C. Thomas.

Dinkmeyer, D. (1988). Marathon family counseling. *Individual Psychology: The Journal of Adlerian Theory, Research, and Practice, 44,* 210–215.

Dinkmeyer, D., Pew, W., & Dinkmeyer, D. Jr. (1979). *Adlerian counseling and psychotherapy.* Monterey, CA: Brooks/Cole.

Dreikurs, R., & Soltz, V. (1964). *Children: The challenge.* New York: Hawthorn/Dutton.

Ellis, A. (1997). Must musterbation and demandingness lead to emotional disorders? *Psychotherapy, 34,* 95–98.

Flanagan, D., & Miranda, A. (1995). Best practices in working with culturally different families. In A. Thomas & J. Grimes (Eds.), *Best practices in school psychology* (pp. 325–326). Washington: National Association of School Psychologists.

Horney, K. (1950). *Neurosis and human growth.* New York: Norton.

Kohn, A. (1999). *Punished by rewards: The trouble with gold stars, incentive plans, A's, praise, and other bribes.* Boston: Houghton Mifflin.

Kottman, T. (1997). Adlerian play therapy. In K. O'Connor & L. M. Braverman (Eds.), *Play therapy theory and practice: A comparative presentation* (pp. 310–340). New York: Wiley.

Kottman, T., & Johnson, V. (1993). Adlerian play therapy: A tool for school counselors. *Elementary School Guidance and Counseling, 28,* 42–51.

Manly, L. (1986). Goals of misbehavior inventory. *Elementary School Guidance and Counseling, 21,* 160–161.

Mosak, H. (1991). Where have all the normal people gone? *Individual Psychology, 47,* 437–446.

Mosak, H. (1992, July 21). Personal communication.

Mosak, H., & Maniacci, M. (1998). *Tactics in counseling and psychotherapy.* Itasca, IL: F. E. Peacock.

Mosely-Howard, G. (1995). Best practices in considering the role of culture. In A. Thomas & J. Grimes (Eds.), *Best practices in school psychology* (p. 326). Washington: National Association of School Psychologists.

Myer, R., & James, R. (1986, February). *Confrontation: A strategy for counseling.* Paper presented at the Tennessee Association for Counseling and Development state conference, Gatlinburg, TN.

Myer, R., & James, R. (1991). Using early recollections as an assessment technique with children. *Elementary School Guidance and Counseling, 25,* 228–232.

Pew, M. (1989). Brief marriage therapy. *Individual Psychology: The Journal of Adlerian Theory, Research, and Practice, 45,* 191–200.

Shulman, B., & Mosak, M. (1977). Birth order and ordinal position: Two Adlerian views. *Individual Psychology, 33,* 114–121.

Stiles, K., & Wilborn, B. (1992). A lifestyle instrument for children. *Individual Psychology, 48,* 96–105.

Terner, J., & Pew, W. (1978). *The courage to be imperfect: The life and work of Rudolf Dreikurs.* New York: Hawthorn.

# Chapter 12

# Family Counseling

*Inappropriate helpfulness fosters helplessness.*
—Murray Bowen

*Life is interrelated. We are caught in an inescapable network*
*of mutuality; tied in the single garment of destiny. Whatever*
*affects one directly, affects all indirectly.*
—Martin Luther King Jr.

*It's surprising how many persons go through life without ever*
*recognizing that their feelings toward people are largely determined*
*by their feelings toward themselves, and if you're not comfortable*
*within yourself, you can't be comfortable with others.*
—Sydney J. Harris

## HOW DOES FAMILY COUNSELING DIFFER FROM INDIVIDUAL COUNSELING?

The principal difference between family and individual counseling is that the focus in family counseling is on the family and its members' interactions and relations. Often, individual counseling tends to separate individuals and their problems from the family setting. Family counseling or family therapy, by contrast, almost always involves interventions to alter the way an entire family system operates. The family counseling and therapy label covers a wide variety of arrangements: It may be individual, husband and wife, parent and child, or the entire family, including all who live in the home.

Another key difference between individual and family counseling is problem diagnosis. Family therapists use a circular causality diagnosis, whereas individual therapists tend to rely on linear causality. For example, a linear causality diagnosis might be as follows: Alice fails to turn in homework to her teacher and therefore suffers a lower grade. A circular causality diagnosis might include how the teacher's reaction to Alice then influences how Alice reacts to her teacher, as well as to her parents. Mom nags Alice about not doing her homework; Alice, in turn, gets the attention, albeit negative, that she wants. The teacher sends home a failing note to Alice's parents, who, in turn, both start to nag Alice, who resists homework even more than before. In other words, a circular causality diagnosis involves the roles each family member plays. In fairness to all the theorists discussed in the previous chapters, however, they all believed their own approaches to be effective for working with families.

## WHAT DEFINES A FAMILY?

Definitions of *family* range from the nuclear family of breadwinner father, homemaker mother, and two children to multiple families living together. Between these extremes are at least eight types of families: extended, blended, common-law, single-parent, communal, serial, polygamous, and cohabitational. Families are also defined by their organizational structure, characterized by degrees of cohesiveness, love, loyalty, and purpose. High levels of shared values, interests, activities, and attention to the needs of its members serve to distinguish the functional family group from other organizational groups and teams.

Perhaps the most all inclusive, politically correct definition of *family* can be found in *Webster's Third New International Dictionary* where *family* is defined as a group of people: (1) bound together by philosophical, religious, or other convictions, (2) with a common ancestry, and (3) living together under the same roof. Another definition listed there defines *family* as "the basic biosocial unit in society having as its nucleus two or more adults living together and cooperating in the care and rearing of their own or adopted children." Possibly the only person left out of these definitions is the hermit who reportedly lives somewhere near Buck Snort, Tennessee. Then again, when the last town he lived near burned down and everybody left, he had to find a new town to live near.

### How Does General Systems Theory Relate to Families?

Systems are organized wholes or units made up of several interdependent and interacting parts. The whole unit is greater than the sum of its parts, and change in any part affects all other parts. Any family member's graduation from high school or hospital admission has effects on all other family members. Family therapists choose to view the family as a system in which each member has a significant influence on all other members. For significant positive change in an identified client, therefore, family members have to change the way they interact. Most family therapists work with present family relationships rather than with past family relationships and conflicts.

A key point of interest to all family therapists is the balance families maintain between the several sets of bipolar extremes that characterize dysfunctional families. For example, families may struggle to find a healthy balance between overinvolvement in each others' lives (*enmeshment*) and too much detachment from each other (*disengagement*). A family could be viewed as a canoe full of people heading into the current of a river. Some canoes are balanced and stable, but maintaining this balance requires each family member to assume a very uncomfortable position, and a shift by one person necessitates a shift by everyone else for the canoe to remain upright. Other families are paddling balanced canoes while sitting comfortably, allowing them to adapt to the changes all families face as they go through the stages of family development; still other canoes capsize, with family members hanging on the side just trying to survive. Family therapists see their job as righting capsized canoes and making family members comfortable in their canoe-paddling roles. Staying with the canoe metaphor, family therapists see an obvious advantage in working with the whole crew as a group rather than focusing on the identified problem member of the family.

## THE SYSTEMS APPROACH TO FAMILY THERAPY

### Murray Bowen

Family therapy roots reach back to the turn of the century, beginning with Alfred Adler's parent groups and developing through various parent-, family-, and couple-education groups within each decade until the 1950s, when family therapy as we know it today was born. Murray Bowen (1913–1990), an early theorist on family relationships, focused on how family members could maintain a healthy balance between being enmeshed and being disengaged. He believed each family member should develop an individual identity and independence separate from family identity, while also maintaining a sense of closeness and a feeling of togetherness with their families. The task for Bowen was to help people integrate the opposing forces of seeking independence from the family and maintaining a sense of family membership and closeness (Bowen, 1976, 1978).

Murray Bowen (Nichols & Scwartz, 1998) was born and grew up in Waverly, Tennessee, in 1913. He was the firstborn of five children in a cohesive and loving family. Waverly, a small town of 1,000 people in 1913, is located in middle Tennessee in Humphreys County 60 miles west of Nashville. Bowen completed his bachelor's degree at the University of Tennessee in 1934 and his MD degree from the University of Tennessee Medical School in Memphis in 1937. He served 5 years of active duty in the army during World War II from 1941 to 1946. Bowen's war experiences influenced his decision to turn down a fellowship in surgery at the Mayo Clinic to enter psychiatric training at the Menninger Foundation in Topeka, Kansas, in 1946. He spent the next 8 years researching symbiotic relationships of mothers and their schizophrenic children at Menninger, where he developed the concepts of anxious and functional attachment involved in the mother–child relationship. From 1954 to 1959, Bowen served as the first director of the Family Division at the National Institute of Mental Health, where he broadened his research on family attachment to include fathers. In 1959, Bowen joined the Department of Psychiatry at Georgetown University Medical Center, where he directed family programs. He founded and directed the Georgetown Family Center in 1975, where he remained until his death in 1990. Among his many honors, he received the Distinguished Alumnus Award from the University of Tennessee in 1986.

Bowen used process questions designed to help family members shift from reacting emotionally about the negative aspects of other family members to thinking rationally about how they personally contribute to the family's dysfunction and what they can do to improve the situation. Bowen assumed the role of coach or educator, whose job was to create an environment in which the family can function at its best. To accomplish this, counselors need to be aware of the emotional processes working in the family while personally remaining neutral (Dattilio & Bevilacqua, 2000). He focused on (1) relationship between the spouses, (2) differentiation of self, (3) triangles, (4) nuclear family emotional process, (5) family projection process, (6) multigenerational transmission process, (7) sibling position, (8) emotional cutoffs, and (9) emotional process in society.

## The Spousal Relationship

Bowen and his followers gave attention to defining and clarifying the relationship between couples: How well do they move in and out of the various roles healthy couples play? Do they care for and nurture each other? Do they solve problems and make decisions well? Do they play well together? Do they work well together? Do they parent well together? Are they able to differentiate themselves as individuals apart from the couple? Do they enjoy time alone? Do they maintain individual relationships and friendships outside the marital dyad? Do they pursue individual goals, interests, and careers? Most important, how well do individuals handle differentiation within themselves and between other family members?

## Differentiation of Self

Differentiation within oneself refers to the ability to separate feelings from thoughts. For example, in crises does the person put rational thinking on hold and react emotionally to the situation? Lack of differentiation between persons refers to the degree to which people introject the thoughts and feelings of others or do the opposite by automatically reacting against these thoughts and feelings. Differentiation is our struggle to develop a sense of personal identity while still remaining a part of the family. This process is similar to being able to distinguish between thoughts and feelings. Bowen rated his patients' ability to differentiate on a scale of 0 to 100, with 0 being low. Those on the bottom end of the scale were regarded as undifferentiated, and their behavior, guided by their feelings, often left them with chronic anxiety resulting in relationship problems. Because they were undifferentiated from the family, their anxiety spilled over onto other family members. Highly differentiated people handle stress and anxiety better, because they are able to apply rational thought to the problem at hand. They are able to maintain a healthy balance between thinking and feeling. Bowen believed that marriage partners seek spouses with the same level of differentiation. Hence, the trait is passed down through several generations. Bowen believed that schizophrenic children resulted from generations of undifferentiated individuals marrying each other. Thus a primary goal for Bowen was to help people attain higher levels of differentiation from enmeshment in one's family. Differentiation enables people to enjoy meaningful relationships with family members while remaining autonomous and rational without falling back into unhealthy enmeshment with family patterns. Increased differentiation by one family member is likely to lead other family members to become more differentiated.

Self-differentiation was Bowen's principal goal of family therapy. He believed that progress toward self-differentiation had to be self-motivated rather than directed by the therapist. Serving in the role of educator, the therapist's job was to move clients toward an intellectual processing of the couple's family system rather than falling into the trap of responding to the emotional tone of the content brought to counseling. Also, Bowen observed that in providing too much "help," therapists could make the family situation worse. Bowen (1976) stated that *inappropriate helpfulness fosters helplessness.*

## Detriangulation of Self from the Family Emotional System

Triangulation, another important concept in Bowen's theory, refers to the practice of two family members bringing a third family member into conflictual situations. Therapists attend to the extent a husband or wife involves one of their children in a problem situation that the two of them should handle. Another example of triangulation is involvement of a person outside the marital dyad, such as a lover, to fill unmet needs in the marriage. A form of triangulation was discussed in Chapter 10 in reference to games and the roles people play in them; for example, one family member may take the role of prosecutor, another the victim, and the third a rescuer. All three roles are needed to maintain the game, and a shift in role by any one of the three alters the roles of the other two. Many of these dysfunctional interactions are similar to dances, where it takes two people to keep the dance going and one to stop it. Bowen believed there was no such thing as a two-person system because a third party is always drawn in when there is increased anxiety. As mentioned previously, third parties can be from inside or outside the family and even can be the memory of a departed loved one. The shifting set of alliances and reactive behaviors that occur with third parties makes it more difficult to resolve the conflict between the original two parties.

## Nuclear Family Emotional Process

The nuclear family emotional process refers to how the family system operates to handle anxiety and stress in times of crisis. Several symptoms are indicators of how the system works. Emotional distance, when one family member avoids or gives the silent treatment to another, is an early symptom of family trouble. A second symptom could be transfer of a family problem to a child when a mother displaces her anxiety on the child by becoming worried and overly concerned about how the child is doing. A third symptom occurs when two family members become blamers, pointing their fingers at each other as the cause of the problem. Finally, a fourth symptom surfaces when one partner develops a disability or becomes dysfunctional. The second partner is forced to adapt to the dysfunctional partner by taking more control, making decisions, and handling responsibilities for the "dysfunctional" partner. Over time, the increased workload may be resented by the partner in charge as the dysfunctional partner becomes even more dependent and develops more symptoms. Such situations are generally headed toward major blowups.

## Family Projection Process

The family projection process refers to how parents pass good and bad things on to their children. In one example mentioned previously, undifferentiated parents distract themselves from solving their conflicts by focusing intently on a child and the child's situation to the point that the child becomes more undifferentiated and dependent, thus blocking normal development toward becoming an autonomous person.

## Multigenerational Transmission Process

Multigenerational transmission process refers to how a family passes its good and bad baggage from one generation to another. The bad baggage is the tendency of families to become less differentiated as this trait is handed down. Families become more vulnerable to stress, anxiety, and problems as they become less differentiated, and this became the point where Bowen directed his method of family therapy for changing the way family members respond to each other in times of crisis.

## Sibling Position

Bowen took the Adlerian position that birth order is a significant factor in how we develop our lifestyles. We refer you to Chapter 9 for a detailed discussion of birth order traits. Bowen held that birth order traits and behaviors carried to an extreme could lead to dysfunction in children. For example, a controlling firstborn may lead to a younger sibling's overly dependent behavior. As the younger child gets more service from the older child, dependence on the older child is increased, and developmental progress toward independence is blocked. Bowen was also concerned that trouble might arise when people of the same birth order married and each tried to maintain such respective birth order behaviors as leaders or followers.

## Emotional Cutoff

As mentioned before, when a marriage partner's method for handling anxiety and stress is to distance oneself from others, problems do not get solved. Emotional cutoffs (sometimes referred to as pouting) are thought to be ways of dealing with unresolved attachment to parents. Whatever the cause, emotional distancing can achieve the ultimate distancing goal of divorce.

## Emotional Process in Society

Bowen saw parallels in how family members react within the family and within society. Undifferentiated people typically react emotionally rather than rationally in times of conflict, stress, crisis, and general anxiety. They do this within the family and carry forth their emotionality when they react in society. Unfortunately, the evidence in present society is that emotionality seems to trump rationality as the people's choice in solving the problems of the day.

In teaching clients about family systems and the intergenerational transmission process, Bowen used genograms and questions to move his clients to the intellectual level in discussing how their own family system had been influenced by material and baggage inherited from prior generations of the family. The genogram provides a generational map of the family including dates of marriages, births, and deaths; cultural and ethnic origins; socioeconomic status; work life; education; hobbies; religious affiliations; politics; and family relationships. In short, the genogram describes *who* makes up your family, *how* they got to be family (birth, marriage, adoption), *when* they arrived (birth date, birth order, marriage dates), *what* they did (work, hobbies), *what* they valued (religion, politics), and *when* they left the family (death, divorce, or separation). (See Figures 12-1 and 12-2.)

Bowen (1980) included data from at least three generations in his genograms. He began by gathering as much information as he could (during the first interview) from the couple he was counseling. All family names and ages from at least three generations are listed on the genogram with the dates of marriages, births, deaths, and other significant life events. Notes explaining the significant events are added to the genogram. Completing the missing data can become a homework assignment for the couple to complete before the second session.

Thomas (1992) suggested the following questions that might be used in a genogram interview:

1. Can you tell me the names of the family members for at least three generations on both sides of the family?

2. When were these individuals born, married, separated, or divorced?

3. Which family members have died? When? Of what?

4. What jobs did the family members hold?

5. What were the family members' educational levels?

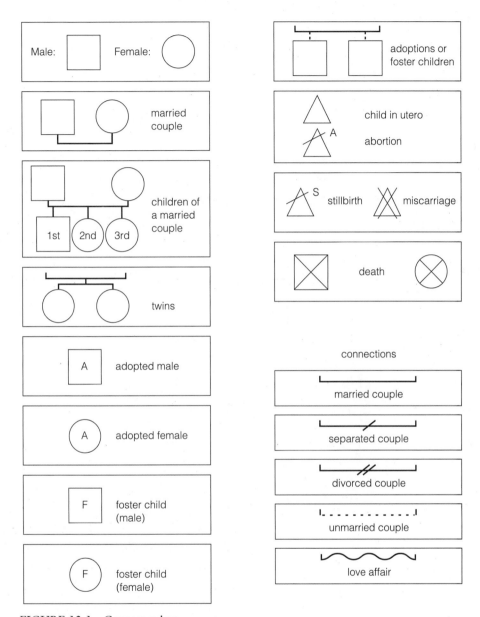

FIGURE 12-1   Genogram key

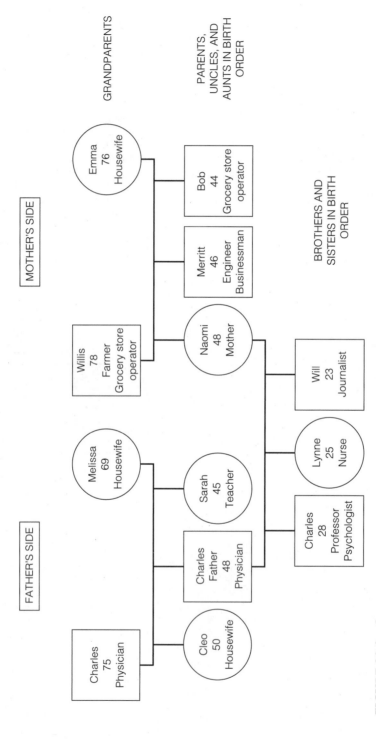

FIGURE 12-2   Genogram

6. What were the ethnic/cultural, religious, and political values of the family members? How were these traditions passed on in the family?

7. Where did the family members live (city and state)? When, where, and why did they move?

8. How did people get along in the family? Who was close to whom? Did anyone not speak to another family member? What happened in these cases?

9. Which family members were very successful at what they did?

10. Which family members used alcohol or drugs, were arrested, had mental problems, committed suicide, or had other serious problems?

11. What illnesses are found in the family? How did family members cope with them?

12. Can you tell me any special life events that happened—positive, neutral, and negative?

13. Tell me about the stories that have been passed down through the generations of your family.

14. Tell me about the family themes that seem to repeat in your family. If your family had a motto, what would it be?

15. If you were an elder in the family, what advice would you give to a younger member of the family?

Thomas (1992) offered the following 10 questions to aid the family counselor in writing a genogram analysis:

1. *Health:* How healthy were the family members? What were the most common health problems? What was done to prevent or treat these health problems?

2. *Structure:* What types of family structure were repeated in the genogram (single parent, nuclear, extended, blended)?

3. *Themes:* What family themes have been carried through the generations?

4. *Occupations:* Which occupations occur most frequently in your family?

5. *Stages:* What stages in the life cycle have been easier for your family to handle? Most difficult?

6. *Events:* Which life events have affected family functions throughout generations of your family?

7. *Triangles:* Where are the triangles present in the genogram? Which relationships are close, distant, conflicted, or fused? Where are the emotional cutoffs?

8. *Patterns:* What patterns are repeated, such as educational or work success, religious commitment, political activity, alcohol or drug use, or other behaviors?

9. *Size:* How large are the families in the genogram? Which families stand out as larger or smaller than the genogram norm? What stresses might have occurred due to the family size or family imbalance?

10. *Contract:* What values and behaviors passed on to you by your family have worked so well for you that you plan to keep them and even pass them on to your children? What family values and behaviors have not worked well for you, and what do you plan to do with them? Are there some family patterns that bother you, and, if so, what could you do to change them?

## Emotional Systems of the Family

Understanding family emotional systems and how they work is also central to Bowen's theory. Once again, failure to achieve differentiation between family members results in unhealthy family relationships that recycle from one generation to the next unless some helpful intervention interrupts. Bowen might well have envisioned himself as a cycle breaker, which is not a bad role for a counselor to take. In fact, Bowen often assumed the role of educator in teaching people about family emotional systems. Once again, when the family of origin lacks differentiation, children have either totally absorbed their parents' feelings and emotions or have totally detached themselves. These children often seek out mates who are also undifferentiated, thus providing fertile ground for future family conflict and discord. Undifferentiated people typically do not develop close, lasting relationships. They do not solve problems or resolve conflicts, and they often develop psychosomatic symptoms in an attempt to meet their needs. In addition, undifferentiated people tend not to take responsibility for their behavior. Many of these consequences are in concert with what Glasser has written about people who have not developed or have not had healthy and caring relationships in their lives (see Chapter 4).

## Modeling Differentiation

Bowen favored modeling for teaching differentiation to his patients. He did this by using "I" statements and taking ownership of his own thoughts, feelings, and behaviors; for example, he'd say, "I think the best thing for me to do is to confront my colleague about his behavior, but thinking about doing it gives me an uneasy feeling." In addition to owning one's thoughts and feelings, this statement lends some help for separating feelings and thoughts.

## STRUCTURAL FAMILY THERAPY

Structural family therapy is closely related to Bowen's family systems theory. Structural family therapists also operate on the assumption that the individual client should be treated within the context of the family system. The therapist does not see the client as a sufficient source of information about the problems brought to counseling or the only source of causes of the problem. Changes resulting from individual counseling are not stable enough to stand against the pressures a dysfunctional family brings to bear. Therefore, the overall goal of structural family therapists is to alter the family structure to empower the dysfunctional family to move toward functional ways of conducting or transacting family business and family communications.

Structural family therapy is also based on the assumption that families are evolving, hierarchical organizations with rules and behavior patterns for interacting across and within the family subsystems. Families get into trouble when their members become either overly enmeshed in each other's business or totally disengaged. Family members should feel a sense of belonging to the family that does not destroy their sense of being unique individuals within and outside the family context. In other words, functional families are characterized by each member's success in finding the healthy balance between belonging to a family and maintaining a separate identity.

One way to find the balance between family and individual identity is to define and clarify the boundaries between the subsystems; for example, a family may have a spousal subsystem, a sibling subsystem, and a parent–child subsystem. Each subsystem contains its own subject matter that is private and should remain within that subsystem. Spouses have matters they need to discuss that do not belong in the context of the parent–child and child–child subsystems. Such topics might include their sex life, financial concerns, and interpersonal conflicts. Dysfunctional families often discuss and play out these topics in an open family forum. Boundaries between subsystems range from rigid to diffuse. Private subject matter from one subsystem that leaks out to other subsystems indicates diffuse, poorly established boundaries. Diffuse boundaries can lead to family members becoming overly enmeshed in the private business of other family members; rigid boundaries allow too little interaction between family members, resulting in disengagement from the family. Once again, the secret to developing functional families is finding the right boundary balance between too rigid and too diffuse; boundaries need to be clearly defined. For example, parents need to provide, on the one hand, enough love and support and, on the other hand, enough room for children to develop independence. A parent–child subsystem and a sibling subsystem also have communications and subject matter that belongs to and is unique to those subsystems. Families who understand and respect differences between healthy and unhealthy subsystem boundaries and rules function successfully; families who do not understand and respect these differences find themselves in a dysfunctional state of conflict, either disengaged from or enmeshed in the family business. Structural family therapy is directed toward changing the family organizational structure as a way of resolving the presenting problem or changing a family member's behavior patterns. For example, in a particular session, Dad might be asked to give up being in charge of the children's homework assignments. The structural therapist actively directs the session and participates as a family member. The therapist may even take over the family ruler role as a way of sidetracking the dominant family member.

## Salvador Minuchin's Contributions to Structural Family Therapy

Salvador Minuchin is considered the founder of structural family therapy as it is practiced today. He was born in 1921 to Russian Jewish parents in a small Argentinian town. According to Simon (1984), Minuchin benefited from a multicultural childhood and became an activist early in life. As a university student, he joined a Zionist organization and was arrested for taking part in a protest against Juan Perón in 1943. After spending 3 months in jail, Minuchin was expelled from the university and studied in Uruguay for a time. Later he completed his medical degree in Argentina. Next came a residency in child psychiatry and an 18-month tour of duty as a doctor in the Israeli 1948 war. Minuchin came to the United States with the intention of working with Bruno Bettelheim in Chicago's Orthogenic School; however, he met Nathan Ackerman in New York and eventually decided to work in Ackerman's child-development center. Minuchin sandwiched in 3 years of work with African and Asian immigrant children in Israel before receiving more analytic training and becoming director of family research at the Wiltwyck School for Boys in New York.

Minuchin's best training did not come from books and classes. As so many therapists have noticed, traditional psychoanalytic methods do not often work with populations such as delinquent boys. The recidivism rate seemed to be close to 100%, with the young men repeating their delinquent behaviors upon their release. Noticing that some families produced several delinquent children, Minuchin concluded that families must be making a significant contribution to the problem. Therefore, he began to develop an approach for working with families who did not have the verbal skills for traditional psychotherapy, instead focusing on the nonverbal communication, a standard practice in individual, group, and family therapy.

Much of what Minuchin learned about families was by observation through a one-way glass and in collaboration with his colleagues at the school. In a method similar to the Adlerian method for working with families, Minuchin and his colleagues developed a three-step approach: Two counselors met with the entire family; then one counselor met with the parents, and the other with the children. The process culminated in a final stage in which everyone gathered to share information and plans for change. Further observation and study led to a language for describing family structure and a system of interventions designed to change unhelpful and even harmful patterns of family organization. Just as Glasser wrote his first successful book based on his experience at the Ventura School for Girls, Minuchin wrote *Families of the Slums* (1967) based on his experiences at Wiltwyck.

Minuchin's next project was transforming the Philadelphia Child Guidance Clinic into a model family therapy center. He had a flair for the dramatic and was highly critical of seminar case presentations that did not meet his standards. As a practicing family therapist, he set the family scene, assigned roles, started and stopped the action, and took a leading or supporting role himself.

Working with Jay Haley, Minuchin developed the clinic's family orientation and the Institute for Family Counseling, which was designed to train paraprofessionals. Perhaps his most notable accomplishment during this period was the treatment he developed for psychosomatic families, particularly those of anorexics. He wrote *Families and Family Therapy* (1974) during his 10 years as director of the clinic. After stepping down as director, Minuchin served as head of the training center until 1981. His next book, *Psychosomatic Families,* was published in 1978. Since then, Minuchin has continued family research with "normal" families, written several plays, and written a book for the lay public, *Family Kaleidoscope* (1984).

Minuchin has been praised for rescuing family therapy from intellectuality and mystery. His pragmatic approach contributed both to understanding how families function and to productive interventions for correcting malfunctions in them. Minuchin worked with children and families written off by the psychiatric community as unsuitable for treatment. His achievements are rooted in his philosophy of putting clients first and in his total commitment to their cases.

Once Minuchin diagnosed a flaw in the family system, he appeared willing to go to any length to bring about a needed change. His techniques ranged from gentle persuasion to outright provocation and confrontation. He viewed psychosomatic illness as a symptom brought on and maintained by the family and successfully treated eating disorders, asthma, and uncontrolled diabetes. As mentioned previously, Minuchin's structural family therapy approach is directed toward changing the family structure or organization as a way of modifying family members' behavior. The counselor makes interventions by becoming an active "family" member.

Minuchin described traditional psychotherapy as a magnifying glass and structural family therapy as a zoom lens that can focus on the entire family or zoom in for a close-up of any family member. The structural therapist works with the family belief system to effect behavior changes between people. Rule changes may be the immediate goal as the family explores three questions: (1) How do family members relate to one another? (2) Who is allied with whom against whom? (3) What is the nature of the parental dyad? The idea is to change the immediate context of the family situation and thereby change the family members' positions. The cognitive dissonance principle operates much the same way.

For example, Minuchin (1978) described the case of a 12-year-old girl with psychosomatically triggered asthma. She had a history of heavy medication, missed school, and several trips to the emergency room. During the first family interview, the counselor directed the family's attention to the eldest sister's weight problem, and the family's concern then shifted to the newly identified patient. The result for the asthmatic was fewer symptoms, less medication, and no lost school time.

Minuchin referred to the preceding case as the foundation of family therapy. The family structure had changed from two parents protectively concerned with one child's asthma to two parents concerned with one child's asthma and one child's obesity. The asthmatic child's position in the family changed, and that changed her experience.

As with all counseling approaches, the counselor's first step is to establish a trusting relationship with the family. Minuchin recommended three ways: (1) *tracking,* or demonstrating interest in the family by asking a series of questions about the topics they bring up; (2) *mimicry,* or adapting the counselor's communication style to fit the family's; and (3) *support,* which includes the first two ways, plus acceptance of the problem as presented by the client.

Minuchin's style was to get the family to talk briefly until he identified a central theme of concern and the leading and supporting roles in it. At this point, he operated like a play director or group dynamics consultant in determining the roles being played, what was interrupting the flow, what was silencing communication, and what diverting maneuvers were blocking family interaction.

Next, the counselor examines boundaries or family rules, which define (1) who participates in what and how, (2) areas of responsibility, (3) decision making, and (4) privacy. When rules have been broken, the family works on them with the help of "stage directions." The counselor may ask a family member to observe the family interaction but not interfere. Minuchin paced the family by adopting their mood and tempo and gradually changing it as the interview proceeded. He asked questions in the enactive mode: not "Why doesn't your mother talk to you?" but "See if you can get your mother to talk to you."

The counselor might assign tasks related to the manipulation of space, such as ask a child to move his chair so he cannot see his mother's signals or ask a husband to sit next to his wife and hold her hand when she is anxious. Assigned tasks can dramatize family transactions and suggest change.

Minuchin (1974) shared a case about an anorexic girl and her family to illustrate how he conducts family therapy. Once again, like a play director, he set the stage. The family of six and Minuchin sat down at the table to have lunch.

Minuchin began to develop the crisis in the family by announcing that Sally must eat or soon die. He assigned her father the task of helping her eat. The father tried bribery with ice cream and a soft drink, to no avail, and was "rewarded" by a minor tantrum from Sally.

Next, having received the assignment to help Sally eat, the mother tried pleas, guilt inducements, and lectures that went unheeded except for more tantrum behavior in the corner of the room (including slapping the mother).

Minuchin began a new stage in the process by standing up and ordering Sally to sit at the table. At this point, the family is exhausted and searching for a way to solve the problem. The reality therapy philosophy that no one stops any behavior until thorough disgust sets in may come into play at this stage.

The therapist offered a way out of the trap: a negotiation model that allowed Sally to negotiate with a pediatric resident, who presented several choices from all the required food groups, from which Sally was to select her daily meals. The therapist blocked any attempt by the parents to intervene in the process and developed a separation between Sally and her parents and a therapeutic dyad between Sally and the therapist. The one rule of the game remained: Sally must eat. The strategy of offering alternatives empowered Sally with control over her life that she had attempted to achieve through not eating. In 1 month, she returned to her normal weight.

In summary, Minuchin's approach to structural family therapy was both active and directive. The first task is to shift the family focus from the identified client to the therapist, which allows the identified client to begin the process of rejoining the family as a regular family member. The shift in focus to the therapist occurs when the therapist joins the family and becomes part of the family system. When treatment is complete, the therapist moves outside the family structure and leaves the family intact and connected without the loss of individual family member identities (see Figure 12-3).

## STRATEGIC FAMILY THERAPY

Following the popularity of structural family therapy in the 1970s, strategic family therapy dominated the 1980s, led by Milton Erickson, Jay Haley, and Cloé Madanes.

Strategic family therapy is based on the assumption that family members' behavior, which is ongoing and repetitive, can be understood only in the family context. The family's ineffective problem solving develops and maintains symptoms. The counselor's role is to design a strategy for solving the presenting problem. Haley (1973) defined *strategic family therapy* as any therapy in which the therapist initiates what happens in therapy and designs a plan for solving each problem. It is characterized by its brief duration, generally no more than 10 sessions. The therapist takes on a very high activity level by giving specific directives for behavior change that are carried out as homework assignments. Many of the therapists' directives are paradoxical interventions and solution-focused brief counseling methods (discussed in Chapter 5).

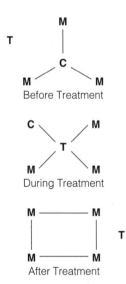

Key  M – Family Member
     C – Identified Client
     T – Therapist

FIGURE 12-3   Stages of structural family therapy

## Paradoxical Interventions

Paradoxical interventions harness the strong resistance clients have to change and to taking directives from the therapist. Rather than working against the client's resistance, the therapist uses it to bring about the changes in behavior needed to correct the problem and repair the family system. The client is in the double-bind position of either obeying the therapist, which the client does not want to do, or stopping the problematic, "uncontrollable" behavior. The client soon discovers that the behavior is controllable and stops the undesirable behavior. For example, the counselor tells an insomniac to see how long the person can go without sleep, maybe even enter a stay-awake contest or go for the world's record, or tells a tantrum-throwing child to have more tantrums and the child's parents to provide a private room for the tantrums. The counselor might also tell children who lose their tempers and commit aggressive acts to do so between 4 P.M. and 5 P.M. daily in a room equipped with a punching bag and tell their parents to remind the children when it is time to vent anger.

In another paradoxical intervention, the counselor takes a "one-down" position, encouraging the client not to do too much too soon. Clients often play the wooden-leg game, described in Chapter 10, which highlights the client's disabilities and the reasons why the client cannot function properly. In the one-down position, the counselor emphasizes all that the client is already doing despite problems and suggests that the client must have great inner strength even to show up for counseling.

Clients who handicap themselves through anticipatory anxiety over activities such as making speeches, taking tests, or meeting new people are directed to practice all the symptoms they fear, such as blushing, speaking in a trembling voice, stuttering, passing out, or completely failing the test. They often tell test-anxious people to take practice tests and fail each one.

Madanes (1981) often asked children to pretend doing the symptom the family was trying to prevent. The other family members were directed to play along with and encourage the child to act out the symptoms. Counselors often treat displays of inadequacy and learned helplessness with directives to the child to act more helpless more often and with directives to other family members to overhelp by providing too much service.

Although strategic or brief therapy is directed toward symptom removal, counselors distinguish between first-order and second-order changes. First-order change occurs when the symptom is temporarily removed, only to reappear later because the family system has not been changed. Haley (1976) pointed out that the behaviors of family members do not occur in isolation. Rather, family behaviors occur in a sequence in which one member's behavior is both the result of and the catalyst for other members' behaviors. Fixing the symptom while failing to fix the system does not fix the family. First-order change is typical for dysfunctional families who work very hard to maintain the status quo.

Second-order change occurs when symptom *and* system are repaired and the need for the symptom does not reappear. For example, Mom and Dad quarrel, the children start a fight, Mom and Dad stop their quarrel to deal with their children, and a period of family peace is achieved. Until Mom and Dad find a better way to resolve conflicts, the sequence repeats frequently and the peace is only temporary. Healthy families with an adaptive facility for repairing the family system when it is broken engage in second-order change.

## Contributions of Milton Erickson, Jay Haley, and Cloé Madanes to Strategic Family Therapy

Jay Haley, director of the Family Therapy Institute of Washington, D.C., was a longtime colleague and student of Milton Erickson. He described Erickson as his mentor and major source of ideas about therapy. Since Erickson's death in 1980, Haley perhaps has been his best interpreter. Haley also worked closely with Salvador Minuchin at the Philadelphia Child Guidance Clinic. For the past several years, Haley's work has been closely associated with that of his wife, Cloé Madanes. They founded the Family Therapy Institute and now conduct lectures and workshops on strategic family therapy.

To strategic family therapists, the term *strategic* refers to the development of a specific strategy, planned in advance by the therapist, to resolve the presenting problem as quickly and efficiently as possible. Erickson promoted the idea that insight, awareness, and emotional release are not necessary for change. Rather, people need to solve their immediate problems and eliminate bothersome symptoms in order to move ahead with their lives. Followers of Erickson's approach do not have the client's personal growth and development as a primary therapeutic goal. Problem solving through minimal intervention is the key goal for the strategic group. It is important to note that strategic interventions often foster changes in the family structure when structural interventions fail.

Erickson's approach incorporated three principles in addition to discounting the importance of achieving insight: (1) The therapist uses the client's reality rather than attempting to fit the client to the views of the world, or even to those of the therapist; (2) both the therapist and client play active roles in the action-oriented process; and (3) minimal change must occur in one or more areas of the client's life for change in the family system to result. Eclecticism is alive and well in family therapy practice as the therapist works to construct strategies to implement the needed changes.

A typical example of an Erickson case concerned a mother and her 61-pound anorexic daughter, Barbie, who was limiting her daily diet to one oyster cracker and a glass of ginger ale. Initial treatment began with routine questions for Barbie, which her mother answered. Erickson allowed the mother's behavior to continue for 2 days as a way of building rapport and establishing a pattern before initiating an intervention. The next stage began with Erickson's scolding the mother in front of Barbie for answering all of Barbie's questions. Barbie developed a new perspective on her mother. The next step was to punish Barbie for keeping her mother awake at night with her whimpering. The punishment was forcing Barbie to eat scrambled eggs—acceptable to her because she viewed eating as punishment. In the next stage, Erickson used storytelling as a way of indirectly replacing Barbie's maladaptive behavior patterns with good associations of food in various social settings. He altered her role as victim by placing her in other roles in the stories, such as rescuer or persecutor. Barbie's treatment was successful and remained so during a lengthy follow-up period (Erickson & Zeig, 1985).

In a similar treatment approach for anorexia nervosa, the therapist viewed the illness as originating from an overprotective family, leading to suppression of autonomy in the adolescent, Cathy, and surfacing in the form of an illness rather than outward rebellion. The therapist used two interventions: (1) Cathy's refusal to eat was termed "disobedient behavior" and was dealt with as unacceptable by the parents, and (2) parental intervention in her eating habits was prevented. Cathy's defiance of the parental rules surfaced in her eating habits. She controlled the family by manipulating her eating behavior. Therapy with the entire family focused on discussing, negotiating, and resolving difficult family issues. The children gained more autonomy and responsibility for their decisions, and the parents spent more time with each other. Any weight gain Cathy showed was reinforced by allowing her more autonomy. Weight loss was punished by loss of new privileges. In other words, Cathy's eating behavior now controlled only her own autonomy and the number of privileges available to her.

Haley (1976) combined a strategic and structural approach to treat a young boy's fear of dogs. A problem of family dynamics was that the boy was close to his mother but disengaged from his father. Haley's first step was to get father and son to interact by having them talk about the dangers of dogs in the neighborhood. When the mother tried to interrupt, Haley neutralized her by explaining that this was Dad's area of expertise. The second step was to get a dog into the home to help in three areas: (1) to continue the father–son interaction, (2) to achieve systematic desensitization of the dog phobia, and (3) to stimulate change in the family dynamics. Haley accomplished Step 2 by asking the boy to pick out a dog who was afraid and to work with his father on teaching the dog not to be afraid.

The preceding case illustrates a common malfunction in a child-centered family structure. Generally one or more overinvolved dyads exist, one of which usually includes the "problem" child. Haley (1973) described three ways to handle the overinvolved dyad: (1) act on the relationship between the child and the mother (neutralize mother); (2) modify the relationship between father and child (interact about the dog); and (3) change the relationship between spouses (bring the dog into the home for the son to care for and teach with the father's help). Haley (1984), in another application of the same three steps, described an intervention for misbehaving children as "ordeal therapy." When all else fails, the counselor might present the father of a teenage son with the following directive:

> When Bill misbehaves at school, he will be sent to me with a note of explanation. I will call you, Dad, at your office to pick up Bill, take him home, and supervise his digging of a 3- by 3- by 3-foot hole in your flower bed. Upon completion of the digging, Bill is to place one of his CDs in it, fill the hole, tramp it down, clean the shovel, and return the shovel to the garage. You will then return Bill to me, and I will return him to his class.

At the end of the day, you, Dad, are to have a talk with your wife about Bill's behavior for that day.

Dysfunctional symptoms in a family system might be evidenced in several ways. Intensive criticism between children and parents in families highly resistant to change could result in anything in children from suicidal depression to refusal to attend school. Strategic family counselors often fix both problems by prescribing more criticism and putting the family in the double bind of having to choose between obeying the counselor or disobeying by doing the "right" thing of stopping the criticism. Family resistance against counseling and the counselor is harnessed to work for the good of the family as they refuse to criticize each other.

DeShazer and Molnar (1984) described a useful team approach for prescribing four common interventions in their practice of solution-focused brief family therapy. The therapy hour is divided as follows: (1) a 40-minute interview with the family, (2) a 10-minute consultation with the team, and (3) a 10-minute delivery of the intervention message and closing of the session. The first intervention, designed for families who focus on the perceived stability of their problem pattern, requires family members to observe one another between sessions so that "you can tell us next time what happens in your family that you want to continue to have happen." The second intervention is for families who are bankrupt of ideas about how to solve the problem. The therapist requests that they "do something different." The third intervention is for clients who believe their problem is out of their control. The therapist asks them to "pay attention to what you do when you overcome the temptation or urge to _____." The fourth intervention works well for clients who are convinced they are doing the only logical thing. The therapist responds, "A lot of people in your situation would have _____." All four interventions are designed to help clients experience changing.

Chasin, Roth, and Bograd (1989), in an article on action methods in strategic therapy, presented another solution-focused brief family counseling method. In an approach to therapy that involves de-emphasizing the problems, their main focus was on looking for clients' strengths and using various action strategies to open up new perspectives and discussions. The authors provide a five-step outline:

1. Therapists and clients contract to promote safe, voluntary participation. The clients have the right to disclose at the level they choose and can refuse to answer any question or participate in any activity.

2. Each participant is invited to list his or her individual strengths and the strengths of the relationship.

3. Participants enact three dramatizations. First, the couple enacts what would happen if the goals for the relationship were reached. Second, each client enacts a painful past experience. Third, each client enacts the painful past experience "as it should have been." The partner's roles in this enactment are preventive, protective, and/or resolving.

4. Each participant states what he or she perceives to be the problem in the relationship.

5. The therapist recommends the next step (homework, follow-up appointment, and so on) based on what happened during the session.

A final example of strategic family therapy is the use of metaphor in bringing about rapid change: Parents bring an 8-year-old girl to family counseling with the problem that she is spoiled, stubborn, argumentative, and whiny. While the parents obviously view this behavior as bad, their daughter does not. The counselor asks her age, and the child says she is 8. The counselor looks incredulously at the mother and father, shakes his head, and says to the parents, "This can't be, for this girl is 8 and this behavior you described is the behavior of a 6-year-old." With a puzzled look, the counselor asks the girl how old she was on her last birthday and how old she will be on her next birthday. The counselor notes that the behavior she is exhibiting during the session is that of an 8-year-old, and he asks the parents to keep a log of the child's behavior for 1 week. The direct challenge of age appeals to children's desire to look their age or older.

In summary, the job of the strategic family therapist is fourfold: First, the hierarchical structure of the family must be identified. "Who is in charge of whom and what?" and "What role does each family member play?" are the critical questions to be answered. Confusion about who is in charge and about role identity is characteristic of dysfunctional families. Second, the sequence of behaviors that causes and maintains the problem symptom needs to be identified. For example, what is the presenting problem, and what family conditions create and maintain the problem? Third, the therapist develops an intervention plan to serve as a directive for how family members are to change certain behaviors. Fourth, the therapist and family evaluate the plan's effectiveness in removing the symptom and repairing the family system. Haley (1976) distinguished between advice and directives. Giving advice is telling people what they ought to do, what job to take, or what person to marry. Giving a directive is like assigning behavior homework or writing a behavior prescription designed to alter family interaction sequences.

Haley (1976) described four stages of a typical strategic therapy first interview:

1. Stage 1, the *social stage,* accomplishes three tasks: building rapport, observing family communication patterns and alliances, and forming tentative hypotheses about how the family functions.

2. In Stage 2, the *problem stage,* the main task is obtaining a clear statement of the problem that meets with each family member's agreement. Haley suggested involving reluctant participants first in the problem discussion and the identified client last, a procedure followed in most family therapies to bring everybody into the discussion without focusing on the identified client as the scapegoat for the family's dysfunction.

3. Stage 3, the *interaction stage,* accomplishes two tasks: Everybody should discuss the problem, and everybody should interact with all other family members. During Stage 3, the therapist does not become personally involved in the family interaction because the family interaction patterns require full attention. The therapist directs the family to discuss their disagreements and to role-play or act out a

typical family problem such as deciding who does what family chores. We prefer to observe how a typical family meeting might operate, even if the family is not accustomed to holding them. All these interactions provide valuable information about problem sequences, communication patterns, and the lines of authority in the family hierarchy.

4. In Stage 4, *goal setting,* the obvious task is to define the goal for therapy in concise, observable behavioral terms. For example, in a family that does not discuss family conflicts, an acceptable goal might be weekly 30-minute family meetings to clear the air of conflicts. The therapist could add a paradoxical directive encouraging the family not to resolve any of the conflicts during the meetings. Again, complete clarity and agreement on the goals are necessary if the family is to have ownership in the therapy process and the resulting cooperation and commitment to make therapy work. Todd (2000) describes a successful adaptation of strategic family therapy as it was applied to a parent-education class for rearing challenging teens.

## THE COMMUNICATIONS APPROACH TO FAMILY THERAPY

Our discussions of systems, structural, and strategic approaches to family therapy have highlighted several commonalities and overlap between methods as well as specific differences. Perhaps the common thread that unites the field of family therapy is the focus on how family members communicate. Communication is the very heart of the two methods presented next in our discussion: John Gottman's behavioral family therapy and Virginia Satir's conjoint family therapy.

### John Gottman's Behavioral Interview Method

Gottman's behavioral family therapy (1979, 1990) has much more in common with traditional family therapy than it does with the behavioral counseling and therapy discussed in Chapter 9. The therapist in Gottman's system functions more as an educator than as a healer, as is true for most of the practitioners of the theories and systems presented in this book.

Family therapists following a communications approach to family therapy naturally hold the view that accurate communication is the key to solving family problems. All families are faced with problems; however, some families solve more of their problems than other families. Families that are good at problem solving hold several traits in common. They communicate in an open and honest manner rather than relying on phony or manipulative roles when trying to meet their needs or resolving family crises. In addition, these family members match the intent and impact of their communication. For example, a wife may want more cooperation from her husband on household chores. She stated her request in clear terms and listened empathically to her husband's response about his needs; the intent of her communication achieved the desired impact. Had she been sarcastic, the impact of her message may have resulted in less cooperation from her husband. Dysfunctional families have low success rates in matching the impact with the intent of their communications.

Gottman built his approach around matching the intent and impact of communication (Gottman, 1979, 1994; Gottman, Notarius, Gonzo, & Markman, 1976). He designed his behavioral interviewing method to teach people about what they are doing that is not working and to help them correct the situation by learning how to get the impact they want from their communication:

Stage I: How a couple or family made the decision to seek therapy is explored. The therapist also determines the level of commitment to therapy and who, if anyone, might be a reluctant client. The dynamics give the therapist an opportunity to view the family interaction pattern firsthand. Areas of family or couple agreement and disagreement surface during this stage.

Stage II: The goals each person has for therapy, some of the fears they have about coming to therapy, and fears about what could go wrong are identified. The therapist asks clients what their situation would be like if all their goals were attained; in other words, how would they be behaving differently, and how would an observer know they had met their goals? More specifically, what would their typical day be like if they achieved their goals? Couples in counseling often state their goals (for treatment) in terms of what they want for each other; a better focus would be the goals the couple wants for the partnership. The therapist can facilitate goal setting by presenting each client with a list of possible goals—improve communication, have more fun, do more things together, become more of a team, become better parents, end fighting, manage finances better, improve love-making, cooperate more on household jobs—and instructing them to select just one goal each. The clients then elaborate on their choices and explain why the goal is important to them. The second task in Stage II is to identify any fears or inhibitions the couple might have about counseling. A good introduction to the subject is asking the couple the worst possible thing that could happen from counseling. The therapist can use this opportunity to explain how treatment is conducted and the roles of the therapist and clients. If the couple is having a problem with finances, for example, the therapist's role is not to solve the money problem per se; rather, the therapist focuses on the couple's communications. Better and more effective communication should provide the means to solve problems more efficiently, including handling finances better.

Stage III: The counselor asks the couple to articulate their perceptions of their marital issues or problems. Again, the couple completes a checklist of several marital issues and rates each issue for its severity on a scale of 1 to 10, with 10 being most severe. The typical list of issues approximates the goals list used in Stage II: for example, house and yard chores, fighting, finances, sex, in-laws, communication, cooperation, parenting, time together, and addictions. Again, the couple's discussion of their marital issues affords the therapist another opportunity to observe the couple's communication pattern.

Stage IV: The therapist asks the couple to select one issue to discuss, just as they might try to resolve it at home, and then observes the free interaction to note how well the intent of each communication is getting the desired impact.

Stage V: A play-by-play analysis of the couple's interaction focuses on miscommunications in which the intent of the speaker's message did not get the desired impact. In fact, the miscommunication often gets an effect opposite the intended meaning. The intent might be to get a partner to help out around the house more, but the result is that the other partner is helping even less than before. After pointing out the differences between intent and impact for a series of communications, the therapist might ask one partner to assume the role of a play director to describe how the other partner could have responded better to the statement just made. Then the couple compares the desired response with the one actually made. As in reality therapy, the couple can decide whether what they are doing is getting the desired response, and they can stop or change what they are doing. The receiver of the message can validate the impact of the sender's message, and the sender then analyzes the receiver's return message for intent and impact. Step V might require the therapist to lecture on the intent and impact equation: *Good communication occurs when intent equals impact.* The therapist explains that choice of words, nonverbal communications, and the sender's and receiver's value filters can distort the intent of the message and lead to an undesired impact. Restating and clarifying the sender's message before reacting can often help. In other words, the couple may have to pass the message back and forth before the receiver understands it the way it was intended. Even with a clear message, the sender may not get the intended impact of the message and need to alter it to get the desired response. The receiving partner can help by stating how he or she wishes to be approached on the presenting issue.

Stage VI: The therapist concludes the session by negotiating a contract with the couple on what goal(s) they will try to achieve and the method of treatment they will use. The clients' job is to decide on the objective, and the therapist's job is to supply the process. Again, as is true with most counseling approaches, the principal goal is to teach people a communication process that enables them to solve more of their problems.

## VIRGINIA SATIR'S CONJOINT FAMILY THERAPY

When Virginia Satir (1916–1988) was 5 years old, she decided to become a detective to help children figure out parents. She was not sure what she would be looking for, but even at this age she knew that more strange things were going on in families than met the eye. More than half a century later, after working with thousands of families, Satir reported that she still found a lot of puzzles in families.

Satir viewed family life as an iceberg. Most people are aware of only one tenth of what is happening in the family—the tenth that they can see and hear. Like the ship that depends on the captain's awareness of the total iceberg, the family must depend on the total awareness of the family structure to survive. Satir referred to the hidden 90% as the family's needs, motives, and communication patterns. In four books, Satir shared some of the answers she found to the puzzles over the years: *Conjoint Family Therapy* (1967), *Peoplemaking* (1972), *Helping Families to Change* (Satir, Stachowiak, & Taschman, 1975), and *Step by Step* (Satir & Baldwin, 1983). According to Satir, she embellished some of the early concepts in *Conjoint Family Therapy* as a result of her work with the Gestalt concepts presented by Fritz Perls and the body-awareness work of Bernard Gunther.

Virginia Satir earned excellent qualifications as a parent detective: formal academic training in psychological social work at the University of Chicago and work as a teacher, consultant, and practitioner in psychiatric clinics, mental hospitals, family service centers, growth centers, and private practice. In 1959, she joined with two psychiatrists to form the initial staff of the Mental Research Institute in Palo Alto, California. She also served as the first director of training at the Esalen Institute in Big Sur, California, and lectured in most parts of the world. She was a visiting professor to at least 10 universities and a consultant to the Veterans Administration and to several other agencies and schools. As is true about many theorists presented in this book, she was more effective demonstrating her methods than lecturing about them.

Satir cited several contributors to the development of her system—including Harry Stack Sullivan's interpersonal theory of the 1920s (an individual's behavior is influenced by his or her interaction with another) and the growth of group therapy, whose major contributors were J. L. Moreno and S. R. Slavson, also during the 1920s. Gregory Bateson and Murray Bowen began to look at families to discover why individuals became "schizophrenic." They believed that one person could represent the family situation.

Bateson, of the Mental Research Institute, contributed the idea of the double-bind communications that occur when one person sends a conflicting, double message to another person; for example, Mom says, "Jane, if you really loved me, you would make better grades at school."

Much of Satir's theory has roots not only in classic theories of clinical psychology and psychiatry but also in her past research at the Mental Research Institute and the National Institute of Mental Health. Satir synthesized older with newer theories and added original techniques.

## The Nature of People

Satir had a positive view of human nature. After studying 12,000 families in depth, she was convinced that, at any time, whatever people are doing represents the best they are aware of and the best they can do. She believed that people are rational and have the freedom and ability to make choices in their lives. Although Satir viewed people as basically free, she considered the extent of their knowledge as the biggest limitation on personal freedom. People can learn what they do not know and change their ways of interacting with others. People can also make themselves healthier by freeing themselves from the past. Like Maslow, Satir believed that people are geared to surviving, growing, and developing close relationships with others. Although some behavior may be labeled psychotic, sick, or bad, Satir saw it as an attempt to reach out for help.

Self-esteem plays a prominent role in Satir's system. She believed that self-esteem and effective communication beget one another. Conversely, low self-esteem and dysfunctional communication are also correlated. Satir saw self-esteem—the degree to which people accept both their good and their bad points—as the basic human drive. Self-esteem is a changing variable that fluctuates within a healthy range, depending on the amount of stress one is experiencing. It is related to one's participation in the family interaction. When individual family members experience stress, their ability to communicate openly, give and receive feedback, and solve problems depends on the collective self-esteem of the family. Family members may try to block communication to protect their own self-esteem under stress or in crises. Family members with low self-esteem are likely to create disturbances to make the others feel as bad as they do. For example, parents guilty of child abuse often have low self-esteem and may unconsciously internalize: "One way to punish myself for my wasteful ways is to punish that same behavior in one of my children."

Behavior, according to Satir, is directly related to one's family position and view of it. Good or bad feelings about ourselves are probably communicated to others. Satir viewed people as mature and functional when they behave in acceptable and helpful ways and take responsibility for their actions. Satir (as well as Adler and Glasser) saw irresponsibility and poor communication as symptoms of low self-esteem.

Satir made the point that a person needs a high degree of self-esteem to qualify as a good marriage partner. People with healthy self-concepts view their partners as enhancing their own self-esteem. However, people who have low self-esteem look to their partners as extensions of themselves. A marital relationship is dysfunctional if one partner looks to the other to supply what is missing in the self. In this dysfunctional couple relationship, a person sees the marriage or partnership as a place for getting and not giving. For example, someone may marry as a type of therapy for strengthening an inadequate personality. However, the general outcome of a "taking" relationship is disappointment and an even lower sense of self-esteem.

By the same token, parents with low self-esteem may compensate for feelings of inferiority by having a child. The child may be used to demonstrate the parents' worth to the community and their self-worth as parents, as well as an extension of themselves. Unconsciously, they seem to be thinking, "If I did not fulfill many of my life's aspirations, perhaps I can relive them through my child." In such situations, parents never see children as individuals with separate worth, value, and identities. Children of parents deficient in self-esteem have a heavy, difficult burden to bear: to live out their parents' fantasies. They see success and failure from the vantage point of the parent. Children who show individuality and different points of view may be accused of not loving their parents by such comments as "After all I have done for you, how could you do this to me?" or "If you loved me, you would practice the piano more."

Satir (1967) held that children are the third angle of the family triangle. As such, their position may be intolerable, similar to the persecutor–victim–rescuer triangle described in transactional analysis (see Chapter 10). Parents in conflict consider any direction the child turns as a turn for or against one of the parents. Given this state of affairs, Satir wrote, children who seem to side with one parent run the risk of seeming not to love the other parent. Because children need both parents, making such a choice inevitably hurts them. Both parents have interlocking roles to play in the process of educating children emotionally, and the failure of one angle of the family triangle (one parent) disturbs the entire system; frequently, the result is disturbed children.

A further complication in the triangle is that the child has already established an identity with the same-sex parent, and the hurt of taking sides is further compounded by the stunted or stifled psychosexual development that may occur. Children need the opposite-sex parent to admire, respect, and love and the same-sex parent as a good role model. When the parents are divided, arguing, and fighting, children cannot achieve these identity and interpersonal goals. In a family with no parental coalition—cooperation between father and mother to fulfill their respective roles as man and woman and husband and wife—the child may need counseling to fulfill unsatisfied wishes. Satir conceptualized this child as the *identified client,* even though the entire family is counseled.

Satir did not believe in the concept of triangular relationships; that is, she believed there is no such thing as a relationship "among" three people, only shifting two-person relationships, with the third member in the role of observer. The building blocks of Satir's system are two-person, interacting relationships. The key to success or failure in this system is the relationship between husband and wife. If the system is dysfunctional and they are not acting in a parental coalition, then both mates may look to the child to satisfy their unmet needs.

According to Satir, children who are triangulated into a marital situation in the role of "ersatz mate"—an ally who is wooed seductively by the parent of the opposite sex—are not happy. The child has loyalties to and needs for both parents. Although a child may appear closer to one parent, such an alliance is illusory. Children cannot unambivalently side with either parent.

Satir wrote that people develop self-esteem in the early childhood years. Beyond the obvious physical needs, children need a warm, ongoing, predictable mastery over their world and validation of themselves as distinct and worthwhile people. They also require a sense of what it is to be male or female and an acceptance of this role. If parents consistently show that they consider their children masterful, sexual people and demonstrate a gratifying, functional male–female relationship, their children acquire self-esteem and become increasingly independent. In every way, self-esteem, independence, and individuality go together.

Satir viewed mature people as those who are fully in charge of their feelings and who make choices based on accurate perceptions of themselves and others. The mature person takes full responsibility for choices that have been made. In summary, Satir regarded mature people as (1) being in touch with their feelings, (2) communicating clearly and effectively, and (3) accepting differences in others as a chance to learn.

## Theory of Counseling

Satir believed that four components in a family situation are subject to change and correction: the members' feelings of self-worth, the family's communication abilities, the system, and the rules of the family. The rules are the way things are accomplished in the family. They are the most difficult component to uncover during therapy sessions because they usually are not verbalized or consciously known to all members of the family. Satir wanted all members of a family to understand the rules that govern their emotional interchanges, including (1) freedom to comment, (2) freedom to express what one is seeing or hearing, (3) freedom to agree or disapprove, and (4) freedom to ask questions when one does not understand. The family unit becomes dysfunctional when members do not understand the unwritten rules. Satir told families who were having problems with a member that families have no bad members who cause pain, only bad rules. She believed that what goes on at a given moment is the natural consequence of the experience of one's own life; consequently, anything can change. However, Satir felt that change is not a "have to" but rather one possibility among several. She believed in taking risks, controlling the counseling process, and leaving the outcome to the family.

In family systems theory, the main idea is that the family functions as a unit, with certain rules, expectations, and emotions. Members of the family unit are interdependent; therefore, stress applied to one part of the system or to one family member is felt throughout the system by all members in varying degrees. The family system has both the potential to share and deal with the stress in a healthy, open, and productive way and the potential to close the communication process by focusing blame for the stress on one family member (the identified client).

To bring about changes in a family's functioning, analyzing the interaction processes between the family members and the family system is as important as analyzing the communications content. Questions of who is right and who is wrong border on value judgments that have no place in the process of family growth and further development. The focus is on discovering how individuals can adjust to the various events within the family to achieve satisfaction and avoid withdrawal and other harmful roles.

Satir emphasized the necessity of developing trust before any meaningful change process can begin. Given willingness to take a risk, trust can be assumed. The second step is developing awareness, or knowing what one is doing. With awareness comes understanding and applying this new understanding to effective decision making. At this point, the new decision-making behavior can be put to use. The underlying theme is the development of self-worth and the freedom to comment.

Satir believed that whether a family grows is primarily the responsibility of counselors and their input. They must be able to put clients in touch with themselves at a feeling level. The counselor assumes the role of teacher to reeducate the family to new ways of thinking, feeling, and communicating.

Communication, the most important factor in Satir's system, is the main determinant of the kinds of relationships people have with one another and of how people adjust to their environment, as well as the tie that binds the family together. When a family is operating smoothly, communication among family members is open, authentic, assertive, and received. Conversely, when a family system is in trouble, communication is blocked or distorted in a futile attempt to ward off anxiety and tension.

Fear of rejection is a common source of anxiety. Because people fear rejection, they resort to one response pattern or to a combination of patterns to communicate with others. These universal response roles are the placater, the blamer, the computer, the distractor, and the leveler. The last response, leveling, helps people develop healthy personalities; all the others hide real feelings for fear of rejection. In such situations, people feel and react to the threat of rejection, do not want to reveal "weakness," and attempt to conceal it. Satir (1971) agreed with Gestalt theory on nonverbal behavior: The body expresses your whole integration. Each response pattern is accompanied by a unique body posture and nonverbal behaviors, and each has its own way of dealing or not dealing with the context (or subject matter of the situation), the needs of the other family members, and the personal or self needs of the person playing the particular role.

**Placater.** Placaters placate so others do not get angry. Their motto is "peace at any price." They talk in ingratiating ways to try to please, or they apologize. They never disagree and even take on the air of a yes person. They have low self-esteem. They cannot negotiate solutions of mutual benefit because the process is too threatening. In other words, placaters negate self in the interest of serving others and staying within the context of the situation. Nonverbal behaviors of the placater send the message that "Whatever you want is okay with me; I am just here to make you happy."

**Blamer.** Blamers are the faultfinders, directors, and bosses. They also do not feel good about themselves. They may feel lonely and unsuccessful and attempt to compensate by trying to coerce others into obeying them so they can feel that they amount to something. Blaming is also a good way to create distance and prevent others from getting too close. The blamers are good guilt inducers: "After all I have done for you, how could you do this to me?" Blamers negate others while focusing on the context of the situation and on themselves. Nonverbal behaviors from the blamer send the message that "You never do anything right. What is the matter with you?"

**Computer.** Computers are calm and correct, show no feelings, and speak like a recording. They pretend there is no conflict when there is. Computers are the superreasonable people. Their bodies reflect their rigid personalities. They negate the context of the situation and others to concentrate on getting what they want. They cover up their vulnerability with big words to establish self-worth. Nonverbal behaviors from the "computer" send messages that "I am cool, calm, and collected." They may also take the position of "See it my way" at the expense of others and of the context of the situation.

**Distractor.** Distractors make completely *irrelevant* statements. They change the subject and never respond honestly. Their strong point is evading the issue. They may even resort to withdrawing from the situation to avoid a crisis or conflict. Distractors negate all three elements of reality: self, others, and the context of the situation. Nonverbal behaviors from distractors send messages that "Maybe if I do this long enough, the problem will really go away." Distracting, doing and saying irrelevant things, withdrawing from the family interaction, or a combination of these behaviors function to prevent the family from discussing painful, unresolved issues that should be faced in open and honest discussion.

**Leveler.** Levelers communicate their honest thoughts and feelings in a straightforward manner that addresses self, others, and the context of the situation. Their verbal messages and nonverbal body posture are consistent. Leveling occurs when all aspects of communication are congruent: body, vocal tone, context, and facial expression. Levelers do not cover up or put other people down in the name of being open and honest. They are not phonies. Levelers tell the truth about what they are thinking, feeling, and doing, and they allow others to do the same. Their relationships are free and honest, with few threats to self-esteem. The leveling response is the truthful message for a particular person at a given time. It is direct and to the point with no hidden agenda. There is an openness and a feeling of trust in interactions with a person who is leveling. This response allows people to live as complete persons in touch with their behavior, thinking, and feelings. Being a leveler allows a person to have integrity, commitment, honesty, intimacy, competency, creativity, and the ability to solve real problems. The other four forms of communicating result in doubtful integrity, commitment by bargain, dishonesty, loneliness, incompetence, strangulation by tradition (inability to change traditional patterns), and destructive ways of dealing with fantasy problems.

Our society does not encourage leveling responses. Although people would like to be honest, they are afraid and instead play games. Satir outlined a variety of experiences to help family members become aware that they can choose to change their responses and understand how they can do so. Levelers can choose one of the other four response patterns if they are willing to accept the consequences, but for them such responses would not be the automatic response of people locked into a particular pattern. Levelers can choose to placate, blame, compute, or distract; the difference is that they know what they are doing and are prepared to accept the result of their behavior.

The message of the leveler is consistent. If a leveler says, "I like you," the voice is warm and the eye contact and body speak the same message. If the leveler is angry, the voice is harsh, the face is tight, and the words are clear: "I am angry about what you have done!"

Satir pointed out that every person she has seen with a behavior or coping problem was a member of a family in which all significant communication was double level—that is, phony or hidden (Satir, Stachowiak, & Taschman, 1975). If people learn to recognize harmful communication patterns and level with their family members, then the family has a chance to make its members' lives better and to solve problems more efficiently. As mentioned previously, Satir's system is based on two-person, interacting relationships. However, every couple has three parts: you, me, and us. For the relationship to continue and for love to grow, each part has to be recognized and not dominated by the other two. Although love as a feeling begins a marriage, the process makes it work. The process is the "how," which is what Satir taught her clients.

Satir divided all families into two types: nurturing and troubled. Each type has varying degrees. Her main objective for her clients was recognition of their type and then change from either troubled to nurturing or from nurturing to more nurturing. The nurturing family helps its members develop feelings of self-worth, whereas the troubled family diminishes these feelings. In every family, factors to be considered include feelings of self-worth, communication, rules, and links to society.

According to Satir (1972), aliveness, honesty, genuineness, and love mark nurturing families. These families have the following characteristics:

1. People are listened to and interested in listening to others.

2. People are not afraid to take risks because the family understands that mistakes are bound to happen when taking risks.

3. People's bodies are graceful, and their facial expressions are relaxed.

4. People look at one another and not through one another or at the floor.

5. The children are friendly and open, and the rest of the family treats them as people.

6. People seem comfortable about touching one another and showing their affection.

7. People show love by talking and listening with concern and by being straight and real with one another.

8. Members feel free to tell one another how they feel and what they think.

9. Anything can be discussed—fears, anger, hurt, criticism, joys, achievements.

10. Members plan, but if something does not work out, they can adjust.

11. Human life and feelings are more important than anything else.

12. Parents see themselves as leaders and not as bosses. They acknowledge to their children their poor judgment as well as their good judgment, and their hurt, anger, or disappointment as well as their joy. Their behavior matches their teaching.

13. When nurturing, parents need to correct their children. They rely on listening, touching, understanding, and careful timing and are aware of children's feelings and their natural wish to learn.

14. Nurturing parents understand that children learn only when they are valued, so they do not respond in a way that makes the child feel devalued.

## Counseling Method

The counseling method of conjoint family therapy involves the entire family and is based on communication, interaction, and general information. The approach Satir taught to families was both physical and emotional. Counselors who prefer to work less with emotions and more with behavior find the Adlerian method more comfortable.

Satir's goals for family counseling were to establish the proper environment and to assist family members in clarifying what they want or hope for themselves and for the family. She wanted them to explore the present state of the family and who plays which roles. She sought to build everyone's self-esteem. Satir also worked to help families operationalize their definitions of words such as *respect* and *love*. For example, she asked clients, "What would be happening that would let us know you were getting the respect and love you desire?" or "What must be done for you to make you feel respected and loved?" Satir also used reframing to turn negatives into positives and thus allow clients to view difficult situations in a better light and see possibilities for cooperation, conflict resolution, and change.

Satir led the family in role playing both family situations and each other's actions and reactions to the happenings in a typical day. She used some Gestalt techniques of "sculpting" a family argument or interaction; she believed that the body is often a more honest reflection than the verbal message. Satir used videotape replay to teach communication, and her role-play dramas used various props, such as ropes and stepladders, to demonstrate and analyze the types of family interactions. She staged these dramas to help family members learn how to level with each other, express their emotions, and use honest, direct language. Satir examined the family history by drawing family trees to look at how past and immediate family styles are passed on from parent to child. She used ropes to demonstrate the complicated process of communication between parents and children.

Even with a multitude of techniques, Satir proposed no formula for therapy because therapy involves human feelings and the ability to respond on a human level. Satir viewed the family as a "people-making factory" in which people are made by a process that is crude at best and destructive at worst. Loeschen (1998) pointed out that Satir viewed parents as children themselves who have learned "the rules" from their own families and brought those rules forward to their current families.

## An Example of Satir's Method

A 40-year-old woman sits in a fetal position on the floor, hiding behind a sofa. Her husband, sitting in a chair, points an accusing finger at her from across the room. One daughter, with arms outstretched, tries to make peace. Two children sit with their backs to the group, and a fourth child rubs his mother's back. Satir breaks the silent role play, rests her hand on the father's shoulder, and asks how he feels right now. She has asked the family to act out silently how they each feel during a family argument. This sculpting method is excellent in creating awareness of personal feelings as well of the feelings of other family members.

Satir reported research data indicating blood pressure, galvanic skin response, and electroencephalograms were significantly affected when people changed their stance and body posture and held them for at least 10 seconds during role-play demonstrations with double-level, verbal, and nonverbal communication. For example, assuming the blamer posture caused a physiological response as well as an emotional response after 10 seconds. In other words, people engaging in harmful role behavior over a given time period have the potential to make themselves physically ill.

## The Importance of Including Children

Including children is imperative for family counseling success in Satir's system. Satir advocated inclusion of all the children, not just the child who has a problem, because all are part of the family homeostasis—a process by which the family balances forces within itself to achieve unity and working order. Satir operated from the assumption that all members feel dysfunction within the family in some way. Therefore, the counselor works with all members of the family to help them redefine their relationships. Family members have their own perceptions of what is going on in the family, and each member's input is vital in building a functional family. The counselor works with the family's interpersonal relationships to discover how the members interact so that they can strengthen their bonding.

Satir suggested meeting with the marital pair before bringing in the children. She made the couple aware of themselves as individuals as well as mates and parents. She also suggested preparing the parents in the initial interview for bringing the children into the counseling sessions. After the parents agreed that the children's role in family counseling was important, the children were included.

Working with children means the counselor needs to be fully aware of the children's capabilities and potential. The counselor can plan the length of sessions according to the children's ages. Children have short attention spans, and the counseling process must hold their interest. Counselors confronted with these obstacles can work within them and make the counseling process beneficial, productive, and enjoyable for all.

The counselor should begin by recognizing all the children and repeating their names, ages, and birth order to let the children know they are being heard. The counselor also sets rules for the sessions; for example, no one may destroy property within the room, no one may speak for the others, all must speak so they can be heard, and everyone must enable others to be heard. When the ground rules have been established, in-depth discussion can begin.

The counselor should set the mood by asking questions in a warm, specific, matter-of-fact way. The setting should encourage people to take the risk of looking clearly and objectively at themselves and their actions. Satir suggested many questions, but those the children are able to answer. During this time, the counselor must be sure the children understand what is happening and what the family is striving to gain. The children need to feel comfortable and be aware of themselves as individuals who are different from one another. They need to know the importance of communicating with one another—for example, to feel free to agree or disagree with other family members, to say what they think, and to bring disagreements out in the open. The children need to know that the counselor will treat them as people with perceptions and feelings.

The counselor should demonstrate individuality by speaking to each child separately, differentiating each child, and restating and summarizing what each child says. Counselors need to convey their sincerity by honoring all questions from each child and demonstrating that questions are not troublemaking and illegitimate—that all should ask questions about what they do not know or are unsure about. Counselors who convey their expectations of the children increase the likelihood that the children will rise to meet them. Children listen, are interested, and contribute to the discussions.

The counselor has to ask the children their ideas about why they are in counseling and then repeat what each child says to make sure the child's meaning is understood. The counselor may proceed by asking the children where they got their ideas about why they are there, who told them, and what was said. From this exchange, the counselor can gain insight into communication within the family. The counselor encourages the children to talk about themselves and their feelings in relation to each family member. The counselor also helps the children express frustration and anger and has the children ask their family members for answers to any questions they may have. The counselor may use confronting questions to provoke thought in the child. As the counseling sessions advance, questions concerning family rules and roles arise. After establishing good rapport and a comfortable atmosphere, the counselor may begin to bring out underlying feelings and confront people concerning the family's dysfunction. The basis for further probing and confronting must be established between counselor and parent, counselor and child, parent and child, and counselor, parent, and child in the initial interviews. From the initial interviews, the counselor must gain the child's confidence to move forward.

The counselor wants to see each child's place in the family unit. In the beginning, to build the children's self-esteem, the counselor focuses on them—not ignoring the parents, but having the parents respond intermittently. Counselors help children understand their parents as parents and people and themselves as children and people. Lurn, Smith, and Ferris (2002) describe a youth suicide intervention model based on the principles of Satir's model listed previously. They point out a suicide could have been averted had the adolescent had the benefit of family counseling with Satir's orientation.

## Three Keys to Satir's System

Satir's approach to family counseling focused on three key ingredients:

1. Increase the self-esteem of all family members by facilitating their understanding of the family system and teaching them to implement changes toward open systems and nurturing attitudes and behaviors.

2. Help family members better understand and analyze their encounters with each other and learn the leveling response so that they can improve and open communication patterns.

3. Use experiential learning techniques in the counseling setting to help the family understand present interactions and encourage family members to take personal responsibility for their own actions and feelings.

Satir viewed the counselor as a facilitator, a change agent who assists in the process of moving toward a more open family system and a more nurturing family. The counselor is not the expert but the one who helps family members become the experts on the family's problems and growth.

## Satir's Technique

Family therapists use a variety of techniques to assist the family in self-discovery. Satir's method was designed to help family members discover what patterns do not work and how to better understand and express their feelings in an open, level manner. Rather than have them rehash past hurts, Satir had the family analyze its "systems" in a present interaction in the counseling setting. Among the many ways to accomplish this analysis are the following:

1. The counselor asks the family to describe a situation that causes the difficulties that have brought them to counseling or asks them to describe a typical situation from their recent experience that usually results in the problem. Family members enact the situation.

2. The counselor has the family sit in a circle in chairs to simulate a family decision, such as deciding where to go on their next vacation.

3. The family participates in a family sculpture, as in the example presented earlier. The counselor asks someone to describe a typical family argument and then has that person "sculpt" the argument by placing each family member in appropriate positions—complete with gestures, facial expressions, and touching. The counselor might then ask each of the other members how he or she would change

it and allow each to make the changes. Discussion aimed at leveling and participation by each family member follows.

4. Each family member takes some long ropes, one for each of the others in the family, and ties all of them around his or her waist. Next, the counselor instructs each of them to tie one rope to each of the other family members. Discussion of the resulting tension and mass of ropes can help the family better understand its complex relationships and crossed transactions.

5. Role playing and reverse role playing stimulate family discussion.

6. Videotaped family sessions and discussions help family members achieve a better understanding of all members' reactions and responses.

7. Games include (a) the simulated family game, (b) the systems game, and (c) communication games.

Satir's games, which are used for counselor training as well as family therapy, are based on her definition of a *growth model,* which assumes that an individual's behavior changes as a process that is represented by transactions with other people. People function fully when they are removed from the maladaptive system or when the system is changed to promote growth. This model differs greatly from the *sick model,* which proposes that a client's thinking, values, and attitudes are wrong and therefore must be changed, and from the *medical model,* which purports that the cause of the problem is an illness located in the patient.

Satir developed games to deal with the family's behavior when family members operate within these three models. All family members are present during the family counseling process, including the games.

## The Simulated Family Game

In the simulated family game, various family members simulate each other's behavior; for example, the son plays the mother. The therapist may also ask family members to pretend that they are a different family. Following this enactment, the counselor and family members discuss how they differ from or identify with the roles.

## Systems Games

Systems games are based on either open or closed family systems; learning and insight can be obtained from both family types. Satir believed that emotional and behavioral disturbances result directly from a member's being caught in a closed family system. The closed system does not allow any individual the right to honest self-expression. The family views differences as dangerous, and the overriding "rule" is to have the same values, feelings, and opinions. In the open-system family, honest expression and differences are received as natural occurrences, and open negotiation resolves such differences by "compromise," "agreeing to disagree," "taking turns," or finding win–win solutions.

One set of games entails having family members take roles revolving around the five interactional patterns of behavior discussed earlier: (1) the placater, (2) the blamer, (3) the distractor, (4) the computer, and (5) the leveler. On the basis of these interactional patterns, various games have been constructed.

1. *Rescue game.* Behaviors 1, 2, 3, and 4 are played. Who plays each role is variable, but each member must remain in this role throughout the session.

2. *Coalition game.* Behaviors 1 and 2 are played. Two people always disagree and gang up on a third person.

3. *Lethal game.* Behavior 1 is used. Everyone agrees.

4. *Growth vitality game.* Each person includes himself or herself and others by honest expression and by permitting others to express themselves (leveling).

These techniques can be broadened beyond the initial family triad by incorporating all family members into a prescribed family situation and assigning various roles to each member. These sessions are vital for younger children who have been ruled by the adage "Children should be seen but not heard." The games aid families in understanding the nature of their own family system. They also allow family members to experience new interactional patterns through identification of their current behavior and insight into possible alternatives. By using the growth vitality game and the leveling role, families can experience movement from a pathological system of interaction to a growth-producing one.

## Communication Games

These games are aimed at establishing communication skills. Satir believed that an insincere or phony message is almost impossible to deliver if the communicator has skin contact, steady eye contact, or both forms of contact with the listener. One communication game involves having two members sit back to back while they talk. Next they are turned around and instructed to stare into each other's eyes without talking or touching. Satir (1967) reported that this type of interaction leads to many insights concerning the assumptions that each makes about the other's thoughts and feelings. Next, the participants continue to stare and then touch each other without talking. This process continues in steps until each partner is talking, touching, and "eyeballing" the other. Assuming these positions, they are asked to disagree, which Satir found was nearly impossible. People either enjoy the effort or are forced to pull back physically and divert their eyes to get angry.

The counselor's role is an important part of these games. Throughout and after each session, the counselor intervenes and discusses each member's responses, feelings, and gut reactions to himself or herself and to other family members.

## The Counselor's Role

In Satir's approach to family counseling, the counselor is a facilitator who gives total commitment and attention to the process and the interactions. The counselor does not take charge and must be careful not to manipulate the participants' reactions and verbalizations. By careful and sensitive attention to each family member's interactions, transactions, and responses (or lack of responses), the counselor can intervene at certain points to ask whether the messages are clear and correct and how a particular person is feeling. Each person thus has a chance to interact or make corrections. For example, the counselor might interrupt the dialogue when one person makes a statement about how another feels or thinks by asking the second person if the statement is accurate and how he or she feels at that moment.

In short, the counselor intervenes to assist leveling and taking responsibility for one's own actions and feelings. The counselor also intervenes to give quieter family members permission to talk and be heard. Analyzing a present interaction in the counseling setting should help family members understand past hurts and problems. Understanding what patterns produced the trouble also helps family members. With experience in openness and leveling, family members can change their communication, and growth can occur. The family is then better able to continue the discussions, come to new insights, and implement appropriate changes.

## CASE STUDIES

People's ability to assume other roles in the family group situation supports the idea that people can change their response roles and that families can change their ways of interacting and solving problems. Family members need to learn to share both positive and negative feedback in ways that do not hurt or belittle others. The following is a family role-play transcript in which the leveling response is omitted:

> *Don [father/husband, blaming]:* Why isn't our dinner ready?
>
> *Sandy [mother/wife, blaming]:* What are you yelling about? You've got as much time as I have.
>
> *Bill [son, blaming]:* Aw, shut up. You two are always yelling. I don't want any dinner, anyway.
>
> *Don [blaming]:* You keep your trap shut. I'm the one who makes the rules around here because I'm the one who pays the bills.
>
> *Sandy [blaming]:* Says who? Besides, young man, keep your nose out of this.
>
> *Don [placating]:* Maybe you'd like to go out to dinner for a change?
>
> *Sandy [computer]:* According to the last issue of *Woman's Day,* they say eating out is cheaper than cooking the same things at home.
>
> *Don [placating]:* Whatever you would like to do, Dear.
>
> *Bill [placating]:* You always have good ideas, Mother.
>
> *Sandy [computer]:* That's right. I have a list of the restaurants offering specials this week.

Perhaps one good leveling response by any of the family members could have helped these short exchanges. Perhaps Sandy could have said that she needed a rest from a long, hard day and would like to have dinner out. Don could have made a statement rather than asking a phony question. Perhaps a leveling remark by Don might have informed Sandy that he was wondering what she wanted to do about dinner tonight. Bill could have changed his remark to "I really worry when we argue and fight in this family, and I would like this to stop." The counselor's job is to rehearse these leveling responses until the problem is solved in the role-playing setting and then make plans to try the leveling response in real life.

In a second family session with the counselor present, the Frazier family is seated clockwise around the counselor: Jody, the wife–mother, 43 years old; Frank, the 11-year-old son; Larry, the husband–father, 44 years old; Joyce, the 14-year-old daughter; and Kathy, the 16-year-old daughter.

*Kathy:*   Mom, just say yes or no. Am I going to be allowed to go out on week-days or not?

*Jody:*   Why don't you do what you want? You always do anyway.

*Counselor [to Kathy]:*   How does this make you feel?

*Kathy:*   Angry. I'd like to be able to do what the rest of the kids are doing, but I know Mom and Dad don't approve.

*Counselor:*   That sounds funny because I heard your mom say it was up to you. [To Jody] Is that what you said? Maybe it was the expression on your face and the way you spoke your message to Kathy that made her think you didn't really mean "Do what you want to do."

*Kathy:*   Yes, her stern face said "no."

*Counselor:*   What did she do with her face to tip you off?

*Kathy:*   Well, she squinted her eyes and wrinkled up her nose.

*Counselor:*   It's hard to read your mom's mind, but I am guessing that she thinks nobody listens to her very much. We can check this with her later. But I'm wondering if you have ever felt this way.

*Kathy:*   Sometimes.

*Counselor [to Jody]:*   Do you ever have this feeling?

*Jody:*   I think maybe we've hit on something new.

*Counselor:*   Do you think no one listens to you?

*Jody:*   I have a rough day just keeping house for this family. Larry comes home from work too tired to talk, and all I ever talk to the children about are their fights and arguments. I have to handle all the family problems.

*Larry:*   Well, my job is all I can handle.

*Jody:*   See, no one listens to my side of the story.

*Counselor [to Larry]:*   Were you aware of what Jody was saying when she said that? What did it feel like, Larry?

*Larry:*   It irritates me that everybody thinks it's my fault that things don't go better in our family.

*Counselor:*   Hold it one minute. Frank is doing something over here.

*Larry [to Frank]:*   Settle down over there and shape up.

*Counselor:*   Let's take some time out and find out what's going on with Frank. I haven't been paying much attention to Frank and Joyce. [To Frank] How did you feel about what was going on over here?

*Frank:*   Well, I, uh. . . .

*Joyce [blaming Frank]:*   You weren't even paying attention.

*Kathy:*   Frank, if you move over here with me, we can get along better.

*Jody [to Larry]:*   Can't you do anything to make him mind me? It's all your fault he acts like he does.

*Counselor [to Kathy and Larry]:*   An interesting thing happened before Frank started acting up. I was wondering, Kathy, how you felt when your father said to your mother, "It's all my fault that things don't go better in our family."

In this short segment, the counselor attempts to look at present communication patterns and the feelings these patterns conceal. After achieving awareness of the communication blocks, the family can begin to practice leveling as an alternative way of communicating.

Virginia Satir's method could fit very well into a systems, structural, or communications approach for counseling families. She focused on developing better family communication by making family members aware of how others in the family react to their communication styles. Satir saw improved communication skills as leading to better family conflict resolution and problem solving.

Shortly before her death, Satir contributed to an article on family reconstruction and sculpting in group counseling (Satir, Bittner, & Krestensen, 1988). The therapists created a drama around each group member, with members starring in their own dramas. Scripts for each drama were developed from family maps, family life fact chronologies, and the family wheel of influence. Core moments of each member's family drama were reenacted in a psychodrama with group members as family players in the drama. Role players enacted verbal and nonverbal behaviors of the family members in each person's family.

## PLAY THERAPY WITH FAMILIES

Play therapy has the advantage of helping children communicate their story to the therapist. Engaging the family in play therapy activities offers a rich observational field for evaluating the family system in action. A principal therapeutic effect from play therapy is the opportunity to help children move from dysfunctional enmeshment with a parent to functional individualization. Likewise, overly rigid family boundaries might be relaxed to allow for a healthy sense of family cohesion. Similar breakthroughs in family therapy with children have been reported for storytelling, art therapy, and outdoor adventure programs.

Interventions combining family and play therapy have been used in prevention programs in elementary schools (McDonald & Morgan, 1997) and in working with the difficulties of alcoholism (Carmichael & Lane, 1997). Gladding (1993) encouraged families to play but in a manner that is fair, tolerant, and trusting. His admonition was to set up cooperative play environments where everyone shares and wins. Several theorists have provided models for promoting that type of play therapy with families.

## Dynamic Family Play Therapy

Harvey (1997) explained dynamic family play therapy. This type of play therapy engages family members in creative activity by using natural play. The counselor's goal is to help the family develop and increase spontaneity. Creating metaphors about the difficulties in relationships is another goal. In this style of family play therapy, a counselor uses art, drama, movement, and video making to encourage family play. As family members engage in creative play moments, the counselor guides them into initiating interactive play in which metaphors emerge. The metaphors help them experience a mutual catharsis, understanding, and sense of mastery in their experiences with each other.

By helping family members engage in play, counselors help families develop or restart their own natural play with each other. Over the progression of therapy, painful and conflicting issues emerge through the play. Counselors can guide family members to generate the naturally creative playful spirit that will produce trust and affiliation. Then counselors can focus on the content of play to help family members reconstruct their relationships. The counselor begins by issuing directive activities such as tug-of-war, scribble war, or follow-the-leader. The counselor remains alert to avoidance, interference, and resistance. The family members evolve into more elaborate and flexible interactions, eventually developing their own unique style of play episodes (Harvey, 1997).

## Filial Therapy

Filial therapy is a play therapy method in which the parents are directly involved. Filial therapy is based on the principles of child-centered therapy. Guerney (1997) believed that children's adjustment problems were caused by parents' failing to learn how to understand their children. She defined these problems as learning problems and thought that teaching parents to conduct child-centered play sessions might overcome parental shortcomings. Parents are so important to their children that she felt acceptance from them would be extremely meaningful for their children.

The goals of filial therapy are to reduce the children's problem behaviors, to help parents gain the skills of the child-centered play therapists to use when relating to their children, and to improve the parent–child relationship. Using learning theory and behavioral therapy for the parent training principles, the training proceeds by completing the following steps:

1. Introduce parents to methods for conducting client-centered play therapy.

2. Consider the other demands of parents' lives, and assure them they are expected to practice these skills only in the play sessions.

3. Model the behaviors as complete tasks. Wachtel (2001) sees the counselor's role as coaching and modeling helpful parent interactions and behaviors with the child. For example, having parents say, " I am noticing how you are helping yourself to not be scared" rather than "You were brave" promotes more positive self-esteem in the child.

4. Reduce each task to small, separate components and practice each component.

5. Reassemble the complete tasks and role-play without children.

6. Encourage parents to conduct sessions observed by the counselor or held at home and reported to the counselor.

7. Gradually increase the length of the sessions and have home play weekly.

As in child-centered play therapy, the child is encouraged to express his or her needs, thoughts, and feelings. Optimally, during the process children and parents perceive each other in a more positive light as they learn how to play and talk together more effectively.

## Strategic Family Play Therapy

Ariel (1997) explained strategic family play therapy as a form of counseling in which all family members and the counselor play. The play is free, imaginative, and make-believe. Toys, costumes, and props may or may not be used. Ariel reported that strategic family play therapy has been practiced successfully with a wide range of problems and is applicable to families of various cultural and social backgrounds.

Ariel (1997) continued by describing the integrated theory that is based on information processing and the theory of signs. The hypothesis is that the processing of information is aided if the information is associated with the person's central emotions. The information related to the central emotion will be overrepresented in make-believe play, allowing the counselor and player an arena for addressing the themes of the intense emotions. Make-believe play is a moderator, helping family members conduct their transactions and conflicts in a nonthreatening way. The family initiates its play themes, and the counselor then watches and tries to identify unhealthy interactions. Next, the counselor begins play moves, weaving into the family's play but gently steering the activity in well-chosen directions. Those choices are based on the curative properties of play, or what Ariel calls "bug-busters" because they remove or weaken the difficulties in the family's programs.

## Theraplay

Theraplay is a treatment method modeled after the healthy parent–child interaction. Koller and Booth (1997) explain this intensive, short-term approach as a therapy in which parents are involved as observers and then as cotherapists. Jernberg (1993) distinguished theraplay from other approaches by noting it is playful, requiring no toys and few props. The person using this approach avoids questions and focuses on health. The adult structures the sessions, and physical contact is encouraged. The agenda of the sessions is designed to meet the child's needs, encouraging regression and enhancing the parent–child attachment. Theraplay integrates the elements of structure, challenge, intrusion/engagement, and nurture. Theraplay employs activities that require building trust between children and their parents through physical touch and caring. Some examples are holding hands with the child and looking into the child's eyes, having the child jump off a chair into the parent's arms, and trust falls, which require children to fall backward, trusting that the parents will be there to catch them. Other activities could include playing patty-cake and stacking hands (putting one hand on top of the other, alternating between the parent's and child's hands). The adult enforces structure by clearly stating safety rules.

## CROSS-CULTURAL APPLICATIONS OF FAMILY COUNSELING

Richeport-Haley (1998) pointed out that many different cultures are represented in the United States and that counselors are finding many of these people coming to their offices for family counseling. So, in addition to understanding psychopathology, counselors need to familiarize themselves with the customs, styles, symbols, and standards of behavior of these diverse groups. Family counselors are not expected to become experts on all cultures, but rather, as mentioned in Chapter 15, they can be open to understanding the uniqueness of every family they counsel, how that family's behavior matches its culture, and how it adapts to American culture.

Yaccarino (1993) presented some helpful guidelines for adapting structural family therapy to families from different cultures. Using Italian American families as an example, he detailed several points defining family norms for this culture. For example, individuality is secondary to family obligations; family roles are clearly defined, with the husband–father earning the money, wife–mother maintaining the home, and children working to help with the family finances; and acceptance by the family is a measure of one's accomplishment. He described Italian American families as tending toward enmeshment, which could support unhealthy symptoms within the family system.

As with any counseling method, family therapists must have thorough knowledge of cultural family norms and communication patterns to be effective in their assessment and treatment of families from unfamiliar cultures. Tamura and Lau (1992) made many of these same points in their research of Japanese families, as did Szapocznik, Kurtines, Santisteban, and Rio (1990) with Hispanic families, Soto-Fulp and Delcampo (1994) with Mexican American families, and Becvar and Becvar (2000) with African American families. Jen Der Pan (2000) found Satir's model used in group counseling to be effective in working with Taiwanese college students who were experiencing family problems.

Richeport-Haley (1998) suggested two models available to family counselors for adapting treatment to multicultural differences. The first model is the directive family approach developed by Jay Haley and based on the work of his mentor, Milton H. Erickson. Focusing on the structural changes within the family, the directive approach minimizes ethnicity as a factor for change in therapy. The directive approach encourages behaviors that help the family to become mainstream with their new culture within the context of their cultural belief system. The example given was a couple new to the United States from a culture where the husband is the breadwinner of the home. The wife finds a better job than the husband, which causes a conflict between the two. The family counselor's role is to know how to intervene to resolve the conflict. The key is to reframe the situation with respect to the clients' roots and solve the problem without molding the couple to behave like the dominant culture.

Richeport-Haley's (1998) second model is a culture-focused approach in which counselors train in cultural sensitivity. Having completed the training, the counselor has four options when faced with clients holding an alternate belief system.

Option 1 is to minimize the alternate belief system. If a couple moves to the United States from a country where wife beatings are the norm, the legal system can be involved to stop the violence. New and legal behaviors can be practiced during counseling without using the alternate belief system.

Option 2 is to use parts of the alternate belief system. One East Indian couple believed they were being followed by an evil spirit. Working with the couple's belief in spirits, the counselor was able to change the meaning of the spirit from evil to good.

Option 3 is the referral of the client to a recognized healer.

Option 4 is collaborating with the healer to bring about needed change.

With the possible exception of Option 1, the first model seems to offer the chance for helping families from diverse cultures to adapt to American culture. Perhaps the cultural training combined with the directive model offers the best option available to counselors for meeting the cross-cultural challenge.

## FAMILY COUNSELING AND MANAGED HEALTH CARE

Practitioners of family counseling will do well under managed care if they use approaches that meet the managed care guidelines listed in Chapter 2. Short-term family counseling will find favor with managed care organizations (MCOs) if it helps clients reach specific, measurable goals in 10 to 15 sessions. Goal attainment at termination and maintenance of goal attainment at follow-ups are important criteria, as well as client satisfaction and low cost of treatment (Anderson, 2000).

Lee (1997) and Nichols and Schwartz (1998) observed that the limited mental health coverage under managed care has resulted in the rush to short-term therapy. They favored solution-focused brief family therapy because, as mentioned in Chapter 5, the focus is on finding solutions and gives minimal attention to defining or understanding threatening problems. The goal is to help clients do something different by changing their interactive behaviors or their interpretations of behaviors and situations to develop a solution. The paradoxical strategies mentioned in Chapter 5, as well as reality therapy, rational-emotive-behavior therapy, cognitive-behavior therapy, and behavioral methods, could be employed in family counseling and meet managed care guidelines.

In general, MCOs favor working with the entire family to remediate causes of problems and to prevent future problems. Remediation and prevention limit future costs. In cases in which the MCO covers only individual counseling, it is recommended that the counselor treat the identified client while using the rest of the family members as consultants.

## SUMMARY

Although this chapter is focused on differences between the schools and proponents of the various family therapies, similarities do exist. First, all agree that families are like engines with interdependent parts. When one part malfunctions, the total engine is adversely affected; that is, one malfunction may cause other parts to break down as well. For lasting behavior change, therefore, the entire family may need to change. Second (to change the analogy), the family is like a canoe floating downstream—that is, maintaining its balance only because one member of the family is leaning way out over the right side and two other members are tilted slightly to the left. In other words, the canoe *is* balanced, but uncomfortably so. The goal of family therapy is to relieve the pain by finding a more comfortable balance without upsetting the canoe. Families often say, "Stabilize us, but do not change anything." Third, to bring about successful change, the counselor may need to tip the canoe; the counselor's job is to ensure that the emergency process is a safe one. Fourth, all family therapy approaches borrow heavily from the material discussed in the previous chapters, as well as from sources outside this book. Once again, as with other theories, eclectic and integrative themes continue in the current literature on family therapy. Family therapy has branched out to include more nontraditional problems, including delinquency, anxiety disorders, schizophrenia, mood disorders, family violence, family abuse, and addictive disorders. Traditionally, family therapists had been mainly concerned with marital, sexual, and child concerns. Storytelling helps the family talk about the painful topics that are disrupting the continuation of the larger family story. Loss of a family member through death or divorce is a painful event that is difficult to talk about, yet talking is a great healing method.

Storytelling can provide the means to speak the unspeakable. Many therapists use storytelling to assess the family system before and after treatment; people think in metaphors and in storytelling formats, and, as we all know, people listen better to stories than to lectures. Riley (1993) made some of the same points for art therapy as a means of illustrating the family story. From a social constructivist position, art therapy can be used to obtain each family member's invented reality of the family and the world. Art therapy can be a method of assessment, treatment, and evaluation. It provides an opening into unspoken thoughts, feelings, and perceptions and can be a bridge across cultural and perceptual boundaries.

An appropriate concluding statement for this chapter on family counseling is Satir's view of the family and the nature of people. Satir believed everyone had untapped potential and a need for growth and change. Families, viewed as incubators for people, could either block or facilitate the growth of their members.

## W E B S I T E S for Family Therapy

Allyn & Bacon, Family Therapy, Bowen
www.athealth.com
www.abacon.com/famtherapy/bowen.html
www.georgetownfamilycenter.org/pages/murraybowen.html

Family Re-Union website
www.familyreunion.org

Psychwatch
www.psychwatch.com

## W E B S I T E S for Family Parenting

Father's World—Resource for single fathers
www.fathersworld.com/fatherhood/index.html

Single Rose—Resource for single mothers
www.singlerose.com

Stepfamily Foundation—Info on successful stepparenting
www.stepfamily.org/content.html

www.aacap.org/web/aacap/info_families/index.htm
www.parent.net
www.positiveparenting.com
www.tnpc.com

## REFERENCES

Anderson, C. (2000). Dealing constructively with managed care: Suggestions from an insider. *Journal of Mental Health Counseling, 22,* 343–353.

Ariel, S. (1997). Strategic family play therapy. In K. O'Connor & L. M. Braverman (Eds.), *Play therapy theory and practice: A comparative presentation* (pp. 358–395). New York: Wiley.

Becvar, D., & Becvar, R. (2000). *Family therapy: A systemic integration.* Needham Heights, MA: Allyn & Bacon.

Bowen, M. (1976). Theory in the practice of psychotherapy. In P. J. Guerin Jr. (Ed.), *Family therapy: Theory and practice* (pp. 42–89). New York: Gardner.

Bowen, M. (1978). *Family therapy in clinical practice.* New York: Aronson.

Bowen, M. (1980). Preface. In E. A. Carter & M. Goldrick (Eds.), *A framework for family therapy* (p. xiii). New York. Gardner.

Carmichael, K. D., & Lane, K. S. (1997). Play therapy with children of alcoholics. *Alcoholism Treatment Quarterly, 15,* 43–52.

Chasin, R., Roth, S., & Bograd, M. (1989). Action methods in systemic therapy: Dramatizing ideal futures and reformed pasts with couples. *Family Process, 28,* 121–136.

Dattilio, F., & Bevilacqua, L. (2000). *Comparative treatments for relationship dysfunction.* New York: Springer.

DeShazer, S., & Molnar, A. (1984). Four useful interventions in brief family therapy. *Journal of Marital and Family Therapy, 10,* 297–304.

Erickson, M., & Zeig, J. (1985). The case of Barbie: An Erickson approach to the treatment of anorexia nervosa. *Transactional Analysis Journal, 15,* 85–92.

Gladding, S. T. (1993). The therapeutic use of play in counseling: An overview. *Journal of Humanistic Education and Development, 31,* 106–115.

Gottman, J. (1979). *Marital interaction: Experimental investigations.* New York: Academic Press.

Gottman, J. (1990). Finding the laws of close personal relationships. *Methods of Family Research, 1,* 249–263.

Gottman, J. (1994). *What predicts divorce?* Hillsdale, NJ: Lawrence Erlbaum.

Gottman, J., Notarius, C., Gonzo, J., & Markman, H. (1976). *A couple's guide to communication.* Champaign, IL: Research Press.

Guerney, L. (1997). Filial therapy. In K. O'Connor & L. M. Braverman (Eds.), *Play therapy theory and practice: A comparative presentation* (pp. 131–159). New York: Wiley.

Haley, J. (1973). *Uncommon therapy.* New York: Norton.

Haley, J. (1976). *Problem-solving therapy.* New York: Harper & Row.

Haley, J. (1984). *Ordeal therapy: Unusual ways to change behavior.* San Francisco: Jossey-Bass.

Harvey, S. (1997). Dynamic family play therapy: A creative arts approach. In K. O'Connor & L. M. Braverman (Eds.), *Play therapy theory and practice: A comparative presentation* (pp. 341–367). New York: Wiley.

Jen Der Pan, P. (2000). The effectiveness of structured and semistructured Satir model groups on family relationships with college students in Taiwan. *Journal for Specialists in Group Work, 25,* 305–318.

Jernberg, A. (1993). Attachment formation. In C. E. Schaefer (Ed.), *The therapeutic powers of play* (pp. 241–265). Northvale, NJ: Jason Aronson.

Koller, T. J., & Booth, P. (1997). Fostering attachment through family theraplay. In K. O'Connor & L. M. Braverman (Eds.), *Play therapy theory and practice: A comparative presentation* (pp. 204–233). New York: Wiley.

Lee, M. (1997). A study of solution-focused brief family therapy: Outcomes and issues. *American Journal of Family Therapy, 26,* 77–90.

Loeschen, S. (1998). *Systematic training in the skills of Virginia Satir.* Pacific Grove, CA: Brooks/Cole.

Lurn, W., Smith, J., & Ferris, J. (2002). Youth suicide intervention using the Satir model. *Contemporary Family Therapy, 10,* 139–159.

Madanes, C. (1981). *Strategic family therapy.* San Francisco: Jossey-Bass.

McDonald, L., & Morgan, A. (1997). Families and schools together (FAST): Integrating community development with clinical strategies. *Families in Society, 78,* 140–156.

Minuchin, S. (1967). *Families of the slums.* New York: Basic Books.

Minuchin, S. (1974). *Families and family therapy.* Cambridge, MA: Harvard University Press; London: Tavistock.

Minuchin, S. (1978). *Psychosomatic families.* Cambridge, MA: Harvard University Press.

Minuchin, S. (1984). *Family kaleidoscope.* Cambridge, MA: Harvard University Press.

Nichols, M. P., and Schwartz, R. C. (1998). *Family therapy: Concepts and methods* (4th ed.). New York: Allyn & Bacon/Longman.

Richeport-Haley, M. (1998). Ethnicity in family therapy: A comparison of brief strategic therapy and culture-focused therapy. *American Journal of Family Therapy, 26,* 77–90.

Riley, R. (1993). Illustrating the family story: Art therapy, a lens for viewing the family's reality. *Arts in Psychotherapy, 20,* 253–264.

Satir, V. (1967). *Conjoint family therapy: A guide to theory and technique* (Rev. ed.). Palo Alto, CA: Science and Behavior Books.

Satir, V. (1971, January). Conjoint family therapy. In G. Gazda (Ed.), *Proceedings of a symposium on family counseling and therapy* (pp. 1–14). Athens: University of Georgia.

Satir, V. (1972). *Peoplemaking.* Palo Alto, CA: Science and Behavior Books.

Satir, V., & Baldwin, M. (1983). *Step by step.* Palo Alto, CA: Science and Behavior Books.

Satir, V., Bittner, J., & Krestensen, K. (1988). Family reconstruction: The family within— a group experience. *Journal for Specialists in Group Work, 13,* 200–208.

Satir, V., Stachowiak, J., & Taschman, H. (1975). *Helping families to change.* New York: Tiffany.

Simon, R. (1984, November–December). Stranger in a strange land. *Family Networker,* 21–31, 66–68.

Soto-Fulp, S., & Delcampo, R. (1994). Structural family therapy with Mexican-American family systems. *Contemporary Family Therapy, 16,* 349–361.

Szapocznik, J., Kurtines, W., Santisteban, D., & Rio, A. (1990). Interplay of advances between theory, research, and application in treatment interventions aimed at behavior problem children and adolescents. *Journal of Consulting and Clinical Psychology, 58,* 696–703.

Tamura, T., & Lau, A. (1992). Connectedness versus separateness: Applicability of family therapy to Japanese families. *Family Process, 31,* 319–338.

Thomas, M. (1992). *An introduction to marital and family therapy.* New York: Merrill (Macmillan).

Todd, T. (2000). Solution-focused strategic parenting of challenging teens: A class for parents. *Family Relations, 49,* 165–168.

Wachtel, E. (2001). *Fostering resiliency through child-in-family therapy.* www.athealth.com/practitioner/newsletter/fpn_4_3l.html. Retrieved September 8, 2002.

Yaccarino, M. (1993). Using Minuchin's structural family therapy techniques with Italian-American families. *Contemporary Family Therapy, 15,* 459–466.

# Chapter 13

# Personality Type

*Zelma Lansford, Ed.D.*

*We should spend less time ranking children and more time helping them to identify their natural competencies and gifts and cultivate these. There are hundreds and hundreds of ways to succeed and many, many different abilities that will help you get there.*
—Howard Gardner

## CARL JUNG

Carl Jung (1875–1961) was born in a small village in Switzerland. The oldest surviving son of a Swiss Reformed pastor and a mother who suffered from "nervous disorders," Jung described himself as a solitary child. Possibly because of his parents' marital problems, young Carl and his father shared a bedroom. As an adult, Jung recalled being frightened by strange, mysterious noises coming from his mother's bedroom during the night. These sounds probably led to his having nightmares and may have contributed to his interest in understanding dreams as a part of his study in later years.

From the age of 11 until he completed medical school, the Jung family lived in Basel. With diverse interests and a solid background in Latin and the classics, young Carl completed his third year of medical school, pursuing interests in surgery and internal medicine. When making the decision for specialization, limited finances and a couple of occult experiences piqued his interests in psychopathology. Jung's professors were disappointed in his decision to jeopardize his potential as a physician in favor of what they believed was the absurd field of psychiatry. Despite a lack of professional respect for the domain at that time, Jung accepted his first professional appointment as an assistant at Europe's famous Burgholzi Mental Hospital in Zurich. Jung never worked in general medicine. Instead, he taught at the University of Zurich and later developed an extensive private psychiatric practice.

378

For a number of years, Jung enjoyed a close personal relationship with Sigmund Freud. After Jung's publication of *The Psychology of Dementia Praecox* (schizophrenia) in 1906, Freud invited Jung and his wife to visit him in Vienna. This visit led to several years of collegial exchange between the two. In one of his frequent letters to Jung, Freud referred to Jung as his adopted son and indicated that he wanted Jung to be his successor to carry on the devotion to his theories. Freud insisted that Jung take the leadership role of the International Psychoanalytic Association and become its first president. Jung, however, became increasingly frustrated by Freud's insistence on the central importance of infantile sexuality. Storr (1983) held that while Freud believed neurosis was invariably rooted in early childhood as a result of incestuous fantasies and desires connected with the Oedipus complex, Jung thought that the cause of neurosis usually lay in the present. He held that the infantile fantasies that Freud detected were secondary phenomena.

The publication of Jung's *Symbols of Transformation,* in which he publicly disagreed with Freud, led to a heated debate during the Fourth Psychoanalytical Congress in Munich in 1912. Freud insisted that the symbol was a distorted expression of inner, unconscious thoughts and was created out of the experience and environment of the individual, whereas Jung believed that the symbol was the psyche's mechanism for transporting information. Although this disagreement contributed to their conflict, Jung's growing dissatisfaction with making "dogma" of childhood sexuality against Freud's insistence on complete obedience was probably the root of their dispute. Accounts of Jung's observations of the relationship between Freud and his wife and Freud and his wife's sister could lead to speculation that Freud's obsession with sex might have been influenced by his "very intimate" relationship with his sister-in-law (Campbell, 1971). In any event, Jung was not a yes man who could be content as a passive advocate for someone else's ideas. Instead, he was flexible, open-minded, and a source of new ideas.

Jung made Zurich his home for most of his adult life. He married in 1903 and lived in a Zurich suburb. Later, he built a country retreat at the far end of Lake Zurich at Bollingen, where he sometimes saw patients but more often retreated to contemplate and write. Jung's use of his wife's money, his lifestyle, and his inference of the role of inherited characteristics have been criticized. However, he was a prolific writer and made numerous contributions to the field of psychology. He worked in the United States, lecturing and delving into Native Americans' religious stories and activities. He also traveled to Africa in pursuit of an understanding of spirituality and myths there. He spent many years in attempts to improve the methods of psychoanalysis, in exploration of humans' inner world, and in advocacy of an improved quality of life through self-understanding.

Perhaps because his writing style is not easily read, or because of his interest in mysticism, Jung's work was not totally appreciated during his lifetime. In the 1980s and 1990s, partly because of the work of Isabel Myers, Katharine Briggs, Joseph Campbell, and others, there was a resurgence of interest in Jung's ideas and his concepts of how personality is defined by preferences and type.

# THE NATURE OF PEOPLE

Jung's view of the nature of people is reflected in his statement that "the sole purpose of human existence is to kindle a light in the darkness of mere being" (Jung, 1961, p. 326). Jung's expansion of Freud's concepts indicated a more positive view of mankind. Freud was a proponent of the scientific concept of *causality*—the idea that everything has a cause. Jung did not reject Freud's attempt to point to the cause of a person's present difficulty in childhood trauma, but he expanded the idea with an orientation of *teleology*—meaning that present behavior is determined by future goals, as well as past events. Although Jung respected the person's past, his reason for not relying on the causal component alone may be found in his reluctance to leave the person with feelings of despair and a sense of being a prisoner of past traumas. He suggested that this concept of teleology can stabilize the present by helping people gain hope in a future they can create, free of the past. He indicated, "I am neither spurred on by excessive optimism nor in love with high ideals, but am merely concerned with the fate of the individual human being—that infinitesimal unit on whom a world depends, and in whom, if we read the meaning of the Christian message aright, even God seeks his goal" (Jung, 1967b, p. 305).

# THEORY OF COUNSELING

After an original association with the Freudian school of psychoanalysis, Jung developed his own system of psychoanalysis, calling it *analytical psychology* and utilizing a variety of theories and methods. It is for this reason that there is no standard Jungian therapy approach. Instead, Jung indicated, "The more deeply we penetrate the nature of the psyche, the more the conviction grows upon us that the diversity, the multidimensionality of human nature, requires the greatest variety of standpoints and methods in order to satisfy the variety of psychic dispositions" (Jung, 1967c, p. 9). One of Jung's major contributions to psychology was through the introduction of new concepts and variations on terms used earlier, which led to increased understanding. The following topics outline the major components of Jungian theory.

## Psyche

Jung used the term psyche to describe the part of the personality that embodies thoughts, feelings, and behaviors—both conscious and unconscious. He did not accept the idea that personality is acquired piece by piece and that one's quest must be to attain wholeness. Instead, Jung believed that humans are born whole but that circumstances sometimes cause an erosion of that whole. He believed that the work of the psychoanalyst was to help patients recover their lost wholeness, strengthen their psyche, and enable the person to face future problems without any threat to loss of the whole.

## Psychic Energy

Jung differed from Freud's belief regarding the libido as representing only sexual drive. He expanded the concept to represent the energy through which the work of the personality is performed. Storr (1983) described Jung's view of the libido as follows:

> When the natural course of a man's development through life was held up, either by misfortune or by his failure to face life's obligations, his libido became turned in upon himself and reactivated the attitudes and feelings of childhood which would normally have been left behind him. (p. 17)

Although he could not prove it, Jung strongly suspected a reciprocal action between physical and psychic energies. He thought that it is possible for psychic energy to become physical energy and vice versa.

## Consciousness

The term consciousness refers to a part of the psyche that is known to the person. Jung developed the concept of four mental functions within the consciousness that he called *thinking, feeling, sensing,* and *intuiting.* In addition, he developed the idea that there are two attitudes that determine orientation of the consciousness, *extroversion* and *introversion.* While Jung believed that all people use these functions and attitudes, the levels to which they consciously use them lead to what he called *individuation,* a process by which uniqueness is attained. He believed that the goal of individuation should be to know oneself as completely as possible. Jung concluded that the process of achieving individuation through the consciousness led to a new element—the *ego.*

## The Personal Unconscious

Jung believed that experiences that did not gain recognition by the ego do not disappear from the psyche but are stored in an adjoining level of the mind—the unconscious. They are available to the consciousness when the ego allows them to pass into greater awareness. Again, this concept emphasizes Jung's concept of the ego as the gatekeeper or the manager of the personality.

## The Ego

In a refinement from Freud, Jung used the term ego to describe the organization of information, feelings, memories, and perceptions. Jung determined that the ego acts as a gatekeeper to the consciousness, and unless the ego acknowledges the approach of a new idea, thought, feeling, memory, or perception, it cannot be brought into consciousness. It is probably for this reason that some people are described as being not really "open to new ideas." Their egos become very selective gatekeepers, not allowing many new ideas to pass into their consciousness. According to Jung, the ego provides identity to the personality through the selection and elimination of any material that is not consistent with the personality and might be too overwhelming.

Jung believed that the dominant function (thinking, feeling, sensing, or intuition) is a major determiner of what the ego gatekeeper will allow to penetrate the consciousness. In essence, if the person has a dominant function for sensing, when facts are presented at the gate, the ego will probably allow them into the consciousness, especially if they are from a very strong experience. Thus, the ego gatekeeper for the sensing preference is likely to be more open to facts, details, and concrete data than for concepts or big-picture ideas. For example, a social studies teacher who is presenting material about the American colonists' decision to separate from England will capture the attention of the sensing types by showing the children a copy of the Declaration of Independence and quotations from what the colonists were saying. The teacher will point to the signatures and talk about the bravery of the men who signed the document. A picture of Thomas Jefferson and information about his role, followed by a look at Independence Hall in Philadelphia and the activities that led up to the declaration on July 4, 1776, will help to captivate the interests of the sensors. The teacher will then emphasize the effect that this document had on the British, their reaction to it, and the reaction of the rest of the world. At this point, the instructor has also achieved comprehension for the intuiting types. Their preference for understanding the whole or the context may mean that their gatekeeper is not fully open to this new information until it can be put into the setting of the world in 1776. The facts of "life, liberty, and the pursuit of happiness" enter through the gate when they fit the whole.

The youthful ego seems to be a gatekeeper who enjoys swinging on the gate to welcome new information, feelings, and perceptions into consideration. If at first the ego does not allow new information to enter, it is also capable of reversing its decision and reevaluating the situation. This is an enormous opportunity for parents, teachers, counselors, and other adults to encourage openness to new learning in the young child. By ensuring psychological safety and security, adults can increase the child's ego strength in managing the personality and widen the child's view to new learning and new experiences.

## The Ego Gatekeeper

Jung also believed that anxiety can increase the ego's intensity, thereby decreasing the ego's openness. In popular parlance, the term *ego* is often used to describe someone whose anxiety or lack of individuation keeps ideas and experiences away by limiting the amount of new material from the consciousness and thereby protects and allows the person to cling to a preferred image of the self. Obviously, to persuade the ego gatekeeper to be open to a new idea or action, it is essential to avoid confronting the ego with anything that might cause anxiety or threaten the image it is protecting. Sometimes in interactions, it is easy to see that another person is becoming defensive about what is being said. This defensiveness arises from the ego's attempt to "defend" the gatekeeping position and resist letting any information through that might not fit with the concepts and ideas that are already embedded in the consciousness. To avoid evoking this defensiveness requires some diplomacy and, usually, carefully chosen words to induce sufficient openness to achieve the purpose. This filtering to "save face" can result in denial of information and lead to faulty decision making, as demonstrated in the investigation of the 1986 explosion of the space shuttle *Challenger*. Despite considerable indication that the launch was risky, several of the engineers involved had ego gatekeepers that denied the validity of the information regarding a possible weather-related malfunction of an O-ring. For them, the ego gatekeeper attempted to avoid humiliation and put a good face on NASA's need to launch. Delving into historical events shows how the role of the ego gatekeeper prevented certain realities from entering the consciousness. It was unthinkable to King George III that the Americans should not comply with the rules for every British colony. With children, it is essential to help them avoid denial and, instead, to develop confidence, which allows the ego gatekeeper to become a wise and informed decision maker.

At times, the ego gatekeeper is more intent on consistency than on effectiveness. The gatekeeper ushers in only the facts and information that are consistent with what is already there, whereas sound decision making requires consideration of a wide range of facts and information to ensure effectiveness. The exclusion of any information that does not fit what already resides in the consciousness can result in a mistaken conclusion. Without any disagreeing facts or pertinent data, the easy conclusion is "This is correct." The results leave one being right but not effective! For example, "That dress is ugly" may be a factual statement. The observer may be right, but the communication is not effective. When the eighth-grader storms out of class saying, "Mr. Smith is boring!" the student may be correct, but the action results in time in detention. Mr. Smith may be a competent teacher, but his gatekeeper has led him to the erroneous conclusion that the current students are the same as those in past years. He may not have recognized the need to be effective in challenging a very bright student who seeks more advanced learning activities. Situations arise in the classroom almost daily where the ego gatekeeper can enable one to be *right*, but not *effective*.

## Complexes

Complexes was Jung's term for describing a large group of ideas or common experiences stored within the unconscious. Jung (1961) indicated that they "interfere with the intentions of the will and disturb the conscious performance; they produce disturbances of memory and blockages in the flow of associations" (p. 393). For example, if the child is bombarded over a period of time with numerous experiences and messages indicating incompetence, then anxiety and the ego will probably be protective and not allow the information to enter the consciousness. Although the information is repressed in the conscious, it is moved to the unconscious. While the child may be unaware of the information of "inferiority," its presence in the unconscious may hinder the child's normal life and may be observable in the child's actions. The child's lack of self-esteem may result in lower classroom performance and hesitance to try new experiences. Jung's view was that psychoanalysis could bring the information of the complexes into the conscious and dissolve it, freeing the person from the dysfunctional grip of this inferiority complex.

## Individuation

Jung used the metaphor of a plant to describe the growth of the individual psyche and ways each person becomes unique. The seed represents a "whole" that is capable of becoming balanced parts of the plant, adapted to specific needs: roots, stems, or leaves. He believed that each person is a whole with balance and unity. Jung's primary developmental concept was *individuation,* a process by which the person becomes a psychological individual, developing specific functions but remaining a balanced whole. This process of individuation takes place through expanding consciousness by knowing and understanding oneself as completely as possible. Jung believed that the purpose of psychotherapy was to help the person find balance and restore "wholeness" through increased self-knowledge. To expand the plant metaphor, the highly individuated person could be compared with a highly complex plant.

## Dreams

For Jung, dreams are the clearest path to the unconscious mind, since they are not under the influence of the will or consciousness. Whereas Freud analyzed single dreams, Jung also saw value in considering recurring themes or dreams in series. He did not believe in using a defined set of symbols to interpret dreams or a "dream dictionary" but preferred to consider the individual circumstances and the condition of the dreamer.

Jung believed that when people encountered difficulty in relationships with others, it would be reflected in their psyche; therefore, it could also be reflected in their dreams. By helping people uncover their internal disharmony, he hoped that the process could lead them toward improved external relationships. In children, frequent nightmares or frightening dreams may be an indication of abuse, trauma, or excessive fears—real or imagined.

## Progression and Regression

Using the term *progression* to refer to a person's psychological adaptation to daily experiences, Jung believed that *regression* describes the backward movement of the libido. He saw that by withdrawing into oneself and into earlier periods, one could possibly be pulled toward activating unconscious material.

## The Collective Unconscious

While his descriptions were somewhat limited by the science and technology of his time, Jung saw the brain as an evolutionary product of many generations of mutations. He saw the result as an increase in humans' chances of survival on the planet. Jung pioneered the idea that the mind is not solely the product of environmental experiences but also contained cumulative genetic contents.

## Archetypes

Jung (1967a) devoted much of the last half of his career to the study of archetypes, which he defined as unconscious images of "patterns of instinctual behavior" (p. 158). He described birth, rebirth, death, power, the hero, the child, the trickster, the demons, the wise old man, the earth mother, the mountains, the rivers, fire, and other objects as "endless repetition which has engraved experiences into the psyche as forms without content." They are not visual images in the mind but prototypes that represent the possibility of a certain type of perception or action. Jung believed that such archetypes are universal, with everyone inheriting the same basic archetypal images and parental and environmental influences determining the variations. Jung (1961) believed that the following four archetypes are a part of every human.

### The Self

A central focus of Jungian psychology is the concept of a total personality or psyche. Jung regarded the psyche as the central archetype in the collective unconscious. He did not believe that the self can become evident until middle age or when the personality is fully developed. Perhaps self-knowledge is the means to self-realization. One cannot fulfill oneself without fully knowing and understanding the self.

### The Anima

Jung called the *anima* the inward feminine side of the male psyche and the *animus* the inward masculine side of the female psyche. These terms describe the traits in both sexes that are not associated with gender. "Since the image is unconscious, it is always unconsciously projected upon the person of the beloved, and is one of the chief reasons for passionate attraction or aversion" (1967c, p. 391). Jung noted that Western civilization has placed value on behavior that is consistent with gender. His emphasis seemed to be not so much on the particular behavior as on the conflict produced by the expectation of conformity.

### The Shadow

An archetype of the same sex, the *shadow* includes everything in the psyche outside consciousness and contains more of a person's basic animal instincts than any other archetypes. For Jung, the shadow represents the hidden, repressed, guilt-laden part of the personality that resides in the unconscious.

### The Persona

Based on the description of a mask worn by an actor in a drama, Jung used the term persona to describe the display of a public facade for the purpose of gaining acceptance in society. He sometimes referred to it as the "conformity" archetype. The persona is a major asset in helping the individual interact with others. Difficulty arises, however, when the individual identifies more with the persona (mask) than with the whole self. The ego's identification with the persona is called *inflation,* thus the common expression "inflated ego" is used to describe one who has an exaggerated sense of self-importance as a facade.

References to an inflated ego have evolved into common usage and are often utilized to describe objectionable behaviors. The term *confident* generally describes one who knows and understands the potential and the limits of his or her abilities and skills. The term *inflated ego* implies an exaggerated sense of self-importance that is not based on a real estimation of abilities and skills. Instead, the facade connotes a fear of inferiority. It could be compared to a Hollywood set that appears to be a row of buildings to the movie camera but is really only a front with nothing behind the doors. Perhaps the facade, with its inflated ego, is an attempt to keep others from discovering that there is something lacking behind this "front." In its inflated state, the ego can never back up and admit a mistake. It is an inflated front that allows very little penetration of new information, only that which fits the fantasized picture of the self—the facade. Real achievement builds genuine confidence and does not seem to inflate the ego.

Fear of failure, a sense of inadequacy, insecurity, and/or abuse can cause the facade to be so inflated that the "ego gatekeeper" becomes a barrier to allowing any new information, ideas, or perceptions to go through the gate and into the conscious. Another hazard of the inflated ego is that it is more difficult to develop trust among people if one or more of them has an inflated ego. Others seem always to suspect the facade. Trust is usually invested only in people who appear to be real and genuine. Since it is difficult to trust someone without really knowing that person, a facade can become a barrier that prevents people from believing that they know and understand the real person. Obviously, a counselor's inflated ego would inhibit the bond that needs to be developed with the child for the counseling to be effective.

When teachers or counselors have inflated egos, they must use their facade of "knowing all of the answers." This can impede learning and effective relations with children. Self-doubt, fear of humiliation, and insecurity also seem to be ego inflators in children. The inflated ego in the child is often an indication of trauma or fear of inadequacy and should be explored by the astute counselor. Indicators of an inflated ego may be fanciful stories, exaggerated accounts of feats of accomplishment, or stories to conceal the child's real circumstances.

## Word Association

Sir Francis Galton had attempted to establish an intelligence test based upon verbal response speed. The subject would be told to respond to each of a series of words with the first word that came to mind. Of course, the test was of little use in determining intellectual capacity, but Jung found that a small adaptation could lend new usefulness. Jung conducted the test in a similar manner but noted response times and any delays. Often, the subjects were unaware of delays. Jung's probing revealed that the word had evoked an emotional response. Later, he studied the expression of emotion in the changes in pulse rate, breathing, and the electrical conductivity of the skin. Jung's work served as a forerunner to the development of the modern polygraph test.

## Psychological Types

Much of the early work of Freud and others in the field of psychology came through their experiences in mental hospitals and in work with abnormal patients. This was also true of Jung's early work. His ideas about type, however, were initiated by his study of people beyond the abnormal and formed a basis for later work, which would distinguish the concept of *type* and make it an especially useful concept for the general public. Jung described the origin of his ideas for writing *Psychological Types* in 1921 in his autobiographical work, *Memories, Dreams, Reflections* (1961).

> This work sprang originally from my need to define the ways in which my outlook differed from Freud and Adler's. In attempting to answer this question, I came across the problem of types; for it is one's psychological type which from the outset determines and limits a person's judgment. My book, therefore, was an effort to deal with various aspects of consciousness, the various attitudes the conscious mind might take toward the world, and thus constitutes a psychology of consciousness. . . . The book on types yielded the insight that every judgment made by an individual is conditioned by his personality type and that every point of view is necessarily relative. (p. 209)

In trying to understand his differences with Freud and Adler, Jung attempted to analyze the conflict between Adler and Freud in order to learn something to apply to his own break with Freud. He realized that his conflict with Freud, like Adler's with Freud, was not a simple matter of a difference of opinion. Instead, he recognized that both were fundamentally different approaches; therefore, he decided to demonstrate how both Freud's and Adler's theories could be applied to actual cases. He carried out this comparative study in great detail over a considerable period. This led to Jung's deduction that Adler's approach was largely internal—the attempt to overcome the childhood feelings of inferiority with feelings of power and superiority. In contrast, he saw Freud's approach as external in the child's response to the Oedipus complex and the child's attitude toward the parent of the opposite sex, coupled with a desire to displace the parent of the same sex. Jung saw these two approaches as the result of an orientation: Freud, the extrovert, was focused on the outer world and responses to it. Adler, the introvert, was focused on the inner world and its responses and reflections.

Kroeger and Thuesen (1988) disagreed with Jung and made a strong case for Freud's being an introvert. As indicated earlier, perhaps Freud's greatest contribution to psychology was his stimulation of others. His actual preference for introversion or extroversion is less important than the concept that his behavior inspired Jung to formulate.

As Jung thought about himself, he recognized that he was also an introvert; however, this concerned Jung as he realized how different he was from Adler. Musing on these differences led Jung to the realization that there are also two pairs of mental processes: *sensing* and *intuiting*, which relate to taking in and using information, along with *thinking* and *feeling*, which relate to drawing conclusions and making decisions. He realized that these are the "tools" for specific mental objectives. Jung continued to work on the development of these concepts for several years through observations of countless patients and other people. He refined and elaborated these conclusions, also developing the idea of *dominant* and *auxiliary* functions, in which there is greater reliance on one function over the others, and he ultimately published *Psychological Types* in 1921.

Although Jung's attempt to understand his differences with Freud was the catalyst for developing the concept, psychological types are a part of his larger theory that describes the progress of consciousness and how individual people have different pathways to development. Jung continued his analysis and research on types during the course of his work with patients. It is an incredibly complex theory that is merely summarized here. Jung's ideas about type were only partially accepted by several decades of psychologists. It was not until two women developed an application for Jung's complexity that his ideas could be implemented as a tool for establishing individual preferences and encouraging effective utilization of the diversity among people. It is helpful to consider this key to Jung's concept in working with parents, teachers, and one's own type. The key to using Jung with children is discussed later.

In 1942, a 44-year-old housewife, encouraged by her mother's interest in writing, began the development of an instrument that would become the key to applying Jung's concept that apparently random behavior is not really random but the result of inborn preferences. Because she wanted to pursue everyday behavior, she used everyday language, thus creating a very simple approach to a highly complex theory. Although she lacked the formal training needed for such research, Myers was a brilliant scholar who relentlessly pursued the knowledge necessary for her project. She had absorbed her father's scientific approach and her mother's devotion to Jung. Myers had accompanied her mother to a meeting with Jung in New York in 1937, when he was giving lectures at Yale University. She attempted a conference with Jung during a 1950 family trip to Switzerland. Unfortunately, Jung was ill at the time, and other subjects had supplanted his interest in type, but he wrote a kind letter to Myers, complimenting the Type Indicator and her work (Saunders, 1991). First published by Educational Testing Service (ETS) and then by Consulting Psychologists Press (CPP), the Myers-Briggs Type Indicator (MBTI), is available only to users who have been qualified through special training or who hold graduate degrees in psychology and related areas. This control is reflective of Myers's fear that the instrument might be misused, as when she saw a bank terminate all of its employees who indicated a preference for intuition, viewing them as troublemakers. Myers and Briggs's intent was that the MBTI would become a positive tool for helping people understand themselves and make better choices, thus improving their decisions. Myers also saw the potential for people to be more understanding and accepting, thus enhancing interpersonal interactions. Although attempts to classify personality date back to the ancient Greeks, interest in Jung's original concepts and perhaps the success of the MBTI have led to additional typology attempts. Because these aspects are something basic in the personality, it is not surprising that other authors have become alert to preferences and type. Although some offer intriguing insights and useful information, even comparing personalities to colors, the decades of research and solid validity of the MBTI makes it the first choice for applying Jung's concepts.

Energizing

Extrovert (E)————————————————|———————————————— Introvert (I)

Gathering Information and Attending

Sensing (S)————————————————|———————————————— Intuition (N)

Deciding

Thinking (T)————————————————|———————————————— Feeling (F)

Living

Judging (J)————————————————|———————————————— Perceiving (P)

## Myers-Briggs Type Indicator

What the mother and daughter were able to achieve was an application for Jung's idea that apparent "chance variation in human behavior is not due to chance; it is in fact the logical result of a few basic, observable *preferences*" (Myers & Mc-Caulley, 1985, p. 11). The MBTI is an inventory based on several assumptions, one of which is that people can give an indication of their preferences that combine to form *type,* directly or indirectly, on a self-report inventory. The questions in the MBTI have no intrinsic good or bad answers or right or wrong answers. The descriptions of type focus on what's right with people. This emphasis on normal and valuable differences makes the instrument especially useful in all kinds of situations, from counseling to education, because it gives the respondents a sense of worth and dignity concerning their own qualities. Many psychological instruments are constructed for the purpose of giving the counselor information about the client—intelligence, psychopathology, or career interests. Whereas most instruments give information back to the person who takes it through a qualified professional, the MBTI information is intended for the person using the Indicator, and complete results are given to the user. The MBTI is available at most career, college, and counseling centers, as well as in many business organizations. Web site addresses at the end of this chapter include qualified sources for using the MBTI and obtaining feedback. Myers and McCaulley (1985) described the purpose of the instrument as follows:

> The main objective of the MBTI is to identify four basic preferences. The indices EI, SN, TF, and JP are designed to point in one direction or the other. They are not designed as scales for measurement of traits or behaviors. . . . While letters indicate the *direction* of the preference, the number indicates the *strength* of the preference. (p. 3)

Myers liked to compare these preferences with the preference that most humans have for using one hand more than the other. People typically use both sides of each preference, although not with equal liking. Myers was adamant that there is no one best preference and no perfect score on the MBTI.

Jung, along with Myers and Briggs, gave special meaning to some words in their classifications. They are as follows:

*Energizing.* The attitude that determines how a person gets renewed psychic energy is called energizing.

Extrovert: Preference for drawing energy from people, the environment, and activities

Introvert: Preference for drawing energy from within, from internal concepts and ideas

*Extrovert* does not mean "talkative," and *introvert* does not mean "shy." Rather, this preference is an attitude that relates to gaining psychic energy or "reenergizing" from an external or internal world. It is observable in the individual's preference to "talk things out" (E) or "think things through before speaking" (I). Because of the focus for reenergizing, it may influence the way in which people prefer to socialize, but neither preference ensures or degrades one's ability to enjoy and be effective with people. For example, an introvert and an extrovert can go to a lively party and interact with many people, having an equally good experience. The introvert will go home and prefer to go straight to bed, exhausted from interacting with so many people. In contrast, the extrovert will go home and need to "unwind," feeling energized by all of the interactions with people. The same is true of children. John, an introvert, is a handsome 8-year-old, the son of an engineer and an artist. At school, John is reserved but talks about his science projects with excitement and animation. When he arrives home, however, John prefers time in his room to tinker with models or wander through the wooded area in the backyard before dinner. With the family, he happily takes his turn describing his day. The conversation follows the solitude John needs to reenergize after he has used energy in the many interactions of the school day. John's mother understands his need for some solitude and does not bombard him with questions or attempt extensive conversation when he first arrives from the school bus. Conversely, Jo, who is an extrovert, needs her mom's attention as soon as she opens the door. She is eager to tell her parents all about her social studies lesson and about the argument that she had on the playground. At home, she engages neighborhood friends for impromptu soccer and play. After dinner, she spends time alone reading, but only after some lively conversation with her parents and sibling. Introvert and extrovert reenergize differently.

*Attending.* Attending is the function of finding out, gathering, and taking in information.

> Sensing: The preference for taking in information through the senses—such as sight, touch, and hearing—leading to a focus on facts, the concrete, and the present
>
> Intuition: The preference for using the facts to make a bigger picture of what is visible beyond the information from the senses, to see connections and possibilities

A major influence on how people learn, accept new ideas, and take actions, the *sensing* (S) and *intuition* (N) preferences have an impact on the ego in its gatekeeper role. How the information is presented affects how readily the gate swings open or remains closed. This function is especially relevant in such situations as the classroom. Sensing types need details and specific facts, whereas those with a preference for intuition want to see the big picture and ways that the issue or event fits into the larger concept. To be effective, people need both the facts and details (S), along with the big picture (N). The attending function is not an either–or matter but rather which is considered first and on which greater reliance may be placed.

This preference for how one takes in information may have a significant influence on success in school. Since many educational institutions must be designed for facilitating the learning of large groups, rather than individuals, the learning preference of each student may or may not be accommodated. It is unfortunate that some children grow into adulthood with a self-concept based on their belief that they are not very smart. In reality, they may be very capable, but they may have had preferences for learning that were not accommodated by their schools. The sensor may be successful in a fact-based high school course where the concrete is emphasized—dates, places and specific facts—but be uncomfortable in a university course that emphasizes big-picture analysis.

In the United States, sensing types are in the majority, estimated to be about 65 to 70%. Sensing types learn best when material is based on experience and proceeds step-by-step with examples and hands-on experiences. Specific facts come easier than the connections between facts and their interpretation. The real is easier for sensors to learn than the symbolic. Intuitive types score somewhat higher on reading tests and appear to read more books. Intuitives are in the majority in programs for the "gifted."

Preference for learning style is related to sensory and intuitive ways of taking in information. This is only one example of how knowledge of type can support course selection. By matching one's preferred means of taking in information to area of study, it is possible to enhance success. Terry knew that he needed a minimum grade of B in history to maintain his college scholarship. He carefully researched the history professors who taught the course and obtained syllabi. Recognizing that one required knowledge of facts—"When did Columbus discover America? Describe the routes of each voyage"—while the other professor required comprehension of significance—"What effect did Columbus's voyage have upon Spain, and how did this period of discovery impact Western Europe?" Knowing that he was an INTP, Terry chose the latter professor to place himself in the best learning environment. Conversely, when such a choice is not possible, it can be reaffirming to understand why one must work harder. When Jamie, an ESTJ, took an art course in sculpture because he thought that he would find the construction and mechanical aspects interesting, he struggled and had to seek assistance with the design aspects. Although he was superb with the logical, detailed composition, he had difficulty seeing the possibilities for the larger designs. Understanding his type kept him from wasting energy or feeling stupid and allowed him to be very open to seeking the teacher's coaching with the design aspects.

Student type distributions vary widely among schools, and sometimes from class to class in the same school. This fact is important for predicting needs for materials, curriculum, and activities.

*Deciding.*   Deciding is the function that is a preference for decision making.

> Thinking: A preference for analytical, logical, objective, "tough-minded" decisions
>
> Feeling: A preference for value-based, person-centered, empathetic decisions

It is important not to regard feeling deciders as "emotional" and thinking deciders as "cold." Rather, they are part of the functions that Jung described and are paths through which people come to conclusions and reach decisions. Both preferences are important for effective decision making. *Thinking* deciders (T) contribute by providing logical, rational analysis and focus on the tasks. *Feeling* deciders (F) provide personal involvement and seek harmony, focusing on the effect that the decision will have on people. The latter may be especially reactive to insensitivity and cynicism.

Considerably more women prefer *feeling* and more men prefer *thinking* as their first consideration for deciding. Probably because this preference also seems to be a part of the gender expectation in many parts of the world, males who have a preference for feeling and females who prefer thinking may not seem typical and may experience frustration in school interactions. Joel, a large, handsome 10-year-old with strong preferences for feeling, felt rejected in many situations because he was constantly told, verbally and through inference, that he needed to keep his emotions under control. As might be expected, he was taunted as being "sissy" because he became teary-eyed at sad situations and overly expressive when excited. It was not until Joel became a soloist with the local boys' choir that he was comfortable using his enthusiasm and passion as an asset. Joel became a student leader in high school. After college, he was recruited by a large sales organization, where he ultimately became vice president. Again, he found a situation in which his preference for feeling was an asset. Conversely, Tina, a small sixth-grader who excelled in math and science, was constantly told by her peers that she was not "soft" enough and that boys would not like her. As an adolescent, Tina dressed in a very feminine style to soften her appearance as she learned to understand her thinking preference and continued to pursue her interest in premed.

Effective decision making is not achieved by using one preference alone. Instead, this preference is about what is considered first. Mature decision makers consider both preferences, but they understand where they begin and on what they rely.

*Living.*   Living is a preference for the person's orientation to the outer world.

> Judging: A preference for external order, organization schedules, systems, planning, and closure
>
> Perceiving: A preference for flexibility, spontaneity, adaptability, and options, with less need for external order

People with a preference for *judging* (J) are decisive (but are not necessarily judgmental) and like reaching closure about how they want to be in the world. They like to live in a systematic, sequential, precise, well-planned environment. They love checklists and timetables. It is as if they have an agenda, and anything that comes into their world must be put on that agenda. Kroeger and Thuesen (1992) assert that "moan time" is necessary before those with the judging preference can insert new data into their agenda. Perhaps that's why Mason whines, "Do I have to do the math now?" He likes math, but he is resisting the change in schedule. Js may not necessarily object to a new idea or information, but they may resist adding anything to their already set agenda. The world of education and much of the world of business fits the J concept. Systems, schedules, order, and follow-through abound. People with a preference for judging usually find this comfortable and are often drawn to such an environment.

In contrast, people with a *perceiving* (P) preference are not necessarily "perceptive," but they like to live with spontaneity, adaptability, and a flexibility that allows them to keep their options open. They have less need for order and schedules and seem to perform most comfortably in less structured environments. They are often curious children who have a much clearer idea of what they do not like than what they actually like. The Ps can often be found in the creative corner, less structured activities, and last in from the playground.

Perhaps this is one of the easier preferences to observe. It may also be an issue in interpersonal friction, affecting parent–child and teacher–student relations as different choices for order collide. The J parent may attempt to force a P child to be neat and decisive. Unfortunately, this puts the child in a world that is not comfortable. The child may prefer to keep options open, but the parent insists on decisions: "Make up your mind and let's move on!" For the P child, this restricts options and seems too final. For the P child, out of sight is out of mind, so the child wants everything stacked on the desk and toys readily accessible. For the parent, this is messy; therefore, "there's a place for everything and everything must be in its place." Conversely, the J child may be seen as obsessive and cajoled to relax and be less of a neatnik. The same kinds of conflicts can take place in the classroom.

It is important to note that the J–P preference is not necessarily about neatness. Js can be sloppy, and Ps can be neat. Rather, it is about the preference for one's orientation to the world. Neither J nor P is good or bad, but it is tragic when one is forced to be different from the preference. This results in the falsification and disrespect of differences that Jung and Myers cautioned against.

Myers extended Jung's model in the Judging–Perceiving scale by "making explicit one aspect of the theory that was implicit but undeveloped in Jung's work" (Myers & McCaulley, 1985, p. 11). To understand Jung's theory, one must comprehend his uses of the terms *judgment* and *perception*. For Jung, perception includes the many ways of becoming aware of things. He considered sensing and intuition to be the two categories of perception. Jung believed that judgment is about all the ways of coming to conclusions about what has been perceived and that thinking and feeling are the two kinds of judgment. Every waking activity is concerned with perceiving and judging. Thus type differences appear in a very wide range of human activities, including learning, communicating, and working.

## The Type Table

Obviously, these four pairs of preferences can be combined in 16 different ways. Myers devised a grid, or type table, in which she arranged the 16 types according to a clever rationale and included a short sketch of each of the types. It is a visual means for people to gain an understanding of Jung's overall concept in the interplay among the various combinations of preferences. A complete profile of each of the 16 types is found in *Introduction to Type* (Myers, 1970/1998). A more detailed description is in Myers and Myers's *Gifts Differing* (1980/1995) and in several other publications on type. Sources for understanding the implications of type in the classroom and in work with children are included in the Murphy-Meisgeier Type Indicator for Children (MMTIC) (Murphy & Meisgeier, 1987).

## Dominance

The incredible complexity of Jung's theory becomes evident in this concept. For each type, Jung assumed that the four preferences have a specific preferred ranking, 1-2-3-4, that reflects a specific attitude. People use their favorite or dominant function most in the world in which they are energized. For example, the extroverts (E) use their dominant function in the outer world of people and experiences, while introverts (I) use their dominant function in the inner world of thoughts and ideas. For the ENTP, intuition is the dominant or most favored function and is expressed in the extroverted world, whereas thinking is the auxiliary or second favored and is expressed in the introverted world. The third and fourth are assumed to be least favored or developed and may be the focus of growth in what Jung called the individuation phase of maturity.

## Temperament

Keirsey and Bates (1978/1984) began their work with the ancient concept of temperament and a somewhat similar interpretation by placing major importance on the preferences of sensation and intuition. Although extroversion and introversion were considered important, they were regarded as minor in comparison to the ways that people think. Keirsey and Bates regarded the preferences of sensation and intuition as the fundamental differences in people, resulting in "the most miscommunication, misunderstanding, defamation, and denigration. *This difference places the widest gulf between people*" (p. 17). By linking the preferred information-gathering function to the deciding function for intuitives and to the living-ordering function for sensors, thus yielding four sets of preferences, Keirsey and Bates arrived at a synthesis they call *temperaments*.

| **NF** | **NT** | **SJ** | **SP** |
|--------|--------|--------|--------|
| Intuitive/Feeling | Intuitive/Thinking | Sensing/Judging | Sensing/Perceiving |

With no acknowledgment of dominant or auxiliary functions and little importance placed on *extroversion–introversion*, this model reduces Jung's concepts considerably; however, it has useful applications in several areas. One is a shortcut to how these four groups may prefer the learning environment to be structured (Table 13-1). Since counseling is often called a process in learning, these considerations are especially useful in structuring the child's counseling environment, regardless of the counseling theory used.

## Usefulness in Counseling

With regard to counseling, Myers and McCaulley (1985) indicated that "people often come to counseling because of a long period of disconfirmation by others. When they see a road toward excellence and happiness which they can travel by discover-

TABLE 13-1   Preferences in learning

| ST | SF | NF | NT |
|----|----|----|----|
| See | Show | Dream | Create |
| Make | Share | Create | Solve |
| Build | Discuss | Choose | Design |
| Show | Explain | Pretend | Write about |
| Touch | Name | Discuss | Discover |
| Do | Visit | Imagine | Explore |
| Name | Help | Explore | Experiment |
| Watch | Touch | Discover | Find a new . . . |
| Suggest | Cooperate | Change | Look at or think about |
| Projects | Show and tell | Help | Find what's wrong |
| Field trips | Group projects | Cooperate | Learning by self |
| Put in order | Videos, movies | Games | Brain twister |
| Computers | Art activities | Experiments | Expert teachers |
| Experiment | Teaching others | Group activities | Investigate |
| Videos, movies | | Art projects | Design and do |
| Collecting things | | Field trips | |

From *Discovering Your Type* published by Center for Applications of Psychological Type, 1999.

ing and following their own intrinsically valuable preferences, they often become hopeful" (p. 63). Even though the MBTI was not developed on the basis of abnormalities but on observations and experiences with a large cross section of normal people, some encounter the MBTI in a counseling situation in the counselor's attempt to understand the person's type and most preferred path to reaching the goals of the counseling need. The nonthreatening implications of the instrument seem to appeal to people who are receiving the feedback from the Indicator. This same aspect, however, is a part of the MBTI that is disliked by a few critics. There seems to be a fear on the part of some that a positive confirmation of the person's type, rather than going straight to the essence of the problem, is a waste of time.

Some people may encounter the MBTI in church or in the workplace as organizations attempt to facilitate a better understanding among people for the purpose of enhancing interactions. The benefit is gained through appreciation of the gifts of other types. Regardless of the source of introduction, it is essential that people have the opportunity and resources for learning about type and the tremendous growth that it can provide—and not just receive the label for their preferences. If people emerge from MBTI sessions with only the type label and without the recognition that this is merely the beginning of a scenic road toward human understanding, there may be little retention.

## Psychological Diversity in Children

One means of enhancing any child's sense of well-being comes from learning about the diversity of types and competencies among other children. An ESTJ child who watches the INTP's approach to solving a puzzle may become discouraged. The ENTP child's visit to the ISFJ's home to see a collection of insects neatly arranged and labeled may generate feelings of inadequacy. When children study type differences, they quickly realize that some of their peers are better at some things, and some are not as good. In an appropriate environment, the child figures out how to learn from those who are better and share with those who need help. Children also become aware of their own experiences of ease and struggles. In recognizing diversity of abilities, it is possible for a child to learn that some tasks may require more effort while others require less effort and that the situation differs for each person. As this awareness grows, the child has greater power over learning and understands how to manipulate the learning environment in order to improve the learning. Ideally, parents and educators support the learning environment through intervention with preferred learning styles when children experience difficulty.

Savvy parents recognize type in children from a very early age. They notice one child's being very expressive and engaging, whereas another is reserved and observant. Since parents and teachers are the primary people in children's lives, it is essential that the differences in psychological type in children be recognized and honored both at home and at school. Type differences appear to have a profound effect on early learning, as well as on almost every area of the child's life. Children's learning and development will be enhanced when those involved in their nurture understand the child's type and are also aware of their own type and the effect that this may have on parenting and learning styles (Meisgeier, 1989). With information as to how each child best perceives and processes information and how each child prefers to interact with the world, parents, educators, and counselors can provide stimulating and effective environments for learning.

One of the most empowering aspects of the child's learning about psychological types is the confirmation and validation that comes from the description of the child's type. When the ISTJ child from a family in which everyone else is extroverted and perceiving has the opportunity to see that his need for structure and quiet is okay, the child experiences enormous growth in self-esteem and confidence. A second confirmation comes when the child's preferred path of learning is accommodated. This makes it possible for the ESFP child, who is not fond of reading, to talk about, touch, and learn through experience. Concomitantly, it is possible for the ENFJ child to realize the need to read about, imagine, and experiment.

Children need to feel psychological safety, at home and in school. When parents, teachers, and counselors adjust their approach to accommodate the child's type, the child's feelings of safety and well-being can be increased.

## Theory of Type Development

Much of the formal training that uses the MBTI seems to be intended for the purpose of identification of the preferred type. The emphasis is on distinguishing and verifying one's preferences. Jung's theory and the MBTI, however, are capable of yielding a much greater depth of information and resources for growth and devel-

opment. Type development is a lifelong process, involving more accurate perceptions and more effective decision making. It is fostered in many applications of the
MBTI. In observing people who are learning about their type, occasionally it is
possible to see a defensiveness arise when the situation includes something other
than their preferences. Many people avoid dealing with anything other than what
is very comfortable for them. Some people tend to confuse areas of strength with
their preferences, probably because they see success when they are operating
within the realm of their type. Conversely, they see areas of the opposite type as
areas of personal weakness. When this happens, some people can get into denial
and defensiveness. Limiting the learning to this initial finding of preferences and
type, however, is to miss much of Myers's and Jung's best work, along with their
attempts to assist people's development. To achieve a continued exploration, it
helps if people have an understanding of the possibilities for development, along
with the facts and details that will help them to achieve greater effectiveness. Instead of identifying strengths and weaknesses, Lansford (2002) found that it was
more conducive to pursue an understanding of areas of personal endeavor that
were developed and areas that were not as developed as needed. Being able to recognize and understand one's preferences is a tremendous nucleus of authenticity
for both children and adults. Both Jung and Myers emphasized repeatedly that the
preferences are a core, not an end.

## COUNSELING METHOD

As noted earlier, there is no standard Jungian method of therapy. While utilizing
an individualized approach, Jungian analysts apply his concepts to enhance the
self-healing potential of the psyche. Two major areas for applications of Jung with
children are in play therapy and in the use of type.

The Jungian approach to play therapy proceeds by building a therapeutic alliance in which the self-healing properties can be activated. Then, children act out
play themes related to their struggles. Allan (1997) described counseling goals as
follows:

1. Activate the self-healing potential.
2. Strengthen the connection and flow between the child's conscious and unconscious.
3. Stimulate creativity and imagination.
4. Heal and transcend wounds.
5. Develop the inner life.
6. Grow a sense of competency and mastery.
7. Build skills to cope with future problems.
8. Understand the complexity of life and be open to change.

The counselor watches the play, provides limits, redirects some activities, and
comments on the action. In the second stage, when the child seems stuck in struggles between characters labeled as good and bad, the counselor puts the struggles

into words and attempts to raise the child's awareness of feeling and issues. When these views are accepted, the counselor offers more sophisticated interpretations that link the play to significant things in the child's life. This process builds a healthy connection between the conscious and unconscious world of the child and between inner and outer realities. The counselor must be consistent in providing regular sessions with the child and link the counseling sessions to life.

Three major stages of this play therapy may be observed: chaos, struggle, and resolution. Children move from projecting their internal emotional state of chaos and confusion onto the toys to more order and structure in play as the ego begins to gain a sense of control and mastery. As the need for counseling reaches a conclusion, children often enact themes of construction, reparation, and healing. The struggle between opposites is a central theme in Jungian theory. Generally, this is the recognition that each child lives in two worlds: the outer world of school, family, and friends and the inner world of feelings, desires, and impulses. Healthy people have developed the ego to bring the two worlds into a workable relationship. This idea is important to the counselor, who, as a Jungian therapist, balances the needs of the child with the needs of the school and/or the family, or of both. The success of the intervention relates not only to the working alliance of the child and counselor but also to a positive alliance with significant others in the child's life (Allan, 1997).

The second opportunity for utilizing Jung's work with children is in the application of type. Jung's conceptual system for describing certain individual differences is extremely complex and can consume a lifetime of study. Myers, with her mother's inspiration, developed an instrument for adults that can be used to unlock the preferences and value diversity. Murphy and Meisgeier (1987) developed an instrument for identifying type in children. The MMTIC may be appropriately used from grades 2 to 8. With a format similar to the MBTI, the MMTIC is a series of 70 questions with two possible choices and measures the same four preferences. It utilizes a second-grade reading level and may be read aloud to younger children or to those who have reading or test-taking difficulties. Sample items from the MMTIC and the preferences that they measure are as follows:

*Extroversion/Introversion*
Having lots of people around:
    A. Gives you someone to talk to (E)
    B. Makes you tired after a while (I)

*Sensing/Intuition*
You prefer:
    A. Doing things you have learned to do (S)
    B. Creating new projects (N)

*Thinking/Feeling*
When your team loses, you:
    A. Plan how you can win next time (T)
    B. Try to cheer everybody up (F)

*Judging/Perceiving*
You like to:
   A. Know what will happen next (J)
   B. Try new things (P)

While it is useful for the child to complete the MMTIC and be given the feedback and materials, it is possible to utilize Jung's concepts by observing for type and responding appropriately. Thus, one of the most effective applications of Jung's work is the study and utilization of Myers's work by the adults in the child's life—counselors, teachers, and parents. As the adults understand their own type, they begin to honor differences in the children. An example of applying Jung's type theory to children and utilizing the MMTIC is in the following case study.

## CASE STUDY

### Identification of the Problem

Andrea was an 8-year-old girl who was referred to the counselor at the end of second grade by her teacher because she seemed depressed.

### Individual and Background Information

*Academic.*   Andrea's school records indicated that she had demonstrated excellent performance in kindergarten and had straight As in first grade and for the first quarter of second grade. The subsequent grading periods showed a steady deterioration in grades, primarily because many assignments were either late or incomplete. An IQ score of 142 indicated that Andrea was highly capable of academic performance.

*Family.*   Andrea is the only child of an ophthalmologist and a registered nurse who was working on a graduate degree. They lived in an upper-socioeconomic neighborhood, seemed to have a very stable relationship, and provided a nurturing environment for the child.

*Social.*   Classroom and playground observations, along with an interview with her teacher, indicated that Andrea was frequently sought as a playmate by her peers, was helpful to others, and seemed to enjoy many friends. Her interactions in play groups and on the playground appeared to be age appropriate. She rarely had conflicts, and when she did, she seemed to generate alternatives and achieve resolution without intervention.

### Counseling Method

The Jungian objectives are to stabilize the present and gain hope in a future that the child can create. The basic steps are to (1) establish a relationship, (2) analyze the present situation, (3) increase the client's awareness of the present situation, and (4) help the client gain awareness of herself that will enable her to effectively manage future situations. The following transcript illustrates the Jungian objectives.

*Counselor:*   Good morning, Andrea, I enjoyed watching you paint yesterday when I visited your classroom.

*Andrea:*   I like to paint, but we don't get to do it often enough.

*Counselor:*   Painting is fun, and you'd like to do it every day.

*Andrea:*   (smiling) Yeah, every day.

*Counselor:*   What else do you enjoy as much as painting?

*Andrea:*   Not much. I like the playground, free time, the puzzle corner, the puppets, and I used to like writing.

*Counselor:*   Tell me about the writing when you used to like it.

*Andrea:*   Well—Ms. Brown, my teacher last year, used to let us use puppets to tell stories. Then she would help us write what we wanted, draw pictures about it, and she would help us make it into a book and we could take it home.

*Counselor:*   And it was fun to share your stories and your drawings with Mom and Daddy.

*Andrea:*   Yeah, and I liked showing them what I had done.

*Counselor:*   Talk about what you write in second grade.

*Andrea:*   Well, we don't write stories. No, we just write. See, we have to write sentences and practice our cursive letters, so we don't write stories, we just write. Ms. Jones doesn't have time to do stories very much, so we just write sentences, do math, work in our books—and sometimes, we get to paint.

*Counselor:*   And you miss making up your own stories and writing about what you are thinking.

*Andrea:*   Yeah, how did you know that?

*Counselor:*   Well, Andrea, do you remember when you came here on Tuesday, and you did an activity with me where I asked you to answer some questions about what you like—about how you feel and think about things? Let's look at how your answers came out.

*Andrea:*   Did I make a bad grade? Are you gonna be upset with me like Ms. Jones?

*Counselor:*   No, Andrea. There are no good or bad grades on this activity. It just tells about what you prefer, and something about you. [Showing Andrea the child's MMTIC results form] Your answers to the questions described someone with the description in this box (ENFP). Would you like for me to read it to you?

*Andrea:*   [Eagerly taking the form] No, I can read it! "Friendly, ready to help anyone with a problem. Have good imaginations. Can do almost anything that they are interested in." [with an enthusiastic smile] Yep, that's me! [Continuing] "Often wait till the last minute to do things. Have lots of new ideas. Want to do new things." That's me, too! "Enjoy talking. Tend to think positively about life." Wow! How did you know this about me and put all of that in this paper?

*Counselor:* Andrea, I didn't do this. You gave this description of yourself by the way that you answered the questions. You see, this is an instrument that helps us understand ourselves and how we are different from each other.

*Andrea:* That part about the talking, that's what gets me into so much trouble with Ms. Jones. She expects me to do my work and sit quietly, but I forget, and I want to tell Jason about what I've read. Then, I get points.

*Counselor:* And that makes you feel like Ms. Jones doesn't like you.

*Andrea:* Right! She doesn't like me.

*Counselor:* Actually, Andrea, Ms. Jones likes you very much. She just gets concerned when you don't do your assignments.

*Andrea:* Are you sure? Do you think Ms. Jones really likes me?

*Counselor:* I'm certain of it, Andrea. And now that you understand Ms. Jones's concerns, let's look at what you can do to complete your assignments.

*Andrea:* OK, but what?

*Counselor:* We can look at the kinds of things that are easy for you and that you like to do. Then, we can look at the things that are not so easy and find ways to make it more fun.

*Andrea:* And not so boring.

*Counselor:* Sure, Andrea, you like making everything fun. When you come to see me next week, we'll talk more about this. Today, I'm going to send these papers (*MMTIC Parents' Guide*) to your mom and dad so that they can know about the activity that you did. If it's okay with you, I can also talk with Ms. Jones about it.

*Andrea:* Sure, I'm glad she likes me.

*Counselor:* And I like you, too.

*Andrea:* See you next week. [as she skips down the hall]

## Case Summary

While Andrea's sad face, falling grades, and lack of participation were signals of depression in children, the immediate problem was lack of intellectual challenge, boredom with the curriculum, and a lack of understanding of the teacher's (ISFJ) type. The counselor recognized that, for the ENFP, anything that disrupts the relationship threatens the child's learning.

The counselor arranged a session with the teacher to help her understand Andrea's type and her classroom needs. Together, they recommended that Andrea be assigned to a third-grade classroom that utilized an individualized program and a less structured classroom environment. They also recommended that Andrea participate in enrichment classes for the gifted. In addition, the counselor arranged a session with the parents to provide understanding of Andrea's needs. Subsequently, the parents completed the MBTI to understand how their type influenced their parenting style. They also joined a parents' support group for gifted children.

◆

## CROSS-CULTURAL APPLICATIONS OF JUNG

Jung was intrigued by the human attributes and myths that transcend culture. One of his easiest concepts to apply to different cultures is that of type. The tool for identifying and applying type is the MBTI. It has been used by millions of people and has been translated into different languages around the globe. It has also been a part of several thousand books, articles, theses, dissertations, and studies. It has been used in research from numerous perspectives, from the way people pray and learn to the ways they choose work or fall in love. New forms of the original instrument are developed by the publisher to maintain relevance to current society and reflect ongoing research into the original work. Much of the structure and approach of play therapy can be applied to children from various cultures, especially when there is no language barrier between the counselor and the child.

## SUMMARY

A resurgent interest in Jung may be attributed to the recognition of the validity and usefulness of several of his concepts. Jungian institutes are located around the world, even in some small cities. It is possible to see similarities in the work of later psychologists, such as the related themes of Myers's ISTJ type to Berne's parent (see Chapter 10). One can also find corresponding ideas in some work done on communication styles, such as connecting extroversion and introversion to gender, such as the talkative wife and the silent husband (Gray, 2001; Tannen, 1990)

Jung's work is highly complex, as complicated as the task of developing a system of understanding human personality. Myers and Briggs gave normal people the usefulness of Jung's ideas. Because of their lifelong pursuit of type, today, many people smile and understand situations that, without MBTI learning, could have caused frustration and emotional injury. Further utilization of the MMTIC and classroom use will afford children the same understanding and opportunities to build their confidence. Perhaps the greatest implication for education is in the utilization of type in accommodating varied learning styles in order to increase individual development and enhance each child's self concept. Future developments will probably lead to greater understanding of Jung's work and of the human psyche.

## W E B S I T E S for Personality Type

Association for Psychological Type
www.aptcentral.org

Center for Applications of Psychological Type
www.capt.org

Consulting Psychologists Press (CPP)
www.cpp-db.com

International Association for Analytical Psychology
www.iaap.org

# REFERENCES

Allan, J. (1997). Jungian play psychotherapy. In K. O'Connor & L. M. Braverman (Eds.), *Play therapy theory and practice: A comparative presentation* (pp. 100–130). New York: Wiley.

Campbell, J. (Ed.). (1971). *The portable Jung.* New York: Penguin.

Gray, J. (2001). *Men, women, and relationships.* New York: Fine Communications.

Jung, C. G. (1921/1971). *Psychological types.* Princeton, NJ: Princeton University Press.

Jung, C. G. (1961). *Memories, dreams, reflections.* New York: Random House.

Jung, C. G. (1967a). *Collected works: Vol. 9. The archetypes and the collective unconscious.* New Jersey: Princeton University Press.

Jung, C. G. (1967b). *Collected works: Vol. 10. Civilization in transition.* Princeton, NJ: Princeton University Press.

Jung, C. G. (1967c). *Collected works: Vol. 16. The Practice of Psychotherapy.* Princeton, NJ: Princeton University Press.

Keirsey, D., & Bates, M. (1978/1984). *Please understand me.* Del Mar, CA: Prometheus Nemesis Books.

Kroeger, O., & Thuesen, J. M. (1988). *Type talk.* New York: Doubleday.

Kroeger, O., & Thuesen, J. M. (1992). *Type talk at work.* New York: Doubleday.

Lansford, Z. (2003). *Psychology for normal people.* Unpublished manuscript.

Meisgeier, C. (1989). *Parent's guide to type.* Palo Alto, CA: Consulting Psychologists Press.

Murphy, E., & Meisgeier, C. (1987). *Murphy-Meisgeier Type Indicator for Children.* Gainsville, FL: Center for Applications of Psychological Type.

Myers, I. (1970/1998). *Introduction to type.* Palo Alto, CA: Consulting Psychologists Press.

Myers, I., & Briggs, K. (1975/2000). *Myers-Briggs Type Indicator.* Palo Alto, CA: Consulting Psychologists Press.

Myers, I., & Myers, P. (1980/1995). *Gifts differing: Understanding personality type.* Palo Alto, CA: Davies Black.

Myers, I., & McCaulley, M. H. (1985). *A guide to the development and use of the Myers-Briggs Type Indicator.* Palo Alto, CA: Consulting Psychologists Press.

Saunders, F. W. (1991). *Katharine and Isabel: Mother's light, daughter's journey.* Palo Alto, CA: Consulting Psychologists Press.

Storr, A. (1983). *The essential Jung.* Princeton, NJ: Princeton University Press.

Tannen, D. (1990). *You just don't understand.* New York: William Morrow.

# PART THREE

# COUNSELING WITH CHILDREN: SPECIAL TOPICS

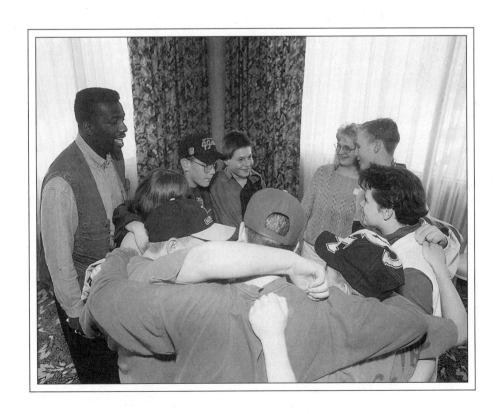

# Chapter 14

# Play Therapy

*You can discover more about a person in an*
*hour of play than in a year of conversation.*
—Plato

Rather than Freud's "talking cure" as a descriptor of therapy, Kaduson, Cangelosi, and Schaefer (1997a) proposed "playing cure" as more appropriate to describe therapy with children. Play is "the child's natural medium of self expression," according to Virginia Axline (1947, p. 9) in her classic book *Play Therapy: The Inner Dynamics of Childhood*. Others concur with her premise (Landreth, 1991; Moustakas, 1998; Schaefer, 1993). Landreth (1993) explained that play is children's symbolic language and provides a way for them to express their experiences and emotions in a natural, self-healing process. "A child's play is his talk and toys are his words," proposed Ginott (1994, p. 33). Orton (1997) stated that play assists in establishing a relationship with a child, helps the child state his or her concerns, aids in the assessment process, and promotes healing and growth.

## DEFINING PLAY THERAPY

Schaefer (1993) has identified common characteristics of play. He stated that play is pleasurable and, therefore, intrinsically motivating. During play, the child is more concerned with the play itself than with the end result, and the child is often engrossed in it. Play is not literal—it has a make-believe quality. Play is flexible. It has the power to enhance normal development and alleviate abnormal behavior. The child feels comfortable when playing. Play is a natural way for children to express themselves, to act out sensitive material, to gain security, and to increase their self-confidence (Bradley & Gould, 1993). Another significant attribute of play is that it is free from evaluation and judgment by adults, and children are safe to make mistakes (Sweeney, 1997).

Cattanach (1995) provided a multidimensional model of play therapy based on these concepts:

- The central place of play is the child's way of understanding the world

- The developmental aspect of play and the recognition that in therapy children move back and forth along a developmental continuum as they discover and explore their identities
- The symbolism inherent in play, through which children can experiment with imaginative choices and maintain a distance from the consequences of those choices in real life
- The special place and time for play, which is both a physical space and a therapeutic space (p. 224)

## ADVANTAGES OF PLAY THERAPY

Albon (1996) stated that facilitating play into therapy "powerfully facilitates development" even with minimal verbal interactions. Besides this general benefit, incorporating play into counseling has several other advantages:

- The child is given freedom to make choices.
- Play evokes fantasies and unconscious feelings.
- Play offers familiar tools for children to use.
- The only limits required are to keep the child and others safe from harm.
- Play therapy allows the child a safe place to act out feelings, to gain understanding, and to change. (Bradley & Gould, 1993)

Kottman (2001) explained the advantages of play therapy for counselors. Play helps counselors establish rapport with children as well as understand the children, the way they interact, and their relationships. Play also allows the teaching of social skills.

The Association for Play Therapy (1997) defines *play therapy* as the "systematic use of a theoretical model to establish an interpersonal process in which trained play therapists use the therapeutic powers of play to help clients prevent or resolve psychosocial difficulties and achieve optimal growth and development" (p. 4). Schaefer (1993) outlined 14 therapeutic powers of play and the beneficial outcome of each, which Sweeney (1997) and Kottman (2001) interpreted. They are as follows:

1. *Overcoming resistance:* Play draws children into a working alliance with the counselor. Many children do not make the choice to enter counseling, so play provides a way to establish a working alliance with them.

2. *Communication:* Play provides a natural medium of self-expression. Counselors convey their respect by being willing to "speak" in the child's language. Watching the child's activity and choices provides the counselor with a quick and smooth understanding.

3. *Competence:* Play satisfies the need to explore and master, thereby building self-esteem. Counselors build confidence by pointing out that the child is working hard and making progress.

4. *Creative thinking:* Problem-solving skills are encouraged so that innovative solutions to dilemmas can occur. Play provides opportunities for creativity and imaginative solutions.

5. *Catharsis:* Children can release strong emotions they have had difficulty confronting. The sense of relief can be an experience that leads to growth for the child.

6. *Abreaction:* In play, children can process and adjust to difficulties by symbolically reliving them with appropriate emotional expression. Play gives children a place to reenact and gain a sense of mastery over the negative experience.

7. *Role playing:* Children can practice new behaviors and develop empathy for others.

8. *Fantasy:* Children use their imagination to make sense of painful reality. They can also experiment with the possibility of changing their lives, a process that instills hope.

9. *Metaphoric teaching:* Children gain insight by facing their conflicts and fears through the metaphors generated in play. Stories, playing, and artwork can be used to look at situations differently.

10. *Attachment formation:* Children develop a bond with the counselor and learn to increase their connections with others.

11. *Relationship enhancement:* Play enhances the positive therapeutic relationship, allowing children to move toward self-actualization and grow closer to others. The children begin to believe they are worthy of love and positive attention.

12. *Positive emotion:* Children enjoy playing. They can laugh and have a good time in an accepting place.

13. *Mastering developmental fears:* Repeated play activities help reduce anxiety and fear. By working with toys, art supplies, and other play media, children can recognize their skills for coping with fear and for taking care of themselves.

14. *Game play:* Games help children socialize and develop ego strength. They have opportunities to expand their interaction skills.

Cangelosi (1997) discussed these therapeutic factors in working with children of divorce, and Kaduson (1997) recognized them in working with children with attention deficit–hyperactivity disorder (ADHD). Henniger (1995) proposed that play could serve as an antidote to childhood stress, and Albon (1996) recognized that play allows children to expose and explore troublesome emotions. Fall (1999) investigated client-centered interventions in the school setting for children with poor coping skills for learning. She reported that the use of six sessions of play therapy increased support for the children. Bratton and Ray (2000) provided further support in their review of the case study research in this field. They summarized 82 studies and presented the effectiveness of play therapy with several specific issues and populations.

## CROSS-CULTURAL APPLICATIONS OF PLAY THERAPY

An additional benefit of play therapy is its applicability across cultural groups. Henderson and Gladding (1998) argued that using the creative arts could enhance multicultural counseling. Certainly, the links between play therapy and creative arts are ample reasons to extend that hypothesis to multicultural counseling and play therapy. All children play. One of the barriers in multicultural counseling is language; play is a natural way to overcome that difficulty. Cochran (1996) proposed play and art therapy as methods to help students who are culturally diverse overcome barriers to school success, particularly in aiding communication and increasing self-esteem. For all these reasons, the use of play therapy with children of different cultures seems to be a promising practice. Coleman, Parmer, and Barker (1993) and Glover (2001) provided the following specifics for working with children from multicultural populations:

- Respect the historical, psychological, sociological, and political aspects of the child's culture. The counselor may gather information about and experience of the culture. Play materials should be chosen to express respect for cultural differences.
- Investigate the role of play in diverse populations in order to avoid comments or interpretations that may violate the culture. Stock the playroom with toys appropriate for the self-expression of a child in that particular group.
- Become familiar with the values, beliefs, customs, and traditions of a child's culture, paying particular attention to language differences.
- Recognize the ongoing process of becoming multiculturally competent.
- Examine the appropriateness of the philosophical basis of the play therapy theory to determine whether there is a mismatch with cultural values.
- Be aware of personal cultural biases, values, beliefs, and attitudes.
- Interact with multicultural populations.

The counselor will want to ask parents about their background, such as their traditions, celebrations, and religion. Gonzalez-Mena (1998) provided one way of understanding a home environment by discussing two opposing goals of parenting styles: individualism versus connectedness. Parents who value individualism will work to help the child develop autonomy and self-help skills. The parent may encourage the idea of passion, making choices, and expression of feelings. Independence, self-assurance, competence, and a sense of specialness may be emphasized with this type of parenting. Parenting to maintain connections emphasizes interdependence as the greatest value. Parents may promote peace and harmony among family members rather than independence and autonomy. Humility and humbleness are valued. Worthiness is connected to fitting in, belonging, and putting others first. You may refer to the discussion on children of different cultures in Chapter 15 for more guidelines in working with children from diverse cultures.

The counselor who uses play therapy must begin by considering personal characteristics that may indicate the counselor's suitability for that type of intervention. Then, by considering the varying theoretical approaches to play therapy, the counselor can construct an understanding of that process. Awareness of the stages of play therapy, criteria for the selection of play materials, and examples of play therapy techniques will contribute to a foundation for integrating play into counseling practices.

# PERSONAL QUALITIES OF A PLAY THERAPIST

Some researchers (Barnes, 1996; Kottman, 2001; Landreth, 1991; Schaefer & Greenberg, 1997) identify the personal characteristics and personality of the counselor as key elements in the play therapy process. According to Kottman (2001), the effective play therapist has the following qualities:

- Appreciation of children, treating them with a respectful, kind manner
- A sense of humor and willingness to laugh at self
- Playful and fun-loving attitude
- Self-confidence and self-reliance
- Openness and honesty
- Accepting
- Willingness to use play and metaphors as communication tools
- Flexibility and ability to deal with ambiguity
- Comfort with children and experience interacting with them
- Ability to set limits and maintain personal boundaries
- Self-aware (pp. 12–13)

# THEORIES OF PLAY THERAPY

In the second part of this book are descriptions of play therapy that are directly related to the theories presented. Some other approaches to working with children and play are summarized in the following section.

## Ecosystemic Play Therapy

In *Advances and Innovations,* the second volume of *The Handbook of Play Therapy,* O'Connor & Schaefer (1994) explained a model of ecosystemic play therapy. O'Connor and Ammen (1997) expanded this description and provided a workbook for counselors to use in implementing this type of play therapy. The model is an integration of several theories of psychotherapy and developmental concepts. The child's interactions and experiences in the world, as well as the internal, symbolic world of the child, are emphasized in this type of play therapy. The model contains a comprehensive model of case conceptualization and intervention.

One key element of the theory is the ecosystemic worldview, the perspective that community and environment form nested systems in which an individual exists. The basic unit of the model, however, is the individual rather than the system. The counselor considers all the systems when conceptualizing the child's problem and the treatment plan. The goal of the intervention is to help children have their needs met without interfering with other people's ability to get their needs met. The strategies that are used are aimed at altering the problem, the child's view of the problem, and the child's response to the problem. O'Connor and Schaefer (1994) further explained working on complementary levels of experience–behavior and cognition–emotion to help the child. As children become reflective about their behavior in the relationship systems, they may choose alternative ways of behaving. Symbolic play facilitates this reflective process.

The counselor assists in the process by providing interventions that allow children to (1) recognize their own needs, (2) identify potential resources for meeting those needs, (3) develop strategies for activating the resources, (4) tolerate frustration, and (5) value and accept gratification when they are successful. Children must learn to recognize the needs of others and to balance those needs against their own.

O'Connor (2000) explained that children will progress through five steps of this therapy. The first is an introduction and exploration in which the relationship is established. During the next stage, tentative acceptance, children have accepted the process and seem to be cooperative but are anxious. Once the children begin to resist the therapy, the next stage, negative reaction, has begun. The reactions may be overt or may be very mild and difficult to detect. After at least one difficult session, children move into the fourth phase—growing and trusting. In this phase, active problem solving is initiated. The final phase is termination, which includes a review of the therapy, the problems faced, and the strategies used (O'-Connor & Ammen, 1997).

In ecosystemic play therapy, the most important goal is to help the children resume normal lives, having their needs met without infringing on others. Specific treatment objects are developed after extensive assessments. Working with parents is stressed (O'Connor, 2000). That may include exchanging information, consulting about management strategies or parenting skills, and problem solving.

## Jungian Play Therapy

Jung (1961) believed in the self-healing potential of the psyche. The Jungian approach to play therapy proceeds by building a therapeutic alliance in which the self-healing properties can be activated. Then children act out play themes related to their struggles. The counselor watches the play, provides limits, and redirects some activities, as well as comments on the action. In the second stage, children seem stuck in struggles between characters labeled good and bad. The counselor puts the struggles into words, attempting to raise the child's awareness of feelings and issues. When these views are accepted, the counselor offers more sophisticated interpretations that link the play to significant things in the child's life.

This process builds a healthy connection between the conscious and unconscious world of the child and between inner and outer realities.

Allan (1988) and Allan and Berry (1987) observed a trend of three major stages in working phases of Jungian play therapy: chaos, struggle, and resolution. Children move from projecting their internal emotional state of chaos and confusion onto the toys to more order and structure in play as the ego begins to gain a sense of control and mastery. As the need for counseling reaches a conclusion, the children often enacted themes of construction, reparation, and healing. The struggle between opposites is a central theme in Jungian theory. Generally, this is the recognition that each child lives in two worlds: the outer world of school, family, and friends, and the inner world of feelings, drives, desires, and impulses. Healthy people have developed the ego to bring the two worlds into a workable relationship. This idea is important to the counselor who, as a Jungian therapist, balances the needs of the child with the needs of the school and/or family. The success of the treatment relates not only to the working alliance of the child and counselor but also to the positive alliance with significant others in the child's life (Allan, 1997).

Allan (1997) explained the counseling goals as follows: (1) activate the self-healing potential, (2) strengthen the connection and flow between the child's conscious and unconscious parts, (3) stimulate creativity and imagination, (4) heal and transcend wounds, (5) develop the inner life, (6) grow a sense of competency and mastery, (7) build skills to cope with future problems, and (8) understand the complexity of life and be open to change. Variables that are important to achieving these goals are building a positive relationship with the child, meeting at a regular time and place, providing effective interpretations that deepen the child's understanding, maintaining a file of the child's pictures and drawings, and linking counseling sessions to life.

## GROUP PLAY THERAPY

Children age 2 to 12 with similar problems or experiences affecting their behavior may benefit from a play therapy group. O'Connor (1991) stated that the children should display a range of functioning both to avoid competition for attention and to provide models. He suggested no more than 6 children per adult in the group, and no more than 10 children in a group with two adults. Children should be within a 3-year age span among members, come from similar socioeconomic status and ethnic background, and have no more than 15 IQ points separating them.

The advisability of mixing boys and girls in one group depends on the age of the members, the type of group, and the group goals. Using play in group counseling is similar to using it with individuals; the previously mentioned theoretical approaches guide a counselor in those decisions. Landreth and Sweeney (2001) identified many advantages to using group play therapy. Children will have experience that helps them learn to function well, explore their actions, develop tolerance, and find joy in working with others.

Schaefer, Jacobsen, and Ghahramanlou (2000) explained a play group for children with social skills deficits. They noted the significance of social relationships in childhood and cite Hartup (1992), who concluded that IQ, school grades, and classroom behavior were not predictors of adult success. The way a child gets along with others is the single best predictor of adult adaptation. The social skills training program includes 10 sessions that focus on specific social skills for elementary children. Their discussion includes the curriculum for that group activity.

## PRESCRIPTIVE PLAY THERAPY

Schaefer, Jacobson, and Ghahramanlou (2000) explained that counselors who use prescriptive play therapy tailor their interventions for each child. To do this, they must have both conceptual and practical knowledge bases about the many theories of play therapy. That knowledge will allow the counselor to understand the child and the child's problems. Kaduson, Cangelosi, and Schaefer (1997a) outlined the responsibilities of counselors who use prescriptive play therapy:

- Know every approach to play therapy, including the theory's philosophical foundations, constructs, and strategies
- Have skill in applying the constructs and strategies
- Understand the psychological and emotional issues related to childhood disorders
- Be capable of identifying the short- and long-term needs of children with specific diagnoses to form treatment plans for those needs
- Know the current outcome research in order to choose the most effective treatment for the specific problem

Kaduson, Cangelosi, and Schaefer (1997a) provided details about this approach to play therapy in their book.

## PLAY THERAPY WITH FAMILIES

Interventions combining family and play therapy have been used in prevention programs in elementary schools (McDonald & Morgan, 1997) and in working with the difficulties of alcoholism (Carmichael & Lane, 1997). Johnson, Franklin, Hall, and Prieto (2000) discussed the use of play therapy to work with a child who had attention difficulties. These authors coached parents in the relationship-building techniques with a successful outcome for the child and parents. Gladding (1993) encouraged families to play but in a manner that is fair, tolerant, and trusting. His admonition was to set up cooperative play environments where everyone shares and wins. Rotter and Bush (2000) also emphasized the importance of families playing together in therapy. Several theorists have provided models for promoting that type of play therapy with families.

### Dynamic Family Play Therapy

Harvey (1997) explained dynamic family play therapy. This type of play therapy engages family members in creative activity by using natural play. The counselor's goal is to help the family develop and increase spontaneity. Creating metaphors about the difficulties in relationships is another goal. In this style of family play therapy, a counselor uses various art, drama, movement, and video making to encourage family play. As family members engage in creative play moments, the counselor guides them into initiating interactive play in which metaphors emerge. The metaphors help them experience a mutual catharsis, understanding, and sense of mastery in their experiences with each other.

By helping family members engage in play, counselors help families develop or restart their own natural play with each other. Over the progression of therapy, painful and conflicting issues emerge through the play. Counselors can guide family members to generate the naturally creative playful spirit that will produce trust and affiliation. From this development, counselors can focus on the content of play to help family members reconstruct their relationships.

The counselor begins by issuing directive activities such as tug-of-war, scribble war, or follow-the-leader. The counselor remains alert to avoidance, interference, and resistance. The family members evolve into more elaborate and flexible interactions, eventually developing their own unique style of play episodes (Harvey, 1997).

## Filial Therapy

Bernard and Louise Guerney developed filial therapy, a play therapy method in which the parents are directly involved. Filial therapy is based on the principles of child-centered therapy. Louise Guerney (1997) believed that children's adjustment problems are caused by parents' failing to learn how to understand their children. She defined these problems as learning problems and thought that teaching parents to conduct child-centered play sessions might overcome parental shortcomings. Parents are so important to their children that she felt acceptance from them would be extremely meaningful for their children.

The goals of filial therapy are to reduce the children's problem behaviors, help parents gain the skills of child-centered play therapists to use when relating to their children, and improve the parent–child relationship. Using learning theory and behavioral therapy for the parent training principles, the training proceeds by completing the following steps:

1. Introduce parents to methods for conducting client-centered play therapy.
2. Consider the other demands of parents' lives and assure them they are expected to practice these skills only in the play sessions.
3. Model the behaviors as complete tasks.
4. Reduce each task to small, separate components and practice each component.
5. Reassemble the complete tasks and role-play without children.
6. Encourage parents to conduct sessions observed by the counselor or held at home and reported to the counselor.
7. Gradually increase the length of the sessions and have home play weekly.

VanFleet (2000) suggested that a counselor needs these skills to use filial therapy: structuring skills, empathic listening skills, imaginary play skills, and limit-setting skills. As in child-centered play therapy, the child is encouraged to express his or her needs, thoughts, and feelings. Optimally, during the process children and parents change their perceptions of each other.

Johnson (1995) listed the benefits of filial therapy as providing a bridge between individual child treatment and family therapy, as empowering parents, and as a springboard to addressing many family issues. Filial therapy has been described as helpful with children who have tendencies toward perfection (VanFleet, 1997), with single parents (Bratton, 1994; Ray, Bratton, & Brandt, 2000), with grandparents (Bratton, Ray, & Moffit 1998), and with incarcerated fathers (Lobaugh, 1992).

## Strategic Family Play Therapy

Ariel (1992, 1997) explained strategic family play therapy as a form of counseling in which all family members and the counselor play. The play is free, imaginative, and make-believe. Toys, costumes, and props may or may not be used. Ariel reported that strategic family play therapy has been practiced successfully with a wide range of problems and is applicable to families of various cultural and social backgrounds.

Ariel (1997) continued by describing the integrated theory that is based on information processing and the theory of signs. The hypothesis is that the processing of information is aided if the information is associated with the person's central emotions. The information related to the central emotions will be overrepresented in make-believe play, allowing the counselor and player an arena for addressing the themes of the intense emotions. Make-believe play is a moderator, helping family members conduct their transactions and conflicts in a nonthreatening way. The family initiates its play themes, and the counselor then watches and tries to identify unhealthy interactions. Next, the counselor begins play moves, weaving into the family's play but gently steering the activity in well-chosen directions. Those choices are based on the curative properties of play, or what Ariel calls "bug-busters" because they remove or weaken the difficulties in the family's programs.

## Theraplay

Theraplay is a treatment method modeled after the healthy parent–child interaction. Koller and Booth (1997) explain this intensive, short-term approach as a therapy in which parents are involved as observers and then as cotherapists. The goal of the therapy is to foster attachment, self-esteem, trust, and joyful engagement.

Jernberg (1993) distinguished theraplay from other approaches by noting it is playful, requiring no toys and few props. The therapist using this approach avoids questions and focuses on health. The adult structures the sessions, and physical contact is encouraged. The agenda of the sessions is designed to meet the child's needs and enhance the parent–child attachment. Theraplay integrates the elements of structure, challenge, intrusion–engagement, and nurture. The adult enforces structure by clearly stating safety rules.

The duration of theraplay is usually 8 to 12 sessions. During that time, the counselor explains the process, describes activities, and elaborates on the process for parents. The counselor also coaches parents and gives support and encouragement (Kottman, 2001).

## CONSIDERATIONS IN PLAY THERAPY

### Therapist

Cattanach (1994) commented on the various ways to be a play therapist. Whatever theoretical choice a counselor makes, keeping the child safe in the play therapy process is the top priority. She recognized that because the counselor is responsible for the process, he or she should seek training and continuing supervision, needs to understand the developmental processes of the child, and needs to learn to play in ways that stimulate the child's participation. The counselor's style of interacting depends on the children with whom he or she works, the personality and skills of the counselor, and the level of his or her training.

Harris and Landreth (2001) identified the principles that guide a client-centered play therapist and seem applicable across several theoretical approaches. The guidelines include the therapist being interested in the child, as well as warm, caring, and accepting. The therapist creates an environment of safety and allows the child opportunities to express freely. The therapist attends to the child's feelings, trusts the child's inner directions, and respects the child's capacity to act responsibly.

### Appropriate Clients

Kottman (2001) identifies most play therapy clients as children between 3 and 11 years of age, although some younger (as young as 2) and older children (12–15) may participate. He suggests that counselors ask the children whether they would rather sit and talk or play with toys.

Anderson and Richards (1995) directed counselors to begin by assessing the following capabilities of the potential client:

- The ability to tolerate/build/use a relationship with an adult
- The ability to tolerate/accept a protective environment
- The capacity to learn new ways of coping
- The potential to gain new insight and the motivation to try
- The attention span and cognitive organization to participate

Those authors also admonish counselors to consider whether play therapy is an effective way to address this particular child's concern and whether conditions in the child's environment will impede the play therapy process. A limited ability in the five things mentioned in the list or a negative answer to the other considerations suggest that play therapy would not be the appropriate choice for that child.

## Effectiveness of Play Therapy

Different studies have focused on the effectiveness of play therapy. In a meta-analysis, Leblanc and Ritchie (1999) concluded that two variables affected the outcome of play therapy. Effective play therapy was more likely to include the active participation of parents in the process and to have lasted for 30 to 35 sessions. These authors (Leblanc & Ritchie, 2001) confirmed these same findings in a meta-analysis of play therapy outcome. They stated that play therapy is as effective as nonplay therapies when working with children who have emotional difficulties. Bratton and Ray (2000) looked at the results of play therapy case studies. Their synthesis supported play therapy as a treatment choice for children with the following: social maladjustment, conduct disorder, problem school behavior, emotional maladjustment, anxiety/fear, poor self-concept, or physical, mental, or learning disabilities.

Kottman (2001) has provided an extremely useful summary of the categories of problems amenable to play therapy. His conclusions are based on research studies and anecdotal reports. The categories include instances (1) in which play therapy would be the treatment of choice, (2) in which certain approaches of play therapy have been helpful, (3) in which play therapy is effective when combined with other interventions, and (4) in which play therapy would not be the treatment of choice. Table 14-1 is a shortened version of his summary.

## Play Stages

Gumaer (1984) stated that the use of play media by a counselor must be attended by purposeful interaction to allow maximal effectiveness. Orton (1997) presented an integrated approach to the therapeutic play process that moves through five stages: (1) relationship, (2) release, (3) re-creation, (4) reexperiencing, and (5) resolving. Through this process, a strong relationship is built in which the child feels accepted and understood. The child uses play to release feelings and to ease tension through cathartic release. As the relationship grows, the child begins to explore significant events or relationships that trigger uncomfortable thoughts and feelings. Children begin to understand the links between past events and to connect that knowledge with current thoughts, behaviors, and feelings. The final stage is reached when children are able to act on the understanding and to experiment with various solutions.

Bradley and Gould (1993) discussed a three-stage process. Stage 1 is relationship building. The counselor focuses on emotions evident in the child's playing and responds to them. At the same time, the counselor develops hypotheses about the child's problems or needs. In the second stage, the relationship is well established, and the counselor becomes more assertive in directing the child's play. While reviewing the hypotheses and determining one that seems most crucial, the counselor encourages play with specific toys or in specific ways that are likely to evoke feelings and behaviors related to the hypothesis. The counselor may initiate deeper exploration of the feelings and behavior the child demonstrates during play.

TABLE 14-1    Play therapy

| Play therapy (regardless of the approach) would be treatment of choice | Certain approaches to play therapy have been useful in treating these children | Play therapy can be an effective intervention when combined with other interventions | Play therapy would not be the treatment of choice for these children |
|---|---|---|---|
| Adjustment disorder | Attachment disorder (theraplay & thematic play) | Attention deficit–hyperactivity disorder | Severe conduct disorder |
| Posttraumatic stress disorder | | Major depressive disorder | Severe attachment disorder |
| Dissociative disorder | Selective mutism (cognitive-behavioral play therapy & client-centered play therapy) | Separation anxiety disorder | Manifest signs of psychosis |
| Depressive episodes | | | |
| Specific fears and phobias | | | |
| Aggressive, acting-out behavior | | | |
| Anxiety and withdrawn behavior | | Enuresis or encopresis | |
| Abuse and/or neglect | Moderate to severe behavior problems (filial therapy, Adlerian play therapy, and ecosystematic play therapy) | Learning disabilities | |
| Divorce of parents | | Mental retardation | |
| Family violence and other family problems | | Physical handicaps | |
| Grief issues | | | |
| Adoption and foster care–related issues | | | |
| Severe trauma (e.g., earthquake, car wreck, war, or kidnapping) | | | |
| Hospitalization | | | |
| Chronic or terminal illness | | | |

SOURCE: Kottman, T. (2001). *Play therapy: Basics and beyond.* Alexandria, VA: American Counseling Association, pp. 16–18. © ACA. Reprinted with permission. No further reproduction authorized without written permission of the American Counseling Association.

If the hypothesis seems incorrect, the counselor should redirect the play to another area. During the third stage, the counselor is more active and engages the child in structured play sequences that encourage the child to confront the problem area.

Rasmussen and Cunningham (1995) described a similar model that integrates focused play and nondirective play. As in the stages discussed by Orton (1997), these authors suggest that play therapy should proceed from nondirective to more directive play. Across all the sessions, the counselor should respond to feelings, clarify behavior, and use open-ended questions to encourage the child to talk. Fall (1997) examined the transcripts of 186 play therapy sessions with elementary students. She reported four descriptive categories of children's play. During the sessions, all the children at some time exhibited play that was characterized as "connected" and "safe play." The other two categories were "unsafe play" and "resolution." Those categories of play have direct implications to counselors, who may use them to help in monitoring the progress through the stages proposed earlier. Cattanach (1995) suggested that children exhibit sensory play, projective play, and dramatic play, and that the most satisfying play contains elements of all types.

## Play Therapy and Managed Health Care

Barnes (1991) suggested criteria for assessing progress toward the goals of play therapy:

- The child comes to the sessions looking more hopeful and relaxed.
- The child appears to have increased confidence.
- The child can summarize what has happened and what has been learned.
- The child's interactions with parents appear more relaxed.
- Play patterns, interactions, and/or body language has changed.
- The child openly raises a problem or concern.

These criteria could be used to help formulate outcomes for the goals of the play therapy, allowing counselors to document the effectiveness of play therapy for themselves, for their clients, and for managed care purposes. The previous discussion of managed care in Chapter 2 offers further guidelines on this type of documentation.

## PLAY THERAPY MEDIA AND STRATEGIES

The materials and props a counselor may use in the play therapy session are play media. These tools can help capture children's interest and provide them with a way to express themselves. Play media should be chosen based on the following criteria:

- Facilitating the relationship between the counselor and child
- Encouraging the child's expression of thoughts and feelings
- Helping the counselor gain insight into the child's world
- Providing the child with an opportunity to test reality
- Providing the child with an acceptable means for expressing unacceptable thoughts and feelings

The material should be selected carefully rather than merely accumulated (Landreth, 1993). Barlow, Strother, and Landreth (1985) detailed three categories of play media: real-life toys, acting-out and aggressive-release toys, and creative-expression and emotional-release toys. Bradley and Gould (1993) suggested the following specific examples for each of those categories:

Real-life toys: doll house and furniture, dolls, doll clothes, doll buggy, bendable doll family, rag doll, household items (iron, ironing board, play kitchen, dishes), telephone, cars, farm animals and buildings, medical kit, school kit, play money, plastic fruit, purse, jewelry

Acting-out and aggressive-release toys: handcuffs, balls, dart gun and suction darts, dart board, suction throwing darts, pounding bench and hammer, drum, blocks, toy soldiers and military equipment, rubber knife, toy gun, masks, inflatable punching toy

Creative-expression and emotional-release toys: colored chalk and eraser, sandbox and sand pencils, paints and brushes, felt-tip pens, white and colored paper, easel, crayons, tape, paste, blunt scissors, Play-Doh clay or plasticine, pipe cleaners, hats and costumes, rags or old towels, hand puppets (p. 87)

Neil and Landreth (2001) listed items for a portable play bag used by a traveling play therapist in a school. Gil (1991) emphasized the use of sunglasses in her work with abused children, noting that children believe they are invisible when they put on sunglasses. She also noted the use of therapeutic stories in her therapy. Kottman (2001) included toys for older children, such as craft supplies, carpentry tools, office supplies and equipment, and more sophisticated games.

The strategies a counselor uses with the media will depend on the theoretical approach that is being followed. Rasmussen and Cunningham (1995) stated that both directive and nondirective techniques have advantages. They suggested that in choosing strategies, the counselor should consider (1) the characteristics of the child, (2) the child's problem(s) and needs, and (3) the stage of the counseling process. Gumaer (1984) defined the play therapy process as being controlled by the counselor. It is related to these factors:

- The counselor's ability to build a helpful relationship with the child
- The goals of counseling, which include the counselor's ability to understand the child's problem
- The counselor's planning skills and use of play material
- The counselor's facilitative responding skills
- The time available for spending with the child

As an example of the use of different media, Fall (1994) incorporated clay, puppets, and beanbag chairs in a school counseling practice. Some common techniques and media useful in communicating with children are art, puppets, and sand play. These are further explored as examples of play therapy techniques in the next section. Counselors and children engaging in play therapy have many other possibilities from which to choose. The books *101 Favorite Play Therapy Techniques* (Kaduson, Cangelosi, & Shaefer, 1997b) and *Windows to our Children* (Oaklander, 1988), as well as many others, contain valuable examples of the use of storytelling, drama, poetry, games, and other techniques.

## Art

Gladding (1998) noted that visual arts offer five benefits for counselors. One is access to the unconscious. A second advantage is the symbolizing of emotions in tangible ways. A third benefit is that visual arts help people become more self-aware.

Fourth, the visual arts are a nonthreatening method that is open to self-interpretation. Finally, they can easily be combined with other play methods.

Orton (1997) stated that art helps establish a relationship, helps children express and resolve their conflicts, and promotes self-expression, problem solving, and confidence.

Naumburg (1966) and Kramer (1971) developed art therapy. Naumburg's psychoanalytic understanding included the interpretation of art as a window to the unconscious, insight as central to the process, and obtaining the client's interpretation of the symbols as crucial to therapy. Kramer focused on the healing power of the act of creating. She explained that process and product are ways of releasing conflict, reexperiencing and rechanneling it, and resolving it.

Art is soothing and can serve as a lubricant for communicating thoughts and feelings (Rubin, 1988). Children should have their choice of media, and counselors can be directive or nondirective about leading them to a certain subject. Landgarten (1981) suggested giving themes for children to address in their artwork, such as emotions, wishes, dreams, plans, self-image, fantasies, families, and situations. Time at the end of the counseling session should be devoted to a discussion of the children's work (Nader & Pynoos, 1991).

Art materials can include crayons, fingerpaint, felt-tip markers, paints, clay and Play-Doh, paper, scissors, paste, glue, and glitter. Gladding (1998) also suggested using published pictures and photography. Campbell (1993a, 1993b) suggested a school counselor might keep an easel with paper, paint, and brushes available for children to use while talking with the counselor.

For counselors to use the "magic art" technique, they need to have a range of colors of construction paper and assorted colors of liquid tempera paint with very small openings in the tops. The child is allowed to select a piece of paper and at least three colors of paint to make a magic picture. The counselor tells the children to draw lines, dots, or any figure they like. After the picture is finished, the child is asked to fold the paper lengthwise. The counselor says, "Magic picture, what will [child's name] draw today?" Then the child unfolds the paper to reveal the new "picture." The counselor asks the child to describe what she or he sees in the picture and is questioned about what makes it look like that (Walker, 1998). Another strategy for counselors is to use yarn to create drawings. Leben (1997) stated this alternative to paper-and-pencil drawing is more appealing to children with low self-esteem.

Berger and Tyler (1994) practiced a model called the "color-emotive brain." Children illustrate their brain, visualizing their level of emotion, then move to a deeper level of disclosing and increased motivation to reach their goals. Shelby (1997) described extensive use of visual arts in her work with children who had survived a disaster. Steinhardt (1995) reported the use of art with a boy who was diagnosed with a borderline disorder. This case study includes the child's response to drawing, masks, and clay. The author noted the effectiveness of providing an environment in which the child discovered his suppressed emotions while playing.

Clay is an art medium that can be used in play therapy. Some activities using clay can be connected to some therapeutic goals. Children can roll clay into a ball and then smash it down. They can also squeeze the clay through their fingers with varying degrees of pressure. To use clay as an activity for self-awareness, children can create a personal mobile. They may use different amounts of clay to represent the value they place on decision points. Clay can also be used to help children clarify goals, build communication skills, and develop time-management strategies.

A final example of the use of art as therapy is provided by Hanes (1997), who presented a case study of a child with aggressive behavior, uncontrollable tantrums, and other behavioral problems. The child produced "messy mixtures" with art materials as she progressed through therapy, eventually improving enough to be released from the hospital.

## Puppets

Axline (1947) suggested that puppets provide opportunities for children to play out their feelings, to reenact events that produced anxiety, and to try out new behaviors. Puppets also allow children to develop communication skills, overcome isolation, build self-esteem, release emotions, and make decisions (Jewel, 1989).

Children can use puppets to tell stories and play out their fantasies. They can act out feelings and deal with their thoughts through puppetry. The child can create a separate person who communicates things too difficult for the child to express directly. Finally, the puppet may be the target of the child's strong emotion, an object of displacement so that anger can be expressed in a healthy way (Bromfield, 1995; Orton, 1997). Gil (1991) identified a benefit of puppet play as the child creating a story anonymously, using characters to enact hidden concerns. Puppet play is also an effective activity for large or small groups of children.

Puppets can be bought or made. Carter and Mason (1998) explained some practical guidelines for selecting puppets. Some of the guidelines are also useful in selecting dolls. Counselors should determine how they intend to use the puppets and should have a variety for the children's choice. The puppets should be chosen to represent a range of emotions, such as aggression, friendship, and neutrality. Puppets should also be representative of family and cultural groups. Other categories for puppets are occupations, symbolic types (witch, pirate), and wild and tame animals. The collection of puppets should relate symbolically to the problems of children. James and Myer (1987) listed these other important selection considerations:

- Ease of manipulation
- Lack of universal symbolism (not Santa Claus)
- Ability to fit both children's and adults' hands
- Unless ventriloquist's dummies or marionettes, soft and cuddly rather than firm and rigid
- Can be cleaned

The final selection consideration is whether the puppet has a "personality" to which the counselor responds with an engaged imagination (Carter & Mason, 1998).

The counselor who plans to use puppets does not have to be a ventriloquist. Basic skills are developing a voice for the puppet's personality, keeping the puppet active enough to engage and hold the child's attention, and knowing when to talk to the child and when to talk to the puppet. To use puppets successfully, counselors must become transparent, real, and courageous. The puppet should look up and out. Only the lower jaw of the puppet should move. Counselors should practice creating emotional expressions and other "moves" in front of a mirror to achieve a realistic presentation (Bradley & Gould, 1993; Carter & Mason, 1998; James & Myer, 1987).

Irwin (1991) used puppets in the following process: First, the child is offered a selection of puppets and invited to tell a story by using them as characters. The child chooses the puppets and creates the story as the counselor observes the child's coping skills in dealing with this experience. The child introduces the puppets as "characters" in the show and "enacts" the story. After the play, the counselor asks the puppets about the plot and themes of the story, extending the make-believe. For the final step, the child is invited to discuss the story and the experience with the counselor. Gil (1991) suggested allowing the child to sit behind a sheet so that the play can be conducted with the child hidden.

The use of puppets with groups of children has been examined. Herring and Meggert (1994) discussed using puppets in working with Native American children. The authors reported that puppetry is beneficial because of the Native American children's love of humor, the importance of clownlike figures in their folklore, and their love of storytelling. Aiello (1988) provided information about the puppet program "Kids on the Block." The puppets in this program represent children who are disabled, as well as those who are not disabled. The goal of the program is to aid in understanding and appreciating differences.

## Sand

Bradley and Gould (1993) considered sand play a self-healing process for the child. Kalff (1981) identified the counselor's role in sand play as being a respectful witness. Gil (1991) suggested that children enjoy the experience of touching, molding, and shaping sand, as well as letting it run through their fingers. She concluded that some children feel nurtured, calmed, or soothed by sand play. Other children use sand play to "make a world," as first discussed by Lowenfeld (1935/1991) as "the World Technique." Kalff (1981) stated that the child resolves conflicts and traumas by externalizing and developing a sense of mastery and control when using sand play. Vinturella and James (1987) believed that sand play is more beneficial than other approaches because no skill is required.

The sand tray is a container with the general dimensions of 20 by 30 by 3 inches. Some counselors use two trays, one for dry sand and one for wet sand; others use only a dry tray. The interior of the tray is painted blue to simulate water.

Carmichael (1994) suggested a transparent plastic storage container with a blue top that can be placed under the tray to provide the blue color. Some dry materials that can be substituted for sand are cornmeal, dried beans or peas, rice, popcorn, and aquarium gravel. The child is offered a choice of miniatures in the following categories:

- Buildings: houses, schools, churches, castles
- People: domestic, military, fantasy, mythological
- Animals: domestic, wild, zoo, prehistoric, marine
- Vehicles: land, air, water, space, war machines
- Vegetation: trees, bushes, shrubs, plants, vegetables
- Structures: bridges, fences, gates, doorways, corrals
- Natural objects: shells, driftwood, stones, bones
- Symbolic objects: wishing well, treasure chests, jewelry (Allan, 1988; Stermback, 1991)

In addition to these miniatures, Allan (1988) indicated that families of items be included—for example, three dinosaurs, four snakes, or a doll family.

The process begins with an invitation to create a miniature world. The counselor provides unconditional positive regard, empathy, warmth, and genuineness (Allan & Berry, 1987; Carmichael, 1994; Landreth, 1993; Stermback, 1991). Allan and Berry (1987) described "the sand as the process, the sand tray as the medium, and the world as the product" (p. 301). DeDomenico (1988) stated that the session should progress without adult interference. The counselor is an attentive observer in the process (Carmichael, 1994).

According to Allan and Berry (1987), three stages occur in sand play: chaos, struggle, and resolution. In the chaos stage, the child imposes no order on the toys or sand. During the struggle phase, battles are waged. At the beginning, no winner emerges. As the sessions progress, the fighting may become more intense and organized, and struggles may become more balanced. A hero emerges, who wins the fight against the dark side. The child who demonstrates resolution restores order and balance in the sand play. The toy figures are in place, and completion and wholeness are apparent (Allan & Berry, 1987; Kalff, 1981).

Tennessen and Strand (1998) compared sand play therapy to principles of Ericksonian psychology. In directed sand play, the child may be told to play with certain pieces or be asked about a certain object. The techniques used are questions to cue clients about change, directives to change the sand tray, directives to create specific scenarios, instructions to work with particular pieces or to bring in a new piece, and use of symbols and metaphors. These authors hypothesized that nondirective sand play may be used to help access emotions and directive play can help manage the impact. They concluded that sand play provides the ideal vehicle for children who have been disempowered, traumatized, and exposed to overwhelming affect.

Mulherin (2001) provided a case study using the sand tray with a mother and child. She discussed the processes of separation, individuation, rapprochement, and recovery that occurred during the stage of treatment. She provided pictures to illustrate how the child represented his emotional states. Vaz (2000) also presented pictures to chronicle the process of sand play. Vaz surveyed other therapists who use sand play. She concluded that most therapists consider the sand play process complete when the images used in the tray reflect the client's return to a more effective approach to life.

Sand trays have been used as a nonviolent method of helping children deal with emotional distress (Wheat, 1995). Each child in an early childhood group was allowed 30 to 60 minutes a week with the sand trays. Teachers who observed the process commented that the children worked through feelings of sadness, anger, and disappointment, returning to the classroom group in a more relaxed state. The teachers were very supportive of the sand play.

This brief overview of using art, puppets, and sand trays shows the possibilities of play media. Counselors are encouraged to investigate others, as well as create their own ways of incorporating play materials into their counseling practice. The following case study illustrates one additional method.

## CASE STUDY*

### *Identification of the Problem*

Amos is a sixth-grade student in a rural middle school. His teacher referred him to the school counselor because his grades had dropped since the beginning of the school year and he was frequently distracted in class.

### *Individual and Background Information*

*Academic.*   School records indicate that Amos's ability is in the average range. He received good grades in elementary school, and teachers noted his positive disposition and quiet nature. End-of-grade tests indicate that his math skills are much stronger than his verbal skills.

*Family.*   Amos lives with his mother and stepfather. He has an older half-brother who is in eighth grade at the same school and a younger brother in the third grade at a nearby elementary school. Although Amos has not told the counselor, she knows his older brother was in a serious accident during the past summer and has recently had an operation. The brother has not returned to school.

*Social.*   According to teachers' reports, Amos is well liked and easily forms friendships. He is involved with several school sports teams and clubs. He enjoys interacting with his classmates.

### *Counseling Method*

After meeting with Amos initially to assess the problem, the counselor decided he might benefit from an alternative method of counseling rather than verbal interactions only. She decided to use a nondirected play therapy approach.

---

*The case of Amos was contributed by Margery Peskin.

*Transcript*

*Counselor:* Hi, Amos! How are you doing today?

*Amos:* Fine.

*Counselor:* Last time we met, you mentioned you had a basketball game that night. How did it go?

*Amos:* Okay.

*Counselor:* How did you think the game went?

*Amos:* Pretty good.

*Counselor:* That sounds positive. Today I thought we could try something a little different than what we've been doing. I laid out on the table here some supplies. You can see I've got colored paper, markers, crayons, glue, yarn, scissors, clay, and watercolors.

*Amos:* I love clay. I work with clay at home all the time.

*Counselor:* Great. It sounds like you've had some experience with some of these materials. Here's what I'd like you to do. Using any combination of the materials here, create something that shows me what you have been thinking about the most over the past few days. You can use just one kind of material or as many as you want. Also, I want you to understand that there is not a "right" or "wrong" way to do this; create anything you want. Remember that our relationship is confidential, so I'm not going to show what you've made to anyone else unless you ask me to. Any questions?

*Amos:* No.

*Counselor:* Okay.

[After some time has passed]

*Amos:* I'm done.

*Counselor:* I wonder if you'd tell me what you've made.

*Amos:* Well, the two clay figures are my parents. See my mom has long blond hair, so this one has yellow string on the top, and my dad has short blond hair, so this one has a short yellow string. This rectangle of paper on the table is a hospital bed, and this clay is my brother because he's been really sick and had an operation on his neck.

*Counselor:* It must be hard that your brother is so sick. One thing I notice is that you're not in this scene.

*Amos:* Well, I would have made myself, but there wasn't enough clay.

*Counselor:* You're feeling left out.

*Amos:* Lots of time I think they have forgotten me.

*Counselor:* So it sounds like your parents are spending a lot of time with your brother in the hospital.

*Amos:* Yeah, they go there every afternoon, so when I get home from school no one is at home.

*Counselor:* That must be pretty difficult because you are worried about your brother but feel lonely, too.

*Amos:* Yeah, sometimes.

*Counselor:* I'm wondering if you ever feel guilty because you wish your parents weren't spending so much time with your brother so they might have more time to spend with you.

*Amos:* Exactly. But I feel really bad about that.

*Counselor:* It sounds like there are a lot of different things for you to be worried about that might be making it hard to concentrate in school.

*Amos:* Usually I like school, but right now I'm sad all the time. I keep wondering if the doctors have found out anything about my brother, and then I wonder if my mom or dad will be home after school and then I feel bad because my brother needs them, too.

*Counselor:* You have lots of different things fighting for your attention. Maybe we can figure out some ways to help you relax a bit. Let's meet again on Wednesday to see what we can try.

*Amos:* That sounds good.

## SUMMARY

In their review of the play therapy literature related to children who are abused or neglected, White and Allers (1994) concluded that research deficits exist. Although they believe in play therapy as an important clinical technique, they nevertheless agreed with Phillips (1985) that no systematic program of research has been defined for play therapy. The scarcity of empirical evidence on the effectiveness of play therapy with children is an unfortunate discrepancy in otherwise vibrant endorsements of this approach. Perhaps practicing counselors will soon begin to answer this call for evidence and begin to gather the data to support the practice of play therapy.

Lowenfeld (1935/1991) and her staff at the Institute of Child Psychology in London recorded and classified the play of 229 children between the years of 1928 and 1934. Her book documents the classification of the children's play as bodily activity, repetition of experience, demonstration of fantasies, realization of the environment, and preparation for life. She concluded that play served four purposes for children:

- Play is children's means for making contact with the environment in a way similar to the social aspect of work in an adult's life.
- Play helps children bridge consciousness and emotional experience as conversation, introspection, philosophy, and religion do for adults.
- Play represents to the child the overt expression of emotional life as does art for an adult.
- Play serves the child as relaxation and amusement. (Lowenfeld, 1935/1991, p. 232)

She argued that play is an essential function of moving from immaturity to emotional maturity. Counselors strive to enhance the development of children; play therapy is a significant way of influencing that growth.

W E B S I T E S for Play Therapy

Association for Play Therapy, Inc.
www.iapt.org

Canadian Play Therapy Institute
www.playtherapy.org

Kid Power Play Therapy, Counseling and Therapy
www.snowcrest.net/kidpower/play.html

## REFERENCES

Aiello, B. (1988). The kids on the block and attitude change: A 10-year perspective. In H. E. Yucker (Ed.), *Attitudes toward persons with disabilities* (pp. 223–229). New York: Springer.

Albon, S. L. (1996). The therapeutic action of play. *Journal of the American Academy of Child and Adolescent Psychiatry, 35,* 545–547.

Allan, J. (1988). *Inscapes of the child's world: Jungian counseling in schools and clinics.* Dallas: Spring.

Allan, J. (1997). Jungian play psychotherapy. In K. O'Connor & L. M. Braverman (Eds.), *Play therapy theory and practice: A comparative presentation* (pp. 100–130). New York: Wiley.

Allan, J., & Berry, P. (1987). Sandplay. *Elementary School Guidance and Counseling, 21,* 300–306.

Anderson, J., & Richards, N. (1995, October). *Play therapy in the real world: Coping with managed care, challenging children, skeptical colleagues, time and space constraints.* Paper presented at the first annual conference of the Iowa Association of Play Therapy, Iowa City.

Ariel, S. (1992). *Strategic family play therapy.* New York: Wiley.

Ariel, S. (1997). Strategic family play therapy. In K. O'Connor & L. M. Braverman (Eds.), *Play therapy theory and practice: A comparative presentation* (pp. 358–395). New York: Wiley.

Association for Play Therapy. (1997). Play therapy definition. *Association for Play Therapy Newsletter, 16,* 4.

Axline, V. (1947). *Play therapy: The inner dynamics of childhood.* Boston: Houghton Mifflin.

Barlow, K., Strother, J., & Landreth, G. (1985). Child-centered play therapy: Nancy from baldness to curls. *The School Counselor, 32,* 347–356.

Barnes, M. (1991). *The magic of play therapy: A workshop on specialized therapeutic skills with children.* Kingston, Ontario, Canada: Mandala Therapeutic Services.

Barnes, M. (1996). *The healing path with children: An exploration for parents and professionals.* Kingston, Ontario: Viktoria, Fermoyle & Berrigan.

Berger, S. N., & Tyler, J. L. (1994). The color-emotive brain: Gone a long journey. *International Journal of Play Therapy, 33,* 57–70.

Bradley, L. J., & Gould, L. J. (1993). Individual counseling: Creative interventions. In A. Vernon (Ed.), *Counseling children and adolescents* (pp. 84–117). Denver: Love Publishing.

Bratton, S., & Ray, D. (2000). What the research shows about play therapy. *International Journal of Play Therapy, 9,* 47–88.

Bratton, S., Ray, D., & Moffit, K. (1998). Filial/family play therapy: An intervention for custodial grandparents and their grandchildren. *Educational Gerontology, 24,* 391–407.

Bratton, S. C. (1994). Filial therapy with single parents *Dissertation Abstracts International, 54* (08). p. 2890.

Bromfield, R. (1995). The use of puppets in play therapy. *Child and Adolescent Social Work Journal, 12,* 435–444.

Campbell, C. A. (1993a). Interview with Violet Oaklander, author of *Windows to our Children. Elementary School Guidance and Counseling, 28,* 52–61.

Campbell, C. A. (1993b). Play, the fabric of elementary school counseling programs. *Elementary School Guidance and Counseling, 28,* 10–16.

Cangelosi, D. M. (1997). Play therapy for children from divorced and separated families. In H. G. Kaduson, D. Cangelosi, & C. E. Schaefer (Eds.), *The playing cure: Individualized play therapy for specific childhood problems* (pp. 119–142). Northvale, NJ: Jason Aronson.

Carmichael, K. D. (1994). Sand play as an elementary school strategy. *Elementary School Guidance and Counseling, 28,* 302–307.

Carmichael, K. D., & Lane, K. S. (1997). Play therapy with children of alcoholics. *Alcoholism Treatment Quarterly, 15,* 43–52.

Carter, R. B., & Mason, P. S. (1998). The selection and use of puppets in counseling. *Professional School Counseling 1,* 50–53.

Cattanach, A. (1994). *Play therapy: Where the sky meets the underworld.* Bristol, PA: Jessica Kingsley.

Cattanach, A. (1995). Drama and play therapy with young children. *The Arts in Psychotherapy, 22,* 223–228.

Cochran, J. L. (1996). Using play and art therapy to help culturally diverse students overcome barriers to school success. *School Counselor, 43,* 287–298.

Coleman, V., Parmer, T., & Barker, S. (1993). Play therapy for a multicultural population: Guidelines for mental health professionals. *International Journal of Play Therapy, 2,* 63–74.

DeDomenico, G. (1988). *Sand tray world play: A comprehensive guide to the use of the sand tray in psychotherapeutic and transformational settings.* San Francisco: San Francisco State University.

Fall, M. (1994). Physical and emotional expression: A combination approach for working with children in the small areas of a school counselor's office. *School Counselor, 42,* 73–77.

Fall, M. (1997). From stages to categories: A study of children's play in play therapy. *International Journal of Play Therapy, 6,*1–21.

Fall, M. (1999). A play therapy intervention and its relationship to self-efficacy and learning behaviors. *Professional School Counseling, 2,* 194–205.

Gil, E. (1991). *The healing power of play: Working with abused children.* New York: Guilford.

Ginott, H. G. (1994). Quotation. C. E. Schaefer & H. Kaduson (Eds.), *The quotable play therapist: 238 of the all-time best quotes on play and play therapy.* Northvale, NJ: Jason Aronson, p. 33.

Gladding, S. T. (1993). The therapeutic use of play in counseling: An overview. *Journal of Humanistic Education and Development, 31,* 106–115.

Gladding, S. T. (1998). *Counseling as an art: The creative arts in counseling.* Alexandria, VA: American Counseling Association.

Glover, C. J. (2001). Cultural considerations in play therapy. In G. L. Landreth (Ed.), *Innovations in play therapy: Issues, process, and special populations* (pp. 31–42). Philadelphia: Brunner-Routledge.

Gonzalez-Mena, J. (1998). *The child in the family and the community* (2nd ed.). Upper Saddle River, NJ: Merrill.

Guerney, L. (1997). Filial therapy. In K. O'Connor & L. M. Braverman (Eds.), *Play therapy theory and practice: A comparative presentation* (pp. 131–159). New York: Wiley.

Gumaer, J. (1984). *Counseling and therapy for children.* New York: Free Press.

Hanes, M. (1997). Producing messy mixtures in art therapy. *American Journal of Art Therapy, 35,* 70–73.

Harris, T. E., & Landreth, G. L. (2001). Essential personality characteristics of effective play therapists. In G. L. Landreth (Ed.), *Innovations in play therapy: Issues, process and special populations* (pp. 23–31). Philadelphia: Brunner-Routledge.

Hartup, W. W. (1992). *Having friends, making friends, and keeping friends: Relationships as educational contexts.* Urbana, IL: Eric Clearinghouse on Elementary and Early Childhood Education. (ERIC Document Reproduction Service No. ED345854)

Harvey, S. (1997). Dynamic family play therapy: A creative arts approach. In K. O'Connor & L. M. Braverman (Eds.), *Play therapy theory and practice: A comparative presentation* (pp. 341–367). New York: Wiley.

Henderson, D. A., & Gladding, S. T. (1998). The creative arts in counseling: A multicultural perspective. *Arts in Psychotherapy, 25,* 183–187.

Henniger, M. L. (1995). Play: Antidote for childhood stress. *Early Child Development and Care, 105,* 7–12.

Herring, R. D., & Meggert, S. S. (1994). The use of humor as a counseling strategy with Native American Indian children. *Elementary School Guidance and Counseling 29,* 67–75.

Irwin, E. C. (1991). The use of a puppet interview to understand children. In C. E. Schaefer, K. Gitlin, and A. Sandgrund (Eds.), *Play diagnosis and assessment* (pp. 617–642). New York: John Wiley.

James, R. K., & Myer, R. (1987). Puppets: The elementary school counselors' right or left arm. *Elementary School Guidance and Counseling 21,* 262–265.

Jernberg, A. (1993). Attachment formation. In C. E. Schaefer (Ed.), *The therapeutic powers of play* (pp. 241–265). Northvale, NJ: Jason Aronson.

Jewel, D. L. (1989). *Confronting child abuse through recreation.* Springfield, IL: Charles C. Thomas.

Johnson, B., Franklin, L. C., Hall, K., Prieto, L. R. (2000). Parent training through play: Parent–child interaction therapy with a hyperactive child. *Family Journal, 8,* 180–187.

Johnson, L. (1995). Filial therapy: A bridge between individual child therapy and family therapy. *Journal of Family Psychotherapy, 6,* 55–70.

Jung, C. G. (1961). *Memories, dreams, reflections.* New York: Random House.

Kaduson, H. G. (1997). Play therapy for children with attention-deficit hyperactivity disorder. In H. G. Kaduson, D. Cangelosi, & C. E. Schaefer (Eds.), *The playing cure: Individualized play therapy for specific childhood problems* (pp. 197–228). Northvale, NJ: Jason Aronson.

Kaduson, H. G., Cangelosi, D., & Schaefer, C. E. (1997a). *The playing cure: Individualized play therapy for specific childhood problems.* Northvale, NJ: Jason Aronson.

Kaduson, H., Cangelosi, D., & Schaefer, C. (Eds.). (1997b). *101 favorite play therapy techniques.* Northvale, NJ: Jason Aronson.

Kalff, D. M. (1981). *Sandplay: A psychotherapeutic approach to the psyche.* Boston: Sigo.

Koller, T. J., & Booth, P. (1997). Fostering attachment through family theraplay. In K. O'Connor & L. M. Braverman (Eds.), *Play therapy theory and practice: A comparative presentation* (pp. 204–233). New York: Wiley.

Kottman, T. (2001). *Play therapy: Basics and beyond.* Alexandria, VA: American Counseling Association.

Kramer, E. (1971). *Art as therapy with children.* New York: Schocken.

Landgarten, H. B. (1981). *Clinical art therapy: A comprehensive guide.* New York: Brunner/Mazel.

Landreth, G. L. (1991). *Play therapy: The art of the relationship.* Bristol, PA: Accelerated Development.

Landreth, G. L. (1993). Child-centered play therapy. *Elementary School Guidance and Counseling, 28,* 17–29.

Landreth, G. L., & Sweeney, D. S. (2001). Child-centered group play therapy. In G. L. Landreth (Ed.), *Innovations in play therapy: Issues, process, and special populations* (pp. 181–202). Philadelphia: Brunner-Routledge.

Leben, N. Y. (1997). The yarn drawing game. In H. Kaduson & C. Schaefer (Eds.), *101 favorite play therapy techniques* (pp. 61–63). Northvale, NJ: Jason Aronson.

Leblanc, M., & Ritchie, M. (1999). Predictors of play therapy outcomes. *International Journal of Play Therapy, 8,* 19–34.

Leblanc, M., & Ritchie, M. (2001). A meta-analysis of play therapy outcomes. *Counselling Psychology Quarterly, 14,* 149–164.

Lobaugh, F. A. (1992). Filial therapy with incarcerated parents. *Dissertation Abstracts International, 53* (04), 2046.

Lowenfeld, M. (1935/1991). *Play in childhood.* London: MacKeith.

McDonald, L., & Morgan, A. (1997). Families and schools together (FAST): Integrating community development with clinical strategies. *Families in Society, 78,* 140–156.

Moustakas, C. (1998). *Relationship play therapy.* Northvale, NJ: Jason Aronson.

Mulherin, M. A. (2001). The Masterson approach with play therapy: A parallel process between mother and child. *American Journal of Psychotherapy, 55,* 251–272.

Nader, K., & Pynoos, R. S. (1991). Play and drawing techniques as tools for interviewing traumatized children. In C. E. Schaefer, K. Gitlin, & A. Sandgrund (Eds.), *Play diagnosis and assessment* (pp. 375–389). New York: Wiley.

Naumberg, M. (1966). *Dynamically oriented art therapy.* New York: Grune & Stratton.

Neil, B., & Landreth, G. L. (2001). Have toys—will travel: A traveling play therapist in the school setting. In G. L. Landreth (Ed.), *Innovations in play therapy: Issues, process, and special populations* (pp. 349–360). Philadelphia: Brunner-Routledge.

Oaklander, V. (1988). *Windows to our children: A gestalt therapy approach to children and adolescents.* Highland, NY: Center for Gestalt Development.

O'Connor, K. (1991). The practice of group play therapy. In *The play therapy primer: An integration of theories and techniques* (pp. 143–156). Northvale, NJ: Jason Aronson.

O'Connor, K. (2000). *The play therapy primer* (2nd ed.). New York: Wiley.

O'Connor, K., & Schaefer, C. (1994). *The handbook of play therapy: Vol. 2. Advances and innovations.* New York: Wiley.

O'Connor, K. J., & Ammen, S. (1997). *Play therapy treatment planning and interventions: The ecosystemic model and workbook.* New York: Academic Press.

Orton, G. L. (1997). *Strategies for counseling with children and their parents.* Pacific Grove, CA: Brooks/Cole.

Phillips, R. D. (1985). Whistling in the dark? A review of play therapy research. *Psychotherapy, 22,* 752–760.

Rasmussen, L. A., & Cunningham, C. (1995). Focused play therapy and nondirective play therapy: Can they be integrated? *Journal of Child Sexual Abuse, 4,* 1–20.

Ray, D., Bratton, S. C., & Brandt, M. A. (2000). Filial/family play therapy for single parents of young children attending community colleges. *Community College Journal of Research and Practice, 24,* 469–487.

Rotter, J. C., & Bush, M. V. (2000). Play and family therapy. *Family Journal, 8,* 172–177.

Rubin, J. A. (1988). Art counseling: An alternative. *Elementary School Guidance and Counseling, 22,* 180–185.

Schaefer, C. (Ed.). (1993). *The therapeutic power of play.* Northvale, NJ: Jason Aronson.

Schaefer, C., & Greenberg, R. (1997). Measurement of playfulness: A neglected therapist variable. *International Journal of Play Therapy, 6,* 21–32.

Schaefer, C. E., Jacobsen, H. E., & Ghahramanlou, M. (2000). Play group therapy for social skills deficits in children. In H. G. Kaduson, & C. E. Schaefer (Eds.), *Short-term play therapy for children* (pp. 296–344). New York: Guilford.

Shelby, J. S. (1997). Rubble, disruption, and tears: Helping young survivors of natural disaster. In H. G. Kaduson, D. Cangelosi, & C. E. Schaefer (Eds.), *The playing cure: Individualized play therapy for specific childhood problems* (pp. 143–170). Northvale, NJ: Jason Aronson.

Steinhardt, L. (1995). Long-term creative therapy with a borderline psychotic boy. *American Journal of Art Therapy, 34,* 43–50.

Stermback, S. (Ed.). (1991). *Sandplay studies.* Boston: Sigo.

Sweeney, D. S. (1997). *Counseling children through the world of play.* Wheaton, IL: Tyndale House.

Tennessen, J., & Strand, D. (1998). A comparative analysis of directed sandplay therapy and principles of Ericksonian psychology. *Arts in Psychotherapy, 25,* 109–114.

VanFleet, R. (1997). Play and perfectionism: Putting fun back into families. In H. G. Kaduson, D. Cangelosi, & C. E. Schaefer (Eds.), *The playing cure: Individualized play therapy for specific childhood problems* (pp. 61–82). Northvale, NJ: Jason Aronson.

VanFleet, R. (2000). *A parent's handbook of filial therapy: Building strong families with play.* Boiling Springs, PA: Play Therapy Press.

Vaz, K. M. (2000). When is a sandplay psychotherapy process completed? *International Journal of Action Methods: Psychodrama, Skill Training, and Role Playing, 53,* 66–81.

Vinturella, L., & James, R. (1987). Sand play: A therapeutic medium with children. *Elementary School Guidance and Counseling, 21,* 229–238.

Walker, R. (1998). Magic art. In H. Kaduson & C. Schaefer (Eds.), *101 favorite play therapy techniques* (pp. 61–63). Northvale, NJ: Jason Aronson.

Wheat, R. (1995). Help children work through emotional difficulties—Sand trays are great! *Young Children, 51,* 82–83.

White, J., & Allers, C. T. (1994). Play therapy with abused children: A review of the literature. *Journal of Counseling and Development, 72,* 390–394.

# Chapter 15

# Counseling with Children
# from Different Cultures

*To have one's individuality completely ignored is like being pushed
quite out of life. Like being blown out as one blows out a light.*
—Evelyn Scott

## INTRODUCTION

Our nation has a changing demographic profile. Figure 15-1 shows the total number of children under 18 during the last three decades to 2010. Henderson (2000) further extends those figures and projects that in 2050 the number of Hispanics in the United States will have moved from 31.4 million to 98.2 million, African Americans from 34.9 million to 59.2 million, and Asians, from 10.7 million to 37.6 million. He suggests that more than 50% of the nation's workforce will include immigrants and people from ethnic groups some classify as minority.

Certainly, these population changes indicate that counselors will have increasing opportunities to work with children who may have cultural practices and beliefs that the counselors may not know. Baruth and Manning (2003) list the following challenges counselors may face in those situations:

- Communication difficulties
- Misunderstanding the culture and the impact of the culture on the process of counseling
- Mistaken assumptions about cultural assimilation
- Different social class values and orientations
- Stereotypical generalizations
- An assumption of cultural bias
- Inability to understand the worldview of the client (p. 20).

Pedersen (1997) includes other cautions: Cultural beliefs influence diagnosis and treatment; diagnoses differ across cultures, clients express symptoms differently across cultures, diagnoses may vary according to categories found most of-

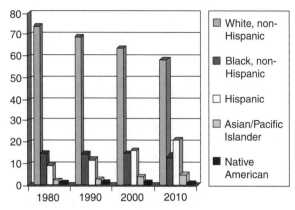

FIGURE 15-1   Percentage of children under 18 by race and ethnicity. (Adapted from Federal Interagency Forum on Child and Family Statistics [2001]. *America's children: Key national indicators of well-being, 2001,* Tables POP1 and POP3. Washington, DC: U.S. Government Printing Office)

ten in the majority populations, and finally most counselors are members of the majority population, whereas most clients are members of the minority.

All counselors in some ways work with culturally diverse people. Rather than be daunted by the challenges, we recommend that counselors make a commitment to continuous renewal and vigilance, increase their awareness of self, and refine and deepen the knowledge and skills needed to be an effective counselor in an increasingly pluralistic world. This chapter is intended only as an overview of some considerations necessary in counseling across cultures. We will use the terms *diversity, cross-cultural, multicultural,* and *pluralistic* as synonyms for the concept of working with someone who has a cultural heritage different from that of the counselor.

## COMPETENCE

Pedersen (2002) explains that training in multicultural competence has focused on three areas. A beginning part involves increasing one's awareness of culturally learned attitudes, beliefs, and values. A second component focuses on knowledge of culturally relevant facts. The third part of the sequence concentrates on developing skills for interventions that are culturally appropriate. Arredondo and Glauner (1992) propose a personal identity model based on the premises that (1) all people are multicultural, (2) all have personal, political, and historical culture, and (3) all are affected by sociocultural, political, environmental, and historical events.

Pederson (1994) suggested the following goals for the multiculturally skilled counselor:

- Is aware of the other cultures
- Is willing to receive information about other value systems and voluntarily selects articles and books about a different culture

- Responds to instructional materials about a different culture by asking questions and offering comments
- Obtains satisfaction from responding to information about another culture
- Accepts the idea that knowing and understanding people of other cultures is good
- Prefers the previous idea to any competing dogma, rejecting cultural isolationism
- Is committed to the value of international understanding and cooperation
- Conceptualizes this value into the total value system by weighing alternative international policies and practices against the standard of international understanding rather than against narrow special interest (p. 209)

Skills and information Pederson (1994) suggests for counselors also include:

- Knows much of the history, customs, language, and geography of one or more cultures other than his or her own
- Knows contributions of various cultures of the world
- Knows where and how to find additional information about other cultures
- Demonstrates constructive ability to solve problems involving international understanding
- Sees the implications in data regarding social and economic circumstances
- Understands that people are more alike than different
- Applies general ideas regarding culture to a popular cultural context
- Analyzes a culture into component parts
- Forms generalizations from cultural data and observes exceptions
- Observes differences in wealth, values, and behavior between cultures and understands the reasons for the differences
- Sees the necessity of world trade and the value of world travel
- Understands the causes for changes in alliances among nations
- Sees the implications of shortened travel and communication time between countries
- Understands the nature of international interdependence
- Evaluates ideas based on how they affect world harmony (pp. 209–210)

Butter and Molidor (1995) described issues they believe may interfere with culturally sensitive counseling. These include the following:

- Professional self-awareness—an understanding of one's own internal states, as well as how one is seen as a professional
- Clients' inconsistent attendance and participation—due to factors such as fear of confronting issues in counseling, financial distress, lack of transportation, or other personal issues (e.g., alcohol abuse)
- Different priorities that place emphasis on other tasks considered to be more important
- A lack of trust—perhaps from suspicion of the institution or based on a bad previous experience
- Differing cultural values that are not understood or accepted

- Motivation—especially those clients for whom services are mandated, such as juvenile delinquents

Let us now consider more detailed information about counseling competencies and working with selected groups.

## Multicultural Counseling Competencies

Multicultural counseling competencies based on this model have been articulated by Arredondo and her colleagues (1996) and clearly outline the attitudes and beliefs, knowledge, and skills that counselors should develop in becoming aware of their own cultural values and biases, their clients' worldview, and appropriate intervention strategies. The competencies deserve intense study and ongoing practice. Lee (2001) suggested that counselors who succeed with clients from a variety of ethnic backgrounds employ a perspective that "acknowledges human differences and celebrates human similarities" (p. 583). Multicultural counseling competencies guide counselors in achieving that perspective and the resulting skills.

### Awareness

Self-awareness involves gaining an understanding of the specific things that influence one's psychological, emotional, and cultural attributes. Baruth and Manning (2003) and Lee (2001) suggested that counselors investigate their own cultural background and the impact it has on their beliefs, attitudes, and values. Washington (1994) outlined a three-step process to clarify cultural knowledge. His chapter includes questions and a process that may be adapted for a cultural inventory, both for the counselor and for those with whom one works.

As well as knowledge of self, counselors must develop extensive awareness of racism, sexism, and poverty; individual differences; other culture(s); and diversity (Locke & Parker, 1994). Building an awareness of how culture influences educational opportunities, cognitive development, and the interpretation of history (Arredondo, 1996) is another desired outcome of the awareness process. The questionnaire in Table 15-1 could serve as a self-check on the awareness, knowledge, and skills needed to work with a multicultural population.

### Knowledge

Pedersen (2002) explained that "all behaviors are learned and displayed within cultural contexts" (p. 3). He stated that a counselor who considers the cultural context will be able to measure behavior more accurately, define personal identity more clearly, understand problems more fully, and counsel more meaningfully. The concept of cultural context incorporates variables such as social class, gender, ethnicity, race, religion, language, age, and exceptionalities among other things.

TABLE 15-1 Criteria for counseling with ethnic minority children

| Skills | Yes | No | Needs improvement |
|---|---|---|---|
| Do you constantly assess your values, attitudes, and beliefs and refrain from imposing them on children? | | | |
| Do you frequently attend training or skill sessions for working with a culturally diverse population? | | | |
| Are you familiar with the strategies that promote equity in a pluralistic society? | | | |
| Are you able to recognize the child's reality, including the effect of racism and poverty? | | | |
| Do you have an awareness and understanding of both verbal and nonverbal language patterns of different ethnic groups? | | | |
| Are you able to discuss openly racial/ethnic differences and issues? | | | |
| Do you have high expectations for all and help them gather resources and opportunities necessary for success? | | | |
| Do you have the ability to understand the child's help-seeking, including the child's idea of the problem and solution? | | | |
| Do you consider the links between the systemic problems and the child's individual concerns? | | | |
| Can you consider the implications of a suggested solution in relation to the child's cultural reality? | | | |
| Are you able to determine and select from three goal categories: Situational stress (isolation, poverty); Cultural transition (conflictual family–school practice); Transcultural patterns (developmental difficulties)? | | | |
| Can you help the child form a goal that is problem or growth oriented, structured, realistic, concrete, practical, and achievable? | | | |
| Do you have the skills to apply new strategies consistent with the needs and problem of the child, the degree of acculturation, and the motivation for change? | | | |

NOTE: Adapted from Greenberg, J. M., and Shaffer, S. (1991). *Elements of equity: Criteria for equitable schools.* The Mid-Atlantic Equity Consortium, www.maec.org (Retrieved August 25, 2002) and Ho, M.K. (1990). *Minority children and adolescents in therapy.* Thousand Oaks, CA: Sage Publications (pp. 28–29). Reprinted by permission of Sage Publications, Inc.

Baruth and Manning (2003) point out that culture should not be considered as fixed but as fluid. Laird (2000) further clarifies culture as intersections of class, race, ethnicity, experiences, and other variables. All these authors remind us that we must recognize the impact of the world in which a child lives as we build and maintain a helpful counseling relationship.

Lee (2001) proposed various knowledge bases needed for planning, delivering, and evaluating counseling services. Counselors should understand the impact of economic, social, and political systems on ethnic groups. Counselors should accumulate information about the history, customs, and values of various groups in an effort to understand the intersection of ethnic contexts with the person. He suggests counselors use media, the Internet, and personal experiences with diverse groups to gain the knowledge needed.

Among some of the important terms in the field of cross-cultural counseling that counselors need to understand are *race, ethnic, ethnicity, worldview, ethnic identity development,* and *acculturation.* Some explanations of those terms occur in the following paragraphs. Hernandez (1989) explained that *race* refers to a concept from anthropology used for classifications of people according to physical characteristics. Mio, Trimble, Arredondo, Cheatham, and Sue (1999) defined *race* as a classification system based on "hair texture, skin color, eye color, and facial features" that is used to categorize people into four groups: Asian, Black, White, or American Indian. They contend that these racial classifications are scientifically meaningless.

An ethnic group refers to a population with members that have a collective identity and heritage. *Ethnic,* according to Mio and colleagues (1999), refers to the various situations in which group members have lived and acted together, values, and a shared style of life. Using these definitions, Lee (2001) concluded that the "personality characteristics among people that become reinforced through association over time . . . these long-standing dynamics of thinking, feeling, and behaving that form the cultural basis of *ethnicity* or an *ethnic group*" (p. 582). He suggested using terminology that captures the realities of ethnic group membership such as Irish American, Korean American, Lakota, and Jamaican American.

*Worldview,* according to Sodowsky and Johnson (1994), consists of an individual's experiences and the social, moral, religious, educational, economic, and political influences of one's group. Lonner and Ibrahim (2002) contend that worldview constitutes the source of personal values, beliefs, and assumptions—one's dominant cognitive framework (Baruth & Manning, 2003). Some authors (Grieger & Ponterotto, 1995; Ibrahim, Roysircar-Sodowsky, & Ohnishi, 2001) assert that worldview is the most important variable in multicultural counseling. A contemporary definition of multicultural counseling reflects this:

> Any counseling relationship in which the counselor and the client belong to different cultural groups, hold different assumptions about social reality, and subscribe to different worldviews. (Das, 1995)

Sue, Ivey, and Pedersen (1996, p. 7) suggested that "multicultural psychologists have also noted that theories of counseling and psychotherapy represent a variety of worldviews, each with its own values, biases, and assumptions about human behavior." They listed several definitions of the term *worldview,* with most focusing on a person's perception of his or her relationship with the world and the way one understands the world, including individual attitudes, values, opinions, and concepts that influence how a person thinks, makes decisions, and behaves. They pointed out that if our present counseling theories represent different worldviews, it is very possible that a counselor's theoretical orientation could clash with the client from a different culture. Sue, Ivey, and Pederson (1996) proposed a theory (metatheory) of multicultural counseling and therapy with a number of propositions and corollaries and described its implications for practice, training, and research.

Trevino (1996) drew on the works of Sue and Ibrahim regarding the worldview of counseling to develop her model of the change process in cross-cultural counseling. She contended that "worldviews are formed out of personal experience through interaction with members of an individual's culture" (p. 200). These experiences can be shared, or common to all members, or they can be unique, particular to one's personal and family history. Trevino believed that these worldviews are organized into general views or basic understandings of the world and that specific views represent particular perceptions (e.g., specific views of marriage, illness, or companionship). She wrote that "without an understanding of how their clients are perceiving and understanding the world, counselors would be unable to understand and assess client problems, establish a therapeutic alliance, or formulate effective strategies for intervention" (p. 199). The counselor's role is to work with the client to find a better way of understanding and interacting with the world through cognitive, behavioral, or affective techniques. Trevino postulated that both congruency and discrepancy facilitate change—congruency enhances understanding and the relationship, whereas discrepancy facilitates change. According to Trevino, her model, while needing further research, is a "powerful way of understanding and operationalizing the process of seeing the world through the eyes of another human being" (p. 212).

Fischer, Jome, and Atkinson (1998), however, suggested that there are common factors in counseling that can bridge the gap between "culturally specific" counseling and "universal approaches." They contended these common factors, combined with a thorough knowledge of the client's culture, can serve as a framework for understanding multicultural literature on counseling, can have empirical support, and may be useful in serving as a guide for future research, training, and practice. Fischer, Jome, and Atkinson (1998) proposed four common factors as essential to the success of all counseling, including multicultural:

- The therapeutic relationship—a positive, trusting, and healing relationship between the counselor and client is supported by Western integrationists and transcultural literature
- A shared worldview—a common framework from which counselor and client conduct their work together
- Client expectations—based on a shared worldview that increases the client's positive expectations that counseling will be helpful
- Rituals or interventions—effective techniques are believed by both client and counselor to be appropriate for positive outcomes

## Ethnic Identity Development

Ho (1992) explained the difference between ethnicity and ethnic identity. *Ethnicity* refers to the person's sense of membership in a group and the associated thoughts, feelings, and behavior. In other words, ethnicity denotes group patterns. *Ethnic identity* refers to the person's incorporation of those patterns, accepting the beliefs, feelings, and actions as one's own. Ethnic identity would shape beliefs about mental health and illness, styles, coping, and help-seeking. Lee (2001) calls this the "interior vision," a foundation of social forms and personality dimensions.

*Ethnic identity development* has been described as a series of stages (Atkinson, Morten, & Sue, 1993; Cross, 1995) and as personality statuses (Helms, 1995). Helms (2003) proposed three interacting components that influence a person's ethnic identity: personal, affiliative, and reference group. The personal component relates to self-concept, "Who am I?" The affiliative component relates to the degree to which the person believes that he or she shares whatever happens to other members of his or her ethnic group. The reference group component includes the person's level of conforming to the norms of the group. She explained that young children probably reflect the identity climate of their home. During the school years, their understandings become more complex, and they may struggle with exclusion in their schools and communities. To help meet these challenges, Washington and his colleagues (2003) detailed a developmental group process that helps young people recognize their cultural identity group and develop confidence and pride.

### Acculturation

Acculturation is the process of becoming like another culture. Garrett (1995) described levels of acculturation. In the traditional level, a person embraces traditional beliefs and values. A person in the transition level holds onto the traditional mores and those of the dominant culture. This person may not accept all of either culture. At the bicultural level, the person accepts and is accepted by both the dominant culture and the traditional culture. The fourth type of acculturation is assimilation—accepting only the dominant cultural beliefs and values. Ho (1992) suggested that group counseling is most appropriate for minority children who are experiencing difficulties related to acculturation, ethnic identity, and/or bicultural skills.

## Skills

Counseling involves the ability to aid people in resolving problems or in making decisions. Culturally competent counselors have skills to accomplish this in a way that is consistent with the client's culture. Counselors begin by acknowledging the reality of cultural influences rather than ignoring that aspect of the client. Counselors recognize differences as differences, not as deficiencies. Third counselors avoid stereotypes and an ethnocentric perspective. They affirm individuals within an ethnic context. Counselors develop a repertoire of helping approaches to incorporate ethnic views and practices. Through those approaches, the counselor respects these concepts: kinship influences, language preferences, sex-role socialization, religious or spiritual influences, and help-seeking attitudes and behavior (Lee, 2001).

Kincade and Evans (1996) looked more closely at the process of selecting appropriate counseling interventions in a multicultural counseling context. They pointed out that when a counseling relationship begins, boundaries are established between the counselor and client, which may differ with clients from different cultures. As an example, the amount of physical space between counselor and client may need to vary, depending on the culture. In the United States, 3 feet is usually considered comfortable; however, Latinos prefer about half that distance for conversation. Latin American and Arab individuals are less comfortable with variation in distance than closeness, whereas U.S. clients are more comfortable with distance. Kincade and Evans (1996) suggested discussing with clients how comfortable they are with the room arrangement.

Kincade and Evans (1996) also cautioned that emotional boundaries—distance and closeness in relationships—are present in multicultural counseling contexts and are more difficult to observe. For example, the Indo-Chinese tend to discuss problems with only family members; therefore, the relationship with the counselor must be redefined. The authors pointed out that the client may ask the counselor personal questions or give the counselor small presents to make the relationship more like a family.

Kinship terms may not mean the same thing in all cultures, according to Kincade and Evans (1996). In Asian and African American cultures, terms such as *Aunt* or *Uncle* may be honorary rather than indicate actual relationships.

One important point emphasized by Kincade and Evans (1996) is related to the client's hierarchy of needs. They pointed out that clients who are worried about fulfilling their hunger or safety needs will not be receptive to counseling techniques not considering these issues. Issues of daily survival may be especially important and overwhelming to children from low-income homes.

Trust is the last issue addressed by Kincade and Evans (1996). Many children, especially those who are members of oppressed groups, have been taught not to trust others. Thus, Kincade and Evans encouraged counselors to openly and honestly address differences in cultures in order to be truly genuine and build trust.

General guidelines for multicultural counselors suggested by Kincade and Evans (1996) include the following:

- Make no assumptions—gather information and reevaluate your biases often.
- Learn about clients' culture from sources other than the client, such as the library, tapes, brochures, novels, poems, and other literature.
- Admit your ignorance about the client's culture—be willing to ask questions and learn.
- Look for similarities in order to connect—find common ground to share.
- Be sensitive to client expectations and needs—together define what counseling is and is not.

This overview of the components of multicultural counseling competencies provides some guidance for practicing with clients from a culture different from that of the counselor. The following sections contain information more specific to working with children from different cultures.

## CHILDREN

Children who have ethnic or social class backgrounds different from those of the majority may face challenges related to not being accepted, receiving unfair treatment, being ridiculed, and being subjected to lower expectations. The socioeconomic status of a family contributes sometimes favorably and sometimes unfavorably to the activities, friends, educational attainment, lifestyle, occupational aspirations, and social roles of the family members. All of those variables may also create stressors for children.

Blum (1998) examined the school experience of children from ethnic groups and concluded it may be punctuated by stresses of several types. The students may experience difficulties in combining the roles and values of their specific culture with those of the dominant culture. Children may incorporate roles and values from another culture more quickly than other family members, thereby creating clashes at home. They may also contend with more limited opportunities to succeed. The adolescent struggle for identity will include another variable as teens struggle with defining self and meaning. Children and adolescents may be subjected to verbal rejection, discrimination, and perhaps even physical attacks. They may suffer social isolation and derisive labels. Children of different ethnic groups may face these and other possible stresses.

Gibbs and Huang (1989) have suggested three perspectives to use in examining the influence of ethnicity on children. A developmental perspective helps counselors consider the role an ethnic group has had on a child's growth. The ecological perspective provides counselors with a means to investigate the interaction of systems such as family, school, government, social and economic policies, and the impact on available risks and opportunities for the child. Finally, the cross-cultural perspective compares the child's culture of origin and the dominant culture.

Bernal, Knight, Garza, Ocampo, and Cota (1993) explained a model of children's ethnic identity development. Although the five components were discussed in terms of Hispanic children, the model can be used to help understand the process as it occurs with other children.

1. *Ethnic self-identification:* Children categorized themselves as members of an ethnic group.

2. *Ethnic constancy:* Children develop knowledge that their ethnic characteristics are constant across time and place.

3. *Ethnic role behavior:* Children take part in behaviors that reflect cultural values, customs, and language.

4. *Ethnic knowledge:* Children understand that some role behaviors, traits, styles, traditions, and language are relevant to their ethnic group.

5. *Ethnic feelings and preferences:* Children's emotional response to their ethnic group.

Garrett (1999) emphasized the importance of assessing cultural identity and level of acculturation before deciding on interventions. He stated that the client's cultural frame of reference and mode of communication are essential considerations in working with ethnic children.

Ho (1992) wrote about working with ethnic minority children. He suggested individual counseling when the child's problem is related to the stresses of immigration and acculturation, developmental tasks, past traumatic reaction, self-identity problems, and serious behavioral problems. The goals of individual therapy would be strengthening the child's self image, helping the child acquire coping skills in a bicultural world, improving the child's interpersonal relationships, and modifying inappropriate behavior patterns. He recommended short-term supportive therapy, cognitive-behavioral therapy, music therapy, and play therapy for intervention choices. Ho (1992) stated that group therapy would be beneficial for minority youth who are struggling with the acculturation process, their ethnic identity, bicultural socialization skills, and feelings of isolation. More specific information about the counseling process with selected ethnic groups follows.

Fascoli (1999) and Kottman (2001) recommend that counselors who work with children investigate the following for the child and family:

- What is the country of origin and cultural identity of the child and family?
- Which generation of family emigrated?
- What languages are spoken? Where are the languages spoken?
- What English knowledge do the parents have? Can they understand the written word? The spoken word? How adequately can they express themselves in English?
- What are the sleeping and eating patterns at home?
- What are the expectations for children in the culture?
- What is the level of acculturation?
- Which are important holidays, celebrations, and cultural responsibilities?
- What is the attitude of the family about play?
- Who are playmates of the child at home and in the community?
- With what materials does the child play? What are the child's play activities?
- What are family members' attitudes toward discipline?
- What are the patterns of discipline?
- What responsibilities and expectations at home does the child have?

We want to remind counselors to be aware that stereotypes may interfere with their perspective of other-culture clients. Counselors need to strive to avoid being influenced or biased by overly generalized descriptions of individuals and groups. Children who have been reared in American cultures have a great deal in common with one another and with other cultures; however, counselors should not overlook possible differences between subcultures and should work to understand both the similarities and the differences.

## African American Children

African American children represent 15% of the juvenile population in the United States (Child Trends, 2002). Their heritage may be from Africa, the Caribbean, or other places. Many are descendants of the slaves. African American children are overrepresented in the foster care and child welfare system, constituting about 45% of all children in foster care and more than half of the children awaiting adoption (Surgeon General, 2002).

Baruth and Manning (2003) suggested that African American children may experience some problems that warrant counseling interventions. Failing to develop a strong cultural identity, being subjected to the adverse effects of racism and inappropriate value judgments, and being unable to overcome the perception of being "problem children" may cause these children difficulties. Interpersonal relations, autonomy, academic performance, and future plans may also be concerns African American young people bring to counselors.

Jones, Forehand, Brody, and Armistead (2002) investigated different models of assessing the impact of risk factors on African American children in families with single mothers. They suggested looking at the multiplicity of risk factors as predictors of difficult adjustment in children and noted a possible "trigger point" that occurs between three and four risks. Another way to consider risk factors is offered by Vontross (1995), who emphasized the many ways young African American males may be overwhelmed by the world they inhabit and the unhelpful habits they may develop to survive. He instructs counselors to reconsider their role and lists these recommendations. Counselors should use group and individual sessions to help the young men understand themselves better and relate more effectively with others. Recognizing the impact of racism on the lives of African Americans, counselors refrain from denying its existence but work on modifying any system that maintains the barriers.

Sue and Sue (1990) pointed out that many people of color are reluctant to seek counseling because they see it as a sociopolitical force. African American families sometimes are required to go for counseling as a consequence of encounters with the law or their interactions with other community agencies. Counseling may be perceived as a punishment rather than as a helpful process. According to Allen and Majidi-Ahi (1989), the traditional clinical or medical model, which focuses on a person's weaknesses or deficits, is not appropriate for working with African American children because many of them adjust well despite poverty, prejudice, and other barriers to their development. Allen and Majidi-Ahi prefer a socioecological approach with an emphasis on understanding how economic status, education, health care, housing, racism, and other ecological factors affect the child.

Akande, Akande, and Odewale (1994) argued strongly for focusing on the self-concept of African American children in order to improve both academic achievement and personal adjustment. As clinicians and researchers, they saw a close tie between parental competence, the teacher's influence and emotional functioning, and children's success in life.

Locke (1989) and Lee and Bailey (1997) identified the following as specific guidelines for counselors in working with African American children:

- Counselors should be open and honest.
- They should demonstrate respect and appreciation of cultural differences.
- Counselors should participate in activities of the community.
- Counselors reject prejudice and racism.
- Counselors question the child about his or her culture.
- Counselors hold high expectations for the child.
- Counselors are developmental in nature.
- Competent adult African American resources are identified for the young person.
- Counselors should incorporate the strengths of the family and the culture into the counseling process.

Counseling African American adolescents necessitates the counselor understanding the young person's historical status and experiences (Howard-Hamilton & Behar-Horenstein, 1995). Wade and Okesola (2002) conducted research on racial peer group selection of African American adolescents in schools. Their findings support the importance of assessing the racial identity ego statuses of these young people in order to understand their relationship choices. Locke (1995) recommends the following steps to build an understanding: First, encourage young people to talk about themselves, their families, and their experiences. The counselor should focus on the strengths evident in these stories. Counselors should ask about social class status rather than make assumptions about it. Asking young folks to describe holiday celebrations, kinship networks, and the role of religion in their lives helps counselors appreciate those aspects. Counselors should solicit the concerns of the young person. Using music and dance as areas of special interest will also help the counseling process, according to Locke.

Bradley (2001) summarized a six-session group for African American adolescent males. The group moved from an introduction to understanding prejudice and racism. The young men learned about challenges within the educational system and then developed survival skills. Bradley concluded that the group sessions helped the participants clarify concerns about race and successfully navigate some challenges in the environment and school.

Vontross (1995) and Belgrave, Chase-Vaughn, Gray, Addison, and Cherry (2000) support gender- and culture-specific interventions for adolescents. Belgrave and her colleagues worked with adolescent African American females and concluded that a group intervention designed around Afrocentric values, gender, and ethnic identity benefited the participants. One example of this work was provided by Woodard (1995), who worked with boys in an inner city school to teach them traditional African values and reported the success as a reduction in fighting and suspensions among the children.

Another idea was given by Richardson (1991), who wrote that counseling professionals must recognize nontraditional means for providing services to their clients. He suggested that the African American church can be helpful in bolstering the self-esteem of its members who have been negatively affected by racism and oppression. The church provides means for self-expression, gaining self-respect and community recognition, and achievement through holding church offices, titles, and responsibilities. Richardson provided guidelines for counselors as they attempt to develop relationships with African American churches for the benefit of clients.

Parham (1996) argued that traditional psychology has been oppressive to different cultures and has ignored the influence of African ideas on Western civilization, citing research that suggests that psychiatry and psychology have increased oppression among African Americans, as indicated by higher rates of mental illness, misdiagnosis of psychological conditions, and mistreatment in the mental health system. Parham cautioned that multicultural counselors "must avoid dancing around the issues of environmental oppression and call them what they are: Racism! Sexism! Classism!" (p. 187). He wrote that multicultural counseling cannot be relevant to African Americans if it does not teach clients, families, and children to confront and understand racism. He urged that the African personality, including its spiritual aspect, must be defined, and that the appropriate human functioning must be redefined in terms of a "culturally centered frame of reference." Finally, he called for specific interventions that will help African Americans achieve a greater congruency with their cultural essence.

## Native American Children

Within American Indians and Alaska Natives, the Bureau of Indian Affairs recognizes 561 tribes (Surgeon General, 2002) with more than 252 different languages (Garrett, 1999). These children are about 1% of the U.S. juvenile population (Child Trends, 2002). Although these children are a small proportion of the total population, their problems are significant. The suicide rate for Native Americans is 1.5 times the national rate. It is estimated that 8% of Americans who are homeless are American Indians. Also the rate of violent victimization is more that twice the national average.

Baruth and Manning (2003) recommend that counselors acknowledge the diversity in American Indian children and the differences between the many tribes. One way of achieving that understanding has been researched. Salzman (2000) described a cross-cultural mentorship project that allowed educators to better serve the needs of Native Americans. The expanded understanding of the European Americans contributed to their increased effectiveness.

Lazarus (1982) suggested that counselors working with Native American children be aware of their particular values in order to prepare them for the difficulties of growing up in the present-day world. Each Native American tribe is different, but Lazarus (1982) listed general guidelines for understanding values:

- Children are respected to the same degree as adults.
- Cooperation and harmony are valued.
- Generosity and sharing are important, and individuals are judged on their contributions.

- Competition is encouraged if it does not hurt anyone.
- Native Americans live in the present, with little concern for planning for tomorrow.
- The school culture for children is strange; some behaviors are considered ill mannered (loud talking and reprimands).
- Older people are respected for their wisdom and knowledge.
- Ancient legends and cultural traditions are important.
- Peace and politeness are essential; confrontation is rude. (p. 84)

Native Americans traditionally hold a worldview that is more spiritual, holistic, harmonious, and collective. Wellness is seen as harmony and lack of wellness as disharmony in spirit, mind, and body (LaFromboise & Jackson, 1996).

Herring (1991) reminded readers that the history of Native Americans is characterized by military defeat, ethnic demoralization, and forced displacement—forces that negatively influence Native American youth. The Native American family is often faced with overwhelming poverty and unemployment, family dissolution due in part to federal government policies, and educational failure.

LaFromboise and Jackson (1996) stated that knowledge of and respect for the Native American worldview, especially an understanding of the culture, social contexts, and roles that helpers play, is essential for counseling Native American clients. A client's world must be considered in the light of the community, because an individual's problem becomes a problem of the community. All members of the community try to understand the client and find ways to integrate him or her back into the group.

Herring (1997) outlined recommendations for building a counseling environment for Native American youth:

- The counselor demonstrates sensitivity and openness by openly addressing the issue of ethnic dissimilarity. Dufrene and Coleman (1992) identified the frank discussion of distrust as a key to their success.
- The counselor considers ethnic identity and degree of acculturation of the young person. Dress, daily activities, family involvement, body language, participation in tribal functions, friendship patterns, and eye contact provide information about these.
- The counselor should allow flexibility in the schedule, as American Indians may prefer open-ended sessions free from time constraints.
- Counselors may want to include family members and tribal elders in the counseling process and perhaps hold sessions in the home. Johnson and Johnson (1998) also recommend the involvement of kin.
- Creative arts such as art, dance, and music are suggested interventions. Other recommendations include humor (Herring, 1994), storytelling, story reading, puppetry, and games (Herring & Meggert, 1994).
- Counselors should include natural healing practices in individual treatment. Herring (1997) suggests four circles, talking circle, and sweat lodge ceremonies (pp. 61–62).

LaFromboise and Jackson (1996) also suggested that cognitive behavior interventions may be more appropriate than psychodynamic or client-centered therapy because it can (and should) be adapted to the culture and community. They stated that one of the most important goals for a counselor of Native American clients is to facilitate *conscientizacao*—helping clients see themselves in relation to the familial and cultural influences on development—and to help them see their many strengths, uniqueness, and resources. They cautioned that conventional Western theories alone cannot prepare counselors to understand the cultural world of Native Americans and work effectively with them. Given the collective identity of Native Americans, it is suggested that respected community leaders, traditional leaders, extended family, elders, and other supportive groups be included in the helping process.

One other caveat was noted by Herring (1991), who cautioned that young clients evaluate the counselor from the first moment—his or her manner of greeting, appearance, communication style, and knowledge of Native American culture. He also suggested that community and tribal leaders can be a valuable source of help in counseling Native American youth, as can bias-free media resources that show realistic, accurate portrayals of Native American culture.

## Asian American Children

Asian Americans and Pacific Islanders include 43 ethnic groups with more than 100 languages and dialects (Surgeon General, 2002). Around 35% live in households of limited English proficiency. Children represent 4% of the U.S. juvenile population, and this figure is predicted to increase to 6% by 2020 (Child Trends, 2002). Asian Americans may have roots in China, Japan, Korea, Vietnam, Cambodia, or elsewhere in Asia. Although they come from different countries, Lee and Richardson (1991) believed all Asian American groups are influenced by old religious traditions that are passed down through the generations, including issues related to moderation of behavior, self-discipline, patience, humility, honor, and respect. However, Leong (1996) emphasized strongly that the phrase *Asian American* represents a diverse set of ethnic groups and cautioned counselors to avoid stereotypes and be aware of between-group differences as well as within-group variations. He urged counselors to determine the degree of cultural identity and assess the depth of acculturation as they work with clients. Stereotypes of Asian American culture would have us believe that all adults are hardworking and successful and all children are high achieving (Sue & Sue, 1990); however, some Asian American families live in poverty and feel the stresses of discrimination (Huang & Ying, 1989). To visit a counselor for help with problems may be viewed as shameful and embarrassing and produce a sense of failure; therefore, the number of clients in treatment is low, and research on effective therapeutic interventions is limited.

Counselor credibility can be an issue with Chinese American children because it is often based not only on therapeutic skills but also on cultural roles related to age and gender. Counselors must communicate thoroughly with Chinese American families about what is going on in counseling in order to enlist their support (Huang & Ying, 1989). Sue and Sue (1990) advised counselors that "issues such as independence, the necessity of eliciting emotional reactions, and the equality of family members must be seen from a cultural perspective and not as a given" (p. 89).

Much of the Japanese culture evolved from the philosophies of Confucianism and Buddhism. These teachings continue to influence the lives of Japanese Americans and are factors that must be recognized in counseling (Tomine, 1991):

- The family is more important than the individual.
- The family roles and rules for behavior are formalized, and adherence to these roles and rules is expected in order to avoid shame and loss of face.
- The father is the leader and authority; the mother is the nurturing parent.
- Communication is usually indirect, and confrontation is avoided.
- Problems are kept within the family, and all problems are solved within the family unit.

In addition to possible acculturation concerns and problems of coping with prejudices, Japanese American children may be dealing with lingering anger over World War II internment issues in the family. They may also feel the impact of other political and economic decisions that affect American–Japanese relationships (Nagata, 1989). Tomine (1991) cautioned counselors to attend carefully to the personal, cultural, and defensive factors that influence the coping mechanisms of Japanese clients.

Some authors (Chandras, Eddy, & Spaulding, 1999; Hartman & Askounis, 1989; Omizo & Omizo, 1989) have provided several recommendations for working with Asian American children:

- Counselors need to ascertain individual strengths and weaknesses.
- Counselors should determine degree of acculturation.
- Counselors should recognize the difficulty in self-disclosure and the meaning of restraint as an attribute of emotional maturity. They need to acknowledge the belief that having problems may be seen as shaming the entire family. Mercado (2000) adapted family systems theory for working with young people who are substance abusers and their families.
- Questions should be relevant to the problem, and counselors should refrain from asking too many personal questions.
- Confrontational, emotionally intense counseling approaches may be inappropriate. Active and direct counseling is recommended. Competition should be minimized.
- Therapy should be limit in time and focused on resolutions.
- Yeh (2001) admonishes counselors to learn to recognize common concerns of Asian American children because of their reluctance to reveal emotional difficulties.
- Counselors are encouraged to ask about the culture of the client.
- Counselors should focus on the present time.
- Counselors work to gain an understanding of nonverbal skills.

Berg and Miller (1992) outlined other techniques to use with Asian American clients. Counselors can ask the client to talk about exceptions to the problem. Counselors may use relationship questions to discover information about social interactions. Asking a client to describe a miracle that would solve the problem helps generate goals and solutions. Probing for coping strategies can help the counselor and the client highlight strengths.

Certainly, the counselor needs a wide range of skills to adapt to the client's needs. Counselors deal carefully with expression of feelings by encouraging children to express only a little more than their comfort zone allows. Because of the strong family orientation, family members may serve as a nontraditional means of providing counseling, but the family may also hinder the process by preferring to solve problems within the nuclear structure.

Lee and Cynn (1991) contended that Korean Americans have cultural values similar to those of Chinese Americans and Japanese Americans. The primary adjustment problems of children from this group may be due to the rate of acculturation. Young persons adopt American values and behaviors more quickly than parents who have only recently immigrated. Lee and Cynn called on counselors to recognize this problem and the expectations both the old and new cultures place on children. Calling adjustment problems a normal part of the acculturation process can save face for the family and enable them to continue counseling with a positive attitude. Counseling strategies must be consistent in degree of acculturation and stage of ethnic-identity development.

Leong (1996) recommended that counselors learn about culture-specific variables in their clients' lives, such as the importance of harmony in interpersonal relationships, the need to avoid loss of face, preferences for more subtle forms of communication, and individualism versus collectivism. These values may affect the counselor–client relationship negatively, especially if they are misunderstood and confuse or frustrate the client.

## Latino Children

In 2000, Latino children represented 16% of the U.S. juvenile population, and this number is expected to increase to 23% by 2020 (Child Trends, 2002). Mexican Americans represent about two-thirds of the Latino population, with the others being Puerto Rican or of Cuban, South American, Central American, Dominican, and Spanish roots (Surgeon General, 2002). According to Baron (1991), labels have psychological meaning for groups. He used the terms *Chicano* and *Mexican American* interchangeably in his writings. Arredondo (1996) wrote that "Latina(o)s in the United States are of African, Asian, European, and Indian heritage, of many shades of skin color and phenotype . . . various levels of acculturation, urban and rural lifestyles, many educational and economic backgrounds, and varied English/Spanish language proficiency. Most government institutions use the label *Hispanic* to try to easily categorize multiple nationalities that have roots in Latin-American countries and Spain" (p. 220).

Latino young people experience more anxiety-related and delinquency behaviors, depression, and drug use than non-Hispanic white youth. In 1997, Latino youth reported more suicidal ideation and attempts than other young people (Surgeon General, 2002).

Gloria and Rodriguez (2000) listed questions to use with Latino clients:

- How do you identify yourself (Hispanic, Chicano, Latino American)?
- What does that word(s) mean to you?
- How hard has it been for you to maintain your cultural values here?
- What is your primary language?
- Who are your friends?
- What holidays and traditions do you celebrate?
- What does your family expect from you?
- Who helps you at home?

Baruth and Manning (1992) pointed out that Hispanic American children tend to be less competitive to avoid standing out in their group. They usually adhere to different male and female gender roles. Attributes such as warmth, dignity, masculine pride, and respect for authority are important in their lives. These children tend to stand close to others, like to touch, but avoid eye contact. Counselors must also understand family behaviors of Hispanic American homes, including a strong family commitment, parental styles that emphasize obedience, and the assumption of important family responsibilities early in the child's life. Because of the Hispanic American emphasis on the family, family counseling can be an effective tool. Arredondo (1996) added that loyalty to family comes first, authority figures such as teachers (and counselors) are highly respected and not questioned, pride and dignity are strongly promoted, and gender roles are clearly defined with *machismo* being valued, but there is a reverence for motherhood.

Religion—mainly Roman Catholic—and spirituality strongly influence the beliefs of Latin Americans; they believe that moral character is related to one's health or lack of it, according to Arredondo (1996). Illness may also be caused by environmental or supernatural causes. These beliefs also influence the types of interventions the client believes to be effective.

Arredondo (1996) also pointed out that most Latin American countries have a history of political struggle with the United States, and this perceived oppression may influence the counseling relationship. Latin Americans are also the most economically disadvantaged group in the United States and tend to underutilize health and mental health services. Poverty, feelings of oppression, and lack of care all combine to make Latin Americans a high-risk group. Arredondo urged that counseling theories and practices focus on "inclusion, value, self-definition, strengths (not just deficits), differences balanced with commonalities, and history to inform the present and the future" (p. 233).

Arredondo (1996) recommended that the counselor make every effort to understand the client's belief system as well as symptoms, determine the degree of acculturation and experiences, and learn more about the roles of economics and institutional racism, language differences, or other discriminatory factors on the client's beliefs and behaviors.

## Biracial Children

The stresses of an interracial marriage can be severe, and the pressure on children of these marriages to understand and adapt to the history and culture of each parent may increase confusion and stress in their lives. In addition to having unusual characteristics and the potential for problems because of their dual ancestry, Gibbs (1989) noted that biracial children may have identity problems related to their ambiguous ethnicity. They may encounter difficulties with family approval, acceptance in the community, discrimination, and isolation.

Gibbs (1989) enumerated their conflicts as the following:

- Racial-ethnic identity: "Who am I?"
- Social marginality: "Where do I fit?"
- Sexuality: "What is my sexual role?" (with regard to orientation, gender identity, and sexual activity)
- Autonomy: Parents may have attempted to protect or isolate children from reality.
- Educational and occupational aspirations: "Where am I going?" and whether children's expectations are realistic in the light of prejudices and discrimination

Gibbs encouraged counselors to assist children in exploring their ancestry and recognizing the impact of their heritage on themselves.

Herring (1992) also stated that biracial children may have issues in the development of self-identity. First, they must integrate two racial and cultural backgrounds while developing their own self-identity. In addition, during adolescence they must deal with the task of developing peer relations and deciding their sex roles and sex preferences. Difficulties with racial identity may lead the child to experience conflicts over separation from parents and to have concerns about career choices.

Herring (1997) advised counselors to (1) develop a positive, trusting relationship with the child; (2) understand that the child's presenting problem may cover a deeper ethnic identity concern; (3) be aware that biracial children usually identify with the minority culture, believing that the white culture is not willing to accept them; (4) become familiar with the customs of all their students in order to serve them better; (5) permit the children to ventilate their feelings about their identity and its meaning in society; (6) assist in building the children's self-esteem through supportive techniques; (7) see the link between their confusion over ethnic and cultural background and other developmental concerns; and (8) involve the entire family to promote individual and family growth.

## SUMMARY

This chapter has provided an overview of the awareness, knowledge, and skills needed for multicultural counseling. The characteristics and needs of some of the many cultures that professionals may encounter when they work with children have been discussed. Research on the counseling needs of culturally different clients is limited. Counselor-education training programs have only begun to prepare more culturally aware professionals. Materials and resources are limited, although books, media, and special programs are beginning to appear. The number of minority group members living in the United States will continue to grow in the 21st century. Counselors must be prepared to bridge cultural gaps and adopt techniques and procedures to meet the needs of many different children and families.

## W E B S I T E S for Counseling with Children from Different Cultures

Mental Health: Culture, Race and Ethnicity: A link to multiple sources of information on working with culture, race and ethnicity
www.surgeongeneral.gov/library/mentalhealth/cre

Multicultural Assessment Standards: A Compilation for Counselors; Standards from the Association for Assessment in Counseling
aac.ncat.edu/documents/mcult_stds.htm

Peace Corps: Materials on cross cultural communication
www.peacecorps.gov/wws

Tolerance: From Southern Poverty Law Center, this web site includes many resources for working with children and diversity.
www.tolerance.org

## REFERENCES

Akande, A., Akande, B., & Odewale, F. (1994). Putting the self back in the child—An African perspective. *Early Child Development and Care, 103,* 103–115.

Allen, L., & Majidi-Ahi, S. (1989). Black American children. In J. Gibbs & L. Huang (Eds.), *Children of color: Psychological interventions with minority youth* (pp. 148–178). San Francisco: Jossey-Bass.

Arredondo, P. (1996). MCT theory and Latina(o)-American Populations. In D. W. Sue, A. Ivey, & P. Pedersen (Eds.), *A theory of multicultural counseling and therapy* (pp. 217–235). Pacific Grove, CA: Brooks/Cole.

Arredondo, P., & Glauner, T. (1992). *Personal dimensions of identity model.* Boston: Empowerment Workshops.

Arredondo, P., Toporek, R., Brown, S. P., Jones, J., Locke, D. C., Sanchez, J., & Stadler, H. (1996). Operationalization of the multicultural counseling competencies. *Journal of Multicultural Counseling and Development, 24,* 42–78.

Atkinson, D. R., Morten, G., & Sue, D. W. (1993). *Counseling American minorities: A cross-cultural perspective* (4th ed.). Madison, WI: Brown & Benchmark.

Baron, A. (1991). Counseling Chicano college students. In C. Lee & B. Richardson (Eds.), *Multicultural issues in counseling: New approaches to diversity* (pp. 171–184). Alexandria, VA: American Association for Counseling and Development.

Baruth, L., & Manning, M. (1992). Understanding and counseling Hispanic American children. *Elementary School Guidance and Counseling, 27,* 113–122.

Baruth, L. G., & Manning, M. L. (2003). *Multicultural counseling and psychotherapy: A lifespan perspective* (3rd ed.). Upper Saddle River, NJ: Merrill.

Belgrave, F. Z., Chase-Vaughn, G., Gray, F., Addison, J. D., & Cherry, V. R. (2000). The effectiveness of culture- and gender-specific intervention for increasing resiliency among African American preadolescent females. *Journal of Black Psychology, 26,* 133–147.

Berg, I. K., & Miller, S. (1992). Working with Asian American clients: One person at a time. *Families in Society, 73,* 356–363.

Bernal, M. E., Knight, G., Garza, C. Ocampo, K., & Cota, M. K. (1993). *Ethnic identity: Formation and transmission among Hispanics and other minorities.* Albany, NY: State University of New York Press.

Blum, D. J. (1998). *The school counselors' book of lists.* West Nyack, NY: Center for Applied Research in Education.

Bradley, C. (2001). A counseling group for African-American males. *Professional School Counseling, 4,* 370–373.

Butter, L., & Molidor, C. (1995). Cultural sensitivity in social work practice and research with children and families. *Early Childhood Development and Care, 106,* 27–33.

Chandras, K. V., Eddy, J. P., & Spaulding, D. J. (1999). Counseling Asian Americans: Implications for training. *Education, 99,* 239–247.

Child Trends. (2002). Racial and ethnic composition of the child population. www.childtrendsdatabank.org. Retrieved August 9, 2002.

Cross. W. E. (1995). The psychology of Nigrescence: Revisiting the Cross model. In J. G. Ponterotto, J. M. Casas, L. A. Suzuki, & C. M. Alexander (Eds.), *Handbook of multicultural counseling* (pp. 93–122). Thousand Oaks, CA: Sage.

Das, K. D. (1995). Rethinking multicultural counseling: Implications for counselor education. *Journal of Counseling and Development, 74,* 45–52.

Dufrene, P., & Coleman, V. (1992). Art and healing for Native American Indians. *Journal of Multicultural Counseling and Development, 22,* 145–152.

Fascoli, L. (1999). Developmentally appropriate play and turtle hunting. In E. Dau (Ed.), *Child's play: Revisiting play in early childhood* (pp. 53–59). Sydney, Australia: Maclennan & Petty.

Fischer, A., Jome, L., & Atkinson, D. (1998). Reconceptualizing multicultural counseling: Universal and healing conditions in a culturally specific context. *Counseling Psychologist, 26,* 525–588.

Garrett, M. T. (1995). Between two worlds: Cultural discontinuity in the dropout of Native American youth. *School Counselor, 42,* 186–195.

Garrett, M. T. (1999). Soaring on the wings of the eagle: Wellness of Native American high school students. *Professional School Counseling, 3,* 57–64.

Gibbs, J. (1989). Biracial adolescents. In J. Gibbs & L. Huang (Eds.), *Children of color: Psychological interventions with minority youth* (pp. 322–350). San Francisco: Jossey-Bass.

Gibbs, J. T., & Huang, L. N. (1989). A conceptual framework for assessing and treating minority youth. In J. T. Gibbs & L. N. Huang (Eds.), *Children of color: Psychological interventions with minority youth* (pp. 10–29). San Francisco: Jossey-Bass.

Gloria, A. M., & Rodriguez, E. R. (2000). Counseling Latino university students: Psychosocial issues for consideration. *Journal of Counseling and Development, 78,* 145–154.

Grieger, I., & Ponterotto, J. G. (1995). A framework for assessment in multicultural counseling. In J. G. Ponterotto, J. M. Casas, L. A. Suzuki, & C. M. Alexander (Eds.), *Handbook of multicultural counseling* (2nd ed., pp. 357–374). Thousand Oaks, CA: Sage.

Hartman, J. S., & Askounis, A. C. (1989). Asian American students: Are they really a "model minority"? *School Counselor, 37,* 109–111.

Helms, J. E. (1995). An update of Helms's White and People of Color racial identity models. In J. G. Ponterotto, J. M. Casas, L. A. Suzuki, & C. M. Alexander (Eds.), *Handbook of multicultural counseling* (pp. 181–198). Thousand Oaks, CA: Sage.

Helms, J.E. (2003). Racial identity in the social environment. In P. B. Pedersen & J. C. Carey (Eds.), *Multicultural counseling in schools: A practical handbook* (2nd ed., pp. 44–58). Boston: Allyn & Bacon.

Henderson, G. (2000). Race in America. *National Forum, 80,* 12–15.

Hernandez, H. (1989). *Multicultural education: A teacher's guide to content and practice.* Upper Saddle River, NJ: Merrill.

Herring, R. (1991). Counseling Native American youth. In C. Lee & B. Richardson (Eds.), *Multicultural issues in counseling: New approaches to diversity* (pp. 37–47). Alexandria, VA: American Association for Counseling and Development.

Herring, R. (1992). Biracial children: An increasing concern for elementary and middle school counselors. *Elementary School Guidance and Counseling, 27,* 123–130.

Herring, R. D. (1994). The clown or contrary figure as a counseling intervention strategy with Native American Indian clients. *Journal of Multicultural Counseling and Development, 22,* 153–164.

Herring, R. D. (1997). Counseling indigenous American youth. In C. C. Lee (Ed.), *Multicultural issues in counseling: New approaches to diversity* (2nd ed., pp. 53–70). Alexandria, VA: American Counseling Association.

Herring, R. D., & Meggert, S. S. (1994). The use of humor as a counselor strategy with Native American Indian children. *Elementary School Guidance and Counseling, 29,* 67–76.

Ho, M. K. (1992). *Minority children and adolescents in therapy.* Thousand Oaks, CA: Sage.

Howard-Hamilton, M. F., & Behar-Horenstein, L. S. (1995). Counseling the African American male adolescent. *Elementary School Guidance and Counseling, 29,* 198–205.

Huang, L., & Ying, Y. (1989). Chinese American children and adolescents. In J. Gibbs & L. Huang (Eds.), *Children of color: Psychological interventions with minority youth* (pp. 30–66). San Francisco: Jossey-Bass.

Ibrahim, F. A., Roysircar-Sodowsky, G., & Ohnishi, H. (2001). Worldview: Recent developments and needed directions. In J. G. Ponterotto, J. M. Casas, L. A. Suzuki, & C. M. Alexander (Eds.), *Handbook of multicultural counseling* (2nd ed., pp. 425–456). Thousand Oaks, CA: Sage.

Johnson, C., & Johnson, D. (1998). Working with Native American families. *New Directions for Mental Health Services, 77,* 89–96.

Jones, D. J., Forehand, R., Brody, G., & Armistead, L. (2002). Psychosocial adjustment of African American children in single-mother families: A test of three risk factors. *Journal of Marriage and Family, 64,* 105–116.

Kincade, E., & Evans, K. (1996). Counseling theories, process and intervention in a multicultural context. In J. L. DeLucia-Waack (Ed.), *Multicultural counseling competencies: Implications for training and practice* (pp. 89–112). Alexandria, VA: Association for Counselor Education and Supervision.

Kottman, T. (2001). *Play therapy: Basics and beyond.* Alexandria, VA: American Counseling Association.

LaFromboise, T., & Jackson, M. (1996). MCT theory and Native American populations. In D. W. Sue, A. Ivey, & P. Pedersen (Eds.), *A theory of multicultural counseling and therapy* (pp. 192–203). Pacific Grove, CA: Brooks/Cole.

Laird, J. (2000). Gender in lesbian relationships: Cultural, feminist, and constructionist's reflections. *Journal of Marital and Family Therapy, 26,* 455–467.

Lazarus, P. J. (1982). Counseling the Native American child: A question of values. *Elementary School Guidance and Counseling, 17,* 83–88.

Lee, C. C. (2001). Defining and responding to racial and ethnic diversity. In D. C. Locke, J. E. Myers, & E. L. Herr (Eds.). *The handbook of counseling* (pp. 581–588). Thousand Oaks, CA: Sage.

Lee, C. C., & Bailey, D. F. (1997). Counseling African American male youth and men. In C. C. Lee (Ed.), *Multicultural issues in counseling: New approaches to diversity* (2nd ed., pp. 123–154). Alexandria, VA: American Counseling Association.

Lee, C. C., & Richardson, B. L. (1991). Promise and pitfalls of multicultural counseling. In C. C. Lee & B. L. Richardson (Eds.), *Multicultural issues in counseling: New approaches to diversity* (pp. 3–10). Alexandria, VA: American Association for Counseling and Development.

Lee, J., & Cynn, V. (1991). Issues in counseling 1.5 generation Korean Americans. In C. Lee & B. Richardson (Eds.), *Multicultural issues in counseling: New approaches to diversity* (pp. 127–140). Alexandria, VA: American Association for Counseling and Development.

Leong, F. (1996). MCT theory and Asian-American populations. In D. W. Sue, A. Ivey, and P. Pedersen, *A theory of multicultural counseling and therapy* (pp. 204–216). Pacific Grove, CA: Brooks/Cole.

Locke, D. C. (1989). Fostering the self-esteem of African American children. *Elementary School Guidance and Counseling, 23,* 254–259.

Locke, D. C. (1995). Counseling interventions with African American youth. In C. C. Lee (Ed.), *Counseling for diversity: A guide for school counselors and related professionals* (pp. 21–40). Boston: Allyn & Bacon.

Locke, D. C., & Parker, L. D. (1994). Improving the multicultural competence of educators. In P. Pedersen, & J. C. Carey (Eds.), *Multicultural counseling in schools: A practical handbook* (pp. 39–58). Boston: Allyn & Bacon.

Lonner, W. J., & Ibrahim, F. A. (2002). Appraisal and assessment. In P. B. Pedersen, J. G. Draguns, W. J. Lonner, & J. E. Trimble (Eds.), *Counseling across cultures* (5th ed., pp. 355–380). Thousand Oaks, CA: Sage.

Mercado, M. M. (2000). The invisible family: Counseling Asian American substance abusers and their families. *Family Journal, 8,* 267–272.

Mio, J. S., Trimble, J. E., Arredondo, P., Cheatham, H. E., & Sue, D. (1999). *Key words in multicultural interventions: A dictionary.* Westport, CT: Greenwood.

Nagata, D. (1989). Japanese American children and adolescents. In J. Gibbs & L. Huang (Eds.), *Children of color: Psychological interventions with minority youth* (pp. 67–113). San Francisco: Jossey-Bass.

Omizo, M. M., & Omizo, S. A. (1989). Counseling Hawaiian children. *Elementary School Guidance and Counseling, 23,* 282–288.

Parham, T. (1996). MCT theory and African-American populations. In D. W. Sue, A. Ivey, & P. Pederson, *A theory of multicultural counseling and therapy* (pp. 177-191). Pacific Grove, CA: Brooks/Cole.

Pedersen, P. B. (1994). *A handbook for developing multicultural awareness.* Alexandria, VA: American Counseling Association.

Pedersen, P. B. (1997). The cultural context of the American Counseling Association Code of Ethics. *Journal of Counseling and Development, 76,* 23–28.

Pedersen, P. B. (2002). Ethics, competence, and other professional issues in culture-centered counseling. In P. B. Pedersen, J. G. Draguns, W. J. Lonner, & J. E. Trimble (Eds.), *Counseling across cultures* (5th ed., pp. 3–28). Thousand Oaks, CA: Sage.

Richardson, B. (1991). Utilizing the resources of the African American church: Strategies for counseling professionals. In C. Lee & B. Richardson (Eds.), *Multicultural issues in counseling: New approaches to diversity* (pp. 65–75). Alexandria, VA: American Association for Counseling and Development.

Salzman, M. (2000). Promoting multicultural competence: A cross-cultural mentorship project. *Journal of Multicultural Counseling and Development, 28,* 119–123.

Sodowsky, G. R., & Johnson, P. (1994). Worldviews: Culturally learned assumptions and values. In P. Pedersen & J. C. Carey (Eds.). *Multicultural counseling in schools: A practical handbook* (pp. 59–79). Boston: Allyn & Bacon.

Sue, D., & Sue, D. W. (1990). *Counseling the culturally different: Theory and practice* (2nd ed.). New York: Wiley.

Sue, D. W., Ivey, A., & Pedersen, P. (1996). *A theory of multicultural counseling and therapy.* Pacific Grove, CA: Brooks/Cole.

Surgeon General. (2002). Mental health: Culture, race, ethnicity. www.surgeongeneral.gov Retrieved August 9, 2002.

Tomine, S. (1991). Counseling Japanese Americans: From internment to reparation. In C. Lee & B. Richardson (Eds.), *Multicultural issues in counseling: New approaches to diversity* (pp. 91–105). Alexandria, VA: American Association for Counseling and Development.

Trevino, J. (1996). Worldview and change in cross-cultural counseling. *Counseling Psychologist, 24,* 198–215.

U.S. Census Bureau. (2000). *Statistical abstracts of the United States: 2000.* (120th ed.). Washington, DC: Author.

Vontross, C. (1995). The breakdown of authority: Implications for counseling young African American males. In J. G. Ponterotto, J. M. Casas, L. A. Suzuki, & C. M. Alexander (Eds.). *Handbook of multicultural counseling* (pp. 457–473). Thousand Oaks, CA: Sage.

Wade, J. C., & Okesola, O. (2002). Racial peer group selection in African American high school students. *Multicultural Counseling and Development, 30,* 96–109.

Washington, E. D. (1994). Three steps to cultural awareness: A Wittgensteinian approach. In P. Pedersen & J. C. Carey (Eds.), *Multicultural counseling in schools: A practical handbook* (pp. 81–102). Boston: Allyn & Bacon.

Washington, E. D., Crosby, T., Hernandez, M., Vernon-Jones, R., Medley, R., Nishamura, B., & Torres, D. (2003). Cultural identity groups and cultural maps: Meaning making in groups. In P. B. Pedersen & J. C. Carey (Eds.), *Multicultural counseling in schools: A practical handbook* (pp. 26–43). Boston: Allyn & Bacon.

Woodard, S. L. (1995). Counseling disruptive African American elementary school boys. *Journal of Multicultural Counseling and Development, 23,* 21–28.

Yeh, C. J. (2001). An exploratory study of school counselors' experiences with and perceptions of Asian-American students. *Professional School Counseling, 4,* 349–357.

# Chapter 16

# Consultation, Collaboration, Teamwork

*You must be the change you wish to see in the world*
—Mahatma Ghandi

Counselors may expand their opportunities to improve children's lives by engaging in cooperative relationships with other adults. The processes of consultation, collaboration, and teamwork provide ways to build those types of working relationships. These related kinds of interactions allow counselors to serve children indirectly. Dettmer, Dyck, and Thurston (1999) explained that consultation, collaboration, and teamwork have these common characteristics:

- Addressing a problem
- Interacting
- Using specialized information to achieve goals
- Sharing resources
- Stimulating change or improvement

For purposes of our discussion, we will use some arbitrary parameters to differentiate the three. Consultation will be considered a method of sharing expertise. Collaboration will be used as a term for an interactive relationship of conferring and collective problem solving. Teamwork will be a group that works together for the good of the whole in which each person contributes a specific effort to a plan of action. The following more specialized definitions, models, and examples will allow counselors to determine ways to incorporate each of these methods in working for children. That discussion is followed by examples of some specific consultation interventions.

## CONSULTATION

Consultation is a process in which the consultant (counselor) works with the consultee (parent, teacher, administrator) with the goal of bringing about a positive change in the client (child). Kurpius and Fuqua (1993) summarized: "In general, consultants help consultees to think of their immediate problem as part of the larger system, and not only to understand how problems are solved but also to understand how they were developed, maintained, or avoided" (p. 598).

459

Dougherty (2000) further reported that human service professionals may be asked to consult with adults who work and live with children and that the young people are ultimately the beneficiaries of the services. He suggested that consultants work with principals to discuss the concerns of students. Consultants may be asked to consult about a particular school program, or they may be involved in organization development. Consultants also work with teachers to enhance professional skills in areas such as effective parenting, enhancement of children's self-concepts, choosing of instructional materials, and conflict resolution. Consultants may meet with parents to help them understand more about children's growth and development or behavior, although they do not engage parents as frequently as might be expected or as may prove beneficial. Dougherty suggested that the range of roles in which a consultant may practice includes advocate, expert, trainer–educator, collaborator, fact finder, process specialist, and less common roles.

According to Glosoff and Koprowicz (1990), consultation directed primarily toward children typically involves the following:

- Conducting professional development workshops and discussions with teachers and other school personnel on subjects such as substance abuse or child abuse
- Assisting teachers in working with individual students or groups of students
- Providing relevant materials and resources to teachers, especially relating to classroom guidance curriculum
- Helping to identify and develop programs for students with special needs
- Participating in school committees that address substance abuse, human growth and development, school climate, and other guidance-related areas
- Designing and conducting parent education classes
- Interpreting student information, such as results of standardized tests for students and team members
- Consulting regularly with other specialists such as social workers, psychologists, and other representatives from community agencies

Behring, Cabello, Kushida, and Murguia (2000) studied the modifications of school-based consultation. They used the following components to identify consultation approaches: models of consultation (mental health, organizational, behavioral), levels (direct or indirect), stages (initiation, problem identification, goal setting, plan implementation, evaluation, and termination), and the people involved. Their research, as well as that of Goldstein and Harris (2000), indicated that current consultation approaches may require modifications if the consultant and the consultee have different cultural backgrounds, a topic addressed in the following sections. First we will consider different models of consultation.

## Models of Consultation

### Mental Health Consultation

Mental health consultation focuses on primary prevention and involves helping professionals as well as nonprofessionals. Caplan and Caplan (1993) explained mental health consultation as a "process of interaction between two professionals—the consultant, who is a specialist, and the consultee, who invokes the consultant's help in a current work problem that he believes is within the consultant's area of specialized competence" (p. 11). In this model, the consultant, considered an expert, diagnoses a problem and provides a solution. However, the consultant has no responsibility for carrying out the recommended changes.

The model proposed by Caplan and Caplan (1993) consists of four ways of approaching the consultation relationship. In client-centered case consultation, the consultant helps the consultee with a client. The consultant assesses the problem and recommends a plan for the consultee to implement. The consultant's responsibilities include performing an accurate diagnosis and suggesting an effective intervention that focuses on the client. In consultee-centered case consultation, the consultant helps the consultee gain the knowledge, skills, self-confidence, and/or objectivity needed to work with a particular client. In this case focusing on the consultee's behavior and attitude, the consultant facilitates change. A consultant using program-centered administrative consultation focuses on the area of planning and administration, such as the development of a program or the improvement of an existing project. The consultant collects information about the organization and suggests solutions, with the goal of prescribing an effective course of action. Finally consultee-centered administrative consultation focuses on remedying difficulties among consultees that interfere with their abilities to perform their work. These problems may be the individual difficulties noted in consultee-centered case consultation, or they may be the result of poor leadership, authority difficulties, communication blocks, and other group problems. Table 16-1 provides a comparison of these four types of consultation.

## Process Consultation

Edward Schein (1988) proposed a model of consultation he labeled *process consultation*. He defined it as a "set of activities on the part of the consultant which help the [consultee] to perceive, understand, and act upon process events which occur in the [consultee's] environment" (p. 11). This type of consultation focuses on how problems are solved and on the system in which the problems occur. The consultant and consultee examine six different areas: (a) communication patterns, (b) group member roles, (c) group problem solving and decision making, (d) group norms and growth, (e) leadership and authority, and (f) intergroup cooperation and competition (Keys, Bemak, Carpenter, & King-Sears, 1998). The consultant may operate as a catalyst in helping the consultee find a solution or as a facilitator who aids the consultee through a problem-solving process (Dougherty, 2000).

## Behavioral Consultation

For school or mental health counselors interested in a more structured model of consultation, behavioral consultation may be appealing. Wallace and Hall (1996) stated that "consultants are attracted to behavioral consultation approaches because

TABLE 16-1   Mental health consultation

| | Client-centered case consultation | Consultee-centered case consultation | Program-centered administrative consultation | Consultee-centered administrative consultation |
|---|---|---|---|---|
| Focus | Focuses on developing a plan that will help a specific client. | Focuses on improvement of the consultee's professional functioning in relation to specific cases. | Focuses on improvement of programs or policies. | Focuses on improvement of consultee's professional functioning in relation to specific programs or policies. |
| Goal | To advise the consultee regarding client treatment. | To educate consultee using his or her problems with the client as a lever. | To help develop a new program or policy or improve an existing one. | To help consultee improve problem-solving skills in dealing with current organizational problems. |
| Example | School psychologist called in to diagnose a student's reading problem. | School counselor asks for help in dealing with students' drug-related problems. | Nursing home director requests help in developing staff orientation program. | Police chief asks for help in developing ongoing program to deal with interpersonal problems between veteran and new officers. |
| Consultant's Role and Responsibilities | Usually meets with consultee's client to help diagnose problem.<br><br>Is responsible for assessing problem and prescribing course of action. | Never, or rarely, meets with consultee's client.<br><br>Must be able to recognize source of consultee's difficulties and deal with them indirectly. | Meets with groups and individuals in an attempt to accurately assess problems.<br><br>Is responsible for correctly assessing problem and providing a plan for administrative action. | Meets with groups and individuals in an attempt to help them develop their problem-solving skills.<br><br>Must be able to recognize source of organizational difficulty and serve as catalyst for action by administrators. |

NOTE: Reprinted from Duane Brown, Walter B. Pryzwansky and Ann C. Schulte (2001). *Psychological Consultation: Introduction to Theory and Practice*, 5e. Published by Allyn and Bacon, Boston, MA. Copyright © 2001 by Pearson Education. Reprinted by permission of the publisher.

they offer well-defined methods of problem solving and are relatively standardized with respect to theories of human behavior and behavior change technologies." Bergan and Kratochwill (1990) outlined behavioral consultation and therapy as the application of systems theory and principles of learning to a problem-solving process. The consultant gathers information from the consultee and then defines the problem in concrete terms and identifies the environmental conditions that maintain it (Brack, Jones, Smith, White, & Brack, 1993). The consultant tries to help the consultee solve the problem by changing the client's behavior, the consultee's behavior, or the system in which the client and the consultee exist. Dougherty (2000) outlined the sequence of behavioral consultation as follows:

1.  Problem identification: After a detailed analysis is performed, the problem is formulated in succinct, behavioral terms.

2.  Problem analysis: A functional analysis of the problem is studied within its framework; antecedents and consequences are identified, as well as task demands (cognitive, time, educational, and others).

3.  Selection of a target behavior: The focus of the consultation is chosen.

4.  Behavior objectives: Specific goals of the intervention are generated.

5.  Plan design and implementation: A behavior plan is developed and applied.

6.  Evaluation of the behavior change program: Behavioral outcomes are measured in relation to goals established (pp. 272–273).

This model emphasizes operant conditioning—reinforcement, punishment, and shaping of behavior. Other behavioral techniques, such as those described by social learning theory and cognitive behavior theory (see Chapters 8 and 9), can also be applied in the consultative setting. Most models of behavioral consultation rely on a problem-solving process that describes the client's problem in behavioral terms, looks at the antecedents and consequences, selects a target behavior to change, generates behavioral objects, implements a behavioral plan for change, and evaluates outcomes (Dougherty, 2000). MacLeod, Jones, Somers, and Havey (2001) investigated the effectiveness of school-based behavioral consultation. Their findings support the importance of consultant skills and the quality of consultation to successful outcomes.

Brown, Pryzwansky, and Schulte (2001) developed general interview guidelines for behavioral noncrisis and crisis consulting. The consultant in a noncrisis situation (developmental interview) focuses on the following:

1.  Establishing clear general objectives
2.  Reaching agreement with the consultee in the relationship between general objectives and more specific ones
3.  Generating clearly defined, prioritized performance objectives with the consultee
4.  Deciding how accomplishment of performance objectives will be assessed and recorded
5.  Deciding on follow-up meetings

In a crisis or problem-centered interview, the outline focuses on the following:

1. Identifying and describing problematic behavior(s) by collecting data from several sources concerning the nature of the problem.

2. Determining the conditions under which these behaviors occur, their antecedents, and their consequences; the consultant and consultee analyze either the setting or interpersonal factors that contribute to the problem or the client's skill deficits.

3. Deciding on assessment procedures; the consultant and consultee design a plan to deal with the problem by identifying objectives, selecting behavioral interventions, considering barriers to be overcome, and evaluating progress.

4. Scheduling future meetings. (pp. 52–53)

MacLeod, Jones, Somers, and Havey (2001) concluded that intervention planning was positively correlated to student outcome. Teachers reported that a step-by-step plan, adherence to the treatment plan, and the comparison of baseline and treatment data related to student behavior change.

Keys, Bemak, and Lockhart (1998) stated that school counselors who consult with parents and teachers typically use the models of client-centered or consultee-centered mental health consultation (Caplan & Caplan, 1993) or behavioral consultation (Bergan & Kratochwill, 1990). Counselors may choose the organizational consultation model, the program-centered administrative process, or the consultee-centered administrative process to work for systemic change.

## Multicultural Consultation

Sheridan (2000) identified considerations of multiculturalism to the behavioral consultation process. She recommends particular attention to the awareness and sensitivity of the consultant, as well as the ability to consider various perspectives and procedures in order to include those qualities into the consulting process. She also discussed factors that may enhance the multicultural consultative relationship, such as trusting, acknowledging diversity, avoiding technical jargon, and considering the effect of interpreters. Although specific to behavioral consultation, her suggestions are also applicable to other models of consultation.

Ingraham (2000) offered a summary of her ideas about components of multicultural consultation. She emphasized methods for supporting consultee and client success that a consultant should consider employing. Consultants should value multiple perspectives and create emotional safety and support. The support provided by the consultant should be balanced with new learning that arises from interventions on principles of mastery. Systems that support learning and development should be part of a consultant's strategy. Those strategies would include cross-cultural learning, bridging, methods matched to the consultee's style, building confidence and self-efficacy, and working to increase knowledge, skill, and objectivity. For the consultant's development, she suggested continuing to learn, engaging in professional development, seeking feedback, and finding cultural teachers.

Ramirez, Lepage, Kratochwill, and Duffy (1998) reviewed multicultural issues in school-based consultation. They discussed ways that culture may affect consultation and how consultants may adapt, during each stage of the process, to be more responsive to cultural differences. Able consultants will work to become proficient at multicultural consultation.

## Consulting Process

Kurpius, Fuqua, and Rozecki (1993) contended that consultation takes place in six stages, whether the process is a short-term individual consultation or a long-term organizational consultation. Dougherty (2000) suggested four stages. The following is a summary of the sequence, tasks, and goals of the consulting process at the steps suggested by those authors.

### *Preentry*

In preentry, consultants look at themselves to see if they are right for the task and what services they can provide.

Consultants may consider these questions. As a consultant, how do you view humans? Are you more attracted to some than to others? How do you listen and respond to leaders at the top of the organization as compared with workers at the bottom? What do you think and feel when consultees disagree with you and confront you or your ideas? What about your espoused theories versus your theories-in-use? (Kurpius, Fuqua, & Rozecki, 1993, p. 601). Dougherty (2000) stated that effective consultants must possess a personal and professional growth orientation, knowledge of consultation and human behavior, and consultation skills. How do you rate yourself on those requirements?

The American Counseling Association (ACA), in its revision to its Code of Ethics and Standards of Practice (1995), addressed consultant competency: "Counselors are reasonably certain that they have or the organization represented has the necessary competencies and resources for giving the kind of consulting services needed and that appropriate referral resources are available" (Section D.2.b). Section D.2.a warns counselors to "avoid placing the consultant in a conflict of interest situation that would preclude the consultant being a proper party to the counselor's efforts to help the client." Kurpius, Fuqua, and Rozecki (1993) also encouraged consultants to define clearly their conception of consultation.

What models, processes, theories, and paradigms do you draw on to conceptualize your mode for helping? How do you define consultation to the consultee and consultee system? When is visioning, looking into the future, and planning a better intervention than cause-and-effect problem solving? What about acting as a judge and evaluator of your consultee? (Kurpius, Fuqua, & Rozecki, 1993, p. 601).

Lippitt and Lippitt (1986) suggested four questions that help consultants focus on their competence: (1) What can I do, given this situation? (2) What is the right thing to do in this situation? (3) Do I have the ability to do the right things? and (4) What is the right thing to do that is in the best interests of the consultee and of the organization?

### Entry, Problem Exploration, and Contracting

During the initial contact, the consultant needs to learn about the presenting problem, the persons involved, the interventions that have been tried, and the expectations of the person or organization seeking consultative services. At this point, the consultant must decide if he or she can be helpful and establish a contract. Kurpius, Fuqua, and Rozecki (1993) recommended, for any work other than individual consultation, a written contract describing the purposes, objectives, ground rules, expectations, resources needed, and time lines for consultation; individual consultation, such as between a counselor and a classroom teacher or another helping professional, should have a brief written agreement, even if it is only a memorandum of understanding. Dougherty (2000) summarizes these steps of the entry stage as exploring the needs of the organization, contracting, and then physically and psychologically entering the system.

### Information Gathering, Problem Confirmation, and Goal Setting

Kurpius, Fuqua, and Rozecki (1993) encouraged consultants to spend enough time to gather valid and reliable data, both qualitative and quantitative, in order to ensure delivering high-quality services. Accurate data are important for defining the problem and attributing ownership—essential steps to establishing the problem as a goal to be reached. Without agreement about the ownership of the problem (the teacher, parent, child, other child, or adult), interventions the consultant suggests are not effective because no one takes responsibility for implementing the plan. The diagnosis stage includes gathering information, defining the problem, setting goals, and generating possible interventions, according to Dougherty (2000).

Wagner (2000) identified four processes that consultants use in their conversations to promote change. One thing the consultant does is help externalize the problem so that the person sees the difficulty differently. The consultant also allows the consultee to gain a larger, more detached view of the problem. According to Wagner, that process allows a paradigm shift, recognition of the complex patterns between the focus and the features of the situation, as well as the possibilities of change. Finally, Wagner remarked that the process of consultation encourages the consultee to engage in self-reflection, recognize her or his own role, and avoid the dynamics of blame.

## Solution Searching and Intervention Selection

Consultants must avoid seeing all problems in the light of their favorite paradigm or counseling theory. Pointing out that human services organizations tend to see human factors as the cause of most problems and that industry and businesses most often see their problems coming from structural causes, Kurpius, Fuqua, and Rozecki (1993) suggested that consultants carefully consider both the human and structural factors (the school or other systems in the child's life) as possible causes of the problem and as areas for intervention. Therefore, this implementation stage includes choosing an intervention, developing and implementing the plan, and then evaluating the success of the intervention (Dougherty, 2000).

Kahn (2000) proposed a model of solution-focused consultation that shifts the consultation emphasis to solutions and strengths. The model rests on the assumptions of a future orientation, and the helper is seen as a facilitator or coach. Little time is spent exploring the problem before a goal is set. The goal is stated in positive language. The helper and the helpee explore exceptions to the problem, choose the best solutions, and create a plan to implement them. The helper also encourages trying something different to change the problem. Kahn encouraged counselors to consider her propositions as another model of consultation in the schools.

## Evaluation

As with any counseling task, evaluation ensures professional effectiveness. Kurpius, Fuqua, and Rozecki (1993) suggested asking certain questions to evaluate the outcomes of consulting services: Have the consulting goals been achieved, and to what degree? How well have interventions worked? Were there unexpected outcomes, and have they been addressed effectively? Evaluation should give the consultant information about how each step in the process worked. Outcomes may include the changes in the client or in the system in which the client exists. Dougherty (2000) concluded that three ways to evaluate a plan's outcome are individual goal-attainment measures (see Chapter 2 for examples), standardized outcome-assessment devices, and consumer satisfaction surveys. Hughes, Hasbrouck, Serdahl, Heidgerken, and McHaney (2001) tested an instrument, the Consultant Evaluation Rating Form (CERF), that could also be used.

## Termination

When the consultant and consultee agree that the process should be terminated, the consultant should review with the consultee each step in the process, describing what was successful or not successful. If the work was successful, this review process provides an opportunity for clarification, recognition of successes, and reflection on how the process brought about improvements. If the consultation process was not successful, the session helps all members understand the reasons for the failure. Brown, Pryzwansky, and Schulte (2001) provided several instruments that can be used to assess all aspects of the consultation process.

This review has outlined models of consultation as well as processes involved in that form of interacting. Counselors may determine that other types of partnerships with adults would be more appropriate for the situation. Collaboration and teamwork are discussed as alternatives for working with other adults.

## COLLABORATION

Friend and Cook (2000) define *collaboration* as "a style for direct interaction between at least two coequal parties voluntarily engaged in shared decision making as they work toward a common goal" (p. 6). They note that this definition conveys how the process occurs—as a partnership. These authors identify defining characteristics of collaboration to clarify their definition. First, they emphasize that collaboration is voluntary. Collaboration requires parity among participants. In other words, each participant has a voice equal to any other participant, and all contributions are valued equitably. The parties involved in collaboration base their work on mutual goals, and they share responsibility for the process and the outcomes. They also share their resources and decision making. O'Loony (1996) defined *collaboration* as an informal process that involves sharing goals, values, ideas, and joint activity.

Porter, Epp, and Bryant (2000) stated that collaboration among school professionals is a necessity, a process of connecting schools, families, and communities (Taylor & Adelman, 2000). Niebuhr, Niebuhr, and Cleveland (1999) presented a rationale for collaboration between principals and counselors, and Shoffner and Williamson (2000) discussed a preservice seminar devoted to that type of collaboration. Geroski, Rodgers, and Breen (1997) listed examples of ways school counselors may work on a collaborative service-delivery team. School counselors may be alert for the typical problem behaviors of young people, provide interventions and support services, and extend referrals to other services as appropriate. Becicka (2000) discussed collaborating with teachers to promote the social and emotional competence of students. Sink (2000) exhorts school counselors to model collaboration for both the school and the larger community.

Keys, Bemak, Carpenter, and King-Sears (1998) suggested that a collaborative consultation model can result in a "more comprehensive and integrated program" to address the complex problems of youth and families (p. 123). They pointed to the increasing number of youths and families facing serious problems, such as poverty, family instability, substance abuse, physical and sexual abuse, violence, and other societal issues, and concluded that new ways of helping require service integration through collaboration. According to the writers, "Collaborative consultation is a model that actively involves parents, educators, youths, and counselors as equal participants and experts in problem solving a specific issue. . . . it is the sharing and transferring of knowledge and information between and among all team members that enables the group to determine and carry out a more comprehensive plan" (p. 127). Their five stages of problem solving for collaborative consultation involve the following:

1. Coming together—establishing a commitment among all participants to collaborate on a certain issue
2. Defining a shared vision—sharing knowledge and information, building trust, and defining vision, goals, and objectives
3. Developing a strategic plan to accomplish goals and objectives
4. Taking action on the plan
5. Evaluating progress by determining if specific objectives are accomplished

The authors called for school and community mental health counselors to redefine their roles to see themselves as a part of the broader community.

Some authors (Porter, Epp, & Bryant, 2000; Taylor & Adelman, 2000) suggest that collaborative efforts may involve nurturing relationships to increase resources, to enhance effectiveness, to decrease fragmentation, and for cost efficiency. Their ideas of "school–community" collaborative include agencies; organizations that provide services and programs, such as health and human services, juvenile justice, and economic development; those that share facilities, such as schools, parks, and libraries; and other entities, such as young people, families, religious groups, civic groups, and businesses. Porter, Epp, and Bryant (2000) argued that collaboration among school mental health professionals must occur and provided examples of collaborative programs that have been successfully implemented.

Bemak (2000) called for counselors to collaborate with school personnel, communities, and families. Within the school, collaborators work with school administrators to collect and share data on school performance, develop programs to overcome barriers, design strategies for school problems, and emphasize a healthy school climate. Collaborators work with teachers to improve classroom performance, understand cultural learning styles, and develop group skills and conflict resolution strategies. Otwell and Mullis (1997) outlined a staff-development model to accomplish those goals. Bemak (2000) further suggested that with community agencies collaborators can help with coordination of services and with outreach. Working with families would revolve around linking schools and homes and building cooperative relationships.

Lusky and Hayes (2001) described collaborative consultation for program evaluation. The collaborator used action research to implement a needs–assessment process. They presented the method for developing instruments to be used for determining the effectiveness of programs. Their case example provides details to recreate the process.

Dougherty (2000) suggested guidelines to determine whether consultation or collaboration should be chosen. First, one should determine how the two services are viewed by the consumer. Next, the consultant should reflect on personal reactions to the two services and comfort with the assumptions of each. Dougherty suggests that collaboration may be the method to choose if the parameters of consultation cannot be met. The consultant's skill level and the consultee's (or collaborator's) skill level also influence the decision. Fundamental to the choice are the nature of the problem, the context in which it occurs, and the skills of everyone involved.

Some activities have been proposed by Dettmer, Dyck, and Thurston (1999) to advance collaborative discussions and build interactive formats. Three are described here.

> **Jigsaw.** Jigsaw means the group decides on an issue and several subtopics. The large group divides into smaller groups. Each small group researches one of the subtopics and shares what is learned by teaching it to the others.
>
> **Compare and Contrast.** In compare and contrast, a small group identifies terms and phrases that represent different perspectives of an issue. The group's work is combined with all in the larger group to result in a broad list of ways of thinking about an issue.
>
> **Circle response.** For circle response, a small group sits in a circle. A leader begins by introducing or by repeating a topic. Moving clockwise, each person takes a turn responding to the issue or by saying, "I pass." At the end of the time, the ideas are summarized and integrated into the larger group.

## TEAMWORK

Azar (1997) defines a *team* as a group of "two or more people who interact dynamically, interdependently, and adaptively and who share at least one common goal or purpose" (p. 14). Kormanski (1999) explained that teams are groups of people who have shared goals. Teams stress their interdependence and require commitment by the team members to the team effort. Finally, Kormanski noted that teams are accountable. Basham, Appleton, and Lambarth (1998) also identified the characteristics of effective teams. They noted that team members are committed to building and maintaining constructive relationships among themselves. Effective teams have goals and identified roles. Each person on the team is aware of the focus of the team, the responsibilities of the members, and the plan for accomplishing the task of the team.

Henderson and Gysbers (1998) recognized the advantages of teamwork. They noted that when people help in an effort, the level of support for both the work and for each other increases. Additionally, the team forum allows members to be challenged, to take risks, to be creative, and to be contributors. Another advantage occurs as the team accepts responsibility for their accomplishments.

Teams may be identified by their setting, such as work, sports, or schools; by their tasks, such as problem solving or a special purpose; or by what they do, such as recommend a strategy (Gladding, 2003). Teams are a special kind of task or work group. Friend and Cook (2000) identify characteristics of teams. They state that individuals must be aware of their membership on a team. A team has an organized system of behavior that is regulated by a common set of norms. They also stress the interdependence of team members, the unique skills and perspectives of team members, and their shared goal of effective service delivery. Productive teams result when these factors combine:

- Team members trust, rely on, and respect each other.
- Members have skills in solving problems, resolving conflicts, and building relationships.
- Members feel accountable for influencing the work and for accomplishing the goal.
- Members encourage and help every other person's efforts. (Henderson & Gysbers, 1998)

Some authors (Friend & Cook, 2000; Kormanski, 1999; Kormanski & Mozenter, 1987) have suggested that teams experience stages of development, with tasks and relationship outcomes specific to each. In the forming or awareness stage, team members examine their task, discover more about each other, and clarify their purpose(s). The goal is for members to commit to the task and accept each other. The leader helps members get acquainted, set goals, and organize their work, as well as clarify the group's values. During the storming or conflict stage, members work out issues of leadership, procedures, and goals. The goals are clarifying and belonging. The leaders use active listening, flexibility, creativity, conflict management, and assertiveness to guide at this stage The norming or cooperation stage involves members establishing role relationships and defining roles and procedures for accomplishing their work. The goals are involvement and support, and leaders use communicating, feedback, affirmation, humor, and networking to help at this stage. In the performing or productivity stage, the members work toward the accomplishment of the goals, with the task outcome of achievement and the relationship outcome of pride. A leader will encourage this by using decision making, problem solving, multicultural awareness, mentoring, and rewarding. When the work is complete, the adjourning or separation stage occurs. The task outcome is recognition of the accomplishment, and the relationship outcome would be satisfaction. A leader would help by evaluating, reviewing, celebrating, and bringing closure to the team experience. Gladding (2003) suggested that effective teams emphasize continuous improvement on interpersonal, process, and product levels.

Johnson and Johnson (2000) identified the following as necessary ingredients for structuring and nurturing productive teams:

- Encourage the team to define a mission and goals that match the mission.
- Have frequent opportunities for members to interact and to promote each other's success.
- Pay attention to the first meetings and to clear "rules of conduct" for members.
- Measure the progress of the team as a whole and individually.
- Identify movement toward goals.
- Supply applicable information and facts to "help them redefine and enrich their understanding of their mission, purpose, and goals."
- Provide training needed for the work and for team skills.

- Commemorate members' contributions to the success of the team.
- Ensure sessions in which the team can examine its work and ways to improve. (pp. 553–555)

Kline (2001) provided a model to test team performance. She hypothesized that the context of the team, individual characteristics of each member, team characteristics, and the process the team uses to accomplish its task would predict team satisfaction and outcome effectiveness. She successfully tested the model and emphasized the importance of looking at several dimensions of a team in facilitating and assessing.

## COMBINATIONS

Myrick (1997) explained a model of consultation that may also serve as framework for the processes of collaborating and teamwork. His systematic facilitative approach for practice involves the following steps:

1. Identify the problem clearly after careful discussion and listening
2. Continue to clarify the situation by determining
   a. The emotional and value components
   b. The specific behaviors involved
   c. The expectations of the people involved
   d. What has been done previously
   e. The strengths of the people and/or systems
   f. The resources available
3. Determine the desired goal or outcome in specific (preferably behavioral) terms
4. Gather any needed information for further clarity
5. Develop a plan of action and determine the responsibilities for implementing it
6. Evaluate and revise as needed, and discuss the next steps

Persi (1997) proposed a set of questions to encourage discussion in a consulting relationship. His questions mirror Myrick's consultation model.

1. How have these problems affected you?
2. What has worked well for you with these problems?
3. What has not worked?
4. What type of support do you need?
5. Is there anything I can do for you?
6. Have we left anything out?
7. May I come back for a follow-up visit? (p. 347)

The tasks of consultation as described by Kurpius, Fuqua, and Rozecki (1993) are, in summary, assessing one's own competency, collecting data, defining the problem, setting a goal, selecting interventions, evaluating results, and terminating the relationship—all activities with which counselors are familiar. To ensure high-quality consultative services, however, counselors inexperienced in consulting should work with a colleague or seek supervision as they begin their consultative work, and all counselor–consultants should periodically evaluate the effectiveness of their professional services.

## CONSULTATION INTERVENTIONS

Consulting can help counselors reach more children by teaching adults (parents, teachers, and other significant persons in the children's lives) to behave in more helpful ways. Providing indirect services to children through consultation, collaboration and/or teamwork can be an important part of the counselor's role. Ideally the impact of those procedures could extend beyond the individual child to other children in the classroom, school, or family, thus expanding the potential for positive change. The following discussion includes some techniques that may be useful in efforts with adults. Each intervention should be chosen only after a careful consideration of each child's uniqueness and special needs

### Role Shift

Simply changing one's own behavior may elicit a behavior change in another person. Adults who change their responses to children's behaviors may cease to reinforce them or may present children with an unexpected response that causes change.

Counselors might want to ask adults to list *everything* they have tried with the child that has been effective and ineffective. The counselor then asks them to commit themselves to dropping the ineffective techniques with this child. The list should be kept as a reminder of what not to do with the child, as well as what responses work.

When the child has behaved inappropriately, adults can stop and ask themselves, "What response does this child expect?" Does the child expect the adult to be shocked, outraged, or angry? For instance, Glen reacted to his mother's scolding by drawing grotesque pictures of her and placing them around the house. He took great delight in watching her reactions when she found the pictures.

She decided that Glen enjoyed her outrage. The next time she found a picture, she calmly commented to him, "I must have really made you angry when I scolded you for you to draw me like this." She left the picture up and went on with her work. Glen quietly removed his pictures later in the day. This technique seems to work best when the child expects to get attention, elicit shock (as with curse words or dirty language), cause frustration or anger, or get revenge.

## Listing of Behaviors

A technique similar to the descriptive discussion is listing behaviors. For instance, Mr. Jones told the counselor that Sherry was a crybaby who cried at everything that did not go her way. The counselor asked Mr. Jones to keep an exact count of the times that Sherry cried during the next week. The next week Mr. Jones admitted that, according to his count, Sherry had cried only three times that week—once when she fell, once when she was told to go to bed, and once when she was refused a request. Mr. Jones began to change his perception of Sherry as a crybaby.

Listing the number of times a behavior occurs can also provide a baseline count to determine if an intervention has reduced an inappropriate behavior or increased an appropriate one.

## Logical Consequences

Proponents of Adler's individual psychology advocate allowing children to experience the natural or logical consequences of their behavior, rather than punishment, as the preferred form of discipline (see Chapter 11). They suggest that adults who punish children become authority figures and lose the friendship of the child. They also point out that natural or logical consequences are reality oriented and teach the child the rules of society, whereas punishment may teach unwanted lessons such as "power is authority." Obviously, adults cannot allow children to experience the consequences of all their behavior; children cannot learn that busy streets are dangerous by playing in them. However, a thoughtful adult can find ways for children to see the consequences of inappropriate behavior. When Peter colors on the walls instead of on paper, for instance, he is responsible for using the sponge and cleanser to remove the coloring. The natural consequence of being late is to miss an event or a meal. The logical consequence of damaging someone's property is to earn enough money to replace it. The logical consequence of behaving inappropriately in a group is usually rejection by the group or isolation. Discipline with logical consequences very quickly teaches children the order and rules of society.

## Isolation Techniques

At times, children's behaviors become so unacceptable that isolation techniques are used, meaning they must be removed from the group (the classroom, family, or peer group). For many years, parents sent children to their rooms when they acted out. Our society isolates adults who behave inappropriately by ostracism and, in extreme cases, by imprisonment. Isolation techniques are a form of logical consequences (see Chapter 11). Children with minor problems of maintaining attention can go to a seat away from the group, in a quiet place but not out of sight. Children who are not attending to the task of the group may be quietly reminded that their present seat is for working on science, participating in a group discussion, and the like. If they choose to continue their nonattentive behavior, they must go to their quiet corner and can return when they want to participate in the group's task.

The second step of isolation is the quiet corner. Some children are highly distractible and highly distracting to their peers. They must be completely screened from the group to accomplish their work. A quiet corner can be made with screens, study carrels, bookshelves (books facing outward), or large, decorated furniture cartons. The quiet corner should contain a desk, chair, books, puzzles, and other quiet materials and no windows or doors. When a child misbehaves, the adult quietly signals the child that the behavior is not appropriate and asks the child to go to the quiet corner. Children choose to return to the group when they are ready to participate more acceptably. The adult may have to impose a short time limit of 10 to 15 minutes before allowing children this choice.

Counselors can suggest a time-out room for more severe problems, when children need to be completely away from the group. Time-out should be used not as a punishment but as a cooling-off time. The adult can instruct the child to make a plan for avoiding the trouble in the future while in the time-out room.

When children's problem behaviors are so severe that the first three isolation procedures have not worked, the adult can quietly ask the child to leave the premises (school, church, club, recreational center) and come back tomorrow to try again. The children should be aware of what behaviors are acceptable and unacceptable, as well as of the conditions for remaining in the group. Because this procedure often requires the assistance of parents, school personnel, or other community workers, establish a written agreement among all parties. Many schools use in-house suspension to provide a place where children who cannot remain in the group can go for supervised study. Other community resources that provide youth services may cooperate in arranging for supervision.

Followers and students of Adlerian psychology have suggested that parents who find themselves as referees in children's conflicts with others take a time-out in the bathroom. Their contention was that children try to involve adults in their conflicts to get attention, that children learn to settle their differences (and learn the consequences) more effectively without relying on adults, and that only danger of physical harm or property damage requires adult intervention. Dinkmeyer and Carlson (2001) provided specific consultation procedures to help adults implement these and other Adlerian interventions with children.

Isolation techniques teach children the logical consequences of their behavior. Acceptable and unacceptable behaviors should be clearly defined for children. When using the procedures, adults should not nag, lecture, or scold. Isolation techniques should be viewed as a positive method of discipline rather than as punishment.

## Assessment as a Consulting and Counseling Intervention

In their attempts to understand children's developmental and other critical problems, counselors often use a variety of tools, such as self-report surveys, interviews, tests, case histories, and behavioral observations. Sattler (1998) created a comprehensive volume that outlines procedures, forms, and issues related to interviewing children and families. Counselors also need to be familiar with standardized tests, understand their results, and use them effectively in counseling and in consulting with other professionals. Some of the more commonly used assessment tools are discussed in the following section.

## *The Interview*

Counselors are usually very comfortable with interviewing their child clients and can obtain much information through this procedure. Counselors are adept not only in listening to what is being said but also in noting how it is said and the accompanying behaviors. Typically, the interviewer seeks to learn something about the child (name, age, family information) and the presenting problem. While interviewing the child, the counselor has an opportunity to observe if the child can make good eye contact and is outgoing or shy, attentive or distracted, overactive or lethargic, talkative or reluctant to speak, confused or thinking clearly, and anxious or depressed. Some counselors prefer structured interviews; others allow clients to reveal themselves at their own pace. Some counselors use self-report surveys that ask children open-ended questions (my best friend _____; I like it when my mother _____). Counselors can learn much through observation of appearance, behaviors, affect, and the verbal and nonverbal communications of children.

One interview, the Mental Status Examination (MSE), may be used to provide an inventory of the person's behavior. Hohenshil and Getz (2001) outlined the following types of observations to be included:

*General Appearance, Behavior, and Attitude.*   Counselors note whether the child's appearance and dress are appropriate to the situation. Observations may also include posture, odd mannerisms, activity level, and facial expression. Whether the client is cooperative, sullen, assertive, impulsive, dependent, evasive, or friendly may also be noted.

*Speech Characteristics and Thought Process.*   Hohenshil and Getz (2001) noted that speech indicates thought processes. Characteristics of verbal activity such as the pattern of speech, the amount of detail, the goal of speech, fragmented ideas, loosely connected phrases, and silences are included.

*Emotional Status and Reactions.*   What the person says and how he or she behaves provide evidence of emotional status. The counselor observes facial expressions, whether flushed, and whether the affect is appropriate to the situation.

*Content of Thought.*   This involves a determination of whether the client's thought patterns are within normal limits. Delusional thinking, rigidly held false beliefs, and obsessions are examples of thoughts beyond the normal range.

*Orientation and Awareness.* The counselor ascertains whether the client is oriented to time, place, and person. This is a critical element of a MSE and may be chosen to begin the interview. The counselor may ask the client the setting, his or her name, and the day, month, and year. This may need to be modified to the cognitive ability of the child.

*Memory.* The counselor may ask the person to talk about the previous day, a birthday, or some past life experience.

*General Intellectual Functioning.* A child may be asked to demonstrate an academic skill relevant to his or her grade level to assess general knowledge. Judgment and reasoning might include something like "What would you do if you saw a fire?" or "How are a cat and dog alike?"

*Insight.* The counselor tries to determine how much the client understands about the current problem situation.

*MSE Summary.* The counselor summarizes the observations and may include recommendations for further assessment (Hohenshil & Getz, 2001, pp. 272–273).

## CASE HISTORIES

A case history gives professionals complete biographical information about the child client. Interviewing the child and his or her parents and other family members and reviewing school records and the records of other professionals (doctors, speech therapists, special teachers, and others) working with the child provide data for the case history.

### Behavioral Observations

In certain cases, the counselor will need to observe children in their work and play situations in order to understand more about their functioning and relationships with others through behavioral observations. Personal observation can tell the counselor if a child's behavior is appropriate, any circumstances that stimulated certain responses, and how others around the child respond. Counselors may use published checklists or develop their own methods for recording behavioral observations.

### Formal Psychological and Educational Tests

Children referred for learning and behavior problems often take a battery of tests to help professionals understand more about their level of functioning. Psychologists working with the child usually decide the tests to be included in the battery.

## *Intelligence Tests*

Intelligence is a difficult concept to define, but most agree that it is related to a person's general mental ability. Tests for children usually include some measure of knowledge, concept formation, and reasoning. Many tests tap both verbal and nonverbal abilities. Some of the more popular tests for measuring children's intelligence are the Stanford-Binet Intelligence Scale, 4th edition; the Wechsler Intelligence Scale for Children–Revised (WISC-III); the Wechsler Preschool and Primary Scale of Intelligence (WPPSI-R); the Otis-Lennon School Ability Test; and the California Test of Mental Maturity. The Stanford-Binet and Wechsler scales must be administered individually by a trained professional; the Otis-Lennon and California tests can be administered in the classroom to groups in grades 1 through 12. The tests yield a numerical intelligence quotient, the IQ score, with 100 being the mean or average and a 15- to 16-point standard deviation to indicate how far above or below the mean the child scores.

For special groups of children, counselors may wish to consider alternative assessments, such as Multiple Assessment for Multiple Intelligences by David Lazear. A quick estimate of intelligence can be obtained with the Peabody Picture Vocabulary Test–Revised (PPVT-R). Children respond by pointing to the picture that best describes the word read by the administrator. The test taps only one area of the child's ability and therefore is not considered to be a measure of general intelligence. A newer test of intelligence and achievement is the Kaufman Assessment Battery for Children (K-ABC). The developers of the K-ABC define *intelligence* in terms of a child's information-processing skills and problem-solving abilities. The test has been a helpful diagnostic tool for both normal and exceptional children. Persons using either the PPVT-R or the K-ABC need training and supervision in the administration and interpretation of these instruments. Children are often labeled or classified by intelligence test results, and extreme care is needed to avoid harming any child through the misuse of assessment measures. Hohenshil and Getz (2001) caution counselors in interpreting results across ethnic and cultural groups.

## *Projective Techniques*

Professionals sometimes ask children to respond to an unstructured stimulus, a picture, or a story to learn more about their thoughts and feelings. One projective technique, the Children's Apperception Test (CAT), uses animals as stimuli for children age 3 to 10. An alternative form, the CAT-H, uses human figures. The administrator asks the children what they see when they are shown each card.

Trained professionals can use Machover's Draw-a-Person and the Kinetic Family Drawing tests to learn more about the child's psychological functioning. They ask children to draw a person or their family on a blank sheet of paper, and these pictures reveal how children feel about themselves and the relationships among family members.

Counselors do not ordinarily administer, score, and interpret projective instruments; however, counselors may need to be familiar with the tests to consult effectively with other professionals about their clients and their families.

## Achievement Tests

Achievement tests are educational assessments that measure the accomplishment of learning. These tests focus on the level of knowledge, skill, or accomplishment in a particular area—what the person currently knows or can do (Hohenshil & Getz, 2001). A battery of achievement tests covers more than one academic area (reading, mathematics, language, and others). Some of the more popular group tests used in kindergarten through grade 12 are the California Achievement Test, Metropolitan Achievement Test, SRA Achievement Test, Comprehensive Test of Basic Skills, Iowa Tests of Basic Skills, Wide Range Achievement Test, and Stanford Achievement Test Series (Aiken, 1997). The Peabody Individual Achievement Test (PIAT) is individually administered. The results of achievement tests can be used for placement of children or to determine educational areas of strengths and weaknesses.

## Aptitude Tests

Aptitude tests are similar to achievement tests but are given to predict learning or behavior—for example, school readiness or reading readiness. The Metropolitan Readiness Test (MRT) measures children's school readiness in reading and mathematics. The System of Multi-Cultural Pluralistic Assessment (SOMPA) was designed to be a measurement of aptitude that would be culturally fair; however, the test has been controversial, and many critics have attacked its validity.

## Other Tests

Counselors may want to administer other tests, surveys, or scales to learn more about a child's interests, values, study habits, or social acceptance by peers or the age appropriateness of their behaviors. Follow-up diagnostic testing in mathematics or reading may be helpful after the results of an initial intelligence or achievement test have been obtained. Special tests are available for children with exceptional conditions—the learning disabled, the hearing or visually challenged, the mentally challenged, and others. The Murphy-Meisgeier Type Indicator for Children and the Myers-Briggs Type Indicator, both self-report instruments, may help students with self-awareness and self-acceptance. The tests selected depend on the nature of the child's problem and the counseling objectives to be accomplished.

Before selecting any test for administration—and before accepting the results of any test—the user of assessment data should know whether the test is a good measure. At least two concepts give counselors an indication of the "goodness" of a particular instrument: validity and reliability. *Validity* is the extent to which a test measures what it is supposed to measure—intelligence, interests, achievement, or aptitude. A test that measures the child's current level of achievement in grade 2 is not a measure of the child's aptitude or intelligence; the test is valid only for measuring achievement. The *reliability* of a test indicates the consistency with which the test measures. Are the results of an intelligence test similar when the test is administered to the same child 2 days, 2 weeks, or 2 months apart? Correlation coefficients indicate the degree to which tests are valid and reliable. Counselors also need to know the type of population used in the norming process. A test with normative data for children under 5 years is not appropriate for administering to a 6-year-old. Complete information on validity and reliability, as well as a description of the norm group, can be found in the technical manuals that accompany tests, or the counselor can consult other references such as catalogs, journal reviews, *Tests in Print,* or *The Mental Measurement Yearbook.*

Counselors must be cautious in working in the area of assessment. Most are trained in interviewing, development of case histories, and behavioral observation. However, their training in assessment procedures varies, and counselors should administer and interpret only those tests for which they have received instruction. In addition, counselors can consult books such as Sattler's *Assessment of Children: Revised and Updated* (3rd edition) and other literature on assessment to keep current about new and revised instruments. Professionals can refer to their appropriate professional code of ethics to determine their role in assessment and appraisal.

## SUMMARY

Although problems exist with theoretical foundations and evaluative research on consultation, we should not overlook the technique as a possible means for helping children in need. Helping techniques presented to significant people in children's lives through small groups, psychological education, outreach programs, and preventive education may reach children to whom a lone counselor's direct services would not be available. For our purposes, consultation refers to the one-to-one interaction between the counselor and a significant adult in the child's life or to a counselor-led group of significant adults, with the purpose of finding ways of assisting children to function more effectively. Counselors will also have opportunities to work collaboratively with other health services and educational professionals, as well as other people who influence a child's life. Additionally, the use of teamwork allows counselors to contribute to cooperative efforts on the behalf of young people.

### W E B S I T E S  for Consultation, Collaboration, Teamwork

Association for Supervision and Curriculum Development
www.ascd.org

SchoolCounselor.com
www.schoolcounselor.com

School Counselor Resources
208.183.128.8/guidance/

## REFERENCES

Aiken, L. R. (1997). *Psychological testing and assessment.* Boston: Allyn & Bacon.

American Counseling Association. (1995). *Code of ethics and standards of practice.* Alexandria, VA: Author.

Azar, B. (1997, July). Teambuilding isn't enough: Workers need training, too. *APA Monitor, 28,* 14–15.

Basham, A., Appleton, V., & Lambarth, C. (1998). The school counselor's role in organizational team building. In C. Dykeman (Ed.), *Maximizing school guidance program effectiveness: A guide for school administrators & program directors* (pp. 51–58). Greensboro, NC: ERIC/CASS.

Becicka, C. (2000). Promoting social and emotional competence through teacher/counselor collaboration. *Education, 120,* 668–675.

Behring, S. T., Cabello, B., Kushida, D., & Murguia, A. (2000). Cultural modifications to current school-based consultation approaches reported by culturally diverse beginning consultants. *School Psychology Review, 29,* 354–367.

Bemak, F. (2000). Transforming the role of the counselor to provide leadership in educational reform through collaboration. *Professional School Counseling, 3,* 323–331.

Bergan, J. R., & Kratochwill, T. R. (1990). *Behavioral consultation and therapy.* New York: Plenum.

Brack, G., Jones, E., Smith, R., White, J., & Brack, C. (1993). A primer on consultation theory: Building a flexible worldview. *Journal of Counseling and Development, 70,* 487–498.

Brown, D., Pryzwansky, W. B., & Schulte, A. C. (2001). *Psychological consultation: Introduction to theory and practice* (5th ed.). Boston: Allyn & Bacon.

Caplan, G., & Caplan, R. B. (1993). *Mental health consultation and collaboration.* San Francisco: Jossey-Bass.

Dettmer, P. A., Dyck, N. T., & Thurston, L. P. (1999). *Consultation, collaboration and teamwork for students with special needs* (3rd ed.). Boston: Allyn & Bacon.

Dinkmeyer, D. Jr., & Carlson, J. (2001). *Consultation: Creating school-based interventions* (2nd ed.). Philadelphia: Brunner-Routledge.

Dougherty, A. M. (2000). *Psychological consultation and collaboration in school and community settings* (3rd ed.). Pacific Grove, CA: Brooks/Cole.

Friend, M., & Cook, L. (2000). *Interactions: Collaboration skills for school professionals* (3rd ed.). New York: Longman.

Geroski, A. M., Rodgers, K. A., & Breen, D. T. (1997). Using the DSM-IV to enhance collaboration among school counselors, clinical counselors, and primary care physicians. *Journal of Counseling and Development, 75,* 231–239.

Gladding, S. T. (2003). *Group work: A counseling specialty* (4th ed.). Upper Saddle River, NJ: Merrill.

Glosoff, H., & Koprowicz, C. (1990). *Children achieving potential: An introduction to elementary school counseling and state-level policies.* Washington, DC: National Conference of State Legislatures and American Association for Counseling and Development.

Goldstein, B. S. C., & Harris, K. C. (2000). Consultant practices in two heterogeneous Latino schools. *School Psychology Review, 29,* 368–377.

Henderson, P., & Gysbers, N. C. (1998). *Leading and managing your school guidance program staff.* Alexandria, VA: American Counseling Association.

Hohenshil, T. H., & Getz, H. (2001). Assessment, diagnosis, and treatment planning in counseling. In D. C. Locke, J. E. Myers, & E. I. Herr (Eds.), *The handbook of counseling* (pp. 269–285). Thousand Oaks, CA: Sage.

Hughes, J. N., Hasbrouck, J. E., Serdahl, E., Heidgerken, A., & McHaney, L. (2001). Responsive systems consultation: A preliminary evaluation of implementation and outcomes. *Journal of Educational and Psychological Consultation, 12,* 179–201.

Ingraham, C. L. (2000). Consultation through a multicultural lens: Multicultural and cross-cultural consultation in schools. *School Psychology Review, 29,* 320–343.

Johnson, D. W., & Johnson, F. P. (2000). *Joining together* (7th ed). Boston: Allyn & Bacon.

Kahn, B. B. (2000). A model of solution-focused consultation for school counselors. *Professional School Counseling, 3,* 248–255.

Keys, S. G., Bemak, F., Carpenter, A., & King-Sears, M. (1998). Collaborative consultant: A new role for counselors serving at-risk youths. *Journal of Counseling and Development, 76,* 123–133.

Keys, S. G., Bemak, F., & Lockhart, E. J. (1998). Transforming school counseling to serve the mental health needs of at-risk youth. *Journal of Counseling and Development, 76,* 381–388.

Kline, T. J. B. (2001). Predicting team performance: Testing a model in a field setting. *Journal of Specialists in Group Work, 26,* 185–197.

Kormanski, C. (1999). *The team: Explorations in group process.* Denver: Love Publishing.

Kormanski, C. L., & Mozenter, A. (1987). A new model of team building: A technology for today and tomorrow. In J. W. Pfeiffer (Ed.), *The 1987 annual: Developing human resources* (pp. 255–268). San Diego: Pfeiffer & Co.

Kurpius, D., & Fuqua, D. (1993). Fundamental issues in defining consultation. *Journal of Counseling and Development, 70,* 598–600.

Kurpius, D., Fuqua, D., & Rozecki, T. (1993). The consulting process: A multidimensional approach. *Journal of Counseling and Development, 70,* 601–606.

Lippitt, G., & Lippitt, R. (1986). *The consulting process in action* (2nd ed.). La Jolla, CA: University Associates.

Lusky, M. B., & Hayes, R. L. (2001). Collaborative consultation and program evaluation. *Journal of Counseling and Development, 79,* 26–38.

MacLeod, I. R., Jones, K. M., Somers, C. L., & Havey, J. M. (2001). An evaluation of the effectiveness of school-based behavioral consultation. *Journal of Educational and Psychological Consultation, 12,* 203–216.

Myrick, R. D. (1997). *Developmental guidance and counseling: A practical approach* (2nd ed.). Minneapolis: Educational Media Corporation.

Niebuhr, K. E., Niebuhr, R. E., & Cleveland, W. T. (1999). Principal and counselor collaboration. *Education, 119,* 674–679.

O'Loony, J. (1996). *Redesigning the work of human services.* Westport, CT: Quorum.

Otwell, P. S., & Mullis, F. (1997). Counselor-led staff development: An efficient approach to teacher consultation. *Professional School Counseling, 1,* 25–30.

Persi, J. (1997). When emotionally troubled teachers refer emotionally troubled students. *School Counselor, 44,* 344–352.

Porter, G., Epp, L., & Bryant, S. (2000). Collaboration among school mental health professionals: A necessity, not a luxury. *Professional School Counseling, 3,* 315–322.

Ramirez, S. A., Lepage, K. M., Kratochwill, T. R., & Duffy, J. L. (1998). Multicultural issues in school-based consultation: Conceptual and research considerations. *Journal of School Psychology, 36,* 479–509.

Sattler, J. M. (1998). *Clinical and forensic interviewing of children and families: Guidelines for the mental health, education, pediatric and child maltreatment fields.* San Diego: Author.

Schein, E. (1988). *Process consultation: Its role in organization development* (2nd ed, vol. 1). Reading, MA: Addison-Wesley.

Sheridan, S. M. (2000). Considerations of multiculturalism and diversity in behavior consultation with parents and teachers. *School Psychology Review, 29,* 344–353.

Shoffner, M. F., & Williamson, R. D. (2000). Engaging preservice school counselors and principals in dialogue and collaboration. *Counselor Education and Supervision, 40,* 128–140.

Sink, C. A. (2000). Modeling collaboration through caring communities of learners. *Professional School Counseling, 3,* ii–iii.

Taylor, L., & Adelman, H. S. (2000). Connecting schools, families, and communities. *Professional School Counseling, 3,* 298–307.

Wagner, P. (2000). Consultation: Developing a comprehensive approach to service delivery. *Educational Psychology in Practice, 16,* 9–18.

Wallace, W. A., & Hall, D. L. (1996). *Psychological consultation: Perspective and applications.* Pacific Grove, CA: Brooks/Cole.

# Chapter 17

# Group Counseling with Children

Many counselors suggest that groups are more natural than individual counseling for working with people. Children and adults function as members of groups in their daily activities—in the family, the classroom, the work setting, or the peer group. Our personal beliefs and our perceptions of self are formed from the feedback of significant people in groups—especially our family, friends, and peers. Psychologists such as Alfred Adler emphasized that people are social beings and that their development is significantly influenced by the groups around them; therefore, group counseling is more reality oriented than individual counseling. Different types of groups appear to be increasing in popularity as loneliness and separation from family and friends increase in our society. At one time, group counseling was considered an effective method of counseling because the counselor could help a number of children more economically. More important, groups provide a place where children can unlearn inappropriate behaviors and learn new ways of relating through interaction and feedback in a safe practice situation with their peers. Robinson and Jones (1996) noted that the effectiveness of group counseling has a sufficient research base. Some literature reviews (DeLucia-Waack, 1997; Shechtman, 2002) identified the outcome and process variables that contribute to that evidence. Clearly, these outcomes suggest that counselors will want to include groups in their practice.

This chapter is not intended to train counselors in conducting groups. Complete books have been written about group counseling, and most counselors have coursework and supervised practicums to help them develop skills in this area. In this chapter, an overview of working with children in groups is presented, with suggestions for those who already possess the knowledge and skills to conduct groups or who intend to pursue further training.

## DEFINITION OF GROUP

Gladding (2003) defined a *group* as "a collection of two or more individuals who meet in face-to-face interaction, interdependently, with the awareness that each belongs to the group and for the purpose of achieving mutually agreed-on goals"

(p. 497). His definition captures the concepts Johnson and Johnson (2000) identified as related to several definitions of groups: goals, interdependence, interpersonal interactions, perceptions of membership, structured relationships, mutual influence, and motivation. Those characteristics allow members in groups to deal with their own concerns, as well as help other participants develop.

Dye (2002) identified assumptions basic to group work. One assumption maintains that social behavior is learned; therefore, new experiences can produce new understandings. Another foundation is that people have reasons for their actions. Bringing about a change of behavior is the goal of counseling, a learning experience. The elements of group counseling are goals, membership, roles, methods and techniques, and interactions.

## TYPES OF GROUPS

Groups function in many ways, depending on the goal. The main goal of group work is creating opportunities for children to increase their knowledge and skills, enabling them to make and accomplish their choices (Bergin, 1999). Here are explanations of some common types of groups to allow counselors to determine which might be most appropriate to the situation and population with which they are working.

Psychoeducational groups emphasize using educational methods to obtain information and develop meaning and skills (Brown, 1997, p. 1). In these groups, children often learn to strengthen their coping skills, as well as their self-esteem (Conyne, 1996). This growth occurs through their new knowledge. The groups may focus on such topics as attitudes, beliefs, working together, communicating, and building friendship skills. According to Boutwell and Myrick (1992), the social interaction in the group helps the members gain a sense of well-being that can lead to the prevention of future problems. Some psychoeducational groups occur as classroom guidance activities in schools. Furr (2000) provided a format for designing a psychoeducational group: stating the purpose, establishing goals, identifying objectives, determining content, choosing exercises, and conducting evaluation. Her outline and examples can help counselors plan and deliver these groups.

Stoiber and Kratochwill (1998) believed that schools are in a strategic position to respond to mental health and healthcare needs, and have special opportunities for both prevention and intervention. They suggested that children and families are more likely to take advantage of school-based services because there is less stigma attached. In addition, Stoiber and Kratochwill wrote that the dramatic changes in U.S. economic, social, and demographic structures have created an urgent need for community-based services to address individual, community, and environmental issues relevant to mental health. They concluded that the schools and the community must collaborate to address the complexity and multitude of problems that exist for children and families. Bemak and Keys (2000) agreed with these points and provided specific skills for working with violent and aggressive young people.

Counseling groups are also growth oriented. Each person's behavior and development is the focus. The members of counseling groups are generally normal people who are experiencing some stress in their lives. The interaction with others in groups may revolve around concerns with interpersonal relationships, social skills, study skills, values, problem solving, or making decisions (Dansby, 1996). Arman (2000) suggested that counseling groups help children reduce their sense of social isolation and their negative emotions. The groups may also be designed for children who are facing transitions in their lives, such as divorce of parents, a death of a loved one, or school problems. Children with behavior problems may also benefit from counseling groups. Orton (1997) listed the benefits of the group as trust, caring, understanding, and support. Counseling groups may be held in schools, institutions, or mental health agencies.

Group therapy deals with unconscious motivations, with the goal of personality change for the group members. These groups are held for the remediation and treatment of people who are severely disturbed, who are suffering from deep psychological problems, or who are exhibiting socially deviant behavior.

## THEORETICALLY ORIENTED GROUP COUNSELING

The number of group counseling methods almost equals the number of counseling theories, most of which can be adapted to a group counseling setting.

Adlerian counselors used group work in their child guidance center in the early 1900s for group discussions involving parents (see Chapter 11). Adlerians believe that people are essentially social and need to belong to a community or group; consequently, they see group counseling as a natural environment for helping children see the reality of the situation and meet their needs through social interactions in the group. As in individual counseling, Adlerian group counselors rely on investigation and interpretation of the child's life by establishing the relationship, exploring the dynamics operating in the child's life, communicating back to the child an understanding of self, and reorienting the child's behavior in new directions (Corey, 2000).

Adlerian groups emphasize the interpretation of a person's early history so that group members recognize and understand the ways they have created their own lifestyles. Adlerian groups also include the practice of having individual, interpersonal, and group process goals throughout the duration of the group. Gladding (2003) explains that individual goals involve developing insight, interpersonal goals revolve around becoming socially oriented and involved, and group process goals entail promoting and experiencing a cooperative group environment. Adlerian group leaders focus on understanding the current patterns of behavior of group members and challenging them to modify those patterns. When working with children in groups, the leaders may use encouragement to imply their faith in the child's ability to change. They may also emphasize natural consequences of behavior. Wick, Wick, and Peterson (1997) used Adlerian adventure therapy with a group of elementary school children. The group was given unfamiliar, noncompetitive, and cooperative tasks to teach social interest and responsibility to the participants.

Reality therapy (see Chapter 4) was originally used more extensively in groups than with individuals. The principles adapt effectively to group work because the group is a microcosm of the real world. The psychological needs of belonging, power, freedom, and fun can all be met by group members in that setting. Also, the members provide feedback about the reality of their behavior and their plans for change. They reinforce one another in their commitments and check on the completion of homework assignments. The group leader focuses on helping the group members take responsibility for what they do, find better ways to have their needs met, and change their inappropriate or destructive behaviors (Glasser & Breggin, 2001). Reality therapy has been a popular method for helping groups of children and adolescents in schools, those confined to correctional institutions, substance abusers, and those with handicaps.

The principles of behavioral counseling (see Chapter 9) are also used in groups when the clients' goals are similar or members can help one another by providing feedback, support, or reinforcement to alter maladaptive behaviors, learn new behaviors, or prevent problems. Relaxation training, assertion training, modeling techniques, and self-management programs to control overeating or other negative behaviors are examples of behavioral techniques that can be used effectively in group settings. Corey (1995) pointed out that because behavioral group counseling is a type of education, leaders must assume an active, directive role in the group, applying their knowledge and skills to the resolution of problems. Leaders emphasize current experiences, learning, and defining goals specifically. Leaders choose group procedures that are adapted to member's needs and that are scientifically verified. Gladding (2003) noted the prevalence of the use of positive reinforcement, extinction, desensitization, and modeling in behavioral group counseling.

Rational-emotive-behavior therapy (REBT) (see Chapter 8) attempts to teach people to think rationally about events and to assume responsibility for their feelings. The techniques of this theory can be applied very effectively in groups. Members are encouraged to recognize and confront their irrational thoughts and feelings, take risks, try new behaviors, and use others' feedback to learn new social skills. Members are taught to apply REBT principles to one another. REBT leaders provide information, discuss problem-solving strategies, and may use many cognitive and/or emotive techniques. The group leader should be a role model for responsible and reality-oriented behavior, show care and respect, and teach participants to evaluate their present behaviors as well as those planned. Sommers-Flanagan, Barrett-Hakanson, Clarke, and Sommers-Flanagan (2000) discussed a school group designed to improve social and coping skills of middle school students. Based on cognitive-behavioral theory, the groups included interventions to help students understand moods, identify pleasant events, reduce tension and increase strength, and solve problems.

Transactional analysis (TA, see Chapter 10) is an ideal counseling method for groups; in fact, most counselors adhering to the principles of TA prefer treatment in groups. This method focuses on analysis of life scripts, games, and interactions among people, and the ideal setting for this teaching and learning is within a group that simulates life's interactions. Group members facilitate the counseling process by representing other individuals with whom past and present transactions can be analyzed.

Gestalt therapy (see Chapter 7) focuses on the here and now and on maintaining personal awareness. Some Gestalt counselors ask for volunteers and focus on one client at a time within the group; for example, the hot seat technique requires the counselor to work with one person in the presence of the other group members. Structured interaction between other group members may be encouraged at certain times. Gestalt group leaders must be skillful enough to find the appropriate technique to help children gain awareness.

Other counseling methods have their place in group work but do not adapt to it as readily as those already mentioned. The relationship skills set forth by person-centered counselors are appropriate in an individual or group setting. The therapeutic relationship is an essential ingredient for all clients to feel free enough to explore their world and make changes.

## GROUP LEADERSHIP SKILLS

In groups for children and adolescents, counselors primarily work as facilitators of the group process. Counselors assess the needs for a group, define the purposes of the group, select participants, arrange permission for participants, organize the schedule, plan the activities, and arrange for materials and space to meet. According to the Association for Specialists in Group Work (1991), to create effective groups, leaders must use the following 16 skills:

1. Encourage the participation of group members.
2. Observe and identify group process events.
3. Pay attention to and acknowledge the behavior of group members.
4. Clarify and summarize statements.
5. Begin and end group sessions.
6. Give information when needed.
7. Model effective behavior.
8. Engage in appropriate self-disclosure.
9. Receive and deliver feedback.
10. Ask open-ended questions.
11. Empathize with members.
12. Confront group members' behavior.
13. Help members recognize the meaning of an experience.
14. Help group members integrate and apply what they learn.
15. Demonstrate ethical and professional standards.
16. Keep the group focused on accomplishing its goals. (p. 14)

Corey (2000) contended that the group leadership's personal characteristics and skills cannot be separated from techniques used. He stated that "leaders bring to every group their personal qualities, values, and life experiences. . . . the most effective group direction is found in the kind of life the group members see the leader demonstrating and not in the words they hear the leader saying" (p. 53). He suggested the following personal characteristics as essential to a group leader:

Presence—genuine caring in "being there" for clients
Personal power—self-confidence and awareness of one's power
Courage—ability to take risks and be vulnerable
Willingness to confront oneself—being honest and aware of self
Sincerity and authenticity—sincere interest in the well-being of others and behaving without pretense
Sense of identity—knowing one's values, strengths, and limitations
Belief and enthusiasm for the group process
Inventiveness and creativity—open to new ideas and experiences

The professional skills needed by group leaders as identified by Corey (2000) include the following: active listening, restating, clarifying, summarizing, questioning, interpreting, confronting, reflecting feeling, supporting, empathizing, facilitating communication, initiating direction, setting goals, evaluating, giving feedback, suggesting, protecting, self-disclosure, modeling, linking (looking for themes), blocking (stopping counterproductive behavior by confronting it), and terminating. (See Chapter 2 for a detailed discussion of these counseling skills.) Gladding (2003) explained that three specific skills are significantly different in group counseling. He said that leaders in groups facilitate by helping group members communicate among themselves. Group leaders protect members by barring unnecessary attacks from others in the group, a skill unnecessary in individual counseling. A related skill, blocking, entails a group leader intervening in a group activity to stop counterproductive behavior. Group leaders also encourage participation, keep the group on task, and move the group in the direction of the stated objectives (Greenberg, 2003).

## GETTING STARTED

### Group Focus

Counselors determine the logistics of a group based on the type of group being held. Some groups may include materials that relate to a wide range of individuals. Others may be focused on specific areas such as divorce or grief. Additionally, resources chosen for a group may be predicated on the age of the participants. The counselor could identify a topic by his or her perception of what is needed, from the results of a needs assessment, or by the special needs of the school or community (Greenberg, 2003). The topics will vary according to the children's ages and the settings in which the groups are to be held.

Gazda, Ginter, and Horne (2001) recommended that children under 12 should take part in groups that include play and action, with counselors using techniques such as sociodrama, child drama, and psychodrama. Gladding (2003) cited Ginott as recommending the use of watercolors, finger paints, clay, and sand for children under age 9. Therefore, groups for children and young adolescents may be more action oriented than groups for children 13 and older. Carroll, Bates, and Johnson (1997) suggested that structured exercises may help individuals in adolescent groups form trust and cohesion and become more open in their communication. Theme-oriented groups may also help adolescent groups. Gladding (2003) suggested having the young people check off a list of interests and/or problems to determine a theme for a group.

Bergin (1999) provided explanations and examples for three types of groups. He listed developmental, problem centered, and topic specific as categories of groups for children and adolescents. He noted some elements basic to all groups. Groups must have purposes that are defined and reflected in the goals and objectives prepared before group participants are selected. The goals direct the group process, and the objectives clarify that focus by outlining anticipated outcomes for group members. The objectives also help the counselor determine the activities and discussion procedure to use, as well as how to determine if the purpose has been attained. He continued by noting that all groups must have requirements for membership. Finally, he stated that counselors incorporate structured activities to stimulate group interaction and self-reflection.

Greenberg (2003) classified groups as remedial, support, or preventive groups. Remedial groups concentrate on the problems faced by most students, such as study skills, listening skills, and overcoming test anxiety. Support groups deal with more personal problems and allow children to realize that others face similar challenges. Examples include groups about parental divorce, stopping a habit, or being new to the school. Preventive groups focus on avoiding difficulties. Problem solving, anger management, and handling stress could be topics of preventive groups. Wilson and Owens (2001) explained that prevention groups have focused on preventing psychological disorders, difficulties in relationships, failure in roles, failure in work groups, and physical distress. Kulic, Dagley, and Horne (2001) outlined concepts and methods for counselors who use prevention groups with children and adolescents.

The developmental groups described by Bergin (1999) involve helping young people meet their challenges in the process of growing. Examples of these challenges include personal identity, relationships, emotional and behavioral development, academic achievement, and career planning. The groups are oriented to growth and to the development of behaviors and skills to enhance a person's ability to be independent and responsible. Activities in these groups may incorporate videos, books, games, worksheets, simulations, and role playing. Bergin suggested these topics for children:

- Listening and other communication skills
- Recognizing and dealing with emotions
- Social skills and friendship
- Academic achievement
- Self-concept
- Career awareness
- Problem solving and/or decision making

And these for adolescents:

- Communication
- Assertiveness training
- Managing stress
- Social skills and making friends
- Personal identity
- Career exploration and planning
- Problem solving and/or decision making

According to Bergin (1999), problem-centered groups are more open-ended, with topics determined by the concern of the group participants at the time of the meeting. These groups focus on the here-and-now experience. Members have the opportunity to engage every other member in exploring their problems, examining potential alternatives and the consequences of those possibilities, and deciding on a course of action. These groups may be more appropriate for older children who have the ability to state their concerns and to attend to others. Some topics that may concern elementary students include relationships with family and friends, conflicts with authority figures, peer groups, and moving into middle school. Adolescents may be troubled by relationships, dating, sexual matters, teachers, homework and school, balancing commitments, and planning for the future.

Topic-specific groups focus on the needs of young people who have a situational difficulty that is causing negative feelings and stress (Bergin, 1999). The group members share some serious, immediate concerns. The group setting allows members to understand the issue in depth, explore feelings, and find coping strategies. This type of group may arise from a crisis event, such as a death. In that case, the group purpose is to provide support in dealing with the crisis. The following concerns may be addressed by topic-specific groups:

- Physical abuse
- Grief and loss
- Sexual abuse
- Aggressive behavior
- Divorce and separation
- Fear and stress
- Children of alcoholics
- Suicide
- Teen parenting

The topic of groups will determine the criteria for selecting members to participate. Some general guidelines for that process are included in this section.

## Selecting Group Members

Some counselors, such as Adlerians, hold that anyone who wishes to participate in a group should be allowed to do so, given similar, age-related levels of interest and intellectual abilities. Other counselors attempt to select members for either heterogeneity or homogeneity. Homogeneity may be desirable for groups focusing on common problems, such as children whose parents are divorced. However, a homogeneous group of underachievers or drug users probably would be counterproductive because no peer model and peer reinforcement for improved behaviors would be present. For children who act out or withdraw, a heterogeneous group provides active discussion and role models. The counselor should seriously consider the possible consequences of including children with highly dissimilar interests or maturity levels and extremely dominating, manipulative, gifted, or mentally retarded children. Children with extreme behaviors may be better candidates for individual counseling, especially during the initial stages of therapy. Most counselors prefer a balance of boys and girls in the same group unless the presence of the opposite sex would hinder discussion (on some sex education topics, for example).

## Forming a Group

Counselors may begin by recruiting members for groups. Ritchie and Huss (2000) suggested that counselors avoid labeling groups with names that imply a diagnosis or dysfunction. Children may be identified by offering adults a behavioral checklist, having children volunteer, or providing responses to needs assessments.

Reports of people being verbally attacked and hurt in groups that use extreme methods may leave parents or children with reservations about participating in a group. Counselors should fully explain the purpose of the group and the experiences planned to allay fears and clarify possible misconceptions. By providing this information to children before starting the group, the counselor can inform the children of their roles and what is expected of them and explain the role and expectations of the counselor as well. Explaining the process provides the structure needed to facilitate interaction once the group begins. The following is an example of an informative statement:

> We are forming a group made up of young people about your age to talk about things that bother or upset us. Many of us have similar concerns, and it is often helpful to share these worries and help each other try to find ways of solving them. Each member will be expected to talk about what bothers him or her and try to figure out what can be done about these situations. In addition, members will be expected to listen carefully to each other and to try to understand the other members' worries and help them solve their problems. The counselor, too, tries to understand what all the members are saying or feeling, to help them explain and clarify their thoughts and feelings, and to find solutions to their concerns.
>
> Most group members learn they can trust the others in the group and feel free to discuss things that worry them. Members are free to talk about anything or anyone that bothers or upsets them. However, the group will not be a gripe session, a gossip session, or a chatting session. We will be working together to find solutions to what is upsetting you. There may be very personal information or feelings that you would prefer not to discuss in the group. You should not feel pressured to disclose these feelings or thoughts to the group. Whatever is said in the group cannot be discussed with anyone except the counselor. If there is anyone you would rather not have in a group with you, discuss this with the counselor.

## Screening Interview

Many group leaders prefer to hold a screening interview—that is, an individual conference or intake interview—with prospective members before forming the group. Other group leaders think that anyone should be eligible to join a group and that the intake interview is unnecessary. An intake interview allows the leader an opportunity to talk privately with prospective members, to learn a little about them and their concerns, and to define some possible goals. The leader also has an opportunity to determine if the child will benefit from a group experience or if individual counseling would be more helpful. The group leader would begin by identifying the characteristics of the group members that would be beneficial to the process as well as criteria that would signify the person should be excluded (Ritchie & Huss, 2000). Children who are overly aggressive or overly sensitive to criticism would probably not benefit from group counseling. Overly angry, hyperactive, self-centered, unstable children should also be helped with other types of interventions (Ritchie & Huss, 2000; Shaffer, Brown, & McWhirter, 1998).

During the screening interview, the counselor can check the young person's willingness to engage in self-improvement, desire to help others, commitment to group progress, and compatibility with other group members (Bergin, 1999). Greenberg (2003) stated other criteria for group members. The child should have the language skills to communicate with other group members and be willing to participate in group interactions. The young people should be prepared to share their individual feelings and experiences. They should accept and abide by group rules and be committed to the group members. Greenberg suggested that counselors ought to ask potential group participants about each of these areas.

Holcomb-McCoy (2003) emphasized the importance of counselors being attuned to cultural beliefs and how culture affects the child's concerns. She suggested asking potential group members to discuss their perceptions of counseling and their expectations of the group. Group activities and structure could be modified accordingly. Reeder, Douzenis, and Bergin (1997) led small-group counseling sessions with second graders. The group focused on the racial attitudes of the second grade members. The authors concluded that the children benefited from the cultural awareness they gained from the meetings.

Ritchie and Huss (2000) listed these as possible screening questions:

How does this concern affect you at school, at home, at play?
Do you spend time worrying about this concern?
Would you like to talk with someone about this issue?
Do you feel comfortable talking about your feelings in a group? (p. 150)

## Size of Group

The number of children in the group depends on age, maturity, and attention span. Children who are 5 and 6 years old have very short attention spans and are unable to give much attention to others' concerns. Counselors may want to limit group size at this age to three or four and to work with the children for only short time periods at frequent intervals—for example, 20 minutes twice a week. Counselors can work with a larger number of older, more mature children for longer periods—for example, six children, ages 10 and 11, for 30 minutes twice a week. The maximum number of children in a group that functions effectively seems to be eight.

## The Group Setting

A room away from noise and traffic provides the best group setting. In addition, children should not fear being overheard if they are expected to talk openly about their concerns. Groups should be conducted with all members sitting in a circle so that everyone can see everyone else's face. Some counselors prefer to have the children sit around a circular table; others think tables are a barrier to interaction. Many counselors prefer to have groups of children sit in a circle on a carpeted floor, which provides easy access for counselors to move the group into play therapy.

## Group Stages

The interactions in groups change as the group continues to meet. Several authors have explained these different group stages, and most include a movement through the stages of beginning, transition, working, and leaving.

Gladding (2003) and Corey (1995) identified four stages of group counseling. The initial stage—orientation and exploration—is one of getting acquainted, determining the structure of the group, and exploring the members' expectations. The members learn how the group functions, define their goals and expectations, and find their place in the group. Members are somewhat tentative and reserved at this point; therefore, the leader should focus on making sure they feel included and on developing trust. The leader and the group establish ground rules and group procedures. In almost all groups, the leader should clarify the purpose of the group and the responsibilities of the group members. The leader should emphasize the need for confidentiality and other crucial guidelines. Some common procedures for groups with children include having only one person speak at a time, listening to the speaker, taking turns, and not making fun of each other. During the beginning of the group, the goal is for members to build rapport and learn to participate in the group.

The transition phase of the group involves members testing each other. Corey (1995) characterized this phase as one of dealing with resistance, in which feelings of anxiety may increase and the group leader may be challenged. The members will test the leader to determine if the counselor can be trusted and decide whether to get involved. The leader structures the group, clarifies the purpose, and models trust.

As the members begin to accept each other, they move to the working stage. This is the stage of cohesion and productivity. During this stage, the members are focused on identifying their goals and concerns and are willing to work both in the group and outside to address these concerns. As they focus on the issues on which they are working, they explore and clarify the concerns, set goals, and practice new behaviors.

In the last stage of group work, the members evaluate what has been accomplished and exit the group experience. The final stage—consolidation and termination—is extremely important, according to Corey (1995), because consolidation of learning takes place and members must be able to transfer what they have learned to other situations outside the group. There may be some anxiety and reluctance to terminate; therefore, the leader must deal with these feelings and any other unfinished business and then prepare members to use their new skills in their daily lives. The leader should make arrangements for some follow-up and evaluation of the group process to determine the effectiveness of the group and its effects on the member. A final group session, an individual session, or a questionnaire may be used for this purpose.

Jones and Robinson (2000) created a model for choosing topics and exercises appropriate for the different group stages. Their framework involves generating activities appropriate for the group theme and then matching the activities to the goals and stages of the group. They discuss intensity, creating a climate of work, and building relationships through all the phases of group work.

## THE GROUP COUNSELING PROCESS

### The First Session

Part of the first group counseling session will be devoted to establishing ground rules and agreeing on some guidelines for the group. The group or the leader determines the frequency of the meetings, the length of each meeting, the setting, and the duration of the group. Members also need to discuss confidentiality and what might be done if confidentiality is broken by a member, what to do about members who do not attend regularly, and whether to allow new members, should a member drop out.

Confidentiality is an important concept to discuss with children. They often do not understand the necessity for "keeping what is discussed in our group" and not talking to others about what happens. The leader can provide specific instances of other children asking about their group and have participants role-play their responses.

The group leader also has to remind members to listen carefully to one another, to try to understand one another's feelings and thoughts, and to help one another explore possible solutions to problems. The children can be encouraged to wait until members seem to have explored and discussed their concerns thoroughly before changing the subject. The group leader can provide the role model for listening and reflecting feelings and content and then reinforce these behaviors in group members.

By establishing ground rules and structuring the group during the initial session, the group leader defines expected behaviors. When inappropriate behaviors occur, the leader can ask the group, "What was the ground rule?" or present the problem to the group for discussion and resolution.

Group members may be reluctant to begin by bringing up concerns or worries for discussion, especially if the participants are not acquainted. The leader can reflect their feeling of reluctance and, if appropriate, try an icebreaker counseling technique; for example, the leader might ask members to introduce themselves and describe themselves with three adjectives, or members might be asked to introduce themselves and complete a statement such as "If I had three wishes, I would wish _____." Another icebreaker is to complete the statement "I am a _____, but I would like to be a _____," using animals, vegetables, automobiles, flowers, or other nonhuman categories; for instance, "I am a dandelion, but I'd like to be a long-stemmed rose." These activities can be done in the entire group or in dyads; either method eases the tension of the first session and promotes interaction.

Building cohesiveness and trust is important for counselors. Children have had little experience with listening to one another and trying to help one another solve problems. Unless these behaviors are taught, the group experience can become little more than unstructured play and chatter.

## Guidelines for the Remaining Sessions

Before the second group session, the counselor reviews thoroughly the content of the first meeting (names, behaviors, concerns, other personal information) and develops a plan for guiding the second meeting. At this point, the counselor should have tentative goals in mind for each member, based on the initial interview, and should be aware of who in the group will facilitate the group process—a good listener, encourager, or problem solver—and who will distract—dominating, too talkative, silly, or confrontational. The counselor may want to develop plans for dealing with distracting behaviors, should they occur.

The second session opens with a brief summary of the initial meeting. If homework was assigned, the results should be shared. The group is then ready to address a member's concerns, either one that was identified earlier or a situation that occurred between meetings that may be concerning a member. If no one volunteers to discuss a problem or concern, those identified in the pregroup interviews can be suggested by the counselor: "When we talked in our interview before the first meeting of the group, some of you shared with me that you were worried because you're going to high school next year. Who would start by telling the group about what frightens you about that change?"

Just as in individual counseling, a group leader establishes a therapeutic counseling atmosphere by demonstrating the facilitative skills of empathetic understanding, genuineness, and respect for group members. Counselors can demonstrate their caring by being nonjudgmental and accepting and by providing encouragement, support, and guidance. Counselors need to be adept at identifying, labeling, clarifying, and reflecting group members' feelings and thoughts. This process becomes difficult as the group size increases. The counselor–facilitator must be concerned about and aware of the reactions of each child in the group. As the leader models facilitative behaviors, group members begin to participate in the helping process and become more effective helpers for one another.

The group counseling process closely follows the format for individual counseling:

1. Establishing a therapeutic relationship
2. Defining the problems of the member or members
3. Exploring what has been tried and whether it has hurt or helped
4. Deciding what could be done and looking at the alternatives
5. Making a plan (goal setting)
6. Trying new behaviors by implementing the plan
7. Assigning homework
8. Reporting and evaluating the results

Also as in individual counseling, the counselor–facilitator is responsible for helping children identify and define their problems and the accompanying feelings and thoughts. The process of defining what is happening in the child's life and looking at alternatives for solving the conflict is enhanced in the group setting because of the other group members. Ideally, the child has several counselors to listen, understand, and help search for solutions while enjoying the acceptance, encouragement, support, and feedback of a number of helpers. The counselor must be skilled in facilitating these interactions and suggesting appropriate interventions. The counselor must also possess information about group dynamics and counseling skills to intervene and facilitate progress through the various steps of the counseling process.

## Implications for Different Ages

The role of the group counselor varies with children of different ages. For instance, elementary school counselors work with children who are in their formative years. Group counseling can help these children acquire social skills and shape a positive attitude toward school. Littrell and Peterson (2002) discussed a case study of establishing group work in an elementary school. Gilbert (2003) suggested topics that should be routinely offered to this age group: children dealing with divorcing parents, children with attention deficit–hyperactivity disorder, friendship, loss, academic achievement, and single-parent homes. She provided outlines for these groups. Kizner and Kizner (1999) outlined a group counseling process for adopted children to help them with their questions and concerns. Groups for elementary students have been used to help children build skills in empathy (Akos, 2000), reduce aggression (Shechtman, 2001), and live with a cancer patient (Stanko & Taub, 2002).

Drucker (2003) reminded counselors that young people in preadolescent years are unsettled in many areas. Group counseling could support them. She listed some fundamental group topics for these children as getting along with family, dealing with peer pressure, and managing anger. Rainey, Hensley, and Crutchfield (1997) provided a procedure for delivering a support group for elementary and middle school students. Their writing contains session outlines and materials. Portman and Portman (2002) presented a group intervention to develop social justice awareness, knowledge, and advocacy skills in middle school students. Their eight-session group format ends with the students completing a social justice project.

Wilson (2003) suggested those topics for high school students, as well as making choices, stress, and aggression. Ripley and Goodnough (2001) outlined the steps for planning and implementing groups in high schools. The escalating problem of eating disorders was addressed in school group counseling interventions (Daigneault, 2000; Van Lone, Kalodner, & Coughlin, 2002) that resulted in improved attitudes and expanded understanding. Zinck and Littrell (2000) had similar success with at-risk adolescent girls, and incarcerated juvenile offenders improved their behavior (Claypoole, Moody, & Peace, 2000).

Brantley, Brantley, and Baer-Barkley (1996) paired counselor interns with children in impoverished public school districts in Michigan. Each group consisted of five or six students and two interns. Each group had no more than three acting-out children, two model children, and one child who behaved "normally." The sample was divided into structured groups, unstructured groups, and a control group. The experimental groups met weekly for 45 to 50 minutes for approximately 8 weeks. Teachers were asked to complete a behavior checklist after each group. Analysis on those students classified as acting out showed that they learned positive behavior skills, positive interactions with adults, and conflict-resolution skills. Those in the structured group received slightly more positive ratings. Both counseling interns and students found the project to be profitable as well as enjoyable.

Nelson, Dykeman, Powell, and Petty (1996) developed a three-stage group intervention strategy to help students who exhibited externalizing behavior. During the first stage, the focus is on helping children take responsibility for themselves, emphasizing the idea that everyone has choices about how he or she will respond to interpersonal problems. Students are asked to identify their problems and the benefits of taking responsibility for themselves. Stage 2 includes identifying problems, establishing goals, generating alternatives, and predicting outcomes. Students are asked to make a commitment to achieving their goals. Stage 3 builds on the social problem-solving skills learned in Stage 2. Students are asked to model behaviors and to self-monitor and self-evaluate their performance. The results indicated the group counseling intervention led to improved behavior adjustment.

Reeder, Douzenis, and Bergin (1997) used small-group counseling techniques to improve racial relationships among second grade students. The students were chosen because they tended to be overly sensitive to race issues, had difficulty getting along with peers of a different race, and did not appear to have the skills necessary to interact with peers of another race. The groups consisted of five males—two African American, two Caucasian, and one Hispanic student. The group met for 1 hour a week for 8 weeks. The teachers and counselors noted a change in racial attitudes and behavior after the group sessions, and positive results were obtained on a racial relations survey administered as a pretest and posttest.

Garrett and Crutchfield (1997) stated that the "unity model" is effective as a comprehensive approach to helping children develop the dimensions of self-esteem, self-determination, body awareness, and self-concept. The unity model is based on an idea from the Native American culture and emphasizes that the whole is greater than the sum of its parts. In other words, persons are not separate in their dimensions of mind, body, heart, and other parts, and we need to find balance among all parts of our world. The medicine wheel represents this interrelationship: east represents self-esteem, or how the child feels about self and his or her ability to grow; south represents self-determination, or one's ability to explore and develop potentials; west represents body awareness, or how one experiences one's physical presence; and north represents the self-concept, or what one thinks about self and one's potential. The "talking circle" models this interrelationship and is a reminder that it is acceptable to express one's thoughts and feelings in an atmosphere of acceptance. The "talking stick" represents truth and understanding. Group members may speak only when they have the stick. The authors described a seven-session plan addressing the four interrelated areas that has worked effectively for them in group counseling with children.

## Evaluation of Groups

The effectiveness of group work can be measured in many ways. Questions that can guide these decisions include the following: What did we set out to accomplish? How did the participants respond? What participant behavior changed outside the group? How effective was the leader?

What did we set out to accomplish? The purpose of the group determines the type of group being led. During the planning process, the goal of the group is identified, as well as the means for determining whether the goal was met. For example, in a friendship group the goal may be for each member to initiate a conversation with a stranger. For an educational group, an assessment of the change in the participants' knowledge about the subject would be an evaluation possibility.

How did the participants respond? Feedback from the group members helps the leader monitor the progress and adapt the procedures as needed. Participants can respond to open-ended questions, rating scales, and summary statements to sum up their reflections and reactions.

What behaviors changed outside the group setting? The group leader may involve other adults in assessing changes in children who participated in groups. Teachers and parents may be asked to complete behavioral observations before, during, and after the group. They may be given a rating sheet about the behaviors that have been targeted. The group leader can interview the adults and ask for observations about the child's behavior.

How effective was the leader? One way to assess the group leader's effectiveness is to consider the answers to the previous three questions. Observations by colleagues, self-reflection, and input from the group members on rating scales or other instruments can also provide useful data. Bruckner and Thompson (1987) provided a model for evaluating weekly group counseling sessions with children in

the elementary school that could be adapted for use with group counseling programs in any setting. They developed an instrument containing the following six
incomplete statements and two forced-choice items:

1. I think coming to the group room is _____.
2. Some things I have enjoyed talking about in the group room are _____.
3. Some things I would like to talk about that we have not talked about are
   _____.
4. I think the counselor is _____.
5. The counselor could be better if _____.
6. Some things I have learned from coming to the group room are _____.
7. If I had a choice, I (would) (would not) come to the group room with my
   class.
8. Have you ever talked with your parents about things that were discussed in
   the group? (yes) (no)

Some of these items may be used as a needs survey for future group sessions.

Two independent persons rate student responses on a 5-point scale, ranging from
5 for statements showing an outright positive, accepting attitude toward the item, to
a rating of 1 for statements showing an outright rejecting, negative attitude toward
the item. A rating of 3 is awarded to neutral, ambivalent, or evasive responses.

Limited positive and negative responses receive ratings of 4 and 2, respectively.
Raters should reach 85% levels of agreement and generally experience little difficulty in obtaining agreement on the remaining 15%.

The process and techniques used in individual counseling (such as role playing,
role rehearsal, play therapy, homework assignments, and contracting) are just as
appropriate for group counseling. In fact, individual counseling is often conducted
in groups, as the following example shows.

Karen, Susan, Peggy, Mark, Ken, and Mike are 11-year-olds in their fourth session in a counseling group.

*Counselor:*   Last time we met, Susan told us about the misunderstanding she
   was having with her neighbor, Mrs. Jackson. As I remember, Susan, you were
   going to offer to use your allowance to replace the storm window you broke
   playing baseball or offer to baby-sit free of charge for her until the bill was
   paid. Can you bring us up to date on what's happened?

*Susan:*   Well, she decided she would rather have me baby-sit for her to pay for
   the window. I baby-sat 1 hour last week. We are keeping a list of the times I
   sit and how much will go toward the cost of the window.

*Counselor:*   It sounds as though you and Mrs. Jackson have worked things out
   to the satisfaction of both of you.

*Susan:*   Yeah, she really liked the idea of my baby-sitting to pay for the window.

*Counselor:*   Good. Is there anyone else who has something they would like to
   discuss today?

*All six children:*   Mr. Havens!

*Counselor:*   You all sound pretty angry at Mr. Havens. Could one of you tell
   me what's happened?

*Ken:* We were all going on a trip to the ice-skating rink next week. Yesterday, somebody broke some equipment that belonged to Mr. Havens. No one would tell who did it, so he is punishing us all by not letting us go ice-skating.

*Counselor:* You think Mr. Havens is being unfair to punish everyone because of something one person did. You'd like to find out who broke the equipment.

*Karen:* That's right. We didn't break his equipment, so why should we have to miss the trip?

*Counselor:* Have you thought of anything you could do to work this out?

*Mike:* Yeah, break the rest of his old equipment!

*Counselor:* How would that help you get to go skating?

*Mark:* It wouldn't. It would just make him madder.

*Peggy [timidly]:* We could tell him who did it.

*Other five children:* You know who did it? Who?

*Peggy [very upset]:* If I tell, I'll be called a tattler, and no one will like me. Besides, I don't want to get anyone in trouble.

*Counselor:* Peggy, it sounds as though you are really feeling torn apart by this. You just don't know what to do. If you don't tell, the whole group will miss the skating outing. If you do tell, you'll get someone in trouble, and your friends might think you're a tattler and not want you around.

*Peggy:* Yeah, I don't know what to do!

*Counselor:* What do you think you could do?

*Peggy:* Well, I could tell who did it.

*Counselor:* What would happen if you told? [Silence.] Let's help Peggy think of all the things that could happen if she told who broke Mr. Havens's equipment.

The group thinks of all the possible positive and negative results of Peggy's telling who broke the equipment: The group might still get to go skating, the person might beat up Peggy or try to get back at her in some other way, she might not be believed, the person could deny it and say Peggy broke the equipment, and so on.

*Counselor:* We've listed all the things that could happen if Peggy told. What will happen if Peggy does not reveal who broke the equipment?

*Karen:* We won't get to go skating, and the person will get away with it!

Other possibilities—such as Mr. Havens's distrust of the whole group and the person thinking he or she "can get away with anything"—are discussed.

*Counselor:* Can anyone think of any alternatives to solve this other than Peggy telling or not telling Mr. Havens?

*Ken:* She could write him an anonymous letter telling him who did it.

*Counselor:* What would happen if she did?

*Mike:* He probably wouldn't believe an anonymous letter.

*Counselor:* What do the rest of you think about that? [They all agree by nodding their heads that Mike is probably right.]

*Counselor:* Is there anything else you could do to straighten this out?

*Susan:* Peggy could tell you [the counselor], and you could tell Mr. Havens.

*Counselor:* How would my telling Mr. Havens help you all solve your problem?

*Mark:* Mr. Havens would believe you, and we'd get to go skating!

*Counselor:* I would have to tell Mr. Havens how I knew and give him some details to assure him that I was right. I really think this is the group's problem. What can you do to work it out?

*Karen:* Seems like it's up to Peggy, then.

*Counselor:* You all think it's up to Peggy to decide whether or not to tell.

[The group agrees it is Peggy's decision.]

*Counselor:* Peggy, we have looked at the consequences of your telling on the other person and not telling, and we've tried to think of other alternatives. Have you made any decision about what to do?

*Peggy:* No, I still don't know.

*Counselor:* So far, it seems that we have come up with two possible alternatives —to tell on the person or not to tell. I wonder if you can think of any other alternatives that might help Peggy. [Silence.] Well, our time is about up for today, but this is really important. Let's meet together tomorrow and try to help Peggy come to some decision at that time. Peggy, I wonder if you would go over the list of alternatives and think about them before tomorrow. [Peggy agrees.] How would the rest of you feel about trying to put yourselves in Peggy's place and think of what you would do if you knew who broke Mr. Havens's equipment? Also, you might think about how you would feel if you were the person who broke the equipment. What would you want Peggy to do? [The group agrees and adjourns.]

The counselor checked on the results of the last homework assignment for the group, listened, and reflected the group members' angry feelings that Mr. Havens was being unfair. The counselor then helped them clarify and define the problem, look at possible alternatives, and consider the consequences of these alternatives. No decision has been reached, but the group has agreed to a homework assignment of thinking further about the problem. Possibly the next session will bring new ideas and a resolution.

## GROUP CRISIS INTERVENTION

Two classmates are killed in a fiery car wreck.

A 12-year-old puts a gun to his head and commits suicide.

The mother of a 9-year-old dies of cancer.

The father of a 7-year-old is murdered.

War breaks out, and the television shows bombings on 24-hour newscasts.

Economic recession hits, and many parents lose their jobs.

Reports of an earthquake forecast send feelings of fear and panic throughout the population.

A hurricane devastates an entire section of the state.

In recent years, professionals have been asked to provide crisis counseling to children in schools, churches, and clubs. Incidents such as these stimulate fear, helplessness, loss, sadness, and shock. Children worry about the loss of their parents (their security), their friends ("Could it happen to me? Why did it happen?"), and their security ("Where will I go if I lose my home?"). In some cases, their parents may be coping with their own loss or grief and be unable to help the children. In other cases, the situation may be related to the school, church, or an organizational group, and children may feel that their parents do not really understand the situation. Some parents may not realize their children are worried; some children are not able to verbalize their pain.

Those who work with children recognize that young people cannot learn or perform their daily activities with these fears and concerns. They become irritable and restless, moody, or agitated. They have difficulty concentrating and sleeping. They may experience physical symptoms such as nausea or diarrhea. Someone has to help them cope, which is usually effected through group discussion and group counseling.

Gilliland and James (1997) proposed six steps for crisis counseling that are similar to the reality therapy model described in previous chapters of this book: (1) defining the problem, (2) ensuring the client's physical and psychological safety, (3) providing support through verbal and nonverbal means, (4) examining alternatives, (5) making plans—definite action steps, and (6) obtaining the client's commitment to take positive action. They urged counselors to evaluate the severity of the crisis in the clients' eyes; appraise clients' thinking, feelings, and behaviors; determine the danger and the length of time in a crisis mode; look for contributing factors; and evaluate resources, coping mechanisms, and support systems. Gilliland and James (1997) suggested that counselors may want to begin sessions with a nondirective approach but shift to more directive counseling as the need arises.

Suicide may be a possibility in a crisis situation, and factors in the child's family and emotional history, as well as the seriousness of the thought and plan, help counselors determine the possibilities of such an action. (See "Suicidal Behaviors" in Chapter 17.) Crisis counseling is short term, and counselors should carefully consider some children's need for referrals or other arrangements to ensure that each client successfully copes with the crisis in the days and weeks to follow.

Graham (1990) presented a plan for helping children after a trauma, such as a hurricane or plane crash, that affects the families of numerous children. Incorporating ideas presented by Graham with those of Gilliland and James (1997), we suggest the following outline for group crisis counseling:

I. Introductory phase
   A. Ask members to introduce themselves and tell why they are in the group.
   B. Help members clarify their goals regarding what they would like to accomplish in the meeting.
   C. Discuss confidentiality—what group members talk about stays in the group. Get a commitment from all members to maintain confidentiality.
   D. Discuss basic rules:
      1. Take a bathroom break first because no one can leave the room after the group begins.
      2. Encourage group members to stay the entire time. The group generally runs for 2 hours; the time depends on the ages of the children.

      3. Elect or appoint a coleader or a peer leader to keep the gate (that is, not let people in or out).

      4. Remind the group that no group member holds rank over any other group member and that everyone's participation is valued equally.

II. Fact phase

    A. Focus on discussing what happened.

    B. Encourage everyone to participate.

III. Feeling phase

    A. Ask, "What happened then?"

    B. Ask, "What are you experiencing now?"

IV. Clients' symptoms

    A. Ask, "How is this affecting you?" (Is the member having trouble sleeping or studying, or is the member worrying too much?)

    B. Ask, "How is this affecting your grades, your studies, your health?"

V. Teaching phase

    A. Explore the common responses to this incident.

    B. Brainstorm about how people have been responding to the incident.

    C. Discuss how each response is helpful or not helpful to people.

VI. Summary phase

    A. Raise questions and provide answers.

    B. Summarize what has been learned and shared.

    C. Develop action plans for individuals and/or the group, if needed.

    D. Provide support for group members to ensure their physical, emotional, and psychological safety. An action plan should be made to protect any group member needing protection.

    E. Conduct a follow-up meeting in 3 to 5 days to see how well the group members are coping.

    F. Arrange individual counseling sessions for group members who need further assistance.

## SUMMARY

In conclusion, group counseling can be a highly effective method for changing children's lives or, better still, preventing excess stress and conflict in their lives. Finding their place in a group and helping one another are rewarding for children. Watching the children grow and develop into caring, functioning group members is rewarding for the group counselor. Group counseling is an effective, efficient intervention to improve children's worlds.

## REFERENCES

Akos, P. (2000). Building empathic skills in elementary school children through group work. *Journal for Specialists in Group Work, 25,* 214–223.

Arman, J. F. (2000). In the wake of tragedy at Columbine High School. *Professional School Counseling, 3,* 218–220.

Association for Specialists in Group Work. (1991). *Professional standards for the training of group workers*. Alexandria, VA: Author.

Bemak, F., & Keys, S. (2000). *Violent and aggressive youth: Intervention and prevention strategies for changing times*. Thousand Oaks, CA: Corwin.

Bergin, J. J. (1999). Small-group counseling. In A. Vernon (Ed.), *Counseling children and adolescents* (pp. 299–332). Denver: Love Publishing.

Boutwell, D. A., & Myrick, R. D. (1992). The go for it club. *Elementary School Guidance and Counseling, 27,* 65–72.

Brantley, L., Brantley, P., & Baer-Barkley, K. (1996). Transforming acting-out behavior: A group counseling program for inner city elementary school pupils. *Elementary School Guidance and Counseling, 31,* 96–104.

Brown, B. M. (1997). Psychoeducational group work. *Counseling and Human Development, 29,* 1–16.

Bruckner, S., & Thompson, C. (1987). Guidance program evaluation: An example. *Elementary School Guidance and Counseling, 21,* 193–196.

Carroll, M., Bates, M., & Johnson, D. (1997). *Group leadership* (3rd ed.). Denver: Love Publishing.

Claypoole, S. D., Moody, E. E. Jr., & Peace, S. D. (2000). Moral dilemma discussions: An effective group intervention for juvenile offenders. *Journal for Specialists in Group Work, 25,* 394–411.

Conyne, R. K. (1996). The Association for Specialists in Group Work training standards: Some considerations and suggestions for training. *Journal for Specialists in Group Work, 21,* 155–162.

Corey, G. (1995). *Theory and practice of group counseling* (4th ed.). Pacific Grove, CA: Brooks/Cole.

Corey, G. (2000). *Theory and practice of group counseling* (5th ed.). Pacific Grove, CA: Brooks/Cole.

Daigneault, S. D. (2000). Body talk: A school-based group intervention for working with disordered eating behaviors. *Journal for Specialists in Group Work, 25,* 191–213.

Dansby, V. S. (1996). Group work within the school system: Survey of implementation and leadership role issues. *Journal for Specialists in Group Work, 21,* 232–242.

DeLucia-Waack, J. L. (1997). Measuring the effectiveness of group work: A review and analysis of process and outcome measures. *Journal for Specialists in Group Work, 22,* 277–293.

Drucker, C. (2003). Group counseling in the middle and junior high school. In K. R. Greenberg (Ed.), *Group counseling in K-12 schools: A handbook for school counselors* (pp. 81–96). Boston: Allyn & Bacon.

Dye, A. (2002). Designing a counseling group. *Group Work Practice Ideas, 7,* 9–12.

Furr, S. R. (2000). Structuring the group experience: A format for designing psychoeducational groups. *Journal for Specialists in Group Work, 25,* 29–49.

Garrett, M., & Crutchfield, L. (1997). Moving full circle: A unity model of group work with children. *Journal for Specialists in Group Work, 22,* 175–188.

Gazda, G. M., Ginter, E. J., & Horne, A. M. (2001). *Group counseling and group psychotherapy: Theory and applications*. Boston: Allyn & Bacon.

Gilbert, A. (2003). Group counseling in an elementary school. In K. R. Greenberg (Ed.), *Group counseling in K-12 schools: A handbook for school counselors* (pp. 56–80). Boston: Allyn & Bacon.

Gilliland, B., & James, R. (1997). *Crisis intervention strategies*. Pacific Grove, CA: Brooks/Cole.

Gladding, S. T. (2003). *Group work: A counseling specialty* (4th ed.). Upper Saddle River, NJ: Merrill.

Glasser, W., & Breggin, P. R. (2001). *Counseling with choice theory.* New York: Harper-Collins.

Graham, C. (1990, November). *A normal response to an abnormal situation: The crisis debriefing.* Paper presented at the meeting of the Southern Association for Counselor Education and Supervision, Norfolk, VA.

Greenberg, K. R. (2003). *Group counseling in K-12 schools: A handbook for school counselors.* Boston: Allyn & Bacon.

Holcomb-McCoy, C. C. (2003). Multicultural group counseling in the school setting. In K. R. Greenberg (Ed.), *Group counseling in K-12 schools: A handbook for school counselors* (pp. 150–164). Boston: Allyn & Bacon.

Johnson, D. W., & Johnson, F. P. (2000). *Joining together: Group theory and group skills* (7th ed.). Boston: Allyn & Bacon.

Jones, K. D., & Robinson III, E. H. (2000). Psychoeducational groups: A model for choosing topics and exercises appropriate to group stage. *Journal for Specialists in Group Work, 25,* 356–365.

Kizner, L. R., & Kizner, S. R. (1999). Small group counseling with adopted children. *Professional School Counseling, 2,* 226–229.

Kulic, K. R., Dagley, J. C., & Horne, A. M. (2001). Prevention groups with children and adolescents. *Journal for Specialists in Group Work, 26,* 211–218.

Littrell, J. M., & Peterson, J. S. (2002). Establishing a comprehensive group work program in an elementary school: An in-depth case study. *Journal for Specialists in Group Work, 27,* 161–172.

Nelson, R., Dykeman, C., Powell, S., & Petty, D. (1996). The effects of a group counseling intervention on students with behavior adjustment problems. *Elementary School Guidance and Counseling, 31,* 21–31.

Orton, G. L. (1997). *Strategies for counseling with children and their parents.* Pacific Grove, CA: Brooks/Cole.

Portman, T. A. A., & Portman, G. L. (2002). Empowering students for social justice. *Journal for Specialists in Group Work, 27,* 16–31.

Rainey, L. M., Hensley, F. A., & Crutchfield, L. B. (1997). Implementation of support groups in elementary and middle school student assistance programs. *Professional School Counseling, 1,* 36–40.

Reeder, J., Douzenis, C., & Bergin, J. J. (1997). The effects of small group counseling on the racial attitudes of second grade students. *Professional School Counseling, 1,* 15–19.

Ripley, V. V., & Goodnough, G. E. (2001). Planning and implementing group counseling in a high school. *Professional School Counseling, 5,* 62–65.

Ritchie, M. H., & Huss, S. N. (2000). Recruitment and screening of minors for group counseling. *Journal for Specialists in Group Work, 25,* 146–156.

Robinson, F. F., & Jones, E. N. (1996). Research on the preparation of group counselors. *Journal for Specialists in Group Work, 21,* 172–178.

Shaffer, J., Brown, L. L., & McWhirter, J. J. (1998). Survivors of child sexual abuse and dissociative coping: Relearning in a group context. *Journal for Specialists in Group Work, 23,* 74–94.

Shechtman, Z. (2001). Prevention groups for angry and aggressive children. *Journal for Specialists in Group Work, 26,* 228–236.

Shechtman, Z. (2002). Child group psychotherapy in the school at the threshold of a new millennium. *Journal of Counseling and Development, 80,* 293–299.

Sommers-Flanagan, R., Barrett-Hakanson, T., Clarke, C., & Sommers-Flanagan, J. (2000). A psychoeducational school-based coping and social skills group for depressed students. *Journal for Specialists in Group Work, 25,* 170–190.

Stanko, C. A., & Taub, D. J. (2002). A counseling group for children of cancer patients. *Journal for Specialists in Group Work, 27,* 43–58.

Stoiber, K., & Kratochwill, T. (1998). *Handbook of group intervention for children and families.* Boston: Allyn & Bacon.

Van Lone, J. S., Kalodner, C. R., & Coughlin, J. W. (2002). Using short stories to address eating disturbances in groups. *Journal for Specialists in Group Work, 27,* 59–77.

Wick, D. T., Wick, J. K., & Peterson, N. (1997). Improving self-esteem with Adlerian adventure therapy. *Professional School Counseling, 1,* 53–56.

Wilson, C. (2003). Group counseling in the high school. In K. R. Greenberg (Ed.), *Group counseling in K-12 schools: A handbook for school counselors* (pp. 97–111). Boston: Allyn & Bacon.

Wilson, F. R., & Owens, P. C. (2001). Group-based prevention programs for at-risk adolescents and adults. *Journal for Specialists in Group Work, 26,* 246–255.

Zinck, K., & Littrell, J. M. (2000). Action research shows group counseling effective with at-risk adolescent girls. *Professional School Counseling, 4,* 50–59.

Chapter 18

# Counseling Children
# with Special Concerns

*I have found the paradox that if I love until it
hurts, then there is no hurt, but only more love.*
—Mother Teresa

In Chapter 1, we described some of the difficulties inherent in our complex society—
difficulties with which children must cope during their major years of growth and development. Counselors obviously cannot supply all the answers to these problems;
however, several pressing concerns are seen frequently by counselors. In this chapter,
we suggest methods for working with children with these special needs and problems.
The suggestions should be incorporated into a caring, accepting counseling atmosphere and modified to meet the unique needs of the child and the presenting concern. Appendixes A and B provide special procedures to handle the problem behaviors that may accompany these societal problems. We will look at the following
problems: child abuse, AIDS, alcoholism, cults, death and dying, depression and suicidal behaviors, divorce and separation, gangs, homeless children, latchkey children,
single-parent homes, stepfamilies, and violence.

## CHILD MALTREATMENT

*Child maltreatment* is a general term that includes several kinds of abuse. According to government statistics (U.S. Department of Health and Human Services,
2000), in 1998 there were 903,000 victims of child maltreatment. That represents
almost 13 children out of 1,000. In those cases, child neglect was most prevalent
(58%), followed by physical abuse (21.3%), sexual abuse (11.3%), and psychological abuse and neglect (6%) (Chalk, Gibbons, & Scarupa, 2002). Some cases included multiple forms of maltreatment. Children age 1 year and under account for
14% of child maltreatment victims; children from 2 to 5 years old, for 24%; children from 6 to 9, for 25%; and those from 14 to 17, for 15% (Child Trends,

2002). Definitions (Berk, 2001; Edgeworth & Carr, 2000; Miller-Perrin, 2001) of maltreatment follow:

Physical abuse: Use of inappropriate physical actions, such as beatings, striking a child with an object, burning a child, poisoning, or some other action that results in substantial risk of physical or emotional harm to the child. Johnson (1990) described physical abuse as the use of an instrument on any part of the body, tissue damage beyond simple redness from a slap, and injury from heat, caustic substances, chemicals, or drugs.

Sexual abuse: The use of a child for sexual gratification. Sexual abuse may vary in intrusiveness (from viewing to oral, anal, or genital penetration) and frequency (from a single incident to frequent abuse). The U.S. National Center on Child Abuse and Neglect has defined *sexual abuse* as an act perpetrated on a child by a significantly older person with the intent to stimulate the child sexually and satisfy the aggressor's sexual impulses (cited in Moeller, Bachmann, & Moeller, 1993).

Psychological abuse: Actions such as intentional and frequent rejection, criticism, punishment for minor infractions, belittling, and threatening that damage the child cognitively, emotionally, or in their social interactions. Moeller, Bachmann, and Moeller (1993) provided six categories of emotional abuse: (1) chronic denigration of the child's qualities, capacities, desires, and emotional expressiveness; (2) isolation; (3) terrorizing; (4) excessive age-inappropriate demands; (5) witnessing extreme parental violence (including excessive use of drugs and alcohol); and (6) not providing services for a seriously emotionally handicapped child.

Physical neglect: Failing to provide a child's basic needs, such as food, clothing, shelter, medical attention, supervision, and hygiene.

Emotional neglect: Failure to provide children's needs for affection and emotional support.

All statistics underestimate the prevalence of child maltreatment. Those miscalculations are caused by variations in definitions of child abuse across the nation, as well as the fact that many incidents of child abuse are unreported or misreported. Additionally, as the *Harvard Mental Health Letter* ("Child Abuse," parts I and II, 1993, p. 1) pointed out, "Not all families have the same rules about disciplining children or the same attitudes toward nudity, touching, and kissing." Two government reports from the U. S. Department of Health and Human Services (1996) provided national statistics on child abuse and neglect for the year 1995. They estimated about 2 million reports of maltreatment of almost 3 million children. Furthermore, more than half of these reports of possible maltreatment came from professionals such as educators, medical or mental health professionals, social services workers, or child-care providers. Among the confirmed victims of abuse and neglect, more than 50% were 7 years old or younger, about 26% were 8 to 12, and about 21% were 13 to 18. Slightly more girls than boys were victims.

Child abuse occurs at all levels of social, economic, and educational status. In a large number of cases, the offender is a male relative or friend of the family. The offender may use bribes, threats, guilt, or coercion to ensure secrecy. To protect the family and this relative or friend, the abuse may be ignored or hushed up in a variety of ways, the incidents are never reported or recorded, and the child and family never confront the issue or receive treatment.

Several hypotheses have been advanced to explain the causes of child abuse. Currently, the origins of child abuse are understood as the interacting variables of the family, community, and culture (Belsky, 1993). The families are often rigid, authoritarian, and isolated from one another and the outside world. They may be experiencing marital, financial, or parent–child relationship problems but lack the resources and skills to cope with them. Poverty, unemployment, parents who were victims of abuse themselves, and stressful changes such as moving or marital separations are often associated with abuse. The community may be one of social isolation with few gathering places such as parks, child-care or recreational centers, and churches to serve as family supports. Societal factors such as the acceptance of domestic violence and corporal punishment may also contribute to the incidence of child abuse. The abused child is usually thought of in negative terms and may be isolated, rejected, ignored, or even terrorized.

## Psychological Maltreatment

The destructive effects of psychological maltreatment on the lives of children have been well documented through experience and research. Disparaging remarks, threats, or punishment by parents, teachers, and other adults or bullying by adults or other children may all contribute to the problem. Strong evidence indicates that psychological maltreatment results in serious emotional problems, behavioral disorders, or both. Counseling techniques such as marital counseling, family therapy, parent–child interventions, methods for working with socially isolated families, and educating the public are suggested to assist the professional working with psychological maltreatment.

Since abused children often have emotional and behavioral problems that make them a challenge in the classroom, it has been suggested in the literature that the educational system may perpetuate child psychological maltreatment. Teachers may be abusive through disparaging remarks, threats, and punishments; the curriculum may be structured to overemphasize academic goals while neglecting social development; and school bullies are a significant factor in the psychological victimization of children. When working with children experiencing emotional and behavioral problems, counselors should always be aware of the possibility of abuse.

Victims of child maltreatment are a diverse group with varying responses. Miller-Perrin (2001) summarized the signs and symptoms associated with various forms of maltreatment. Table 18-1 contains her summary.

Counselors should be aware that the exact link between experiences of abuse and mental health outcomes has yet to be determined. The counselor may see constellations of symptoms that cross several areas of a child's functioning.

## Physical Abuse

The *Harvard Mental Health Letter* ("Child Abuse," parts I and II, 1993) concluded that the long-term effects of physical abuse are not fully understood; the effects of abuse and those of other familial or environmental effects are difficult to distinguish. However, it estimated that "at least 25% of physically abused children have serious psychiatric problems, including chronic anxiety and depression and sometimes neurological damage" (p. 3). Kurtz, Gaudin, Wodarski, and Howing (1993) reported that the physically abused children in their study displayed an overwhelming set of problems in school, such as dropping out, teen pregnancy, institutionalization, low scores on standardized tests of language and math, and repeating one or more grades. They had lower educational aspirations and more behavior problems in the classroom than other children.

Academic failure was the most obvious factor among children classified as neglected; however, this group did not experience significant behavior problems in class or display significant adjustment difficulties, as do children who are physically abused.

## Child Sexual Abuse

According to Schoen and Davis (1998), results from a survey of adolescent boys documented that one in eight high school boys (13%) had been physically or sexually abused or both. Most (66%) of those who reported the abuse on the survey said the abuse happened at home, and 68% stated the abuser was a family member. Almost half of the boys said they had told no one about their abuse. One in five high school girls reported abuse on the survey, with 53% stating it had happened at home and 20% reporting they had not told anyone of the abuse. According to Green (1993), reporting of sexual abuse cases in the United States substantially increased during the 1980s. Sexual abuse of girls is reported more often than abuse of boys. Boys are more likely to be approached by strangers, and girls are more likely to be victims of incest ("Child Abuse," parts I and II, 1993). Children in frequent contact with their abusers have additional problems in maintaining the relationship, as well as coping with the trauma of the abuse.

In his review of the literature, Green (1993) found that the short-term symptoms of sexually abused children usually include fearfulness and anxiety, sleep disturbances, insomnia, nightmares, phobic avoidance, somatic complaints, and others similar to those of posttraumatic stress disorder. The symptoms of sexually abused boys may include conduct disorder, such as lying, stealing, vandalism, and assaults on other children ("Child Abuse," parts I and II, 1993). Children with more severe abuse may dissociate, with early symptoms that include periods of forgetfulness, excessive fantasizing and daydreaming, sleepwalking, blackout, and imaginary friends, according to Green (1993). He pointed out that multiple personality disorder appeared for the first time in children during this decade and that these children are almost always victims of severe physical or sexual abuse. Low self-esteem, depression, and suicidal behaviors may be observed in older children

TABLE 18-1  Potential signs and symptoms of maltreatment

| | Sexual abuse | | Child neglect | Physical abuse | | Psychological maltreatment |
| --- | --- | --- | --- | --- | --- | --- |
| | *Children* | *Adolescents* | | *Children* | *Adolescents* | |
| Physical complications: | Genital bleeding, pain, odors; eating or sleep disturbances; somatic complaints; enuresis or encopresis | Somatic complaints, eating disturbance, sleep disturbance | Failure to thrive | Bruises; head, chest, and abdominal injuries; burns; fractures | | |
| Affective-behavioral problems: | Anxiety and fears, nightmares, guilt, anger/ hostility, depression, low self-esteem, sexualized behavior and preoccupation, aggression, regression/ immaturity, hyperactivity | Anxiety, anger, depression, guilt, suicidal ideation, low self-esteem, social withdrawal, self-injurious behavior, sexualized behavior, delinquency, running away, substance abuse | Low self-esteem, aggression, anger, frustration, conduct problems | Aggression, hopelessness, depression, low self-esteem, fighting, noncompliance, defiance, property offenses, arrests | | Aggression, self-abusive behavior, anxiety, shame, guilt, anger and hostility, pessimism, dependency |

| | | | | | |
|---|---|---|---|---|---|
| **Cognitive deficits:** | Learning difficulties, poor attention and concentration, declining grades | Learning difficulties, poor concentration and attention, declining grades | Language deficits, academic problems, intellectual delays, poor problem solving | Decreased intellectual and cognitive functioning; deficits in verbal faculty, memory, problem solving, perceptual-motor skills, and verbal abilities; decreased reading and math skills; poor school achievement; increase in special education services | Academic problems, deficits in cognitive ability, poor problem solving |
| **Social deficits:** | | | Disturbed parent–child attachment and interactions, deficits in prosocial behavior, social withdrawal and isolation | Delayed play skills, infant attachment problems, poor social interaction skills, difficulty making friends, deficits in prosocial behaviors and deficits in social competence with peers, avoidance of adults | Violent interpersonal behavior, delinquency, violent offenses, substance abuse   / Insecure attachments, poor social adjustment |
| **Other:** | | | | | Attention problems, depressed school performance, increased daily stress, low self-esteem |

Reprinted from Miller-Perrin, C. L. (2001). Child maltreatment: Treatment of child and adolescent victims. In E. R. Welfel, & R. E. Ingersoll (Eds.), *The mental health desk reference.* New York: Wiley, p. 170. This material is used by permission of John Wiley & Sons, Inc.

who have been abused. Disturbances in sexual behavior are not unusual and may take the form of acting out or sexual inhibition.

Green (1993) concluded that no specific behavior patterns in children indicate sexual abuse and that some cases might show no symptoms; diagnosis must be based on a variety of data, including a history, assessment of the reliability of the child's disclosure, psychiatric evaluation, physical examination, evaluation of the child's prior psychological functioning, and assessment of the family's functioning.

The *Harvard Mental Health Letter* ("Child Abuse," parts I and II, 1993) concluded that treatment of children who are victims of sexual or physical abuse follows no accepted formula. It suggested that crisis intervention and counseling may be helpful for a single incident but that more severe forms require years of treatment for the child and other family members.

Miller-Perrin (2001) outlined some ways of intervening with children who have been victims of abuse. She noted that the family should be included, as well as the child. One goal suggested was to help the child learn to manage the negative cognitions and emotions associated with the incident(s). Emotions such as guilt, shame, anger, stress, stigma, and fear occur as a result of abuse. Relaxation training, anger management, problem-solving skills, positive coping statements, and imagery are possible techniques. Cognitive-behavioral approaches are useful in helping victims change their ideas about being different from other children, as well as feeling as they are somehow responsible for the abuse. Group therapy to counter such beliefs and to confront secrecy is helpful to children who are able to discuss their abuse with peers who have also been abused.

Edgeworth and Carr (2000) reviewed treatment studies and concluded that for physical abuse and neglect, residential treatment, therapeutic day care, and resilient peer therapy are effective interventions. Therapeutic day treatment often includes group activities, opportunities to interact with peers, and learning experiences to enhance development. Miller-Perrin (2001) noted that prevention training in self-protection is an important component of treatment. Teaching children to identify harmful situations and move to a safer location is an example that may be included in that intervention. Other suggested techniques for working with abused children include empathic listening, clarifying the child's words and sentences ("What do you mean?"), discussing "good" and "bad" touching, emphasizing the child's right to say no to inappropriate touching, and encouraging the child to talk to a trusted adult about any incident that causes him or her to feel uncomfortable.

Sexually abused children are probably more difficult clients than physically or emotionally abused children. They, too, have learned not to trust people; they have been deeply hurt by those they love. The counselor may have a difficult time developing a relationship of trust in order to help the child. Edgeworth and Carr (2000) suggested individual or group therapy over 12 to 36 sessions.

Parent-focused interventions for physically abusive and neglectful parents have involved these parts:

- Teaching parents about normal child development to correct unrealistic expectations

- Educating parents about appropriate discipline procedures and other child-management strategies
- Practicing anger-control techniques and coping skills
- Discussing stress-management techniques (Schellenbach, 1998)

The *Harvard Mental Health Letter* ("Child Abuse," parts I and II, 1993) was not positive about its review of prevention programs. It noted that the time spent on the program is short and that the concepts presented can be difficult, especially for young children. They cited studies showing only a 10% increase in the number of correct answers after a single presentation and stating that 11-year-olds were likely to give the wrong answers when asked if the abuser could be someone they knew or if breaking a promise was all right in this case. Other studies, according to the *Letter,* suggested that the children would still be too frightened or embarrassed to tell and that the programs may create anxiety. The writers concluded that no one knows how to teach children preventive techniques because abuse comes in so many different forms and because the research is so limited. However, James and Burch (1999) suggested some activities that can be conducted in schools.

- Prepare school personnel by teaching about normal sexual development, symptoms of abuse, state law, school policy, and reporting procedures.
- Deliver an abuse-prevention program at school that educates children to danger signs, prevention skills, and the importance of telling adults about abuse.
- Develop a network of professionals to build assessment skills and a knowledge base of ways to work with abused children. The network should include child protection workers, other counselors, therapists, and agencies that diagnose and treat victims.
- Have toys, books, and games in the counseling office to ease discussions of family, feelings, or trauma.
- Have resources about testifying in court.
- Keep accurate professional records that are clear and objective. (p. 216)

## GENERAL COUNSELING STRATEGIES FOR WORKING WITH ABUSED CHILDREN

Society's first priority has traditionally been to punish the offender. Until recently, society forgot the victim once medical attention had been given for the physical problem and the child had been removed from the abuser's custody. Recently, victims of abuse have gotten more assistance because of educational information in churches and schools, reporting and information provided by the news media, and the victims' increased willingness to tell their stories in the hope that they will help another victim.

Abused children are not easy clients. They have learned not to trust themselves, other people, or their environment. The world and the people in it are inconsistent and hurt them. Withdrawal from this painful world is safer than chancing relationships. Building friendship and trust may be difficult. The child needs to ventilate feelings, ask questions, and replay abusive incidents in order to resolve issues. Children have been taught that caregivers and other adults in their lives act in a child's best interest and cannot understand that people who are supposed to love and care for them can also harm them. Their dependency on parents and other adults for care and security intensifies the conflict. Many children believe they deserve the punishment they receive. Their level of cognitive development may not allow them to recognize and deal with the fact that their parents are not kind and loving. Specific suggestions for counseling with abused children are summarized next.

1. In counseling all abuse victims, counselors must be prepared to become totally involved with the child client, including the child's repeated testing of their caring.

2. Relaxation and visualization may help the child develop a more positive attitude toward herself or himself and toward life.

3. Encourage good physical appearance and a self-confident stance in both verbal and nonverbal interactions.

4. Play therapy may help abused children communicate their thoughts and feelings.

5. Sexually abused children require extra consideration, understanding, and support from the counselor. Often the children are initially unable to discuss the problem with the counselor because of intense feelings of guilt; they believe that somehow they provoked the attack or could have done something to prevent it. They may feel worthless and ashamed of having been used or abused in such a manner. They may be more affected by the questions and reactions that follow than by the act itself, and they often feel intense guilt at having gotten a parent or other adult in trouble, in jail, or barred from the home because the child "told." Empathetic listening and clarification of words and nonverbal expressions are essential.

6. Specific techniques such as bibliocounseling, role playing, play therapy, or group counseling may be considered, depending on the child's maturity. Placing sexually abused children in groups requires caution, especially if the trauma is very recent. The child may not be ready to share intense feelings.

7. Children may need information about what is appropriate and inappropriate touching or treatment and may need to be assured that certain parts of their bodies are private. They may need to be told that the adult's sexual or punishing behavior was inappropriate. Because of children's limited cognitive development and understanding, and to allay the anxiety surrounding the topic, most programs designed to teach children about child abuse use role playing, puppets, coloring books, filmstrips, movies, and so on. The vocabulary used is not explicit but instead refers to *touching* and *private areas*. The programs are designed not for sex education but to give children information and strategies for coping with abusive situations.

8. Assertiveness training that focuses on how to say no or handle potentially abusive situations may be necessary. The child needs help to determine the warn-

ing signs of abuse and to plan ways for coping with the situations—for example, calling a special person when the father or mother begins to drink. Role playing of these strategies prepares children to handle such situations more effectively. Counselors need to do a careful assessment of the child's situation so that the new skills would not place the child at an increased risk.

9. Encourage children to tell someone right away when an abusive situation occurs. Adults who abuse children sexually often warn the children to keep "their secret." Children need help in discerning when they should tell a secret and when information should be kept confidential and in deciding whom they should tell and what to do if the adult does not believe their story.

10. Counselors must deal with issues of trust at some point in work with abused children. Developmental theorists have emphasized that children must develop trust in people and their interactions in order to live effectively, yet children receive a multitude of daily messages, designed to protect them, that imply that the world and the people in it are dangerous.

11. Ratican (1992) cautioned that some models of therapy are inappropriate and perhaps harmful for abuse survivors; she quoted some writers who suggest throwing away the textbook and listening to the client! Ratican called for an eclectic combination of techniques: guided imagery, hypnosis, exploration and ventilation of feelings, journal keeping, letter writing, cognitive restructuring to correct distorted messages, empty chair technique, psychodrama, art, music, and dance.

Childhood abuse is a part of an overall pattern of abusive behavior, and the family network, as well as the personality of the abuser, must be considered. In addition, family reactions to the child who has been abused will enhance or interfere with counseling treatment and progress. Counselors ought to consider family therapy at an appropriate time in their treatment plans.

Counselors working with abused children must be prepared to provide understanding and support for all persons involved. The natural reaction is anger at anyone who hurts a child; however, these feelings must be recognized and resolved for the counselor to work effectively with the child and the family, particularly the abuser. Counselors who are overly sympathetic with abused children lose objectivity and their ability to help the child; counselors who are extremely angry and judgmental toward the family of an abused child (for allowing this to happen) or toward the abuser can never establish the relationship necessary to help these individuals. Before beginning counseling with victims of abuse, counselors may need to examine their own feelings and views about the case.

## Children's Memories of Abuse

Although most professionals report a high percentage of valid child abuse reports, some are skeptical of certain reports because experiments and experience have shown that young children are particularly susceptible to suggestion or misleading information given to them after an event. They believe that this suggestibility arises in part from children's desires to please an adult.

Loftus (1993) suggested two sources that could contribute to false memories: popular writing and counselors' suggestions. Although children may not have read the materials Loftus described, they often hear accounts of child abuse reported in news media or discussed by adults. In addition, adults may repeatedly warn them about the possibility of encountering an abuser. Loftus (1993) also reported that the therapist or counselor can unintentionally contribute to a client's false memories through suggestions made during therapy. Some counselors believe the possibility of child abuse must be discussed openly, regardless of the symptoms; others may push the client, interpret dreams as showing signs of abuse, question the client in such a manner as to suggest abuse, or reinforce their suspicions in other ways. Loftus suggested that counselors lack the tools to distinguish true memories; therefore, they should avoid zealous interventions in favor of techniques that are less potentially dangerous—clarification, compassion, empathy, and gentle confrontation.

James and Burch (1999) caution counselors to avoid contamination of a child's story—leading questions, feeding information, providing details, asking many questions, or pressuring. Yapko (1993) listed guidelines for professionals working with the possibility of child abuse:

- Do not jump to conclusions.
- Do not ask leading questions.
- Get external corroboration when the situation is ambiguous.
- Be conservative in suggesting any method of limiting communication with the client's family.
- Do not rely on your own memory, especially if sensitive information is discussed.

James and Burch (1999) offered these suggestions for interviewing a child who may be abused:

1. Use statements and questions such as "Tell me about a time something happened to you that made you feel uncomfortable" or "Tell me what happened to you" or "Has anyone tried to touch your private parts?" (Counselors can define as parts of the body covered by a bathing suit.)

2. Pay attention to the child's body language as the interview progresses. The child may tell more nonverbally than with words.

3. Let the child tell his or her own story.

4. Be empathic but neutral.

5. Use clarification and summary skills.

6. Employ the child's terms when paraphrasing. (p. 215)

Child maltreatment is a tremendous problem in our world. Children who have been victims need extra care and attention to overcome the effects of their trauma.

Counselors can be instrumental in protecting the child's safety and providing helpful interventions for enhancing the child's life.

## CHILDREN OF ALCOHOLICS

Children living in alcoholic families receive little attention in our society. They are often left out of an alcoholic parent's treatment, even though the entire family is affected. Yet O'Rourke and Worzbyt (1996) quoted statistics indicating that about 43% of American adults have lived in an alcoholic family and that approximately 7 million children under age 18 now live in an alcoholic family. Wilson and Blocher (1990) cautioned that sons of alcoholics are five times more likely to become alcoholics than others and that daughters of alcoholic mothers are three times more likely to become alcoholics than girls living in a nonalcoholic environment.

The children of alcoholic parents frequently do not have their physical or psychological needs met in the family. Money needed for food and shelter may be spent on alcohol; even if there is money, the parents may be too preoccupied with alcohol to attend to the child's physical needs. Parents who have lost control of their lives and frequently dislike themselves cannot meet the child's need for love, belonging, and security. Children who live in homes whose rules are consistently broken and whose family members cannot be relied on to provide love and nurturance cannot be expected to grow and develop into fully functioning, well-adjusted individuals.

These children frequently are the victims of abuse and neglect, have little structure in their lives, receive inconsistent discipline, and cope with constant conflict in the home. Alcoholic households are often described as turbulent and lacking in parental warmth and affection (Campo & Rohner, 1992). Children adopt the roles they need to survive in this environment and often fail to learn the variety of roles children from homes with open communication and consistent lifestyles master (James & Gilliland, 2001).

Wilson and Blocher (1990) described children in alcoholic homes as under considerable stress as a result of family quarreling, abuse or neglect, inconsistent discipline, inadequate or unpredictable environments, disruption of family holidays or rituals, early assumption of adult roles, denial of reality that makes understanding the real world difficult, isolation, shame, and embarrassment. The adverse effects of conflicted home environments are seen in behavior such as school absenteeism, poor academic performance, isolation from peers, physical symptoms such as headaches and stomachaches, psychological symptoms (fears, moods, regressive behaviors), and "people-pleasing behaviors" (O'Rourke & Worzbyt, 1996).

Additionally, several writers (Black, 1981; Glover, 1994; Muro & Kottman, 1995) have outlined dysfunctional roles children of alcoholics may assume to cope with their parents' dependence: family hero (overly responsible, mature), scapegoat (one who is blamed for all problems), lost child (scared and isolated), placaters ("people pleasers"), or mascot (the clown). Researchers have described children of alcoholics as having conduct problems, difficulty with communication and interpersonal relationships, and psychological difficulties (Jones & Houts, 1992; Sher, 1991).

As well as these roles children assume, they also learn the family's unspoken rules. Those guidelines for surviving in an alcoholic family have been summarized by Doweiko (1999), Black (1981), and James and Gilliland (2001):

Don't talk; don't have problems. This stems from the denial of the problem of alcoholism as well as the lack of recognition of the child's problem. Doweiko (1999) explained that the family makes it clear that no problem exists and you better not discuss it. Black (1981) further explains the belief that if one does talk, bad things will happen.

Don't trust. Children cannot depend on the drinking parent and often cannot depend on the nondrinking partner who is so busy meeting the needs of the alcoholic (Black, 1981).

Don't feel. Children learn that expressing fear, guilt, anger, sadness, or other feelings will bring more pain to the family.

Don't behave differently. Shifting roles is not allowed.

Don't blame chemical dependency. Blame is typically assigned to people, situations, or things outside the family. Denial of personal responsibility for actions is the norm.

Do behave as I want. A child who does not comply with the wishes of the alcoholic may be threatened with losing love and support, with abuse, or with increased drinking.

Do be better and more responsible. No matter what a family member does, it will never be enough to satisfy the alcoholic.

Don't have fun. Broken promises, angry recriminations, embarrassment of the family situation, unpredictable outbursts, and exhaustion keep children from enjoying life.

Growing up in an alcoholic family has different effects on children, according to Jones and Houts (1992). They classified families of the subjects participating in their research as "regular problem drinking," "occasional problem drinking," "minor problem drinking," or "non-problem drinking." Young adults who grew up in homes where drinking was a regular problem said they received less positive regard and less attention to their feelings from their parents. The researchers did not find significant differences among the problem-drinking groups for the parents' level of criticism of the child or emotional support. They conclude that to understand the impact of growing up in an alcoholic family, it is important to describe specific characteristics of the family and conceptualize these characteristics as interacting with problem drinking to create a family environment that influences developmental processes. At the same time, the results suggest that it is inappropriate to assume that growing up in an alcoholic family has comprehensive and maladaptive outcomes for young adult children (p. 55).

Seilhamer, Jacob, and Dunn (1993) also pointed out that many factors can determine the effects of parental drinking on children, "including the presence and severity of other parental psychopathology, the ability of the non-drinking parent to act as a buffering influence and the availability of extra-familial sources of support" (p. 197). Additionally, the parent's ability to deliver consistent discipline, a predictable environment, emotional support, and social modeling may be more important than drinking-related variables.

Reich, Earls, Frankel, and Shayka (1993) reported that children of alcoholics may be more at risk for oppositional or conduct disorders. They called for early intervention in these children's lives. They noted that the logical place to provide early assistance and intervention for children from alcoholic homes is the school. They described identification procedures and step-by-step guidance lessons to help these children understand alcoholism as a family problem and the necessity for all members to seek help. Ferquist (2000) hypothesized that the chronic stress in families with chronic drinking could contribute to youth suicide.

One method to screen children of alcoholics is the CAST (Children of Alcoholics Screening Test; Jones, 1985). This 30-item inventory measures negative life events associated with alcoholic families, such as emotional distress, marital discord, attempts to control parental drinking, efforts to escape from alcoholism, exposure to drinking-related violence, and desire for help. CASTD (Pidcock, Fischer, Forthun, & West, 2000) is the shortened version of the instrument with 14 items, which has been adapted to include other types of substance use. Both of these are useful diagnostic tools.

Brake (1988) stated that children of alcoholics need a counselor to help them understand that they can love their parents without liking their behavior and that these children need help in feeling worthwhile as individuals. She suggested group counseling preceded by an individual session. Films and books may be needed to encourage talking because these children have learned to avoid conflict by not talking.

Time and patience are required to build trust. Wilson and Blocher (1990) suggested developmental support groups incorporating bibliotherapy, role playing of problem situations, rational-emotive-behavior techniques for assessing behavior and coping more effectively, Gestalt activities to express feelings, assertiveness training to express needs and rights, and relaxation techniques to reduce stress. O'Rourke (1990) provided an outline for a children's support group that includes attention to the preceding needs and provides information about alcoholism for young participants. These children also need activities to improve their self-esteem, assertiveness training to teach them to say no to drugs and alcohol, and help with developing problem-solving and decision-making skills. Excellent drug education programs are now available to counselors working with these children. O'Rourke and Worzbyt (1996) cautioned that prevention programs should respect the conditions under which the children of alcoholics live and understand that they live in a world with limited choices. They encouraged counselors to focus on strengthening self-esteem and building strengths, resources, and resiliencies.

## CHILDREN IN CULTS

Although the typical young person involved in cults or satanic rituals is usually an adolescent, Rudin (1990) noted that the satanically involved can be as young as 11 years old. Clifford (1994) also believed that children and adolescents are quite vulnerable to being lured into satanic cult practice. In addition, some children are born into satanic cults that have been practicing rituals for generations.

Schwartz (2001) acknowledged the increased numbers of children born to cult members as one of the changes that has occurred in the past two decades. He reported that the children born into a cult are raised by the group. Often the ways to discipline children, the activities that are encouraged, and what is taught may be dictated by the cult leader (Langone & Eisenberg, 1993). The children may be subjected to psychological and physical abuse, as well as medical and other physical neglect. Rudin (1990) warned that child abuse is prevalent in cults because children are not valued. These children may or may not attend school. Schwartz noted that some of the children have been enslaved and suffer deprivations if they do not meet expectations. Children raised in cults live in isolation and have little knowledge of the world. Often their schooling is so poor that they are illiterate. If they do attend a public school, they may be ridiculed for their limited range of experiences (Holmes, 1995).

Malcarne and Burchard (1992) discussed the difficulties of investigating charges of child abuse in cults. They noted that cult members and state authorities often disagree on what constitutes abuse. Another identified difficulty is that removing a child from the cult to state custody may create conflicts of interest between the protection of the child and the maintenance of the family unit and the right to practice religion freely. Schwartz (2001) noted the complication that ritual child abuse often leads to serious psychological trauma.

Some adolescents and young adults choose to join cults. Schwartz (2001) listed common factors of these recruits: little experience in decision making, a need for peer acceptance and a place to belong, being naïve, difficulty with a new situation such as moving, and breakdowns in the family. According to her, the majority are idealistic, bright, lonely, middle class, and vulnerable to the overtures and charismatic leadership of the cult. Rudin's (1990) description mirrored those characteristics: the typical cult member as very intelligent, idealistic, and high achieving.

The typical youth involved in devil worship is troubled and alienated from his or her significant groups. The young person who might be attracted to the drug culture is also a prime candidate for the occult. The young person involved in satanic worship is also intelligent and curious but is usually an underachiever. Clifford (1994) stated that most susceptible adolescents and children include boys or girls with low self-esteem, children with vague or confused religious and moral values, and the young person with lots of idle time who is not actively involved in activities at school or church. These young people have feelings of powerlessness, have few friends, and are often isolated from their families. They are drawn to negative groups because of their need for friendships and power. Rudin (1990) cautioned school personnel to watch for black clothing; jewelry with satanic symbols; drawings or symbols of demons, death, and mutilation; satanic literature; and other paraphernalia. Counselors may want to consult their local police department to learn more about clothing, literature, music, and symbols that are current indications of cult membership. Rudin strongly recommended that school personnel learn the signs of satanic involvement and schedule educational programs for staff and students. The International Cult Education Program (P.O. Box 2265, Bonita Springs, FL 34133 http://www.csj.org/rg/rgprevedu/rgpreved_icep.htm) provides speakers, literature, resource lists, and other materials to assist with educational programs.

Counselors will want to help young people understand their motivation for involvement in cult activities and find new and better ways to meet these needs. Clifford (1994) recommended that mental health workers gain an understanding of the signs, symbols, and activities of cults; explore the individual and family dynamics and developmental issues that led the child to want to join the cult; develop a treatment plan to distance the child from the cult while teaching more positive values and beliefs; and develop support groups for the child. Family counseling is helpful because most children feel alienated from parents and other family members.

Children deeply involved in satanic rituals or the occult may need to be removed from all contact with their present environment and provided with intense, continuing efforts to improve their self-esteem, to help them find positive relationships within their families and peer groups, and to establish some control over their lives. Young people sometimes have a casual interest in reading about the occult; however, parents, teachers, counselors, and friends should become concerned when the young person retreats from more positive group relationships and shows changes in behavior that indicate alienation and withdrawal.

Counselors working with children involved in the occult need to be aware of their feelings of alienation, powerlessness, and low self-esteem. Counselors need to listen to such children intently to understand all the underlying reasons for their involvement.

## DEATH AND BEREAVEMENT

Death has been a taboo subject for discussion in our society. Asked about death or dying, most adults try to avoid the subject or excuse themselves by expressing their inadequacy to discuss such a subject with young people. Discussions about death seem to be accompanied by a great deal of adult discomfort, anxiety, vagueness, and avoidance behavior. Only recently has the realization set in that talking about death may help people accept it as a part of life and cope with the feelings that accompany it. Children are often affected by the death of pets or grandparents, if not by the loss of parents, friends, or siblings. Counselors need to be prepared to help children accept the reality of death as a part of life. To work effectively with children on the issue of death, counselors must first examine their own attitudes toward death. A counselor in conflict cannot provide the support and understanding the child needs.

Children have trouble understanding death for many reasons. As Piaget (Piaget & Inhelder, 1969) pointed out, children are limited in their understanding by the stage of their cognitive development. Young children are unable to understand the finality and irreversibility of death; they feel they are immortal and have trouble understanding how others are not. As children grow, they begin to question death and its causes. They may recognize it as inevitable and final, but comprehending the process is still difficult for children. Children often believe that only old people die.

Many factors in the child's environment may encourage other faulty concepts concerning death. The mass media often portray death violently. Children may also be exposed to a media figure dying one week and then appearing the next in another program. Adults in the child's life may react negatively to death. Often they attempt to protect the child from death by refusing to discuss the subject and by hiding their own feelings. Understanding adult reactions may be difficult for children. They may think they caused or contributed to the death in some way or decide that death is a punishment for something bad they have done. Unfounded fears and anxieties arise out of these misunderstandings. Euphemistic explanations often cause misconceptions in children. If told that the person is "only asleep" or that "God has called her," children can learn to fear sleep or fear that God will call them away from their world.

For the most part, children have difficulty learning effective ways of handling death. Adults may not provide the answers needed or demonstrate appropriate behaviors. Unresolved grief can result in personal, interpersonal, or social problems in the future.

From her work with terminally ill patients, Kübler-Ross (1969) defined the stages that most patients and their families go through in facing death. The first reaction is denial: "This is not happening to me." Second, the patient and family experience anger over the situation: "Why did this have to happen to me and not to somebody else?" The next stage includes bargaining. People may try to make a bargain with God to be a better person if God will let them or their loved one live. When the inevitability of death must be faced and the pressures become a harsh reality, depression is common. Eventually the patient comes to the realization of the inevitability of death and often a peaceful acceptance.

O'Rourke and Worzbyt (1996) wrote that "how children view loss and death is a matter of development, personal experiences, adult guidance, and innate abilities" (p. 303). They reported that there is limited understanding of responses to death for children under age 3. Children from 3 to 5 years of age consider death a temporary condition, and they may show little reaction to or understanding of it. Children from 6 to 8 begin to understand the finality of death and become curious about the details, but it may not hold a personal meaning. By age 10, most children understand the finality of death but still may be limited in their experience with it. The authors stated that children progress through stages of grieving similar to those described by Kübler-Ross (1969). Reactions may include (1) shock, denial, disbelief, and numbness; (2) apparent lack of feelings; (3) physiological changes (tiredness, lack of appetite, headache, and other somatic symptoms); (4) regression; and (5) explosive emotions, acting out behavior, guilt, self-blame, and other strong emotions.

Freeman (2001) discussed the grief experience as a progression through 10 stages. The person moves from shock, to an emotional release, to depression, and often to physical symptoms of distress. The bereaved shows anxiety, hostility, and then guilt and fear. The last two stages include healing through memories and acceptance of the death. He stated that the tasks of mourning involve expressing the reality of the death, tolerating the suffering, and converting the relationship from presence to memory. The final tasks are developing a new identity of self without the deceased and finding some meaning in grief. Moore and Carr (2000) provided examples (see Table 18-2) of a child's statements that might indicate these stages.

O'Halloran and Altmaier (1996) reviewed the literature concerning death awareness and understanding among three groups: healthy, chronically ill, and terminally ill children. They reported that children with life-threatening diseases seem to understand death concepts such as irreversibility and finality more than healthy or chronically ill children because of their own experience. They also suggested that greater understanding of these concepts may come from life-threatening circumstances such as war. They believed that understanding the death awareness of dying children can help counselors work with them more effectively. Open communication about the child's disease and diagnosis may help the child to feel freer to discuss his or her fears and anxieties and to assist counselors in clarifying inaccurate concepts. Parents of dying children also need information about how to communicate at the appropriate cognitive level about death.

From his study of children's grief patterns after the death of a parent, Worden (1996) found that the initial effects include sadness and crying, with a large number of children continuing to experience these emotions up to 2 years after the death. Fears and anxiety, centering on the safety of a remaining parent, were also present, especially in girls. Physical responses included illness, headaches, and stomachaches; these children appeared to be more accident prone than their peers who had not experienced loss.

Worden (1996) listed four tasks for grieving children to accomplish: (1) accepting the reality of the loss, (2) experiencing the pain or emotional aspects of the loss, (3) adjusting to an environment in which the significant one is missed, and (4) relocating the person within one's life while finding ways to memorialize the person.

Tonkins and Lambert (1996) evaluated the effectiveness of the group process with 16 grieving children. Evaluations of the group effectiveness were completed by parents, and all had positive responses, indicating that the group had been either moderately effective or extremely effective in helping their child.

Moore and Carr (2000) suggested a six-session family therapy process that focuses on grief work for all family members to improve the child and parent adjustment. Webb (1993) listed several advantages of family counseling: the counselor has the opportunity to observe the child's role in the family and to assess the availability of other family members to the child, the reality of death is shared with other family members, and the family has the opportunity to understand the pace and form of the child's grieving process. The disadvantages include the possibility that the child is not focused on because of grieving adults in the family and that the family may be so grief stricken they cannot empathize with the child.

In summary, counseling strategies for helping children who have experienced loss through death include the following:

1. Listen carefully to children's thoughts, feelings, and concerns, and respond clearly and objectively with statements at the child's level of understanding. Clarify children's questions or statements that may have a double meaning or suggest a hidden concern. Be aware of the child's cognitive level of development.

TABLE 18-2  Themes underlying children's grief

| *Grief process* | *Underlying theme* | *Behavioural expressions of grief processes* |
|---|---|---|
| Shock | • I am stunned by the loss of this person | • Complete lack of affect and difficulty engaging emotionally with others<br>• Poor concentration and poor school work |
| Denial | • The person is not dead | • Reporting seeing or hearing the deceased<br>• Carrying on conversations with the deceased |
| Yearning and searching | • I must find the deceased | • Wandering or running away<br>• Phoning relatives |
| Sadness | • I am sad, hopeless and lonely because I have lost someone on whom I depended | • Persistent low mood, tearfulness, low energy and lack of activity<br>• Appetite and sleep disruption<br>• Poor concentration and poor school work |
| Anger | • I am angry because the person I needed has abandoned me | • Aggression, tantrums, defiance, delinquency<br>• Conflict with parents, siblings, teachers and peers<br>• Drug or alcohol abuse<br>• Poor concentration and poor school work |
| Anxiety | • I am frightened that the deceased will punish me for causing their death or being angry at them. I am afraid that I too may die of an illness or fatal accident | • Separation anxiety, school refusal, regressed behaviour, bedwetting<br>• Somatic complaints, hypochondriasis and agoraphobia associated with a fear of accidents<br>• Poor concentration and poor school work |
| Guilt and bargaining | • It is my fault that the person died so I should die | • Suicidal behavior |
| Acceptance | • I loved and lost the person who died and now I must carry on without them while cherishing their memory | • Return to normal behavioral routines |

NOTE: Reprinted from Moore, M. and Carr, A. (2001). Depression and grief. In A. Carr (Ed.) *What works with children and adolescents? A critical review of psychological interventions with children, adolescents, and their families.* Andover, UK: Routledge, p. 209. Reprinted with permission.

2. Allow children to express their grief, talk freely, and ask questions. Play therapy, the use of puppets, role playing, creative artwork, bibliocounseling, a visit to a nursing home, videos on dealing with loss, family drawing, relaxation and imagery, letter writing to say goodbye, the open chair technique, and individual or group discussions may be helpful counseling techniques for working with these children. Counselors can also recommend books, pamphlets, or other resources to the adults who provide support for these children. Children experiencing a loss through death may feel abandoned or insecure and need extra amounts of time, energy, and reassurance.

3. Help the child learn more about death and dying by talking about the death of an animal or a plant (Costa & Holliday, 1994).

4. Children sometimes have trouble understanding concepts such as heaven and eternity. They may be confused about why "God takes away" loved ones. Counselors may want to consult with the family's clergy for assistance in dealing with this sensitive topic. Avoid half-truths such as death is "sleeping."

5. Counselors are often asked if children should attend the funeral of someone who has died. The answer depends on the child's age, the kinship of the deceased, and the child's reaction to the death. Children need to learn that death is part of the natural order of life. They need the opportunity to say goodbye to a close loved one. However, consider as well the child's reaction to death and his or her concern about attending the funeral.

6. Work to reduce the stress in the child's life. Try to maintain as much familiar structure as possible. Be aware that the child may regress to behaviors of an earlier developmental stage or manifest physical symptoms of distress (Costa & Holliday, 1994). Family counseling may be indicated.

7. Watch for triggers of grief—birthdays, holidays, the anniversary of the death (Costa & Holliday, 1994).

There is little information in the literature describing effective methods for counseling with children and their reactions to death and dying, especially empirical studies. Perhaps researchers avoid the subject, as do parents and other adults. The severity of pain associated with the death and dying of a loved one indicates a need for study of both the short- and long-term effects of the trauma.

## DEPRESSION AND SUICIDE

A popular misconception is that children's lives are so carefree that they do not have suicidal thoughts and do not commit suicidal acts. Professionals working with children know otherwise. Suicide is the third leading cause of death among teenagers age 15 to 19. In 2001, the percentage of youth who reported they had seriously considered committing suicide was 19%. Those who reported attempting suicide represent 8 to 9% of that population (Child Trends, 2002). Herring (1993) stated that nearly 200 children younger than 14 commit suicide each year. According to the National Center for Health Statistics (1993) 266 children between 5 and 14 years old committed suicide in the United States in 1991 (Jacobsen et al., 1994, p. 439). In a survey Nelson and Crawford (1990) conducted, counselors in one state indicated they had made contact with 187 elementary grade students considering suicide, 26 of whom had actually attempted the act.

Most researchers question the statistics relative to the incidence of child suicide, pointing out that they are probably underestimates because of society's reluctance to admit that children commit suicide. Nelson and Crawford (1990) noted that the stresses once identified with adolescence have now become prevalent in the lives of children. Increases in stress also increase anxiety, depression, and suicide ideation. Parental loss through separation or divorce was cited as the number one cause of childhood suicide. Mentioning many of the stressors children face, Herring (1993) stated that depression stands apart from other psychological disorders in that suicide is often its tragic outcome.

Hart (1991) cited studies that show a 20% rate of depression among school-age children (ages 5 to 12). More than one-quarter of students in grades 9 to 12 report feeling sad and hopeless over an extended period of time (Child Trends, 2002). A 51% to 59% depression rate was cited for child-psychiatric settings. From the contemporary psychodynamic view, the child's depressive difficulties relate to loss of self-esteem from feelings of helplessness or loss. Losses range from loss of contact with a primary caregiver to less traumatic losses, both actual and perceived. Children often respond to feelings of helplessness and loss by swallowing their anger. Depression is the result of anger turned inward.

Signs of depression include the following: sadness that persists, hopelessness, loss of interest in normal activities, changes in eating or sleeping habits, school absenteeism or poor performance, aches and pains that do not get better with treatment, and thoughts about death or suicide (SAMHSA's National Mental Health Information Center, 2002). The *Harvard Mental Health Letter* ("Depression in Children," 1997) outlined symptoms for young children: being accident prone and subject to phobias, extreme self-reproach, clinging behavior, avoiding new people and challenges, and excessive worry. Adolescents may seem to be angry rather than sad. Mellin and Beamish (2002) provided a treatment protocol using interpersonal theory for working with adolescents with depression.

Emslie (1997) estimated an incidence of about 6.2% for mood disorders in children and adolescents and 4.9% for major depressive disorders. According to Emslie, the incidence is approximately the same for boys and girls in childhood, but increases to a 2:1 ratio of girls to boys during adolescence. The three common symptoms presented are irritable, oppositional, and negative behavior; excessive unexplained physical complaints such as headaches or stomachaches not related to clear causes; and hyperactivity—impulsivity with severe aggression accompanied by a denial that anything is wrong. The occurrence of these symptoms may be episodic. Emslie recommended multimodal treatment that could include individual counseling (cognitive-behavioral or interpersonal), family counseling, education, or pharmacological treatment.

Herring (1993) suggested that child suicide attempts are often silent. Parents and physicians may conceal the suicide to avoid embarrassing the family. Many accidents are actually child suicides (Stefanowski-Harding, 1990). Children sometimes run in front of vehicles or jump off high places when they want to commit suicide (Herring, 1990). Stefanowski-Harding (1990) also reported an increasing number of children under age 12 who are treated for accidental overdoses. She pointed out that children rarely leave suicide notes because they cannot write or are not in the habit of writing their communications.

Why a child attempts suicide is a complex question. Beautrais (2000) reviewed risk factors for youth suicide in Australia and New Zealand. She identified social and educational disadvantages, childhood and family adversity, mental disorders, personal vulnerability, stressful life events and circumstances, and contextual factors as risks. Some researchers believe that suicidal children are highly sensitive, have a low tolerance for frustration, and have feelings of depression, guilt, hostility, and anger that they are unable to express (Stefanowski-Harding, 1990). Popenhagen and Qualley (1998) contended that some young people "are just confused and do not know what to do" (p. 30). Nelson and Crawford (1990) asked counselors to indicate factors they thought contributed to suicidal attempts and completions in the group they saw. They rated family problems such as divorce, separation, and parental alcoholism as highly probable contributors. Peer pressure and pressure to achieve academically were ranked second and third, respectively. Drug abuse, physical handicap, and economic stress were ranked very low. Stefanowski-Harding (1990) also found several researchers who indicated that family problems related to death, divorce, separation, physical assault, rejection, or a suicidal parent were probably factors related to child suicide. Herring (1993) reported that children with a family history of suicide are nine times more likely to take their own lives than those who do not have this history. Boys are more likely than girls to complete the suicidal act because they use more violent means in their attempts. Stefanowski-Harding (1990) cautioned that children with learning disabilities or other learning difficulties that cause constant frustration are more likely to attempt suicide and that gifted children may attempt suicide because their advanced intellectual ability makes relating to children their own age difficult.

Thoughts of suicide and attempts to commit it often accompany a poor self-concept and feelings of hopelessness, worthlessness, depression, or guilt. A depressed or suicidal child may be extremely quiet and withdrawn or highly active and agitated. Depression may be masked by overactivity, gaiety, or acting-out behavior. Feelings of depression leading to self-destructive attempts frequently follow the death of loved ones, significant personal or material losses, events that profoundly affect self-esteem, or other traumatic life crises. Clues may include chronic sleeplessness, loss of appetite, withdrawal, or any extreme behavioral change.

Wise and Spengler (1997) suggested that myths and misconceptions about childhood suicide make it difficult for mental health counselors to assess childhood risk potential and make accurate reports of occurrences. They pointed out that children *do* commit suicide, although the data are incomplete and may be inaccurate. Wise and Spengler reported the base rate for suicide in children under 14 years is 0.8 per 100,000 and that childhood suicide is up 267% from 15 years ago.

They also believed that reported rates may be underestimated because many childhood suicides may be reported as accidents.

Another myth counselors must address is a widespread belief that children do not understand the finality of death; therefore, childhood suicide is impossible. Wise and Spengler (1997) cited research showing children's growing realization about death from 5 to 12 years of age, with most kindergartners through third-graders having a fairly clear understanding of the concept. (See the section on Death and Bereavement on p. 523 for additional research and information on children's understanding of death.) Wise and Spengler also discussed the faulty belief that children are unable to commit suicide because they lack the size, strength, motor coordination, and ability to obtain the materials necessary to perform it. They cited research that indicated that most 6- to 12-year-old children who commit suicide do so by methods such as jumping from heights, drowning, stabbing, running in front of moving vehicles, hanging themselves, or using fire.

In considering risk factors, Wise and Spengler (1997) concluded that the single best predictor of suicide is persistent suicidal ideation. Suicidal attempts are a high risk indicator also, but the fact that attempts may be misclassified as accidents must be considered. Parental suicide, depression, marital discord, family violence, child abuse and neglect, and poor academic performance were all identified as risk factors. Wise and Spengler recommended that evaluations include interviews with the child and family; observations of play, looking for developmentally inappropriate activities, dangerous or reckless behaviors, or activities indicating death or violence fantasies; discussions about what the child is thinking and feeling; and perhaps psychological testing on instruments such as the Child Suicide Potential Scale. While it is difficult to determine the factors associated with children's potential for suicide, guidelines such as these give counselors some basis for assessment of risks.

Strategies for counselors working with suicidal children include:

1. If you feel a child could be seriously contemplating suicide, suggest to the parents that they consult a doctor or psychiatrist.

2. Never hesitate to consult with someone thoroughly trained in suicide prevention—suicide-prevention centers, clinics, or psychiatrists—or refer suicidal children to them.

3. Use techniques to enhance the self-concept of children who exhibit suicidal tendencies. Children with self-destructive or self-mutilating tendencies, such as head banging, breath holding, and hair pulling, have responded to behavior modification techniques in which acceptable behaviors are rewarded and destructive tendencies punished by penalties such as withdrawing privileges or ignoring the behaviors. Children with symptoms this severe will probably need to be treated in an institutional setting.

4. Never ignore threats, hints, and continued comments about destroying oneself, "leaving this world," "you're going to miss me," or "life's not worth living." These comments may be attention getting, but children who use these techniques to get attention need help. Follow up the threat immediately with active listening in an attempt to discover the feelings or events that brought on the self-destructive feelings.

5. At a time of crisis, listen to the child carefully in a nonjudgmental manner. Have the child tell you *everything* that has happened during the previous few hours or days. You may gain some understanding or knowledge of factors contributing to the depression.

6. Suicidal children need permission to call—and the phone number of—a person (the counselor or another close and understanding friend) they feel they can talk with in times of distress.

7. The parents of a suicidal child should be made aware of the child's feelings and thoughts and helped to understand the situation without panic or guilt. Counsel with them about how to listen to and talk with the child. Consult with them concerning danger signals, and make a plan for handling crises, should they arise.

8. If you suspect a child has suicidal tendencies, confront the child with your thoughts and feelings. You are not placing the thought in the child's mind, but you may provide an opening and opportunity for the child to discuss the troublesome thoughts and feelings.

9. Talk with suicidal children about what has happened in their lives recently. Losses of loved ones, pets, and other significant objects in the children's lives; feelings of personal failure; feelings of extreme shame or grief; and other traumatic events contribute to suicidal thoughts. Allow children to express their feelings without being judgmental, glossing over, or denying their right to these feelings.

10. If suicidal children admit to self-destructive thoughts, ask about their plan. A well-thought-out plan is a significant danger signal.

11. Ask suicidal children to tell you about their fantasies or dreams. Ask them to draw a picture or write out their thoughts. These techniques often give the adult some insight into the child's thoughts and feelings.

12. Often children do not understand death as final and irreversible; therefore, any child who is seriously disturbed or depressed needs careful attention. Greene (1994) pointed out that preschoolers link death to separation, which is temporary. Five- to 7-year-old children begin to develop concepts related to death— irreversibility and causality—and may be able to see the final meaning of death.

13. The months following the threat are also crucial, and careful attention should be continued until the conflict is completely resolved. A sudden recovery after severe depression may be a warning signal that means the client has made a decision to end one's life.

Jacobsen et al. (1994) suggested questions such as the following, among others, to interview children about suicidal ideation and behaviors:

1. Did you ever feel so upset that you wished you were not alive or wanted to die?
2. Did you ever do something that you knew was so dangerous that you could get hurt or killed?
3. Did you tell anyone that you wanted to die or were thinking about killing yourself?
4. What would happen if you died? What would that be like?

5. How do you remember feeling when you were thinking about killing yourself or trying to kill yourself?
6. Has anything happened recently that has been upsetting to you or your family?
7. Have you had a problem with feeling sad, having trouble sleeping, not feeling hungry, losing your temper easily, or feeling tired all of the time recently? (p. 450)

Roberts (1995) found that interventions made after a youth suicide can be preventive as well as assist the grieving process. He recommended that a "psychological autopsy" be performed to try to understand all the factors that contributed to the child's decision to commit suicide, to determine why the death occurred at a particular time, to provide information to prevent other suicides, and to aid in the grieving process. Roberts urged schools to develop "postvention" plans to deal with a child's suicide during the school year and during vacation.

Many writers in this area suggested psychological education and peer-group counseling as preventive measures. In addition to forming peer-counseling groups, Herring (1993) advocated psychological education as part of the middle school curriculum, involvement of parents in training sessions to help them understand the issue of suicide, and counselors as consultants, providing information and knowledge about what to do and where to refer clients.

Siehl (1990) suggested that all schools should have a disaster plan to use in the event of a suicide, just as they have a plan for hurricanes, tornadoes, earthquakes, and other traumatic events. Some of Siehl's suggestions include:

1. Developing a team of resource people to handle the emotional crisis
2. Presenting in-service training programs to the entire staff on the causes of suicide, warning signs, and sources of help for suicidal persons
3. Establishing a network to inform all faculty of the facts of the tragedy
4. Designating special crisis centers for children needing additional help
5. Developing a checklist of activities to be included in the classroom announcement
6. Planning for cautions about the dangers in the days following a suicide
7. Carrying out home visits
8. Developing guidelines for media coverage
9. Developing procedures to continue alertness for several months

Because helping professionals are aware that children may imitate other children who commit suicide, such a plan, along with psychological education and group counseling, is appropriate for counselors to consider.

## FAMILY STRUCTURES

### Children of Divorce

The incidence of divorce has increased rapidly in the United States during the past several decades, and the National Center for Health Statistics reports that at the present time about one of every two marriages ends in divorce (Wendel, 1997).

This means that about 1 million children, or about one-third of the nation's children, will experience the divorce of their parents. Divorce or marital separation is traumatic and painful for all involved. Adults frequently seek help to cope with the hurt associated with divorce through individual and group counseling or through organized helping groups such as Parents Without Partners. In past years, children of divorce got little direct help; in fact, in most instances, the children were told as little as possible about family affairs and were instructed to keep the breakup secret for as long as possible. Recently, because of the noticeable effects of family separation on children, more attention has been directed to the needs of children going through this traumatic event.

The lives and relationships of children in a divorcing family are profoundly affected—socially, economically, psychologically, and even legally. Children must adjust to separation from one parent and formation of a new and different relationship with the other. A change in the family's economic status, possibly a change in the home and school environment, different parenting styles, custody battles, and sometimes a totally different lifestyle create feelings that may be positive or negative. Often, mothers who were totally involved in the care of children and home may go to work; many are unskilled and accept low-paying jobs. Children may be torn by conflicting loyalties or learn to manipulate the parents to get their own way. Children of divorced parents may be asked to assume the role of the absent parent and to fulfill physical or emotional responsibilities beyond their maturity level.

Several leading researchers (Hetherington, Cox, & Cox, 1978; Wallerstein & Blakeslee, 1989; Wallerstein & Kelly, 1980) have attempted to follow children to determine the long-term effects of divorce on their growth and development. Wallerstein and Kelly (1980) noted that the "central hazard of divorce" is adverse effects on the child's development. Numerous studies have suggested that the child's developmental level is related to the reaction that follows the separation. Wallerstein and Kelly (1980) and Wallerstein and Blakeslee (1989) suggested that infants respond mainly to the emotional reactions of their caretaker; for example, mothers or fathers under stress convey their feelings to the infant through their handling and verbal communication. Very young children seem to have many of their needs met, regardless of the stress of the caretaker. They are dependent and demand attention to their needs. Preschoolers (age 3 to 5) have only a vague understanding of the family situation because of their limited cognitive development; thus, they often feel frightened and insecure, experience nightmares, and regress to more infantile behaviors. School-age children, who have more advanced cognitive and emotional development, see the situation more accurately. However, children age 6 to 8 often believe the divorce was their fault ("If I had not been bad, Dad would not have left"), and children at this age often hold unrealistic hopes for a family reconciliation. They may feel loss, rejection, guilt, and loyalty conflicts. Age 9 to 12 is a time when children are developing rapidly and rely on their parents for stability. They may become very angry at the parent they blame for the divorce or may take a supportive role as they worry about their troubled parents. Because of their anxiety, they may develop somatic symptoms, engage in troublesome behaviors, or experience a decline in academic achievement. The parents' divorce during children's adolescent years brings a different set of developmental problems. Young people at this age are striving for independence and exploring their own sexuality. They need structure, limits, and guidance in dealing with their sexuality. They also may worry about their own relationships and the possibility of repeating their parents' mistakes.

The results of research relating risk to age have been contradictory. Hetherington, Cox, and Cox (1978) thought that younger children suffer more detrimental effects of a divorce. In her 10-year follow-up, Wallerstein (1984) found that children who were very young at the time of the divorce seem to have suffered less—they remembered less about that time in their lives. A multitude of factors other than developmental level may influence the effects of divorce on the child, including the amount of tension and conflict in the home, the length of time the child has lived with the conflict, the parents' reactions to the conflict, and the parents' personal adjustment to divorce and the resumption of parenting roles.

Wallerstein (1983) and Wallerstein and Blakeslee (1989) described "psychological tasks" that children of divorce must successfully resolve:

Children should acknowledge the reality of the marital rupture. Young children often experience terrifying fantasies, feel abandoned, and tend to deny the reality of the family situation. Because of their own stress, parents often fail to reassure children and help them understand the situation and their future. Older children, too, may experience fantasies of disaster, reduced ability to think and cope, and even psychosomatic symptoms indicating their anxiety. Supportive counseling techniques, including listening, reflection, clarification, and problem solving, and perhaps stress-reduction techniques such as relaxation or guided imagery are appropriate for children working through this task. Oehmen (1985) asserted that the child should be confronted with the situation quickly and forcefully and given an opportunity to discuss, process, and resolve his or her feelings about the divorce to avoid being overwhelmed by negative feelings.

Wallerstein and Blakeslee (1989) stated that the most critical factor in helping children through divorce is parental support. Both parents should talk with all the children together about the decision to divorce several days before one parent leaves the home. Children should be provided with a clear explanation about why their parents are divorcing, although they need not be told the details of an infidelity or other sexual problems. The parents should convey that, unfortunately, they have made a mistake in their marriage, but they remain committed to the family. According to the authors, understanding the divorce and its consequences is the first psychological task for children of divorcing families. Some specific difficulties follow.

*Disengaging from parental conflict and distress and resuming customary pursuits.* The resolution of this task calls for the children to distance themselves from the crisis in their household and resume their normal learning tasks, outside activities, and friendships. Parents must work to help children keep their lives in order and not let the divorce overshadow all their activities. As has been reported by other researchers, Wallerstein (1983) saw a significant decline in academic achievement in more than half of her sample of children age 7 to 11 following a marital separation. Group counseling and individual techniques directed toward improving academic achievement (for example, contingency contracting) may assist children at this level. Consultation sessions with teachers to plan for a structured class environment may bring stability to the child's life and encourage achievement.

*Resolution of loss.* Divorce brings not only loss of a parent but also often loss of familiar surroundings and possibly a different lifestyle. Wallerstein (1983) noted that the task of resolving these losses may be the most difficult: "At its core this task demands that the child overcome his or her profound sense of rejection, of humiliation, of unlovability, and of powerlessness which the one parent's departure so often engenders" (p. 237). Wallerstein and Blakeslee (1989) suggested that a consistent pattern of visitation by the absent parent and an emphasis on building a new and positive relationship can help children through this stage. Unfortunately, many children do not have this relationship with the absent parent and remain disappointed for years. They feel rejected by the absent parent and thus unlovable and unworthy. Role playing, puppetry, writing, drawing, feelings, charades, and other techniques can encourage children to express their feelings. Individual and group sessions focusing on building self-esteem may be helpful—for example, strengths testing, peer teaching, finding the child a "buddy," and the techniques of cognitive restructuring.

*Resolving anger and self-blame.* Because divorce is a voluntary decision by one or both parents, children tend to blame them for being selfish and unresponsive to their needs, or children may blame themselves for the breakup of the family. Intense anger at one or both parents is characteristic of the children of divorce, especially older children. The researchers found that the child's ability to forgive himself or herself for the divorce or lack of reconciliation was a significant step toward forgiving the parents and reconciling the relationship. There are some excellent children's books that can help them understand the divorce process and the reality that they are not to blame for the divorce. Most of these books emphasize that sometimes adults just cannot live together or resolve their differences.

Counselors can recommend specific books for the developmental level of their clients and discuss the books with the children. The child's intense anger often results in acting-out behavior. A consistent, structured environment at home and at school provides some of the security the child needs during this period of turmoil and change. Group counseling that focuses on role playing, play therapy, drawing, and writing can help children express their anger and feelings of guilt. Group problem-solving discussions help children find constructive ways of handling their feelings.

*Accepting the permanence of the divorce.* Wallerstein (1983) pointed out that the fantasy of a reunited family persists tenaciously for children of divorce, even after the parents marry other partners. Whereas losing a parent through death has a finality about it, the fact that both partners are alive contributes to the continuing fantasy of restoring the intact family. Reality therapy may help the child accept the permanence of divorce. Group counseling with other children who are going through divorce or who have experienced it may also help. Drawings of the family before the divorce and at the present time, good and bad family changes since the divorce, and filmstrips and books about divorce and other family lifestyles (the stepfamily or single-parent family) often stimulate excellent discussions.

*Achieving realistic hope regarding relationships.* During the adolescent years, the child of divorce must resolve issues surrounding relationships—learning to take a chance in relationships while knowing full well that they might be fulfilling or that they might fail. Doing so requires that the child feel lovable and worthy. Children often feel rejected, unlovable, and unworthy because they feel guilty over the divorce or because they believe that one or both parents rejected them and cared little about their feelings and welfare. Wallerstein and Blakeslee (1989) noted that some adolescents engage in acting-out behavior (promiscuity, alcohol or drug abuse, and the like) that indicates low self-esteem. An important task for adolescents is realizing they can love and be loved. They must learn to be open in relationships while knowing that divorce or a loss is possible. According to Wallerstein and Blakeslee, effective resolution of this last psychological task of "taking a chance on love" leads to freedom from the psychological trauma of divorce and provides second chances for children of these families. Wallerstein and Blakeslee concluded that the effects of divorce are much more pervasive and longer lasting than originally thought. In earlier research, Wallerstein and Kelly (1980) had reported that boys showed more signs of trauma from the divorce during their developmental years than girls did. Wallerstein and Blakeslee (1989) found a sleeper effect—the girls' problems became more apparent as they entered young adulthood. Twenty years after Wallerstein began her initial research, she found parents' continuing anger still a factor in their children's lives. Many of the sample of children, now adults, were underachievers or drank heavily; a few had been involved in serious crimes. One third of the girls had relationship problems.

Wendel (1997) reported that Wallerstein stated, as a result of a 25-year follow-up of her longitudinal study of 131 children, begun in 1970, that the effects of the divorce seem cumulative and that its impact increases over time. She found that about half of the 131 children were involved with drugs and/or alcohol; that girls were most inclined to become sexually active; that one-third of the youngest participants (age 2 to 6 years at the time of the separation) did not continue their education after high school, although 40% did eventually graduate from college; and that many were distrustful of relationships, fearing they would repeat the failures of their parents.

Wallerstein's longitudinal study has been criticized because she used the interview technique, her sample was mostly white and middle class, and there were other research flaws; however, Wendel (1997) concluded that "one point is undeniably clear—divorce makes children's lives more difficult" (p. 35). McConnell and Sim (2000) reported on a successful innovative counseling service offered to children of divorce or to children and custodial parents. The authors emphasized thorough assessments to determine the most effective way to intervene.

There is growing concern about the lack of a father in the home. Divorce alters the parent–child relationship, and when the father is not present in the family, a bond may never be formed or it may be damaged severely—to the detriment of the child. In fact, a number of studies indicate that boys from single-parent homes (whether from divorce or out-of-wedlock birth) are more likely to end up in the juvenile justice or adult penal system (Whitehead, 1993). Laws requiring noncustodial fathers to assume financial responsibility for children have been strengthened, but the physical presence of the father is equally important to the development of children, especially males.

Counselors working with the parents of children involved in a divorce can be of assistance by providing consultative advice. Counselors can offer parents some of the following suggestions:

1. Talk with the child about the divorce at his or her cognitive level. (Counselors may want to rehearse this with the parents.) Explain what has happened at the child's level of understanding, and try to relate the experience to one that the child may have had. Emphasize that the child is not at fault. Keep the lines of communication open so that the child's misconceptions or fears are recognized immediately. Avoid blaming or criticizing the other parent and relating all the unpleasant details.

2. Plan for ways to make the child's life as stable and consistent as possible, even though changes may be necessary. Household routines, school schedules, and consistent discipline help children understand that their world is not completely wrecked. Involve teachers, counselors, ministers, grandparents, and other support systems.

3. Avoid using the children as go-betweens to carry messages ("The child support check is late!") or to find out about the other parent's life ("What does the apartment look like?"). Children love both parents and are already torn by conflicting loyalties.

4. Arrange for regular visits from the absent parent to assure the children that they are loved by both parents. Children are sometimes disappointed by absent parents who fail to call or come for a visit. Custodial parents need to provide a lot of love and reassurance at these times.

5. Talk with the children about the future. Involve them in the planning without overwhelming them with problems. They need to know what to expect.

6. Children experiencing a divorce in their family are still children at a particular developmental level. Avoid asking them to assume responsibilities beyond their capabilities—being the man of the family, baby-sitting younger children, or taking on excessive household chores.

Although many children of divorce do experience increased risks of social, emotional, and academic difficulties, others have successfully adjusted to the disruption and do not display significant signs of distress as a result of the experience. Gately and Schwebel (1992) found some areas in which the children experienced favorable outcomes:

1. Maturity, because they tended to assume greater responsibility for chores
2. Improved self-esteem, because they coped effectively with their changing life's circumstances
3. Empathy, due to increased concern for family members
4. Androgyny, as a result of seeing models not confined by stereotypical sex roles

Positive factors in their lives that contributed to the development of these attributes were positive personality, supportive family environment, and supportive social environment (Gately & Schwebel, 1992).

In their comprehensive article attempting to link intervention to basic research on children of divorce, Grych and Fincham (1992) also suggested helping parents understand how their behavior affects their children's adjustment and assist them in minimizing the effect of the divorce on children. Parents and counselors need to remember that adjustment after a divorce takes a child time and requires continuing understanding and reassurance. Parent-group meetings can help parents understand the problems their children are experiencing, learn new methods for communicating with their children, try new methods of discipline, and resolve some of their own frustration.

As in counseling about any problem in which values, beliefs, and attitudes may affect the counselor's objectivity, counselors may want to assess their feelings about divorce and their potential reactions to both the parents and the child. Children who are the victims of divorce have been hurt by adults they trusted and are quick to detect uneasiness, anxiety, or insincerity in the counselor's behavior.

## Children in Stepfamilies

For years, the intact nuclear family has been considered the ideal or norm. With the present rate of divorce and the number of adults remarrying each year, this idealized view of the family must be adjusted. Wendel (1997) reported that, according to the National Center for Health Statistics, about 45% of children born in

1983 will experience parental divorce and 35% of their parents will remarry, with 20% of these couples going through a second divorce.

Joining two families into one presents children with another set of unique problems with which to cope at a time when the effects of the biological parents' divorce may still be troublesome. With the number of stepfamilies increasing, mental health professionals are becoming more involved with stepfamilies and the problems of the adults and children in them. Kantrowitz and Wingert (1990) stated that, until the 1970s, researchers focused their attention on nuclear, intact families. Stepfamilies or single-parent families were virtually ignored, but researchers have shown that these families are very different in structure, interactional modes, and functioning from nuclear, intact families.

Because the stepfamily is not considered a "normal" family, expectations and relationships are more ambiguous and complex. Not only are cultural and social guidelines unclear but also children who are members of two households, moving in and out, have ambiguous and complex home guidelines and schedules. Adults and children experience changes in roles, alliances, parenting arrangements, household responsibilities, rules, expectations, and demands. For children who are attempting to regain stability after the first family breakup, this lack of structure may bring additional stresses and strains.

Zeppa and Norem (1993) tested the generally accepted conclusion that stepfamilies have more stress than do first families. While acknowledging their study's flaws, the authors concluded that significantly fewer differences divide first families and stepfamilies than had been thought. Their results showed that stepfamilies experience more stress, but they suggested that the idea that stepfamilies are different from first families and have more problems may be due to socioeconomic factors or bias against stepfamilies.

Often stepparents and stepchildren have a weak sense of attachment; stepparents find it more difficult to love and relate to stepchildren than to their biological children. A 1991 study by the National Commission on Children (Whitehead, 1993) found that stepparents were less likely to be involved in the lives and activities of their stepchildren than either intact or single-parent families.

It has been a generally accepted conclusion that children in stepfamilies have more difficulties than children growing up in nuclear families, and they are often labeled delinquent or thought not to be well adjusted because of the crisis of divorce and development of the new family. Coleman and Ganong (1995) pointed out that stepfamilies must deal with cultural stereotypes that may interfere with the establishment of good relationships in the family. Stepparents are often perceived as unloving or abusive—the "wicked stepmother," for instance. *Stepchild* is a word often used to describe someone who is rejected or unwanted. Love and acceptance of a new father or mother, of brothers and sisters, does not occur instantly. The child may be angry at the "replacement" of a parent and the intrusion of other children into his or her life. The adjustment may be particularly difficult for adolescents, who are dealing with their own sexuality, growing maturity, need for independence, and search for identity. Visher and Visher (1995) recognized that stepfamilies often experience disorganization and dysfunction but warn against "over-pathologizing" their needs.

Papernow (1995) outlined the following stages of stepfamily development:

1. Early stage
   a. Fantasy stage—There is the dream that the new family will be ideal and everyone will love each other
   b. Immersion stage—Reality indicates that something in the family is different and may not be right
   c. Awareness stage—Identifying a new position in family structure and clarifying understanding of associated feelings
2. Middle stage
   a. *Mobilization*—More conflict may emerge as the new family begins to move toward a new structure
   b. *Action stage*—The new family reaches consensus on the family structure and operation
3. Later stages
   a. *Contact stage*—Deeper stepfamily relationships are formed
   b. *Resolution stage*—Step relationships become more intimate and solid; family norms and procedures are established

Families and individual members proceed through these stages at varying rates. Papernow (1995) believed counselors must assess the family and individual dynamics to really understand the developmental levels of members and the structure of the stepfamily.

Counselors need to help both parents and children in the stepfamily to find their appropriate roles and clearly define the expectations of all members. Defining these new roles requires time and patience. Thoughts and feelings must be expressed and clarified, routines and expectations established, visitations with other parents planned, and discipline guidelines agreed on. Play therapy is especially helpful for counseling with younger children. Drawings, journals, bibliocounseling, and group counseling with other children in stepfamilies may assist older children in working through their feelings and concerns. Family counseling is encouraged to help the newly organized family increase awareness and acceptance of each other and individual differences, facilitate problem solving, and build support for each other.

We have suggested that counselors need to periodically examine their own attitudes and beliefs about certain clients in order to maintain the highest levels of objectivity and efficiency. Since negative stereotypes of stepparents are common, people in the helping professions may sometimes unwittingly adopt stereotypical thinking and evaluate stepparents or stepchildren clients in the light of these negative stereotypes.

In addition, schools need to evaluate their activities in light of their effects on stepfamilies. Do policies and activities allow stepparents' participation in the child's school life? Do special occasions like Mother's Day and Father's Day include references to stepparents? Are living arrangements and name differences clearly indicated in records in order to avoid embarrassment? School may be the one place a child in a new stepparent home finds structure and familiarity. Counselors can help school personnel make the environment more comfortable and accepting for children in a changing world.

## Children in Single-Parent Homes

It has been pointed out in a previous section that about one-third of children born in the 1980s will spend some time in a single-parent home as a result of divorce before they reach the age of 18 years. These statistics do not include the number of single-parent homes created because of out-of-wedlock births. In the 1950s and early 1960s, only 5% of the nation's births were to unmarried mothers. By 1990, this rate had climbed to 27% (Whitehead, 1993). There are indications at this time that the rate is leveling off.

Single mothers are very vulnerable economically because their earnings are usually low and many do not receive child support from the father. Single motherhood appears to be strongly related to poverty, and never-married mothers are particularly apt to end up on welfare. Poverty, of course, has a strong correlation with children's low academic achievement, conduct disorders, and even juvenile crime.

Richards and Schmiege (1993) were concerned that most of the literature on single-parent homes focuses on the negative effects for children experiencing divorce and not living in the ideal two-parent household. They studied 60 single-parent mothers and 11 single-parent fathers to learn more about the problems faced in the homes and the strengths identified by the parents. The single-parent mothers most often said that money was their biggest problem area, with role and task overload following. Social life and problems with their ex-spouses were rated third and fourth. Single-parent fathers rated role and task overload and problems with ex-spouses as first and second on their list of problems, with financial problems ranking last. Both single-parent mothers and single-parent fathers rated their parenting skills as their main strength. Family management (being organized, dependable, and able to coordinate schedules) was second for both groups, and both groups also rated good communication and personal growth as strengths. The authors suggested that, given the likelihood of young women and men living in a single-parent household, a stronger emphasis on family education is necessary. They encouraged their readers not to accept negative stereotypes and to acknowledge that single-parent homes do have strengths.

Downey (1994) compared the school performance of children from single-mother and single-father families with the performance of children living with both parents. The single fathers were better educated than single mothers in the sample, but the children of single fathers did not earn higher grades. Neither group performed in school as well as the children from two-parent families. Economic problems may be affecting the children in single-parent homes, especially single-mother households. The researchers suggested that single fathers spend less time talking to the children, and less parental involvement in the children's school and play activities may be a significant factor.

Counseling strategies to help children in single-parent homes are similar to many described for children of divorce. The counselor must deal with the child's feelings of loss, whether the loss resulted from divorce, separation, or death. Emotions must be recognized and discussed. These children need stability, security, and consistency in their lives. Therefore, counselors may want to recommend to the child's parent and other family members that they join a support group to help the family reorganize effectively after the loss. Counselors in schools can provide group activities for children of single-parent homes to help them discuss their fears, concerns, and feelings about having only one parent in the home. Crosbie-Burnett and Pulvino (1990) described a classroom guidance program for children in nontraditional families that focused on eight aspects of nontraditional families and included topics such as having less money, feelings of anger or sadness, questions friends ask, and time alone.

As stated previously in this section, considerable research substantiates that children from single-parent homes have a higher rate of conduct disorders and other adjustment problems than children from intact homes. However, well-adjusted children live in single-parent homes. Counselors must be careful not to allow generalizations or personal bias to interfere with their objectivity in working with these children.

## Homeless Children

Many communities have concerns about the increasing number of homeless families. Families with children represent the 40% of the homeless population, and children are approximately one-fourth of the homeless population (National Coalition for the Homeless, 1998). According to Schmitz, Wagner, and Menke (1995), hopelessness has a very negative impact on a child's physical, educational, and emotional development. The children's lives lack continuity, consistency, privacy, cleanliness, permanency, and belonging, which may result in unacceptable behaviors such as acting out, fighting, restlessness, depression, moodiness, and low frustration tolerance. Based on her review of the literature, Dail (1990) described these families. Most homeless people in the past were male; a growing number today are single-parent families headed by women. Approximately 50% of the women heading homeless families are between 17 and 25 years of age; the majority have never been married or are separated or divorced. Most have some high school education, and a few attended postsecondary education. These mothers have few social or family support systems and tend to distrust people. About 50% of homeless children are under 5 years old. They are typically undernourished, and many show delayed development, with symptoms of acting-out behavior and physical problems. They may have difficulty with language and paying attention, physical coordination problems, and symptoms of anxiety. More than half of the children over 5 years old need mental health treatment. School performance is low because of poor attendance and confused lives. These children may be abused physically or psychologically because of their parents' stress (Dail, 1990).

Children of homeless parents are often prohibited from entering school because of requirements such as residency, proof of age, communication, and lack of school records. Other barriers include transportation and other enrollment requirements (Strawser, Markos, Yamaguchi, & Higgins, 2000).

If the children do enter school, placement and support services may be inadequate. Remediation and tutoring in basic skills are the most frequently identified educational needs of homeless children, according to Rafferty (1995). Congress passed a law in 1987 requiring schools to admit homeless children and integrate them into the present public educational system. Homeless children must also receive services comparable to those received by other children, such as transportation, meals, and programs for the disabled or gifted (Rafferty, 1995). Counselors should also be aware of the need for day care, counseling, and nutritional and educational support for homeless children.

Daniels (1992) stated that school can provide a "reprieve from the frightening realities of wandering the streets" (p. 104), as well as a sense of normalcy in a child's life. She suggested interventions based on Maslow's hierarchy of needs and the developmental guidelines of Erik Erikson (see Chapters 1 and 2). Daniels developed a six-session group counseling unit to increase self-esteem and address developmental concerns; its activities include an assessment of self-esteem, drawing a family portrait of those with whom the children live as well as where they live, drawings of feelings, sharing an accomplishment of which they are proud, identifying stress and worries in their lives, and, finally, drawing a group mural. These and other group activities can increase self-esteem and promote peer acceptance and appreciation. Strawser et al. (2000) identified other direct and indirect ways school counselors can help homeless children.

Counseling tasks include facilitating the child's entrance into school, helping the child and his or her family find some kind of stability in their lives, assisting the child in overcoming excessive fears and distrust of people, and being alert to the possibility of abuse. Counselors need a variety of referral resources to help the child meet physical needs such as shelter, food, and medical care. Assessing the child's educational level and helping him or her develop social skills requires time, energy, and patience.

Masten, Miliotis, Graham-Bermann, Ramirez, and Neemann (1993) compared 159 homeless children with 62 low-income children living in a home. As would be expected, the homeless children experienced more stress and disrupted schooling and friendships than did the low-income children in homes. The researchers concluded that homeless children's behavior problems are related more to parental distress and adversity than to housing conditions or income.

Vostanis, Tischler, Cumella, and Bellerby (2001) investigated mental health problems and social supports among homeless mothers and children. They emphasized the need for multiple levels of social support.

The counselor must avoid being influenced by generalizations about the homeless, such as that they are mentally ill, are unmotivated, could find a job if they wanted to, or abuse alcohol or drugs. Education is the best method for overcoming the problems of the homeless, but it requires a broad spectrum of services within the school and community. The counselor may be called on to coordinate these services and act as an advocate for the child.

## Latchkey Children

Children left at home unsupervised while parents work are called latchkey children because they carry a key to lock the house as they leave after their parents in the mornings and to unlock the house when they return before their parents in the afternoon. Some professionals believe that 15% to 20% of young elementary schoolchildren carry their own latchkey and that approximately 45% of late elementary schoolchildren are unsupervised for some period in the day (Peterson & Magrab, 1989). The developmental implications of children's self-care are uncertain because of the lack of research in this area.

Some researchers believe that about one-third of all children between ages 5 and 13 are latchkey children. The numbers are probably increasing annually because of many factors, including the increasing number of single-parent families, the cost of child care, and different school and work schedules (O'Rourke and Worzbyt, 1996). O'Rourke and Worzbyt (1996) researched the literature to learn more about the positive and negative consequences of being a latchkey child. They found that some children have inadequate peer socialization, fears, feelings of isolation, and loneliness. These children were also concerned about being hurt, being kidnapped, and getting into fights. Other children worried about getting bored, wasting time, and not completing tasks or chores. The more positive outcomes of being a latchkey child include increased independence, feelings of competence, and assumption of responsibility.

Latchkey children may be taught better self-care responsibilities in order to care for themselves and cope with emergencies. O'Rourke and Worzbyt (1996) suggested a series of group activities for latchkey children that focus on rules and responsibilities, things the children can do to keep themselves and their home safe, handling emergencies, dealing with feelings and boredom, and "what if" situations (fire, strangers, etc.).

The children's activities while on their own can be problematic because of the risk of injury, emotional reactions to being alone, and poor selection of activities (Peterson, 1989). Peterson concluded from her review of the literature that children are more likely to be injured when an adult is not present in the home; that although research is not clear on children's emotional reactions to staying alone, many experience negative feelings (anxiety, worry, fear); and that children spend their unsupervised hours watching too much television, not getting enough physical exercise, snacking inappropriately, and postponing homework and chores until later in the evening. She suggested as alternatives programs for preparing children for self-care, "neighborhood mothers," activities in or near the school, and expanded child care in schools or businesses. In addition, Peterson provided a checklist for ensuring that the home is secure from strangers, fire, and poisoning and for the safe use of equipment.

Society has generally felt that being a latchkey child negatively affects the child's development. Peterson and Magrab (1989) pointed out that some indict "working mothers" for leaving their children but that communities must recognize the changing values and lifestyles of the present and find ways to support working families. Research by Lovko and Ullman (1989) comparing latchkey children with others indicated no differences in levels of anxiety, social ability, or behavior problems. Any variance in the two groups' adjustment levels was accounted for by the demographic and background variables of sex, income, and interaction with other children. The researchers were quick to point out their study's limitations and suggest that adjustment depends on many variables still not clearly defined.

Counseling with latchkey children may include listening for fears and anxieties about being left alone and helping the child cope with these feelings. The child may have concerns about what to say when the phone or doorbell rings, who will care for the child if he or she gets hurt or sick, or what to do about boredom or loneliness. Group discussions with role play provide an opportunity for children to voice their concerns and to practice appropriate techniques for answering the door or phone, reacting to emergency and nonemergency situations, and coping with other problems that may arise.

## CHILDREN AND VIOLENCE

In a 1993 commentary (Graves, Zuckerman, Marans, & Cohen), the *Journal of the American Medical Association (JAMA)* reported that more than 90% of a sample of New Orleans elementary school children had seen violence—70% had seen weapons used and 40% had seen a dead body. Los Angeles researchers believed that children see from 10% to 20% of the homicides committed in that city. In Boston, 10% of children at a Boston City Hospital clinic had seen a stabbing or shooting before the age of 6 years. James and Gilliland (2001) pondered the reasons for violence in schools and listed multiple causes: poor parenting, disenfranchised students, lack of role models, hate crimes, bullying, media violence, and others.

Despite medical or psychiatric causes of violence and violence that may be associated with war, poverty, oppression, or political rebellion, violence may also be learned in our culture. The *Harvard Mental Health Letter* ("Violence and Violent Patients," 1991) reported that children who watch a lot of television are more aggressive and see the world as more violent than it is. In another article in this same newsletter, Comstock (1990) concluded from research on the effects of television violence that numerous studies have clearly shown a relationship between television violence and aggression, especially in boys. Viewers are more apt to become less sensitive to violence and to begin to think of the world as more threatening. Grossman (1995) talked about the classical conditioning at work when one watches mayhem on television, operant conditioning at video games that reward killing and maiming, and social learning with models such as Freddie Kruger, who slashes throats.

The writers of the *JAMA* commentary on children and violence (1993) suggested that children need an opportunity to talk about the violence they witness and that mental health professionals should obtain specialized training to treat children who witness violence and experience symptoms of stress. They also urged society to ensure a safe environment for children to grow and develop.

Osofsky (1995) surveyed children and mothers exposed to violence and found that there is an impact on young children, even though they may not verbalize their feelings. Young children exposed to violence are more apt to exhibit nonverbal reactions such as behavioral or adjustment problems, which may be the result of witnessing violence or of parental fears of violence and severely limit the child's activities.

School-aged children exposed to violence often experience anxiety, have sleep disturbances, have difficulty paying attention and concentrating, and are less likely to explore and play freely. Soriano, Soriano, and Jimenez (1994) pointed out that the chances of children becoming victims of violent crime are greater than being hurt in a traffic accident, and youth of color are at greater risk. These writers suggested that racism, classism, sexism, and racial privilege are related to school violence and are influenced by socioeconomic variables such as poverty, lack of affordable housing and health care, adult joblessness, overcrowded schools, racial stereotypes, and economic exclusion.

The increasing incidence of juvenile violence, particularly in school settings, is becoming an issue of growing concern across the nation. The Center to Prevent Handgun Violence estimates that more than 100,000 youths take guns to school each day (Pietrzak, Petersen, & Speaker, 1998). Morrissey (1998) cited March 1998 statistics from the National Center for Education Statistics indicating that 57% of 1,234 public schools surveyed last year reported at least one crime incident and that 10% reported at least one serious crime incident (defined as murder, sexual assault, suicide, physical attack with a weapon, or robbery). Fifty-nine percent of these incidents occurred in urban schools and 41% in rural schools. It was suggested that rural schools have fewer problems than urban, but they also are underserved in terms of their services for families and children. The 1999 incidents of violence in Arkansas, Mississippi, Kentucky, Pennsylvania, Oregon, Texas, Oklahoma, and other states appear to support the contention that problems exist in rural American schools as well as in urban settings.

Hunter (1999) pointed out that a potentially violent child is not always a child who continually acts out in an aggressive manner. He described the young person at the bottom of the social ladder—the "geek" or "nerd" who is the brunt of jokes over the years. One day he brings a gun to school and threatens to kill anyone who comes near him. Hunter contends that abuse has been going on for months or years—and that teachers, administrators, and students knew. They just did not act to help this young person.

Stephans (1994) reported that many educational professionals believe that the increase in school violence is not due to the educational process but reflects factors such as societal changes, the breakdown of the family unit, and role modeling of violence in the media. The 10 things perceived as being the most likely contributors to the rise in violence were lack of rules or family structure, lack of parental supervision and involvement, modeling parental acting-out behavior, drug and alcohol abuse, violence in movies, violence on television, student poor self-esteem or emotional disturbance, gang activities, violent games, and changes in the traditional family. However, Pietrzak, Petersen, and Speaker (1998) found in their survey of elementary and middle school personnel that those responding not only feared students but also feared their parents. Thirty-two percent indicated they were worried about verbal threats and attacks from students' parents, and 21% were concerned or very concerned.

McRary (1998) interviewed Helen Smith, who at that time was writing *Killer Kids: Why Kids Kill and What We Can Do to Stop It*. Smith indicated that youth who kill feel deeply alienated, believe no one cares about them, and feel that no one else has rights. Smith suggested that it is not because these young people have low self-esteem that they kill, but rather they kill because they have inflated self-esteem and blame everyone but themselves for problems. Smith cautioned that warning signs show up as early as the preschool years and suggested looking for signs such as head banging and screaming uncontrollably, fire setting or a fascination with fire, and torturing or killing animals.

Dealing with violence as a result of societal change may require that the role of the school be reexamined, according to Pietrzak, Petersen, and Speaker (1998). They suggested that the school may need to take a more central role in the socialization of many children, including parent education programs, parent involvement activities, before- and after-school programs, and use of the school as the center of community services for families and children.

Morrissey (1998) reported that schools often contact the National School Safety Center for assistance after a violent incident. The officials of this center make the following recommendations, according to Morrissey (1998):

- Establish clear behavior standards.
- Provide adequate adult presence and supervision.
- Enforce the rules fairly and consistently.
- Supervise closely and sanction offenders consistently.
- Cultivate parental support.
- Control campus access.
- Create partnerships with outside agencies.
- Believe they can make a difference. (p. 36)

Hiring security guards and installing metal detectors and surveillance cameras is not seen as particularly effective in preventing violence. The Schools Without Violence program developed by the International Alliance for Invitational Education and codirected by William Purkey has reported success with its program focusing on the five Ps that make up a school system—processes, programs, places, people, and policies. According to Purkey (in Morrissey, 1998), the goal of the program is to make school a more exciting, satisfying, and enriching experience for all.

Morrissey's article summarized suggestions from a 1996 publication of the U.S. Department of Justice, Office of Juvenile Justice and Delinquency Prevention, entitled "Creating Safe and Drug-Free Schools: An Action Guide." The publication urged a partnership between school and community leaders and enumerates the following "essential ingredients for creating safe, orderly, drug-free schools":

- Make school safety a high priority on the educational agenda.
- Involve parents and citizens in the planning, implementation, and evaluation of the plan.
- Build and develop a team that includes parents, educators, students, law enforcers, community and business leaders, probation and court representatives, social service and health care providers, and other youth-serving agencies.
- Assess specific issues and concerns important to the community.
- Review the law to make sure legal issues are addressed correctly.
- Develop a safe school action plan outlining the processes and objectives necessary to achieve the goals.
- Create a backup plan for crises and emergencies.
- Engage students in developing and implementing solutions.
- Communicate the message in a variety of ways.
- Evaluate and modify the plan as necessary.

Osofsky (1995) offered public policy initiatives for dealing with children and violence. She recommended a national campaign to change attitudes toward violence and tolerance of violent behaviors that would require politicians and media leaders to cooperate in bringing about change. In addition, she recommended a family- and community-centered approach to addressing violence prevention and additional education about the negative effects of violence and the dangers of firearms.

In addition to treatment, children need the tools to resolve their difficulties without resorting to violent behavior. Children who learn problem-solving skills or conflict resolution are less impulsive and aggressive and tend to be more rational and patient. The basic principles of conflict resolution are similar to the problem-solving strategies described previously: Listen objectively to the other person, identify the problem, brainstorm for alternatives, agree on common grounds, and find a win–win solution. Most programs discuss the nature of the conflicts encountered by children, incorporate rules for attacking the problem (not the person) and treating others with respect, and emphasize accepting responsibility for one's behavior. Participants may also discuss issues related to diversity, power, and anger control. Role plays, simulations, stories, and discussions provide practice for children in learning the new skills required for conflict resolution.

Peer mediators are sometimes trained to facilitate the conflict-resolution process. Lane and McWhirter (1992) described a peer mediation model for elementary and middle school children with 19 steps for the mediation. Peer mediators learn very specific actions concerning introductions, listening, ascertaining "wants," and finding solutions. Peer mediators are trained in the steps and must make a complete report of all interactions at the completion of the process.

Johnson and Johnson (1994) believed that all students should learn to negotiate and mediate and have the experience of serving as a mediator. They cited studies showing that conflict-resolution and mediation training result in fewer student–

student conflicts and increased student management of their conflicts witout adult intervention.

Johnson and Johnson (1996) conducted a comprehensive review of the literature describing conflict resolution and peer mediation programs in elementary and secondary schools. They described the types of programs found: those that train a small number of students or the total student body to be mediators; conflict resolution programs that are preventive and curriculum based, designed to teach students alternatives to violent behavior; conflict resolution and peer mediation programs that teach students interpersonal and small-group skills to resolve conflicts; academically oriented programs that teach the cognitive skills necessary for conflict resolution; and structural change approaches that emphasize team building in the school. The most common types of conflicts addressed in these programs were verbal harassment, arguments, rumors and gossip, physical fights, and dating and relationship issues. Although they found methodological problems with the research reviewed, they concluded that "conflict resolution and peer mediation programs do seem to be effective in teaching students integrative negotiation and mediation procedures. After training, students tend to use these conflict strategies, and constructive outcomes tend to result" (p. 498).

Carruthers, Sweeney, Kmitta, and Harris (1996) also reviewed the literature on conflict resolution programs. They found reports of higher levels of student academic performance associated with the integration of conflict resolution principles and practices into the curriculum, learned prosocial attitudes, and the generalization of skills in actual conflict situations. While admitting there are theoretical and methodological problems with many studies, the writers encouraged practitioners to continue to conduct limited studies. They concluded that many researchers sharing their results will yield useful information that can add to the understanding of the field.

Messing (1993) cautioned that "mediation is not a replacement for short-term counseling or crisis intervention" (p. 71) but suggested that it can be used in addition to counseling "in situations when there is not a great imbalance of power between parties or when there is no clear right and wrong position or a serious crime has not been committed" (p. 71).

## GANGS*

Parks (1995) suggested that gang-related behavior is a "major sub-problem" of the youth violence issue but admitted that there is little empirical evidence for a causal relationship between school violence and youth gang-related behaviors. Although it is difficult to determine the number of gangs in the United States because there is no agreement on a definition of gangs and limited research in the area, Parks estimated there are approximately 1,439 gangs and about 1.5 million

*Sincere appreciation is expressed to Donna Maxwell Casteel, the University of Tennessee, for her contribution to the material on gangs and gang membership.

members in 2,100 American towns and cities with a population of 10,000 or more. James and Gilliland (2001) announced that gangs are in all geographic locales, all socioeconomic environments, and all ethnicities. They describe five types of gangs. The homegrown copycats and wannabes constitute one type. Another type is the homegrown survivalist, Aryan nation, neo-Nazi, or extreme right-wingers based on political and/or religious philosophies. Transients from a mega-gang are offshoots from large metropolitan groups who have relocated. Mega-gangs opening new territory may occur when the groups try to find new territory to sell their drugs or other wares. Finally, James and Gillilard discuss the small gangs, started for a variety of reasons, which the authors call smorgasbord home-boys.

Strong (1998) believed that critical socioeconomic factors encourage the development of gangs: (1) the erosion of the family, including growth in the number of teen parents, no family or social support systems available to the young person, and the development of values from the media; (2) community depersonalization, or the loss of community attachment and sense of responsibility; (3) and economic malaise, resulting in poverty and hopelessness. Strong contended that society must focus on risk factors predictive of gang involvement; encourage "protective factors" such as positive relationships with family, teachers, and other adults; and intervene early with multiple prevention and intervention strategies.

Scheidlinger (1994) has studied adolescent group violence since the 1960s. He found that adolescent peer groups differ today from the organized crime of the past, in which group loyalty was common. Today, group identity is lacking, which Scheidlinger attributes to deindividuation caused by a lack of self-awareness and of self-inhibition. Scheidlinger contended that preventive intervention efforts may be difficult because of this deindividuation, as well as the other psychological factors present in these groups.

The Tennessee Law Enforcement Training Academy (Welch, 1997) profiled the typical gang member, focusing on both individual and cultural characteristics. They found that the average gang member came from a single-parent or unstable family structure, received no discipline or overly harsh discipline in the home, had poor relationships with parents and peers, could not express emotion appropriately, achieved poorly in school and in other endeavors, had a history of abuse, and was usually average or above average in intelligence.

Nawojczyk (1998) cautioned parents that they should be concerned about their child's involvement with gangs if he or she:

- buys or is obsessed with one particular color of clothing or shows a desire for a particular logo
- wears sagging pants
- wears excessive jewelry and distinctive designs and wears them only on the right or left side of the body
- is obsessed with gangster-influenced music, videos, and movies and imitates talk or lifestyle observed through media
- withdraws from family with an accompanying attitude change

- associates with undesirables and breaks curfew rules
- develops an unusual desire for privacy and secrecy about peers
- uses hand signs or there is evidence of peculiar drawings or language on school books, clothing, or the body
- has unexplained cash or goods, such as clothing and jewelry
- possibly uses alcohol and drugs with attitude change

Obviously, parents and teachers should look for these signs as a part of an overall behavior pattern—their consistency and numbers. A student wearing baggy pants to school one day may means his pants were purchased a size too big or that he prefers that style, rather than that he is a gang member.

Parks (1995) reviewed the literature on school-related gangs and reported that gangs operate at every level of school, including at the elementary level. She found that a newly developed form of gang activity revolved around providing "protection" from threats or assaults—giving "permission" to enter or leave the school or pass through an area or to use a certain school facility, which is extortion. Arthur and Erickson (1992) reported that school gang activities include drug sales and use, graffiti to indicate "owned" territory, roaming of hallways, class disruptions, assaults (especially on female students), and possession of weapons.

Wang (1994) attempted to determine if self-esteem and prejudice were related to gang membership. He hypothesized that gang members would have lower self-esteem and display greater ethnocentrism and that the absence of a parental role model would influence gang membership. Wang found that gang members of Caucasian and African American groups had lower levels of self-esteem than the control group, that ethnicity alone is not an indicator of self-esteem, that gang members were not more prejudiced than non-gang members, and that the best predictor of gang membership, particularly among the youth of ethnic minorities, was the absence of a parental role model.

Bender and Leone (1996) interviewed leaders and others who worked with youth and gangs. Among the opinions expressed about how street gangs can be controlled were to send a message to youth that violence never resolves issues and to the general society to unite against "thugs," eradicate poverty and despair by providing jobs and other opportunities, toughen laws on gangs while providing support for victims and protection for witnesses, utilize data-tracking systems, intercede in schools and communities, and pass laws dealing with specific gang problems.

Another person interviewed by Bender and Leane opposed toughening laws and advocated prosecuting the crime because of the broad and vague definition of gangs and suggested that a return to high principles and moral responsibility was necessary. Still another person interviewed made a strong argument for guiding and empowering youth in order to overcome their need to join a gang. The differing opinions found in these interviews underscore the conclusion that society does not know enough about gangs to be able to develop effective prevention and intervention programs (Bender & Leone, 1996). The best solution may be different for differing groups and may require a combination of techniques working together.

Suggestions for controlling gangs include creating a more culturally relevant structure and curriculum for students, encouraging in-school gang mediation programs, and offering after-school activities as alternatives to gang membership (Parks, 1995). Parks recommended obtaining community agreement about the nature of gang incidents and organizing external advisory groups from the community, including religious organizations. Parks also believed that parents, families, and teachers must be involved as reinforcing groups in order to change gang behavior. They need instruction in understanding, monitoring, and correcting violent behavior.

Strong (1998) suggested similar procedures for addressing gang behavior. He recommended providing experiences to promote understanding of other cultures and values, developing conflict resolution or peer mediation procedures to handle conflict, providing training about gang issues for parents, encouraging involvement in the gang reduction program, developing reentry programs for suspended students that provide structure and positive role models, and avoiding the use of fear or intimidation tactics with individuals in gangs.

Huesman (1994) doubted the effectiveness of prevention programs. He looked at programs in 60 cities reporting gang activity and found that most were ineffective. Huesman attributed this lack of effectiveness to the failure of the programs to implement an actual intervention plan, a lack of intensity, a lack of follow-through between procedures and outcomes, a lack of individualization, and a lack of comprehensiveness. Huesman concluded that comprehensive program planning was necessary to deal with the current problems and that it must be individualized to meet specific needs. Active input from previous gang members was crucial to understanding the need for youth's involvement with gangs.

James and Gilliland (2001) touted the SARA (scanning, analysis, response, assessment) model. This program involves people such as parents, service clubs, businesses, churches, the justice system, and other community agencies and organizations. They trade information and work for change in the school and the community. They begin by identifying problems and publicizing their findings. The information is analyzed and presented in concrete, measurable terms. The response phase involves developing options based on the gathered information and selecting and implementing a response. The phase of assessment gauges the effectiveness of the response. The comprehensive program may well lead to safer schools.

## W E B S I T E S for Counseling Children with Special Concerns

Children of divorce: All kinds of problems
www.divorcereform.org/all.html

National Benevolent Association Tennyson Center for Children at Colorado Christian Home
www.childabuse.org

Parent News—General News, Articles and Links for Parents
www.parentnews.com

The National Association for Children of Alcoholics (NACoA)
www.nacoa.org

# REFERENCES

Arthur, R., & Erickson, E. (1992). *Gangs and schools.* Holmes Beach, FL: Learning Publications.

Beautrais, A. L. (2000). Risk factors for suicide and attempted suicide among young people. *Australian and New Zealand Journal of Psychiatry, 34,* 420–436.

Belsky, J. (1993). Etiology of child maltreatment: A developmental-ecological analysis. *Psychological Bulletin, 114,* 413–434.

Bender, D., & Leone, B. (1996). How can street gangs be controlled? In C. Cozic (Ed.), *Gangs: Opposing viewpoints* (pp. 91–131). San Diego, CA: Greenhaven.

Berk, L. E. (2001). *Development through the lifespan* (2nd ed.). Boston: Allyn & Bacon.

Black, C. (1981). Innocent bystanders at risk: The children of alcoholics. In G. Lawson, J. Peterson, & A. Lawson (Eds.), *Alcoholism and the family.* Rockville, MD: Aspen.

Brake, K. (1988). Counseling young children of alcoholics. *Elementary School Guidance and Counseling, 23,* 106–111.

Campo, A., & Rohner, R. (1992). Relationships between perceived parental acceptance–rejection, psychological adjustment, and substance abuse among young adults. *Child Abuse and Neglect, 16,* 429–440.

Carruthers, W., Sweeney, B., Kmitta, D., & Harris, G. (1996). Conflict resolution: An examination of the research literature and a model for program evaluation. *School Counselor, 44,* 5–18.

Chalk, R., Gibbons, A., & Scarupa, H. J. (2002, May). The multiple dimensions of child abuse and neglect: New insights into an old problem, [Electronic version]. *Child Trends Research Brief.* www.childtrends.org/PDF/ChildAbuseRB.pdf. Retrieved August 6, 2002.

Child abuse, parts I and II. (1993, special supplement). *Harvard Mental Health Letter,* 1–6.

Child Trends. (2002). Child Trends Data Bank. http://www.childtrendsdatabank.org/health. Retrieved August 6, 2002.

Clifford, M. (1994). Social work treatment with children, adolescents, and families exposed to religious and satanic cults. *Social Work in Health Care, 20,* 35–59.

Coleman, M., & Ganong, L. (1995). Insiders' and outsiders' beliefs about stepfamilies: Assessment and implications for practice. In D. Huntley (Ed.), *Understanding stepfamilies: Implications for assessment and treatment* (pp. 101–112). Alexandria, VA: American Counseling Association.

Comstock, G. (1990). Television violence: Is there enough evidence that it is harmful? *Harvard Medical School Mental Health Letter, 6,* 8.

Costa, L., & Holliday, D. (1994). Helping children cope with the death of a parent. *Elementary School Guidance and Counseling, 28,* 206–213.

Crosbie-Burnett, M., & Pulvino, C. (1990). Children in nontraditional families: A classroom guidance program. *School Counselor, 37,* 286–293.

Dail, P. (1990). The psychosocial context of homeless mothers with young children: Program and policy implications. *Child Welfare League of America, 69,* 291–307.

Daniels, J. (1992). Empowering homeless children through school counseling. *Elementary School Guidance and Counseling, 27,* 104–112.

Depression in children, part I. (2002). *Harvard Mental Health Letter, 18,* 1–4.

Doweiko, H. E. (1999). *Concepts of chemical dependency* (4th ed.). Pacific Grove, CA: Brooks/Cole.

Downey, D. (1994). The school performance of children from single mother and single father families: Economic or interpersonal deprivation? *Journal of Family Issues, 15,* 129–147.

Edgeworth, J., & Carr, A. (2000). Child abuse. In A. Carr (Ed.), *What works with children and adolescents? A critical review of psychological interventions with children, adolescents and their families* (pp. 17–48). Philadelphia: Brunner-Routledge.

Emslie, G. (1997). Children and depression. *Treatment Today, 9,* 10–11.

Ferquist, R. M. (2000). Problem drinking in the family and youth suicide. *Adolescence, 35,* 551–559.

Freeman, S. J. (2001). Death and bereavement. In E. R. Welfel & R. E. Ingersoll (Eds.), *The mental health desk reference* (pp. 38–43). New York: Wiley.

Gately, D., & Schwebel, A. (1992). Favorable outcomes in children after parental divorce. In *Divorce and the next generation.* Binghamton, NY: Haworth.

Glover, J. (1994). The hero child in the alcoholic home: Recommendations for counselors. *School Counselor, 41,* 185–190.

Graves, B., Zuckerman, B., Marans, S., & Cohen, D. (1993). Silent victims: Children who witness violence (commentary). *Journal of the American Medical Association 269,* 262–264.

Green, A. (1993). Child sexual abuse: Immediate and long-term effects and intervention. *Journal of the American Academy of Child and Adolescent Psychiatry, 32,* 890–902.

Greene, D. (1994). Childhood suicide and myths surrounding it. *Social Work, 39,* 145–147.

Grossman, D. (1995). *On killing: The psychological cost of learning to kill in war and society.* Boston: Little, Brown.

Grych, J., & Fincham, F. (1992). Interventions for children of divorce: Toward greater integration of research and action. *Psychological Bulletin, 111,* 434–454.

Hart, S. (1991). Childhood depression: Implications and options for school counselors. *Elementary School Guidance and Counseling, 25,* 277–289.

Herring, R. (1993). Suicide in the middle school: Who said kids will not? *Elementary School Guidance and Counseling, 25,* 129–137.

Hetherington, E., Cox, M., & Cox, R. (1978). Play and social interaction in children following divorce. *Journal of Social Issues, 35,* 26–49.

Holmes, K. (1995, January 16). Hare Krishna movement faces loss of the young faithful. *The Philadelphia Inquirer,* B1, B5.

Huesman, R. (1994). *Aggressive behavior.* New York: Plenum.

Hunter, D. (1999, March 2). There are deeper reasons why kids bring weapons to school. *Knoxville News-Sentinel,* A7.

Jacobsen, I., Rabinowitz, I., Popper, M., Solomon, R., Sokol, M., & Pfeffer, C. (1994). Interviewing prepubertal children about suicidal ideation and behavior. *Journal of the American Academy of Child and Adolescent Psychiatry, 33,* 439–452.

James, R. K., & Gilliland, B. E. (2001). *Crisis intervention strategies* (4th ed.). Pacific Grove, CA: Brooks/Cole.

James, S. H., & Burch, K. M. (1999). School counselors' roles in cases of child sexual behavior. *Professional School Counseling, 2,* 211–217.

Johnson, C. (1990). Inflicted injury versus accidental injury. *Pediatric Clinics of North America, 37,* 791–814.

Johnson, D., & Johnson, R. (1994). Constructive conflict in the schools. *Journal of Social Issues, 50,* 117–137.

Johnson, D., & Johnson, R. (1996). Conflict resolution and peer mediation programs in elementary and secondary schools: A review of the research. *Review of Educational Research, 66,* 459–506.

Jones, D., & Houts, R. (1992). Parental drinking, parent–child communication, and social skills in young adults. *Journal of Studies on Alcohol, 53,* 48–56.

Jones, J. W. (1985). *Children of Alcoholics Screening Test.* Chicago: Camelot Unlimited.

Kantrowitz, B., & Wingert, P. (1990, Winter-Spring). Step by step. *Newsweek special issue, 114,* 24–28.

Kübler-Ross, E. (1969). *On death and dying.* New York: Macmillan.

Kurtz, P., Gaudin, J., Wodarski, J., & Howing, P. (1993). Maltreatment and the school aged child: School performance consequences. *Child Abuse and Neglect, 17,* 581–589.

Lane, P. S., & McWhirter, J. J. (1992). A peer mediation model: Conflict resolution for elementary and middle school children. *Elementary School Guidance and Counseling, 27,* 15–24.

Langone, M. D., & Eisenberg, G. (1993). Children and cults. In M. D. Langone, (Ed.), *Recovery from cults: Help for victims of psychological and spiritual abuse* (pp. 327–342). New York: W. W. Norton.

Loftus, E. (1993). The reality of repressed memories. *American Psychologist, 48,* 518–537.

Lovko, A., & Ullman, D. (1989). Research on the adjustment of latchkey children: Role of background/demographic and latchkey situation variables. *Journal of Clinical Child Psychology, 18,* 16–24.

Malcarne, V. L., & Burchard, J. D. (1992). Investigations of child abuse/neglect allegations in religious cults: A case study in Vermont. *Behavioral Sciences and the Law, 10,* 75–88.

Masten, A., Miliotis, D., Graham-Bermann, S., Ramirez, M., & Neemann, J. (1993). Children in homeless families: Risks to mental health and development. *Journal of Consulting and Clinical Psychology, 61,* 335–341.

McConnell, A. R., & Sim, A. J. (2000). Evaluating an innovative counseling service for children of divorce. *British Journal of Guidance and Counselling, 28,* 75–87.

McRary, A. (1998, June 18). Kids who kill: Psychologist says watch for warning signs. *Knoxville News-Sentinel,* B1–2.

Mellin, E. A., & Beamish, P. M. (2002). Interpersonal theory and adolescents with depression: Clinical update. *Journal of Mental Health Counseling, 24,* 110–126.

Messing, J. (1993). Mediation: An intervention for counselors. *Journal of Counseling and Development, 72,* 67–71.

Miller-Perrin, C. L. (2001). Child maltreatment: Treatment of child and adolescent victims. In E. R. Welfel & R. E. Ingersoll (Eds.), *The mental health desk reference* (pp. 169–176). New York: Wiley.

Moeller, T., Bachmann, G., & Moeller, J. (1993). The combined effects of physical, sexual, and emotional abuse during childhood: Long-term health consequences for women. *Child Abuse and Neglect, 17,* 623–640.

Moore, M., & Carr, A. (2000). Depression and grief. In A. Carr (Ed.), *What works with children and adolescents? A critical review of psychological interventions with children, adolescents and their families* (pp. 203–232). Philadelphia: Brunner-Routledge.

Morrissey, M. (1998). Mitigating school violence requires a system-wide effort. *Counseling Today, 40,* 36–37.

Muro, J., & Kottman, T. (1995). *Guidance and counseling in the elementary and middle school: A practical approach.* Dubuque, IA: Brown & Benchmark.

National Coalition for the Homeless. (1998). NCH fact sheet #3: Who is homeless? www.nationalhomeless.org/who.html. Retrieved August 6, 2002.

Nawojczyk, S. (1998, Winter). Warning signs of possible gang involvement. *Help & hope: News for the at-risk professional.* Public interest video, Cardiff, CA.

Nelson, R., & Crawford, B. (1990). Suicide among elementary school-aged children. *Elementary School Guidance and Counseling, 25,* 123–128.

Oehmen, S. (1985). Divorce and grief: Counseling and the child. *Elementary School Guidance and Counseling, 19,* 314–317.

O'Halloran, C., & Altmaier, E. (1996). Awareness of death among children: Does a life threatening illness alter the process of discovery? *Journal of Counseling and Development, 74,* 259–262.

O'Rourke, K. (1990). Recapturing hope: Elementary school support groups for children of alcoholics. *Elementary School Guidance and Counseling, 25,* 107–115.

O'Rourke, K., & Worzbyt, J. (1996). Coping with death, grief and loss. In *Support Groups for Children* (pp. 301–343). Washington, DC: Accelerated Development.

Osofsky, J. (1995). The effects of exposure to violence on young children. *American Psychologist, 50,* 782–788.

Papernow, P. (1995). What's going on here? Separating (and weaving together) step and clinical issues in remarried families. In D. Huntley (Ed.), *Understanding stepfamilies: Implications for assessment and treatment.* (pp. 3–24). Alexandria, VA: American Counseling Association.

Parks, C. (1995). Gang behavior in the schools: Reality or myth? *Educational Psychology Review, 7,* 41–68.

Peterson, L. (1989). Latchkey children's preparation for self-care: Overestimated, under rehearsed, and unsafe. *Journal of Clinical Child Psychology, 18,* 36–43.

Peterson, L., & Magrab, P. (1989). Introduction to the special section: Children on their own. *Journal of Clinical Child Psychology, 18,* 2–7.

Piaget, J. & Inhelder, B. (1969). *The psychology of the child.* New York: Basic Books.

Pidcock, B., Fischer, J. L., Forthun, L. F., & West, S. (2000). Hispanic and Anglo college women's risk factors for substance use and eating disorders. *Addictive Behaviors: An International Journal, 25,* 705–723.

Pietrzak, D., Petersen, G., & Speaker, K. (1998). Perceptions of school violence by elementary and middle school personnel. *Professional School Counseling, 1,* 23–29.

Popenhagen, M., & Qualley, R. (1998). Adolescent suicide: Detection, intervention, and prevention. *Professional School Counseling, 1,* 30–35.

Rafferty, Y. (1995). The legal rights and educational problems of homeless children and youth. *Educational Evaluation and Policy Analysis, 17,* 39–61.

Ratican, K. (1992). Sexual abuse survivors: Identifying symptoms and special treatment considerations. *Journal of Counseling and Development, 71,* 33–38.

Reich, W., Earls, F., Frankel, O., & Shayka, J. (1993). Psychopathology in children of alcoholics. *Journal of the American Academy of Child and Adolescent Psychiatry, 32,* 995–1002.

Richards, L., & Schmiege, C. (1993). Problems and strengths of single-parent families: Implications for practice and policy. *Family Relations, 42,* 277–285.

Roberts, W. Jr. (1995). Postvention and psychological autopsy in the suicide of a 14-year-old public school student. *School Counselor, 42,* 322–330.

Rudin, M. (1990). Cults and Satanism: Threats to teens. *NASSP Bulletin, 74,* 46–52.

SAMHSA's National Mental Health Information Center, The Center for Mental Health Services (1997). Major depression in children and adolescents. www.mentalhealth.org/publications/allpubs/CA-0011/default.asp. Retrieved August 5, 2002.

Scheidlinger, S. (1994). A commentary on adolescent group violence. *Child Psychiatry and Human Development, 24,* 3–10.

Schellenbach, C. J. (1998). Child maltreatment: A critical review of research on treatment for physically abusive parents. In P. K. Trickett & C. J. Schellenbach (Eds.), *Violence against children in the family and the community* (pp. 251–268). Washington, DC: American Psychological Association.

Schmitz, C., Wagner, J., & Menke, E. (1995). Homelessness as one component of housing instability and its impact on the development of children in poverty. *Journal of Social Distress and the Homeless, 4,* 301–317.

Schoen, C., & Davis, K. I. (1998). *The health of adolescent boys: Commonwealth Fund survey findings.* New York: Commonwealth Fund.

Schwartz, L. L. (2001). The cult phenomenon: A turn of the century update. *American Journal of Family Therapy, 29,* 13–23.

Seilhamer, R., Jacob, T., & Dunn, N. (1993). The impact of alcohol consumption on parent–child relationships in families of alcoholics. *Journal of Studies on Alcohol, 54,* 189–193.

Sher, K. (1991). *Children of alcoholics.* Chicago: University of Chicago Press.

Siehl, P. (1990). Suicide postvention: A new disaster plan—What a school should do when faced with a suicide. *School Counselor, 38,* 52–57.

Soriano, M., Soriano, F., & Jimenez, E. (1994). School violence among culturally diverse populations: Sociocultural and institutional considerations. *School Psychology Review, 23,* 216–235.

Stefanowski-Harding, S. (1990). Suicide and the school counselor. *School Counselor, 37,* 328–336.

Stephans, R. (1994, January 15). Gangs, guns and school violence. *USA Today,* A7.

Strawser, S., Markos, P. A., Yamaguchi, B. J., & Higgins, K. (2000). A new challenge for school counselors: Children who are homeless. *Professional School Counseling, 3,* 162–172.

Strong, K. (1998). *Gangs and schools.* Presentation to the Governor's Conference for a Safe and Drug-Free Tomorrow, Nashville, Tennessee.

Tonkins, A., & Lambert, M. (1996) A treatment outcome study of bereavement groups for children. *Child and Adolescent Social Work Journal, 13,* 3–21.

U.S. Census Bureau. (1998). U.S. Census Bureau: The Official Statistics. www.census.gov/hhes/poverty/poverty96/pv96estl.html. Retrieved September 13, 2002.

U.S. Department of Health and Human Services. (1996). HHS releases new statistics on child abuse and neglect as child abuse and neglect prevention month begins. www.hhs.gov/news/press/1996pres/96041a.html. Retrieved March 3, 2003.

U.S. Department of Health and Human Services, Administration on Children, Youth, and Families. (2000). *Child maltreatment 1998: Reports from the states to the National Child Abuse and Neglect Data System.* Washington, DC: U.S. Government Printing Office.

Violence and violent patients: part 1. (1991). *Harvard Mental Health Letter, 7,* 1–4.

Visher, E., & Visher, J. (1995). Avoiding the mind fields of stepfamily therapy. In E. Huntley (Ed.), *Understanding step-families: Implications for assessment and treatment* (pp. 25–34). Alexandria, VA: American Counseling Association.

Vostanis, P., Tischler, V., Cumella, S., & Bellerby, T. (2001). Mental health problems and social supports among homeless mothers and children victims of domestic and community violence. *International Journal of Social Psychiatry, 47,* 30–41.

Wallerstein, J. (1983). Children of divorce: The psychological tasks of the child. *American Journal of Orthopsychiatry, 53,* 230–243.

Wallerstein, J. (1984). Children of divorce: Ten-year follow-up of young children. *American Journal of Orthopsychiatry, 54,* 444–458.

Wallerstein, J., & Blakeslee, S. (1989). *Second chances.* New York: Ticknor & Fields.

Wallerstein, J., & Kelly, J. (1980). *Surviving the breakup: How children and parents cope with divorce.* New York: Basic Books.

Wang, A. (1994). Pride and prejudice in high school gang members. *Adolescence, 29,* 279–291.

Webb, B. (1993). Counseling and therapy for the bereaved child. In B. Webb (Ed.), *Helping bereaved children* (pp. 43–58). New York: Guilford.

Welch, J. (1997). *Street gangs and youth violence.* Presentation at the Tennessee Law Enforcement Training Academy, Nashville, Tennessee.

Wendel, P. (1997). Counseling children of divorce. *Counseling Today, 40,* 6, 35, 56.

Whitehead, B. (1993, April). Dan Quayle was right, [Electronic version]. *The Atlantic Monthly,* www.theatlantic.com/politics/family/danquayle.html. Retrieved September 13, 2002.

Wilson, J., & Blocher, L. (1990). The counselor's role in assisting children of alcoholics. *Elementary School Guidance and Counseling, 25,* 98–106.

Wise, A., & Spengler, P. (1997). Suicide in children younger than age fourteen: Clinical judgment and assessment issues. *Journal of Mental Health Counseling, 19,* 318–335.

Worden, J. (1996). *Children and grief.* New York: Guilford.

Yapko, M. (1993). Suggested guidelines for professional counselors. *Guidepost, 36,* 11.

Zeppa, A., & Norem, R. (1993). Stressors, manifestations of stress, and first-family/stepfamily group membership. *Journal of Divorce and Remarriage, 19,* 3–23.

# Chapter 19

# Counseling with Exceptional Children

*The miracle is not that we do this work, but that we are happy to do it.*
—Mother Teresa

## THE SITUATION OF THE EXCEPTIONAL CHILD

Exceptional children are different in some way from their peers. They deviate from what is considered to be normal or average in physical appearance, learning abilities, or behavior. They may be exceptionally gifted, or they may be exceptionally limited in their abilities to learn or to function in life. Unfortunately, many societies throughout history have not readily accepted people with disabilities and instead viewed them as evil omens, demons, or even witches. At one point in history, people with disabilities were court jesters or on display in public streets or parks. In our not-too-distant history, people with disabilities were hidden in institutions that provided inadequate care. During the Middle Ages especially, a mentally or physically "defective" person was often considered possessed by evil spirits. Some have felt that children with disabilities were God's punishment for the sins of the parents. Some Native American tribes murdered children who had disabilities; other tribes, however, worshiped them as gods, loving and protecting them. In recent years, society has been recognizing the special needs of these children and treating people with disabilities more humanely.

Society has placed more emphasis on meeting these children's physical, psychological, and educational needs in a nonrestrictive environment (outside an institution) and on providing support for the families through groups, associations, and legislation. Although all of us deviate from the average to some degree—in height or weight, introversion or extroversion, the amount of happiness or sadness in our lives—myths concerning exceptional individuals still pervade our society. These individuals continue to be stereotyped, shunned, rejected, pitied, or wrongfully institutionalized.

Smith (1998) believed the main question is more about the way exceptional people are treated, limiting their independence and opportunities. She suggested that "being handicapped" may be more the result of society's perceptions than most of us would like to accept. Smith cited as an example the English settlers from Kent who lived on Martha's Vineyard. Deafness was very prevalent among these settlers, but because the community was skilled in both oral and sign language, the deaf were integrated into all activities. As a result, a high percentage married both deaf and hearing partners and earned average or above-average incomes. No one perceived their deafness as a handicapping condition.

Too often, counseling with the exceptional child has been limited to assessment, assigning a vague diagnosis, and perhaps suggesting a prognosis. Parents and children then cope with the developmental and adjustment problems as best they can. Usually, the parents or children get no thorough explanation of the condition. They do not learn what to expect in terms of learning, social, or behavior problems, and counselors do not help the parents and children adjust to and cope with the handicapping condition. Doctors, nurses, teachers, and counselors are inadequately prepared to work with the problems of being different in a society that has little tolerance for and understanding of the different.

Being a special child presents problems to both the parents and the special child. Parents are confused about the disability. They have fears concerning their child's present and future life. They may experience feelings of guilt ("Did I cause this?"), self-pity ("Why did it have to happen to me?"), or even self-hate. Parents who are confronted with the fact that their child is disabled do not all react in the same manner.

Hardman, Drew, Egan, and Wolf (1993) suggested that most parents initially react with shock, which may be accompanied by feelings of anxiety, guilt, numbness, confusion, helplessness, anger, disbelief, or denial. Realization follows and may be characterized by self-pity or self-hate and withdrawal. The parent may enter a defensive retreat stage in order to avoid facing reality. When parents move on to the acknowledgment stage, they are able to participate in the treatment process and may even become advocates for the cause (Hardman et al., 1993). Parenting special children necessitates paying for medical specialists, diagnostic tests, special schools or teachers, and special therapies. It causes a strain on personal resources and family relationships. Often the children must have extra attention and care. The time and energy required may take away the pleasure that could be derived from relationships with husband or wife, other children, or friends.

What are the personal thoughts and concerns of the special child? From an early age, these children begin to realize they are different in some manner. This difference is often interpreted to mean "not as good as" other children. They cannot ride a bike like the kid next door; they look different from the child down the street; they do not understand jokes or what is going on in their surroundings; and they are not accepted by the gang and are called *weirdo, dumb, retard,* or a multitude of other hurtful names. Even gifted children bear the burden of nicknames such as *weirdo* or *brain* and may feel rejection because of their exceptionality. The same messages are sometimes subtly conveyed to the children by parents and other significant adults. From verbal and nonverbal signals and interactions, the children are soon assured by the world that being different means being odd, inferior, or worthless.

Growth and maturity bring special problems to both child and parents. Upon entering school, some exceptional children have academic problems. The child may compensate for problems by withdrawing from the school world physically or psychologically, or the child may become a behavior problem. After all, better that others think "I do not want to learn" than "I cannot learn." Social relationships may be a disaster; peers often do not understand the exceptionality. No one discusses exceptionalities with other children because society is uncomfortable with the idea of difference. This lack of understanding interferes with friendship, and classmates tend to isolate, reject, and taunt the special child. School can be a very painful place.

At home, things may not be much better, especially at report card time and when notes come home from the teacher or principal: "Johnny is not doing well in school; he must study harder." "Johnny is misbehaving in class; we simply cannot tolerate disruptive behavior." No one seems to understand that these learning and behavior problems may have underlying causes. Because most parents are ego involved with their children's academic achievement, they may pressure the child to study harder or behave more appropriately. Perhaps Johnny has been working hard but still cannot meet the expectations of parents and school. He may decide, "What's the use? I can't please them no matter how hard I try." Unless someone intervenes, society may have lost the opportunity to help Johnny become a productive citizen and a happy adult.

## HISTORY

Progress toward helping exceptional children become accepted members of society has been slow. The 1880s saw the first steps toward recognizing the needs of persons with disabilities: the establishment of the first schools for the deaf and the blind. In the mid-1930s, Congress passed the Crippled Children Act, authorizing financial aid to the families of people with orthopedic handicaps. President Franklin D. Roosevelt, whose polio caused him to be disabled, undoubtedly gave impetus to this legislation. President John F. Kennedy, who had a sister with mental retardation, urged that attention be given to children's developmental disabilities, including mental retardation and learning disabilities. In 1961, the President's Panel on Mental Retardation was established, and in 1963 the National Institute of Child Health and Human Development was founded. The child advocacy movement of the late 1960s and early 1970s resulted in the formation of the National Center for Child Advocacy. During the 1970s and 1980s, legislative appropriations and federal committees and agencies increased. In 1975, President Gerald Ford signed the Education for All Handicapped Children Act, Public Law 94-142. This law provided that all handicapped children receive free educational experiences designed to meet their particular needs. It described specific procedures for identification and placement and for designing educational programs for children with certain disabling conditions.

In 1977, the Education of the Handicapped Act was amended to define *learning disabilities,* and in 1978 the Gifted and Talented Children's Education Act provided money to states for planning, training, program development, and research. Amendments in 1983 extended the act to provide additional services to secondary school students and children from birth to 3 years. The Education for All Handicapped Children Act was renamed Individuals with Disabilities Education Act (IDEA) in 1990, and two new categories of disability were added: autism and traumatic brain injury (Hardman et al., 1993). The U.S. Department of Education (2001) reported that the number of students ages 6 to 21 with disabilities who received services under the IDEA was 5,683,707 in 1999–2000, 8.3% of the child population.

In 1990 President Bush extended the 1973 Rehabilitation Act (Section 504), which prohibited discrimination against qualified individuals in federally funded programs and protected the rights of students with disabilities to free and appropriate public education, when he signed the Americans with Disabilities Act (ADA), which prohibits discrimination against persons with disabilities in employment, transportation, public services, public accommodations, and telecommunications, regardless of federal funding (Hardman et al., 1993; Smith & Luckasson, 1995). Smith (1998) pointed out that Section 504 and ADA have a broader definition of disabilities than does the IDEA. Section 504 and the ADA provide the "right to accommodations" to qualified persons, whether or not they need special education. Henderson (2001) compared the purpose, eligibility requirements, educational implications, due process, placement, and evaluation procedures for the federal acts related to children with disabilities (Table 19-1).

Parette and Holder-Brown (1992) stated that counselor involvement with school-age children with disabilities is mandated by Public Law 94-142, now IDEA. They pointed out that counselors are required by law to participate with multidisciplinary teams to develop individualized educational plans (IEPs). Collaboration with families is required by Public Law 99-457 of the Education of the Handicapped Act (EHA) of 1986 to implement an individualized family service plan (IFSP).

## CATEGORIES OF EXCEPTIONALITY

A controversy exists over the categorizing or labeling of children. Many professionals believe that children who are so categorized may be permanently stigmatized, rejected, or prevented from developing in a healthy manner. These children, especially if they are minority children, may be assigned to inferior educational programs or institutionalized. Furthermore, classification of a child can encourage the behaviors characteristic of the label. On the other hand, classification may be necessary to obtain services for exceptional children. Children who do not neatly fit into categories may have trouble obtaining diagnostic services and treatment.

Smith (1998) differentiated "classification" and "labeling," stating that classification "refers to a structured system that identifies and organizes characteristics to establish order," whereas labeling "identifies individuals or groups according to a category assigned to them" (such as learning disabled) (pp. 10–11). Smith admitted that labeling can be stigmatizing and harmful but pointed out that it provides

*Text continued on p. 567*

TABLE 19-1   An overview of ADA, IDEA, and Section 504: update 2001

| *Americans with Disabilities Act of 1990 (ADA)* | *Individuals with Disabilities Education Act (IDEA), amended in 1997* | *Section 504 of the Rehabilitation Act of 1973* |
|---|---|---|
| | *Type/purpose* | |
| A civil rights law to prohibit discrimination solely on the basis of disability in employment, public services, and accommodations. | An education act to provide federal financial assistance to state and local education agencies to guarantee special education and related services to eligible children with disabilities. | A civil rights law to prohibit discrimination on the basis of disability in programs and activities, public and private, that receive federal financial assistance. |
| | *Who is eligible?* | |
| Any individual with a disability who (1) has a physical or mental impairment that substantially limits one or more life activities; or (2) has a record of such an impairment; or (3) is regarded as having such an impairment. Furthermore, the person must be qualified for the program, service, or job. | Children and youth aged 3 through 21 who are determined through an individualized evaluation and by a multidisciplinary team (including the parent) to be eligible in one or more of 13 categories and who need special education and related services. The categories are autism, deaf-blindness, deafness, emotional disturbance, hearing impairment, mental retardation, multiple disabilities, orthopedic impairment, other health impairment, specific learning disability, speech or language impairment, traumatic brain injury, and visual impairment including blindness. Children aged 3 through 9 experiencing developmental delays may also be eligible. Infants and toddlers from birth through age 2 may be eligible for early intervention services, delivered in accordance with an individualized family service plan. | Any person who (1) has a physical or mental impairment that substantially limits one or more major life activities, (2) has a record of such an impairment, or (3) is regarded as having such an impairment. Major life activities include caring for oneself, performing manual tasks, walking, seeing, hearing, speaking, breathing, learning, and working. The person must be qualified for the services or job; in the case of school services, the person must be of an age when nondisabled peers are typically served or be eligible under IDEA. |

*continued*

TABLE 19-1    An overview of ADA, IDEA, and Section 504: update 2001    *(Continued)*

| *Americans with Disabilities Act of 1990 (ADA)* | *Individuals with Disabilities Education Act (IDEA), amended in 1997* | *Section 504 of the Rehabilitation Act of 1973* |
|---|---|---|
| *Responsibility to provide a Free, Appropriate Public Education (FAPE)?* | | |
| Not directly. However, ADA provides additional protection in combination with actions brought under Section 504 and IDEA. ADA protections apply to nonsectarian private schools but not to organizations or entities controlled by religious organizations. Reasonable accommodations are required for eligible students with a disability to perform essential functions of the job. This applies to any part of the special education program that may be community based and involve job training/placement. Although not required, an individualized educational program (IEP) under IDEA will fulfill requirements of Title II of the ADA for an appropriate education for a student with disabilities. | Yes. A FAPE is defined to mean special education and related services that are provided at no charge to parents, meet other state educational standards, and are consistent with an IEP. Special education means "specially designed instruction, at no cost to the parents, to meet the unique needs of the child with a disability." Related services are those required to assist a child to benefit from special education, including speech–language pathology, physical and occupational therapy, and others. A team of professionals and parents develop and review at least annually, an IEP for each child with a disability. IDEA requires certain content in the IEP. | Yes. An "appropriate" education means an education comparable to that provided to students without disabilities. This may be regular or special education. Students can receive related services under Section 504 even if they are not provided any special education. These are to be provided at no additional cost to the child and his or her parents. Section 504 requires provision of educational and related aids and services that are designed to meet the individual educational needs of the child. The individualized educational program of IDEA may be used to meet the Section 504 requirement. |
| *Funding to implement requirements?* | | |
| No, but limited tax credits may be available for removing architectural or transportation barriers. Also, many federal agencies provide grants to public and private institutions to support | Yes. IDEA provides federal funds under parts B and C to assist state and local educational agencies in meeting IDEA requirements to serve infants, toddlers, children, and youth with disabilities. | No. State and local jurisdictions have responsibility. IDEA funds may not be used to serve children found eligible only under Section 504. |

*Procedural safeguards/due process*

The ADA does not specify procedural safeguards related to special education; it does not detail the administrative requirements, complaint procedures, and consequences for noncompliance related to both services and employment. The ADA also does not delineate specific due process procedures. People with disabilities have the same remedies that are available under Title VII of the Civil Rights Act of 1964, as amended by the Civil Rights Act of 1991. Thus, individuals who are discriminated against may file a complaint with the relevant federal agency or sue in federal court. Enforcement agencies encourage informal mediation and voluntary compliance.

IDEA provides for procedural safeguards and due process rights to parents in the identification, evaluation, and educational placement of their child. Prior written notice of procedural safeguards and of proposals or refusals to initiate or change identification, evaluation, or placement must be provided to parents. IDEA delineates the required components of these notices. Disputes may be resolved through mediation, impartial due process hearings, appeal of hearing decisions, and/or civil action.

Section 504 requires notice to parents regarding identification, evaluation, and placement, and before a "significant change" in placement. Written notice is recommended. Following IDEA procedural safeguards is one way to meet Section 504 mandates. Local education agencies are required to provide impartial hearings for parents who disagree with the identification, evaluation, or placement of a student. Parents must have an opportunity to participate in the hearing process and to be represented by counsel. Beyond this, due process is left to the discretion of local districts. It is recommended that they develop policy guidance and procedures.

*continued*

TABLE 19-1   An overview of ADA, IDEA, and Section 504: update 2001   *(Continued)*

| Americans with Disabilities Act of 1990 (ADA) | Individuals with Disabilities Education Act (IDEA), amended in 1997 | Section 504 of the Rehabilitation Act of 1973 |
|---|---|---|
| | *Evaluation/placement procedures* | |
| The ADA does not specify evaluation and placement procedures; it does specify provision of reasonable accommodations for eligible students across educational activities and settings. Reasonable accommodations may include, but are not limited to, redesigning equipment, assigning aides, providing written communication in alternative formats, modifying tests, reassigning services to accessible locations, altering existing facilities, and building new facilities. | With parental consent, an individualized evaluation must be conducted using a variety of technically sound, unbiased assessment tools. Based on the results, a team of professionals (including the parent of the child) determines eligibility for special education. Reevaluations are conducted at least every 3 years. Results are used to develop an IEP that specifies the special education, related services, and supplemental aids and services to be provided to address the child's goals. Placement in the least restrictive environment (LRE) is selected from a continuum of alternative placements, based on the child's IEP, and reviewed at least annually. IEPs must be reviewed at least annually to see whether annual goals are being met. IDEA contains specific provisions about IEP team composition, parent participation, IEP content, and consideration of special factors. | Section 504 provides for a placement evaluation that must involve multiple assessment tools tailored to assess specific areas of educational need. Placement decisions must be made by a team of persons familiar with the student who understand the evaluation information and placement options. Students with disabilities may be placed in a separate class or facility only if they cannot be educated satisfactorily in the regular education setting with the use of supplementary aids and services. Significant changes to placement must be preceded by an evaluation.<br><br>Section 504 provides for periodic reevaluation. Parental consent is not required for evaluation or placement. |

Henderson, Kelly. (March 2001). *An overview of ADA, IDEA, and Section 504: update 2001.* ERIC Clearinghouse on Disabilities and Gifted Education. www.ericec.org/digests/e606.html. Retrieved September 16, 2002.

a common language to describe a disability. She believed that classification systems enable professionals to identify and differentiate disabilities and communicate effectively about the condition, describe the disability and needs of persons with a particular condition effectively for research purposes, help citizens form special interest groups to enhance services for persons with the disability, and facilitate planning for the treatment of a special disability.

Smith and Luckasson (1995) agreed, noting that a classification system for special education "enables us to name disabilities, to differentiate one from another, and to communicate in a meaningful and efficient way about a specific disability" (pp. 9–10). In addition, a classification system is useful because it is necessary for research, for lobbying for improved services, and for relating specific treatments to specific disabilities.

The IDEA includes 13 different categories of disabilities under which a person age 3 to 21 would be eligible to receive services if the disability affected educational performance. Based on information provided by the National Information Center for Children and Youth with Disabilities (NICHCY, 2002), the following section contains a list of categories and their brief descriptions:

Autism: A developmental disability that significantly affects verbal and nonverbal communication and social interaction

Deaf-blindness: The combination of hearing and visual impairments

Deafness: Severe hearing impairment

Emotional disturbance: One or more of five problems described in a following section over a long period of time and to a marked degree

Hearing impairment: Hearing impairment not included under "deafness"

Mental retardation: Significantly subaverage general intellectual functioning

Multiple disabilities: Concurrent impairments, such as mental retardation–blindness

Orthopedic impairment: Severe orthopedic impairment

Other health impairment: Limited strength, vitality, or alertness due to chronic or acute health problems

Specific learning disability: Disorder in one or more of the processes involved in understanding or in using language that causes difficulties in listening, thinking, speaking, reading, writing, spelling or doing mathematical calculations

Speech or language impairment: Communication disorder such as such as stuttering, impaired articulation, or voice impairment

Traumatic brain injury: An acquired injury to the brain caused by an external physical force that results in total or partial functional and/or psychosocial impairment

Visual impairment including blindness: Impairment in vision (NICHCY, pp. 1–3)

The U.S. Department of Education (2001) reports the number of children receiving special education services for specific disabilities each year. The most common categories of those receiving services are as follows:

Specific learning disability 50.5%

Speech or language impairment 19.2%

Mental retardation 10.8%

Serious emotional disturbance 8.3%

Discussing each area of exceptionality individually is beyond the scope of this chapter; therefore, it includes a general discussion of gifted, mentally retarded, learning disabled, and physically handicapped children, as well as children categorized as having behavioral disorders. These conditions seem to be the most generally recognized exceptionalities and the conditions counselors are most apt to encounter daily. Although attention deficit disorders are not among the exceptional conditions listed by the U.S. Department of Education, this condition is included here because of its increasing diagnosis.

Counselors, parents, teachers, and children may need clarification on the process that is followed to identify children who may need special education and related services. The Office of Special Education Programs (2000) has outlined these steps.

1. The child is referred as possibly needing services.

2. The child is evaluated in all areas related to the suspected disability.

3. A group of qualified professionals and the parents consider the results of the evaluation and determine whether the child is eligible for services.

4. If the child is found eligible, within 30 calendar days, a team meets to write an individual educational plan (IEP) for the child.

5. IEP meeting is scheduled. Parents are invited.

6. IEP meeting is held and the IEP is written. The plan includes accommodations, modifications, and supports to be provided to the child. Parents must consent to services and placement.

7. Services are provided. The school monitors the plan to determine whether it is being implemented as written.

8. Progress is measured and reported to the parents.

9. IEP is reviewed at least once a year.

10. The child is reevaluated at least every 3 years. (pp. 4–7)

Often counseling is included in IEPs. We have defined *counseling* as a therapeutic relationship, a problem-solving process, a reeducation, and a method for changing behavior. We have also discussed counseling as a method for helping children cope with developmental problems and as a preventive process. Who more than exceptional children, constantly faced with rejection and failure, need an accepting relationship, someone to listen, assistance in setting present and future goals, guidance for improving interpersonal relationships, and, perhaps most important, help in building a strong self-concept and confidence? Counseling with the exceptional child requires no magic formula; however, it does require counselor dedication to the philosophy that all individuals are unique and capable of growth to reach their potential.

Counseling literature has suggested many ways of counseling with children's developmental and behavioral problems, but not enough research has been conducted in the area of counseling with the special problems of exceptional children. Even less research has been done with families of exceptional children.

## METHODS FOR COUNSELING WITH EXCEPTIONAL CHILDREN

Some recent literature has addressed the topic of counseling the exceptional child. However, the results of much of this research are inconclusive, many studies contain methodological problems, and many of the articles offer opinions or suggest methods of counseling without citing research to support their efficacy. A few articles focus on counseling with the families of exceptional children; others suggest methods for working with children who are gifted or who have learning disabilities or behavioral disorders. The suggestions for counseling exceptional children in this chapter are a combination of research and theory published in the literature. As is true with most counseling methods, the counseling strategies should be incorporated into a positive, accepting counseling relationship.

To understand the world of the exceptional child, counselors need to have a basic knowledge of the disabling condition. What are the symptoms and general characteristics of a child with this exceptionality? What are the child's limitations? What are the child's strengths and potentials? All children have some developmental and psychological needs in common, but are there other needs specific to the exceptional condition that must be considered? The counselor does not need to become an expert in the teaching techniques of special education, but knowledge of the needs and characteristics of these children is necessary for effective counseling.

Counselors should ask themselves if they have taken the time to get to know the child as an individual—not as a "child with a disability." The following questions are helpful:

Has my counseling assisted the child in developing good relations with classmates?
Has my counseling focused on helping the child to solve his or her own problems?
Has my counseling helped the child to feel better about himself or herself?
Has my counseling with the parents and teachers of the child helped them find ways of interacting that enhance the child's self-esteem and feelings of self-sufficiency?

Perhaps the primary concern of the counselor working with exceptional children should be the child's self-concept. A person's self-concept begins to form early in life, based on the feedback of significant persons in the child's world. In daily interactions, parents, friends, teachers, and peers send verbal and nonverbal messages to children about their worth and abilities. Exceptional children, even the gifted, often receive negative messages. Parents of children with disabilities may feel guilty or overprotective, friends and peers may pity these children or see them as a burden, and teachers may resent having to work with them. "Normal" people feel uncomfortable with "different" children for a variety of reasons. Because most exceptional children experience some type of rejection and failure, many have negative self-concepts.

In the professional's attempts to diagnose and find help for a child with special problems, the child as a person is sometimes forgotten in the proliferation of testing, diagnosing, and planning. These procedures that are designed to aid the child may increase self-doubts and fears. Testing, diagnosing, and planning are necessary, but they cannot replace a good relationship—one in which the child feels free to express fears, anxieties, doubts, and insecurities. A person who is listened to is being respected. It may begin the process of developing or restoring a more positive self-evaluation. Building a better self-concept includes helping exceptional children see themselves as people who can and do perform and accomplish goals. Unfortunately, most people tend to focus on such children's limitations rather than emphasize their strengths and what they can do, encourage them to take responsibility for decisions about their own lives, and assist them in finding ways to live productive lives.

## The Gifted Child*

Much of the discussion of exceptionality has focused on children with disabilities or some handicapping condition. Children who are gifted, however, are also considered to be exceptional. They face unique problems related to their exceptionality and are not always completely accommodated by mainstream educational programs. Smith (1998) contended that children who are gifted or talented do not face the barriers that their peers with disabilities do but instead are handicapped by society and our educational systems that do not challenge them. In addition, parents, teachers, and others sometimes inadvertently discourage the gifted from achieving their potential. Many people believe that the bright person can solve almost any problem and find a way without help. The gifted child may have difficulty in relationships with friends because of advanced intellectual or creative interests. While such children possess knowledge beyond their years, they may lack the emotional ability to cope with this knowledge. The pressures that parents, teachers, peers, and society place on gifted and talented children may be strong and overwhelming.

Describing all of the characteristics of a person considered to be gifted is difficult. Terman and Oden (1947) attempted to describe the characteristics of the gifted in their studies during the early 1930s. They dispelled many of the myths concerning the gifted, but their studies focused primarily on the academically gifted. The characteristics identified do not seem adequate to describe the gifted or talented child of today. Because the definition of giftedness covers many differ-

---

*We owe appreciation to Zelma Lansford, Ed.D., for her contribution to this section.

ent areas, a restrictive list of traits that could screen out a gifted student or talented child seems unfair. In addition, certain kinds of giftedness are difficult to identify. Schools often use intelligence and achievement tests, tests of creativity, teacher recommendations, and parent, peer, and self-referrals. Although none of these methods alone is adequate, used in combination, they contribute to the identification process utilized by many school systems.

Most definitions of gifted children include criteria such as high performance capability on general intellectual aptitude, specific academic ability, creative or leadership ability, or capabilities in the visual and performing arts. According to Smith (1998), the concept of "talent development" is gaining acceptance. She identified talent development as "the process of translating ability into achievement" by the family, teachers, experts, and others (e.g., mentors). Talent development focuses not only on intelligence and academic skills but also on all areas of human development. This is an especially useful technique to include children from minority populations in programs for the gifted.

The incidence of gifted and talented children in the population is difficult to determine because of the lack of a generally accepted definition of giftedness, but most estimates range from 2% to 5% of the population. It is also difficult to draw conclusions from the numbers of children in school programs for the gifted because of the variety of criteria that various states have adopted and the variability of funding for such programs. As can be seen in the report of special education services provided, the states do not report to the federal government the number of gifted children receiving services (in that this category is not funded by the IDEA), and no other national reporting mechanism exists. In addition, not all school systems provide programs for the gifted. Hardman et al. (1993) reported that from 3% to 15% of students in school may be described as gifted. Davis and Rimm (1994) estimated that 3% to 5% of the school population should receive gifted educational services. Renzulli and Reis (1997) believed that the number should be increased to 10% to 15%.

Because schools see gifted and talented children as outstanding in many ways (especially academically), teachers have not recognized that these children may also need the counselor's intervention to cope with social or emotional problems. The gifted child often feels isolated and alienated because he or she has no one to relate to who has similar interests and reacts to the world in a similar way. It is essential that the gifted child develop a peer relation between the ages of 5 and 7 with someone who has equivalent intellect and shares comparable curiosities. Without intervention, the child may experience low self-esteem and become an underachiever. It cannot be assumed that teachers of the gifted will completely fulfill this task, as they have an extensive agenda. The counselor can provide a critical addition to programs for the gifted.

The counselor can support the gifted child in several important ways. The counselor can help the child understand his or her giftedness, ways the child is different from others, and that it is all right to be different. The counselor can help the child understand that the differences are neither good nor bad, perhaps preventing the child from developing an attitude of superiority and helping in the development of a positive self-concept. Gifted children may need help in recognizing their strengths and limitations, as well as the abilities and limitations of others. Badolato (1998) urged school counselors to identify the special needs of gifted girls by providing support groups and career development groups for them. This will be an invaluable key to forming good peer relationships.

Counseling with gifted and talented children presents a challenge to the counselor. These children are often very independent and may want to solve their own problems. They are also bright enough to compensate or to disguise many of their feelings and concerns. They are also perceptive and recognize insensitivity or inconsistencies immediately. At the same time, their intellectual capacities may increase their fear of failure, leading to their becoming perfectionistic and reacting negatively to any criticism or lack of success.

Effective ways to help the gifted child develop relationships are through inclusion in heterogeneous groups for sports and activities, along with discussions of hobbies and other mutual interests. The gifted may be included in homogeneous groups to discuss areas of mutual concerns. Bibliocounseling may help gifted children solve problems in their lives, especially if the story is discussed with the children and they are assisted in understanding its meaning and application. Technology is a particularly useful tool for working with the gifted. Computers allow the gifted child to work independently, study a subject in more depth, and research a potential solution for a particular problem.

The counselor can also help the children in recognizing career options open to them. One of their assets is that the gifted may possess the ability to perform well in a variety of jobs. However, because they can excel at many things, they can struggle at finding the best fit for a college major, a field of study, or the right career.

According to Smith and Luckasson (1995), the gifted child may exhibit the ability to reason abstractly, conceptualize, process information well, solve problems, and learn quickly. The child may demonstrate intellectual curiosity, show wide interests, avoid drill and routine, demonstrate unevenness at times in learning, generalize learning, remember large amounts of material, demonstrate high levels of verbal ability, and perhaps prefer learning in a quiet environment. The child may or may not show leadership qualities, be concerned about ethical issues, or be nonconforming. Socially and emotionally, the child may be the chronological age, or the child may be advanced and prefer older peers and playmates.

The essential elements for the counselor are in helping the child understand himself or herself and ways to cope with school and the world. Remembering that these children may be the future scientists, scholars, and business executives, with minimal effort the astute counselor can enable the gifted child to realize the gifts and become a happy, contributing member of society.

According to Smith (1998), the concept of "talent development" is gaining acceptance. She defined talent development as "the process of translating ability into achievement" by the family, teachers, experts, and others (e.g., mentors). Talent development focuses not only on intellect and academic skills but also on all areas of human development.Socially and emotionally, the gifted child criticizes self, empathizes, plays with older friends, persists, is sensitive to others' feelings, exhibits individualism, has strength of character, shows leadership qualities, is concerned about ethical issues, takes risks, is independent and autonomous, has a mature sense of humor, and is nonconforming—characteristics that can be of help to a gifted child. Because of their gifts and talents, gifted children can be responsive clients.

## Children with Emotional or Behavioral Disorders

Problems exist in defining an emotionally disturbed (ED) child or one considered to have a behavioral disorder (BD). NICHCY (2002) reported that IDEA has adopted the term *serious emotional disturbance* as follows: "a condition exhibiting one or more of the following characteristics over a long period of time and to a marked degree that adversely affects a child's educational performance:

- an inability to learn that cannot be explained by other factors such as intellectual, sensory, or health problems
- an inability to form satisfactory interpersonal relationships with peers and teachers
- inappropriate displays of feelings or behavior
- pervasive unhappiness or depression
- a tendency to develop physical symptoms or fears associated with personal or school problems." (www.nichcy.org/pubs/factshe/fs5txt.htm)

The condition must have been present to a marked extent over a period of time and must substantially interfere with the child's educational achievement. The term includes schizophrenic children but excludes those whose problems result from social maladjustment.

In the 1999–2000 school year, 470,111 children with an emotional disturbance received services in the public schools (U.S. Department of Education, 2001). Brandenburg, Friedman, and Silver (1990) suggested that the number of children in this category receiving special education is less than one-third of those who need such programs, probably because of the ambiguity of the criteria and definition.

Historically, emotional and behavior disorders were attributed to causes ranging from evil spirits to subconscious factors, but recent researchers have focused on "inappropriate learning and complex interactions that take place between individuals and their environments" (Hardman et al., 1993, p. 147). NICHCY (2002) discussed factors such as heredity, brain disorder, diet, stress, and family functioning as possible causes but acknowledged that research does not support those causes. The children may exhibit some of these behaviors:

- Hyperactivity (short attention span, impulsive)
- Aggression/self-injury (acting out, fighting)
- Withdrawal (does not initiate social contact, retreats from social exchanges, excessive fear)
- Immaturity (inappropriate crying, temper tantrums, poor coping skills)
- Learning difficulties (performing below grade level)

- With severe emotional disturbances may have distorted thinking, excessive anxiety, bizarre actions, and abnormal mood swings. Some have been diagnosed with schizophrenia or severe psychosis. (www.nichcy.org/pubs/factshe/fs5txt.htm)

Smith (1998) suggested there may be biological reasons for anorexia and bulimia and genetic bases for mood disorders, depression, schizophrenia, and attention deficit disorders. She also pointed out that children who might be stable under normal conditions sometimes become emotionally disturbed in homes or communities when they experience negative conditions such as abuse, turmoil, poverty, illness, and other traumatic conditions for long periods. Counselors are cautioned to note the frequency and intensity of such behaviors to make sure they are extreme and not a part of normal childhood development.

Children with mild to moderate problems ordinarily function relatively well in the home environment and are educated in public school. More severe disorders such as psychoses usually require treatment by psychiatrists and possibly institutionalization.

Smith and Luckasson (1995) listed the possible indicators of behavioral and emotional disorders as few or no friends, problems with family relationships, problems with teacher relationships, hyperactive behavior, aggression to self or others, impulsivity, immature social skills, feelings of depression and unhappiness, withdrawal into self, anxiety or fearfulness, expression of ideas of suicide, distractibility, and inability to pay attention for an appropriate length of time. Furthermore, they stated that the children usually have lower academic performance than expected for their age, social skills deficits, and the obvious behavior problems and internal conflicts described. They recommended behavior modification strategies, individual and family counseling, moral education, and character training. The counselor should be in contact with other professionals working with these children—teachers, medical doctors, specialists, and others—in order to coordinate all services for the ED–BD child.

These children need love and understanding, and they need a counselor who can provide security and stability. The counselor who is effective with ED–BD children can detect and reflect the feelings and frustrations of the children, discuss these feelings, and decide how to manage them effectively. Much of the success achieved from working with the emotionally disturbed has been due to the relationship between adult and child as well as to the technique used. These children have often experienced inconsistency in their relationships and may be suspicious of adults because of past experiences with hurtful people. The counselor needs to be strong enough to place consistent limits on the children and require them to assume responsibility for their behavior.

Smith (1998) outlined effective educational accommodations for ED–BD children that included creating a positive climate, communicating carefully, establishing expectations, maintaining consistency, encouraging success, avoiding power struggles, and giving choices to children. These would be equally effective counseling strategies for ED–BD children. Ruth (1996) found that a high and consistent success rate can be obtained for children with emotional and behavioral difficulties with the use of behavioral contract and goal setting (see Chapter 9). Patton (1995) used rational-emotive-behavior therapy with a group of ED–BD young adolescents to increase effective rational thinking and appropriate social behaviors.

To bring consistency and stability to the life of the ED–BD child, the counselor can discuss expected and appropriate behaviors with the child. Writing out what is considered inappropriate and the consequences of this behavior is often helpful.

The counselor can define expected behaviors by such methods as contracting. The counselor, parents, teachers, and all significant people in the child's life must be willing to set limits and consistently maintain the rules. Behavior modification techniques emphasizing positive reinforcement have been effective. Relaxation exercises, talking therapy, physical activities, writing, drawing, or games may be scheduled into the child's day to provide outlets for tension and other emotions. Changes in the environment, expectations, stimulation, and conflicts should be as minimal as possible. Tarver Behring, Spagna, and Sullivan (1998) suggested that counselors help teachers with social skills strategies and classroom programs on problem solving, conflict resolution, anger management, and making friends. Peer groups can be effective reinforcers who provide models for appropriate behavior.

The tasks of the counselor of an ED–BD child can be summarized as:

1. Forming a counseling relationship with the child that includes well-defined responsibilities and limits

2. Working to change the child's image and expectations through counseling and consultation with family and other significant people in the child's world

3. Conducting individual and group counseling to deal with feelings and behaviors, teach social skills, and improve academic performance

4. Assisting parents and teachers in structuring the child's physical environment and schedule, establishing rules for behavior, and providing encouragement, reinforcement, and logical consequences for misbehavior

## The Child with a Learning Disability

A learning disability (LD) is a general term for different kinds of learning problems, most often skills related to reading, writing, listening, speaking, reasoning and doing math (NICHCY, 2002). Boudah and Weiss (2002) stated that individuals with LD usually have average or above average intelligence yet often do not achieve on the same level as their peers. The most basic characteristic of learning disability is that weaker academic achievement. The U.S. Department of Education (2001) estimated that 1 of every 5 people have a learning disability. About 3 million children with learning disabilities receive special education services in schools. More than 50% of the children who receive special education services are identified as youth with learning disabilities. The term includes such conditions as perceptual handicaps, brain injury, minimal brain dysfunction, dyslexia, and developmental aphasia. The term does not include children who have learning problems that are primarily the result of visual, hearing, or motor handicaps; mental retardation; emotional disturbance; or environmental, cultural, or economic disadvantage (U.S. Office of Education, 1992, cited in Smith & Luckasson, 1995).

The National Joint Committee on Learning Disabilities proposed a slightly different definition that is not as medically oriented. *Learning disabilities* is a general term that refers to a heterogeneous group of disorders manifested by significant difficulties in the acquisition and use of listening, speaking, reading, writing, reasoning, or mathematical abilities. These disorders are intrinsic to the individual, presumed to result from central nervous system dysfunction, and may occur across the life span. Problems in the self-regulatory behaviors, social perception, and social interaction may exist with learning disabilities but do not by themselves constitute a learning disability. Although learning disabilities may occur concomitantly with other handicapping conditions (for example, sensory impairment, mental retardation, serious emotional disturbance) or with extrinsic influences (such as cultural differences or insufficient or inappropriate instruction), they are not the result of those conditions or influences (National Joint Committee on Learning Disabilities, 1988; cited in Smith & Luckasson, 1995, p. 246).

Children with learning disabilities usually have a measured intelligence in the normal range but are achieving academically well below an expected level. This discrepancy is not due to a visual, hearing, or motor handicap; mental retardation; emotional disturbance; or environmental, cultural, or economic disadvantages. In general, the literature in this area has cited as indicators of a learning disability such characteristics as hyperactivity, distractibility, impulsiveness, motor problems, poor problem-solving skills, poor motivation, overreliance on others for help with class assignments, poor language skills, immature social skills, and a general disorganization in learning approaches (Smith & Luckasson, 1995).

Glasser (1998) wrote that the label *learning disabilities* implies that students have something wrong with their brains. He contended that having a learning disability is not a matter of having an abnormal brain but rather a matter of excessive schooling. He stated: "Our brains are not set up to memorize information we do not use, and we are certainly not given brains that can even remotely compete with a calculator. What many of these students do is take schooling and with it, a lot of essential schoolwork, such as reading and writing, out of their quality worlds" (p. 255). He believed that often the parents of these children accepted their own schooling and performed well and now see nothing wrong with the current procedures. They are puzzled about their child's poor performance and accept the diagnosis of "learning disabled" as an explanation for poor performance in school.

Smith (1998) suggested possible signs or characteristics of learning disabilities might include a significant discrepancy between potential and actual academic achievement, distractibility or inability to pay attention, hyperactive behavior exhibited as excessive movement, inattentiveness during class, impulsiveness, poor motor coordination and spatial relation skills, inability to solve problems, poor motivation, dependence on others for work, poor language and/or cognitive development, immature social skills, general disorganization in learning, and substantial delays in academic achievement.

Although the specific causes of learning disabilities are not known, researchers believe they include biological, genetic, and environmental factors. Biological factors include a variety of causes such as minimal brain dysfunction, biochemical disturbances (allergies to certain food, for instance), developmental delay of the nervous system, and nutrition. Some evidence suggests that heredity is a factor in the prevalence of LD, and some educators now feel that a poor or inadequate learning environment may contribute to LD problems. Smith and Luckasson (1995) reported that about 5% (or 2.5 million) of the school-age population have been classified as learning disabled.

Frost and Emery (1996) estimated that approximately 3% to 6% of all school-age children have a neurocognitive deficit or developmental reading disability—dyslexia. Almost 50% of children classified as having a learning disability are dyslexic, according to these writers. This deficit, primarily related to phonological core processes, affects reading and spelling abilities, even though the children are very capable in other intellectual domains. Definitions of dyslexia have remained vague over the years, and school psychologists usually classify children according to federal and state guidelines for placing children with learning disabilities (Frost & Emery, 1996).

As in counseling with other exceptional children, the counselor begins by recognizing and reflecting the feelings of the child with an LD. Because their characteristics tend to create an unstable world, these children have often experienced failure, rejection, isolation, and confusion. Perceptions of their world change, their visual perception plays tricks on them, their impulsivity causes them trouble with authority figures, they may have communication difficulties because of poor auditory or language skills, and they are often clumsy and awkward. These and the other behaviors that accompany their disability do not endear them to teachers, parents, or peers, and emotional problems often result.

Some children with LD lack social perception and skills and perform poorly in social situations. They may lack good judgment and appear to be insensitive tattlers. They may have trouble making friends and forming good relationships in their families. Activities for building body image and self-perception, sensitivity to other people, social maturity and skills, self-esteem, and emotional well-being may enhance these areas.

Thompson and Littrell (1998) suggested brief solution-oriented counseling for adolescents with learning disabilities. The four-step model they used involved building rapport and then helping the student identify, describe, and define a specific problem or concern. In Step 2, the counselor and student considered what had been tried previously, what has worked, and any new possible solutions. During Step 3, the counselor helped the student decide on a specific, concrete, measurable, and attainable goal. Often this step included using the miracle question, "Suppose a miracle happened and the problem was solved. What would be different?" The fourth step was the generation of a specific task to help the student reach a goal. The counselors checked with the student 3 and 4 weeks later. These authors reported success in 90% of the research participants.

Boudah and Weiss (2002) identified direct instruction of specific skills and learning strategy instruction as the best instructional practices for children with

LD. The children should be taught with a step-by-step approach with appropriate modeling, practice, and feedback. Smith (1998) suggested that teachers use instructional tactics that actively involve children with LD, use advance organizers and concrete examples, demonstrate concepts as necessary, help children focus on the task at hand, teach problem-solving skills, help children understand the connection between effort and success, and teach them to predict consequences of their behavior. Since counseling is a form of teaching, these suggestions seem very appropriate for counselors as well.

Counseling goals include enhancing social skills, helping overcome a sense of failure, and promoting a positive attitude toward learning. Cognitive behavioral approaches (see Chapter 8) may be helpful with those goals. One task of a counselor working with a child with LD may be to coordinate diagnostic services in order to pinpoint the child's specific strengths and weaknesses and plan an educational program based on these findings. A typical diagnostic evaluation includes physical, educational, and psychological assessments and perhaps the opinions of other specialists, such as speech pathologists or ophthalmologists. These data must be shared with all those working with the child to ensure a well-organized remediation plan and to avoid overlap or omission of services.

In recent years, medical specialists have used drugs to control the attention span, distractibility, and behavior of children with LD. The practice is controversial, and the counselor is involved only in observing the effects of the drug and reporting these effects to the parents. Other therapies, such as diet control, megavitamins, and motor training, are still highly controversial. Most have little research support for their use in helping children with LD.

Emotional problems, caused primarily by feelings of failure and worthlessness, often compound the problems of children with LD. Any program planned for these children should include individual or group counseling. Counseling for the entire family may be necessary to deal with the feelings and reactions of all family members. Behavior modification procedures, implemented both in the home and in school, provide structure and stability that help children with LD navigate in a world of turmoil. Relaxation training can help children with LD cope with tensions and anxieties; talking therapy can provide an outlet for expression of pent-up feelings and exploration of doubts. The counselor's job is to build an improved self-concept, help children learn social skills, assist them in learning to cope with environmental demands, and guide them in planning ways to realize their potential.

## Attention Deficit–Hyperactivity Disorder and Attention Deficit Disorder

The cluster of problems known as attention deficit–hyperactivity disorder (ADHD) forms an extremely complex childhood problem and elicits the most frequent referrals for professional help, according to Goldstein and Goldstein (1990). They summarized the symptoms of this disorder as including inattention, over-arousal, hyperactivity, impulsivity, and difficulty with delay of gratification. Children with ADHD may have trouble sitting still, controlling their behavior, and paying attention. Three to 7% of schoolchildren may have this behavioral disorder (NICHCY, 2002). Three types of ADHD have been found:

- *Inattentive:* The person cannot focus or stay focused on a task or activity, does not pay attention to details, cannot maintain focus on play or school work, does not complete work, has trouble organizing tasks and activities, and gets distracted and loses things.
- *Hyperactive-impulsive:* The person is very active and often acts without thinking. The child is in constant motion and acts before thinking, such as running into danger and being surprised to find herself or himself there. Children may fidget, squirm, run around, climb, leave seats, talk too much, have trouble playing quietly, blurt out answers, have trouble waiting for their turn, interrupt, and butt into games
- *Combined:* The person is inattentive, impulsive, and too active; these children have symptoms of both of the previous types (American Psychiatric Association, 2000, p. 92).

The American Psychiatric Association (2000) cautioned that for a child to be classified as hyperactive-impulsive, some symptoms must have been present before the age of 7 years, must persist for at least 6 months, must be present in multiple settings and inconsistent with the child's developmental level, and must clearly impair functioning.

Goldstein and Goldstein (1990) presented what they called a commonsense definition that included four components: inattention and distractibility, over-arousal, impulsivity, and difficulty with gratification. Smith and Luckasson (1995) stated that the condition is confusing in that not all children diagnosed as having attention deficit disorders (ADD) are in special education programs; some are diagnosed as learning disabled, and others may be classified as having behavior disorders, emotional disturbance, or other disabilities.

Goldstein and Goldstein (1990) saw a reasonable incidence rate for attention deficit as only about 1% to 6%. They pointed out that the disorder occurs more frequently in lower socioeconomic areas (which may be a result rather than a cause of the disorder) and occurs 5 to 9 times more often in boys than girls, although the latter finding is being questioned. Fottrell (1998) reported that ADHD occurs much more frequently in boys than in girls, probably a 9:1 ratio. She suggested that the ADD incidence for boys to girls is a 2:1 to 3:1 ratio.

Goldstein and Goldstein (1990) argued that attention deficit disorder with and without hyperactivity are different disorders and cited research that children with attention deficits and hyperactivity are more aggressive and unpopular and have greater trouble with their behavior. Other researchers have found attention deficit children without hyperactivity to be shy, socially withdrawn, not very popular, and not adept in sports, a state some have called "undifferentiated attention deficit disorder." A national nonprofit organization, Children with Attention Deficit Disorders, reported that children might have ADD if they fidget, squirm, or seem restless; have trouble remaining seated, playing quietly, waiting their turn, following instructions, or sustaining attention; talk excessively; are easily distracted; blurt out answers; shift from one uncompleted task to another; interrupt others; do not seem to listen; often lose things; frequently engage in dangerous behavior; act without thinking; have a low self-esteem; have frequent, unpredictable mood swings; and get angry and lose their temper easily (de la Cruz, 1994). However, many of these characteristics may be normal behaviors for a child's particular developmental level, or they could be characteristics of other problems. One must consider the intensity and duration of the symptoms, as well as how they fit into the child's overall developmental pattern.

Hardman et al. (1993) described two subcategories of ADD: attention deficit–hyperactivity disorder (ADHD) and undifferentiated attention deficit disorder (UADD), both of which have the primary characteristic of inability to concentrate for a long period. The authors reported disagreement about the causes of ADD; factors such as genetic inheritance, neurological injury during birth, vitamin deficiencies, and food additives have all been suggested.

Goldstein and Goldstein (1990) contended that common sense dictates a multidisciplinary, multitreatment model. Usually, such teams are composed of professionals such as physicians, psychologists, psychiatrists, counselors, and speech and other educational specialists. A physical examination must be a part of the diagnostic process; then professionals must supervise medications as necessary. Medications such as Ritalin, Cylert, and Dexedrine continue to be the most common form of treatment. However, these drugs have unwanted side effects for some small children, and medication as a sole treatment is not recommended by most professionals. Teachers, parents, and other adults who work with children on medication must be aware of the treatment in order to provide feedback about its effects.

As with other children's problems that involve hyperactivity, overarousal, and inappropriate behaviors, behavioral techniques work well with children with ADD. They respond to a structured environment with limited stimuli and a consistent schedule. Counselors should work with parents and teachers to develop behavior modification programs and to apply rules at home and school. The children should know the rules and the consequences for not following them *before* infractions occur. All adults must remain patient, calm, and consistent while applying both positive and negative consequences. To help them deal with their activity level, children with ADD may need planned physical activities at intervals, although they may not be adept at sports and other games requiring coordination.

Cognitive restructuring techniques may teach the child more positive ways of thinking as well as self-monitoring of behavior. Group counseling to teach more effective social skills may be helpful at some point during treatment; however, counselors must carefully assess the child's readiness to benefit from this interaction and to function as a group member. Nigg and Rappley (2001) concluded that multimodal intervention produces the broadest benefit in ADHD. The services provided from different agencies and people need to be coordinated with follow-up to refresh parents on behavior management as well as to update school plans.

According to Kottman, Robert, and Baker (1995), parents of children with ADHD in their study expressed a great deal of concern about their children's self-esteem, future adjustment, and lack of social skills, as well as the stress of parenting these children. They called for more communication and cooperation with the school. Counselors can be the vital link between children with ADHD, their parents, and the school system. They can provide educational seminars for teachers and parents focusing on behavioral techniques to decrease impulsiveness and increase appropriate behaviors. Counselors can serve as coordinators of the many professionals working with the child during the assessment and intervention stages. In addition, they can develop referral lists that include physicians and other helping professionals familiar with ADHD, as well as local groups offering parenting classes or support groups. Schwiebert, Sealander, and Tollerud (1995) suggested that bibliotherapy, support groups, a parent group, and family counseling may be helpful to parents, especially during the initial assessment period and while the parent is dealing with feelings about the child's condition. Kottman, Robert, and Baker (1995) recommended a parent training program that includes general information about ADHD, its causes, and possible treatment plans; self-esteem development suggestions; training in parent listening and encouragement skills; dealing with parent stress; suggestions for working with the child's school; and suggested means of social support for parents. Finally Erk (1999) provided extensive, helpful suggestions for working with individuals with ADHD.

## The Child with Mental Retardation

The most commonly accepted definition of *mental retardation* was developed by the American Association on Mental Retardation (AAMR): Mental retardation refers to substantial limitations in present functioning. It is characterized by significantly subaverage intellectual functioning, existing concurrently with related limitations in two or more of the following applicable adaptive skill areas: communication, self-care home living, social skills, community use, self-direction, health and safety, functional academics, leisure, and work (as cited in Smith & Luckasson, 1995, p. 136). The limitations in skills will cause someone to learn and develop more slowly than normal (NICHCY, 2002). Mental retardation manifests before age 18. Smith and Luckasson (1995) noted that this definition emphasizes three major themes: intellectual function, adaptive skill areas, and the developmental period.

After the diagnosis, the child's functioning in four areas is studied: intellectual and adaptive skills, psychological and emotional concerns, physical functioning and health, and the current environment and the environment that would be optimal for the growth of the individual (Wicks-Nelson & Israel, 2000). Services and support are based on the level of intensity of need. Hardman et al. (1993) suggested that the child may need help with adaptive skills such as coping in school, developing interpersonal relationships, developing language skills, coping with emotional concerns, and taking care of personal needs. As many as 3% of children may have mental retardation (The Arc, 2001). More than 614,000 children have some form of mental retardation, and 10% of those who receive special education services have some form of mental retardation (U.S. Department of Education, 2001).

Smith (1998) reported that under the old classification system for the mentally retarded, individuals who scored between 50 and 80 on IQ tests were labeled as educable children with mental retardation (EMR). Individuals scoring between 25 and 50 were categorized as trainable mentally retarded. More recently, educators have contended that all individuals can learn; therefore, the newer definition gave rise to a new classification system with the following categories: intermittent, limited, extensive, or pervasive. Those who require support on an "as needed basis" are classified as intermittent, those needing consistent and more intense support services are classified as limited, regular involvement and long-term support in some to most environments is needed for individuals with extensive retardation, and constant, high-intensity supportive services are needed for those with pervasive retardation (Smith, 1998).

The causes of mental retardation vary. Smith and Luckasson (1995) and Smith (1998) summarized the various factors in four categories: socioeconomic and environmental factors, injury, infection and toxins, and biological causes. Poverty, with its associated factors such as pollution, poor nutrition, and inadequate health care, is the leading cause suspected in most cases with no organic basis. Head and brain injury may occur at birth or at other times (car or bicycle accidents). Mental retardation caused by infection or toxin may be the result of viral infections (rubella, measles), sexually transmitted diseases (syphilis, HIV), or toxins such as alcohol, other drugs, or tobacco used by the mother during pregnancy. Down syndrome and Tay-Sachs disease are examples of mental retardation caused by biological factors. NICHCY (2002) lists the common causes as genetic conditions, problems during pregnancy, problems at birth, and health problems.

The counseling techniques in this section are geared to those children categorized as intermittent or limited, the groups most likely to face societal problems and pressures. These children have physical and psychological needs similar to those of other children, but the added handicap of their exceptionality interferes with their adjustment. The AAMR definition suggested that children may need help in 10 "adaptive skill" areas: communication (understanding and expression), self-care, home living, social interactions, understanding the community, self-direction (making choices), health and safety, obtaining functional academic skills (reading, writing, everyday mathematics), effectively using leisure time, and developing employment skills (Smith, 1998).

Counseling goals include improving social interactions, enhancing skills, developing interpersonal relationships, and promoting a positive self-image (Parette & Hourcade, 1995). Peer feedback and peer modeling can be highly effective counseling techniques. Group counseling can help the child learn and rehearse effective ways of behaving. Behavior modification techniques, such as the token system or contingency contracting, have been found to work effectively with individuals who have mental retardation. The counselor ought to be clear and concise in communications, limit the number of directions, display respect, and provide encouragement (Parette & Hourcade, 1995).

Counselors will need to work with the parents and other significant people in the child's life to help them understand and encourage the child's abilities. Special attention should be paid to teaching the child independent living skills as well as personal and social skills. The child and parents also need guidance and assistance in planning for the child's educational and vocational future.

Studies about the value of counseling and psychotherapy for the children with mental retardation are inconclusive; obviously, however, the counselor can provide valuable services in personal and social development and in helping the family deal effectively with adjustment and behavior problems.

## The Child with a Physical Disability

Hardman et al. (1993) described physical disorders as "impairments that may interfere with an individual's mobility and coordination. The impairments may also affect his or her capacity to communicate, learn, and adjust" (p. 340). They may include cerebral palsy, spina bifida, spinal cord injuries, amputations, muscular dystrophy, epilepsy, diabetes, cystic fibrosis, sickle cell anemia, adolescent pregnancy, and cocaine addiction.

IDEA refers to orthopedically impaired children as having a condition that adversely affects educational performance. The term includes impairments caused by congenital anomaly (e.g., club foot, absence of some member), impairments caused by disease (e.g., poliomyelitis, bone tuberculosis), and impairments from other causes (e.g., cerebral palsy, amputations, and fractures or burns that cause contractures) (NICHCY, 2002).

IDEA further described children with other health impairments as having limited strength, vitality, or alertness resulting from chronic or acute health problems such as a heart condition, tuberculosis, rheumatic fever, nephritis, asthma, sickle cell anemia, hemophilia, epilepsy, lead poisoning, leukemia, or diabetes, all of which adversely affect a child's educational performance (U. S. Department of Education, 1992, in Smith, 1998, p. 370).

Many children have more than one disability, and some conditions have overlapping symptoms. Knowing the characteristics, physical problems, symptoms, and prognosis of the child with a physical disability helps counselors understand the child's world. Counselors also want to know the child's strengths. Lack of knowledge and fear of the unknown can make the counselor apprehensive, which the child can sense. The children's needs vary according to the type of disability— some may need help with basic functioning, and others may need help in building relationships and dealing with ridicule.

The child may have anxiety, fears, shame, or other negative feelings because of his or her disability. The children's perceptions of self and their abilities are also determined by their age at the time the disabling condition occurred and the severity of the condition. These reactions may reflect how the child has been treated by others, especially family. Family problems increase when a child has a disability; the demands for energy, time, and financial resources add a heavy burden of stress. Smith (1998) pointed out that families of children with severe physical and health problems may experience fatigue and low vitality, a restricted social life, financial setbacks, and career interruptions, and the family can become preoccupied with the child's illness.

Smith and Luckasson (1995) reported that the research indicates that teachers do not feel prepared to work with children with disabilities in the classroom. They requested help most often with classroom management techniques. Because teachers' attitudes are critical to the success of children with disabilities, counselors should be prepared to work with them in a consultative manner to alleviate their personal concerns and anxieties about teaching disabled children and assist them in developing whatever skills are needed.

The counselor who works with children who have disabilities needs to be able to work with all agencies, professionals, parents, and other significant persons in the child's life. Coordinating services, rearranging physical environments, removing barriers and inconveniences, and securing special equipment and materials may be only the first step to meeting the needs of those with physical disabilities.

The goals of counseling involve helping the student identify his or her strengths and encouraging the student to become a self-advocate. Counselors should focus on building feelings of self-worth and healthy attitudes. The child may need to be encouraged to express and recognize his or her feelings toward the disability, helped to learn social or personal skills, counseled in the area of independent living, and assisted in making vocational plans for the future. Adlerian counseling (see Chapter 11) may help a child recognize strengths. More important than the physical limitation is the fact that each child is a unique individual who has capabilities and potential; the counselor's role is to facilitate growth toward reaching this potential.

## General Guidelines

Simpson (1998) lauded behavior modification as one of the most effective tools in working with children with special needs. He outlined the most important features of behavior modification programs: The first essential task is the clear identification, definition, and measurement of an appropriate target behavior. The second step includes the identification of where, when, with whom, and under what conditions the target behavior happens. Next, the professional investigates factors that cause or maintain the target behavior. Finally, the professional uses appropriate interventions to modify the target behavior. Simpson's guidelines help counselors teach parents and teachers as well as work with children to modify some inappropriate habits.

Deck, Scarborough, Sferrazza, and Estill (1999) recounted some of the issues of school counselors working with students with disabilities. They discussed using small-group counseling, classroom guidance, individual counseling, after-school counseling, and collaborating with teachers and parents. Another summary of the tasks of the counselor working with any type of exceptional child might include the following:

- Recognizing that the child is a *person* first
- Working toward an understanding of the child's specific exceptionality and the unique social, learning, or behavioral problems that may accompany this exceptionality
- Counseling to enhance self-concept
- Facilitating adjustment to exceptionality

- Coordinating the services of other professionals or agencies working with the exceptional child
- Helping the significant people in the child's life (parents and teachers especially) to understand the child's exceptionality, strengths and limitations, and special problems Carpenter, King-Sears, and Keys (1998) discussed teaming models for special education and the counselor's functions in those teams.
- Assisting in the development of effective, independent living skills
- Encouraging recreational skills and hobbies
- Teaching personal and social skills
- Assisting in educational planning and possibly securing needed educational aids and equipment for the child
- Counseling with the parents
- Acquiring a knowledge of and working relationship with professional and referral agencies

## COUNSELING WITH PARENTS OF EXCEPTIONAL CHILDREN

Interestingly, there is very little research or literature for counselors who want to work with parents of exceptional children. Many parents are able to accept and adjust to their child's condition in a healthy manner; others, even though they love their child, may have trouble dealing with their feelings and the situation. Parents may experience a range of emotions: grief, shock, and disbelief; fear and anxiety about the child's future; helplessness because they cannot change the condition; and disappointment because theirs is not the perfect child they expected. They may resent the burdens the child's disability places on the family. Whatever the feelings, the counselor needs to help the parents work through them. Parents are the child's main support system, and they must be free to accept and support the child in his or her growth and development.

Parents of exceptional children who are gifted do not experience the shame, guilt, or helplessness that parents of other exceptional children may feel. However, they may wish their child was ordinary because coping with the creativity, advanced intellectual development, and precociousness of their child is so hard. Finding adequate, stimulating educational facilities may be frustrating and possibly financially draining.

Parents may overprotect children with disabilities from a world that is cold and hurtful. They may be overwhelmed with pity and express this feeling by becoming a servant to the child's needs. Some become martyrs, giving up their lives and their own needs to devote themselves totally to the child. The children of overprotective parents get the idea that they are not capable of doing anything for themselves because their parents have never allowed them the opportunity.

Parents often need to work through their own guilt feelings about the exceptionality. Mothers often feel that a handicap is the result of something they did while pregnant, such as horseback riding, tennis, or a fall. The parents may see the child's problem as a consequence or punishment for a parent's wrong behavior. Shame concerning the exceptionality may be the parents' primary reaction: "What will other people think?" Parents are often afraid that other people will gossip, accuse, or ridicule. Parents continue to have vague uncertainties about the causes of disabilities and may suspect that neighbors are blaming them for bad genes, poor health care, or ignorance.

Counseling tasks for the counselor working with the parents of exceptional children include the following:

- Encouraging and helping parents to gain knowledge about their child's exceptionality, prognosis, strengths, and limitations
- Assisting the parents in working through feelings and attitudes that may inhibit the child's progress
- Advising parents concerning state, federal, or community resources available for educational, medical, emotional, or financial assistance
- Assisting the parents in setting realistic expectations for their child
- Encouraging the parents to view their child as a unique individual with rights and potentials and the ability to make choices about his or her own life.

The publications of the NICHCY (www.nichcy.org) have current, valuable information for parents, children, and professionals.

Parent groups are probably a good way of helping parents of exceptional youngsters. Through sharing, the parents learn that others have the feelings and problems they are experiencing. They realize they are not alone in their plight; many other parents have children who are different. Parents not only share their feelings in groups but also share methods for problem solving. Others may have lived through the particular crisis one set of parents is facing, and solutions can be discussed. Parent groups provide an atmosphere of understanding, acceptance, and support; they reassure troubled parents that they are not alone and that others care.

Counselors also may want to explore the possibilities of family therapy. Families of exceptional children often experience considerable financial, psychological, and physical stress. Family sessions could explore feelings of anger, frustration, and shame; tendencies to scapegoat, exclude, or overprotect; communication styles or blocks; and effective and ineffective interactions and other problems of families who do not function effectively.

## SUMMARY

The needs of special children and their families have been ignored for too many years. Stereotypes and societal attitudes must change. Further research is needed to counsel special children more effectively. Additional money and resources are needed to provide means for helping these children become productive citizens. Exceptional children can learn, enjoy life, be independent and productive, and fulfill their individual potential, whether they are exceptionally gifted or have disabilities.

Exceptional children are unique individuals, just as "normal" children are unique. They have the same rights to respect and growth as other children, and they have the same needs. The challenge is there for counselors.

## W E B S I T E S  for Counseling with Exceptional Children

American Association of Gifted Children (AAGC)
www.aagc.org/index.html

Children and Adults with Attention Deficit Hyperactivity Disorder (CHADD)
www.chadd.org

Disability Briefing Papers
www.nichcy.org/pubs/factshe/fs17txt.htm

ERIC Clearinghouse on Disabilities and Gifted Education
ericec.org

National Center for Learning Disabilities
www.ncld.org

## REFERENCES

American Psychiatric Association (APA). (2000). *Diagnostic and statistical manual of mental disorders* (4th ed., text revision). Washington, DC: Author.

The Arc (2001). Statistics. www.thearc.org. Retrieved August 8, 2002.

Badolato, L. A. (1998). Recognizing & meeting the special needs of gifted females. *Gifted Child Today Magazine, 21,* 32–38.

Boudah, D. J., & Weiss, M. P. (2002). *Learning disabilities overview: Update 2002* (EC Digest No. E624). Arlington, VA: ERIC Clearinghouse on Disabilities and Gifted Education.

Brandenburg, N., Friedman, R., & Silver, S. (1990). The epidemiology of childhood psychiatric disorder: Prevalence findings from recent studies. *Journal of the American Academy of Child and Adolescent Psychiatry, 29,* 76–83.

Carpenter, S. L., King-Sears, M. E., & Keys, S. G. (1998). Counselors + educators + families as a transdisciplinary team = more effective inclusion for students with disabilities. *Professional School Counseling, 2,* 1–10.

Davis, G., & Rimm, S. (1994). *Education of the gifted and talented* (3rd ed.). Boston: Allyn & Bacon.

Deck, M., Scarborough, J. L., Sferrazza, M. S., & Estill, D. M. (1999). Serving students with disabilities: Perspectives of three school counselors. *Intervention in School and Clinic, 34,* 150–156.

de la Cruz, B. (1994, May 23). Mothers go on attention deficit disorder crusade. *The Tennessean,* p. 4B.

Erk, R. R. (1999). Attention deficit hyperactivity disorder: Counselors, laws, and implications for practice. *Professional School Counseling, 2,* 318–326.

Fottrell, A. (1998). *Mental and physical disorders in the family: How to detect it, treat it, and refer it.* Presentation to the Tennessee Association of Marriage and Family Therapy annual conference, Nashville, TN.

Frost, J., & Emery, M. (1996). Academic interventions for children with dyslexia who have phonological core deficits. *Teaching Exceptional Children, 28,* 80–83.

Glasser, W. (1998). *Choice theory.* New York: HarperCollins.

Goldstein, S., & Goldstein, M. (1990). *Managing attention disorders in children: A guide for practitioners.* New York: Wiley.

Hardman, M., Drew, C., Egan, M., & Wolf, B. (1993). *Human exceptionality: Society, school and family.* Boston: Allyn & Bacon.

Henderson, K. (2001). *An overview of ADA, IDEA, and Section 504: Update 2001* (EC Digest No. E606). Arlington, VA: ERIC Clearinghouse on Disabilities and Gifted Education.

Kottman, T., Robert, R., & Baker, D. (1995). Parental perspectives on attention deficit/hyperactivity disorder: How school counselors can help. *School Counselor, 43,* 142–150.

National Information Center for Children and Youth with Disabilities (NICHCY). (2002). *Factsheets.* www.nichcy.org. Retrieved August 8, 2002.

Nigg, J. T., & Rappley, M. D. (2001). Interventions for attention-deficit/hyperactivity disorder. In E. R. Welfel & R. E. Ingersoll (Eds.), *The mental health desk reference.* New York: Wiley.

Office of Special Education Programs. (2000). The basic special education process under IDEA. www.ed.gov/offices/OSERS/OSEP/Products/IEP_Guide/IEP_Guide.doc. Retrieved September 8, 2002.

Parette, H., & Holder-Brown, L. (1992). The role of the school counselor in providing services to medically fragile children. *Elementary School Guidance and Counseling, 27,* 47–55.

Parette, H. P., & Hourcade, J. J. (1995). Disability etiquette and school counselors: A common sense approach toward compliance with the Americans with Disabilities Act. *School Counselor, 52,* 224–233.

Patton, P. (1995). Rational behavior skills: A teaching sequence for students with emotional disabilities. *School Counselor, 43,* 133–141.

Renzulli, J., & Reis, S. (1997). The schoolwide enrichment model: New direction for developing high end learning. In N. Colangelo & G. Davis (Eds.), *Handbook of gifted education* (2nd ed., pp. 136–154). Boston: Allyn & Bacon.

Ruth, W. (1996). Goal setting and behavior contracting for students with emotional and behavioral difficulties: Analysis of daily, weekly, and total goal attainment. *Psychology in the Schools, 33,* 153–158.

Schwiebert, V., Sealander, K., & Tollerud, T. (1995). Attention-deficit disorder: An overview for school counselors. *Elementary School Guidance and Counseling, 29,* 249–259.

Simpson, R. L. (1998). Behavior modification for children and youth with exceptionalities: Application of best practice methods. *Intervention in School and Clinic, 33,* 219–227.

Smith, D. (1998). *Introduction to special education: Teaching in an age of challenge.* Boston: Allyn & Bacon.

Smith, D., & Luckasson, R. (1995). *Introduction to special education: Teaching in an age of challenge.* Needham Heights, MA: Allyn & Bacon.

Tarver Behring, S., Spagna, M. E., & Sullivan, J. (1998). School counselors and full inclusion for children with special needs. *Professional School Counselor, 1,* 51–56.

Terman, L., & Oden, M. (1947). *The gifted child grows up: Twenty-five years follow-up of a superior group.* Stanford, CA: Stanford University Press.

Thompson, R., & Littrell, J. M. (1998). Brief counseling for students with learning disabilities. *Professional School Counseling, 2,* 60–68.

U.S. Department of Education. (2001). *Twenty-third annual report to Congress on the implementation of the Individual with Disabilities Education Act.* Washington, DC: U.S. Government Printing Office.

Wicks-Nelson, R., & Israel, A. C. (2000). *Behavior disorders of childhood* (4th ed.). Upper Saddle River, NJ: Prentice Hall.

# Chapter 20

# Legal and Ethical
# Considerations for Counselors

*May you live your life as if the maxim of your
actions were to become universal law.*
—Immanuel Kant

Legal, ethical, moral, and professional considerations combine to form daily considerations for counselors. Counselors' frustration may be fueled by the lack of unequivocal answers from ethical or legal guidelines to the dilemmas created in their practice.

Schmidt and Meara (1984) defined the differences among ethical, professional, and legal issues in counseling. Ethical issues "arise from personal and professional standards of moral duty and obligation" (p. 56). Ethical guidelines educate professionals about principled conduct in practice, provide a means of accountability in practice, and create ways to improve the profession (Herlihy & Corey, 1996). Professional issues are technical, procedural, or cultural standards that members of the profession are expected to accept as part of their practice. Daniels (2001) provided a summary of the ways managed care affects professional issues. Finally, legal issues are related to federal, state, and municipal standards of practice as regulated by law. Laws are mandated standards that carry greater punitive sanctions or penalties for not complying than do ethical and/or professional standards. All three sets exist to guide behavior for professionals. If the standards seem contradictory in a particular situation, the counselor is left to determine the most prudent action to protect the best interest of the client. With children those decisions become complex.

Remley and Herlihy (2001) suggested that professional practice is built on three basic elements that they explain as follows: One foundation is intentionality, wanting to do the right thing for those being served. Another element consists of the moral principles of the helping profession. Those shared beliefs that guide our ethical reasoning include:

- Autonomy (respecting freedom of choice)
- Nonmaleficence (doing no harm)
- Beneficence (responsibility to do good)

- Justice (being fair)
- Fidelity (being faithful)
- Veracity (being honest)

Other aspects these authors discussed include the knowledge of ethical, legal, and professional standards and the skills to apply that knowledge. Finally, they challenged counselors to have the courage of their convictions in order to function in an ethical and professional manner.

Meara, Schmidt, and Day (1996) quoted Beauchamp and Childress (1994, p. 4) in defining *ethics* as a "generic term for various ways of understanding and examining the moral life." These authors believed that "morality is concerned with perspectives of right and proper conduct" (p. 6). They pointed out that codes of ethics guide professionals in their work and provide standards to assist when they must defend their actions.

Meara, Schmidt, and Day (1996) were concerned that a code of ethics cannot contain everything one needs to know and that codes and their interpretations change because of a changing society, technology, rules, and public policy. For these reasons, the writers argued that professionals need to be aware of principle ethics, but must also possess "virtue ethics," or character ethics. According to the authors, "proponents of virtue ethics believe that motivation, emotion, character, ideals, and moral habits situated within the tradition and practices of a culture or other group present a more complete account of moral life than actions based on prescribed rules or principles of practice. . . ." (p. 24). The focus of principles has been on duty, laws, rules, obligations; the focus of virtue ethics, on the other hand, is on the human character. Meara, Schmidt, and Day urged the integration of principle and virtue ethics to assist professionals in making difficult decisions and in more fully developing the ethical character of the profession.

Salo and Shumate (1993) wrote that "counseling minor clients is an ambiguous practice" (p. 1). They suggested that absolute guidelines are difficult to determine because statutes and court decisions do not always agree. In addition, conflicts arise between codes of ethics and state and federal laws. An example of the variation in state laws is the different "ages of majority," the age at which a minor becomes an adult. In some states that age is 18, in others, 19, and in still others, 21 (Swenson, 1993).

Lawrence and Kurpius (2000) traced the history of children's rights and crucial court cases that have set precedents for the interpretation of those rights. They concluded that safeguarding basic rights for children involves balancing three social systems:

> The state, which must accept the imperative of maintaining the safety and rights of citizens, including children; the parent or family, interested in their freedom to raise their children without interference; and the minor child, "whose vested interest has been self-protection from perceived harm, preservation of privacy, and maintenance of personal dignity" (p. 133)

They concluded that currently parents and others in positions of authority over children have the balance of power. Although most adults agree on the worth and dignity of children, legally, minors have fewer rights than adults. Linde (2003) has identified minors' rights to ask for health care and other services in each state. A review of her summary, as well as the recognition of the intersecting social systems just discussed, highlights the complexities of the decisions. Consequently, unique concerns arise in counseling children. Lawrence and Kurpius (2000) and Remley and Herlihy (2001) identified counselor competence, parental permission, confidentiality, and child-abuse reporting as ethical issues that consistently emerge when children are counseled.

The American Counseling Association (ACA) *Code of Ethics and Standards of Practice* (1995) outlines the responsibilities of counselors toward their clients, colleagues, workplace, and self. Whereas the *Code* calls for counselors to respect clients and their background, to maintain professional behavior, to practice with the best interest of the client in mind, and to practice within the limits of their competence, the *Standards of Practice* describe the minimal behavioral expectations for carrying out the *Code of Ethics*. The following sections review the particular challenges of counseling children based on the ACA *Code*.

## COMPETENCE

Counselors need particular areas of knowledge and skills to work with children and cannot assume they can generalize from their coursework on adults. Therefore, they should participate in coursework in child counseling before working with young people. Counselors must be thoroughly familiar with child and adolescent development, developmental tasks, family dynamics, and interventions designed for a particular age and stage (Weiner & Robinson Kurpius, 1995). To be competent to counsel children, counselors must participate in specialized education, training, and supervised practice.

To ensure professional competence, counselors should participate in continuing education, not only for renewing credentials and licensure but also to stay current with best practices and updated information about client populations. Counselors maintain accurate knowledge in their areas of expertise. The credentials of the counselor are accurately portrayed, and counselors provide only services for which they have been trained and had supervised practice. Following those guidelines will help a counselor develop and maintain professional competence (Linde, 2003).

## PARENTAL PERMISSION

One goal of the counseling relationship is the creation of a climate of safety and trust. Professionals assume that the protection of information obtained in that relationship increases the potential for that climate to be built. This right to privacy and confidentiality becomes complicated with minors. Informed consent presents the first complication.

The formal permission given by a client for the beginning of counseling is known as *informed consent*. In effect, that permission constitutes a contract that allows treatment. People who are unable to understand the contents in a consent form or who are unable to make a rational decision are also unable to give informed consent (Huey, 1996). Lawrence and Kurpius (2000) noted that "informed consent must be given voluntarily with sufficient knowledge of the treatment and its consequences, and the person must be competent to give it, that is, able to understand the consequences and implications of the choices being made" (p. 133). The ACA (1995) *Code of Ethics* read as follows:

> When counseling clients who are minors or individuals who are unable to give voluntary, informed consent, parents or guardians may be included in the counseling process as appropriate. Counselors act in the best interest of clients and take measures to safeguard confidentiality. (B.3)

Consequently, parental permission may be necessary for children to receive treatment. Remley and Herlihy (2001) explained that unless a federal or state law states otherwise, school counselors do not have an obligation to attain a parent's permission for counseling services. Counselors outside school do need a parent or guardian's consent for a minor to receive counseling. Lawrence and Kurpius (2000) discussed some situations that are exceptions to this practice. One exception is court-ordered treatment. Another exception involves a mature minor, an older adolescent capable of understanding the consent. These authors noted that in some states minors can give consent to treatment in an emergency, when waiting would endanger their lives or health. They also caution care when working with a minor of divorced parents to obtain consent from the custodial parent.

## CONFIDENTIALITY

Stadler (1990) noted confusion concerning the terms *privacy, confidentiality,* and *privileged communication*. She stated that the right to privacy ensures that people may choose what others know about them. Confidentiality refers to the professional responsibility to respect and limit access to clients' personal information. According to Stadler, issues of confidentiality are the ethical problems counselors most frequently encounter. She recommended that counselors be extremely careful to apprise their clients of their limits of confidentiality at the very beginning of counseling.

Linde (2003) provided helpful definitions of *privileged communication,* a legal term used "to describe the privacy of the counselor–client communication. Privileged communication exists by statute and applies only to testifying in a court of law. The privilege belongs to the client, who always has the right to waive the privilege and allow the counselor to testify" (p. 52). She explained that the limits of privileged communication are determined by federal, state, and local mandates and vary in existence and parameters accordingly. Therefore, counselors must know local, state, and federal laws to understand how privileged communication applies.

One assumption on which counseling proceeds is that the promise of confidentiality helps create trust and safety, with both adults and children. For example, research (Ford, Milstein, Halpern-Felscher, & Irwin, 1997) suggests that adolescents are more willing to disclose personal information with the promise of confidentiality. However, children may have parents or guardians who want to know the contents of counseling sessions, and those adults probably have a legal right to know (Remley & Herlihy, 2001). Salo and Shumate (1993) contended, "When a child approaches a counselor without parental knowledge or consent, immediate tension arises between the child's right to privacy and the parent's right—on the child's behalf—to provide informed consent for the counseling" (p. 10). Obtaining parental consent is good practice for counselors unless potential danger to the minor exists. The authors pointed out that early communication with parents concerning the purpose of counseling can prevent later problems. The law generally supports parents who forbid counseling of their minor children unless there are extenuating circumstances. Counselors must balance offering privacy to minors with not only the rights of parents but also the therapeutic goal of engaging parents in helping children. Remley and Herlihy (2001) suggested that counselors consider these facts about children and privacy:

- Younger children have little understanding of confidentiality or a need for privacy. Huey (1996) stated that young children often are much less concerned about confidentiality than the counselor is.
- Preadolescents and adolescents, on the other hand, may have a heightened need for privacy because of their developmental stage.
- Some children may want their parents or guardians to know what has occurred in the counseling session(s).
- Children sometimes disclose something to an adult in hopes that the adult will intervene with other adults.
- Children's reasoning capacity may limit their ability to make decisions in their own best interest.

Accordingly, the 1995 revision of the ACA *Code* endorses counselors using their professional judgment in deciding when to include parents or guardians in the counseling process (Huey, 1996).

To safeguard against confidentiality becoming a possible ethical or legal problem, counselors should inform clients during the first and subsequent interviews (as applicable) that the client holds the rights to confidentiality. When possible, have parents and guardians as well as the minor present in the first session so that all understand the parameters of therapy and the limits of confidentiality. Those limits should be clearly disclosed and explained and should include examples of legally and ethically mandated breaches of confidentiality. This disclosure should be done both verbally in language easily understood by the client and in a written professional disclosure statement that should be signed by the client (and parents, if necessary) and the counselor. All parties should retain a copy of the professional disclosure statement.

Remley and Herlihy (2001) suggested ways to cope with requests when parents want to know about counseling and the minor client has strong feelings about the disclosure not happening.

1. Discuss the request with the child, and ask if the minor is willing to talk to the adult. If the child refuses, proceed with the next step.

2. Try to convince the adult that the nature of the counseling relationship and the importance of confidentiality work for the best interests of the child. Assure the adult that information concerning any danger to the child will be disclosed. If that does not convince the adult, move to the next step.

3. Hold a session with the child and the adult and act as a mediator, hoping that one or the other will acquiesce. Failing that, proceed according to step 4 or 5.

4. Inform the child beforehand, and then tell the adult the content of the counseling session to the adult who has requested the information or

5. Refuse to disclose the information, after having informed your supervisor.

Salo and Shumate (1993) urged that, in cases of parental separation or divorce, the counselor always obtain permission from the custodial parent before revealing information to a noncustodial parent. They advised counselors to obtain written proof of who retains legal custody of the child.

As noted previously, privileged communication is a legal concept designed to protect the rights of the client (rather than for the protection of the counselor's rights) to withhold testimony in court proceedings. Because there is great variation among all 50 states, statutes must specify which professionals (e.g., attorneys, clergy, psychologists, counselors) are included under the umbrella of privileged communication. Since exclusions to this privilege vary by state, it is imperative for the counselor to be thoroughly familiar with the state laws governing counseling practice. It is also the client's right to waive privileged communication that leaves the counselor with no legal grounds for withholding the requested confidential information.

However, professionals are required only to disclose the information requested to the parties specified by the client. Because the right to privileged communication is not absolute, courts may order the release of records, especially in situations where the society's need for information overrides the client's right to privacy. In most states, the legal concept of privileged communication does not extend to groups, couples, or family counseling, nor does it cover disclosures made in the presence of third parties not specified under the umbrella of privileged communication.

Exceptions to the privileged communication right, in which professionals must disclose information, include situations in which:

- The professional is fulfilling a court-ordered role, such as expert witness
- A court mandates the release of information considered to be privileged communication
- A lawsuit against the professional is initiated by the client (e.g., malpractice)
- The client uses his or her mental condition as a defense in a lawsuit

- A professional determines that the client needs hospitalization because of a mental disorder
- A client discloses intent to commit a crime or is assessed to be dangerous to self or others
- A client is a minor and has been or is suspected of being the victim of a crime such as child abuse.

## Confidentiality of Files

A national survey of American Psychological Association (APA) members found that confidentiality was their highest ranked ethical dilemma (Pope & Vetter, 1992). Access to files presented another concern involving confidentiality. There appears to be a move toward allowing clients to see their own records. The federal Family Educational Rights and Privacy Act (FERPA) provided parents and students of legal age the right to inspect their records and to protect unlimited access to their records (Burcky & Childers, 1976). Also known as the Buckley Amendment, the act applies to all educational records collected, maintained, or used by a school the student has attended. Personal logs, treatment records, and directory information are excluded. *Personal logs* are defined as records of instructional, supervisory, administrative, and associated educational personnel. The records must be in sole possession of the individual and not have been shared. *Treatment records* include the records of a physician, psychiatrist, psychologist, or other recognized professional acting in the professional role. The records can be used only in conjunction with the treatment of the student. *Directory information* includes the demographic information, grade or field of study, participation in extracurricular activities, physical descriptions, and dates of attendance (FERPA, 1974; Sealander, Schwiebert, Oren, & Weekley, 1999; Underwood & Mead, 1995; U. S. Department of Education, 2002).

Hughes (2001) summarized the laws regarding the release of student information. Also, the U. S. Department of Education (2002) clarified that schools need written permission from the parent to release information, except as follows:

- To school officials with legitimate educational interests
- To a school to which a student is transferring
- Officials for auditing or evaluation purposes
- In conjunction with financial aid requests
- Organizations conducting research on behalf of the school
- Accrediting bodies
- To comply with a judicial order or subpoena
- Appropriate officials in cases of emergency
- State and local authorities in a juvenile justice system. (p. 2)

Counselors need to know the types of records kept in institutional files. They may not be able to maintain confidentiality if the parents of underage children request access to such files. The counselor may maintain a personal file for confidential notes because personal files do not fall under this law. However, files that have been seen by *anyone,* except a paid secretary, or have been discussed with anyone in the process of decision making are no longer considered personal notes (Salo & Shumate, 1993).

Remley (1990) found no legal or ethical requirement for counselors to keep notes about their counseling sessions in most states. For the counselor who keeps notes, he suggested that factual information concerning actual occurrences in the session should be kept separate from the subjective section in which the counselor records diagnoses and develops future treatment plans. Remley also recommended writing notes carefully, with the thought in mind that they could become public one day and that counselors may want to document questionable or controversial information.

## Breaching Confidentiality

In court cases in states where the clients of counselors and psychologists (or other helpers) are not protected by a licensure law providing for privileged communication, counselors have no recourse except to reveal the information if subpoenaed. Some courts are more tolerant than others, allowing the counselor to share the privileged information with the judge in private to determine if the information is necessary to the proceeding or if public disclosure would be too hurtful to those involved, such as children who are a part of the case.

Examples of legally and ethically mandated breaches of confidentiality include situations in which:

- The client is under the age of 18 years or the recognized age of majority in that jurisdiction. (The parent or legal guardian then has a legal right to the child's counseling records and to be informed of the counseling content, progress, and other information.)
- The client expresses an intent to harm self, others, or property. (Court decisions such as *Tarasoff* v. *Regents of the University of California* [1974] have delineated the counselor's duty to warn and protect others at the expense of breaking client confidentiality.)
- The client discloses acts (either past or present) of verbal, physical, or sexual abuse, or the counselor has reasonable suspicion that such acts occurred or are occurring.
- The counselor is court-ordered to break confidentiality or to provide counseling notes or records subpoenaed or requested by the court.
- An adult client willingly provides written informed consent requesting the counselor to breach confidentiality or to release counseling records.
- The counselor is a student or is being supervised for licensure. The client's written consent to record counseling sessions must be obtained to provide the student counselor with professional supervision or consultation with treatment teams. In these cases, student counselors should disclose only as much confidential information as is required or necessary for professional supervision or consultation.

If breaking confidentiality is necessary, the counselor ought to discuss with the client his or her intention to do so and ask the client for assistance with deciding on the best process. The counselor should explain why confidentiality must be broken, summarize what has to be done or said, and then ask the client to help resolve the dilemma. The child client might prefer to take the lead by calling parents or other authorities or by taking whatever appropriate action is necessary.

Breaching confidentiality when a counselor has a dangerous client requires extreme care. Isaacs (1997) suggested that the *Tarasoff* case, case law in other jurisdictions, legal requirements, and ethical guidelines can confuse counselors on ways to proceed with dangerous clients. She proposed counselors develop protocols for consistency. Among other things, those protocols should include:

- Current standards of care
- List of treatment alternatives
- Full informed consent
- Consultation guidelines with parents, attorneys, school officials, and other counselors
- School policy

She concluded that establishing protocols will prepare counselors to recognize the issues, identify their options, and have ready access to needed information. Isaacs and Stone (1999) also provided similar guidelines.

McFarland and Dupuis (2001) admonished counselors to protect gay and lesbian students from violence by educating others, advocating for safe schools, and implementing prevention efforts. These authors cited emerging case law as mandating this protection for gay and lesbian students.

## Confidentiality in Groups

Corey (1995) was particularly concerned about confidentiality in counseling groups for minors. He urged leaders to "teach members, in terms they are capable of understanding, about the nature, purposes and limitations of confidentiality" (p. 33) and to remind members to discuss their concerns about confidentiality whenever needed. With complete information about the limits of confidentiality, members can decide how much they want to disclose. Salo and Shumate (1993) also noted that "groups, by their very nature, negate the presumption of privacy" (p. 34). They advised counselors to inform all group members about the necessity for confidentiality but also to point out that privileged communication may not apply to group discussion.

## CHILD ABUSE REPORTING

Child welfare agencies receive approximately 3 million reports of child abuse and neglect each year. All states have statutes that require adults who have responsibility to care for and treat children to report suspected abuse of children (Lawrence & Kurpius, 2000). Lawrence and Kurpius stated that unreported suspected abuse is one of the most common breaches of ethical standards. They hypothesize that the reporting may harm the therapeutic relationship and may destabilize the family. They suggest that counselors confer with professional colleagues and get legal advice before a decision is made to refrain from reporting child abuse.

## SUMMARY

In conclusion, Lawrence and Kurpius (2000) proposed the following guidelines for counseling with minors:

1. Practice within the boundaries of your competence as defined by your education, training, and supervised practice.

2. Know state laws regarding privilege. Privilege does not exist unless the state has mandated it (Hendrix, 1991).

3. Explain your policies on confidentiality with both the child and parents at the beginning of the counseling relationship and ask them for cooperation. Provide a written informed consent that everyone signs.

4. Should you decide to work with a minor without the consent of the parent or guardian, ask the child to give informed consent in writing (Hendrix, 1991) and recognize the legal risks involved.

5. Maintain accurate and objective records.

6. Purchase adequate professional liability insurance.

7. Confer with colleagues and have access to professional legal advice when you are uncertain about how to proceed. (Lawrence & Kurpius, 2000, p. 135)

## TEST YOUR ETHICAL KNOWLEDGE*

Although understanding ethical and legal issues is of utmost importance to those who work in the helping professions, training, research, and knowledge in the area seem seriously lacking. As a test of your general understanding of ethical and legal issues, consider the following situations and describe methods and procedures you would use in handling the incident. Many situations have no *right* solution; the final answer depends on your counseling setting, the philosophy of your supervisor, the interpretation of the law by your local or state authorities, potential advantages or disadvantages of the solution, and the risks to the counselor and client. In these situations, *our comments are only our interpretation and not necessarily the right answer.* We refer to the 1995 Ethical Standards of ACA, the Ethical Principles of Psy-

---

*Sincere appreciation is extended to Janet Floyd and Nicole McDonald at the University of Tennessee for their suggestions and ideas in developing many of the ethical situations described in this chapter.

chologists (APA, 1992), and the Code of Ethics for the National Association of Social Workers (1996). Although we understand that other professionals bound by other professional codes encounter these situations, we believe all codes have similarities, and the principles outlined here can be generalized to other professions.

## Situation 1

A master's level intern in counseling psychology is asked to speak at her church on the subject of disciplining children, focusing on the difference between spanking and when physical punishment becomes child abuse. The intern has almost completed her placement in an adult services division of a mental health clinic but has had little experience in working with families and children.

*Response.*   ACA Code of Ethics and Standards of Practice C.2.a states: "Counselors practice only within the boundaries of their competence, based on their education, training, supervised experience, and appropriate professional experience." APA Principle A cautions that psychologists "recognize the boundaries of their particular competencies and the limitations of their expertise. They provide only those services and use only those techniques for which they are qualified by education, training, or experience." The NASW Code of Ethics 4.01(a) states that social workers "should accept responsibility or employment only on the basis of existing competence or the intention to acquire the necessary competence." It would probably be better to decline the invitation and refer the group to someone more experienced. However, if such an experienced person is not available, she may speak in front of the group but disclose her intern status and her limited experience. Most of her speech should be composed of research or writings in the area.

## Situation 2

You are licensed as a professional counselor and have worked with numerous families in your area. At a meeting of the general public composed of families interested in learning more about being more effective, you are introduced as a licensed marriage and family therapist. What should you do?

*Response.*   ACA Code of Ethics and Standards of Practice C.3.c advises that counselors should "make reasonable efforts to ensure that statements made by others about them or the profession of counseling are accurate." APA Ethical Standard 3.02 urges psychologists to "make reasonable efforts to prevent others whom they do not control (such as employers, publishers, sponsors, organizational clients, and representatives of the print or broadcast media) from making deceptive statements concerning psychologists' practice of professional or scientific activities." The NASW Code of Ethics 4.06 warns that social workers should take steps to correct any inaccuracies or misrepresentations of their credentials by others. You should correct your colleague's statement immediately, clarifying your licensure status.

*Situation 3*

You are a counselor in a local mental health clinic and receive a referral for a child with behavioral problems. During the initial interview, you realize this child is the son of your husband's business client. Would this cause a problem with your accepting the referral and working with the child?

*Response.*    The ACA Code of Ethics and Standards of Practice A.6.a warns counselors to "avoid dual relationships with clients that could impair professional judgment or increase the risk of harm to clients." They include examples such as familial, social, business, or close personal relationships. The APA Principles and Ethical Code of Conduct 1.17(a) cautions psychologists to refrain "from entering into or promising another personal, scientific, professional, financial, or other relationship with such persons if it appears likely that such a relationship reasonably might impair the psychologist's objectivity." The NASW Code of Ethics 1.06(c) prohibits social workers from condoning or engaging "in dual or multiple relationships with clients or former clients in which there is a risk of exploitation of or potential harm to the client." It is suggested that knowing the child is the son of a business client of your husband's could interfere with your counseling.

*Situation 4*

You are a counselor in a residential treatment facility for young offenders and hold very stringent codes and beliefs, many of which question the worth of African Americans and other cultural minorities. Many of the residential youth are African American and from other cultures. What would you do?

*Response.*    The ACA Code of Ethics and Standards of Practice A.2.a states that counselors "do not condone or engage in discrimination" based on a multitude of factors that include culture. APA Principles advise psychologists to be "aware of cultural, individual, and role differences" due to many factors and states that psychologists should "try to eliminate the effect on their work of biases based on those factors." The NASW Code of Ethics 4.02 warns social workers not to "practice, condone, facilitate or collaborate with any form of discrimination" on the basis of these same factors. This counselor needs to resign his or her job and seek help to resolve the conflict between counseling philosophy and personal codes and beliefs.

*Situation 5*

Walter is a good student, makes Bs and Cs, enjoys sports, and is involved in many clubs. His parents are pressuring him to make As so that he can earn a scholarship. They have limited income and do not believe they can send him to a "really good" college. Walter is showing some signs of anxiety because of his parents' pressure. What do you do?

*Response.* ACA A.3.b urges counselors to "promote the freedom of clients to choose whether to enter into a counseling relationship." APA Principle D supports the client's right to self-determination and autonomy. The NASW Code 1.02 also urges that social workers "respect and promote the rights of clients to self-determination." You explain to the parents your role as a helping professional in the light of these codes and, with their permission, ask Walter if he would like to talk with you about these concerns. If he does choose to talk with you, you should avoid pressuring him to accept his parents' plans. He should have the right of "self-determination and autonomy."

## Situation 6

You are called to the school after a tornado to participate in crisis counseling for children coping with fears or experiencing anxiety. The teacher asked you to include one child in the group, not because of her anxiety but because she has problems with relationships and her parents have not let her participate in group counseling previously. They have agreed to the crisis counseling because so many other children are participating and it would appear that any problem she was having was related to the tornado.

*Response.* ACA A.9.a states that "counselors select members whose needs and goals are compatible with goals of the group, who will not impede the group process, and whose well-being will not be jeopardized by the group experience." The ethical codes of APA and NASW do not address the screening and selection of group participants but generally emphasize respect for the well-being of clients. Thus, this child's needs do not meet the goals of the counseling group, and teacher and parents should be informed immediately.

## Situation 7

Marcia is a 10-year-old girl in a day treatment facility for children with behavioral and psychological disorders. Marcia reveals that she has been wanting to kill herself by taking an overdose of her parents' pills. She then begs you, her counselor, not to reveal this information to her mother or father. Should you reveal this information to Marcia's parents?

*Response.* ACA B.1.c states that confidentiality does not apply when disclosure is necessary to "prevent clear and imminent danger to the client or others." APA 5.05 says that psychologists disclose information "to protect the patient or client or others from harm," and NASW Section 1.07(c) allows social workers to reveal confidences for "compelling professional reasons." The child's parents should be told and assisted with a plan to help prevent such an action.

## Situation 8

You are head of a mental health clinic and have just increased fees for hourly services. Some of the clinic's clients have been in counseling for years at the lower rate and have limited resources. They have been paying on a sliding scale. Your counselors are concerned about these clients receiving care when it appears treatment is no longer affordable.

*Response.*   ACA Code of Ethics A.10.b advises counselors to consider the financial status of their clients and the locality in establishing fees. APA 1.25 cautions psychologists that if services are limited because of financial reasons, other appropriate services should be arranged (also Standard 4.08). NASW 1.13(b) states that social workers shall set fees that are fair and reasonable and with regard to clients' ability to pay.

## Situation 9

You are subpoenaed to testify in a court case involving the father of a child you are counseling. The defense is trying to establish that the father has excellent character and wants you to testify about the father–child relationship. Your client, the child, is unwilling for you to reveal the content of the counseling sessions, but the father and his attorney are pressuring you for this testimony—it is very important to their case. What do you do in court?

*Response.*   ACA states that "the right to privacy belongs to the clients and may be waived by the client." If the client is unwilling to do so, B.1.d advises counselors that, when courts order the release of confidential information, "counselors request to the court that the disclosure not be required due to potential harm to the client or counseling relationship." NASW has a similar provision [1.07(j)]. APA does not address the situation as directly but gives guidance about maintaining the confidentiality of the counseling interview.

## Situation 10

You are a school counselor leading a group that includes Peter, a sixth grader. Although his parents signed a consent form and indicated that they understood that what was revealed in the group was to be kept confidential, they have recently become suspicious of Peter's behavior and are demanding that you tell them what Peter is discussing in the group. How would you handle this?

*Response.*   ACA B.1.a states that "counselors respect their clients' right to privacy and take steps to avoid unwarranted disclosures of confidential information." ACA B.3 points out that "informed consent, parents or guardians may be included in the counseling process as appropriate." APA points out that "psychologists have a primary obligation and take reasonable precautions to respect the confidentiality rights of those with whom they work or consult, recognizing that confidentiality must be established by law, institutional rules, or professional or scientific relationship." NASW 1.07 (c) maintains that the social worker should share with others confidences revealed by clients, without their consent, only for "compelling professional reasons." Refer back to the section on confidentiality in this chapter for suggestions about handling this case.

## Situation 11

A counselor with whom you work talks about her cases with you in front of staff in the counseling office. What is your responsibility?

*Response.*   The rules for maintaining confidentiality are described in Situation 10. Because this counselor is behaving in an unethical manner, you should attempt to resolve the conflict in an informal manner by discussing the behavior with him or her. If this does not stop the violations of confidentiality, the counselor following the ACA Ethical Code has the obligation to report the behavior to an administrative head, as well as a state or national ethics committee or to a state licensing board (H.1.d and c). APA has similar standards for reporting unethical behavior (8.04 and 8.05). NASW 2.11 (d) encourages the social worker to "take action through appropriate channels" against unethical conduct by any other member of the profession.

## Situation 12

You are working with a child exhibiting a variety of symptoms. The cause of these symptoms is unclear, and you decide that numerous tests are required to help clarify the situation. There are a number of new tests just published that you want to try. You have been trained generally in assessment but not with these particular types of tests. Is it ethical for you to administer and interpret these tests?

*Response.*   ACA E.2.a cautions counselors to "recognize the limits of their competence and perform only those testing and assessment services for which they have been trained." APA 2.06 prohibits the use of "psychological assessment techniques by unqualified persons." NASW does not address assessment. It would be wise to consider your training very thoroughly in light of the chosen test. Consulting with colleagues is also recommended.

*Situation 13*

As an intern in a school setting, you are conducting research about children's social behavior with a new assessment instrument. To have an adequate sample, you ask teachers to allow you to use their classrooms for the research. Have you met all of your ethical responsibilities for the research?

*Response.*   As long as the data are reported in a way to disguise the identity of the participants, you have met ACA research codes B.5.a. and G.3.d.; however, E.3 cautions that the nature and purposes of assessment and the use of results must be explained to the client or legally authorized person. Parental consent should be obtained before the administration. APA 2.08 offers similar advice. NASW does not address assessment but cautions that informed consent must be obtained [see 5.01 (d), (e), and (f)].

*Situation 14*

A counselor in a mental health clinic wants to ask a child psychiatrist to consult with her about the behaviors and ideation of a 6-year-old with whom she is counseling. The counselor feels that progress has not been as good as she would have liked and that the psychiatrist can help her develop a better treatment plan. Is this an appropriate consultation? What precautions should be taken?

*Response.*   ACA B.6.a points out that "information obtained during a consultation is discussed for professional purposes only with persons clearly concerned with the case" and that "every effort is made to protect client identity and avoid undue invasion of privacy." APA 5.06 prohibits psychologists from sharing confidential information that could identify the client without the client's consent and urges psychologists to reveal only necessary information. NASW 2.05 states that the "social worker should seek the advice and counsel of colleagues whenever such consultation is in the best interests of clients." Consultation with colleagues is encouraged, but every effort should be made to protect the identity of the consultee.

## SUMMARY

It is difficult to recommend specific answers to the situations outlined in this chapter because situations, people, and laws vary. References are given to ACA, APA, and NASW codes of ethics to aid readers in formulating their own resolutions. We hope that readers will be stimulated to read the ethical standards thoroughly and to consider the issues in the light of presenting situations and regulations.

   The foregoing situations are by no means all the ethical and legal situations encountered in counseling. Other situations and their resolutions for study appear in the casebooks prepared by ACA and APA. The situations in this chapter are intended only to give readers some indication of their own ethical knowledge and practices. Should uncertainty arise concerning interpretations of ethical practices, counselors have the option of consulting other professionals or local, state, or national professional ethics committees.

## W E B S I T E S for Legal and Ethical Considerations for Counselors

**ACA Code of Ethics and Standards of Practice—Frequently Asked Questions**
www.counseling.org/ctonline/news/aca_ethics.htm

**APA Ethical Principles of Psychologists and Code of Conduct**
www.apa.org/ethics/code.html

**U.S. Department of Education**
www.ed.gov

**Department of Education Office for Civil Rights**
www.ed.gov/offices/OCR

**National Clearinghouse on Child Abuse and Neglect Information**
www.calib.com/nccanch

**National Board for Certified Counselors**
www.nbcc.org

## REFERENCES

American Counseling Association. (1995). *Code of ethics and standards of practice.* Alexandria, VA: Author.

American Psychological Association. (1992). *Ethical principles of psychologists and code of conduct.* Washington, DC: Author.

Beauchamp, T., & Childress, J. (1994). *Principles of biomedical ethics* (4th ed.). New York: Oxford University Press.

Burcky, W. D., & Childers, J. H. Jr. (1976). Buckley amendment: Focus of a professional dilemma. *School Counselor, 23,* 162–164.

Corey, G. (1995). *Theory and practice of group counseling.* Pacific Grove, CA: Brooks/Cole.

Daniels, J. A. (2001). Managed care, ethics, and counseling. *Journal of Counseling and Development, 79,* 119–122.

Family Educational Rights and Privacy Act. (1974). 20 U.S.C.A. §1232g. [Buckley Amendment.] (1991). Implementing regulations 34 C.F.F. 99.3 Fed. Reg. 56, §117, 28012.

Ford, C. A., Milstein, S. G., Halpern-Felscher, B. L., & Irwin, C. E. Jr. (1997). Influence of physician confidentiality assurances on adolescents' willingness to discuss information and seek future health care: A randomized controlled trial. *Journal of the American Medical Association, 278,* 1029–1034.

Hendrix, D. H. (1991). Ethics and intrafamily confidentiality in counseling with children. *Journal of Mental Health Counseling, 13,* 323–358.

Herlihy, B., & Corey, G. (1996). *ACA ethical standards casebook* (5th ed.). Alexandria, VA: American Counseling Association.

Huey, W. C. (1996). Counseling minor clients. In B. Herlihy & G. Corey, *ACA ethical standards casebook* (5th ed.) (pp. 241–245). Alexandria, VA: American Counseling Association.

Hughes, T. (2001, Winter). Releasing student information: What's public and what's not. *School Law Bulletin*, 12–29.

Isaacs, M. L. (1997). The duty to warn and protect: *Tarasoff* and the elementary school counselor. *Elementary School Guidance and Counseling, 31*, 326–342.

Isaacs, M. L., & Stone, C. (1999). School counselors and confidentiality: Factors affecting professional choices. *Professional School Counseling, 2*, 258–266.

Lawrence, G., & Kurpius, S. E. R. (2000). Legal and ethical issues involved when counseling minors in non-school settings. *Journal of Counseling and Development, 78*, 130–136.

Linde, L. (2003). Ethical, legal, and professional issues in school counseling. In B. T. Erford (Ed.), *Transforming the school counseling profession* (pp. 39–62). Upper Saddle River, NJ: Merrill.

McFarland, W. P., & Dupuis, M. (2001). The legal duty to protect gay and lesbian students from violence in the schools. *Professional School Counseling, 4*, 171–179.

Meara, N., Schmidt, L., & Day, J. (1996) Principles and virtues: A foundation for ethical decisions, policies, and character. *Counseling Psychologist, 24*, 4–77.

National Association of Social Workers. (1996). *Code of ethics, adopted by the 1979 NASW Delegate Assembly and revised by the 1993 NASW Delegate Assembly*. Silver Spring, MD: NASW Press.

Pope, K., & Vetter, V. (1992). Ethical dilemmas encountered by members of the American Psychological Association: A national survey. *American Psychologist, 47*, 397–411.

Remley, T. (1990). Counseling records: Legal and ethical issues. In B. Herlihy & L. Golden (Eds.), *Ethical standards casebook* (pp. 162–169). Alexandria, VA: American Association for Counseling and Development.

Remley, T. P., & Herlihy, B. (2001). *Ethical, legal, and professional issues in counseling*. Upper Saddle River, NJ: Merrill.

Salo, M., & Shumate, S. (1993). *The ACA legal series: Vol. 4. Counseling minor clients*. Alexandria, VA: American Counseling Association.

Schmidt, L., & Meara, N. (1984). Ethical, professional, and legal issues in counseling psychology. In S. Brown & R. Lent (Eds.), *Handbook of counseling psychology* (pp. 56–96). New York: Wiley.

Sealander, K. A., Schwiebert, V. L., Oren, T. A., & Weekley, J. L. (1999). Confidentiality and the law. *Professional School Counseling, 3*, 122–127.

Stadler, H. (1990). Confidentiality. In B. Herlihy & L. Golden (Eds.), *Ethical standards casebook* (pp. 102–110). Alexandria, VA: American Association for Counseling and Development.

Swenson, L. C. (1993). *Psychology and the law for the helping professions*. Pacific Grove, CA: Brooks/Cole.

Tarasoff v. Regents of University of California. (1974). 13c. D177; 529 p. 2D553; 118 *California Reporter, 129*.

Underwood, J. K., & Mead, J. F. (1995). *Legal aspects of special education and pupil services*. Boston: Allyn & Bacon.

U.S. Department of Education. (2002). Family educational rights and privacy act (FERPA). www.ed.gov/offices/OM/fpco/ferpa/index.html. Retrieved September 1, 2002.

Weiner, N., & Kurpius, S. E. R. (1995). *Shattered innocence: A practical guide for counseling women survivors of childhood sexual abuse*. Washington, DC: Taylor & Francis.

# APPENDIXES

Appendixes A and B suggest techniques for intervening with specific problem behaviors and are included to stimulate ideas. The lists, of course, are not exhaustive, but we hope they help counselors who are attempting to develop treatment plans for children. At the end of each appendix are some *Diagnostic and Statistical Manual of Mental Disorders (DSM) IV–TR* categories (American Psychiatric Association, 2000) that may be applicable in classifying client behaviors. Use caution in assigning classifications because the categories ordinarily describe mental disorders and are not appropriate for all problematic behaviors that are not a part of a pattern or syndrome of symptoms. At the conclusion of Appendix B is a table of psychotropic medications that may be indicated for different diagnoses.

Appendix C contains computations and T-scores to use with goal-attainment scaling, which is explained in Chapter 2. Appendix D includes some sample questions that might be asked for oral licensing examinations and examples of answers.

# Appendix A

# Children's Conflicts with Others
## Alternatives for Intervention

The suggestions in this appendix are techniques collected from a variety of resources on counseling children with learning and social problems. Some suggestions are used directly with the child; others are consultation techniques to use with parents and teachers. In each case, the procedures must be incorporated into a therapeutic counseling or consulting atmosphere that includes caring, respect, empathic understanding, and acceptance. The techniques presented can be preventive and developmental as well as remedial; no single technique has only one possible application. In any case, the techniques should be adapted to meet the unique needs of children and their behaviors.

## *Fighting*

Fighting is one of the most common behavioral problems of children today. Many children have not learned to settle their misunderstandings through methods other than physical means. Fighting may be a way of gaining attention; a learned behavior from parents, peers, or other significant people in the children's lives; or a way of striking back at a world perceived as cruel and hostile. Adults want children to learn to resolve their disagreements and conflicts in other ways, but the problem of aggressive behavior persists. Following are various suggestions for working with fighting behavior. (See also "Destructiveness," p. 614.)

1. Examine the situation that brought on the encounter. Determine the sequence of events and any particular time, place, or situation in which fights are likely to occur. Become an environmental engineer; rearrange the time schedule or the physical environment. Intervene in the sequence of events to prevent or circumvent fight-arousing conditions.

2. Fighting can be a compensation for feelings of inadequacy, ignorance of social skills, learned behavior from the home, or a means of covering up emotional or learning problems. Investigate these possibilities by becoming a child watcher and listening actively to the child. See Chapter 6 for more information.

3. Use group or family discussions to focus on how fighting helps or hurts the fighter, how others feel about fighting, the consequences of fighting, and ways in which the fighter could resolve conflicts more effectively. Also, encourage children to practice new behaviors before the group, and use their feedback to improve relationships. Be certain the child has opportunities to see effective ways of resolving conflicts.

4. Determine the goal of the fighter. (See Chapter 11 regarding goals of misbehavior.) Is the child seeking attention, power, revenge, or free time? Is the fighting a learned be-

havior? Could the fighting result from a lack of social skills? Intervene in ways that allow the child to meet these needs appropriately.

5. Contract with the fighter to not fight for a short time period (2 hours, 4 hours, 1 day). Continue to renegotiate the contract until the behavior decreases significantly. Rewards for not fighting and consequences for fighting behavior may be included. (See Chapter 9 regarding contingency contracting.)

6. Arrange with the physical education teacher for students to work out their emotions with punching bags or other equipment under supervision. Each time students are found fighting, encourage them to go to the gym and work out for a certain period of time (perhaps 15 minutes). After a cooling-off period, the fighters should be required to write a plan for avoiding future fighting. Children who cannot write may dictate or tape their contracts.

7. Have the fighters write their side of the story or tell it to a tape recorder. Ask the children to read their stories to you, or listen to the tape with them. Plan other ways to resolve such situations in the future.

8. Films, television programs, or stories can stimulate children to think more objectively about fighting and its consequences. Follow the film or story with a family or group discussion examining the causes and consequences of fighting and other ways the situation could have been resolved. Adults should strictly limit the amount of time children spend watching any violence on television or video games.

9. Children and parents or teachers may cooperatively draw up a list of ground rules concerning fighting. Each time the adult notices the child about to become involved in a fight, the adult asks, "What is the ground rule?" Have the child repeat the rule. Early and consistent intervention is necessary. A variation is to clearly define the consequences of fighting and, when fighting is about to occur, ask, "What happens when someone fights?"

10. Encouragement from friends or peers (or other kinds of peer pressure) can help the child control fighting behavior. Find the fighter a good role model with whom to work or play. Ask the child to describe or list the model's behaviors. Rehearse and practice admired behaviors.

11. Isolation techniques such as the quiet corner and time-out rooms are effective for helping children cool off. When the children feel ready to return to the family group or classroom, they may do so without lectures or blame, provided they have a plan for staying out of fights. (See Chapters 11 and 16 regarding isolation techniques.)

12. The adult may quietly ask the fighters to leave the room and develop a plan for solving their conflict. The fighters then report their plan to the adult.

13. Three chairs are placed in a semicircle. The adult sits between the two fighters and asks each person to describe what happened. The adult repeats verbatim to Child A what Child B says, and then to B what A says. This continues until usually everyone ends up laughing. The adults limit themselves to conveying messages between A and B and refrain from making judgments or placing blame. (See Chapter 7.) Discussion of a plan for avoiding future conflicts may follow.

14. Parents can avoid becoming referees by withdrawing to the bedroom or bathroom until the fighting ceases. Parents should take precautions to prevent one child from harming the other if they decide to withdraw.

15. Peer pressure, especially in small groups, is often effective to help fighting children change their behavior. Adults should find appropriate times to encourage a group when the children are playing or working cooperatively.

16. Have the fighting children carry index cards and keep a record of the number of fights that occur each day. Have them role play exactly what happened and the conse-

quences. Discuss alternatives to fighting, rehearse how the situation could have been handled more appropriately, and develop a plan for not fighting in future situations.

17. Build self-esteem so that fighting is not necessary for the child to feel good about himself or herself (see "Poor Self-Concept," Appendix B). Responsibility and praise for a job well done add to a positive self-concept—for example, "I appreciate your help in putting away the games we used during this activity."

18 If excessive punishment or brutality seems to be a factor, consult with the parents to help them learn more effective ways of relating to the child. Parent effectiveness classes or books may be helpful.

19. Strongly confront older children with the reality questions (see Chapter 5), and use these questions every time a fight occurs or is about to occur.

20. For very young children who have trouble with fighting, try play therapy with puppets, art, or drawings to assess feelings that stimulate fighting.

21. Relaxation techniques or music therapy may help angry or anxious children who fight often.

22. Find a quiet place for the child for structured work or play away from peers. This procedure should not be a punishment or isolation, but rather an opportunity for productive work.

## Verbal Abusiveness

Most verbal abusiveness (such as rudeness, sarcasm, impoliteness, and name-calling) is a cover for feelings of inadequacy, a learned behavior from adults or other models, a call for attention, or a way of striking back at an unfriendly world. In this instance, the child needs interactions with adults who are calm, rational, and consistent and who behave maturely. Adults need to be on guard against allowing the child's verbal abusiveness to provoke the same behavior from them. Adults who resort to criticism, belittling, and name-calling have little chance of changing children's behaviors.

1. Determine the goal of the verbal abusiveness. Could it be that the child is seeking attention, revenge, or power? (See Chapter 11.) Become a child watcher and listen attentively to determine these needs and goals. Having defined the goal, the adult can help the child find a more constructive means of meeting this need.

2. Meet privately with rude, sarcastic, impolite, or name-calling children. Explain that you interpret their behavior as a cry for help. Then discuss the reasons they feel it necessary to use verbal abusiveness. Help the children develop a plan for being kinder with words. Build the child's skills and vocabulary for kindness.

3. Contract with children to reduce verbal abrasiveness. Clearly define unacceptable behaviors and their consequences. The contract can also include rewards for appropriate responses (see Chapter 9).

4. Provide opportunities for success. Praise and reinforce nonabusive verbal behavior—for example, "I noticed how understanding you were when Tom had his accident today. That was a nice thing to say to him."

5. Role-play or use films, filmstrips, or books to demonstrate and provide stimuli for group or family discussions. Examine what has occurred and the consequences. Discuss new and better methods of interacting. Behavior rehearsal may help children practice the new behaviors.

6. Call together the parties engaged in the verbal battle and have them write their story or tell it to a tape recorder. Read the story aloud with them or play the tape, and allow the

children to discuss and evaluate what has happened. Ask them to choose three of the most hurtful statements and rewrite or eliminate those words in the story. Ask them to make a plan for avoiding future verbal battles.

7. Encourage the teacher, parents, or other children to ignore the verbal abuser. If the behavior becomes too unacceptable to ignore, use isolation techniques such as the quiet corner or the time-out room (see Chapters 9, 11, and 16).

8. Build self-esteem so the child need not resort to verbal abuse (see "Poor Self-Concept," Appendix B). Avoid criticism, name-calling, and belittling remarks. Encourage and reinforce cooperative behavior, and provide opportunities for children to interact successfully.

9. Give reprimands quietly, firmly, and calmly. Do not attack the child as a person. Focus on the behavior, and admit how the behavior makes you feel—for example, "I get really angry when I hear students talking like that, and I would like you to stop now." Avoid modeling the behaviors for which the reprimand is given.

10. Pair the child with good role models for work and other activities. Discuss with the child the behaviors he or she sees in the models and the positive and negative consequences of these behaviors. Encourage the child to rehearse and practice these behaviors.

11. Every time a child is verbally abusive, quietly place a check on a chart or card. Contract with the child so that if a certain number of checks accumulate, privileges are lost or other consequences previously agreed on are imposed. A child who accumulates fewer checks than the agreed number is rewarded with special privileges chosen by the child. Avoid lecturing, reminding, scolding, or nagging when recording checks, as this attention reinforces that verbal abuse helps get attention.

12. Teach children new and acceptable ways of expressing feelings, and suggest words to say in situations in which they tend to be verbally abusive.

13. Help older children develop a self-management plan. Work with them to use thought-stopping for irrational ideas and the techniques of cognitive restructuring to stop the feelings that accompany verbal abusiveness. Help them develop an alternative plan for expressing their feelings.

14. For older children, try confrontational techniques such as "Could it be . . . ?" questions ("Could it be you want to hurt me by calling me names?") or Glasser's reality questions (see Chapter 4).

15. Ask the child to catch other children being courteous and report on their findings.

### *Physical Abusiveness*

Physical abusiveness, or bullying, can be a compensation for a poor self-concept. Children often hide fears and feelings of inadequacy behind acts of bullying. Children may also be responding to or modeling adult behavior they have observed. Bullying may be an attempt to strike back at an unfriendly world or seek power and attention the child cannot otherwise gain. Bullying children need calm, consistent adult–child interactions. However, because bullying behavior usually provokes anger in the adult, the child may receive only criticism and punishment—increasing the child's feelings of worthlessness and hostility.

1. Give reprimands in a quiet, adult manner without devaluing the child as a person. Focus the reprimand on the behavior. Instead of calling the child a name, such as *bully,* admit your feelings to the child: "I get angry when I see you hit other children like that, and I would like you to stop."

2. Sociograms are helpful in learning which children the bully likes or dislikes. Activities may be organized in which the bully is grouped with liked children and appropriate role

models. Discuss with children the behaviors they see in the models and the positive and negative consequences of these behaviors. Encourage children to rehearse and practice the appropriate behaviors.

3. Have a family or group discussion. Present to the group a hypothetical example similar to an actual incident. Use films, filmstrips, or stories to stimulate discussion. Guide the discussion to explore why children bully, how bullies feel about themselves, how other children feel about bullies, and more appropriate behaviors. Role-play and rehearse the new behaviors. Use feedback and group encouragement to promote changes in behavior.

4. Praise and reinforce friendly and cooperative behavior. For example, if the child helps another, verbally or physically, during play activities or during any social interaction, comment on the appropriate behavior. Catching children in good behavior is an effective intervention for most behavior problems.

5. Contract with the child to reduce specific acts of bullying. Clearly define unacceptable behaviors. Include rewards for success in the contract, along with negative consequences, such as isolation, for breaking the terms of the contract (see Chapter 9).

6. Provide outlets for the child's emotions in supervised activities, such as running, hammering, writing out feelings, drawing pictures, playing games, or talking out feelings.

7. Encourage responsibility by giving children responsible jobs at which they can feel successful—for example, delivering materials or messages, watering plants, or feeding the fish. Avoid drudgery job assignments.

8. Encourage cooperation by finding an interest or ability the bully has. Have the child pursue this interest or ability by helping others or sharing it with others—for instance, sharing a stamp or rock collection, building a science project.

9. Observe the child's environment to determine situations that provoke bullying behavior. Try to engineer the child's activities to reduce opportunities for bullying. Rearrange time schedules or the physical environment, if possible. Intervene before the opportunity for bullying occurs.

10. Determine the goal of the bullying behavior. Could the child be attempting to gain attention, power, or revenge or to strike back at what he or she perceives to be a hostile world? (See Chapter 11.) Could the bullying be a learned behavior or lack of social skills?

11. Use ideas for building a good self-concept (see Appendix B) so that the child does not resort to bullying to cover feelings of inadequacy. Reinforce and praise cooperative behaviors.

12. Teach the child conflict-resolution or problem-solving skills so that he or she can find better ways of reacting to frustrating situations.

13. Teach the child to use a method, such as stop, look, listen, and think, before taking any action.

14. Teach relaxation techniques to the child, such as counting to 10 before acting.

### Cruelty to Peers, Animals, and Others

Cruelty to people or animals is usually a sign of other problems. Extended counseling may be necessary to uncover the underlying reasons for the cruelty. Children who are cruel to peers or animals may be responding to punitive adults in their own lives. Severe cases may require intensive psychotherapy or even residential treatment. (See also suggestions under "Fighting," p. 609, and "Destructiveness," p. 614.)

1. Closely supervise the children in all activities.

2. Give the children releases for emotional tension—for example, varying quiet activities with physical activities frequently. Encourage constructive physical releases, such as

running, playing ball, or cycling. Writing, music, art, and talking may also help. Schedule times for releases regularly throughout the day's activities.

3. Employ group or family discussions that emphasize cooperation with others. Discuss the feelings and events that provoked the cruel acts, and plan ways for coping with these feelings.

4. Encourage cooperation, responsibility, and pursuit of interests by giving children responsible jobs that enable them to feel success—for example, delivering messages or filing materials. Do not place more responsibility on the child than the child can tolerate. Find areas of interests by asking the child what those are, and structure activities and jobs around them.

5. Contracting and isolation techniques may be used to control behavior to some extent (see Chapter 9). Clearly define and explain acceptable and unacceptable behaviors and the rewards and penalties for each.

6. Carefully structure the child's environment and daily activities to provide little or no opportunity for unacceptable behavior. Plan each hour's activity in cooperation with the child, if possible. A daily schedule of work, play, study time, and planned leisure time can be posted in the child's room or school desk.

7. Avoid physical punishment. Strong punishment produces further anger and the likelihood of aggression. It also provides a model for cruel, aggressive behavior. Limit TV viewing to nonaggressive programs. Remove as many models of aggression and cruelty as possible. Focus on the child's strengths, and reinforce cooperative behaviors.

8. Determine the goal of the cruel behavior. Does the child see the world as cruel? Could the child be seeking revenge or power? What needs are not being met? (See Chapter 11.)

9. Diaries, play therapy, fantasy games, sentence completion, and active listening may be used as aids to understanding cruel children. Diaries and play therapy also allow children to vent their thoughts and feelings nondestructively.

10. Interpret the child's cruel behavior as a cry for help and an expression of loneliness and rejection. Ask the child to write out feelings of contempt and cruelty. Discuss the feelings, and make a plan for more constructive ways of handling them. Encourage the child's appropriate behavior.

11. Ask the child to find an admired model and to keep a list of the model's behaviors for a short time. Discuss the behaviors with the child, rehearse new behaviors, and encourage the child to try out new ways of behaving.

12. With the child, draw up a behavioral contract that sets out rewards for appropriate behaviors and the consequences of cruel behavior. Clearly define acceptable and unacceptable behaviors.

### Destructiveness

Destructiveness and vandalism are problems of increasing severity in our society (see also "Fighting," p. 609). One of the counselor's first concerns is to find what is happening in the child's environment to cause such intense feelings and behavior. Is the child angry with someone or about something (school, for instance) to the extent of having an intense need to strike out and hurt that person or place? Could the destructiveness be a result of frustration, feelings of failure, or feelings of revenge because the child feels no one cares? A second concern is gaining the child's trust in order to change this self-defeating behavior—a task that requires time and patience.

1. Determine the goal of the child's destructiveness. Could the motive be attention, feelings of rejection, anger, a need for power, or revenge (see Chapter 11)?

2. Examine the situation that brought on the destructiveness or preceded the act. Does the destructiveness occur most often at a particular place, situation, or time? If so, become an environmental engineer, arranging the circumstances or schedule to avoid the situations.

3. Use logical consequences (see Chapter 11) as punishment or a penalty for destructive behavior. Whatever the child destroys must be paid for or the cost worked off in some manner. Refrain from harsh punishments, which may reinforce the child's idea that the world is cruel and hostile and that destructiveness is the only way of getting back at the world.

4. Have the child write a description of the destructive act; discuss and plan ways for avoiding such behavior in the future. Have the child generate multiple ways of repairing the damage caused.

5. Confront the child nonjudgmentally by interpreting the destructive behavior as a distress signal. Offer to listen and help. Help the child make a plan to avoid destructive behaviors in the future.

6. Start a campaign of "Keep our school (home) clean!" Working together ("we" feelings) to build pride in personal areas is often helpful in preventing vandalism or destructiveness.

7. Determine the child's areas of interest, and involve the child in working with them—not busywork but productive tasks. Peer teaching, peer tutoring, or sharing the interest in another way may be helpful. Guiding the child in pursuing interests and special abilities may be a productive way of diverting the child's behavior toward more constructive actions and building feelings of success.

8. Encourage children to keep a diary of their feelings and thoughts or tell them to a tape recorder. Writing or talking provides a means of catharsis and gives the adult some insight into the child's world. The adult and child can then discuss these feelings and develop a plan for coping with them.

9. Play therapy with toys, Play-Doh, music, or drawing may be used in an effort to understand the feelings underlying the child's destructiveness. This therapy may also be used as a means of catharsis (see Chapter 14).

10. Hold group or family discussions focusing on the consequences of vandalism and destructiveness. Help the children look at what they are doing, the consequences, and alternative ways of behaving. Expect the child to repair damages. Use behavior rehearsal to practice new methods of handling situations.

11. Help the child find a friend and model. Encouragement and peer pressure are effective in helping children redirect their behavior into more constructive paths. Discuss the behaviors of the model, and allow the children to practice and rehearse these behaviors.

12. Refrain from punishing, scolding, lecturing, moralizing to, preaching to, or degrading children. These methods reinforce the children's thinking that the world and the people in it are cruel and uncaring.

13. Use contracting with rewards to help the child change destructive behaviors (see Chapter 9). Be certain the child understands the rules. Define appropriate and inappropriate behaviors clearly, as well as the rewards and consequences of each. Be clear that destructiveness of any kind is unacceptable.

14. A resource person from a local law enforcement agency could discuss laws and penalties for destructiveness and vandalism with the children, but avoid scare techniques and threats.

15. Arrange the child's schedule to allow time during the day to work off energy. Vary the day's activities from quiet to physical. Encourage physical activities (such as running,

football or basketball, and bicycling,) and quiet releases (such as writing, music, art, or talking).

16. Work out a plan with the child and an adult authority so that a child whose tense feelings become overwhelming can signal the adult and report to some agreed-upon place to work out these feelings. For example, assisting the custodians with maintenance and cleaning might help in three ways: (1) to dissipate bad feelings, (2) to develop appreciation for the building, and (3) to create empathy for the custodian, who has to repair damage to the building.

### *Tantrums*

Temper tantrums may cause parents or other adults to experience feelings of anger, frustration, and helplessness. Adults often feel they have completely lost control of the child and the situation when children throw temper tantrums. In some children, tantrums are a learned behavior for getting attention or getting their way. Some children have learned to manipulate adults by throwing tantrums; some seek revenge.

1. Determine the motive for the tantrum. Is the tantrum an effort to gain attention, to cover feelings of inadequacy, to manipulate, or to embarrass or strike out at adults? (See Chapter 11.)

2. Children throw tantrums because it is a learned behavior that works for them. They get their way or what they want. The adult can stop the behavior by not allowing it to work. Ignore the behavior whenever possible; refuse to give in. Eventually the tantrum becomes an unrewarding behavior.

3. If ignoring the tantrum becomes impossible, quietly ask the child to leave the room and make a plan for avoiding tantrums in the future. The child should have the option of returning and behaving appropriately after a cooling-off period. Physically removing the child from the room may be necessary.

4. Provide alternative methods of venting feelings. Ask children to keep a diary of their feelings, write them out on paper, or talk to a tape recorder. Play therapy can help, and fantasy games or storytelling may provide some catharsis and insight (see Chapter 14).

5. Use active listening to understand the child's feelings and the motives behind the tantrums (see Chapter 6).

6. Investigate the possibility of the tantrums being related to a physical problem if the behavior continues over a given time period. Refer the child to a pediatrician for examination.

7. Try to determine the sequence of events before a tantrum. Investigate whether tantrums are most likely to occur at a particular time, place, or situation. Rearrange the environment or schedule to reduce the child's frustrations, if possible.

8. Avoid threats, lectures, scolding, and nagging, which can be reinforcing because they are forms of attention. Define the unacceptable behavior and the consequences for it (see Chapter 9), and consistently carry out the terms of the behavioral contract between the adult and the child.

9. Severely disturbed children often have temper tantrums because they feel insecure. Using techniques of isolation and other forms of strictness may tend to intensify these feelings. In such cases, some tantrum-throwing children become quiet when held affectionately and reassured.

10. Peer pressure can be an effective tool for modifying children's behaviors. Group or family discussions of temper tantrums and their effects on others may help the tantrum-throwing child understand how others react to the behavior.

11. Rehearse and practice the new behaviors.

12. Help the child find a mature model. Ask the child to keep a list of the model's admired behaviors and ways in which the model handles frustrations. Rehearse and practice these ways of behaving.

13. Examine with children the self-messages that make them angry enough to throw tantrums, and try to identify more rational and helpful self-messages (see Chapter 8).

14. Teach the child to communicate his or her unhappiness through more appropriate methods such as problem-solving techniques, role modeling, or other counseling strategies.

## Chronic Complaining

Chronic complaining about feeling ill gains attention or sympathy and avoids unpleasant situations. This behavior can be manifested as an exaggeration of symptoms or fantasies of diseases: "I think I have cancer." Other kinds of hypochondria are consistent headaches, stomachaches, and muscle aches.

1. Recommend to the parents and child that the child be examined by a pediatrician to rule out actual physical illness.

2. Try to determine the motive or goal of the chronic complainer. Are the complaints a result of feelings of inadequacy, fear of failure, a need for attention or sympathy, or an attempt to avoid an unpleasant task? Help the child find ways of meeting this need more effectively.

3. Enlist the cooperation of the pediatrician. Many pediatricians require the children to come straight to their office whenever they feel a pain. Children (and parents) soon tire of repeated trips to the pediatrician.

4. Actively listen to the child's complaints (see Chapter 6). Do not oversympathize, but tell the child you will write a note or call the parents to suggest a trip to the doctor's office to check out the complaint.

5. Ask children to write out their feelings or tell them to a tape recorder. A diary might help determine the circumstances under which the feelings occur.

6. Excessive stress and tension can provoke chronic complaining. Check with parents, teachers, and other significant persons in the child's life. The child may be under pressure from schoolwork, from problems within the home, or from peers. Help the other adults find ways to reduce the tension.

7. Take precautions to ensure that the child is not ill when chronic complaints occur; firmly insist that the complainer attend to the task or return to class. Reassure the child that, should an illness occur, help will be provided. Continue to observe the child closely to assure he or she is not ill.

8. Chronic complaining may result from a lack of interest in the world around the child—school, friends, activities. Help these children find an interest or activity in which they can feel successful. Encourage participation in groups, children's organizations, sports teams, or neighborhood activities.

9. Enlist the aid of a buddy to encourage the complainer to become more involved in the world and to participate in friendships and activities.

10. Actively listen for clues to stresses in the child's life, and plan with the child for more constructive means of coping with the tensions (relaxation techniques, physical activities, talking, writing, play therapy).

11. Have children monitor their own behavior. Give them an index card, and ask them to check it every time they become aware that they are complaining. Catching oneself in the act often increases awareness of the behavior and reduces the incidence.

12. Try to find ways for children to assume more responsibility in their lives. Feeling competent and worthwhile reduces the need to gain attention through sickness.

## *Tattling*

The tattler, like a gossip, is attempting to gain attention and favor, usually with an adult authority figure. Ignoring talebearers is difficult because many times they bring needed information to adults. However, the tattler is usually lonely and rejected by peers.

1. Determine the goal of tattling. Is the child attempting to gain attention, power, or revenge? Confront the child with your hypothesis—for example, "Could it be that you are telling me this to get Warren in trouble?" (See Chapter 11.)

2. Meet privately with the tattler and interpret the behavior as a cry for help to gain acceptance and recognition in the group. Discuss the reasons the child tattles and plan better ways to achieve those goals.

3. Help the child gain acceptance by capitalizing on special abilities and interests such as sports, hobbies, or special knowledge. Encourage the child to share these abilities and interests with others or to peer-teach or tutor another child.

4. The child may need help in learning social skills. Help the child find a model. Have the child list the model's admired behaviors and then rehearse and practice them.

5. Turn your attention elsewhere when the child begins a tale. Say, "Rather than discussing that now, perhaps we should _____."

6. Use tattling as a topic for family or group discussions. Guide the group to look at motives for tattling and the reactions and feelings of others toward a tattler. Films, filmstrips, or stories may provide a stimulus for these discussions. List alternatives to tattling, and rehearse and practice them.

7. Use storytelling, choosing a hypothetical example similar to the child's problem, to show the consequences of tattling and the reactions of others to tattling (see Chapters 6 and 14). Ask the child questions about how the tattler must be feeling and how the child who is being tattled on must feel.

8. Instead of listening to the tattler, ask the child to write a brief note to you explaining what has happened.

9. Ignore the tattling behavior, but praise and reinforce appropriate behaviors. Give attention to the child for the cooperation.

10. When ignoring tattling becomes impossible, draw up a contract with the child with rewards for not tattling. Penalties and rewards for appropriate and inappropriate behavior may be included.

11. Build self-esteem (see Appendix B) so that the child does not have to resort to tattling to gain attention and acceptance.

12. Pair tattlers with good role models for work and other activities. Discuss with the tattlers the behaviors they see in the model and the positive and negative consequences of these behaviors. Encourage the child to rehearse and practice these behaviors.

13. Have children monitor their own behavior. Ask them to check an index card each time they tattle or feel the urge to tattle. Increasing awareness of the behavior may decrease the frequency.

14. Encourage children to problem-solve. Rather than having the adult take over the situation and seek a resolution, say to the child, "I wonder what could be done to straighten this out." Assist the child in seeking alternatives.

## Swearing

Swearing may reflect a need for attention, an effort to shock others or prove to peers that the child is "big," or modeling behavior. Swearing can also be a release for pent-up aggression or tension or an expression of rebellion.

1. Determine the motive for the behavior (see Chapter 11). Is the goal a need for attention or power, an effort to cover feelings of inadequacy, or an emotional release? Does the swearing reflect a lack of social skills?

2. Confront the child, interpreting the swearing behavior as a need to shock or gain attention—for example, "Could it be that you want to shock me by talking in that manner?" (See Chapter 11.) Work with the child to make a plan to avoid swearing in the future.

3. Examine the child's world. Does a certain time of day, a particular situation, or a certain event provoke the swearing? If so, attempt to reduce the frustrations by rescheduling or rearranging the environment.

4. Ignore the behavior, if possible. When this becomes impossible, contract with the child to decrease the swearing systematically (see Chapter 9). Build in rewards for success and consequences for unacceptable behavior. Isolation techniques may or may not be used in the contract, depending on the severity of the problem.

5. Small children may not be aware of the meaning of the words they use. Ask what they think the word means and suggest an alternative. Remind the child that certain words are acceptable in certain places and at particular times, and some words are never appropriate.

6. Have the child write out some dialogue using symbols for swear words. Ask them to substitute strong feeling words that are appropriate for the symbols.

7. Work with the child to find acceptable words to express feelings. Write a contract with the child that states that, when frustrated, the child will use these words instead of the usual swear words. The child can carry the list on an index card for easy reference.

8. Confront the children with an interpretation of the goals of their misbehavior (see Chapter 11) so that they understand why they like to use these words and what they could do instead of swearing to feel important. Discuss alternative methods of expressing emotions (physical activities, art, games, music, new verbal responses). Rehearse these alternatives, and contract with the child to try the new methods of responding to emotions.

9. Hold a family or group discussion focused on the motives for swearing and how others feel about the person who is swearing. Use role playing and role rehearsal to help children see the behavior and its effects on others. Discuss alternatives to swearing, and role-play these alternatives. Have adults eliminate their swearing.

10. Use storytelling (see Chapter 14) with a hypothetical example similar to the child's problem. Ask the child to react to the story.

11. If swearing seems to be a means of releasing tension or aggression, contract with the child to work off these emotions in more acceptable ways—running, writing, talking, or physical exercises. Writing out feelings in a diary or talking into a tape recorder may also help the child vent feelings.

12. Use cognitive restructuring to help angry children who use swearing as an outlet. They may be able to reframe the situation so it does not stimulate swearing.

13. Self-monitoring may help older children become aware of their behavior. Self-reward for *not* swearing should be included in the self-management program.

14. Teach children stress-management techniques, such as deep breathing, to help ward off the feelings that may stimulate swearing. When the child feels an urge to swear, he or she is encouraged to breath deeply instead.

15. Use confrontational techniques, such as the reality questions (see Chapter 4), to encourage responsible behavior.

## Lying

As a part of their normal development, young children often lie because of their inability to distinguish fact from fantasy or because they fear disapproval and punishment. Habitual lying may be caused by feelings of inadequacy, insecurity, or pressure from parents or other significant persons in the child's life. It could also be a learned behavior to escape responsibility or punishment.

1. Determine what needs of the child are not being met (see Chapter 11). Is the child seeking attention or power? Is he or she attempting to evade reality or the consequences of misbehavior?

2. Arrange for successful experiences in learning and in daily interactions with peers. Use praise and other types of reinforcement for appropriate behaviors to build confidence and self-esteem. Lying may not be necessary if the child has self-confidence (see Appendix B). Ignore the lying or fantasy behaviors while reinforcing positive behavior.

3. Avoid trying to trap the child. If you have positive evidence that the child is lying, be quietly direct in your confrontation—for example, "Jeff, I know that you did not do your homework." If you do not have direct knowledge of the truth, admit to the child that you are having trouble understanding the story and ask for more details. This response lets the child know you do not believe all that is being said and gives the child a chance to tell the truth.

4. When the child continues to tell stories that are obviously fantasies, the adult may confront the child in a nonjudgmental manner, using statements such as "You know, I have never seen or heard anything like that, and I'm really having trouble imagining what you are telling me. Could we begin again?" With this technique, you do not call the child a liar, but you convey that you simply cannot accept all that is being said as the truth.

5. Note the areas in which lying seems to occur most often. Is the child lying about schoolwork, parents, money, clothes, or aggressive abilities? If the lying occurs most frequently in one area, examine the possibilities of changing the circumstances in this area to decrease the temptation or pressure to lie.

6. Talk with parents, teachers, and others close to the child. Are the expectations and pressures placed on the child too great? Do parents expect perfect behavior and the highest school marks? Are teachers demanding too much work or work that is too difficult for the child? If so, consult with these adults concerning ways of reducing pressures on the child.

7. Ignore fantasy tales that are meaningless, or ask the child to write the story and give it to you. Caution should be exercised not to ignore the child altogether. Respond to positive behaviors.

8. If the problem seems to stem from excessive pressure, decrease the push toward competition with others and emphasize competition with self: "You did six math problems yesterday. Let's see if you can do eight today."

9. Use the technique of storytelling (see Chapter 14). Choose a hypothetical example involving behaviors similar to those exhibited by the lying child. Ask the child to react to the story, and discuss the reactions.

10. Review the child's academic progress. Does lying compensate for a learning difficulty or cover some other real or imagined failure?

11. Films, filmstrips, stories, and other materials may provide stimuli for a good classroom or family discussion on lying and its consequences. Include in the discussion methods for avoiding lying and better ways of handling situations.

12. Avoid reinforcing the behaviors. Do not pay attention to or respond to lying behavior, fantastic stories, or something that seems exaggerated or incorrect.

13. A child who feels worthwhile, loved, and successful does not have to resort to lying (see also Appendix B). Give the child responsible jobs, such as carrying messages, watering plants, or feeding fish (not drudgery work), to promote feelings of success. Use a sociogram to find admired classmates, and pair the child with these children for group activities.

14. Enlist the aid of a buddy to involve the child in activities. Ask the child to keep a record of a model's behaviors to aid in learning techniques for successful interpersonal relationships. Practice and rehearse these behaviors in a safe atmosphere. Encourage the child to try the new behaviors.

15. Use self-monitoring to increase awareness of the behavior. Have children keep a record of each time they told the truth when they were tempted to lie.

## *Teasing*

Teasing is attention-getting behavior with several possible motives. Children may get attention only when they misbehave, they may be showing friendship for another person, or they may have hostile motivation. Teasing is sometimes the result of a lack of knowledge about how to make friends, how to be a friend, or other social skills.

1. Determine the goal of the teasing (see Chapter 11). Is the motive attention, power, or revenge, or does the teasing come from a lack of social skills? Teasing can be a way of compensating for feelings of inadequacy or a means of covering up learning or emotional problems. Become a child watcher; listen actively to investigate all possibilities (see Chapter 6).

2. Examine the circumstances under which the child teases. What is the sequence of events? Does teasing occur most frequently in a particular time, place, or situation? If so, rearrange the environment or schedule to reduce provoking circumstances.

3. Group or family discussions may help the child see how teasing behavior affects others and produce suggestions and a plan for alternative ways of behaving. Peer pressure in group situations is an effective behavior modifier.

4. Ignore the teasing behavior as long as possible. Then use an isolation technique such as the quiet corner or the time-out room (see Chapters 9, 11, and 16). The teaser should be free to return to the group when the child has worked out a plan for behaving more acceptably.

5. Cooperatively draw up a contract to decrease teasing behaviors. Clearly define unacceptable behavior and the consequences (see Chapter 9). Rewards for appropriate behaviors may also be included.

6. Help the child find other ways to get attention or acceptance. Encourage the child to pursue liked activities, interests, or hobbies and share them with other children. Allow the child to peer-teach or tutor another child. Assign responsible tasks to the child; avoid meaningless work or drudgery jobs.

7. Teasing is often modeling behavior. Check the child's environment to determine if the teaser is modeling an admired person. Help the child find a more appropriate model, observe the model's behaviors, and rehearse new and more acceptable ways of interacting with peers.

8. Teach the child ways to interact with other children. Have her or him practice the engaging behaviors and then try those actions out and report on the reactions received.

9. Talk with the people being teased. Plan ways for these children not to reinforce the aggressor's teasing behavior. Explain to the victims of the teaser that the behavior is not as much fun if the person being teased does not respond. Explain to them that the motivation of the teaser is to get attention, even though it is negative attention. Role-play situations, teaching the victims to respond with new techniques, such as cognitive restructuring or ignoring the teasers.

10. Albert Ellis's ideas of irrational thinking may be incorporated into counseling with the person being teased. (See Chapter 8 for an explanation of cognitive restructuring.) Teach the victim to change internal thinking from "It is terrible to be teased" to "I don't like to be teased, but it is not the end of the world, and I can just ignore the teasing."

11. Children have little need to tease if they feel they are a part of their environment and successful in the world. Find ways of providing successful experiences. Capitalize on the child's interests and abilities. Encourage participation in activities at school, at home, or in the community.

## *Disobedience, Negativism, and Resistant Behavior*

Disobedience, negativism, and resistant behavior are open displays of anger and antagonism toward authority figures. Children exhibiting these behaviors are often highly critical, easily irritated, and sometimes aggressive.

1. Determine the goals of the behavior (see Chapter 11). Actively listen to the child to learn about the child's feelings toward self, family interactions, and school (see Chapter 6). Children tend to strike out when their needs for love and respect are not met. Recognize the child's feelings. Admit that the child has the power to disobey or resist. Avoid threatening the child. Refuse to become involved in a conflict; tell the child you will discuss the matter later.

2. Interpret the goal of the misbehavior to the child with "Could it be . . . ?" questions but not at the time of the conflict (see Chapter 11). Later the adult might ask, "Could it be that you would like to show me that you are boss?" The question opens the door for a nonjudgmental discussion of the child's motives and for planning better ways of meeting these needs.

3. When there is no conflict, discuss with the child the consequences of the negative behavior. Plan alternative behaviors, and rehearse and practice them.

4. Avoid open confrontations with put-downs, threats, and name-calling. Try active listening to learn the reason for the negativism or disobedience (see Chapter 6).

5. Assess the environment in which the child is disobedient, negative, or resistant. Is the child receiving some reinforcement from peers or other significant persons? What circumstances provoke the behavior? Is there a time when negativism, resistance, and disobedience occur most often? Rearrangement of schedules or the environment may decrease the undesirable behavior.

6. Avoid possible conflict situations by allowing the child some choices—for example, "Do you want to complete the assignment now or after lunch?" Make a list of tasks to be done, and cooperatively plan the day's schedule with the child.

7. Specify in advance the consequences for disobedience, negativism, and resistant behavior. Hold a discussion with the child in which you draw up ground rules and the consequences for breaking the rules. Rules made in cooperation with children are carried out more readily.

8. When the child misbehaves, the inappropriate behavior should be clearly explained. Children often do not understand what they have done wrong. After defining the problem, work with the child to draw up a plan or contract to change behavior (see Chapter 9). The plan may include rewards for acceptable behavior and penalties for unacceptable behavior. Rehearse and practice new behaviors to help the child meet the terms of the contract.

9. Ignore the negativism, disobedience, and resistant behavior, if possible. When ignoring the behavior becomes impossible, isolation techniques such as the quiet corner or a time-out room may be effective in changing the behavior (see Chapter 9). Avoid physical punishment; it provides only a model of aggression for the child.

10. Disobedience, negativism, and resistant behaviors are often attempts to cover up a lack of self-confidence, lack of social skills, or inability to find success in school and other areas of life. Attempt to determine if the unacceptable behavior is compensatory behavior for a learning problem, a lack of self-esteem, or some other problem. Look over the child's academic progress to determine if the behavior could be related to a learning problem. Carefully watch the child's interactions with others to determine if the problem is related to difficulties with social relationships. Listen for clues that may help you understand the child's feelings about self and others. (See the discussion of active listening in Chapter 6.)

11. Praise, telephone calls, or notes to the child's home about good behavior, along with other positive reinforcers, may be effective in decreasing negative behavior.

12. Discuss with the child appropriate and inappropriate behaviors. Respond to and reinforce appropriate behaviors while ignoring behavior that is unacceptable.

13. Suggest that parents or teachers leave the room for a few moments to remove themselves from the conflict. This arouses surprise and curiosity in the child about what the adult will do. The action also prevents the adult from entering into a conflict with the child (see Chapter 11).

14. Encourage the child to use constructive methods for releasing negative feelings. Suggest techniques such as talking out or writing out feelings, drawing, music, or physical exercises. Arrange for periodic emotional outlets if necessary.

15. Find the child a model or friend. Ask the child to watch the model and record admired behaviors. Then rehearse and practice these behaviors with the child.

16. Encourage children to pursue interests, hobbies, and abilities and become involved in activities, clubs, or other organizations in which they can feel successful. Enlist the aid of a friend or buddy to involve the child in activities.

### *Stealing*

Children may steal because of the high value society places on material wealth, because of ignorance of ownership rights, because they want to impress others, or because they want to experience the adventure of getting away with something. Although many children try stealing once or twice during their developmental years, persistent, repeated acts of stealing indicate other problems and require an understanding of the motives and needs behind the behavior.

1. Determine the motivation or goal of the behavior (see Chapter 11). Is the child seeking attention, power, or revenge? Is the behavior the result of a dare, an initiation, or peer pressure? Is this the first incidence of stealing, or is there a pattern of behavior? Actively listen to the child to try to understand the motive (see Chapter 6).

2. Investigate whether the child is stealing to meet basic needs for food or clothing, and, if so, contact appropriate agencies to find resources for meeting those needs.

3. Use logical consequences to cope with the stealing child. Have the child replace or make payment for stolen property, through work, if possible.

4. Give the child an opportunity to return the stolen property.

5. Have group or family discussions about stealing, its consequences, and the rights of ownership. Films, filmstrips, books, and newspapers can stimulate such a discussion. Discuss alternatives to stealing. Plan and rehearse appropriate ways of handling situations that might tempt the child.

6. Make certain children are aware of ownership rights. Comments such as "This is school property, but it is our responsibility" remind the child of ownership rights.

7. If stealing occurs in a group, often the children can solve the problem themselves if allowed to do so. Present the situation to the group, and ask them to draw up a plan for resolving the problem. Ask for a discussion of the plan with the entire group, avoiding accusations and blame.

8. Avoid trying to trap the thief or making threats that cannot be carried out, such as "We are all going to stay here until the property is returned." Such threats inevitably end up with the adult having to withdraw the ultimatum.

9. If you have positive evidence that the child is stealing, be quietly direct in your confrontation. Ask the child for a plan to pay for the stolen item and to avoid stealing in the future.

10. Use behavior rehearsal to practice situations in which the child could be tempted to steal. Include instances in which peer pressure might occur. Discuss ways to handle these situations, and practice the behaviors.

11. Use storytelling (see Chapter 14), posing a hypothetical example similar to the child's problem. Ask the child for a reaction to the story. Discuss what might happen to the story character involved in stealing.

12. Children may be stealing to feel more accepted by their peers. Most children who find some success in their lives and feel they belong have no need to behave inappropriately. Find an interest, hobby, or ability (stamp or rock collection, knowledge on a subject of particular interest to children, sports ability) the child possesses. Use this strength to help the child become involved in activities and find friendships.

13. If stealing is a prevalent or persistent behavior, ask a local law enforcement person to talk with the children about the legal consequences of stealing.

14. Encourage the child to focus on "reality, responsibility, right and wrong" through the techniques of reality therapy (see Chapter 4).

## *Possible DSM IV–TR Codes*

**Conduct Disorders:** Fighting; Verbal Abusiveness; Cruelty to Peers, Animals and Others; Destructiveness; Tattlers; Swearing; Lying; Disobedience; Negativism and Resistant Behavior; Stealing; Teasing; and Tantrums

V61.20—Parent-Relational Problem, V61.8—Sibling-Relational Problem
V71.02—Child or Adolescent Antisocial Disorder
309.9.3—Adjustment Disorder with Disturbance of Conduct, 309.9—Adjustment Disorder (unspecified)
312.33—Kleptomania
312.8x—Conduct Disorder
312.9—Disruptive Behavior Disorder Not Otherwise Specified (NOS)
313.81—Oppositional Defiant Disorder

**Anxiety Disorders: Chronic Complaining and Tantrums**

300.02—Generalized Anxiety Disorder (also see other anxiety disorders such as 309.21—Separation Anxiety, 300.23—Social Phobia)

309.24—Adjustment Disorder with Anxiety

316—(Specified psychological factor) affecting . . . (indicate the general medical condition)

## REFERENCE

American Psychiatric Association. (2000). *Diagnostic and statistical manual of mental disorders DSM-IV-TR* (4th ed., text revision). Washington, DC: APA, Inc.

# Appendix B

# Children's Conflicts with Self

As in Appendix A, the following techniques are derived from a variety of resources and methods for counseling with children. The procedures must be incorporated into a caring and accepting counseling or consulting atmosphere, and the techniques should be modified to meet the individual needs of children and their particular social, learning, or behavioral problems.

## Self-Destructive or Suicidal Behaviors

See Chapter 18 for information on suicidal behaviors and suggestions for counseling with children exhibiting these symptoms.

## Poor Self-Concept

Unfortunately, most of children's negative feelings about themselves are formed from adults' evaluations. Adults lecture, scold, moralize, nag, belittle, label, and criticize. Sometimes children decide they really are worthless, stupid, unlovable, and worthy of punishment because of the continued negative judgments adults place on them. Negative feelings about themselves can affect children's motivation, work, interpersonal relationships, and future success. Once formed, a negative self-concept is difficult to reverse; however, these children can be helped.

1. Provide opportunities for success. Encourage the child's efforts and recognize the strengths the child demonstrates. For example, an adult can say, "You worked hard at picking up every piece of paper (straightening the books, throwing that ball, and so on)." Children easily recognize artificial and forced compliments, which are ineffective.

2. Use strengths exercises with children in a group situation. Give each group member a list of the names of other group members. Each child should write a positive adjective or statement beside each name. Have each child read his or her list aloud. Laminate the lists so the child can keep them for a long time.

3. Discuss with the children what they would like to do or accomplish. Working with the children, set up realistic goals and a step-by-step program to guide them toward achieving their goals. Continue this guidance until the children feel they can work toward their goals alone.

4. Allow children with poor self-concepts to help someone else; arrange peer teaching or tutoring. Doing something special for someone else helps the helper feel better about himself or herself.

5. Have the adult working with the children write a list of each child's strengths to help the adult form a more positive conception of the children. Encourage the adult to capitalize on these strengths whenever possible to promote success in each child's life.

6. Ask the children to write 10 positive things about themselves: friendly, can play ball well, can repair a bicycle, can play the piano, and so on. Help the children find ways to use their positive attributes to increase positive feelings about themselves.

7. Supportive counseling with significant adults in the child's life can help these adults understand the child and the inappropriate behaviors that often result from a poor self-concept. Instruction in effective parenting may also be helpful.

8. Have the child list uncomfortable or difficult situations. Discuss ways of behaving in these situations, and role-play new behaviors. Encourage the child to try the new behaviors in realistic situations and report the results to you.

9. Use active listening (see Chapter 6). Teach the child problem-solving skills; being able to solve one's own problems builds self-confidence.

10. Involve the child in group activities at home and at school. Encourage the child to join Scouts, a church group, or a club in which he or she will feel accepted and achieve success. Adults should avoid encouraging participation in groups requiring skills the child does not possess. Give responsibilities or tasks in school and in the home at which the child can feel successful.

11. Use a contract with rewards for attempting new behaviors. Rehearse and practice the new behaviors in a safe atmosphere before trying them in a real-life situation (see Chapter 9).

12. Help the child change thoughts of "I can't" to "I will try." Examine the worst thing that could happen if the child attempted the task. (See Chapter 8 for a discussion of cognitive restructuring.) Encourage positive thinking.

13. Children with a poor self-concept often benefit from assertiveness training (see Chapter 9).

14. Use diaries, drawings, incomplete sentences, fantasy games, storytelling, and play therapy as aids to understanding the child's feelings and thoughts (see Chapter 14).

15. Find an appropriate model or buddy for the child. Ask the child to describe admired behaviors of the model. Rehearse and practice these behaviors with the child.

16. Examine the family constellation (see Chapter 11). Often children form a poor self-concept when they are compared to elder or younger siblings and feel they do not measure up. Work with families in finding ways to value each child.

17. Readers are referred to books, such as *Just Because I Am: A Child's Book of Affirmation* (1994) by Lauren Murphy Payne and Claudia Rohling, published by Free Spirit Publishing, Minneapolis, Minnesota, to help children age 3 to 8 years enhance their self-concept. Many techniques for helping older children are presented by Diane Frey and Jesse Carlock in their book, *Practical Techniques for Enhancing Self-Esteem* (1991), published by Accelerated Development, Muncie, Indiana. Diane Frey also has a more current book, *From Human Being to Human Becoming* (1998), published by Mandela Publishers.

## Cheating

The present school system and society in the United States strongly encourage competition and high grades—values that can contribute to cheating. Students cheat for a variety of reasons, the main one possibly the pressure to achieve. School personnel and parents can place less emphasis on competition with others and more on cooperation with others and competition with self. School personnel and parents can also let students know that they expect honesty.

1. Determine the type of pressures the child may be encountering. Talk with the child and significant adults about their expectations for the child. Often parents and teachers place unrealistic pressures on children to excel in school, sports, or other areas. If this is the problem, consult with the adults and cooperatively plan ways to reduce the stress.

2. Determine the goal of the cheater (see Chapter 11). Is the child trying to impress someone, earn recognition, please parents or teachers, or cover up a learning problem?

3. Talk with cheating children concerning their study habits and preparation for work. Better study skills may increase self-confidence and reduce cheating.

4. Encourage teachers to hold class discussions with students on cheating, explore ways to reduce cheating, and draw up guidelines for consequences should the problem occur. A film, story, or hypothetical example may stimulate a rewarding discussion. Combine your discussion with a sociodrama, role playing, or puppet play about cheating (see Chapter 14 for play techniques).

5. Consult with teachers about reducing temptations to cheat by arranging classroom desks or tables to separate students.

6. Children are often asked by their friends to cheat, and many have trouble handling the situation without losing the friend. A group or family discussion focusing on the problem with a question such as "What would you do if your best friend asked you for the answer to a question during a test?" may help children find an alternative to cheating or helping their friends cheat.

7. Consult with the teacher about testing procedures. Could an open-book test be given? Could the teacher use alternative forms of the test? Is the teacher in the room monitoring the test at all times?

8. If a child is caught cheating, remove the child's paper quietly, and confront the child privately. Tell the child what you saw, and discuss what consequences should be imposed. Ask that a plan be made to solve the present cheating problem and prevent cheating in the future.

9. Refrain from accusing a child of cheating unless there is proof. Do not attempt to force a confession. Avoid name-calling, scolding, lecturing, moralizing, and preaching.

10. Place more emphasis on cooperative behavior and less on competition in interactions with the child. Stress competing with self rather than competing with another person.

11. Relaxation and systematic desensitization (see Chapter 9) may help a cheating child if the behavior is the result of anxiety or test phobia. Suspend competitive and punitive grading practices that create test anxiety.

12. Contract with the child to avoid cheating in the future. Clearly define cheating behavior and the consequences of the behavior (see Chapter 9).

13. Use the reality questions (see Chapter 4) to encourage responsible behavior in the cheating situation.

14. Make sure the children have an opportunity to ask questions for direction or clarification.

### Truancy

*Truancy* is defined as deliberate absence from school without a valid reason. Truants are generally telling the school that they prefer to be elsewhere. Children who do not achieve well or who have other learning problems are often truant because they find school unpleasant. Avoiding the situation is easier than facing failure, rejection, or embarrassment.

1. Pinpointing the reasons for truancy may be difficult. Determine the motive for the behavior (see Chapter 11). Is the child experiencing learning problems, failure, or rejection? Does the child receive encouragement to attend school and find learning relevant? Deter-

mine when truancy seems to occur most often. Is the truancy related to family problems or needs?

2. Personal interest from school personnel may be an effective reinforcer. Actively listen to the child for clues about what is happening in the child's life (see Chapter 6). Many students respond to special attention in the form of invitations from the teacher, other school personnel, or peers to come to school and participate in activities.

3. Look over the truant's class schedule and academic progress. Determine if the classes are too difficult or the assignments are beyond the child's capabilities. Might the child feel more success and find more relevance in other ways of learning?

4. Check into the home situation. Could the truancy be the result of a lack of proper clothing or lunch money or of baby-sitting responsibilities or other job requirements? Enlist the parents' cooperation, and devise a system for keeping in touch with them concerning days present and absent.

5. Hold a group or family discussion about truancy. Discuss with truant children how their presence or absence in school is helping or hurting them in reaching their immediate or long-term goals. Work with them to make a plan to avoid truancy in the future.

6. Contract with the student to attend school the next day. Continue to renegotiate the contract, increasing days in attendance step by step. Include a clause in the contract making the child responsible for all work missed. Rewards and/or penalties for attendance and nonattendance may be worked out cooperatively with the child (see Chapter 9).

7. Older students serving as peer counselors may help devise ways to keep truant children in school. The attention of the older student also serves to motivate the other child to attend school.

8. Involve the child in school activities that require his or her presence—for example, audiovisual or physical education equipment handling, room responsibilities, or a responsibility in an interesting group project.

9. Refrain from critical, sarcastic comments such as "Glad to see you made it today" or "If you had been here, you would have had the assignment." Avoid scolding, lecturing, punishing, and preaching. Concentrate on the child's positive behaviors. School must become a pleasant place for truant children if their behavior is to be changed.

10. Whenever possible, allow the children choices in arranging their daily school activities and learning. Adjustments might also be made in the curriculum to reflect the children's individual abilities and achievement levels.

11. For children who see little relevance in school life, hold a discussion of "What does it take to make it through life?" Ask the children to imagine themselves as adults in their jobs or daily activities. Discuss what abilities and skills they will need to succeed in their imagined adult world.

12. Out-of-school suspension for truancy is seldom effective. The child who is consistently truant does not want to be in school, and suspension is no punishment. Seek ways to make school a pleasant, rewarding place.

13. Reframing or other cognitive-restructuring techniques may help the child see school in a different light (see Chapter 8).

14. Ask the truant to interview selected people who have dropped out of school to see how their lives were affected.

## Carelessness in Work and with Property

A common complaint among teachers and parents is that children are careless with school property, books, the completion of assigned work, and personal property such as coats, sweaters, and other possessions. Lecturing, scolding, preaching, and nagging are seldom effective in changing their habits. Children need to learn responsibility for their own actions and possessions and that an adult will not always be present to assume responsibility for them.

1. Determine the reason for the carelessness. Is the behavior due to a lack of interest or motivation? Could the carelessness be an attempt to cover up a learning or emotional problem or an attempt to get back at parents for some real or imagined wrong? Actively listen to the child for clues that may indicate the motivation for carelessness (see Chapter 6).

2. The careless child can redo the work until it is correct. Children can pay for lost items or property with time or work. Parents should not hurriedly bring forgotten items such as lunches and tennis shoes. The logical consequence of carelessness, forgetting, or losing is that the child must assume responsibility—redo the work, replace the property, or do without the forgotten items (see Chapter 11).

3. Praise and reinforce responsible behavior—for example, "That paper was well written" or "You did a good job cleaning out the basement." Consistently give attention to acceptable behavior.

4. Help the careless child find a model who behaves maturely and responsibly. Pair the child with the model for activities. Ask the child to observe the model's behaviors for several days. Discuss the behaviors of the model with the careless child. Role-play and rehearse these behaviors. Make a plan for the child to try the newly learned behavior.

5. Carelessness may be due to a lack of understanding. Give clear, specific instructions to the child for proper preparation of work and other activities. Have the careless child write down the instructions to eliminate forgetting and mistakes.

6. If carelessness with homework assignments is a problem, ask the child to write down all assignments and take them home. Talk with parents to gain their cooperation in checking assigned work each night. Discontinue the procedure when the child begins to assume responsibility for homework. The parent should be available to assist the child but not do the homework for him or her.

7. If the problem seems to stem from inability to cope with the amount of work or responsibility assigned, reduce the requirements for a time, requiring quality rather than quantity. Gradually work up to the point where the child meets the expected criteria (see Chapter 9).

8. Carelessness may reflect a difference in cultural values. The child's environment may not place a great value on achievement or the possession of property. Hold a group discussion focusing on the value of property and of assuming responsibility for oneself. Help the children to identify acts of carelessness and their consequences, and make a plan for avoiding careless acts.

9. Ask careless children to evaluate their work from your role or to assess consequences as they think you should. Discuss with them the reasons for their evaluations.

10. Encourage responsibility through the use of reality questions (see Chapter 4). Give small assignments designed for success.

### Underachievement

*Underachievement* is usually defined as a discrepancy between the child's ability and actual achievement. It may be related to a poor self-concept, cultural deprivation, lack of family involvement and encouragement, peer pressure, learning or emotional problems, physical illness, or a lack of interest in school subjects and content.

1. Try to determine the causes contributing to underachievement. Become a child watcher, and use active listening to try to understand the child (see Chapter 6). Underachievement is often related to physical problems or other learning difficulties; therefore, a psychological evaluation and checkup with a physician may provide some insight into the problem.

2. Assess the child's academic level, and help the teachers build learning and class assignments from this base. Much new learning is based on old learning; the child must be able to accomplish prerequisite skills before achieving success in new ones. Once the weak link in the chain of learning is identified—a past school experience, physical health, cultural background, or any other factor—counseling can begin, and instructional materials can be designed to promote success.

3. Contract with the child to complete at least a small amount of work each day. Build in rewards for progress. The completion of two problems or questions is better than no progress. Renegotiate the contract periodically, increasing the amount of work expected (see Chapter 9).

4. Try peer teaching or peer tutoring. Students who are in an upper grade can tutor students in lower grades. They can also help peers who are having trouble in areas of their strengths. Both children learn and benefit from the relationship.

5. Capitalize on an area of interest or ability by relating the assignment to it. Situations in math, writing, spelling, and other subjects can often be related to the child's interests, hobbies, and skills.

6. Team teaching may be helpful. Two or more teachers are often able to generate more ideas to stimulate the child. The child may also be able to cooperate with one teacher more readily than with another.

7. Avoid lecturing, nagging, scolding, and threatening the child. Encouragement and a positive attitude produce better results. See "Poor Self-Concept" earlier in this appendix for additional ideas.

8. Vary school activities from physical to quiet to prevent fatigue and boredom. Involve the child in arranging the day's work. Children who have taken part in the planning are likely to cooperate and complete assigned tasks.

9. Teachers can consult with underachieving children for alternative ideas for completing learning objectives. Ask the child to remember a time when learning was easy, and together identify what strategies made that possible.

10. Special arrangements can be made for testing or for completing other class assignments. For example, if the child has problems in reading or writing, oral testing, tape recorders, or typewriters can be used.

11. Help the child find an admired friend and model. Ask the child to talk with the model about study habits and to observe the model's methods of studying. Have the child practice these procedures (see Chapter 9). Allow the two children to work and study together as much as possible.

12. Check on study skills, test-taking procedures, and place and time for studying. Help adults and the child learn ways to arrange an environment conducive to study and learning. A contract incorporating a schedule for studying specific subjects at certain times and places will help the child plan study time more wisely and develop discipline for studying.

13. If the underachievement is related to parental pressure, counsel the parents about how to decrease the pressure yet reinforce studying. Assist parents and the child in determining an appropriate place and time to study. Make a plan to avoid or cope with things that might interfere with study times, such as small siblings, telephone calls, and peers.

14. When homework assignments are not completed at home, the logical consequence is for the child to complete the work during free time at school (see Chapter 11). Avoid nagging, scolding, or lecturing.

15. Focus on and reinforce work improvements; past faults and failures should be forgotten. Emphasize the positive—for example, "Jimmy, you did part of your homework assignment, and it was done very well. Would you be willing to work on these two additional questions?"

16. The parent–child relationship works better if parents do not teach or tutor their own children. If the child asks for help, a parent may provide assistance; however, someone outside the family is a more effective teacher or tutor.

17. For children with special learning problems, plan a consultation session with all resource persons and teachers involved. Cooperatively draw up a learning plan in which the role and objectives of each professional are clearly defined.

18. Underachievers usually respond best to a structured environment for learning. Children who are simply told to do their best set low goals and achieve below their maximal abilities. Teachers and parents need to have high expectations but also give needed support. Give directions for assignments very clearly. A check or reward system may be used for completed work. Learning contracts may be helpful to the underachiever. Some underachievers require additional time to complete all assignments; continue to encourage their completion.

## Daydreaming

Daydreaming is not always bad; it sometimes clears confusion, solves problems, or is creative in other ways. However, excessive daydreaming or daydreaming at the wrong times—in school—can affect the child's academic progress. Adlerian theory suggests that daydreaming children are striving for superiority. These children have no faith in their abilities to achieve success in the real world; therefore, they create fantasies in which they are always great or superior.

1. Periodic eye contact between child and adult may decrease daydreaming. If one cannot make eye contact with the child, a light touch on the shoulder should bring the child back to reality.

2. Interrupt children's fantasies by calling them by name. Avoid embarrassing children by asking them to answer a question they obviously have not heard.

3. Try incomplete sentences, storytelling, a diary, or play therapy to learn more about the child and the possible reason for daydreaming.

4. Channel daydreaming into constructive channels by having the child write about the daydream. The writing could be incorporated into a learning exercise. Find other opportunities to help children display their creativity.

5. Write a contract with the daydreamer for completion of assigned work (see Chapter 9). Contract for only the amount of work the child feels he or she can accomplish. Renegotiate contracts for additional work in a step-by-step plan.

6. Tape an index card to the child's desk. When the child is working on a task, place a check on the card and give verbal reinforcement for the accomplishment. A contract may be made with the child to earn rewards or privileges for a certain number of checks. Ignore the daydreaming; reward on-task behavior.

7. Plan the child's environment and schedule to vary activities from quiet to physical. Assess the day's schedule to determine if activities are interesting, relevant, and appropriate for the child's level of maturity, interest, and ability.

8. Find the child a friend who encourages participation in groups and other activities. Encourage the teacher to include the daydreamer in group activities and projects. Counsel with the parents to plan how to reduce daydreaming at home and encourage participation in activities.

9. Often children retreat to a daydream world because the real one is too painful. Determine if the child is having learning, social, emotional, or physical problems. A psychological evaluation and physical examination may be helpful.

10. Daydreaming may be related to a poor self-concept. See "Poor Self-Concept" earlier in this appendix for additional ideas for working with these children.

### Shyness and Withdrawal

Shyness and withdrawal are attempts to avoid participation in one's surroundings. The child may fear the situation, fear failure or criticism, lack self-confidence, or fear embarrassment or humiliation. The child may also be physically ill. Unfortunately, shy and withdrawn children are usually ignored because they cause less trouble than the attention-seeking child.

1. Try to determine the underlying cause for the reserved behavior. Use diaries, puppets, role playing, incomplete sentences, drawing, storytelling, play therapy, or any similar technique to try to understand the child better. Children often express their feelings through these means when they will not verbalize them.

2. Work on developing trust and good rapport with the child. Try active listening to increase understanding of the child (see Chapter 6).

3. Have the shy child help another student through peer teaching or peer tutoring. Capitalize on any interest or ability to promote sharing and participation.

4. Involve shy or withdrawn children in small-group activities or projects with other children they like. Often a shy child is willing to talk in small groups. Encourage and reinforce these attempts to participate. Send them on errands with another child. A sociogram may determine other liked children.

5. Give the withdrawn child responsibilities such as carrying messages, feeding the fish, watering plants, handing out supplies, or helping the school secretary answer the phone and take messages. Avoid drudgery jobs, and do not ask the shy child to perform tasks that may be embarrassing (such as speaking in front of the class).

6. Make a list with the withdrawn child of things he or she would like to be able to do—for example, join a group of friends, speak to a particular person, or play a game. Have the child select one thing on the list and set a goal to accomplish this behavior. Use behavior rehearsal to help the child practice certain responses or behaviors. Contract with the child to try these new behaviors (see Chapter 9).

7. Avoid embarrassing shy children by teasing them about their shyness or by calling on them to perform in front of a group without first discussing and arranging the activity with them. One technique for encouraging a child to participate in class is to plan a question and answer with the child. The teacher asks the question in class, and the child agrees to answer with the response. When the child feels comfortable answering rehearsed questions, the child and teacher make a contract that the teacher will call on the child only when he or she volunteers to answer. Ask the child to volunteer at least a certain number of times per week. Renegotiate periodic contracts to encourage participation in a step-by-step progression.

8. Find a model for the shy child. Ask the child to observe the model for several days and list admired behaviors. Role-play, rehearse, and contract with the child to try the new behaviors.

9. Withdrawn or shy children may benefit from assertiveness training (see Chapter 9). Have the children list situations in which they would like to be more assertive. Discuss possible ways of meeting each situation. Practice the new behaviors with the children, both individually and in small groups.

10. Use a variety of play techniques, such as hand puppets, games, art, and music, to encourage expression. Pets may be a useful adjunct to therapy.

11. Teach extremely shy children social skills—specifically, conversational skills, asking questions, making and responding to comments, improving eye contact, and displaying warmth. Use modeling and behavior rehearsal to help the child practice new skills.

12. See "Poor Self-Concept" earlier in this appendix for other ideas to encourage more participation in learning and interpersonal situations.

### *Excessive Tension and Anxiety*

A little tension and anxiety may motivate a child, but excessive tension and anxiety interfere with learning and performance. Excessive tension and anxiety may be situational or chronic. The symptoms include continued restlessness and movement, nail biting, tics, frequent blinking, rapid breathing, repeated throat clearing, and similar somatic complaints.

School-related tension and anxiety:

1. Tell highly anxious children that they have a right to fail. Take away the pressure to excel and to be perfect. This technique may ease the anxiety and allow further exploration of conditions causing the anxiety.

2. Highly anxious children function better with a teacher who is warm and understanding but also organized and structured. Suggest that teachers use techniques such as behavioral objectives and learning contracts so that highly anxious students know exactly what is expected of them.

3. Consult with the child's parents and teachers. Determine if the anxiety is a result of pressures and perfectionistic expectations. If so, work with the child and the adults to encourage more realistic expectations.

4. Teachers and parents may help decrease children's tension and anxiety by talking quietly to them about relaxing—for example, "Relax your neck; relax your shoulders." Deep-breathing exercises may also help the child relax (see Chapter 9).

5. Avoid overemphasizing the importance of success on a test or task. Many adults cause anxiety in their efforts to impress the child with the importance of doing well. Provide encouragement for the child's attempts.

6. If the child is highly anxious about tests, use the "study buddy" system. Pair the child with a capable student who is willing to help. Developing better study skills may help reduce anxieties related to school.

7. Encourage teachers to de-emphasize tests and allow the child to demonstrate learning in other ways, such as oral tests, oral reports, projects, and papers.

8. Look over the child's schoolwork and academic progress. Anxiety is often related to learning disabilities.

9. Use cognitive-restructuring techniques to help children feel they can cope with situations. Discover the irrational, self-defeating, anxiety-provoking self-statements that the children are telling themselves, and help them formulate more positive ones (see Chapter 8).

10. Use imagery techniques to help children visualize themselves coping with situations in a relaxed, positive manner.

11. Advise students about good test-taking procedures, such as pacing responses according to the time allotted for the test, narrowing choices by eliminating obviously wrong answers, responding first to questions to which answers are known, giving last priority to questions not known, and being aware of qualifiers such as *always* and *never*.

General anxiety:

1. Some tension and anxiety may be related to fear of the unknown—for example, going to new places or being in new situations. A thorough explanation of the feared situation or a visit to a feared place with a trusted person may reduce situational anxiety.

2. Talk with anxious children and agree on methods, such as physical activity, talking, or writing, for release of these feelings. When children become highly anxious or tense, they could be allowed to signal the teacher or another adult and proceed to carry out the plan previously discussed. Counselors may suggest that anxious children come to their office when they experience intense feelings.

3. Diaries, autobiographies, drawing, puppets, and other forms of play therapy may assist in determining the causes for the anxious feelings (see Chapter 14).

4. Children have less anxiety about situations if they feel competent. Discuss with the child the reasons for anxiety and ways of handling specific situations; rehearse the situations.

5. Relaxation methods and desensitization reduce tension and anxiety (see Chapter 9).

6. If the anxiety appears debilitating, refer the child to a medical specialist for examination.

### Distractibility and Short Attention Span

Being able to focus one's attention on the task to be done and ignore irrelevant stimuli in the environment is necessary for learning school material and new behaviors. Although attention span and the degree of distractibility vary with the child and the situation, these learning problems seem to be increasing in today's classrooms.

1. Determine if the child is actually distracted easily and has a short attention span. The child's inattention may be the result of some other reason, such as the nature of the work the child is asked to do (boring or too difficult), noisy or more interesting surroundings (windows, TV, pictures, bulletin boards), fatigue, or physical illness.

2. Record the time when distractions and inattention seem most frequent. Rearrange the environment or schedule. Vary quiet activities with more physical ones. Limit over-stimulation and distractors, including interesting bulletin boards, teachers' clothing and jewelry, mobiles, and brightly colored pictures.

3. Use seating arrangements or some method of screening the distractible child from excessive stimuli. Consider small carrels or "offices." Bookcases, movable screens, or even large moving cartons that have been painted or decorated can be used to reduce distracting stimuli.

4. Contract for the completion of short assignments. Talk with distractible children about the amount of work they believe they can accomplish—for example, two math problems, one paragraph of English. Write a realistic contract to ensure success. Continue to renegotiate the contract, increasing the assignments as the distractibility decreases.

5. Recommend that highly distractible children be checked by a medical specialist to determine if the behavior is connected to a medical problem.

6. Shorten teaching time and study periods, and schedule the periods more frequently. Visual aids, games, and other teaching aids may add interest and maintain attention.

7. Use techniques such as raising or lowering your voice, placing your hand on the child's shoulder, or catching the child's eye to capture the distractible child's attention and direct it back to the task.

8. Encourage children to monitor their own behavior. Have them make a check mark on an index card when they catch themselves off-task and then immediately focus on the task. Increasing awareness of the problem is often a productive technique in itself. Plan for self-reward when the child can refocus attention to the task.

For additional information on distractibility and short attention span, refer also to the section entitled "Attention Deficit–Hyperactivity Disorder" in Chapter 19.

### *Immaturity and Dependent Behavior*

Dependency may be the result of overprotective or critical parents who have told their children in many ways that they are not capable of functioning or thinking for themselves. Immature or dependent children usually do not achieve well in school because they are not ready to learn the subject matter presented. They may have trouble with interpersonal relationships because of their immature behavior and often become social isolates or discipline problems; alternatively, they may choose their friends from a younger group.

1. Work with the parents on strategies to help them trust the child's abilities and potentials. Suggest methods to develop independent behaviors. Books or parent effectiveness training may help parents understand their children's development and abilities.

2. Have children identify areas in which they would like to be more independent or behaviors they would like to change. Discuss these situations and alternative ways of behaving with the child, and rehearse the situations until the child feels comfortable with the new behaviors.

3. Encourage and praise attempts to become more mature and independent. Ask the child to do jobs or assume responsibilities in the home and classroom to increase his or her confidence. Avoid assigning drudgery jobs.

4. Have the child select a model and observe the model's behavior for several days. Pair children with mature models for group activities. Ask them to keep a list of the model's behaviors they particularly like. Rehearse behaviors the children would like to acquire until they feel confident.

5. Encourage immature or dependent children to join groups such as Little League, Boy or Girl Scouts, clubs, or church groups. The children need support and encouragement to take the first steps and continued counseling to learn social skills for good relationships in the groups.

6. Give children as many choices as possible—for example, whether to complete the reading or the math assignment first, or whether to wear a blue shirt or a red shirt.

7. Learn about the child's abilities, interests, and hobbies. Have the child peer-teach or tutor another student in one of these areas of expertise to build self-confidence. Both children will benefit from the teaching and the relationship.

8. Work with immature or dependent children to teach them problem-solving techniques. Counsel with parents and teachers to encourage these children to attempt to solve their own problems with adult guidance rather than depend on others for solutions.

9. Avoid reinforcing dependent behaviors. Encourage immature children to make decisions and accept responsibilities within their capabilities. Reinforce efforts toward more mature behavior with praise and encouragement.

10. Use active listening to help immature and dependent children express their fears and other feelings (see Chapter 6). Help them develop realistic goals and make a systematic plan for attaining these goals.

### *Perfectionistic Behavior*

Compulsive and perfectionistic children usually perform their tasks and assignments well and therefore often overachieve. This behavior can inhibit everyday functioning; for example, the child takes too much time to complete assignments and feels that everything must be absolutely perfect. Perfectionistic behavior is often accompanied by symptoms of anxiety.

1. Perfectionistic children usually perform best in a well-structured situation in which rules and expectations are clearly defined. Clearly explain all instructions, and use teaching methods such as behavioral objectives and learning contracts to reduce anxiety concerning expectations.

2. Talk with parents and teachers to determine if the pressures and expectations placed on the child are too great. Perfectionistic children often have perfectionistic adults for models. Counsel with adults about normal growth and development and the behaviors that can be expected of the child.

3. Involve the children in individual and group activities that do not require perfect performance. Techniques such as creative drawing or writing de-emphasize perfection and also allow the child to express feelings.

4. Encourage the child to relax. Teach the child breathing exercises and other relaxation techniques (see Chapter 9). Encourage the child to change internal self-talk to recognize that perfection in all areas is not essential (see Chapter 8). "Shoulds" and "have-tos" can be changed to "It might be better ifs"—for example, "It might be better if I make all As, but that is not required for me to be a good person."

5. Use negative rehearsal to help perfectionistic children be less rigid. Observe a situation in which the child appears to be highly perfectionistic. Role-play the same situation with the child while encouraging behavior that is less than perfect. Discuss with the child what would happen if the child were not 100% perfect in the situation. Make a plan with the child to decrease compulsiveness.

6. Allot an amount of time for the child to finish a task. Place a timer within the child's sight. When the timer rings, review the child's progress. If the child has not made sufficient progress, contract with the child to set a new goal the next time.

7. The overly perfectionistic child may be compensating for feelings of inadequacy. See "Poor Self-Concept" earlier in this appendix for further suggestions for working with these children.

8. Plan a self-management program with the child; encourage him or her to monitor perfectionistic behavior and develop alternative ways of responding to situations. Build in self-reward for accomplishments.

9. Anxiety and tension may be related to perfectionistic behaviors. See "Excessive Tension and Anxiety" earlier in this appendix for additional ideas.

### *School Phobia*

School phobia may grow out of unpleasant or embarrassing experiences in school, failure in school, fear of separation from the security of home and parents, fear of the unknown, or other experiences that may have associated bad feelings with school.

1. Actively listen to try to understand the phobic child's underlying feelings and to establish a feeling of trust and security (see Chapter 6).

2. The child can be desensitized by going to school with a parent and staying for a short time, such as 15 minutes the first day, 20 minutes the second day, and 25 minutes the third day. Continue in this manner until the child can remain in school a full day.

3. The desensitization procedure may be used with rewards. Write a contract with the child to provide a reward for staying in school a certain amount of time—for example, 30 minutes (see Chapter 9). Renegotiate the contract for longer time periods as the child is able to stay in school an increasing length of time.

4. If one parent is reinforcing the child's anxiety about school, suggest that the other parent or another adult bring the child to school. A parent may unconsciously be encouraging school phobia by conveying anxiety to the child, verbally or nonverbally—for example, saying "Now, you call me if you get afraid while you are in school," or becoming more nervous and irritable as they approach school.

5. Avoid placing the child in any situation that may increase fear or cause embarrassment. Explain all new situations and expectations clearly. Role playing expected behaviors may help the child feel more confident about meeting the new situation.

6. School phobia may be related to learning difficulties. Review the child's academic progress, and provide needed help. Children who associate school with their personal failure often become phobic.

7. Ask the teacher to involve phobic children in pleasant group projects and activities. The more pleasure the children derive from school, the more they want to attend. Successful learning, good peer relationships, pleasant teachers and other school personnel, and enjoyable activities can be positive reinforcers.

8. Allow phobic children to phone home occasionally or at specific intervals if they feel fearful or insecure. Make arrangements with the parents so that someone is available to answer and reassure the child.

9. Many parents include something from home in the child's lunch box or with books—a picture or some favorite object, for instance.

10. Relaxation and desensitization procedures may be necessary for the extremely phobic child (see Chapter 9).

11. Often school phobia is the result of family interactions in which children become overly dependent on parents. Consultation with the family may provide some insight into the family system and suggestions for treatment.

12. Play therapy for the child with school phobia may allow the child to feel less overwhelmed and provide support while returning to school.

13. See other ideas for working with the phobic child under "Excessive Tension and Anxiety" earlier in this appendix.

### *Possible DSM IV–TR Codes*

#### Self-Destructive and Suicidal Behavior

296.xx—Bipolar I Disorder, Major Depressive Disorder, Bipolar II Disorder, Mood Disorder Not Otherwise Specified (NOS)
300.4—Dysthymic Disorder
309—Adjustment Disorder with Depressed Mood
309.81—Post-Traumatic Stress Disorder
311—Depressive Disorder NOS

#### Poor Self-Concept, Underachievement

V61.21—Abuse of Child—Perpetrator (Physical, Sexual, Neglect)
V62.3—Academic Problem
V62.81—Relational Problems

296.20–296.36—Major Depressive Disorder
300.02—Generalized Anxiety
300.23—Social Phobia
300.4—Dysthymic Disorder
309.xx—Adjustment Disorder
315.3—Learning Disorder NOS
995.52–995.54—Abuse of Child—Victim of Abuse

### Cheating, Truancy, Carelessness in Work and with Property

V62.3—Academic Problem
V71.02—Child or Adolescent Antisocial Behavior
309.3—Adjustment Disorder with Disturbance of Conduct
312.8x—Conduct Disorder
315.9—Learning Disorder NOS

### Daydreaming

V62.3—Academic Problem
314.xx—Attention Deficit Disorder/Hyperactivity Disorder

### Shyness and Withdrawal, Excessive Tension and Anxiety, School Phobia

V62.3—Academic Problem
300.00—Anxiety Disorder NOS
300.02—Generalized Anxiety
309.xx—Adjustment Disorder (309.24—Adjustment Disorder with Anxiety)
311—Depressive Disorder NOS

### Perfectionistic Behavior

300.00—Anxiety Disorder NOS

### Immaturity and Dependent Behavior

V62.89—Phase of Life Problem/Borderline Intellectual Functioning

## REFERENCE

American Psychiatric Association. (2000). *Diagnostic and statistical manual of mental disorders DSM-IV-TR* (4th ed., text revision). Washington, DC: APA, Inc.

TABLE B-1  Medications that may be indicated for childhood DSM diagnoses

| DSM IV Diagnosis | Medications Used | Names of Medications |
|---|---|---|
| Attention Deficit–Hyperactivity Disorder | Stimulants | Ritalin (methylphenidate), Dexedrine (dextroamphetamine), Adderall (mix of amphetamine salts), Cylert (pemoline) |
| | Antidepressants (including Effexor, Wellbutrin, tricyclics) Catapres, Tenex | Effexor (venlafaxine), Wellbutrin (bupropion), Tofranil (imipramine), Pamelor (nortriptyline), Norpramin (desipramine), Catapres (clonidine), Tenex (guanfacine) |
| Major Depression | Selective serotonin reuptake inhibitors (SSRIs) | Zoloft (sertraline), Paxil (paroxetine), Prozac (Fluoxetine), Celexa (citalopram) |
| | Atypical or Unrelated Antidepressants | Effexor, Wellbutrin, Serzone (nefazadone) |
| | Tetracyclic Antidepressants | Remeron (mirtazapine) |
| Mania (acute and for maintenance) | Anticonvulsants | Depakote (divalproex), Tegretol (carbamazepine) |
| | Lithium, antipsychotics, benzodiazepines | |
| Mental Retardation (with severe aggression or self-injurious behavior) | Antipsychotics, lithium, Inderal (propranolol), Trexan (naltrexone) | |
| Pervasive Developmental Disorder | Antipsychotics, Trexan | |
| Conduct Disorder (with aggression) | Antipsychotics, lithium, anticonvulsants, Inderal | |

| Anxiety Disorders | | |
|---|---|---|
| Generalized Anxiety Disorder | Antidepressants, benzodiazepines, BuSpar (buspirone) | Xanax (alprazolam) |
| Obsessive-Compulsive Disorder | SSRIs, clomipramine | Zoloft, Paxil, Prozac, Celexa, Luvox (fluvoxamine), Anafranil (clomipramine) |
| Post-Traumatic Stress Disorder | Antidepressants, benzodiazepines, Buspar, clonidine | |
| Separation Anxiety Disorder | Antidepressants, benzodiazepines | |
| Panic Disorder | Antidepressants, benzodiazepines | |
| Schizophrenia | Antipsychotics | Risperdal (risperidone), Zyprexa (olanzapine), Haldol (haloperidol), Navane (thiothixene), Mellaril (thioridazine), Thorazine (chlorpromazine), Clozaril (clozapine) |
| Intermittent Explosive Disorder | Propranolol, lithium, antipsychotics | |
| Sleep Disorders | Some antidepressants (Remeron, Desyrel) Benzodiazepines Antihistamines | Remeron (mirtazapine), Desyrel (trazodone) Valium (diazepam) |
| Enuresis (not due to medical disorder) | DDAVP, tricyclic antidepressants | DDAVP (desmopressin) |
| Tourette's Syndrome | Haloperidol, pimozide, clonidine, Risperdal | Haldol, Orap (pimozide) |

# Appendix C

# Conversion Tables

Appendix C contains conversion tables for goal-attainment scales that are explained in Chapter 2.

TABLE C-1  Conversion table for goal-attainment scales having one scored scale

| Sum of scale scores | Average scale score | T-scores |
|:---:|:---:|:---:|
| −2 | −2.00 | 30.00 |
| −1 | −1.00 | 40.00 |
| 0 | 0 | 50.00 |
| +1 | +1.00 | 60.00 |
| +2 | +2.00 | 70.00 |

TABLE C-2  Conversion table for goal-attainment scales having two scored scales

| Sum of scale scores | Average scale score | T-scores |
|:---:|:---:|:---:|
| −4 | −2.00 | 25.19 |
| −3 | −1.50 | 31.39 |
| −2 | −1.00 | 37.59 |
| −1 | −0.50 | 43.79 |
| 0 | 0 | 50.00 |
| +1 | +0.50 | 56.21 |
| +2 | +1.00 | 62.41 |
| +3 | +1.50 | 68.61 |
| +4 | +2.00 | 74.81 |

TABLE C-3   Conversion table for goal-attainment scales having three scored scales

| Sum of scale scores | Average scale score | T-scores |
|:---:|:---:|:---:|
| −6 | −2.00 | 22.62 |
| −5 | −1.67 | 27.18 |
| −4 | −1.33 | 31.74 |
| −3 | −1.00 | 36.31 |
| −2 | −0.67 | 40.87 |
| −1 | −0.33 | 45.44 |
| 0 | 0 | 50.00 |
| +1 | +0.33 | 54.56 |
| +2 | +0.67 | 59.13 |
| +3 | +1.00 | 63.69 |
| +4 | +1.33 | 68.26 |
| +5 | +1.67 | 72.82 |
| +6 | +2.00 | 77.38 |

TABLE C-4   Conversion table for goal-attainment scales having four scored scales

| Sum of scale scores | Average scale score | T-scores |
|:---:|:---:|:---|
| −8 | −2.00 | 20.98 |
| −7 | −1.75 | 24.61 |
| −6 | −1.50 | 28.24 |
| −5 | −1.25 | 31.86 |
| −4 | −1.00 | 35.49 |
| −3 | −0.75 | 39.12 |
| −2 | −0.50 | 42.75 |
| −1 | −0.25 | 46.37 |
| 0 | 0 | 50.00 |
| +1 | +0.25 | 53.63 |
| +2 | +0.50 | 57.25 |
| +3 | +0.75 | 60.88 |
| +4 | +1.00 | 64.51 |
| +5 | +1.25 | 68.14 |
| +6 | +1.50 | 71.76 |
| +7 | +1.75 | 75.39 |
| +8 | +2.00 | 79.02 |

TABLE C-5   Conversion table for goal-attainment scales having five scored scales

| Sum of scale scores | Average scale score | T-scores |
|:---:|:---:|:---:|
| −10 | −2.00 | 19.85 |
| −9 | −1.80 | 22.86 |
| −8 | −1.60 | 25.88 |
| −7 | −1.40 | 28.89 |
| −6 | −1.20 | 31.91 |
| −5 | −1.00 | 34.92 |
| −4 | −0.80 | 37.94 |
| −3 | −0.60 | 40.95 |
| −2 | −0.40 | 43.97 |
| −1 | −0.20 | 46.98 |
| 0 | 0 | 50.00 |
| +1 | +0.20 | 53.02 |
| +2 | +0.40 | 56.03 |
| +3 | +0.60 | 59.05 |
| +4 | +0.80 | 62.02 |
| +5 | +1.00 | 65.08 |
| +6 | +1.20 | 68.09 |
| +7 | +1.40 | 71.11 |
| +8 | +1.60 | 74.12 |
| +9 | +1.80 | 77.14 |
| +10 | +2.00 | 80.15 |

TABLE C-6    Conversion table for goal-attainment scales having six scored scales

| Sum of scale scores | Average scale score | T-scores |
|:---:|:---:|:---|
| −12 | −2.00 | 19.02 |
| −11 | −1.83 | 21.60 |
| −10 | −1.67 | 24.18 |
| −9 | −1.50 | 26.76 |
| −8 | −1.33 | 29.34 |
| −7 | −1.17 | 31.93 |
| −6 | −1.00 | 34.51 |
| −5 | −0.83 | 37.09 |
| −4 | −0.67 | 39.67 |
| −3 | −0.050 | 42.25 |
| −2 | −0.033 | 44.84 |
| −1 | −0.17 | 47.42 |
| 0 | 0 | 50.00 |
| +1 | +0.17 | 52.58 |
| +2 | +0.33 | 55.16 |
| +3 | +0.50 | 57.75 |
| +4 | +0.67 | 60.33 |
| +5 | +0.83 | 62.91 |
| +6 | +1.00 | 65.49 |
| +7 | +1.17 | 68.07 |
| +8 | +1.33 | 70.66 |
| +9 | +1.50 | 73.24 |
| +10 | +1.67 | 75.82 |
| +11 | +1.83 | 78.40 |
| +12 | +2.00 | 80.98 |

# Appendix D

# Questions for Licensing

Appendix D contains some possible questions and answers for licensing examinations. These are intended as illustrations of some of the preparations and details someone studying for these tests may encounter. Gay Bera (1997) of the University of Tennessee at Knoxville provided the responses. The authors acknowledge her work with appreciation.

### Possible Question

If you were approached by a young person about age 16 for counseling, and he asked that his parents not be notified, what would be your response to this, and to what degree would you enter into a treatment relationship with him?

*Example of Response.*   This scenario highlights the conflict between a child–client's competence and right to privacy and the parent's right to provide informed consent for their child's counseling. Because "minors lack the capacity to make fully informed, voluntary decisions in the eyes of the law" (Salo & Shumate, 1993, p. 29), parents, legal guardians, or those in loco parentis (i.e., in place of a parent; with a parent's rights, duties, and responsibilities) retain both the privacy rights for their minor children and the primary responsibility for the upbringing of their minor children.

Thompson and Rudolph (1996) state, "No general rule requires counselors to obtain parental consent concerning a child with the ability to make an informed decision, but obtaining parental consent is good practice for counselors unless potential danger to the minor exists" (p. 509). However, most state laws favor the parents' right to control their children's access to counseling services unless extenuating circumstances override parental rights—for example, child reports sexual abuse or intent to commit suicide. Since legal statutes take precedence over professional codes of ethics, this ultimately is a legal matter, with laws varying by state.

Some states (e.g., Virginia and California) have statutes granting "mature" minors the right to seek a specifically defined range of counseling services without parental notification or consent (Fischer & Sorenson, 1996). If, after investigating the state and local laws, such latitude exists, then I would evaluate other factors before rendering the requested services. Such factors would include the competence level of the minor, the severity of the problem, the consequences of the probable treatment, an assessment of risks if treatment is withheld, and the possibility of securing parental consent.

Because the child is 16 years old and either may be an emancipated minor or deemed competent to make informed decisions in the absence of any of the aforementioned extenuating circumstances, I would inform the teen of the state laws plus agency and school guidelines (if applicable) that parental permission for counseling was required. I would suggest that the teen return with a parent for a meeting to discuss what kind of counseling is available to the teen and the possibility of initiating a counseling relationship with the parent's consent.

In a meeting with both the teen and parent present, I would attempt to persuade the parent to grant consent for counseling; detail the need for voluntary, informed consent by both the teen and a parent (per the American Psychological Association's [APA, 1992] Ethical Principles of Psychologists Section A.3.c); treatment disclosure (APA Section A.3.a); family involvement in treatment (APA Section A.1.d); and promotion of the client's best interests and confidentiality issues (APA Section B.3). I would also suggest other counseling agencies or referrals that might be more acceptable to the parent in the hope that the child–client's welfare would prevail in the parent's decision. In the event all alternatives are exhausted and all affiliated agency guidelines are met, I would reluctantly honor the parent's legal right to withhold counseling services. However, I would thoroughly document all meetings, consultations, and personal recommendations and concerns and then refer the matter to my agency supervisor or director to see if additional action (e.g., notification of a child protective service agency) might be merited.

### Possible Question

If a minor were referred to you for examination by a school system, to what degree would you think parental consent was required for you to go ahead with the examination?

*Example of a Response.*    Depending on the age of the minor referred by the school, my first reaction would be to require parental consent before examining the child–client. Some states (e.g., Virginia and California) have statutes granting "mature" minors the right to seek a specifically defined range of counseling services without parental notification or consent. After investigating the state and local laws, and if such latitude exists, then I would evaluate other factors before rendering the requested services. Such factors would include the competence level of the minor, the severity of the problem, the consequences of the probable treatment, an assessment of risks if treatment is withheld, and the possibility of securing parental consent.

Additionally, Thompson and Rudolph (1996) state, "No general rule requires counselors to obtain parental consent concerning a child with the ability to make an informed decision, but obtaining parental consent is good practice for counselors unless potential danger to the minor exists" (p. 509). However, most state laws favor the parents' right to control their children's access to counseling services unless extenuating circumstances override parental rights—for example, child reports sexual abuse or intent to commit suicide. Since legal statutes take precedence over professional codes of ethics, this ultimately is a legal matter determined at the state level.

Counselor responsibility to parents must also be considered. In the American School Counselor Association's (ASCA, 1992) Ethical Standards for School Counselors, a counselor is exhorted, "Respect the inherent rights and responsibilities of parents for their children and endeavor to establish a cooperative relationship with parents to facilitate the maximum development of the counselee" (Section B.1, p. 331). I would also abide by the American

Counseling Association's (ACA, 1995) Code of Ethics and Standards of Practice, Section A.3.c: "When counseling minors or persons unable to give voluntary, informed consent, parents or guardians may be included in the counseling process as appropriate. Counselors act in the best interests of clients and take measures to safeguard confidentiality" (p. 93).

Informed consent is essential in treating clients, especially child–clients. Bray, Shepard, and Hayes (1985) outlined three elements that must be present before a client gives informed consent:

1. Capacity: assumes the client has both the mental and legal ability to make rational decisions; if not, then a parent or legal guardian is responsible for granting informed consent on the client's behalf.

2. Comprehension of information: assumes the client is able to understand information explained in a clear manner by the counselor regarding the treatment's methods, duration, benefits and risks, consequences, alternatives, and possible side effects.

3. Voluntariness: assumes the client is making an informed decision freely and voluntarily without undue duress.

In conclusion, I would require that specific written parental consent and consent from the school district be granted to me as a consultant of the school system before seeing the referred child–client.

## *Possible Question*

Suppose that it came to your attention that another psychologist, counselor, or psychological examiner was indulging in unethical practices—for example, you know that a psychologist is getting young girls in his office and fondling them or having them engage in sexual practices. What is your responsibility, and how would you go about exercising your responsibility?

*Example of a Response.*   In adherence to ACA's (ACA, 1995) Code of Ethics and Standards of Practice, I would have an ethical responsibility in the case described above to take actions prescribed in ACA's Code of Ethics, Section H: Resolving Ethical Issues. Although it appears that my colleague's behavior includes both ethical and legal violations, my first concern is for the safety and welfare of my colleague's young clients. Because federal and state laws mandate the reporting of suspected child abuse, I would be legally justified in breaching confidentiality to protect a person in danger and in reporting my suspicions. I would first consult with other knowledgeable professionals, including my counseling supervisor, agency director, and legal counsel, as to appropriate legal reporting procedures for disclosing my suspicions of sexual child abuse to the appropriate agency or authorities—for example, child services, law enforcement.

## *Possible Question*

What are the rights of the schools or other local organizations to withhold information about a child from his parents?

*Example of a Response.*   The school's decision to withhold information gained during a counseling relationship with a child–client from the child–client's parents is legally governed by the state's right to privacy, privileged communication, and disclosure laws. If the child is a minor under the age of 18, then "privacy rights for minors are generally seen as an extension of the parent's right to privacy: minors do not hold these rights in isolation from their parents" (Salo & Shumate, 1993, p. 28). Therefore, the inquiring parent most probably has a legal right to be informed of the counseling session contents, even if the child–client does not want to disclose the requested information and refuses to grant consent to disclose. Schools or other organizations have few, if any, rights to withhold information from a child's parents as long as that parent is the child's legal guardian.

The Family Educational Rights and Privacy Act of 1974 (FERPA) stipulates that schools receiving federal funding cannot allow others to inspect or disclose a minor student's educational records without the consent of a parent or legal guardian. Such schools must annually notify parents and students of the FERPA law and the provisions allowing parents or students to access their educational files and to register any ensuing complaints.

Exceptions to FERPA do exist, including the definition of *educational files* to exempt "personal files of psychologists, counselors, or professors if these files are entirely private and not available to other individuals" (Fischer & Sorenson, 1996, p. 92). Nor do schools need the written permission of the parent to "comply with a judicial order or lawfully issued subpoena," but the school must attempt to inform the parent and student prior to releasing the records to the court. Other exceptions specified by FERPA include when transferring schools, substantiating requests for educational financial aid, conducting studies on behalf of the school district, and complying with appropriate parties in a safety or health emergency.

Although this legal requirement to disclose seems antithetical to the professional ethical codes promoting the sanctity of trust, confidentiality, and supremacy of the client's best interest in counseling relationships, legal requirements supersede ethical codes or standards. There are ways of responding to disclosure requests that may limit the information divulged while protecting the client. Other options are also available to the school and to the counselor:

1. Refuse to disclose any information and accept the legal consequences of such a refusal.
2. Convince the parent that the child's best interests would be harmed by the request for information.
3. Discuss the request with the child–client to see if voluntary disclosure is possible.
4. Comply with the disclosure request and inform the child–client.

## REFERENCES

American Counseling Association. (1995). *Code of ethics and standards of practice.* Alexandria, VA: Author.

American Psychological Association. (1992). *Ethical principles of psychologists.* Washington, DC: Author.

American School Counselor Association. (1992). *Ethical standards for school counselors.* Alexandria, VA: Author.

Bera, G. (1997). *Issues in professional ethics.* Knoxville, TN: Author.

Bray, J. H., Shepard, J. N., & Hayes, T. R. (1985). Legal and ethical issues in informed consent to psychotherapy. *The American Journal of Family Therapy, 13(2),* 56–60.

Fischer, L. & Sorenson, G. P. (1996). *School law for counselors, psychologists, and social workers* (3rd ed.). White Plains, NY: Longman.

Salo, M. M., & Shumate, S. G. (1993). Counseling minor clients. In T. P. Remley (Ed.), *The ACA legal series* (pp. 26–30). Washington, DC: U.S. Department of Education.

Thompson, C. L. & Rudolph, L. B. (1996). *Counseling children.* NY: Brooks/Cole Publishing Company.

# Name Index

Addison, J., 446, 454
Adleman, H., 468, 469, 483
Adler, A., 76, 298, 304, 327, 387, 388, 404
Ahn, M., 6, 56, 69
Aiello, B., 424, 429
Aiken, L., 470, 481
Ainsworth, M., 18, 28
Akande, A., 445, 545
Akande, B., 445, 545
Akos, P., 497, 504
Albon, S., 409, 429
Alexander, F., 294, 327
Alexander, J., 192, 203
Alioto, J., 230, 232
Allan, J., 398, 404, 412, 413, 425, 429
Allen, L., 445, 454
Allers, C., 428, 433
Altmaier, E., 525, 556
American Counseling Association, 60, 69, 591, 292, 465, 481, 599–604, 649
American Psychiatric Association, 66, 69, 403, 579, 587
American Psychological Association, 21, 28, 595, 599–604, 624, 625, 638, 639, 648
American School Counselor Association, 648
Ammen, S., 411, 412, 432
Anderson, C., 201, 203, 374, 375
Anderson, J., 417, 429
Ansbacher, H., 198, 310, 327, 328
Ansbacher, R., 310, 328
Appleton, V., 470, 481
Arc, The, 581, 587

Ariel, S., 371, 376, 416, 429
Arman, J., 486
Armistead, L., 445
Arredonodo, P., 435, 437, 439, 451, 452, 454, 457
Arthur, R., 551, 553
Askounis, A., 450, 455
Assagioli, R., 186, 203
Association for Play Therapy, 408, 429
Association for Psychological Type, 403
Association for Specialists in Group Work, 488
Atkinson, D., 440, 441, 454, 455
Axline, V., 168, 174, 180, 407, 423, 429
Azar, B., 470, 481

Bachmann, G., 509, 555
Badolato, L., 572, 587
Baer-Barkley, K., 498, 505
Bailey, D., 446
Baker, D., 580, 581
Baldwin, M., 354, 377
Ballou, R., 309, 328
Bandura, A., 260, 263
Banks, S., 236, 263
Barker, S., 410, 430
Barlow, K., 420, 429
Barnes, M., 411, 420, 429
Barrett, P., 225, 232
Barrett-Hakanson, T., 487
Bartholomew, K., 18, 28
Baruth, L., 434, 437–439, 445, 447, 452, 454
Baron, A., 451, 454

Baron, M., 62, 71

Basham, A., 470, 481

Bates, M., 395, 404, 490

Baumgardner, P., 183, 203

Beamish, P., 558, 555

Beauchamp, T., 590

Beautrais, A., 529, 553

Becicka, C., 468, 481

Beck, A., 219, 225, 232

Becvar, D., 373, 376

Becvar, R., 373, 376

Behar-Horstin, L., 446, 456

Behring, S., 460, 481

Beilharz, C., 112, 131

Belgrave, F., 446, 454

Bellerby, T., 543, 557

Belsky, J., 510, 533

Bemak, F., 461, 464, 468, 469, 481, 485, 505

Bender, D., 551, 553

Benson, P., 19, 28

Bera, G., 647

Berchick, R., 225, 232

Berg, I., 134, 156, 451, 455

Bergan, J., 463, 464, 481

Berger, S., 422, 429

Bergin, J., 485, 490, 491, 493, 498

Berk, L., 18, 28, 509, 553

Berkowitz, L., 230, 232

Bernal, M., 443, 455

Bernard, M., 219, 232

Berne, E., 265, 266, 271, 272, 276, 278, 290, 292, 403, 463, 464

Berry, P., 412, 425, 429

Beslija, A., 291, 292

Biever, J., 155, 156

Bingham, R., 200, 203

Bischoff, R., 62, 71

Black, C., 519, 520, 553

Blakeslee, S., 533–536, 557

Blocher, L., 519, 521, 558

Blos, P., 76

Blue, Y., 235

Blum, D., 443, 455

Bogard, M., 370, 376

Booth, P., 372, 376, 416, 431

Boster, L., 224, 232

Boudah, D., 575, 577

Boutwell, D., 485, 505

Bowen, M., 330, 332–336, 340, 354, 376

Bowlby, J., 17, 18, 28

Brack, C., 463, 481

Brack, G., 463, 481

Bradley, C., 446, 455

Bradley, L., 407, 408, 418, 420, 424, 429

Brake, K., 521

Brandenburg, N., 573, 587

Brandt, M., 416, 433

Brantley, L., 498, 505

Brantley, P., 498, 505

Bratton, S., 409, 416, 418, 429, 430, 433

Brazelton, T., 4, 7, 28

Brechman-Touissant, M., 225, 234

Breen, D., 468, 481

Breggin, P., 487

Brennan, K., 18, 28, 29

Bretherton, J., 17, 28

Breuer, J., 75, 93

Brickell, J., 130, 132

Briesmeister, J., 228, 232

Brody, G., 445

Bromfield, R., 423, 430

Bronfenbrenner, U., 11, 28

Brown, B., 485, 505

Brown, D., 462, 463, 468, 481

Brown, L., 493, 560

Brown, S., 437, 454

Bruce, M., 134, 136, 156

Bruckner, S., 499

Bryant, S., 468, 469, 482

Bryne, D., 15, 29

Burch, K., 515, 518, 554

Burchard, J., 522, 555

Burcky, W., 595

Burton, L., 36, 69, 100, 108

Bush, G., 67, 69

Bush, M., 414, 433

Butter, L., 436, 455

Cabello, B., 468, 481

Cade, B., 146, 156

Campbell, C., 196, 203, 422, 430

Campbell, Janet, 149, 156

Campbell, Joseph, 379, 404

Campbell, S., 32, 64, 69, 71, 153, 155, 157, 228, 232

Campo, A., 519, 553
Cangelosi, D., 97, 109, 407, 409, 414, 421, 430, 431
Caplan, R., 460, 461, 464, 481
Cardillo, J., 56, 58, 70
Carkhuff, R., 52, 69, 162, 165, 167, 180
Carlson, C., 326, 328
Carlson, J., 325, 328, 475, 481
Carlson, K., 40, 69
Carlson, M., 325, 328
Carmichael, K., 370, 376, 414, 424, 425, 430
Carpenter, A., 461, 468, 482
Carpenter, S., 585, 587
Carr, A., 509, 514, 525, 526, 554, 555
Carroll, F., 195, 203
Carruthers, W., 549, 553
Carter, R., 423, 424, 430
Cattanach, A., 407, 408, 417, 420, 430
Cattani-Thompson, K., 32, 70
Center for Applications of Psychological Type, 396, 403, 404
Chalk, R., 508, 553
Chandras, K., 445, 455
Charcot, J., 75, 76
Chase-Vaughn, G., 446, 454
Chasin, R., 349, 376
Cheatham, H., 439, 457
Cherry, V., 446, 454
Child Trends, 3, 28, 527, 528, 553
Childers, J., 595
Children's Defense Fund, 4, 28
Childress, J., 590
Clark, A., 83, 108
Clark, D., 225, 232
Clarke, C., 487
Claypoole, S., 498
Clemons, D., 155, 156
Cleveland, W., 468, 482
Clifford, M., 421–523, 553
Cochran, J., 410, 430
Cohen, D., 545, 554
Coleman, J., 22, 28
Coleman, M., 539, 553
Coleman, V., 410, 430, 448, 455
Comstock, G., 545, 553
Conyne, R., 485
Consulting Psychologists Press, 389

Cook, L., 468, 470, 471, 481
Corcoran, J., 155, 156
Corey, G., 486–489, 494, 495, 597, 649
Costa, L., 527, 553
Cota, M., 443, 455
Coughlin, J., 498
Cox, M., 553
Cox, R., 553
Crawford, B., 528, 529, 555
Crawford, T., 209, 232
Crosbie-Burnett, M., 542, 553
Crosby, T., 441, 458
Cross, W., 441, 455
Crutchfield, L., 498, 499
Cumella, S., 543, 557
Cummings, N., 65, 69
Cunningham, C., 419, 421, 433
Cunningham, L., 130, 131
Cynn, V., 451, 457

Dadds, M., 225, 232
Dagley, J., 490
Daigneaulty, S., 498
Dail, P., 542, 553
Daniels, J., 543, 553, 589
Danish, S., 176, 180
Dansby, V., 486, 505
Das, K., 439, 455
Daughhtree, C., 146, 149, 156
Davis, D., 224, 232
Davis, G., 571, 587
Davis, J., 65, 70
Davis, K., 18, 28, 29, 511, 557
Day, J., 590
de la Cruz, B., 580, 587
de Shazer, S., 133–135, 139, 140, 156, 349, 376
Deck, M., 584, 587
Delcampo, R., 373, 377
Delucia-Waack, J., 484
Deming, W., 114, 115, 131
DeOrnellas, K., 323, 328
Dettmer, P., 459, 470, 481
Deutsch, H., 183
DiGiuseppe, R., 213, 225, 232, 234
Dinkmeyer, D., 310, 324, 328, 475, 481
Dobson, J., 91, 108
Dodge, K., 18, 28

Dolliver, R., 188, 203
Donovan, C., 225, 234
Dougherty, A., 460, 461, 463, 465–467, 469, 481
Douzenis, C., 493, 498
Dowd, E., 59, 70
Doweiko, H., 520, 553
Downey, D., 541, 554
Draguns, J., 176, 180
Dreikus, R., 306, 314, 317, 328
Drew, C., 560, 562, 571, 573, 580, 581, 583, 588
Drew, N., 33, 70
Drucker, C., 497
Dryden, W., 206, 213, 232, 233
Duffy, A., 225, 232
Duffy, G., 226, 232
Duffy, J., 465, 483
Dufrene, P., 448, 455
Duncan, B., 146, 157
Dunlap, K., 133, 156
Dunn, N., 520, 557
Dupuis, M., 597
Dyck, N., 459, 470, 481
Dye, A., 485
Dykeman, C., 498

Earls, F., 521, 556
Eddy, J., 450, 455
Edgeworth, J., 509, 514, 554
Edison, T., 110
Educational Testing Service, 389
Egan, M., 560, 562, 571, 573, 580, 581, 583, 588
Eisenberg, G., 522, 555
Elder, J., 149, 156
Eliot, T. S., 31, 70
Elkind, D., 14, 28
Elliot, C., 225, 233
Ellis, A., 117, 176, 188, 205–212, 2314, 218–220, 230–233, 309, 328
Emery, M., 577, 587
Emslie, G., 528, 554
Engle, D., 192, 203
English, S., 63, 65, 70
Epictetus., 206
Epp, L., 468, 469, 482
Erdman, P., 35, 36, 70

Erickson, E., 15–19, 28, 76, 543, 551, 553
Erickson, M., 133, 345, 347, 348, 373, 376
Erk, R., 581, 587
Estill, D., 584, 587
Evans, K., 175, 180, 229, 233, 422
Evans, S., 155, 157
Eyseneck, H., 235
Fall, M., 98, 108, 175, 180, 409, 419, 421, 430, 431
Family Educational Rights and Privacy Act, 44, 70, 595
Fancher, R., 76, 108
Farwell, G., 24, 29
Fascoli, L., 444, 455
Feldman, E., 18, 28
Ferguson, M., 182
Ferquist, R., 521, 554
Ferris, J., 363, 377
Fincham, F., 538, 554
Fisch, R., 133, 157
Fischer, A., 440, 455
Fischer, J., 521, 556
Fischer, L., 647
Flanagan, D., 325, 326, 328
Fleming, J., 146, 154–156
Follensbee, R., 176, 180
Ford, C., 593
Forehand, R., 445
Forthun, L., 521, 556
Forttrell, A., 579, 587
Frankel, J. B., 99, 108
Frankel, O., 521, 556
Frankl, V., 133, 153, 156
Franklin, C., 155, 156
Franklin, L., 414, 431
Freed, A., 280, 283, 292
Freed, M., 280, 283, 292
Freeman, S., 524
Freud, A., 76, 98, 108, 206, 233
Freud, S., 75–80, 85, 94, 107, 108, 110, 116, 130, 133, 183, 232, 379–381, 384, 388, 407
Friedberg, R., 228, 233
Friedman, R., 573, 587
Friend, M., 468, 470, 471, 481
Fromm, M., 184

Frost, J., 577, 587
Fuqua, D., 459, 465–467, 472, 482
Furr, S., 485

Gallagher, D., 149, 459
Galton, F., 287
Ganong, L., 539, 553
Garbarino, J., 7, 28, 48, 70
Gardner, H., 378
Gardner, R., 97
Garmezy, N., 19, 29
Garrett, M., 441, 455, 499
Garza, C., 443, 455
Gately, D., 538, 554
Gaudin, J., 537, 555
Gazda, G., 489
Gerler, E., 33, 70
Geroski, A., 468, 481
Getz, H., 476–479, 482
Ghahramanlou, M., 413, 433
Gibbs, J., 443, 453, 455
Gibbons, A., 508, 553
Gil, E., 421, 423, 424, 430
Gilbert, A., 497
Gilliard, B., 503
Gilliland, B., 519, 520, 545, 550, 554
Ginott, H., 407, 430
Ginter, E., 489
Gladding, S., 31, 70, 370, 376, 409, 410,
    414, 421, 422, 430, 431, 470, 471,
    481, 484, 486, 487, 489, 490, 494
Glaros, A., 22, 28
Glass, G., 32, 71
Glasser, W., 11, 48, 110–131, 126–133,
    157, 487, 576, 588
Glauner, T., 435, 454
Gloria, A., 452, 455
Glosoff, H., 21, 460, 481
Glover, C., 410, 430
Glover, J., 519, 554
Goldstein, B., 460, 482
Goldstein, M., 578–580, 588
Goldstein, S., 578–580, 588
Gonzalez-Mena, J., 410, 430
Goodnough, G., 498
Gordon, T., 165, 180
Gottman, J., 351, 376
Gould, L., 407, 408, 418, 420, 424, 429

Graf, C., 179, 180
Graham, C., 503
Graham-Bermann, S., 543, 555
Grant, D., 146, 149, 156
Graves, B., 545, 554
Grawe, K., 52, 71
Gray, F., 446, 454
Gray, J., 403, 404
Green, A., 511, 514, 554
Greenberg, E., 201, 203
Greenberg, K., 489, 490, 493
Greenberg, L., 191, 192, 203, 204
Greenberg, R., 411, 433
Greene, D., 531, 534
Greenspan, S., 4, 7, 28
Grieger, I., 439, 455
Griffith, M., 175, 180
Grossman, D., 545, 554
Grunbaum, A., 107, 108
Grych, J., 538, 554
Guerney, B., 415
Guerney, L., 370, 376, 415, 431
Guimaraes, B., 291, 292
Gumaer, J., 184
Gysbers, N., 470, 471, 482

Haley, J., 133, 157, 343, 345–348, 350,
    376
Hall, C., 75, 76, 108
Hall, D., 462, 483
Hall, G. S., 76
Hall, K., 414, 431
Halpern-Felscher, B., 593
Hanes, M., 423, 431
Happel, C., 183
Hardman, M., 560, 562, 571, 573, 580,
    581, 583, 588
Hargis, C., 112, 131, 132
Harman, L., 192, 201, 203, 204
Harper, R., 208, 233
Harris, G., 549, 553
Harris, K., 460, 482
Harris, T., 278, 280, 292, 417, 431
Hart, S., 528, 554
Hartman, J., 450, 455
Hartup, W., 413, 431
Harvard Mental Health Letter, 509, 511,
    514, 515, 528, 545

Harvey, J., 463, 464, 482
Harvey, S., 370, 376, 414, 415, 431
Hasbrouck, J., 467, 482
Hauser, S., 19, 29
Havighurst, R., 15–19, 29
Hayashi, S., 176, 180
Hayes, R., 469, 482
Hefferline, R., 183
Heflinger, C., 62, 70
Heidgerken, A., 467, 482
Heikkinen, C., 194, 204
Helms, J., 441, 455
Henderson, D., 409, 410, 431
Henderson, K., 562, 588
Henderson, P., 470, 471, 482
Hendrix, D., 598
Henniger, M., 409, 431
Hensley, F., 498
Herlihy, B., 589, 591–594
Hernandez, H., 439
Hernandez, M., 441, 458
Herr, E., 6, 29
Herring, R., 424, 431, 448, 449, 453,
    527–529, 532, 554
Hetherington, E., 533, 534, 554
Higgins, K., 543, 557
Hill-Hail, A., 177, 180
Hill-Hain, R., 177
Ho, M., 440, 441, 444
Hocutt, A., 62, 70
Hohenshil, T., 476–479, 482
Holbrook, M., 288
Holcomb-McCoy, C., 493
Holder-Brown, L., 562, 588
Holliday, D., 527, 553
Holliman, M., 192, 203
Holmes, K., 522, 554
Holmes, O., 75
Horne, A., 489, 490
Horney, D., 297
Horney, K., 183, 297, 328
Horowitz, L., 18, 28
Hourcade, J., 582, 588
Houts, R., 520, 554
Howard-Hamilton, M., 446, 456
Howling, P., 511, 555
Huang, L., 443, 449, 450, 455
Huesman, R., 552, 554
Huey, W., 592, 593

Hughes, J., 467, 482
Hughes, T., 595
Hunter, D., 545, 554
Huss, S., 492, 493
Hutterer, R., 177, 181

Ibrahim, F., 439, 457
Imber-Black, E., 106, 108
Ingersoll, R., 513, 557
Ingraham, C., 464, 482
Inhelder, B., 12–15, 29, 86, 109
International Association for Analytical
    Psychology, 404
Irwin, C., 593
Irwin, E., 424, 431
Isaacs, M., 597
Israel, A., 581, 588
Ivey, A., 439, 440, 458

Jacob, T., 520
Jackson, M., 448, 449
Jacobsen, E., 251, 263
Jacobsen, H., 413, 433
Jacobsen, I., 528, 531, 554
James, M., 279, 292
James, R., 313, 328, 423, 424, 431, 433,
    503, 519, 520, 545, 550, 554
James, S., 200, 203, 518, 552
Jay, S., 225, 233
Jefferson, T., 382
Jen Der Pan, P., 373, 376
Jernberg, A., 372, 376, 416, 431
Jewel, D., 423, 431
Jimenez, E., 546, 557
Johnson, B., 416, 431
Johnson, C., 448, 509, 548, 549, 554
Johnson, D., 448, 471, 482, 485, 490,
    509, 548, 549, 554
Johnson, F., 471, 482, 485
Johnson, L., 175, 180
Johnson, P., 439, 457
Johnson, R., 509, 548, 549, 554
Johnson, V., 322, 328
Jome, L, 440
Jones, D., 445, 520, 554
Jones, E., 76, 463, 481, 484
Jones, J., 437, 454, 521, 555
Jones, K., 463, 464, 482, 495

Jongeward, D., 279, 292

Journal of the American Medical Association, 545, 546

Jung, C., 76, 79, 378–390, 393–395, 397–400, 403, 404, 412, 431

Kaduson, H., 228, 233, 407, 409, 414, 421, 431

Kahn, B., 467, 482

Kalff, D., 424, 425, 431

Kalodner, C., 498

Kantrowitz, B., 539, 555

Kaplan, K., 278, 292

Kazdin, A., 32, 70

Keat, D., 33, 70

Keirsey, D., 395, 404

Kelly, F., 59, 70

Kelly, J., 533, 536, 557

Kendall, P., 224–226, 233

Kestenbaum, C., 98, 108

Keys, S., 461, 464, 468, 482, 485, 585, 587

Kincade, E., 175, 180, 229, 233, 442

King-Sears, M., 461, 468, 482, 585, 587

Kingston, M., 182

Kiresuk, T., 56, 58, 70

Kirkpatrick, L., 18, 29

Kizner, L., 497

Kizner, S., 497

Kline, M., 98, 108

Kline, T., 472, 482

Kmitta, D., 549, 553

Knell, S., 227, 228, 233

Knight, G., 443, 455

Kobak, R., 18, 29

Kohlberg, L., 120, 132

Kohn, A., 318, 328

Koller, T., 372, 376, 416, 431

Koprowicz, C., 21, 28, 460, 481

Kormanski, C., 470, 471, 482

Kottman, T., 322, 323, 328, 444, 408, 409, 411, 417, 420, 421, 432, 519, 555, 580, 581, 588

Kramer, E., 422, 432

Kratochwill, T., 463–465, 481, 483, 485

Kris, M., 76

Kroeger, O., 388, 404

Kronick, R., 112, 131, 132

Kubler-Ross, R., 524, 555

Kulic, K., 490

Kurpius, D., 459, 465–467, 472, 482

Kurpius, S., 590–592, 598

Kurtines, W., 373, 377

Kurtz, P., 511, 555

Kushida, D., 468, 481

LaFromboise, T., 448, 449

Laird, J., 438

Lambarth, C., 470, 481

Lambert, M., 32, 35, 36, 70, 525, 557

Lampe, R., 35, 36, 70, 228, 234

Landgarten, H., 422, 432

Landreth, G., 174, 175, 181, 407, 411, 413, 417, 420, 421, 425, 429, 431, 432

Lane, K., 370, 376, 414, 430

Lane, P., 548, 555

Langone, M., 522, 555

Lansford, Z., 378, 398, 404

Lau, A., 373, 377

Lawrence, G., 590–592, 598

Lawson, D., 98, 108

Lazarus, A., 32, 70

Lazarus, P., 447

Leben, N., 422, 432

Leblanc, M., 418, 432

Lee, A., 99, 108

Lee, C., 437, 439, 441, 442, 446, 449, 457

Lee, J., 451, 457

Lee, M., 374, 377

Lee, W., 100, 108, 262, 264

Leone, B., 551, 553

Leong, F., 449, 451, 457

Lepage, K., 465, 483

Levenson, H., 155, 157

LeVine, E., 12, 29

Levinson, B., 266

Linde, L., 591, 592

Lippitt, G., 466, 482

Lippitt, R., 466, 482

Littrell, J., 146, 157, 497, 498, 507, 577, 588

Lobaugh, F., 416, 432

Lochman, J., 224, 233

Locke, D., 437, 446, 454, 457

Loeschen, S., 361, 377

Loftus, E., 518, 555

Lonner, W., 439, 457
Lovko, A., 545, 555
Lowenfeld, M., 424, 428, 432
Lowenthal, B., 19, 29
Luckasson, R., 562, 567, 571, 574, 576, 577, 581–583, 588
Lurn, W., 363, 377
Lusky, M., 469, 482
Lyness-Richard, D., 98, 108, 228, 234

Macleod, I., 463, 464, 482
Madanes, C., 345–347, 377
Magellan Behavioral Health, 62, 70
Magrab, P., 544, 545, 556
Majidi-Ahi, S., 445, 454
Malcarne, V., 522, 555
Malcolm, W., 192, 203
Maniacci, M., 317, 328
Manly, L., 308, 328
Manning, M., 434, 437–439, 445, 447, 452, 454
Marans, S., 545, 554
Marino, T., 63, 65, 70
Markos, P. 543, 557
Martin, S., 59, 71
Marvasti, J., 150, 157
Maslow, A., 9–11, 29, 88, 108, 112, 113, 116, 160, 238, 264, 543
Mason, P., 423, 424, 430
Masten, A., 543, 555
Maultsby, M., 219–221, 234
Mazzeetti, M., 292, 292
McCaulley, M., 389, 390, 394, 395, 404
McConell, A., 537, 555
McDonald, L., 370, 390, 394, 395, 404
McFadden, J., 128, 129, 132
McFarland, W., 597
McGinn, L., 219, 234
McHaney, L., 467, 482
McIntosh-Koontz, L., 62, 71
McKinney, J., 62, 70
McLeod, E., 175, 180, 416, 431
McRary, A., 547, 555
McWhirter, J., 493, 506, 548, 555
Mead, J., 598
Meara, N., 82, 109, 589, 590
Medley, R., 441, 458
Meggert, S., 424, 431
Meichenbaum, D., 219, 234

Meisgeier, C., 393, 394, 397–399, 402–404
Mellin, E., 528, 555
Mercado, M., 450, 457
Meggert, S., 448
Menke, E., 542, 556
Mental Status Examination, 476
Messing, J., 549, 555
Miliotis, D., 543, 555
Miller, M., 187, 188, 204
Miller, S., 134, 156, 451, 455
Miller, T., 32, 71
Miller-Perrin, C., 509, 510, 513, 514, 555
Millican, V., 323, 328
Milo, J., 439, 457
Milstein, S., 593
Minuchin, S., 342–344, 347, 377
Miranda, A., 325, 326, 328
Moeller, J., 509, 555
Moller, T., 509, 555
Moffit, K., 416, 429
Mohr, P., 33, 70
Molidor, C., 436, 455
Molnar, A., 134, 349, 376
Montague, M., 62, 70
Moody, E., 498
Moore, K., 155, 156
Moore, M., 370, 377, 414, 432
Morgan, A., 370, 377, 414, 432
Morris, C., 22, 28
Morrissey, M., 546, 547, 555
Morten, G., 441, 454
Mosak, H., 296, 300, 301, 317, 328, 329
Mosely-Howard, G., 326. 328
Moustakas, C., 175, 181, 407, 432
Mozenter, A., 471, 482
Mulherin, M., 425, 432
Mullis, F., 469, 482
Murguia, A., 468, 481
Muro, J., 519, 555
Murphy, E., 394, 404
Murphy, J., 146, 157
Murphy, K., 63, 71
Myer, R., 313, 328, 423, 424, 431
Myers, I., 162, 179, 379, 389–391, 394, 395, 398–400, 403, 404
Myers, S., 162, 179, 181
Myrick, R., 472, 482, 485, 505

Nader, K., 422, 432
Nagata, D., 450, 457
National Association of Social
    Workers, 599, 600–604
National Center for Health Statistics, 528
National Coalition for the Homeless, 542
National Information Center for Children
    and Youth with Disabilities, 567,
    573, 575, 579, 581–583, 588
Naumburg, M., 422, 432
Nawojczyk, S., 550, 555
Nazzettum, N., 291
Neemann, J., 543, 555
Neibuhr, K., 468, 482
Neibuhr, R., 498, 482
Neil, B., 421, 432
Nelson, R., 498, 528, 529, 555
Neubauer, P., 98, 108
Newman, B., 15, 29
Newman, P., 15, 29
Newton, I., 135
Nichols, M., 374, 377
Nigg, J., 580, 588
Nin, A., 265
Nishamura, B., 441, 458
Norem, R., 539, 558
Northrup, D., 62, 70

O'Brien, M., 36, 71, 100, 109
O'Connor, K., 411–413, 432
O'Halloran, C., 525, 556
O'Hanlon, W., 146, 156
O'Hara, M., 64, 71
O'Loony, J., 468, 482
O'Rourke, K., 519, 521, 524, 544, 556
Oaklander, V., 195, 196, 204, 421, 432
Ocampo, K., 443, 455
Oden, M., 570, 588
Odewale, F., 445, 454
Oehmen, S., 534, 556
Office of Special Education Programs,
    568, 588
Ohnishi, H., 439
Okesola, O., 446, 458
Omizo, M., 450, 457
Omizo, S., 450, 457
Open Minds on On-Line News, 62, 71
Oren, T., 595
Orlando, M., 61, 65, 71

Orlinsky, D., 52, 71
Orton, G., 6, 29, 407, 418, 419, 422,
    423, 432, 486
Osofsky, J., 546, 547, 556
Otwell, P., 469, 482
Owens, P., 490
Oz, S., 125, 132

Paivio, S., 191, 204
Papernow, P., 540, 556
Parette, H., 562, 582, 588
Parham, T., 447, 457
Park, E., 154, 157
Parker, L., 437, 457
Parks, C., 549, 551, 552, 556
Parmer, T., 410, 430
Patterson, J., 62, 71
Patterson, L., 19–21, 29
Patton, M., 82, 109
Patton, P., 575, 588
Pavlov, I., 235, 250, 251
Peace, S., 498
Pedersen, P., 434, 435, 437, 439, 440,
    457, 458
Pellar, J., 134, 157
Perl, J., 36, 71, 100, 109
Perls, F., 182–190, 194, 195, 202–204,
    230
Perls, L., 182–184, 202, 204
Persi, J., 472, 482
Peters, H., 24, 29
Petersen, G., 3, 29, 546, 547, 556
Peterson, J., 486
Peterson, L., 543, 545–547, 556
Peterson, N., 497
Petty, D., 498
Pew, M., 324, 329
Pew, W., 310, 312, 328, 329
Pfeffer, C., 528, 531, 554
Phillips, R., 428, 432
Piaget, J., 12–15, 29, 86, 109, 120, 132,
    217, 249, 523
Pidcock, B., 521, 556
Pietrzak, D., 3, 29, 546, 548, 556
Pinderhughes, E., 229, 234
Plaude, J., 251, 264
Ponterotto, J., 439, 455
Pope, K., 595
Pope, M., 155, 157

Popenhagen, M., 521, 556
Poppen, W., 43, 46, 71, 115, 132
Popper, M., 528, 531, 554
Porche-Burke, L., 200, 203
Porter, G., 468, 469, 482
Portman, G., 498
Powell, B., 65, 71
Powell, S., 498
Prieto, L., 414, 431
Pryzwansky, W., 462, 463, 468, 481
Pulvino, C., 542, 553
Putallaz, M., 18, 29
Pynoos, R., 422, 432

Qualley, R., 529, 556
Quinn, R., 178, 179, 181

Radd, T., 171, 174, 181
Rafferty, Y., 543, 556
Rainey, L., 498
Rak, C., 19–21, 29
Ramirez, M., 543, 555
Ramirez, S., 465, 483
Rank, O., 159
Rapee, R., 225, 232
Rappley, M., 580, 588
Rasmussen, L., 419, 421, 433
Ratican, K., 517, 556
Ray, D., 409, 416, 418, 429, 433
Ray, K., 246, 264
Reeder, J., 493, 498
Reich, W., 183, 521, 556
Reis, S., 571, 588
Remley, T., 589, 591–593, 596
Renzulli, J., 571, 588
Richards, L., 541, 556
Richards, N., 417, 429
Richardson, B., 446, 449, 457
Richeport-Haley, M., 372, 373, 377
Rickford, B., 146, 154–156
Riley, R., 375, 377
Rimm, S., 571, 587
Ringel, J., 60, 61, 71
Rio, A., 498
Ripley, V., 498
Ritchie, M., 418, 432, 492, 493
Robert, R., 580, 581
Roberts, W., 532, 581
Robinson, E., 495

Robinson, F., 484
Robinson, J., 291, 293
Robinson, K., 591, 592
Rodgers, K., 468, 481
Rodriguez, E., 452, 455
Rogers, C., 52, 134, 158–160, 162, 163,
    165, 177–179, 181, 187, 188
Rohner, R., 519, 553
Roll, D., 245, 264
Romano, J., 245, 264
Ronen, T., 226, 234
Roth, S., 370, 376
Rotter, J., 414, 433
Roysircar-Sodowsky, G., 439
Rozecki, T., 465–467, 472, 482
Rubin, J., 422, 433
Rudin, M., 521, 522, 556
Rudolph, L., 647, 648
Rund, A., 182

Sallee, A., 12, 29
Salo, M., 590, 593, 594, 596, 597, 647,
    649
Salzman, M., 447, 457
SAMHSA's National Mental Health Infor-
    mation Center, 528
Sanchez, J., 437, 454
Sanderson, W., 5219, 234
Saner, R., 200, 204
Santisteban, D., 373, 377
Satir, V., 184, 353–367, 369, 375, 377
Sattler, J., 476, 483
Saunders, F., 389, 404
Scamardo, M., 155, 156
Scarsborough, J., 584, 587
Scarupa, H., 508, 553
Sceery, A., 18, 29
Schaefer, C., 97, 109, 407–409, 411–414,
    421, 431–433
Scheidlinger, S., 550, 556
Schein, E., 461, 483
Schellenbach, C., 515, 556
Scheon, C., 511, 557
Schmidt, L., 589, 590
Schmiege, C., 541, 556
Schmitz, C., 542, 556
Schulte, A., 462, 463, 468, 481
Schultz, W., 184
Schwartz, R., 374, 377, 522, 557

Schwebel, A., 538, 554
Schwiebert, V., 581, 588, 595
Sealander, K., 581, 588, 595
Seilhamer, R., 520, 557
Selekman, M., 146, 157
Seligman, M., 31, 55, 71
Selman, R., 15, 29
Serdahl, E., 467, 482
Sexton, T., 32, 71
Sferrazza, M., 584, 587
Shahin, J., 267, 293, 297
Shaffer, J., 493
Shapiro, M., 235
Shaver, P., 18, 29
Shayka, J., 521, 556
Shechtman, Z., 484
Shelby, J., 422, 423
Shepard, M., 182, 204
Sheridan, S., 464, 483
Sher, K., 520, 557
Shoffner, M., 468, 483
Shostrom, E., 176, 181, 188, 204
Shulman, B., 300, 301, 329
Shumate, S., 590, 593, 594, 596, 597, 647
Sidney, P., 236
Siebert, A., 179, 181
Siegel, S., 225, 233
Siehl, P., 532, 557
Silver, S., 573, 587
Silverman, S., 225, 234
Sim, A., 537, 555
Simon, J., 149, 156
Simon, R., 342, 377
Simon, S., 88, 109
Simpson, R., 583, 588
Singleton, M., 155, 157
Sink, C., 468, 483
Skinner, B. F., 235–237, 263
Skinner, C., 246, 364
Sklare, G., 134, 139–141, 144, 146, 157
Smith, A., 56, 58, 70
Smith, D., 559, 562, 567, 570–572, 574, 576–578, 581–583, 588
Smith, H., 55, 56, 63, 71
Smith, J., 363, 377
Smith, M., 32, 71
Smith, R., 19, 29, 463, 481
Sodowsky, G., 439, 457
Sokol, L., 225, 232

Sokol, M., 528, 531, 554
Soloman, L., 177, 181
Solomon, R., 528, 531, 554
Soltz, V., 306, 314, 317, 328
Somers, C., 463, 464, 482
Sommers-Flanagan, J., 487
Sommers-Flanagan, R., 487
Sorenson, G., 647, 649
Soriano, M., 546, 547
Soriano, R., 546, 547
Soto-Fulp, S., 373, 377
Spagna, M., 575, 588
Spaulding, D., 450, 455
Speaker, K., 3, 29, 546, 547, 556
Spence, S., 225, 226, 232, 234
Spengler, P., 529, 530, 558
Stachowiak, J., 437, 454, 592
Stanko, C., 497
Santon, E., 110
Steenbarger, B., 55, 56, 65, 71
Stefanowski-Harding, S., 529, 557
Stein, B., 61, 65, 71
Steiner, C., 278, 284, 293
Steinhardt, L., 422, 433
Stephans, R., 546, 557
Stephenson, M., 155, 156
Stermback, S., 425, 433
Stiles, K., 298, 329
Stipsits, R., 177, 181
Stoiber, K., 485
Stone, C., 597
Storr, A., 379, 381, 404
Stott, F., 48, 70
Strand, D., 425, 433
Strawser, S., 543, 557
Strong, K., 550, 552, 557
Strother, J., 420, 429
Strum, R., 60, 61, 71
Sue, D., 154, 157, 200, 203, 229, 234, 439, 440, 441, 445, 449, 450, 454, 457, 458
Sullivan, J., 575, 588
Summerton, O., 274, 293
Surgeon General, 4, 20, 22, 29
Sweeney, B., 549, 553
Sweeney, D., 174, 181, 407–409, 413, 432, 433
Swenson, L., 590
Szapocznik, J., 373, 377

Tamura, T., 373, 377
Tannen, D., 403, 404
Tarasoff v. Regents of University of California, 596
Tarver Behring, S., 575, 588
Taschman, H., 354, 377
Taub, D., 497
Taylor, A., 149, 156
Taylor, L., 468, 469, 483
Tennessen, J., 425, 433
Terman, L., 570, 588
Terner, J., 312, 329
Thebarge, R., 213, 234
Thomas, C., 131, 132
Thomas, M., 336, 339, 377
Thompson, C., 32, 43, 46, 56, 59, 71, 115, 132, 153, 155, 157, 228, 234, 236, 263, 499, 647, 648
Thompson, R., 577, 588
Throckmorton, W., 63
Thuesen, J., 388, 404
Thurston, L., 459, 470, 481
Tischler, V., 543, 557
Todd, T., 351, 377
Tollerud, T., 581, 588
Tomine, S., 450, 458
Tonkins, A., 525, 557
Toporek, R., 437, 454
Torres, D., 441, 458
Trevino, J., 440, 458
Trimble, J., 439, 457
Trivedi, L., 36, 71
Tyler, J., 422, 499

Ullman, D., 545, 555
Underwood, J., 595
U.S. Department of Education, 567, 573, 575, 576, 581, 583, 588, 595, 606
U.S. Department of Health and Human Services, 508, 509, 557
U.S. Department of Justice, 547
U.S. National Center on Child Abuse and Neglect, 509
Uscher, C., 176, 181
Utay, K. 228, 234

VanFleet, R., 228, 234, 415, 416, 433
Van Lone, J., 498, 507
Vasquez, M., 200, 203

Vaz, K., 425, 433
Veach, L., 60
Vernon-Jones, R., 441, 458
Vetter, V., 595, 606
Vinturella, L., 424, 433
Visher, E., 539, 557
Visher, J., 539, 557
Vontross, C., 445, 446, 458
Vostanis, P., 543, 557

Wachtel, E., 371, 377
Wade, J., 446, 458
Wadsworth, B., 12, 30
Wagner, J., 542
Wagner, P., 466, 483
Wagner, W., 26, 29
Walker, R., 422, 433
Wallace, W., 462, 483
Wallerstein, J., 533–537, 557
Walter, J., 134, 157
Wampold, B., 6, 56, 69
Wang, A., 551, 557
Washington, E., 437, 441, 458
Waters, V., 210, 215, 216, 234
Watkins, C., 220, 221, 234
Watson, T., 246, 264
Watzlawick, P., 133, 157
Waxer, P., 176, 181
Weakland, J., 133, 157
Webb, B., 525, 557
Webb, W., 227, 234
Weekley, J., 595
Weiner, N., 591
Weiss, M., 575, 577, 587
Welch, J., 550, 558
Welfel, E., 513
Wendel, P., 532, 536–538, 558
Werner, E., 19, 20, 29
West, S., 521, 556
Wheat, R., 426, 433
White, J., 428, 433, 463, 481
Whitehead, B., 537, 539, 541, 558
Whitson, S., 32, 71
Wick, D., 486, 507
Wick, J., 486, 507
Wicks-Nelson, R., 581, 588
Wilborn, B., 298, 329
Williams, G., 155, 157
Williamson, R., 468, 483

Wilson, C., 498, 507
Wilson, F., 490, 507
Wilson, J., 519, 521, 558
Windholtz, G., 251, 264
Wingert, P., 539, 555
Wise, A., 529, 530, 558
Wodarski, J., 511, 555
Wolf, B., 560, 562, 571, 573, 580, 581, 583, 588
Wolpe, J., 235, 251, 254, 264
Woodard, S., 446, 458
Woods, K., 274, 293
Woody, P., 225, 233
Worden, J., 525, 558

Worzbyt, J., 519, 521, 524, 544, 556
Wright, F., 225, 232
Wubbolding, R., 130, 132

Yaccarino, M., 372, 377
Yamaguchi, B., 543, 557
Yapko, M., 518, 558
Yarbrough, J., 56, 59, 71, 155, 157
Yeh, C., 450, 458
Ying, Y., 449, 450

Zeppa, A., 539, 558
Zinck, K., 498, 507
Zuckerman, B., 545, 554

# Topical Index

Abuse, 509–522, 597–598
Acculturation, 411, 439
Achievement tests, 479
Acting out, 85
Adaptive child, 268
Adlerian family counseling, 323, 324
    Brief marriage therapy, 324
    Interview guidelines, 323, 324
    Marathon family counseling stages, 324
Advice vs. information, 49–51
African Americans, 434, 442
    African American children, 445–447
Aggression, 224
America's children: key national indictors
    of well-being, 435
Americans with Disabilities Act, 563–566
Anima, 385
Anorexia, 261
Anticathexis, 81
Anxiety, 82, 225
Aptitude tests, 479
Archetypes, 385
Asian American, 449
Asian American children, 449–451
Asians, 434, 442
Assertiveness training, 250
Assessment as a consulting and counseling
    intervention, 475
Attending, 389, 391, 392, 394, 395, 399
Attention deficit–hyperactivity disorder,
    226, 578–579
Aversive conditioning, 255, 256

Basic ID model, 32–33
Behavioral counseling, 235–263
Behavioral consultation, 461
Behavioral disorder, 573–575
Behavioral momentum, 245
Behavioral observations, 477
Behavior-practice groups, 247
Biofeedback, 246
Bipolarities, 190
Biracial children, 453
Birth order, 300
    Firstborn children, 300, 301
    Middle children, 301
    Only child, 300
    Second-born children, 301
    Youngest children, 301
Blamer, 358
Brief counseling, 133–157
Bulimia, 20, 261

Case histories, 477
Carkhuff's five response levels, 165
Catharsis, 92, 93
Cathexis, 81
Chicano, 451
Children of alcoholics, 227, 519–521
Children's misbehavior problems brought
    to counseling, 611–639
Child abuse, 508–522, 597–598
Child Trends (2000), 445, 447, 449, 451,
    455
Choice theory, 112–130

Circle response, 470
Classical conditioning, 250, 251
Cognitive behavioral therapy, 114, 218–231
Cognitive development, 12–15
Collaboration, 468
    Activities, 470
    Five stages of problem solving for collaborative consultation, 469
Collective unconscious, 79, 385
Combinations, 472
    Collaborating and teamwork, 472
Communication approach to family therapy, 351–353
Compare and contrast, 470
Compensation, 74, 85
Complexes, 383–384
Computer, 358
Confident, 386
Confidentiality, 592–597
Confluence, 185
Congruence, 163
Conscientizacaco, 449
Conscious, 78
Consciousness, 381
Consultant Evaluation Rating Form, 467
Consultation, 459
Consultation interventions, 473
Consulting Process, 465
    Entry, problem exploration and contracting, 466
    Evaluation, 467
    Information gathering, problem confirmation, and goal setting, 466
    Preentry, 465
    Solution searching and intervention selection, 467
    Termination, 467
Contingency contracts, 243, 244, 257–259
Continuous reinforcement, 241
Control psychology, 112–118, 126
Control theory, 111, 115
Cost-analysis, 125
Counseling, group, 484–507
Counseling, individual, 21–22
Counseling, silences in, 49
Counseling and psychotherapy, compared, 21

Counseling focus scale, 23–25
Counseling goals, 138–142, 146
    Positive goals, 147
    Negative goals, 147
    Harmful goals, 139
    "I don't know" goals, 140
Counseling records, 49
Council for Accreditation of Counseling and Related Educational Programs, 26
Counterconditioning, 255
Crisis intervention, 502–504
Cross-cultural counseling, 106, 129–130, 153, 175–177, 199, 200, 228, 229, 261, 262, 290, 291, 325, 326, 372, 373, 435
Cults, 521

Death and bereavement, 523, 535
Deciding, 389, 392, 395
Defense mechanisms, 83–85
Definition of family, 331
Denial, 84
Depression, 113–114, 118, 126, 225, 527
Differential thinking, 190
Directory information, 595
Displacement, 83
Distracter, 358
Diversity, 435
Divorce, 532–538
Dominance, 395
Dreams, 94, 378, 387, 404
Dreamwork, 194, 195

Early recollections, 312–314
Ego, 80
Ego-gram, 285, 286
Ego states, 268–270
Emotional disorders, 573–575
Empathy, 163–164
Empty chair technique, 191, 192, 196, 201, 203
Energizing, 389–390
Erikson's stages of social development, 15–18
Ethnic group, 439
Ethnic identity development, 440, 441
Ethnicity, 439, 440
Evaluation of counseling, 55–60

Exceptional children, 559–588
Existential theory, 114
Expressive arts, 98
Extinction, 238
Extravert, 388–391, 395

Failure identity, 112
Family atmosphere, 302–304
Family constellation, 299
Family counseling, 330–375
Family environment, 299–301
Family member roles, 358, 359
Family play therapy, 369–372
Fantasy, 84
Feeling, 388, 389, 392–396
Filial therapy, 370
First interviews, 37–42
Five layers of neuroses, 186–187
Fixation, 84
Fixed-interval schedule, 241
Fixed-ratio schedule, 241
Flagging the mine field, 149
Flooding, 254–256
Formal psychological and education tests, 477
Fragmentation, 186
Free association, 92–93
Free child, 268

Games, 274–176
Gangs, 549–552
Gatekeeper, 382, 383, 391
Genograms, 334–340
Gestalt prayer, 185
Gestalt therapy, 182–204
Gifted children, 570–573
Goal attainment scales, 56–60
Goals of behavior, 297
Goals of misbehavior, 306–308, 314–318
Gordon's dirty dozen, 165
Group counseling, 484–507
  Adlerian, 486
  Behavioral, 487
  Defined, 484
  Evaluation, 499–500
  Gestalt, 488
  Goals, 485–486
  Leadership skills, 488–489

Group counseling—cont'd
  Person-centered, 488
  Process, 495–497
  Rational emotive behavior therapy, 487
  Reality therapy, 487
  Stages of, 494–495
  Transactional analysis, 487
Group therapy, 486

Hispanic(s), 434, 451
  Hispanic children, 443
Homeless children, 542–543
Homeostasis, 272
Humor, 95
Hypnosis, 255

"I" language, 188
I'm okay, you're okay, 272, 273
Id, 80
Identification, 83
Implosion, 254
Incomplete sentences, 190
Indicators of well-being, 4
Individual education plan, 128
Individual psychology, 294–329
Individuals with Disabilities Education Act, 563–566
Individuation, 381, 382, 384
Indo-Chinese, 442
Inferiority, 388
Inferiority feelings, 295
Injunctions, 271–274
Instrumental behavior, 238
Intellectualization, 84
Intelligence test, 478
Internal inhibition, 254
Interview, The, 476
  Content of thought, 476
  General appearance, behavior, and attitude, 476
  General intellectual functioning, 477
  Insight, 477
  Memory, 477
  Orientation and awareness, 477
  Speech characteristics and thought process, 476
  Thinking, 381, 382, 388, 389, 391–393, 395, 399

Interventions for children's misbehavior, 611–639
  Carelessness in work and with property, 629–630
  Cheating, 627–628
  Chronic complaining and whining, 617–618
  Cruelty to peers, animals, and others, 613–614
  Daydreaming, 632–633
  Destructiveness, 614–616
  Disobedience, negative attitude, and resistive behavior, 622–623
  Distractibility and short attention span, 635–636
  Excessive tension and anxiety, 634–635
  Fighting, 609–611
  Immaturity and dependent behavior, 636
  Lying, 620–621
  Perfectionistic behavior, 637
  Physical abusiveness, 612–613
  School phobia, 637–638
  Shyness, 633–634
  Stealing, 623–624
  Swearing, 619–620
  Tantrums, 616–617
  Tattling, 618
  Teasing, 621–622
  Truancy, 628–629
  Underachievement, 630–632
  Verbal abusiveness, 611–612
Introvert, 388–391, 395
Intuiting, 381, 382, 388, 389, 391, 394, 395, 399
Irrational thinking, 207–217
Irresponsible behavior, 111–112, 119
Isolation techniques, 474

Jigsaw, 470
Judging, 389, 393–395, 399, 400
Jungian individualized counseling method, 380, 398–400
Jung's concept, 381, 384, 399

Latchkey children, 544–545
Lead manager, 115
Learning disabilities, 575–578
Leveler, 358

Lifestyle, 297, 298
Listing of behaviors, 474
Living, 389, 393–395
Logical consequences, 474

Machismo, 452
Managed health care, 60–68, 130, 154, 177, 178, 200, 201, 229, 262, 291, 326, 327, 373, 374, 420
Masculine protest, 296
Maslow's hierarchy of needs, 9–11, 112–113, 116
Mental attitudes, 381, 387, 395
Mental functions, 381, 382, 384, 388, 391, 392, 395
Mental health consultation, 460
Mental health professionals, 27
  Degree requirements, 27
  Work settings, 27
Mental retardation, 581–582
Mexican American, 451
Miracle question, 140, 147
Modeling, 236, 246
Models of consultation, 460
Mood disorders, 528
MSE summary, 477
Multicultural counseling and therapy, 440
  Multicultural, 435
  Multicultural counseling competencies, 437–443
Multicultural consultation, 464
Muphy-Meisgeier Type Indicator for Children, 394–397, 399–404
Myers-Briggs Type Indicator, 389–400, 402–404
  Use of, 390, 395–397

National Academy for Certification of Clinical Mental Health Counselors, 26
National Board for Certified Counselors, 26
National Center for Learning Disabilities, 587
National Counselor Examination, 26
Natural and logical consequences, 318, 319
Natural child, 268

Natural selection, 236
Need for success, 297
Negative reinforcement, 238
Neglect, 509, 512
Nondirective therapy, 161

Obesity, 226, 227
Operant behavior, 238
Operant conditioning, 236, 238, 245
Ordinal position, 299
Other tests, 479

Parent, adult, child model, 267–270
Paradoxical counseling strategies, 127,
    150
Parental permission, 591–592
Perceiving, 389, 393–395, 397, 400
Persona, 386
Personal logs, 595
    Reporting, 597
Personality type, 378–404
Personal unconscious, 381
Person-centered counseling, 158–181
Physical disabilities, 583–584
Piaget's stages of development, 120
Projection, 83
Placator, 358
Play, therapeutic powers of, 408, 409
Play therapist, personal qualities of, 411
Play therapy, 150, 174, 175, 195, 196,
    227, 228, 322, 323, 369–372,
    378–399, 403, 404, 407–433
    Advantages of, 408, 409
    Appropriate clients, 417
    Considerations in, 417–420
    Cross-cultural applications, 409, 410
    Defined, 407, 408
    Dynamic family play therapy, 414, 415
    Ecosystemic play therapy, 411, 412
    Effectiveness, 418
    Family play therapy, 414–417
    Group play, therapy, 413
    Jungian play therapy, 412, 413
    Play stages, 418–420
    Prescriptive play therapy, 414
    Strategic family play therapy, 416
    Theories, 411–413
    Therapist, 417
    Theraplay, 416, 417

Play therapy media, 420, 421
Pluralistic, 435
Polarities, 186
Population Reference Bureau, (June
    2000), 457
Positive balance, 148
Positive reinforcement, 238
Preferences, 379, 388, 389
    In learning, 396
Privacy, 592–597
Privileged communication, 592–597
Process consultation, 461
Progression, 384
Projective techniques, 478
Psyche, 379–381, 384, 398, 403
Psychic energy, 381, 390
Psychoanalytic theory, 116–117
Psychological autopsy, 532
Psychological types, 387–404
    Development of, 397, 398
    Table of, 394
Psychotherapy, 110, 116
Punishment, 238, 319

Quality schools, 111–112
Quality world, 113–121, 129–130

Race, 439
Rackets, 272, 279, 282, 287
Rational-emotive-behavior education,
    217, 218
Rational-emotive-behavior therapy,
    114,117, 205–217, 228–231
Rationalization, 84
Reaction formation, 83
Reactive inhibition, 254
Reality therapy, 110–132
    Basic needs, 111–113, 116, 126, 129
    Eight steps of, 118–124
    Ten-step consultation model,
        126–129
Records, 595
Regression, 84
Relationships, 111–121
Repression, 83
Resiliency, 19–21
Resistance to counseling, 37–42
Respondent conditioning, 251
Response cost, 260

Role of the ego, 387
Role reversal, 248
Role shift, 473
Role-playing, 248, 249

Scaling, 145
Schools without failure, 112,115
Script analysis, 270, 271, 267–270
Self, 385
Self-esteem, 171–174
Self-management contracts, 244, 245,
    258, 259
Sensing, 381, 382, 388, 389, 391–393,
    395, 399
Sexual abuse, 509–512
Shadow, 386
Shaping, 245
Silences in counseling, 49
Single-parent homes, 541
Social interest, 298, 299
Solution-focused brief counseling (SFBC),
    134–150
Special education, 586
Stepfamilies, 538–540
Stimulus-response, 237
Strategic family therapy, 345–351
Stress inoculation, 219
Structural family therapy, 340–345
Subconscious, 78
Sublimation, 85
Success identity, 112
Suicide, 527–530
Superego, 80
Suppression, 83

Surgeon General (2002), 445, 447, 449,
    451, 452, 458
Systematic desensitization, 251–254
Systems theory, 331–340

Teamwork, 470
Teleoanalytic holistic theory, 310
Temperament, 395
Termination of counseling, 54, 55
Therapeutic alliance, 121
Token economies, 247
Topdog/underdog, 186, 190, 191, 195,
    197, 198
Transactional analysis, 265–293
Transactions, 269, 282, 285
    Complementary, 269, 277, 282, 285
    Covert, 270
    Crossed, 270, 282, 285
    Ulterior, 272, 285
Transference, 95,116

Unconditional positive regard, 163
Unconscious, 78–79,117
Undoing, 85
Unfinished business, 185, 192
U.S. Census Bureau (2000), 458

Variable interval schedule, 241
Variable ratio schedule, 241
Violence, 545–548

Withdrawal, 84
Word association, 387
Worldview, 439

## TO THE OWNER OF THIS BOOK:

I hope that you have found *Counseling Children*, Sixth Edition, useful. So that this book can be improved in a future edition, would you take the time to complete this sheet and return it? Thank you.

School and address: _____

_____

Department: _____

Instructor's name: _____

1. What I like most about this book is: _____

_____

_____

2. What I like least about this book is: _____

_____

_____

3. My general reaction to this book is: _____

_____

_____

4. The name of the course in which I used this book is: _____

_____

5. Were all of the chapters of the book assigned for you to read? ____

    If not, which ones weren't? _____

6. In the space below, or on a separate sheet of paper, please write specific suggestions for improving this book and anything else you'd care to share about your experience in using this book.

_____

_____

_____

OPTIONAL:

Your name: _____ Date: _____

May we quote you, either in promotion for *Counseling Children*, Sixth Edition, or in future publishing ventures?

Yes: _____ No: _____

Sincerely yours,

Charles L. Thompson

Linda B. Rudolph

Donna A. Henderson

**BUSINESS REPLY MAIL**

FIRST CLASS          PERMIT NO. 358          PACIFIC GROVE, CA

POSTAGE WILL BE PAID BY ADDRESSEE

NO POSTAGE
NECESSARY
IF MAILED
IN THE
UNITED STATES

ATTN: Shelley Gesicki, Counseling Editor

**BROOKS/COLE/THOMSON LEARNING**
511 FOREST LODGE ROAD
PACIFIC GROVE, CA      93950-9968